Henry Webb Dunshee

History of the School of the Collegiate Reformed Dutch Church in the City of New York from 1633 to 1883

Henry Webb Dunshee

History of the School of the Collegiate Reformed Dutch Church in the City of New York from 1633 to 1883

ISBN/EAN: 9783337307530

Printed in Europe, USA, Canada, Australia, Japan

Cover: Foto ©ninafisch / pixelio.de

More available books at **www.hansebooks.com**

HISTORY
OF THE
SCHOOL
OF THE
COLLEGIATE REFORMED DUTCH CHURCH

IN THE CITY OF NEW YORK,

FROM 1633 TO 1883.

SECOND EDITION, REVISED AND ENLARGED

BY AUTHORITY OF CONSISTORY.

NEW YORK
PRESS OF THE ALDINE PRESS, 1 VESEY STREET.
1883.

Entered according to Act of Congress, in the year 1883,

BY HENRY W. DUNSHEE,

In the Clerk's Office of the District Court of the United States for the Southern District of New York.

TABLE OF CONTENTS.

	PAGES
Preface to the Second Edition, by Rev. T. W. Chambers, D. D.	v
Preface to First Edition	x
Notes Relative to the Second Edition	xiii
Additions and Corrections	xv
Board of Trustees and Names of Teachers, 1883	xx
Sketch of Parochial School System in Holland, by Rev. Thomas De Witt, D.D.	1

HISTORY, by Henry Webb Dunshee:

Chapter I.—A Brief Outline of the Discovery and Settlement of New Amsterdam, 1609-1633	7
Chapter II.—From the Establishment of the School (1633) to the Capitulation (1664)	12
Chapter III.—From the Capitulation (1664) to the Revolutionary War (1776)	35
Chapter IV.—From the Peace of 1783 to the Present Time	64

APPENDIX:

1. Attendance of the Children on the Sabbath	83
2. Revenue of the School	84
3. Localities of the School	85
4. Present Condition of the School Course of Study, etc.	91
5. Names of School Officers, 1642 to 1883	94
6. Names of Members of the Board of Trustees	103
7. Ancient and Modern Names of Streets	107
8. Catalogue of Scholars since 1790	109
9. Alphabetical List of Scholars, page 217—with NOTES	237
10. Names of Assistant Teachers since 1842	236
11. Addresses delivered on the occasion of the 250th Anniversary of the School	246
12. Addresses at the Re-union on the Unveiling of the Tablet	264
13. Description of the Coat-of-Arms on Tablet	278
Autographs	280
INDEX	281

ILLUSTRATIONS AND MAP.

View of New Amsterdam, the Earliest Locality of the School	iv
" De Witt Chapel, the present School Building	ix
" the City Tavern, Branch School, 1652	xvii
" Old and New Dutch Churches	xviii
" the South Dutch Church	xix
Etching of Henry Webb Dunshee	6
Photograph of Gerrit Van Wagenen	43
" James Forrester	80
The Stuyvesant Pear Tree	249
Seal of the Collegiate R. P. D. Church	263
Coat-of-Arms of John Harpending	276

Map of 1755.

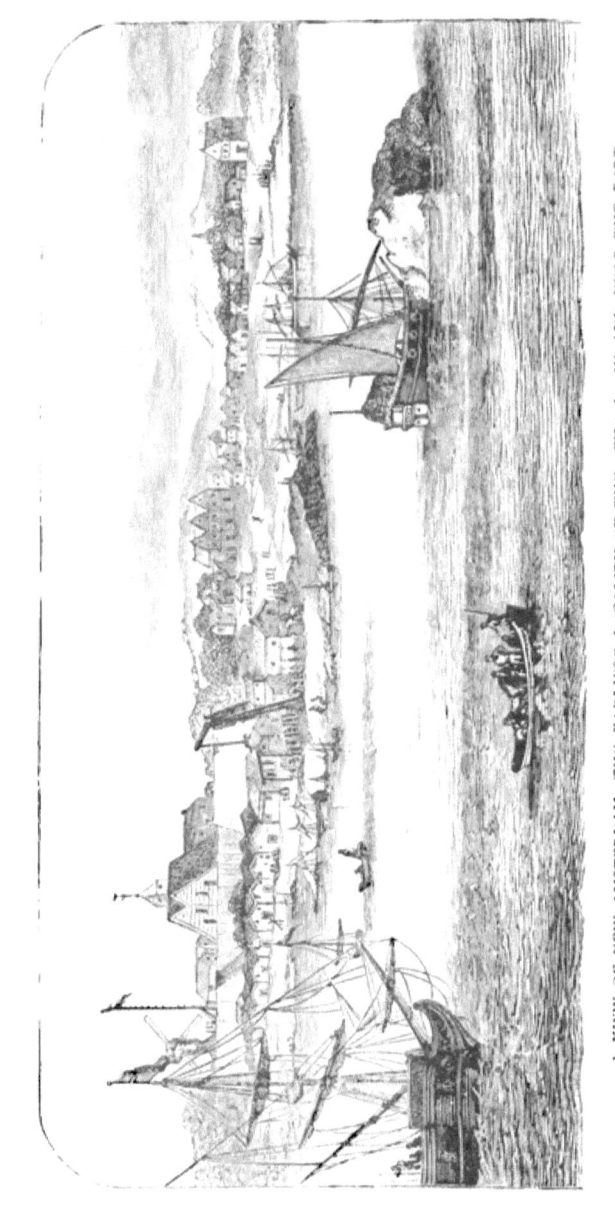

A VIEW OF NEW AMSTERDAM, THE EARLIEST LOCALITY OF THE SCHOOL.—IN AND NEAR THE FORT.

PREFACE TO THE SECOND EDITION.

BY REV. T. W. CHAMBERS, D.D.

THE first edition of this historical memoir was issued in 1853, and served a very useful purpose. The present year completing a quarter of a millennium (since the School was founded), it has been deemed advisable to commemorate the fact by a new edition, with such corrections and additions as further investigation has suggested, and a continuation of the narrative to the close of the quarter-millennial period.

The School is remarkable for the persistency with which it has maintained its existence and its character for two centuries and a half, amid the great and manifold changes which occurred during that lengthened period. The Dutch gave place to the English; the trading establishment became a colony; the colony was transformed into an independent State; the small settlement on the bay grew into a huge metropolis, made cosmopolitan by the influx of strangers from every part of the world; theories and plans of education have succeeded each other in public favor, until now one uniform system extends over the whole State; yet the unpretending School first established in Fort Amsterdam by Wouter Van Twiller, the Director-General, still continues, with the same aims and the same mode of reaching them as at the beginning. Men and times have changed; but the need and propriety of instruction for the young upon a Christian basis have undergone no change.

And so the institution continued faithful to its original purpose, neither rising above it nor falling below it, neither seeking to become an academy or a college, nor degenerating into the empty shell of a school, having the name without the reality. Its one aim was to train its pupils, intellectually and religiously, so that they would be fitted for the duties of life, become useful citizens, and adorn by intelligence and morality whatever station they might come to hold. The sphere of instruction was not large, but it was sufficient. It met the needs of the large class who must always be the bone and sinew of the commonwealth—the multitude who by manual toil earn their daily bread, and who especially need to be guided and restrained by moral forces.

The origin of the School is particularly interesting, as indicating the character of the people from whom it came. When they required those who planted colonies to provide for the education of the young, it was only carrying out what had been their own practice from a very early period. Mr. Motley ("Dutch Republic," i. 84), speaking of Antwerp as it was in the middle of the sixteenth century, says: "The schools were excellent and cheap. It was difficult to find a child of sufficient age who could not read, write and speak at least two languages." Again (*Ibid*, i. 86) he says of the country at large: "Nor was intellectual cultivation confined to the higher orders. On the contrary, it was diffused to a remarkable degree among the hard-working artisans and handicraftsmen of the great cities." This is shown by the literary festivals which were periodically celebrated in all the large towns. The various guilds competed with each other in magnificent processions, brilliant costumes, living pictures, charades and other animated, glittering groups, and in trials of dramatic and poetic skill. The intellectual character of these exhibitions was not of the highest order. They were often coarse and tawdry, or for various reasons offensive to a refined taste. Yet, as Mr. Motley observes: "No unfavorable opinion can be formed as to the culture of a nation whose weavers, smiths, gardeners and traders [and these in so small a country constituted the staple of the population] found the favorite amusement of their holidays in composing and enacting tragedies or farces, in reciting their own verses, or in personifying moral and æsthetic sentiments by ingeniously arranged groups or gorgeous habiliments." (*Ibid*, i. 89.) Luigi Guiccardini (1523-1589), who was a nephew of the great Italian historian, and who lived in the Low Countries for more than forty years and was an author of repute, says that "there was scarcely a peasant who could not read"—a remark which could be truly made of no other country in Europe and, perhaps, least of all in the case of England, where popular education on a large scale has taken a start only in the present century.

It is not an unreasonable supposition that the school system founded in the New England colonies at an early period was suggested by what the Puritan exiles had seen during their twenty years' stay in Holland. It is very certain that nothing of the kind was known in their mother country. But the scholars and gentlemen who came over in the Mayflower had had abundant opportunity to see in the Dutch Republic how closely knowledge and religion were bound together, and how firm a foundation was laid for the maintenance of liberty and religion when the elements of education were made common to all classes. The existing state of things in the Seven Provinces, and their marvellous experience for the previous half century, were a living testimony to the power of intelligence and virtue to establish and preserve a free State even against the most formidable opponents. The Hollanders owed much of their success to their situation and their pursuits; but far more to their sterling patriotism, enlightened by culture and purified by religion.

Mr. O'Callaghan, at the close of the first volume of his "History of New Netherland," speaking of the state of things in 1646, just before General Stuyvesant assumed the government, remarks, that "though a college had been founded in Massachusetts some nine years before, the authorities of New Netherland made little or no effort up to this time to establish a common primary school in any part of this country." But it should be considered that the settlers in Plymouth and Boston came hither on purpose to found a commonwealth which should be a permanent home for themselves and their children, free from the unpleasant restraints which hampered them in England. The immigrants on Manhattan Island, on the contrary, whether their occupation was mercantile or agricultural, regarded Holland as their home from which they had no divided interests. And they had no special inducements to seek for institutions to do what was so well done at Utrecht, Leyden and Groningen. It took more than a century to convince them that the university system should be planted on their own soil. As for popular education, provision was ordered to be made for that in every charter of the West India Company. It is true that the erection of a school-house, though attempted or prepared for on several occasions, was intermitted and delayed for a series of years. Yet there is abundant evidence that a teacher was on the ground from 1633, and that he pursued his calling, doubtless in temporary apartments. Mr. O'Callaghan's reproach, therefore, seems hardly to be merited. Instruction was given to the young from a very early period, and that after the excellent pattern which had been set in the mother country.

This School, which has such a long history and for so many years has been a fountain of living waters, seems to many now to be superseded by the public-school system which prevails throughout the city. It, however, serves a very useful purpose as a relic of bygone days;

a memorial of the founders of the colony, and an abiding testimony to the great truth that religion and education should not be severed ; that the young should be taught and trained in a Christian atmosphere, and that sound morals cannot successfully be inculcated unless they are based upon Biblical truth and enforced by spiritual sanction.

DE WITT CHAPEL, 160 WEST 29TH STREET.
PRESENT SCHOOL BUILDING. *Vid. p. 88.*

PREFACE TO THE FIRST EDITION.

1853.

THE preparation of an inscription for the tablet intended to be placed in the front of the new edifice erected in Fourth Street, in 1847, for the school of the Reformed Protestant Dutch Church, in the city of New York, led to the inquiry: "In what year was the School established?"

To this question no satisfactory answer could be obtained. History, indeed, informed us that the establishment of a school by the Dutch in New Netherland was synchronous with the founding of a colony; and from this circumstance the opinion was entertained by some that the germ of this institution was planted in New Amsterdam at an early period in its history. But the generality of those who were acquainted with the school supposed that the date of its origin could be traced to a period subsequent to the Revolutionary War.

The traditional knowledge of the School leading its Trustees to the belief that it was one of antiquity, that body, on the motion of Mortimer De Motte, Esq., one of its members, requested the Principal to compile such information with regard to it as authentic sources might furnish. The present work is the result.

Identified with the history of the city from its settlement, and with the most ancient church established therein; perpetuated by our worthy ancestors, to whose children and children's children, even to the present day, it has afforded a religious and intellectual training; endeared by associations of a most interesting character to numerous members of the Dutch Church now living, descendants of the original stock and partakers in youth of its benefits; an interest attaches to it, at once peculiar and delightful.

Induced by these considerations, and with the view of preserving in substantial form the history of this, the oldest educational institution existing at present in the Western World, the Consistory of the Collegiate Church, with its accustomed liberality, made provision for its publication.

The materials for this work were principally derived from the Colonial Records of New Amsterdam, preserved in the archives of the city and State governments; the Correspondence of the Classis of Amsterdam; the Consistorial Minutes of the Collegiate Church (the Rev. Dr. De Witt rendering the translation from the Dutch language in the two latter); Brodhead's New York, the Documentary History of the State and the Minutes of the Board of Trustees.

The Author acknowledges with kindness his lasting obligations to Hon. James W. Beekman, E. B. O'Callaghan, M.D.; James B. Brinsmade, Esq., of Albany; A. D. F. Randolph, Esq.; David T. Valentine, Clerk of the Common Council; Theodore Nims, Jr., Esq.; Samuel W. Seton, Esq.; and to the librarians of the Historical Society, Mercantile and Society Libraries of this city, for the facilities they so cordially afforded him in the prosecution of his researches.

EXTRACTS FROM THE MINUTES OF THE BOARD OF TRUSTEES AND OF CONSISTORY.

NEW YORK, May 29, 1848.

On the motion of Mortimer De Motte, it was unanimously

Resolved, That Mr. Henry W. Dunshee be requested to investigate the records of our Church, and gather together from them and from such other sources as may be presented to him, all the facts attainable in connection with and relative to the School of the Reformed Protestant Dutch Church, in the city of New York, for the purpose of preparing its history.

THOMAS JEREMIAH, Sec. Board of Trustees.

Upon the completion of the work, it was approved by the pastors of the Collegiate Church and the Board of Trustees, before whom it was read, May 24, 1852.

At a subsequent meeting of the Board, June 28, Messrs. Van Nest, Oothout and Dunshee were appointed a committee with reference to the publication of the work.

Oct. 25th.—The draft of a memorial was presented at a meeting of the Trustees, by Mr. Van Nest, in behalf of the above committee, and it was on motion

Resolved, That the said memorial, signed by the officers of this Board, be presented to Consistory.

GEO. S. STITT, Sec.

IN CONSISTORY, February 3, 1853.

On the request of the Trustees of the School of the Church, to publish its history for gratuitous distribution.

Resolved, That the sum of six hundred dollars be appropriated for that purpose.

Resolved, That the Rev. Dr. De Witt be requested to aid the Trustees in the said publication.

Extract from minutes. CORNELIUS BOGERT, Clerk.

June 29, 1853.

Resolved, That Messrs. Warner and Beadle be a special committee to superintend the publication of the History of the School.

GAMALIEL G. SMITH, Sec.

RELATIVE TO THE SECOND EDITION.

1883.

TWO hundred and fifty years having elapsed since the School was established, the Trustees resolved to republish its History, incorporating such new material as has been brought to light since the original publication in 1853.

At a stated meeting of the Board of Trustees, held Jan. 28, 1881 — present, Messrs. Bookstaver, Chn. Anderson, Schell, Whiton, Perlee, Van Vechten and Secretary Julien — on motion, it was

Resolved, that the Board requests the Principal, Mr. Dunshee, to gather together all the facts connected with the History of the School of the Collegiate Dutch Church, and the names of its trustees, teachers and scholars, so far as possible, from its foundation, with a view to their ultimate publication at the coming quarter-millennial celebration in 1883.

At a meeting of the Board of Trustees, March 24, 1882, a communication was received from the Principal, relating to the preparation of statistics for the Record of the Schools, shortly to be published.

The matter was referred to the Committee of the Month — Mr. R. N. Perlee — for conference with the Principal and to obtain estimate of the probable cost, and report.

1882, Sept 29.— A report was received from Mr. Perlee, Committee in charge of the estimates for publishing the Quarter-millennial Record, announcing progress, and it was

Resolved, That the suggestions of the Principal be adopted in reference to the headings of the columns of the Record, and that they be, respectively:

No.	Pupil's Name	Age	Admitted	Withdrawn	Parent's Name	Residence	Graduated

as per sample page.

Messrs. Perlee and Van Vechten were appointed a committee to confer with Dr. Chambers in regard to preparing a suitable prefatory history for the Record, either upon the basis of the former one or upon such new basis as he might prefer.

A communication from the Principal in reference to Gen. Henry T. Kiersted was read, and ordered to be incorporated in the minutes of the meeting and to form a part of the material to be published in the Quarter-millennial Record shortly to be issued.

It was also ordered that similar effort be made in the case of Daniel Ayers and others (*Vide Notes*, pages 237-238).

1882, Oct. 27.—The Committee reported that Dr. Chambers had consented to undertake the labor of preparing a suitable prefatory history.

1882, Nov. 24.—

Resolved, That the Board of School Trustees request from Consistory an extra appropriation of $1,000 to cover the expenses connected with the celebration of the quarter-millennial anniversary of the founding of the School and for the publication of the History of the School.

At the suggestion of Mr. R. N. Perlee, it was

Ordered, That the matter of appendices in reference to graduates of the School be referred to a Special Committee, consisting of Messrs. Bookstaver, Hutton and Perlee ;

That obtaining of information from classical records in Amsterdam, about the School, be referred to Mr. Bookstaver, with power ;

That Dr. Chambers be requested to deliver an Historical Address at the 250th anniversary of the School, and that the same committee be appointed to digest the matter of speakers, etc., for that occasion.

1883, March 31.—

Resolved, That the quarter-millennial anniversary be arranged for the latter part of October, upon an evening to be hereafter designated.

When first published, copies of the work were presented to many persons eminent in science or literature, from whom congratulatory responses were received. One of these is so characteristic of the writer that it is given entire :

SUNNYSIDE, Jan. 16, 1854.

DEAR SIR : Accept my sincere thanks for the copy of your History of the School of the Reformed Protestant Dutch Church which you had the kindness to send me.

I have read it with great interest from the many facts it contains concerning the olden time of our city, and the recollections it awakens of the *olden time of my youth.*

There is one historical fact of which you make no mention, and possibly know nothing. A war once raged between the Dutch school and the school to which I belonged (kept by Mr. Benjamin Romaine, on Partition, now Fulton Street, below St. Paul's Church), and more than one doughty battle was fought, in which, on the whole, I rather think we of Partition Street came off the worse. However, these were feuds of the last century, and have long since passed away. I have no longer any pugnacious feelings towards your school, and am, Dear Sir,

Your obliged friend and servant,

WASHINGTON IRVING.

HENRY W. DUNSHEE, Esq.

Since the publication of the *first* edition the Records of the Collegiate Dutch Church have been translated by the Rev. Dr. Chambers, which has proved of invaluable assistance in the preparation of the present volume; and the author would also acknowledge his indebtedness to Rev. Abraham Thompson and Rev. A. H. Bechthold, for the translation of documents recently brought to light, in Albany and New York, which contained important information concerning the School.

The photograph of Gerrit Van Wagenen (schoolmaster 1733-1743), dressed in his official robes as Voorsanger, was obtained through the kindness of one of his descendants, Mr. William F. Van Wagenen, who possesses the original portrait.

The photograph of James Forrester is a tribute of respect from some of those who were under his instruction.

The etching *(page 6)* of the present Schoolmaster is a contribution to this work from his friend, Mr. Louis Delnoce.

ADDITIONS AND CORRECTIONS.

On *page 69* it is recorded that the Deacons had organized *another* school in Cortlandt Street, and had placed it under the supervision of Abraham De La Noy; and on *page 59* it is stated that this school "probably continued until 1776;" but, a journal of the Board of Deacons, recently discovered among the archives of the Church, throws new light upon this subject, and reveals the information that Mr. De La Noy, upon his decease in 1747, was succeeded by William Van Dalsem (a name hitherto unknown in connection with the School), who continued to teach until 1757, when, upon his decease, his scholars were transferred to Mr. Welp, in the new school-building in Garden Street.

The journal referred to, covering the period from 1731 to 1784, on *pages 39, 71 and 90*, records the payments to the different Schoolmasters—Van Wagenen, Bratt, De La Noy and Van Dalsem—from which it appears that the last payment made to De La Noy, was June 25, 1747, and the first made to Van Dalsem, was September 17, 1747.

The payments made to De La Noy and Van Dalsem were as follows:

	£	s.	d.
Nov. 7, 1743, Wood for Abraham De La Noy's School	0	15	6
Jan. 12, 1744, " " " "	1	2	0
May 3, 1744, Paid Abraham De La Noy, for Teaching the School Kinderen	1	15	4
Nov. 8, 1744, Paid Abraham De La Noy, for Teaching the School Kinderen	1	17	6
Nov. 15, 1744, Wood for the Schools of H. Van Wagenen and De La Noy	4	6	2

		£	s	d
Jan. 10, 1745, Paid Abraham De La Noy, for Teaching the School Kinderen...............................		1	17	6
May 30, 1745, Paid Abraham De La Noy, for Teaching the School Kinderen..............................		1	17	6
July 25, 1745, Paid Abraham De La Noy, for Teaching the School Kinderen..............................		1	19	4
Oct. 17, 1745, Paid Abraham De La Noy, for Teaching and Firewood...................................		3	6	8
Jan. 8, 1746, Paid Abraham De La Noy, for Teaching the School Kinderen.............................		1	17	6
April 6, 1746, Paid Abraham De La Noy, for Teaching the School Kinderen............................		3	5	0
July 24, 1746, Paid Abraham De La Noy, for Teaching the School Kinderen............................		1	10	0
Nov. 6, 1746, Paid Abraham De La Noy, for Teaching the School Kinderen.............................		1	10	0
Jan. 8, 1747, Paid Abraham De La Noy, for Teaching the School Kinderen.............................		2	1	3
April 2, 1747, Paid Abraham De La Noy, for Teaching the School Kinderen............................		2	1	3
June 25, 1747, Paid Abraham De La Noy, for Teaching the School Kinderen............................		4	2	9
Sept. 17, 1747, Paid William Van Dalsem, for Teaching the School Kinderen...........................		2	16	3
Jan. 7, 1748, Paid William Van Dalsem, for Teaching 15 Kinderen..................................		2	19	6
March 30, 1748, Paid William Van Dalsem, for Teaching 15 Kinderen................................		3	6	6
June 23, 1748, Paid William Van Dalsem, for Teaching 15 Kinderen.................................		3	15	0
Sept. 15, 1748, Paid William Van Dalsem, for Teaching 15 Kinderen................................		4	2	0
Oct. 6, 1748, Paid William Van Dalsem, for Teaching 15 Kinderen.................................		4	1	6

These payments continued to be made, as above, to Bratt and Van Dalsem during subsequent years, the last payment being made to the former November 6, 1755, when he received £5 3s. 6d. for instructing twenty children, and was superseded by Mr. Welp (*vide* pages 50–51).

During the year 1756 Mr. Van Dalsem received for teaching, in six payments, £19 12s.

April 28, 1757, Van Dalsem was paid for instructing 12 children. £2 18 0
July 21,   "   "   "   "   15   "   3 8 6
Sept. 15,   "   For six weeks instruction of 15 children....... 1 6 0

This last payment was paid to his widow.

As ten of the scholars were transferred provisionally, August 22, to Mr. Welp, it is probable that this branch school was discontinued (*vide* page 51).

Page 44. Van Wagenenen should be Van *Wagenen*.
Page 98. —— Maerschalk should be *Andrew* Maerschalk.
Page 99. —— Hoffman should be *Nicholas* Hoffman.

THE CITY TAVERN,

subsequently used as the Stadt Huys or City Hall, was at the corner of Pearl Street and Coenties Alley. Here was held a branch school, under De La Montagne, in 1652 and subsequent years. *Vide*, **page 24.**

OLD AND NEW DUTCH CHURCHES.

Old Dutch Church.

The Oude Kerke, in Garden Street, built in 1693. The School-house was opposite this Church from 1748 to 1824—seventy-six years. — *Vide* p. 47, and *Greenleaf's* Hist. of the Churches in New York, p. 11.

New Dutch Church.

The New Kerke, in Nassau Street, between Liberty and Cedar, built in 1729—100 feet by 70. It had no gallery and the ceiling was one entire arch without pillars. The pulpit was on the eastern side between the two doors. In 1764 the pulpit was removed to the north end of the church, a gallery was erected on the three other sides and large pillars put up to support the roof. During the Revolutionary War it was used by the British as a riding school for the cavalry.—*Vide Greenleaf*, Hist. as above, p. 12.

SOUTH DUTCH CHURCH, GARDEN STREET,

as rebuilt in 1807. Separated from the Collegiate Church, 1813. Destroyed in the great fire of December 16, 1835.

BOARD OF TRUSTEES

OF THE

SCHOOL OF THE REFORMED PROTESTANT DUTCH CHURCH

IN THE CITY OF NEW YORK.

1883.

HENRY W. BOOKSTAVER, *Chairman.*
FREDERIC R. HUTTON, *Secretary.*
JAMES ANDERSON, *M.D.*
RALPH N. PERLEE.
ROBERT SCHELL.
ABRAHAM V. W. VAN VECHTEN.
AUGUSTUS S. WHITON.

TEACHERS.

HENRY W. DUNSHEE.
MISS MARY P. DUNSHEE.
MISS JESSIE BLOOMFIELD.
MISS SARAH C. MOTT.

A SKETCH

OF THE

PAROCHIAL SCHOOL SYSTEM IN HOLLAND

SUBSEQUENT TO THE REFORMATION.

BY REV. THOMAS DE WITT, D. D.

THIS volume gives the History of the School of the Reformed Dutch Church in this city, as far as it can be ascertained from surviving documents in various sources. This school was coeval with the first settlement by Hollanders here, and has continued, to the present time, an instrument of much good in training the children, especially of the poorer class, under a direct religious influence. It has proved, under the Divine blessing, a nursery to the Church, gathering many into her communion ; and it has introduced a very large proportion as useful members of society. It was the custom, after the Reformation in Holland, to send out with emigrants going to any of its colonies, however few in number, a well-qualified schoolmaster, who was a member of the Church, and accredited by his competence and piety to take charge of the instruction of children and youth. During the absence or want of a minister, he was bound to conduct public worship, by reading a sermon, offering prayers, etc., on the Sabbath and on other occasions. With the earliest agricultural settlement of Manhattan Island and its vicinity, such a schoolmaster and *voorleeser* was sent out, and from the earliest period the School has continued to this day.

The importance of the religious element in early education cannot be too highly estimated in reference to the formation of character, and the direction of the future course of life. Under the Old Testament economy, the Divine direction was : "*These words shall be in thine heart ; and thou shalt teach them diligently unto thy children, and shalt talk of them when thou sittest in thy house, and when thou walkest by the way, and when thou liest down,* and when thou risest up." In the early Christian Church particular attention was paid to the scriptural and religious instruction of youth, and constant reference is made to the office and exercises of catechists and catechumens. The witnesses for the truth in the dark middle ages of the reign of Papal usurpation were remarkable for their faithfulness in the religious instruction and discipline of their children. The excellent and devoted Waldenses were probably indebted, under God, to their peculiar diligence in the discharge of this duty for their remarkable success in keeping their body together, under the influences and persecutions that pressed upon them; in transmitting their testimony from generation to generation, and in remaining continually a beacon-light amid the prevailing darkness, for the admiration and guidance of the Church in future time. History informs us that they bestowed constant and careful attention on the religious instruction of their children and youth, that they were in the habit of preparing excellent and appropriate catechisms and formularies, and that the pastors made the religious training of their youth a leading and unceasing object of their labors.

At the period of the Reformation the different parts of the Protestant Church made this a prominent object of their care and efforts. Formularies of divine truth, and catechisms adapted to different ages, were early introduced. Many of them obtained ecclesiastical sanction and authority, and were directed to be explained in the pulpit and the schools. It would be interesting to trace the history of the introduction and use of catechetical instruction in the churches and schools, from the earliest time of the Reformation, by the Church of England, the Church of Scotland, the Reformed Churches of France, Switzerland, Germany and Holland, etc. Measures were taken in Scotland at an early period of the Reformation, leading to the institution of parochial schools, widely diffused, under the supervision of the churches, and making religious instruction a pervading and distinguishing element.

We can here only make a brief reference to the Church of Holland. Nowhere was the struggle for the principles of the Reformation so severe and (we may say) so crushing. Charles V., who held the crown of Spain, and the patrimonial inheritance of the Netherlands, was elected Emperor of Germany. He found it his policy to treat the Protestant princes, and the professors of the Protestant faith there, with comparative indulgence; while in the Netherlands, hereditarily devolving upon him, he introduced his Spanish armies and the Inquisition. The page of history is replete with the account of the severity and extent of the religious persecutions by Spanish and Papal power. Thousands upon thousands lost their lives, while many more fled for refuge to other parts. But then the Word of the Lord took deep root. The first religious societies of the Reformed faith called themselves "*De Kerken van Christus onder het Kruys :*" "The Churches of Christ under the Cross." In 1566 the first Synod met at Antwerp, minutes of which have not been handed down. The noted and cruel Duke of Alva succeeded to the Viceroyalty of the Netherlands in 1567. He boasted that during his seven years' regency *eighteen thousand* had been put to death by him for heresy. The Reformed held their Synod at Wesel, now in Rhenish Prussia, on the Rhine, in 1568; and at Embden, in East Friesland, in 1571; not being able to find a place of safety in the Netherlands. They called themselves "*Believers under the Cross scattered throughout the Netherlands.*" At these Synods particular reference was made, and provision secured, for the Christian education of the young. At subsequent Synods, held in Holland, before and after the Union of Utrecht, in 1579, the subject was carefully considered and plans adopted. The principles thus adopted became more fully developed and matured in the action of the well-known Synod of Dort, held in 1618 and 1619. In the seventeenth session of that Synod, November 30, 1618, the subject of the instruction and education of youth, and of catechising, was under discussion. In the result the following resolution was adopted and minute made. The whole is inserted, as worthy of being read and well weighed:

In order that the Christian youth may be diligently instructed in the principles of religion, and be trained in piety, three modes of catechising should be employed. I. IN THE HOUSE, BY PARENTS. II. IN THE SCHOOLS, BY SCHOOLMASTERS. III. IN THE CHURCHES, BY MINISTERS, ELDERS AND CATECHISTS ESPECIALLY APPOINTED FOR THE PURPOSE. That these may diligently employ their trust, the Christian magistrates shall be requested to promote, by their authority, so sacred and necessary a work; and all who have the oversight of churches and schools shall be required to pay special attention to this matter.

I. The office of PARENTS is diligently to instruct their children and their whole household in the principles of the Christian religion, in a manner adapted to their respective capacities; earnestly and carefully to admonish them to the cultivation of true piety; to engage their punctual attendance on family worship, and take them with them to the hearing of the Word of God. They should require their children to give an account of the sermons they hear, especially those on the Catechism; assign them some chapters of Scripture to read, and certain passages to commit to memory; and then impress and illustrate the truths contained in them in a familiar manner, adapted to the tenderness of youth. Thus they are to prepare them for being catechised in the schools, and by attendance on these to encourage them and promote their edification. Parents are to be exhorted to the faithful discharge of this duty, by the public preaching of the Word; but specially at the ordinary period of family visitation, previous to the administration of the Lord's Supper, and also at other times by the minister, elders, etc. Parents who profess religion, and are negligent in this work, shall be faithfully admonished by the ministers; and, if the case requires it, they shall be censured by the Consistory, that they may be brought to the discharge of their duty.

II. SCHOOLS, in which the young shall be properly instructed in the principles of Christian doctrine, shall be instituted not only in cities, but also in towns and country places where heretofore none have existed. The Christian magistracy shall be requested that well-qualified persons may be employed and enabled to devote themselves to the service; and especially that the children of the poor may be gratuitously instructed, and not be excluded from the benefit of the schools. In this office none shall be employed but such as are members of the Reformed Church, having certificates of an upright faith and pious life, and of being well versed in the truths of the Catechism. They are to sign a document, professing their belief in the Confession of Faith and the Heidelberg Catechism, and promising that they will give catechetical instruction to the youth in the principles of Christian truth according to the same. The schoolmasters shall instruct their scholars according to their age and capacity, at least two days in the week, not only by causing them to commit to memory, but also by instilling into their minds an acquaintance with the truths of the Catechism. [An elementary small Catechism, the Compendium, and the Heidelberg Catechism are those specified to be used by the different grades of children and youth.] The schoolmasters shall take care not only that the scholars commit these catechisms to memory, but that they suitably understand the doctrines contained in them. For this purpose, they shall suitably explain to every one, in a manner adapted to his capacity, and frequently inquire if they understand them. The schoolmasters shall bring every one of the pupils committed to their charge to the hearing of the preached Word, and particularly the preaching on the Catechism, and require from them an account of the same.

III. In order that due knowledge may be obtained of the diligence of the schoolmasters, and the improvement of the youth, it shall be the duty of the MINISTERS, WITH AN ELDER, and, if necessary, with a magistrate, to visit all the schools, private as well as public, frequently, in order to excite the teachers to earnest diligence, to encourage and counsel them in the duty of catechising, and to furnish an example by questioning them, addressing them in a friendly and affectionate manner, and exciting them to early piety and diligence. If any of the schoolmasters should be found neglectful or perverse, they shall be earnestly admonished by the ministers, and, if necessary, by the Consistory, in relation to their office. The ministers, in the discharge of their public duty in the Church, shall preach on the Catechism. These sermons shall be comparatively short, and accommodated, as far as practicable, to the comprehension of children as well as adults. The labors of those ministers will be praiseworthy who diligently search out country places, and see that catechetical instruction be supplied and faithfully preserved. Experience teaches that the ordinary instruction of the Church, catechetical and other, is not sufficient for many, to instill that knowledge of the Christian religion which should, among the people of God, be well grounded; and also testifies that the living voice has very great influence; that familiar and suitable questions and answers, adapted to the apprehension of each individual, is the best mode of catechising, in order to impress the principles of religion upon the heart. It shall be the duty of a minister to go with an elder to all capable of instruction, and collect them in their houses, the Consistory chamber, or some other suitable place (a number particularly of those more advanced in years), and explain familiarly to them the articles of the Christian faith, and catechise them according to the circumstances of their different capacities, progress and knowledge. They shall question them on the matter of the public sermons on the Catechism. Those who desire to unite with the Church shall, three or four weeks before the administration of the Lord's Supper, be more carefully and frequently instructed, that they may be better qualified and be more free to give a satisfactory account of their faith. The ministers shall employ diligent care to ascertain those who give any hopeful evidence of serious concern for the salvation of their soul, and invite them to them ; assembling those together who have like impressions, and encouraging to friendly intercourse and free conversation with each other. These meetings shall commence with appropriate prayer and exhortation. If all this shall be done by the ministers with that cordiality, faithfulness, zeal and discretion that become those who must give an account of the flock committed to their charge, it is not to be doubted that in a short time abundant fruit of their labors shall be found in growth in religious knowledge and holiness of life, to the glory of God and the prosperity of the Church of Christ.

In the above we find evidence of alliance between Church and State to some extent, from which we are, happily, wholly free. But it suggests sentiments, and marks a course bearing upon the religious education of children and youth, well deserving the attention and approbation of the Church and Christian community. It is deeply to be regretted that with the extension of common school education through the entire community, under the patronage and by the provision of the State, certain influences have successfully operated to divest them of a Christian character. Some time since, the Romanists raised an organized opposition to our common schools as then conducted, demanding the alteration and excision of our school-books, and afterwards proceeded to object to the use of the Bible and the offering of prayer in the schools, until they are deprived of the semblance of religious character. Succeeding in this, they raised the cry that the schools were godless and infidel, and claimed for themselves their proportionate part of the public moneys to support their own denominational schools, confounding the doctrines and rites of their own Church with religion. While the system of universal education, under the patronage of the State, is to be preserved as of the highest importance, and no denominational claim should be allowed, it is most desirable and important that in the Christian community the Bible should be preserved in our schools, and that God should be acknowledged in them. But beyond this, it is the province of the Church, from her own resources and means, to devise the best methods of providing an enlightened, sound, religious education to her children, in a way the most practicable under existing circumstances. The minute extracted from the acts of the Synod of Dort furnishes principles of great value and enduring excellence, which, with some variety in the details caused by a change of circumstances in our position, should be carefully kept in view by the Church, to be faithfully carried into execution. The high importance of selecting or forming schools exerting a religious influence need not be dilated on. Parents should be led with greater fidelity to impart domestic instruction in the great truths of the gospel as embraced in our standards, and should accompany it with salutary guidance and example. Ministers and officers of the Church should pay particular attention to the young, in their early religious training, and seek to win them to the faith and service of the Redeemer. Is it not to be feared that, in the facilities which modern times afford in the spread of universal education, the institution of Sabbath-schools, and the multiplied and cheap issues from the press, there is yet a decline in the careful attention of the Church, in the use of the various means exhibited in the article quoted from the acts of the Synod of Dort, for the acquisition of sound and well-digested religious knowledge found among the children of the Church in earlier days?

This volume, giving the history of the school of our Reformed Dutch Church in this city, is not without its interest to the general reader as a research into the "*olden times,*" and connected with the earliest period of our city's history. But it bears peculiar interest to the friends of our church, and all who feel the importance of the religious training of the children of the Church, particularly of those who might otherwise be neglected. This history has been prepared by the present Principal of the school, after careful investigation of remaining sources of information. It is to be regretted that so few materials as to some periods have been preserved. In the school there has ever been preserved a course of instruction in the branches of knowledge adapted to prepare for practical life, while sound religious instruction has been carefully imparted. The happy and salutary influence of the school has been experienced through its continued existence, and it is now flourishing under the wise and faithful direction of the present Principal, who has prepared this volume at the request of the Board of Trustees appointed by the Consistory.

THOMAS DE WITT.

NEW YORK, Sept. 20, 1853.

Yours truly
Henry W. Dunshee

HISTORY OF THE SCHOOL

OF THE

COLLEGIATE REFORMED DUTCH CHURCH,

IN THE CITY OF NEW YORK.

CHAPTER I.*

A BRIEF OUTLINE OF THE DISCOVERY AND SETTLEMENT OF NEW AMSTERDAM : 1609—1633.

SPECIAL, preconcerted efforts, authorized by Government or induced by religious persecution, led to the settlement by the English of ten out of the thirteen original colonies, extending on the sea-coast from Maine to Georgia, inclusive. How, then, did Holland obtain a foothold on this continent, and how came the Dutch Government, with its Church and School, to be the first established in the Empire State?

A brief outline of the circumstances which led to the discovery and subsequent colonization of New Amsterdam will not only afford a solution to these questions, but also demonstrate the fact that a public school was established therein as soon as the circumstances of the settlers permitted it.

The discovery of America by Columbus, while attempting to reach China and Cathay by a westward passage, did not in the least repress the efforts prompted by the commercial spirit of the age, to accomplish that undertaking. The voyages made for that purpose resulted in the exploration of most of the large rivers and estuaries on the entire eastern sea-board of the continent. The southern route, discovered by Magellan in 1520, affording no advantages over the accustomed route through the Indian Seas, a passage was sought for on the north-west. Foremost and most persevering in this enterprise was England : no

---

* The contents of this chapter were culled from the first eight chapters of Brodhead's New York ; and here, as elsewhere throughout the work, his language has at times been appropriated.

less than thirty voyages, with this design, having been undertaken by British navigators, among whom was Henry Hudson. Failing to achieve the object of his ambition in the two attempts made by him in 1607 and 1608 in behalf of the English "Association for the Discovery of the North-west Passage," he offered his services to the East India Company of Holland ; and, on the 6th of April, 1609, departed in the *Half Moon*, from Texel, with instructions to "explore a passage to China by the north-east or north-west." Prevented by the ice from proceeding eastward toward Nova Zembla, he touched at the island of Faro, sailed thence to the Banks of Newfoundland, ran down the coasts of Nova Scotia, Maine and Massachusetts, and, failing to find an opening to the west, put to sea again. A fortnight after he made land off the capes of the Chesapeake, whence, sailing northward along the coast of Maryland, he entered Delaware Bay. Proceeding thence cautiously up the eastern coast of New Jersey, he entered the Narrows, and, on the 11th of September, anchored in the lower bay. Subsequently, in prosecution of his main design, he passed up the river, which now bears his name, to the vicinity of Albany ; and, having ascertained by soundings that no farther advance could be made, he reluctantly returned to the neighborhood of Hoboken. On the 4th of October he weighed anchor for the last time, and, having re-crossed the ocean, landed, in November, at Dartmouth, in England, whence he communicated to the Company at Amsterdam an account of his discoveries.

"Thus the triumphant flag of Holland was the harbinger of civilization along the banks of the great river of New York. The original purpose of the *Half Moon's* voyage had failed of accomplishment ; but why need Hudson repine ? He had not, indeed, discovered the passage to the eastern seas, but he had led the way to the foundation of a mighty State. The attractive region to which accident had conducted the Amsterdam yacht, soon became a colony of the Netherlands, where, for half a century, the sons and daughters of Holland established themselves securely under the ensign of the republic, transplanted the doctrines of a reformed faith, and obeyed the jurisprudence which had governed their ancestors." *

In 1610, the great "River of the Mountains" was visited a second time by a vessel from Holland, in pursuit of beaver and other valuable furs.

In 1611, Christiaensen and Block made a joint voyage to the river for the purposes of trade ; and the reports which they made of the country on their return to Holland led three influential

* Brodhead, N. Y., 36.

merchants of Amsterdam to dispatch with them, in 1612, two vessels for the purpose of continuing the traffic with the natives.

During 1613, three other trading-vessels visited the island of Manhattan, returning in 1614, freighted with large cargoes of valuable furs. The ship under the command of Block having been burned while he was preparing to return to Holland, he was obliged to build a yacht, which caused him to remain at Manhattan during the winter of 1613-14 ; and the few huts erected by him at this time near the southern point of the island were the first European abodes upon it. Forsaking these temporary structures upon the completion of his yacht, he explored the bays and rivers on the coasts of Connecticut, Rhode Island and Massachusetts. Here he found Christiaensen's ship from Manhattan, in charge of Cornelis Hendricksen ; and having exchanged vessels with him, Block returned to Holland. In the meanwhile, Fort Nassau was built by Christiaensen, on Castle Island, a little below Albany, as a warehouse and military defense for the traders.

Previous to Block's return to Amsterdam, the States-General had passed an Octroy, granting and conceding that "whosoever shall from this time forward discover any new passages, havens, lands or places, shall have the exclusive right of navigating to the same for four voyages." The merchants who had employed Block, encouraged by the results of his voyage, formed an Association, and lost no time in taking the steps necessary to secure to themselves the special privileges guaranteed in the general ordinance. Through their deputies at the Hague, they laid before the States-General a map and report of the newly explored countries, which now (1614), for the first time, received the name of NEW NETHERLAND. Their High Mightinesses having granted their request, they assumed the title of "The United New Netherland Company," and enjoyed for three years, from January, 1615, the exclusive trade "of all lands from the fortieth to the forty-fifth degree of latitude." *

In the spring of 1617, Fort Nassau was destroyed by a freshet, and a new fortified post was erected by the traders on the main land, on a commanding eminence called Tawassgunshee, at the mouth of Norman's Kill, immediately south of the present city of Albany.

On the expiration of the Company's charter in 1618, the trade of the Manhattans was thrown open, and many vessels, heretofore excluded, resorted thither for traffic.

The next important movement affecting the interests of New Netherland, was the establishment by charter, in 1621, of the

---

* Brodhead, N. Y., 60, *et seq.*

Dutch West India Company. The central power of this Association was divided, for the more efficient exercise of its functions, among five branches or chambers, located in the different cities of the Netherlands, the managers of which were styled Lords Directors. That of Amsterdam was the principal; and to it was assigned the management of affairs in New Netherland. The general supervision and government of the Company were lodged in an Assembly or College of nineteen delegates. This Company, with the approbation of the States-General, appointed the Director-General, and all other officers, civil, military, judicial and executive. "The profit and increase of trade" was its main object, although it was expected to promote colonization. Two years elapsed before the company was prepared to go into operation: the trade of New Netherland, however, was constantly increasing.

In 1623, thirty families were dispatched from Holland, and, upon entering Hudson River, eight men were left to take possession of Manhattan Island, and eighteen families were taken to the neighborhood of Albany. The remainder were sent to locate upon the Connecticut and Delaware rivers and the Wallabout. This was the first attempt at colonization.

In 1624, Cornelius Jacobsen May was appointed First Director of New Netherland, and, during his administration, Fort Orange, which had been commenced the year previous, was completed.

During 1625, forty-five new settlers were added to the population of New Netherland: but it was not till 1626 that any permanence was given to the colony at *Manhattan*. In this year Peter Minuit commenced his administration as Director-General, and a council of six individuals was appointed for the administration of affairs. The island, heretofore occupied by mere sufferance, was purchased from the natives for twenty-four dollars. Fort Amsterdam* was commenced near the Battery, and became the head-quarters of the Government: and religious services, in the absence of a regular clergyman, were commenced by the reading of the Scriptures and the Creed, by the Consolers of the Sick. This may be deemed the commencement of a city now unrivalled in the western world.

Compelled by the hostility of the neighboring Indians, the eight families now constituting the colony at Fort Orange, and the settlers on the Delaware, removed to Manhattan; so that, in 1628, the population of Manhattan amounted to two hundred and seventy. But serious causes operated to prevent the pros-

---

* This fort was between Whitehall and State streets, directly facing the Bowling Green. The "Government House" afterwards occupied this site.

perity of the colony. The Indians were unfriendly, difficulties existed between the colony and the settlements in New England and on the Delaware ; and the colonists received but little attention from the West India Company, in consequence of their commercial interest being involved in the war then existing between Holland and Spain. By the Charter of Privileges and Exemptions granted to the Patroons, in 1629, colonies were established beyond Manhattan, and the commerce of New Netherlands was prosperous, the imports, in 1632, amounting to $57,200 ; but the small community located in the vicinity of Fort Amsterdam, being principally engaged in agricultural pursuits, supported themselves, in the absence of supplies from the fatherland, with great difficulty.

Minuit, who was recalled in 1632, had done much for the advancement of trade, to which his attention had been chiefly directed ; but the affairs of the colony were far from possessing any considerable degree of stability. Several families of Manhattan returned with Minuit to Holland, and for twelve months the colony was left without a Director-General ; when the West India Company, learning that the English, who had for some years laid claim to the country, were making preparations to establish settlements in certain portions of the territory under their jurisdiction, sent over Wouter Van Twiller as Director-General, accompanied by one hundred and four soldiers ; the first military force in the colony. A certain degree of security against the encroachments of the Indians and English was now established ; prompt and energetic measures for the more efficient management of the internal affairs of the colony were adopted, and the individual interests and prosperity of the settlers were provided for ; all of which imparted an impetus which enabled the brave and industrious pioneers at Manhattan to overcome all the difficulties from within, and foes from without, with which for many years they were called to contend : and it is at this period we shall, in the subsequent chapter, take up the subject of the establishment of the *oldest school now in existence in America*.

CHAPTER II.

HISTORY OF THE SCHOOL FROM ITS ESTABLISHMENT, 1633, TO THE CAPITULATION, 1664; EMBRACING A PERIOD OF THIRTY-ONE YEARS.

In the "Historical Sketch" we have seen that the Dutch have long been distinguished for their interest in education. "Neither the perils of war, nor the busy pursuit of gain, nor the excitement of political strife, ever caused them to neglect the duty of educating their offspring. Schools were everywhere provided, *at the public expense*, with good schoolmasters, *to instruct the children of all classes* in the usual branches of education; and the Consistories of the churches took zealous care to have their youth thoroughly taught the Catechism and the Articles of Religion." *

Their national prosperity must be attributed, in no small degree, to their moral character; and when, in the course of Providence, they commenced the colonization of New Netherlands, the settlers, noted for their sterling virtues and adherence to the principles which they had embraced, not only brought with them and established, as far as the circumstances of a new colony rendered it practicable, the civil polity to which they had been accustomed, but had secured to them, by legal enactment, the institution of churches and schools.

The West India Company, with whom the work of colonization commenced, bound itself "to maintain good and fit preachers, schoolmasters and comforters of the sick." † "They recognized the authority of the Established Church of Holland over their colonial possessions: and the specific care of the transatlantic churches was early intrusted by the Synod of North Holland to the Classis of Amsterdam. By that body all the colonial clergy were approved and commissioned. For more than a century its ecclesiastical supremacy was affectionately acknowledged; and long after the capitulation of the province to England, the power of ordination to the ministry, in the American branch of the Reformed Dutch Church, remained in the governing Classis of Holland, or was exercised only by its special permission." ‡

* Brodhead, i. 462.   † O'Call. N. N., i. 220.   ‡ Brodhead, i. 614.

The establishment of schools, and the appointment of schoolmasters, rested conjointly with the Company and the Classis of Amsterdam : and it is from this circumstance that much relating to the early history of the school under consideration has been preserved.

When the special Charter of " Freedoms and Exemptions " was granted by the Company to the Patroons, for the purpose of agricultural colonization, they were not only obligated to satisfy the Indians for the lands upon which they should settle, but were to make prompt provision for the support of "a minister and schoolmaster, that thus the service of God and zeal for religion may not grow cool, and be neglected among them ; and that they do, for the first, procure a comforter of the sick there."* Thus religion and learning were encouraged ; and we find accordingly, in the early records, frequent references to the judicial support and maintenance of schools at Fort Orange, Flatbush, Fort Casimir, and other settlements. In the contract made with the Rev. Gideon Schaets, when engaged as minister at Rensselaerswyck, he was required, among other duties, "To use all Christian zeal there to bring up *both the heathens and their children* in the Christian religion. To teach also the *Catechism* there, and instruct the people in the Holy Scriptures, and to pay attention to the office of *schoolmaster* for old and young. And, further, to do everything fitting and becoming a public, honest, and holy teacher, for the advancement of divine service and church exercise among the young and old. And in case he should take any of the heathen children to educate, he was to be indemnified therefor as the Commissioners shall think proper." † This is not the only instance where public provision was made by our ancestors for the education of all classes, including even the children of the natives.

The course most commonly pursued, when a colony was to be established, was to have a schoolmaster accompany the settlers, and, to a certain extent, conduct religious services. After habitations were erected, and the settlement had assumed a warrantable degree of stability, it was provided with a minister. A settlement on the Delaware furnishes a case in point. Settlers were encouraged to proceed to New Amstel by certain conditions, thirty-five in number, the seventh of which was, "The city of Amsterdam shall send thither a proper person for *schoolmaster*, who shall *also read the Holy Scriptures in public, and set the Psalms.*" The eighth article stipulated, "The city of Amsterdam shall also provide, as soon as convenient, for the said school-

---

* *Vide* Charter of " Privileges and Exemptions." O'Call. N. N. i. 119.
† O'Call. N. N. ii. 567.

master." When the population should amount to two hundred, a minister and Consistory were to be appointed. Accordingly, about one hundred and sixty-seven colonists embarked, accompanied by "*Evert Pietersen*, who had been approved, *after examination before the Classis*, as schoolmaster and Zieken-trooster," " to read God's Word, and lead in singing." Notwithstanding disasters at sea, the colony was soon organized under auspices favorable to its prosperity.

"Under date of Aug. 10, 1657, Evert Pietersen, Comforter of the Sick and Schoolmaster in the Colonie established by the city of Amsterdam, on the South (Delaware) River, in New Netherlands," writes to the Commissioners of the Colonie :

"IN FORT AMSTEL, ON THE SOUTH RIVER, N. N.
"We arrived here on the 25th of April. I find twenty families, mostly Swedes, not more than five or six families belonging to our nation. I already begin to keep school, and have twenty-five children, &c., &c.
"Your Honors' most obedient servant,
"EVERT PIETERSEN."*

"The religious instruction of the colonists was superintended by Pietersen," until the arrival, a few months afterwards, of Dominie Everardus Welius, accompanied by about four hundred new emigrants. A church was immediately organized, and two elders were appointed, with "Pietersen as fore-singer, Zieken-trooster, and Deacon," with a colleague. The colony seemed very prosperous, and was augmented by thirty families from Manhattan.†

Creditable in the extreme was this determination of the Dutch to transplant in the New World those institutions which had long been the pride of their native land ; and, notwithstanding the many and formidable difficulties with which these had to contend in those troublous and perilous times, their influence in the community has not yet ceased.

Would that the Dutch descendants of the present generation, the recipients of a noble inheritance, and participants of its resultant blessings, were as ardently attached to these institutions, and as zealous as were their forefathers in sustaining and extending them !

1626.—On the settlement of Manhattan, we find nearly the same course pursued as in the case of New Amstel. When a colonial government was organized, 1626, by Minuit, the first Director-General, we find the place of a clergyman supplied, to a certain extent, by Sebastian Jans Crol, and Jan Huyck, two " Krank-besoeckers," " Zieken-troosters," or " Comforters of the Sick," whom they were to visit and pray with. It was their espe-

* Holland Doc., ii. 17.   † Brod. N. Y., i. 631 633.

cial duty to read to the people, on the Sabbath, "some texts out of the Scriptures, together with the Creeds." "François Molemaecker was at the same time employed in building a horse-mill, with a spacious room above to accommodate a large congregation ; and a tower was also to be erected in which the bells brought from Porto Rico were intended to be hung." *

Thus, coeval with the arrival of the first organized body of colonists we have the introduction of public religious services ; the settlers being exclusively from Holland, and of the Reformed religion.

Exigency of circumstances, in a new settlement, sometimes demanded that the exercise of the functions pertaining to the offices of the minister, the schoolmaster, and the Krank-besoecker, devolved upon the same individual ; so that we might with propriety be justified in claiming the introduction of public education as early as 1626 ; but as the term schoolmaster is not expressly applied to either of the Krank-besoeckers, we will waive the position. It will be observed, however, that this peculiarity of the Reformed Church was introduced into Manhattan previous to any legal enactment of requirement, as it was not until 1629 that the condition was imposed of appointing a "comforter."

1633.— In April (prior to the 12th †), 1633, Wouter Van Twiller arrived at Manhattan, as the second Director-General of New Netherlands. In the enumeration of the Company's officials of the same year, Everardus Bogardus is mentioned as officiating as minister at Fort Amsterdam, and ADAM ROELANTSEN as the *first* schoolmaster. ‡

Here, then, in accordance with the custom of the age, the usage of the home Government, and by charter stipulations, we have the introduction of the first schoolmaster in Manhattan, establishing, as the sequel will prove, the foundation of an institution which the Church has never lost sight of ; and although it is probable that at times the school was kept somewhat irregularly, owing to the unsettled state of affairs arising from Indian depredations, and the hostile attitude and aggressions of the colonists in New England, yet the records furnish direct and indisputable evidence of the efforts made for its support and continuance.

* Memoir on the Colonization of New Netherlands, by J. R. Brodhead, Esq.; collected from "Wassenaar's Historiche Verhael" (Amst. 1621-1632). "The Creed is still read in the churches in Holland by the 'Voorleezers' or clerks, from the 'Doop-huysje' or baptistery, under the pulpit. Until a recent period this custom was kept up in the Reformed Dutch churches in this country." N. Y. H. S. Coll., ii. 363. Brod. N. Y., i. 165. Doc. Hist. N. Y., iii. 42.

† O'Call. N. N., i. 141-143. ‡ Alb. Rec., i. 52.

On the arrival of Van Twiller, he found affairs in a sad condition, the colony having been for a year without an executive officer. "Fort Amsterdam, now dilapidated, was repaired. A guard-house and barrack for the newly arrived soldiers were constructed within the fort ; three windmills were erected ; brick and frame houses were built for the Director and his officers ; small houses were constructed for the corporal, the smith, the cooper and the midwife ; and the 'upper room' in the mill, in which the people had worshipped since 1626, was replaced by a plain wooden building, *the first church edifice of New Netherlands*, situate on the East River, in what is now Broad Street, between Pearl and Bridge Streets ;"* and near this "Oude Kerck," in Whitehall Street, near Bridge, a dwelling-house and stable were erected for the use of the Dominie.†

In an extended list of the officers and servants of the Dutch West India Company, in 1638, Rev. Everardus Bogardus is again mentioned as minister at Fort Amsterdam, *where* Adam Roelantsen was still the schoolmaster.‡ Roelantsen is mentioned also as having a lawsuit this year with one Jan Jansen ; and also as testifying in another suit, at the request of Rev. E. Bogardus.§ The following year he resigned his charge and left the colony, as in the list of settlers arrived in Rensselaerswyck, in 1639, we find the name of "Adam Roelantsen Van Hamelwaard, previously schoolmaster at New Amsterdam."‖ Roelantsen was born about 1606, and was consequently twenty-seven years of age on his arrival at New Amsterdam, where he married a widow.

His stay in Rensselaerswyck was less than two years, for in 1641 he is again in New Amsterdam. On the 22d of June of that year he had a daughter (Tryntje) baptized. While officiating as schoolmaster he resided in the outskirts of the settlement, adjoining or in close proximity to the farm of Jan Damen, the south side of which bordered along Wall Street. This is inferred from complaints made by Roelantsen that Damen's cattle trespassed on his premises.

February 7, 1642, the following agreement was entered into between Adam Roelantsen, from Dockum (a city in Northern Holland), on one side, and John Teunison, carpenter, on the other, respecting the building of a house for said Roelantsen. This was on the north side of Stone Street (then a mere road and unpaved), between Whitehall and Broad streets, and next door but one to the brewery of the celebrated magistrate, Oloff Stevensen Van Cortland. His garden had a frontage of one hundred feet.

---

* Now known as 100 Broad Street. Alb. Rec., x. 335. Benson's Hist. Mem., 42. O'Call. N. N., i. 155. † Val. Man.Com. Coun., 1853, 427 *et seq.*
‡ Alb. Rec., ii. 13-15. § *Ibid.*, i. 43. ‖ O'Call. N. N., i. 438.

The following is a translation of the contract:

John Teunison agrees to build the same of the following dimensions: In length thirty feet, in width eighteen feet, in height eight feet; the beams to be hewn at four sides, the house to be well and tight clapboarded, and roofed with substantial reeden thatch; the floors tight and made of clapboard; two doors, one entry, a pantry, a bedstead, a staircase to go to the garret; the upper part of the chimneys to be of wood; one mantelpiece; the entry to be three feet wide, with a partition. The house to be ready by 1st of May next. All for the sum of three hundred and fifty guilders ($140), to be paid by Roelantsen, one half when the timber is on the ground and the other half when the building is finished.*

In 1643 he was "weighmaster," and purchased a lot for a house and garden.† February 3, 1644, he had a son (Daniel) baptized. After the death of his wife, who left four small children, he went to Holland, July, 1646, returned in November, and in December sold his house to Govert Aertsen.‡ In 1647 he was appointed Provost, and in 1653 was a member of the Burgher Corps of New Amsterdam.§ Subsequent to the latter date neither his name nor that of his descendants is found in the Records.

A successor to Roelantsen was found in Jan Stevensen, *schoolmaster*, to whom the West India Company granted the patent of a lot north of Fort Amsterdam, for a house and garden. ‖ March 9, 1646, shortly after the death of Mrs. Roelantsen, who left four young children, "on application of the Fiscal, Philip Geraedy, Hans Kierstede, Jan Stevensen, *schoolmaster*, and Oloff Stevensen (van Cortland) were appointed curators of the estate and children of Lyntje Martens, late wife of Adam Roelantsen.¶

In 1642, the church on Broad Street having become somewhat dilapidated and reproachful in appearance, an effort was made to procure a new one, and at the same time was commenced the laudable undertaking of *building a school-house* with suitable accommodations. The Vertoogh, after mentioning the efforts made to raise subscriptions for building a new church,

---

* Val. Man., 1863, p. 560. † Reg. Deeds, N. A., 134.
‡ Val. Man., 1863, p. 560. § O'Call. N. N., ii. 569. Alb. Rec., viii.
‖ Cal. Dutch MSS., p. 367. In a map exhibiting the original grants of village lots from the Dutch West India Company to the inhabitants of New Amsterdam, below the present line of Wall Street (Val. Man., 1857), this lot is located at the north-west corner of the "Heere Straat," now Broadway and Morris Street. The dimensions were ten rods and nine feet on Broadway, and extended twelve rods and eight feet towards the river. Immediately adjoining on the north was the Old Church Yard, the first in the city. To the west of these was a parcel of land belonging to Dominie S. Drisius. Upon the land on the map above mentioned is inscribed "Jan Stevensen, schoolmaster, 1643." Andries Hudde, a private schoolmaster quite noted in his day, purchased a lot the same year on the east side of Broadway, about 150 feet south of Exchange Place. His name and date only appear on the map, and not the distinctive term "schoolmaster," which in this and in several other instances was used only when the official schoolmaster was referred to.
¶ Cal. Dutch MSS., p. 99.

adds : " 'The bowl has been going round a long time, for the purpose of collecting money for erecting a *school-house ;* and it has been built with words ; for, as yet, the first stone is not laid ; some materials only are provided. The money, nevertheless, given for the purpose, has all found its way out, and is mostly spent.' The church, however, was commenced in the Fort, by John and Richard Ogden. It was to be built of stone, seventy-two feet long, fifty-two broad, and sixteen over the ground. Joachim Pietersen Kuyter was elected deacon, and with Jan Dam, Captain De Vries, and Director Kieft, formed the *first Consistory* to superintend its erection."* " But in 1646 the church was still unfinished, as the Director-General, being distressed for money, had applied to his own use the funds appropriated ; and, from the same cause, the laudable undertaking of erecting a school-house had failed."†

But New Amsterdam had, indeed, been experiencing troublous times. " Even the poor-fund of the deaconry was sequestered, and applied to the purposes of war." Parties of Indians roved about, day and night, over Manhattan Island, killing the Dutch not a thousand paces from Fort Amsterdam ; and no one dared "to move a foot to fetch a stick of fire-wood without a strong escort." " The mechanics who plied their trades were ranged under the walls of the fort ; all others were exposed to the incursions of the savages." For the protection of the few cattle which remained to the decimated population, "a good solid fence" was ordered to be erected nearly on the site of the present Wall Street. The authorities write : "Our fields lie fallow and waste ; our dwellings and other buildings are burnt. We are burthened with heavy families ; we have no means to provide necessaries for wives or children ; and we sit here amidst thousands of Indians and barbarians, from whom we find neither peace nor mercy." " At Manhattan, and in its neighborhood, scarcely one hundred men, besides traders, could be found." Such being the state of affairs, it is not surprising that the church was unfinished, and the school-house not commenced ; for the money which the impoverished commonalty had contributed to build the school-house had "all found its way out, and was expended for the troops." ‡ Yet, notwithstanding these difficulties, the subject was not forgotten.

1647.—In the following year, 1647, a new feature was introduced in the government of New Amsterdam by the appointment of *Nine Men.* The introduction of this description of tribunal furnishes an additional proof that Holland was the source whence

* Van Der Donck's Vertoogh. ii. N. Y. H. S. Coll., vii. 294. O'Call., i. 260.
† O'Call., i. 395, 396. ‡ Brod. N. Y., i. 397, 374, 392, 398, 410.

New Netherland derived its municipal institutions, and shows how strongly its settlers were attached to those freedoms with which they were so familiar in their fatherland.

The Director and Council, desirous "that the government of New Amsterdam might continue and increase in good order, justice, police, population, prosperity, and mutual harmony, and be provided with strong fortifications, a church, a school, &c.," permitted the inhabitants to nominate eighteen of the most notable, reasonable, honest and respectable citizens, from whom the Director and Council selected nine, "as is customary in Fatherland." *

These *Nine Men* were the Representatives of the people. They were consulted in all matters of importance, were invested with limited judiciary powers, and those who appealed from their decision subjected themselves to a fine. On the organization of this body, Director Stuyvesant, who this year superseded Kieft, called their special attention, November 11, 1647, among other things, "to the condition of the fort and of the church, and to the state of public education ;" informing them that, "owing to the want of proper accommodations, no school had been held for three months." Subsequently, November 14, "he consented to defray, on behalf of the Company, a portion of the expenses necessary for the encouragement of education, and to continue such assistance in future, to 'promote the glorious work.'" "Meanwhile, he informed them that a convenient place for a school-house and dwelling for the schoolmaster would be provided for the winter, either in one of the outhouses of the Fiscaal's department, or any other suitable place that the *Deacons* of the church might approve." "The arrangements for completing the church, and for fostering the school, met with no objection." A plan, however, which he had proposed for repairing the fort was condemned by them. †

It will be observed that when a school is spoken of under the Dutch administration, special reference is invariably made to the official public school, supported by the authorities, and in connection with the Established Church, the schoolmasters whereof were appointed by the West India Company. From the first organization of the school till the year 1808, when a special *Board of Trustees* was appointed, the supervision and management of the school were in the hands of the *deacons ;* hence the reference made to them above.

No private school teachers, as will hereafter be shown, could follow their calling without a license from the civil and ecclesiastical authorities.

The Records furnish the names of some such in the city at

* O'Call. N. N., ii. 37.' † O'Call. N. N., ii. 41, 42.

this period,* but the provision made above is for a school-house and dwelling for the schoolmaster, *under the direction of the deacons;* and, furthermore, the statement that, for want "of proper accommodations, no school had been held for three months," must have reference to the public school in connection with the church, of which Jan Stevensen was then master, and for whom the dwelling (above alluded to) was intended.

July 20, 1647, a Power of Attorney was given by Jan Stevensen, *schoolmaster,* to Luycas Smith, to receive certain moneys from the West India Company at Amsterdam.†

August 13, 1648, a similar Power was given by Jan Willemsen Schut to Jan Stevensen, *schoolmaster,* to receive money due him by the W. I. Co. at Amsterdam.‡ He was then on the eve of his departure for Holland, and as the schoolmaster always "read the Holy Scriptures in public and set the Psalms," temporary provision was made for filling the latter office, as follows:

26 OCTOBER, AO. 1648.—Ter vergaderinge is hooghnoodigh geacht in plaets van Jan Stevensen voorsanger (fore-singer) een ander bequaem persoon te stellen. Soo ist dat voor deesen jegenwoordigen tijt opt Eijlant Manhatans geen bequaemer persoon als Pieter van der Linden hebben connen tot het selve voorleesers (fore-reader) ampt uijt vinden, hebben oversulx denselven Pieter van der Linden als voorleeser aengenomen, ende daer voor jaerlijex toegeleijt ƒ.150, jaerly en dat ter tijt een ander bequaem persoon uyt Holland mocht gesonden worden.§

TRANSLATION.

26 OCTOBER, 1648. At the meeting it was considered highly expedient, instead of Jan Stevensen, fore-singer, to appoint another able person. So it is, that at this present time, no better person could be found upon the Island of Manhatans than Pieter van der Linden to fulfil the post as fore-reader, and have, in consequence thereof, appointed said Pieter van der Linden, with an annual income of ƒ.150 (guilders), until another suitable person might be sent from Holland. ||

August 13, 1649.—"Jan Stevensen, *late Schoolmaster at New Amsterdam,* sold a house and garden north of the fort."¶

The successor of Jan Stevensen was Jan Cornelissen.

1649.—In the year 1649 serious difficulties arose between the Nine Men, on one part, and the Director-General and his Council, in consequence of which a delegation from the Nine Men, at the head of which was Adriaen van der Donck, the President of that body, proceeded to the Hague (October), and laid before

* N. Am. Rec., 102.   Alb. Rec., i. v. 31.   † Cal. Dutch MSS., p. 38.
‡ Cal. Dutch MSS., p. 42.
§ Vol. iv. p. 420 of original Dutch MSS. in Department of Historical Records, Albany.
|| Peter van der Linden and wife arrived at Manhattan, 1639. He was a surgeon and quite a prominent man in the colony. He was the owner of considerable real estate. In 1647 he sold his plantation on Manhattan Island, 't Oude Vraack Kill, and extending along the East River 300 paces. Records of Collegiate R. D. Church, pp. 7, 11, 41, 365.
¶ Cal. Dutch MSS., p. 48.

the States-General a remonstrance, known as the Vertoogh, in which they complain of many grievances existing in the administration at New Amsterdam. Speaking of the Church, they say: "As for its revenue, we know of none. No pains were taken by the Director to create any. There has been a good deal said about the building of a school-house, but, as yet, the first stone is not laid. The funds collected for this object have been misapplied. No provision has been made for the poor, who had to depend entirely on the congregation and a few fines and offerings. But the greater part of the sacred fund had found its way into the Company's hands, on interest, it was pretended, but, as yet, neither principal nor interest was forthcoming. Furthermore, they desire that the school be provided with at least *two* good schoolmasters, so that the youth may be instructed and trained, not only in reading and writing, but also in the knowledge and fear of the Lord." *

Cornelius Van Tienhoven, the Schout or Sheriff of New Amsterdam, proceeded to the Hague and presented a reply to the Vertoogh, November, 1650, and in answer to the above says: "It is true the new school-house has not been built; but this was not the fault of the Director, who is busy collecting materials, but of the churchwardens (or deacons) who had charge of the funds, provided in part by the commonalty and in part by subscriptions." In the meanwhile, *Jan Cornelissen had kept the school*, a place for which had been provided; and then immediately adds: "*Other* teachers† keep school in hired houses, so that the youth are furnished with the means of education," although there is, as yet, no Latin School or Academy. "If," he adds, "the remonstrants be such friends to religion and education as they pretend, let them be leaders in a subscription to such laudable undertakings, and not complain as they did when asked to contribute for the church and school-house."‡

The same year, Dominie Backerus, who had succeeded Bogardus in 1647, by the permission of the Classis, took leave of the Church at Manhattan, with the intention of returning to Holland. Jan Cornelissen, the third master mentioned in connection with the public school under the care of the Church, having signified his intention to resign his situation, Stuyvesant embraced the opportunity of the Dominie's return to write earnestly to the Classis of Amsterdam "for a pious, well qualified, and diligent schoolmaster." "Nothing," he adds, "is of greater importance than the right, early instruction of youth."§

* Hol. Doc., iv. O'Call. N. Y., ii. 114, 120.
† *Vide* N. Am. Rec., v. 31, 150, 169, for names of private schoolmasters from 1643 to 1649.
‡ ii. N. Y. Hist. Soc. Col., ii. 331. O'Call., ii. 123, 126.
§ Cor. Cl. Am. Brod., i. 508.

Subsequent to the departure of Backerus, Dominie Megapolensis arrived in Manhattan, on his way from Rensselaerswyck to Holland, whither his wife had already returned. The Church being vacant, he was solicited by Stuyvesant to remain, as children were every Sunday presented for baptism, "sometimes one, sometimes two, yea, sometimes three and four together." The Dominie being prevailed on to stay, was formally installed.*

1650.— Jacob Pergens and S. Ryckaerts, Directors of the West India Company, in reply to Stuyvesant's letter, state : "We will make use of the first opportunity to supply you with a well-instructed schoolmaster, and shall inform ourselves about the person living at Harlem, whom your Honor recommended." †

The Committee of the States-General, to whom the remonstrance above spoken of was referred, accorded, in 1650, a Provisional Order for the Government of New Netherland, in which they direct that three new ministers shall be called and supported —one for Rensselaerswyck, one for distant parts of the country, and one in and around New Amsterdam — and the youth were to be instructed by good schoolmasters. We accordingly find that the Rev. Samuel Drisius was sent out to assist "that worthy old servant, the Rev. Megapolensis." ‡

In the same year, February 16, Pergens and Ryckaerts again write to the Director-General, and say : "We appoint, at your request, a schoolmaster, who shall also act as Comforter of the Sick. He is considered an honest and pious man, and shall embark the first opportunity." §

In a subsequent letter, April 15, they write : "The schoolmaster that had been sent for came over with the wife of Rev. Megapolensis," || on her return from Holland to Manhattan, where her husband had been induced to remain.

The Classis of Amsterdam, anxious to promote the cause of education and religion in New Netherland, now (January 10) sent out William Verstius, "a good, God-fearing man," as "Ziekentrooster," or Consoler of the Sick, and Schoolmaster at Manhattan. ¶

In 1654 he petitioned the Classis of Amsterdam for an increase of salary.**

1655.— January 26, "William Verstius, Schoolmaster and Chorister in this city, solicited the Council by a petition, as he had completed his service ; and whereas there were now several persons fully competent to acquit themselves in this charge, that he might be favored with his dismission, and permitted to return to Holland in the first ship." On which petition was given the

* Brod. N. Y., i. 508.   † Alb. Rec., iv. 17.   ‡ O'Call. N. N., ii. 134, 191.
§ Alb. Rec., iv. 23. || Ibid., iv. 30.   ¶ Brod., i. 516.
** Cor. Cl. Am., 1654.

apostil, that it would be communicated to the Consistory and Ministers.* His request was granted and a successor appointed, as appears from the following minute :

<small>Whereas, William Verstius, *Chorister and Scholmaster of this city*, hath several times earnestly solicited leave to depart for the Fatherland, so is his request granted him ; and in consequence thereof have the Noble Lords of the Supreme Council, with the *consent* of the respected Consistory of this city, appointed Harmanus Van Hoboocken as Chorister and Schoolmaster of this city, at $g.35$ per month, and $g.100$ annual expenditures ; who promises to conduct himself industriously and faithfully, pursuant to the instructions already given, or hereafter to be given.

Done in Am. N. Neth. 23 March, 1655.
(Signed)   NICASIUS DE SILLE,
La Montagne.†</small>

The appointment of Verstius by the West India Company : his office as Krank-besoecker ; his petition to Classis for a rise of salary, and his formal dismissal by the Council, denote him as the (fourth) teacher of the Reformed Dutch Church School. ‡

1652.—The Vertoogh of 1649 having eventuated in a provisional Order of Government for New Netherland, and to the consequent adoption of such measures as were deemed essential to the promotion of its best interests ; and as among these was reckoned the advancement of religion and education, the vacant churches were supplied with ministers, and a second public school established, in accordance with the desire of the remonstrants, that "at least *two* good schoolmasters may be provided, so that the youth may be instructed and trained, not only in reading and writing, but also in the knowledge and fear of the Lord." §

A seeming necessity existed for this, in the fact that New Amsterdam contained at that time a population of seven or eight hundred souls ; || and, as the result of correspondence between the Director-General and the Company, as to the selection of a teacher, and a suitable place for holding the school, the Directors of the West India Company, April 4, 1652, wrote to Stuyvesant :

<small>* Alb. Rec., x. 6.   † Alb. Rec., x. 29, 30 ; xx. 4, 133.
‡ There were others in the city at this time engaged in teaching private schools. These were licensed by the Council ; and in consequence of the connection between the Church and Government, its sanction was necessary. On the application of Andries Hudde for a license to keep school, the Director and Council informed him that they would first *ask the opinion of the Ministers and the Consistory*. One Jacob Van Corler having arrogated to himself to keep school, is directed to apply for a license, which he did repeatedly, and finally received as answer, "*Nihil actum.*" Permission was granted by the Council for Jan Lubherts to teach reading, writing and arithmetic, "provided he conducted himself as such a person ought to do," and so of others.   Alb. Rec., ix. 304.   N. Am. Rec.
§ *Ante*, p. 21.   Brod. N. Y., i. 548.</small>

"We recommend to you Jan De La Montagne, whom we have provisionally favored with the appointment. Your Honor may appropriate the City Tavern for this purpose, if this is practicable." A few weeks subsequently, they wrote to the Director and Council : "John Montagne is appointed schoolmaster, with a salary of 250 guilders."*

Under the head of "Churches and Clergymen," which sufficiently identifies the school with the Church, we find the following : "On the petition of John Morice De La Montagne, the Director-General and Council command the Comptroller to pay the supplicant three or four months of his wages."†

* Alb. Rec., iv. 68. The City Tavern, subsequently named the Stadt Huys or City Hall, stood on the corner of Pearl Street and Coenties Alley. This spot was occupied in 1775 by Brinckerhoff & Van Wyck ; in 1806 by Abraham Brinckerhoff, and in 1825 by his heirs. Moulton, i. 27. The present site is known as 71 and 73 Pearl Street. For view and description of this ancient edifice, *vide* Val. Man. Com. Coun.. 1852, pp. 378, 403.

† Alb. Rec., vi. 49. While Montagne, as an official schoolmaster, was remunerated from the Government funds, we have Joost Carelse, Adriaen Van Ilpendam, and others, instituting law-suits against individuals, for the payment of tuition in beavers and shillings.—Alb. Rec., x. N. Am. Rec.

The following reminiscences, illustrative of things *as they were*, are deemed worthy of insertion. The quaint and elliptical language in which the latter is given, is characteristic of the author, Judge Benson. In his memoir, read before the New York Historical Society in 1816, speaking of John De La Montagne, ordinarily pronounced, Jan Montagne, sexton of the old Dutch church in Garden Street, he says : "I saw him at the house of my parents ; I in my earliest youth, he approaching to fourscore. He was on his way to collect the Dominie's gelt : for the Dutch always took care the stipend to the minister should be competent, that so he never might be straitened ' to desire a gift.' He told me his father and grandfather before him (the names of all these individuals may be found in the old Directories), the latter probably the same as mentioned in the records, ' Jan De La Montagne, Schoolmaster, with 250 guilders salary,' had been the sexton of the congregation ; so that, as I have it from the relation of others, the successive incumbents, having been as well of the same Christian as surname, the name had, as it were, become the name of the office, like Den Keyser, the Cæsar, the Emperor ; and, accordingly, when the English, having built a church, had also a sexton, the Dutch children, and not impossible some adults, called him, ' De Engelishe Jan Montagne.' He told me his grandfather was the sexton when the church was within the fort. On his (the third Jan's) death, the Consistory appointed his son Jan, who remained sexton till the dispersion of the congregation on the invasion of the city, 1776."

The Judge records also the following : "There was a day always kept here by the Dutch, and the keeping of it delegated by the mothers to their daughters, still at school. Vrouwen Dagh, Woman's Day ; the same with the Valentine's Day of the English, and although differently, still, perhaps, not less salutarily kept. Every mother's daughter, furnished with a piece of cord, the size neither too large nor too small ; the twist neither too hard nor too loose ; a turn round the hand, and then a sufficient length left to serve as a lash ; not fair to have a knot at the end of it, but fair to practice for a few days to acquire the *sleight ;* the law held otherwise, duelling. On the morning of the day, the youngster never venturing to turn a corner without first listening whether

The fact that this second school was commenced and carried on for a brief period is clearly established : but the absence of any subsequent reference to it, leads to the strong inference that its existence was of short duration. The principal school, however, was uninterruptedly conducted by Verstius, from 1650 to 1655.

In 1653, New Amsterdam was incorporated with municipal privileges ; and a court of justice, similar to that of Amsterdam in Holland, consisting of a schout, burgomasters and schepens was instituted. Director Stuyvesant relinquished to the burgomasters the excise license* on condition that they paid out of it the salaries of the Ecclesiastique, to wit : one of the ministers (Megapolensis or Drisius), *one precentor, beadle, or schoolmaster*, and one dog-whipper, now called sexton ; and of the Polity, to wit : the Schout, both the Burgomasters, the five Schepens, the Secretary, and the Court Messenger.†

1654.—The following year, 1654, the Director and Council re-claimed the excise, "inasmuch as the burgomasters had failed to pay the clergyman and schoolmaster or beadle." ‡

This presents another valid proof of the connection existing between the school and the Church. "The schoolmaster was always, *ex-officio*, clerk or beadle, chorister, and visitor of the sick."§

1655-56.—We have recorded the supersedure of Verstius in 1655, by Harmanus Van Hoboocken. The following spring, 1656, the first survey of the city was made, and it was ascertained to possess 120 houses and 1,000 souls ; and "the number of children at the public school having greatly increased, further accommodation was allowed to Van Hoboocken, the school-

---

no warblers were behind it, no golden apples to divert him from the direct course in this race. Schoolboy Hippomenes espied, pursued by Charmer Atalanta ; he, encumbered with his satchel, still striving to outrun, and, to add to his speed, bending forward, thereby giving the requisite roundness to the space between the shoulders ; she, too swift afoot for him, and overtaking him, and three or four strokes briskly and smartly laid on ; he, to avoid a further repetition, stopping and turning ; she, looking him steadfast in the eye, and perceiving it required all the man in him to keep back the tear ; not all the fruit in all the orchards of the Hesperides, and in their best bearing year, to compensate for the exultation of the little heart for the moment.

"The boys requested the next day should be theirs, and be called MANNEN DAGH, *Man's Day ;* but my masters were told, the law would thereby defeat its own very purpose, which was, that they should, at an age and in a way most likely never to forget it, receive the lesson of MANLINESS, *he is never to* STRIKE."

This privilege has been neglected for such a length of time that perhaps it is never again to be recovered.—Ben. Mem., 41.

* This was the first revenue in the treasury of New Amsterdam.—Paulding, 34.   † Val. Man. Com. Coun., 1848, p. 377. O'Call. N. N., ii. 269.
‡ O'Call., ii. 270.   § Watson's Annals, 166.

master."* His school-house having been burned partly down, he addressed the following application to the city magistrates:

"*To the Heeren Burgomasters and Schepens of the City of New Amsterdam:*
"The reverential request of Harmanus Van Hoboocken, schoolmaster of this city, is, that he may be allowed the use of the hall and side-chamber of the City Hall, for the use of his school and as a residence for his family, inasmuch as he, petitioner, has no place to keep school in, or to live in during the winter, it being necessary that the rooms should be made warm, which cannot be done in his own house, from its unfitness. The petitioner further represents that he is burthened with a wife and children, ... so that he is much at a loss how to make accommodation for his family and school-children. The petitioner, therefore, asks that he may use the chamber wherein Gouert Coerten at present dwells. Expecting a favorable answer,
HARM. VAN HOBOOCKEN.†

The reply of the burgomasters to this petition was as follows:

Whereas the room which petitioner asks for his use as a dwelling and school-room is out of repair, and moreover is wanted for other uses, it cannot be allowed to him. But, as the town youth are doing so uncommon well now, it is thought proper to find a convenient place for their accommodation, and, for that purpose petitioner is granted one hundred guilders yearly.
4th *Sept.*, 1656.‡

The burning of the school-house, while the youth were "doing so uncommon well," led to the revival of the question of procuring a suitable edifice; and the magistrates of the city, writing the 7th of the following November to the West India Company, "assert that the only revenue to the city was that arising from the excise of wines and beers, and that this was needed for immediate expenses in repairing the city wall, the Schoeyinge, the City Hall, the watch apartments, *the building of the school-house*, and for several other improvements, and ask thereon the advice of the Company."§ It is not known what answer was returned to this application, but one thing is certain: the condition of the city finances was such, "the old debt made in the time of the English troubles being yet unliquidated," that the school-house was not built.

During the winter of 1658–59, the colony at New Amstel, on the Delaware, experienced great distress. The crops having failed, famine and epidemic fever, induced by the nature of the soil, nearly decimated the population. Among those who fell victims to the prevailing disease, were the surgeon, the commissary, the Director's wife, and six of his household, and the good Dominie Welius. The Director himself died also. In the

---

* O'Call., ii. 540. Brod., i. 623. † Paulding, N. Am. 40.
‡ Paulding, N. Am. 41.
§ Paulding, N. Am. 41. It was in this year that streets were first regulated. The first *tax list* was made out in 1655, to defray the expense of fortifying the city.

midst of these calamities, information was received from Maryland that Lord Baltimore was about to extend his jurisdiction over their territory. This added to the consternation, and many of the settlers sought safety elsewhere, so that in a few months, famine, sickness and desertion had reduced the population from over 600 persons to less than thirty families.* Several of those who left the colony came to New Amsterdam, and among them was EVERT PIETERSEN, who from the first had been their schoolmaster (p. 14). Here he was employed by the Director-General either as a colleague with *Van Hoboocken*, or as his *locum tenens*, while he was disqualified from teaching by sickness.

The period of Pietersen's engagement is not definitely known; but on his return to Holland he petitioned the West India Company for a permanent engagement, the Director-General and magistrates recommending his re-appointment.

The Directors of the Company wrote to Stuyvesant (1660), "We will consider the petition of Mr. Evert Pietersen, *late* schoolmaster and chorister in the colony of the city, to be employed *again* in the Company's service, and return thither with his wife, and inquire about his character, conduct, and abilities, when we shall communicate the result to your honor."†

Subsequently, the following letter, dated May, 1661, was received by Governor Stuyvesant:

The Directors of the West India Company, department of Amsterdam, to the honorable, prudent, beloved, trusty Petrus Stuyvesant, Director-General and Council, make known:

Whereas we have deemed it necessary to promote religious worship, and to read to the inhabitants the Word of God, to exhort them, to lead them in the ways of the Lord, and console the sick, that an expert person was sent to New Netherland in the city of New Amsterdam, who at the same time should act there as *Chorister* and *Schoolmaster;* so is it, that we, upon the good report which we have received about the person of EVERT PIETERSEN, and confiding in his abilities and experience in the aforesaid services, together on his pious character and virtues, have, on your Honor's recommendation, and that of the magistrates of the city of New Amsterdam, appointed the aforesaid person as *Consoler of the Sick, Chorister* and *Schoolmaster* at New Amsterdam in New Netherlands, which charge he shall fulfil there, and conduct himself in these with all diligence and faithfulness; so as we expect that he shall give others a good example, so as it becomes a pious and good *Consoler, Clerk, Chorister* and *Schoolmaster;* regulating himself in conformity to the *instructions which he received here from the Consistory*, and principally to the instructions which he received from us, which he shall execute in every point faithfully; wherefore, we command all persons, without distinction, to acknowledge the aforesaid Evert Pieterson as *Consoler, Clerk, Chorister* and *Schoolmaster* in New Amsterdam in New Netherlands, and not to molest, disturb or ridicule him in any of these offices, but rather to offer him every assistance in their

* O'Call. N. N., ii. 374-388. Brod. N. Y., 652 *et passim.*
† Alb. Rec., iv. 364.

power, and deliver him from every painful sensation, by which the will of the Lord and our good intentions shall be accomplished.

Done by the Department of Amsterdam, on the 2d of May, XVIe and sixty-one.

(Signed), ABRAM WILMERDONCX.
By order of him,
LOWER STOOD. C. VAN SEVENTER.*

In a few days another letter from the same source, dated May 9, 1661, was received, in which Pietersen's salary is fixed, and instructions given with respect to the books he would need as Krank-besoecker.

Honorable, prudent, beloved Trustees :

Our last was of the 11th of April, by the way of Curaçoa, of which we now have enclosed the duplicate ; since which period nothing has occurred here of consequence—*i. e.*, which deserves to be mentioned—as only, that we have engaged, on your Honor's recommendation and that of the magistrates of the city of New Amsterdam, Mr Evert Pietersen as schoolmaster and clerk, upon a salary of *g.*36 per month [$15], and *g.*125 [$52 +] annually for his board, who is now embarked in the ship the *Gilded Beaver*,† but not with his wife, whose indisposition, as he said, prevented her departure. And whereas he solicited to be supplied with some books and stationery, which would be of service to him in that station, so did we resolve to send you a sufficient quantity of these articles, as your honor may see from the invoice. Your honor ought not to place all these at his disposal at once, but from time to time, when he may be in want of these, when his account ought directly to be charged with its amount ; so, too, he must be charged with all such books of which he may be in want as a consoler of the sick, which he might have obtained from your Honor, which afterwards might be reimbursed to him, whenever he, ceasing to serve in that capacity, might return these ; all this must be valued at the invoice price.‡

This correspondence establishes Evert Pietersen as the seventh schoolmaster of the Reformed Dutch Church school.

1660–1661.—Governor Stuyvesant's mansion § was erected on a large "bouwery" which the Director-General purchased in or previous to the year 1649. Settlers gradually located in this vicinity, and the plantation, or the "bouwery," became a sort of "stopping-place and the pleasure-ground of the Manhattans." In the year 1660, arrangements were made for conducting divine service here under the following circumstances : Dominie Selyns was this year installed as the first clergyman of the church in Brooklyn, which consisted of 24 members ; the population of the village being 134 persons. The bounds of the Dominie's charge included "the Ferry, the Waal-bogt, and Gujanes." "As

* Alb. Rec., viii. 321. † Doc. Hist. N. Y., iii. 58. ‡ Alb. Rec., iv. 373.
§ This building stood east of the Third Avenue, between Twelfth and Thirteenth streets. The exact situation of Stuyvesant's estate may be found on a map obtained from Cornelius De Witt, Esq., Val. Man. Com. Coun., 1852, 462. The "old pear tree" stood at the junction of Thirteenth street and the Third Avenue, near the Governor's dwelling. It was imported from Holland by Stuyvesant, 1647 (Lossing, ii. 784), destroyed, 1867.

the people there were unable of themselves to pay his salary, they petitioned the Council for assistance, and Stuyvesant individually agreed to contribute two hundred and fifty guilders, provided Dominie Selyns would preach a sermon on Sunday afternoons at the Director's bouwery, on the island of Manhattan. To this arrangement the Dominie assented." "Thither the people came also from the city for evening service."*

The establishment of church service at the bouwery, and the remote distance which the children in its vicinity were from Pietersen's school, at the lower extremity of the island, rendered it necessary to procure a chorister and schoolmaster. Accordingly, we find the following:

"Order in Council.—Present, the Director-General, Petrus Stuyvesant and the Hon. Johan de Decker.

"Whereas, *Harman Van Hoboocken, before* schoolmaster and chorister, was removed because another was sent to replace him [Pietersen] by the *Lords Directors* and the CONSISTORY, solicits to be employed *again* in one or other manner in the Company's service, so is he engaged as Adelborst [signifying a sergeant, or something above a common soldier], and allowed 10 guilders per month, and *g*. 175 for board from 27th Oct., 1661.

"Nota: Whereas the aforesaid Harman is a person of irreproachable life and conduct, so shall he be employed on the bouwery of the Director-General as schoolmaster and clerk [Voorleeser], with this condition, that the Director-General, whenever his service might be wanted for the Company, as Adelborst, shall replace him by another expert person."† So that from this date, until after the capitulation, there were *two* schools under the care of the Consistory—Pietersen's, at or near Fort Amsterdam, and Van Hoboocken's, on the Bouwery. "The Church at New Amsterdam was now in a flourishing condition under the administration of Megapolensis and Drisius." ‡

The year following, 1662, the burgomasters petitioned the "noble, great and respectful Director-General and Council in New Netherland," to grant a lot of ground in Brewer Street § (in the vicinity of Whitehall and Stone streets), opposite the lot of Johannes de Peyster, for a school-house, and also a lot outside

---

* Brod., 680, 681.
† Alb. Rec., xix. 383. Governor Fish, in a letter to the author, writes: "I have an impression, although it is but vague and indefinite, that Mr. Stuyvesant pointed out to me the location of the old school-house, as situate on what now is the site of Tompkins Market, about the corner of Sixth Street and Hall Place." It is well known that Governor Stuyvesant provided for the education of the colored persons on his extensive bouwery, and it is highly probable that Van Hoboocken had them under his instruction. ‡ Brod., 681.
§ Here were several breweries. This was the first street regulated and paved in New Amsterdam; hence its present name, Stone Street.

the gates for a burying-ground ; and the Director-General and Council "deem it, for various reasons, more proper that the school-house was constructed on a part of the present churchyard,"* *i. e.*, within the fort.

There is no evidence to support the conclusion that the school-house was built as contemplated.

1664.—In 1664 Evert Pietersen still remained as the schoolmaster ;† and on the 17th day of March the Director-General and Council issued an edict, requiring the practice of a custom long known in the Fatherland, and productive of good wherever conformed to, but which, at the present day, with us, has grown into sad desuetude ; to wit, "the public catechising of the children." In view of the beneficial results accruing from it, both to the children and the Church, the immediate revival of this good custom is greatly to be desired.

The first civil ordinance in New Amsterdam *enjoining*‡ this practice was as follows ; and it speaks creditably of the youth-loving and God-loving hearts of its authors :

"Whereas, it is highly necessary and of great consequence that the youth, *from their childhood*, is well instructed in reading, writing and arithmetic, and *principally* in the principles and fundaments of the Christian religion, in conformity to the lesson of that wise King Solomon, '*Learn the youth the first principles, and as he grows old, he shall then not deviate from it ;*' so that in time such men may arise from it, who may be able to serve their country in Church or in State ; which being seriously considered by the Director-General and Council in New Netherland, as the number of children by God's merciful blessing has considerably increased, they have deemed it necessary, so that such an useful and to our [us] God agreeable concern may be more effectually promoted, to recommend the present schoolmaster, and to command him, so as it is done by this, that they [Pietersen, the Principal, and Van Hoboocken, of the branch school on the Bouwery] on Wednesday, before the beginning of the sermon, with the children intrusted to their care, shall appear in the church to examine, after the close of the sermon, each of them his own scholars, in the presence of the reverend ministers and elders who may there be present, what they, in the course of the week, do remember of the Christian commands and catechism, and what progress they have made ; after which the children shall be allowed a decent recreation.

"Done in Amsterdam, New Netherland, this 17th March, 1664, by the Director-General and Council."§

* Alb. Rec., xx. 39, 40. † N. Am. Rec., v. 428.
‡ The custom, introduced from the Fatherland, had previously obtained in New Netherland. § Alb. Rec., xxii. 100.

Five days previous, an event transpired in England which was soon to issue in a change in the name, government and destiny of New Amsterdam, "which now contained a population of 1,500 souls and wore an air of great prosperity," notwithstanding the sad reverses it had experienced. On the 12th of March Charles II. granted to his brother, James, Duke of York, and Albany, the territory lying between the Connecticut and Delaware rivers, including all the possessions of New Netherland.

In August following, the Duke's squadron, under the command of Colonel Richard Nicolls, consisting of four ships carrying 94 guns and 450 soldiers, was off New Amsterdam, opposite to which, just below Brooklyn, was an encampment of volunteers from New England and the Long Island villages. To resist this force, the city was wholly unprepared; for although the fort mounted 24 guns, its single wall of earth rendered it by no means invulnerable. It was garrisoned by only 150 soldiers; and though there were 250 of the citizens able to bear arms, they were not disposed to hazard their lives in a vain resistance. Moreover, "there was scarcely six hundred pounds of serviceable powder in store." Upon the faith of Nicolls' promise to deliver back the city and fort, "in case the difference of the limits of this province be agreed upon betwixt His Majesty of England and the high and mighty States General," Stuyvesant consented to capitulate upon terms which had been mutually agreed upon by commissioners; and on the morning of the 8th day of September the Director-General, at the head of the garrison, having marched out of Fort Amsterdam with all the honors of war, the British took possession of the city. The name of Fort Amsterdam was immediately changed to Fort James. And though New Amsterdam became New York, in name, the ascendancy of the Dutch in numbers and character did not fail to perpetuate that influence which they had originally imparted: so that even now, after a period of more than two hundred years, notwithstanding the vicissitudes which the city has experienced, and the present heterogeneous character of its population, there is not wanting abundant and gratifying evidence of the early presence here of those who brought with them "the liberal ideas, and honest maxims, and homely virtues of their Fatherland; who carried along with them their huge clasped Bibles, and left them heir-looms in their families; who introduced their Church and their schools, their dominies and their schoolmasters."*

* Brod., chap. xx. *passim.*

RECAPITULATION.

At the close of Stuyvesant's administration, in consequence of charter provisions and the efforts of the clergy, "schools existed in almost every town and village" * in New Netherland; of this the records furnish abundant evidence. The whole system was but a counterpart of that to which the settlers had been accustomed in their native land. From the material furnished in this chapter, it is evident that education received a considerable degree of attention in New Amsterdam; and that there was a *public school* therein, *dispensing education gratuitously, the teachers receiving their appointment and remuneration from the constituted authorities*, is undoubtedly established. The following is a summary of facts connected therewith:

Adam Roelantsen, first schoolmaster, 1633-1639.

Efforts made by commonalty to procure suitable accommodations for the school, 1642, 1647, 1652, 1656, 1662.

Jan Stevensen, second schoolmaster, 1639-1648.

Jan Cornelissen, third schoolmaster, 1648-1650.

William Verstius, fourth schoolmaster and Kranck-besoecker, 1650-1655.

Jan Morice De La Montagne, fifth schoolmaster; in City Tavern, 1652-1664 (?).

Harmanus Van Hoboocken, successor to Verstius, sixth schoolmaster, 1655-1664.

Evert Pietersen Keteltas, seventh schoolmaster, 1661-1687 (?).†

Introduction of catechetical exposition to schools of the two last-named schoolmasters—1664.

OTHER FACTS CONNECTED WITH EDUCATION IN NEW AMSTERDAM DURING THE PERIOD OF THIS CHAPTER.

Previous to 1664, the persons who had been engaged in teaching school on their own account, under license from the conjoined civic and ecclesiastical authorities, were—Adriaen Jansen van Ilpendam, 1645-1660; David Provoost, 1647; Joost Carelse, 1649; Hans Steyn, 1652; Andries Hudde, 1654; Jacobus van Corlear, 1657; Jan Lubbertsen, 1658; Jan Juriaense Becker,

---
* O'Call. N. N., ii. 546.

† Oct. 2, 1661, "Evert Pietersen Keteltas, Voorleeser and Schoolmaster," united with the Low Dutch Reformed Church of this city, by certificate from the church at New Amstel, whence he came to New Amsterdam, June 16, 1669, being a widower, he was married to Hillegond Ioris, a widow. Rec. Coll. Ch.

In 1674 he was residing in Stone Street, and his estate was assessed at *fl*2,000. N. Y. Colon. MSS., ii. 699.

The names of all these schoolmasters are found enrolled as members of the Dutch Church; also the *private* schoolmasters. *Vide*, p. 21.

1660-1663 (?); Frans Classen, 1660; Johannes Van Gelder, 1662.*

In addition to the means of education thus afforded by the *free* church schools, and those taught privately, many of the inhabitants desired the establishment of an Academy, Latin or High School.

Dominie Drisius, when appointed as colleague with Megapolensis, in 1652, had called the attention of the West India Company to this subject ; and it is highly probable that the abortive attempt of Montagne, at the City Tavern, was the result.

"The foundation of the first ACADEMY and *classical* school in the city was based upon the following representation, which was transmitted to Holland, 19th September, 1658, as part of a petition of the burgomasters and schepens to the West India Company.

"It is represented that the youth of this place and neighborhood are increasing in number gradually, and that most of them can read and write ; but that some of the citizens and inhabitants would like to send their children to a school, the Principal of which understands Latin, but are not able to do so without sending them to New England ; furthermore, they have not the means to hire a Latin schoolmaster, expressly for themselves, from New England, and therefore they ask that the West India Company will send out a fit person as Latin schoolmaster, not doubting that the number of persons who will send their children to such teacher will from year to year increase, until an academy shall be formed, whereby this place to great splendor will have attained, for which, next to God, the Honorable Company which shall have sent such teacher here shall have laud and praise. For our own part, we shall endeavor to find a fit place in which the schoolmaster shall hold his school." †

In compliance with this petition, the West India Company sent out Dr. Alexander Carolus Curtius, a Latin schoolmaster, from Lithuania. On the 4th of July, 1659 (when about entering upon his duties), he attended the meeting of city magistrates, to learn definitely the terms upon which he was to be employed. The burgomasters proposed to give him, out of the city treasury, five hundred guilders annually, and tendered him fifty guilders, in part thereof, in advance. He was allowed the use of a house and garden, and was permitted to charge six guilders per quarter for each scholar. He was also privileged to practice medicine. In 1660, he in several instances demanded a beaver ‡ (valued at

* Alb. and N. Am. Rec. † Pauld. N. Am., 41.
‡ The currency of New Amsterdam was in general composed of the Indian money called wampum or seawant, and of beaver skins. Seawant consisted of small perforated shells, "loose" or "strung." This was used in trading at

eight guilders), in consequence of which overcharge his annual salary was withheld.

He likewise lacked the *sine qua non* for a schoolmaster, and the parents complained of the want of proper discipline among his pupils, "who beat each other and tore the clothes from each other's backs." He retorted by stating that "his hands were tied, as some of the parents forbade him punishing their children." The result was, the school changed teachers : Curtius returned to Holland, and the Rev. Ægidius Luyck, who had been acting as tutor to Stuyvesant's sons, became Principal of the High School, 1662. Under his charge it attained so high a reputation that children were sent to it from Virginia, Fort Orange and the Delaware, to receive a classical education.*

the market, the grocer's or the baker's. Six white or three black seawants, "loose" or "commercial," were valued at one stuyver, *i. e.* about two cents. The stated value of the "beaver" was eight guilders, or about three dollars. When divided into half-beavers they depreciated in value. Pauld. N. Am., 28.

* Brod., 656 694. Pauld. N. Am., 42. Alb. and N. Am. Rec. Luyck resided in Whitehall Street, near Stone Street.

CHAPTER III.

FROM THE CAPITULATION, 1664, TO THE REVOLUTIONARY WAR, 1776; EMBRACING A PERIOD OF 112 YEARS.

Although at the Capitulation of New Amsterdam, the government of the Dutch as a nation ceased, her people, her Church, her school still remained. By the articles of capitulation, the Dutch had secured to them "the liberty of their consciences in divine worship and church discipline, with all their accustomed jurisdiction with respect to the poor and orphans."*

As no record has been found after the capitulation in 1664, relative to the school of Van Haboocken, on the Governor's Bouwery, the probability is that it was then closed; but Pietersen continued to teach as heretofore, residing near his school, in 1665, in De Bouwer Straat, now Stone Street, and continued teaching for many subsequent years.†

From the Records of the Burgomasters' and Schepens' Court, which was continued until Nov. 10, 1774, we extract the following:

SEPT. 19, 1665.—The petition of Mr. Evert Pietersen, *Schoolmaster* and *Precentor* of this city, being read and considered, requesting that he may have some proper fixed *Salarium*, as he was heretofore paid his wages by the Honorable Company, and has been continued in his employment from that time to the present, is apostilled as followeth: Whereas order shall be shortly made relative to the salary of the *ministers* of this city, under which the *precentorship* also comes, proper order shall then be made herein likewise.‡

MAY 8, 1666.— Captain Steynmets entering demands payment of a year's rent of his house, hired to the city as a city school, due on the first of this month, amounting to the sum of 260 florins. Petitioner is requested to wait yet awhile, as there is at present no money in the chest. §

FEB. 16, 1668 9.—Evert Pietersen, *Schoolmaster* and *Precentor* requests payment of his earned salary, and further allowance for his future services. ‖

In an enumeration of "the best and most affluent inhabitants of this city," Feb. 19, 1674, is found the name of Evert Pietersen (who resides on the south side of Brewer, now Stone Street), and his property was valued at 2,000 florins. ¶

---

* *Vide* Art. of Capit. in full. O'Call. N. N., ii. 532.
† Val. Man., 1850, p. 454. Val. Hist. N. Y., p. 120. Paulding's N. Am., 109.   ‡ N. Am. Rec., vi. 73.   § *Ibid.*, 178.
‖ N. Am. Rec., vi. 436.   ¶ Hol. Doc., ii. 699.

DEC. 12, 1686. Jan De La Montagne (probably the same person who was the Schoolmaster in 1652) was appointed to be present at the public catechising, and at the private catechising held every fortnight on Wednesday afternoon.*

DEC. 16, 1686.—In consequence of the advanced age of Evert Pietersen, Abraham De La Noy was appointed to act as Clerk, Chorister and Visitor of the Sick † (offices, as well as that of Catechist, always included in the duties of the Schoolmaster previous to the Revolutionary War).

Mr. De La Noy asked for the fees for recording baptisms, but Consistory resolved that the yearly allowance of fifty gulden for baptismal fees shall be made until the death of Mr. Evert Pietersen, but when he dies the fees for recording baptisms shall be paid to petitioner.

Being thus relieved from these extra duties, it is safe to conclude that Pietersen was enabled to continue to teach into the following year, at least.

The ecclesiastical organization of the Dutch Reformed Church remaining intact, she still acknowledged the jurisdiction of the Classis of Amsterdam. The school continued, as heretofore, under the direct supervision of the deacons ; and being now deprived of all aid from the treasury of the colonial government, its support wholly devolved upon the Consistory, and the institution had such strong hold on the affections of the Dutch people, that they could not and would not relinquish their jurisdiction over it, even when efforts were made to compel them so to do, as will be presently shown.

The English governors, solicitous to produce uniformity in religion and language, encouraged English preachers and schoolmasters to settle in the colony ; and, although for many years after the Capitulation there were comparatively but few Episcopalians in the city, independent of the Government officers and the military, yet the Dutch, with magnanimous spirit, granted them the occupancy of the church in the fort a portion of each Sabbath. ‡

In the year 1673, England and Holland being then at war, the city surrendered to the Dutch, and Governor Colve, in granting charters to the several towns of Long Island and the Hudson, enjoined, first of all, that the authorities "should take care that the Reformed Christian religion be maintained in conformity to the Synod of Dordrecht." They were also empowered to enact "ordinances for the observance of the Sabbath, erecting churches and school-houses, or similar public works ;"§ but Colve's administration was brief, the province being ceded to the British by the treaty of November, 1674.

Subsequently, 1687, Governor Dongan, in his Report to the Committee of Trade on the Province of New York, states, "Here

---

* Con. Min., Lib. A. 65. *Vide* also Ordinance for catechising (p. 30), and Pietersen's appointment to these offices (p. 27). † Watson's Annals, p. 166.
‡ Doc. Hist. N. Y., i. 186.   § *Ibid.*, i. 655, *et seq.*

bee not many of the Church of England. *The most prevailing opinion is that of the Dutch Calvinists.* It is the endeavour of all Psons here to bring up their children and servants in that opinion which themselves profess."*

During Fletcher's administration, the Assembly passed a law providing for the settlement of ministers of the gospel, *to be chosen by the people.* The Council added an amendment, giving to the Governor the power of approval or rejection. The House, composed in the main of those attached to the Church of Holland, refused to concur in the amendment, when Fletcher, addressing them in an angry speech, prorogued them to the next year.†

The repeated efforts made in behalf of the English Church bore hard at times upon the prospective welfare of that of the Dutch ; but tolerant to all, while watchful for herself, she maintained her position, and continued, as from the first, in the enjoyment of her worship and her school.

But, undoubtedly, the greatest severity which the people of the Reformed Dutch Church experienced, was at the hands of Lord Cornbury.

His imprisonment and amercement (1707) of two Presbyterian ministers, for preaching without his license, and his breaking up by stringent measures the Dutch schools on Long Island, testify to his misguided zeal.‡

Of the Dutch Church in New York, maintaining the ascendency in numbers and influence, he was somewhat wary ; but, on the recurrence of a favorable opportunity, he unhesitatingly gave them to understand that no Dutch minister or schoolmaster would be allowed to exercise his calling without a special gubernatorial license ; and this in direct opposition to the previously-granted charter of incorporation, given by William III. to the Reformed Dutch Church in America.

ACT OF INCORPORATION OF THE REFORMED PROTESTANT DUTCH CHURCH.

And our will and pleasure is, and we do hereby declare, that the Minister o. the said Church shall and may, by and with the consent of the Deacons of the said Church, for the time being, or any four of them, whereof one of the elders to be one, from time to time as need shall require, nominate one or more able Ministers, lawfully ordained, according to the Constitution and Directions aforesaid, to be preachers and assistants to the said Minister and his successors in the celebration of the Divine offices of praying and preaching, and other duties incident to be performed in the said Church, as the Ministers, Elders and Deacons of said Church shall require of him, and *likewise to nominate and appoint a Clerk,* SCHOOLMASTER, *Bellringer or Sexton, and such other officers as they shall stand in need of.*

* Doc. Hist. N. Y., i. 161, *et seq.* † Hale's U. S., 76.
‡ Smith's Hist., published at Philadelphia by Benjamin Franklin & D. Hall, MDCCLV., 114. Hardie, 67. Dunlap, ii. Ap. U. 254. Greenleaf's Hist. of Churches in N. Y., 125.

And, furthermore, we do of our special grace, certain knowledge and meer motion, give and grant unto the said Ministers, Elders and Deacons, by and with the advice and consent of the members in communion of the said Church, or the major part of them, full power and authority to make rates or assessments upon all and every of the members in communion of said Church for the raising of money for the payment of the yearly stipends or salaries of the aforesaid officers of the said Church.

And, lastly, we do, for us, our heirs and successors, ordain and grant unto the said Ministers, Elders and Deacons of the said Reformed Protestant Dutch Church, and their successors by these presents, that this our grant shall be firm, good, effectual and available in all things in the law, to all intents, constructions and purposes whatsoever, according to our true intent and meaning hereinbefore declared, and shall be construed, reputed and adjudged in all cases most favorable in the behalf and for the best benefit and behoof of the said Ministers, Elders and Deacons of the Reformed Protestant Dutch Church in the city of New York and their successors.

In view of this right to the jurisdiction of an institution which they considered of vital importance, and to which they were endeared—a right affirmed at the capitulation, and subsequently—the Consistory, with a spirit worthy of their high trust, took a decided stand in opposition to the Governor's claims; as in their records is a minute referring "to the arbitrary measures of Lord Cornbury, who had taken the regulation of schools into his own hands, and claimed the direct appointment of the schoolmaster."

1705.—A vacancy occurring in the school, a nomination was made and presented in Consistory by Jacobus Goelet and Dr. Johannes Kerfbyl.

A committee of the Consistory remonstrated against the Governor's claim as being contrary to the privilege guaranteed in the Charter. This remonstrance was declined. Whereupon the Ruling Consistory, deeming this a matter of great importance, directed a meeting of the Great Consistory, on January 16, when it was *Resolved*, "that the members of the Great Consistory should have, with respect to this matter, the appointment of the Schoolmaster, not merely an advisory, but also a *deciding* vote with the Ruling Consistory." *

So that, notwithstanding the Governor's mandatory prohibition, so unjustly and disastrously effectual in other parts of the province, the Dutch in New York retained their rights, and continued to call and settle their schoolmasters as heretofore.

The name of the person appointed to fill the vacancy above alluded to is not known.

The subsequent minutes are wanting, until January 5, 1726, when the Consistory engaged† Barent De Foreest to give "instruction not only in the Low Dutch language, but also in the elements of Christian piety;" his salary to commence January 1.

* Consistorial Minutes, Lib. B. 12.
† Con. Min., Lib. A. 422.

By the terms of the contract made with him the school was to be in session—in summer, from 9 o'clock to 11 in the morning, and in winter, from half-past 9 to half-past 12; and, through the year, from 1 to 5 in the afternoon.

On festival days he was to be free, with the knowledge and approval of Consistory; also on Fridays, when there was to be a trial sermon, and on Wednesdays and Saturdays in the afternoon according to custom.

The school was to be opened and closed with prayer and singing, and the children, according to their capacity, were to be taught to spell and read and write and cipher, and also the usual prayers in the catechism.

On Saturday morning they were to be prepared to repeat to the Minister the Lord's-Day portion in the catechism, which was to be subject of discourse the following day, so as to be able to recite it in the church.

Every Monday the scholars were to be publicly catechised—and on Wednesdays, when there was preaching, he and the scholars were to come to church in a body.

The children were to be examined in their studies, four times a year, in the presence of the Consistory or a committee thereof.

None but edifying and orthodox text books were to be used, such as would meet with the approbation of the Reverend Consistory.

If ten of the scholars, or less (of seven years of age or upwards), were unable to pay for their instruction, the Consistory guaranteed to pay the schoolmaster, annually, nine pounds, New York currency. If there were more than ten he was to receive pay in the same proportion.

As to firewood for the children, the Consistory will, in due season, take order and communicate with you.

Under these promises, then, and upon condition that you submit to such orders as the Reverend Consistory shall give concerning the school, whether by altering the foregoing or adding new ones, the Reverend Consistory thus provisionally appoints you for this year.

Thus done in our ecclesiastical meeting at New York, January 5th, A. D. 1725-6.

In the name of the Reverend Consistory,

G. DU BOIS.

p. t. PRAESES.

The foregoing proposal of the Reverend Consistory, the original of which has been delivered to me, I accept in the fear of the Lord, thanking their Reverences for their goodness to me.

BARENT DE FOREEST.

New York, Jan'y 13, 1725-6.

DECLARATION*

of the Reverend Consistory to the Christian Congregation, that Mr. Barent De Forest has been appointed by them, with the Great Consistory to be Schoolmaster for one year beginning with January 1, Anno 1726.

Since we all, under Divine Providence, are subjects of his Royal Majesty, George, the King of Great Britain, our most gracious Sovereign, and we are living in a Province where the English language is the common language of the inhabitants; there cannot but be a general agreement by each and all of us that it is very necessary to be versed in this common language of the people, in order properly to carry on one's temporal calling.

Herewith, also, all who belong to the Low Dutch Reformed Church, and have any regard for God, and prefer the worship of the Low Dutch Reformed Church, cannot but see and acknowledge that every one, be he who it may, must regard it as urgently necessary that since the practice of the Low Dutch Reformed worship, and attendance upon the public exercise of the same, and the devout hearing of pious sermons in the Dutch language, furnish the only hope, under the co-operation of God's Spirit, from time to time, of advancing in the knowledge of the truth, which is according to godliness, to their comfort and salvation, it is equally necesary for them to be versed in the language in which God's worship is conducted and exercised.

What, therefore, can any esteem more fit and proper than that they who are not ashamed to belong to a Church and congregation, where the true doctrine of comfort in life and in death is preached in the clearest and most powerful manner, in the Low Dutch tongue, according to the decrees of the National Synod at Dordrecht, etc., in order to progress in the right knowledge of God's word and the practice of true piety, as we are forgiven by the Most High in Christ, through his Spirit, should cause their children from their youth up to be instructed in the Low Dutch tongue, and not neglect any opportunity for gaining this end.

Therefore, the acting Consistory, having, after calling on God's name, taking the whole weighty subject into mature consideration, have unanimously resolved to appoint Mr. Barent de Forest, Schoolmaster, under their own supervision, and his pledge to obey strictly all such orders as shall be judged necessary for the advancement of the youth in the Netherlandish tongue, and in the first principles of the Christian religion, and in writing and ciphering. And they have likewise thought proper to make known to the Christian congregation this their resolution under these circumstances.

So that your children, whom you may please to send there for instruction, shall be diligently cared for, without omission save in cases of extreme necessity; to which Mr. De Forest has pledged and bound himself to the Rev. Consistory according to articles prepared for that purpose.

Meanwhile, we, Ministers, Elders, etc., have willingly taken it upon ourselves to see that your reasonable expectations may be satisfied so far as possible in respect to the proper instruction of your children, not only in reading and writing but also in the usual prayers and in the Catechism.

For which purpose Mr. De Forest will every week appear with all the children at the public catechising in order that they may be examined as to their proficiency. He will, also, whenever there is preaching on Wednesday, come to church with all the children.

Herewith are the Christian congregation also informed, in respect to those among us who are unable to pay the money required for the teaching of their children, from 7 years of age and upward, that they have only to repair to Mr. De Forest, who will confer with them and receive their children according to the order which he has already received or shall still further receive

* Con. Min., Lib. A. 426.

from the Rev. Consistory, that the school money shall be provided by the Rev. Consistory.

The design is the instruction of the youth and the arousing of the adults to this matter in order to the further propagation of Christ's Kingdom among us, for God's honor and our salvation. This, then, being the only object sought, it is our friendly request that you may so take to heart its importance that one may serve as an example to another and the prompt stir up the slothful. And we with our children will, as members of the true Christian Church, steadfastly serve God and his Son, Jesus Christ, in faith and love.

So that our congregation shall not diminish, but daily increase more and more, like God's people, over the whole earth.

So that even Babylon may fall and the fullness of the Gentiles come in and all Israel be saved, and we altogether receive hereafter the end of our faith in eternal glory. Amen.

Thus done in Christian Assembly at New York. Jan. 5th, A. D. 1725-6.

G. DU BOIS.

p. t. PRAESES.

1725 6.—January 9, being Sunday, the above was read before the congregation after the morning service.

1726. Dec. 1.* Reverend Consistory further appoint you Low-Dutch Schoolmaster for the ensuing year, 1727, on the same conditions with this alteration: When those able to pay apply, take the names of the parents in writing and say to them that you will speak with the Rev. Consistory on the matter, and delay receiving the children at the cost of the Church until you have received the approval of the Rev. Consistory. In teaching the children of the poor, it is agreed you shall draw salary from the Reverend Consistory according to the instruction they receive — so much for one who learns only to read, and so for one who learns only to write, and so for one who, besides, learns ciphering. And in case any child of the poor shall learn writing or ciphering, that must be with the approval of one of the Ministers. Firewood for the school is already provided according to your own proposal — four cords for the whole winter. In case any children remain away from school, you will inquire after the reasons thereof, whether it was with the knowledge of the parents or not and on good grounds, so that the parents may take order thereon; and if any of the children of the poor are often absent, and their parents do not apply a remedy, you shall give notice to the Reverend Consistory.

You will furnish a list of the parents whose children are taught at the expense of the Consistory; and every quarter you will specify their names in the reckoning, and what each one learns, whether to read or also to write and cipher, in order that it may properly appear to the Rev. Consistory, or to the Deacons, for payment.

And it is further earnestly recommended to you to be precise in following these directions. Thus the Reverend Consistory appoints you for Schoolmaster for the coming year, 1727.

Thus done in our Ecclesiastical Assembly at New York, Dec. 27, 1726.

I, the undersigned, accept this appointment, whereof the original has been given to me, in the fear of the Lord, with heartfelt gratitude to the Reverend Consistory.

BARENT DE FOREEST.

New York, Dec. 29, 1726.

* Con. Min., Lib. A. 432.

As his successor was engaged for two years and no longer, but remained for ten years up to the time of his death, so De Foreest continued in the performance of his duties up to December, 1732, as the following payments recorded in Deacon's Minutes will attest :

				£	s.	d.
1726—March 3.	Paid Barent De Forcest, for the Schoolkinderen			1	4	0
July 21.	"	"	"	10	4	0
Nov. 10.	"	"	"	5	17	0
Dec. 8.	"	for Firewood		3	14	0
1727—Feb. 2.	"	for Three Months' Instruction		5	12	6
April 27.	"	"	"	3	1	0
Sept. 14.	"	"	"	3	11	6
Nov. 1.	"	for Firewood		3	14	0
1728—Aug. 5.	"	for School Money and Firewood		18	16	6
Nov. 4.	"	for Firewood		3	14	0
1729 Jan. 20.	"	for Instructing the Children of the Poor		4	15	0
July 14.	"	"	"	"	8	8	0
Sept. 3.	"	"	"	"	10	15	0
Sept. 11.	"	"	"	"	3	6	0
Oct. 9.	"	"	"	"	4	4	0
1730 May 21.	"	"	"	"	8	8	0
Oct. 8.	"	for Firewood		3	0	0
Dec. 7.	"	for Services		15	0	0
1731—Oct. 1.	"	for One Year's Services		15	0	0

In 1732 he was arrested for debt, and on the 19th of December asked Consistory to become responsible for £50 or £60 and continue him in his office, and on his behalf state this by word of mouth, and from time to time take one-half of his salary for the debt and pay him the other half for his support, so long as he discharged his duties well and no longer.

After much consideration it was

Resolved—That the Consistory cannot be answerable for any sum, and still have it in consideration whether to restore Mr. De Forcest to his office or not, even if he is released.
Also—That Mr. Isaac Stoutenburgh, now acting as his helper, shall be asked to continue as such ; if so, he shall be paid at the same rate as Mr. De Forcest, and that from the time when he began, which was *December 3d*, because the Consistory finds it necessary to abide by the resolution to hold the offices of *Clerk* and *Schoolmaster* together for one competent person.

This proposal being made to Mr. Stoutenburgh in the meeting, was accepted by him.*

From this it would appear that Mr. Stoutenburgh, not being qualified to teach, acted as Clerk or Chorister from December 3, 1732, until a person was found capable of performing the duties of both offices ; and it is to be inferred that there was an *interregnum* in the school from the above date until June 1, 1733.

Although Consistory resolved, December 19, 1732, not to be

* Con. Min., Lib. B. 65.

Schoolmeester and Voorsanger
1733 to 1743.

answerable for any sum, yet they seem to have relented in one instance at least, for the records state that, in 1733, they paid to one Gerrit Harssen, for Barent De Foreest, £5 4s.

On the 21st day of March, 1733, the following letter was addressed in the name of the Consistory to Gerrit Van Wagenen, and henceforth the records furnish a full and uninterrupted chain of interesting facts respecting the size and progress of the school, with a complete list of the Schoolmasters up to the present day:

> Since the Old Church of the Low Dutch Reformed Congregation at New York* at present lacks a Foresinger, with a Schoolmaster and Visitor of the Sick, and it is necessary that these offices should be undertaken as soon as possible by a suitable person; the Rev. Consistory, in consequence of the general testimony to your fitness, turned their attention to you, so that on the 20th of March, 1732-3, they unanimously resolved to appoint you to those offices. Therefore, the Consistory of the Low Dutch Reformed Congregation in the city of New York hereby fully appoint you, Mr. Gerrit Van Wagenen (at present Foresinger in the Low Dutch Reformed Congregation at Kingstown) [Kingston], to the aforesaid offices.
>
> And, if you are inclined to accept the same here, we name and commission you as Clerk and Foresinger for the Low Dutch Reformed Congregation of New York, in their so-called Old Church (even as Mr. Van. Arnheim renders the service in the New Church); and also to be the Visitor of the Sick for the whole congregation, and to keep school in the Low Dutch language, and finally to keep the books of the Elders, Deacons and Church Masters.
>
> That is, to express our intention still further—
>
> 1st. To exercise the function of Clerk and Foresinger on all occasions of public worship, both in preaching and in catechising, which now is done on Wednesday mornings.
>
> 2d. Especially do the Consistory expect you to be active and diligent in keeping the school, since nothing is more necessary for those who belong to our congregation; and, in that case, there is no doubt that several others will send their children to you to be taught reading, writing, ciphering, and also the principles of the true Reformed religion, and the Rev. Consistory will secure you, from time to time, at least twelve children from the poor, with payment thereof (presently to be stated), that you may teach them, as all other children in your school, according to their capacity, to read, write and cipher, the usual prayers and the Heidelberg Catechism; and, further, in your school keeping, and the use of books therein, you are to act in all respects as the Consistory shall judge to be most useful, with such additions or alterations as experience shall show to be best.
>
> 3d. As each one of the Schoolmasters has had the duty of Visitor of the Sick, so you are to make no piteous scruples concerning the service (however weighty in itself), but render as the Ministers shall orally direct you.
>
> 4th. To keep the books of Consistory legibly.
>
> To encourage you in undertaking these offices, the Rev. Consistory promise you, for performing the said services, as before written,
>
> First.—As Foresinger and Visitor of the Sick, yearly and every year, to be paid quarterly £15 0
> Second.—For the Schoolteaching of twelve of the children of the poor, to be paid quarterly 10 6
> Third.—For Keeping the Books of Consistory 9 0
> Fourth.—Four Cords of Wood, yearly, more or less.
> Fifth.—To Record the Baptisms in the Old Church.

* Con. Min., Lib. A. 493.

Your salary as Foresinger shall commence from the time that it shall cease at Kingstown [Kingston, N. Y.], and as Schoolmaster from the time school here begins. As to the keeping of the books, if you have no inclination for this, the Reverend Consistory must look out for some one else ; meanwhile

If you carry on your school industriously the Consistory doubts not the citizens here will send you such a number of children, that, altogether, your salary will furnish an adequate support for your family.

Thus the Consistory, heartily desiring that you will readily accept this commission for the aforesaid offices on the conditions expressed, will receive you with sincere affection and show you their favor.

Wherefore they expect and desire, by the first opportunity, a speedy answer that you undertake these services in the fear of the Lord, and your arrival in New York to enter upon them.

With prayer for God's gracious blessing therein upon your person and family.

Thus done in our Consistory, 21st of March, 1733.

GUALTERUS DU BOIS. p. t. PRAES.

N. B.—Besides the foregoing Commission, the Consistory promised to pay Mr. Gerrit Van Wagenen, over and above, for the first two years (and no longer), Six Pounds, yearly, N. Y. currency, for his house rent ; whereupon, on a certain day, he appeared before the Consistory and accepted the proposed services.

G. DU BOIS. p. t. PRAES.

The terms* of the contract made with Mr. Van Wagenen with regard to the school hours and holidays, the catechising of the children and their presence in church on stated occasions, quarterly examinations, &c., were substantially the same as those made with Barent De Foreest, except that the Consistory guaranteed the tuition of *twelve* or more scholars, none of whom were to be under seven years of age.

The contract concludes thus :

You shall also minutely record all the children who are brought to the Old Church for baptism, and conduct therein according to the direction of the Reverend Consistory as the Minister shall announce to you ; for each child that you record, you shall receive at least a half-quarter, and so much more as the parties may present to you.

Your salary, as Foresinger, is to commence from the 15th of May, last, and, as Schoolmaster, from the 1st of June.

The original hereof is given to you, and you are also to sign this.

Thus done in our meeting in New York, June 13th, A. D. 1733.

In the name and authority of the Consistory.

HENRICUS BOEL.

p. t. PRAESES.

The foregoing Commission, and the Farther Explanation by the Rev. Consistory, of which the original was given to me, I undertake in the fear of the Lord, with thanksgiving.

N. Y., June 20th, A. D. 1733.

GERR. VAN WAGENENEN.

* Con. Min., Lib. A. 497.

Publication made from the pulpit in both Churches of the Low Dutch Reformed Christian Congregations here in New York, Sunday Forenoon, June 10, 1733 : *

BELOVED IN THE LORD: The Reverend Consistory, taking to heart the extreme necessity, usefulness and benefit under the Lord's blessing, for this congregation in general, that there should be a Foresinger in the Old Church, and a Visitor of the Sick, and for the youth in particular, that there should be a good Low Dutch Orthodox Schoolmaster maintained among us, has, in testimony of Mr. Gerrit Van Wagenen's good qualifications, called him to these offices and he has accepted the same.

Therefore, Notice is hereby given to the Christian Congregation that Mr. Gerrit Van Wagenen is appointed Visitor of the Sick in our congregation, and Foresinger in the Old Church, just as Mr. Jan Van Arnheim is Foresinger in the New Church, and is to record who are baptized there.

The Christian Congregation will please conduct themselves accordingly.

Further, Notice is given that Mr. Van Wagenen will be Schoolmaster in the Low Dutch, under the inspection and orders of the Consistory, so as best to advance the youth in the Low Dutch language, in the arts of reading, writing and ciphering, and also in the elements of the Low Dutch Reformed religion. He will therefore appear with the school-children at the public catechising in the church, that they may recite the Questions according to their ability, and he may show his diligent performance of all his duties.

The Consistory will also, from time to time, take care that your reasonable expectations as to the good instruction of your children in reading, writing and ciphering, and also in the prayers, the Catechism and catechising in the Low Dutch, are fulfilled.

And as there are in our Congregation persons unable to pay the school money, these shall give notice of their children, of seven years or over, to Mr. Van Wagenen, who will inform the Consistory ; and they, having given their consent, will pay the school money required.

Therefore, the Consistory hopes that all this may prove a desired success for our Church, and that the Christian Congregation will be pleased to support the same for the general good, for themselves and their children, by assiduously, and in good number, sending scholars to Mr. Van Wagenen's School of Orthodoxy.

We justly expect this the more, because, for a long time, we have heard the wish and desire of many for a *good* Low Dutch School among us, according to the language and religion of our Church ; as, also, because it is so absolutely necessary, useful and salutary for the Christian rearing, teaching and training of our youth, in order to gain them, from the earliest period, to the language of our Church, and to a love for the Low Dutch Reformed worship, that the prosperity of our Church may be furthered, with heartfelt prayer to God for his blessing.

Thus done in our Session.

In the name and authority of the Reverend Consistory,

HENRICUS BOEL.

p. t. PRAESES.

The Deacons' Book records the amount paid from year to year to Mr. Gerrit Van Wagenen for his services.

Upon his decease, in the forepart of 1743, his son, Huybert Van Wagenen, was appointed to fill the vacancy.

* Con. Min., Lib. A. 501.

The increasing population had not only rendered necessary the erection, "farther up-town," of a second house of worship, but a second school was to be provided for, as the deacons, in their capacity as trustees, informed Consistory "That, for the encouragement of *another* Dutch school, they had, during this month [November 21, 1743], directed Mr. ABRAHAM DE LANOY to present the names of ten (10) children of poor parents (who lived at too great a distance, particularly in winter, to come to the school of Mr. HUYBERT VAN WAGENEN) to the deacons, in writing, that, after investigation of their cases, they may be approved. Mr. De Lanoy, for instructing them according to the rates prescribed by Consistory, shall receive, in quarterly payments, the same amount of money and firewood which Mr. Van Wagenen received for the same number. Mr. Van Wagenen shall attend to the catechetical instruction of the children in the Old Church [Garden Street], and Mr. De Lanoy in the New Church [the Middle]."

The Consistory hereon declared that they appreciated the excellent aim of the Deacons and approved it, and desired the Deacons to take the matter to heart and act further therein with the Consistory.

HENRICUS BOEL,

p. t. PRAESES.

Accommodations having been secured, the school of Mr. De Lanoy went into operation.* While it existed there was a school to each church; and had the plan been strictly carried out of establishing a school by the side of each Dutch Church subsequently erected, is it not reasonable to suppose that it would have proved a source of rejoicing to our denomination at the present day? May she not awake to a sense of her duty in this respect when it is too late?

In 1746, Consistory *resolved*, "That there should be appropriated to Mr. Huybert Van Wagenen, in *addition* to the sum

---

* Mr. Abraham Brower (born 1753, died 1832) states that, when a lad, " he went to the Dutch school, to his grandfather, Abraham Delanoye (a French Huguenot, *via* Holland), whose school was in *Cortlandt* street" (Wat. An., 172). This being in the vicinity of the Middle Church, was, in all probability, the school organized by the deacons in November, 1743, as above stated.

The late Judge Benson, in his early youth, "attended school at the corner of *Marketfield* and *Broad* streets, *where he learned the Dutch Catechism*. They used in the Dutch churches," he adds, "*an hourglass*, near the clock, to ascertain the length of the sermon, which was always limited to one hour. They made the collections in a bag, with a *bell* to give notice of the approach of the deacons—gatherers"—(*vide* Wat. An., 191). The whole complexion of the Judge's statement, in connection with the statement of the Consistory of that date, "that there was (then) no other suitable school of the Low Dutch in the city," (*post*, 49), renders it highly probable that the *locality* mentioned was the site of Mr. Van Wagenen's labors at this date.

pledged to him for the instruction of the children in the school, *ten pounds* New York currency, for one year, on condition that he should officiate as *chorister* alternately in the Old and New Church, as shall be directed by Consistory. If this should prove satisfactory, the Consistory will take further action."

This was accompanied with resolutions relating to Isaac Stoutenburgh and John Van Aernam, choristers in the Old and New churches, providing for Mr. Van Wagenen taking their places occasionally, and paving the way for his permanent appointment.*

August 6, 1748, the subject of erecting a school and dwelling-house was referred to a Committee of Consistory, consisting of Abel Hardenbroek, Theodorus Van Wyck, J. Turk and Jan Brevoort; and Mr. Huybert Van Wagenen having signified his intention to resign, Consistory engaged "Mr. DANIEL BRATT, chorister in the church of Catskill, to be *chorister* in the New Church for the five subsequent years, for which service he is to receive, in addition to the fees for entering baptisms, £12 10s. He is also to officiate as the *schoolmaster*, for which he shall be provided with a *dwelling-house* and *school-room* by the Old Church, and also with *twelve free scholars*, six in reading and six in writing; for which he shall receive £12 10s., and also a *load of wood for each scholar*, annually, half nut and half oak. His services to commence April, 1749." †

August 15.—"The Committee for preparing a plan for the building of a school and dwelling-house, exhibited one which was unanimously approved; and it was resolved, that the erection of a building, according to such plan, should forthwith proceed."‡

In the year 1691, the Dutch Church purchased, for $450, from the Common Council, a tract of land on *Garden Street*, between William and Broad Streets, "on the north side 175 feet, on the south side 180 feet, more or less." A church was erected here in 1693, on the north side of the street; and opposite this, on the south side, several feet back from the building-line, the *school-house* (with teacher's dwelling attached) was built. §

1751.—November 18, Mr. Daniel Bratt handed a list of free scholars who were found to be three more than Consistory had appointed. He requested payment for these, and also to take more if they offered themselves; both of which were agreed to on condition the number should not exceed twenty. ||

---

* Con. Min., Lib. A. 503. Stoutenburgh, in 1746, was Voorleezer in the Oude Kerke, and Van Aernam in the New Kerke. Rec. Col. Ch.
† Con. Min., Lib. B. 130. ‡ *Ibid.*
§ The exact site of this building is designated on an ancient map of the city, 1763, which is to be found in Val. Man. Com. Coun., 1850, p. 220. This property is now known as Nos. 50 and 52 Exchange Place.
|| Con. Min., Lib. B. 136.

1751.—*December* 12.—"Mr. Van der Sman was appointed Consoler of the Sick and Catechiser." *

Mr. Bratt, from the complexion of the records, had been selected with reference to his abilities as chorister. As an instructor of youth and catechist, he seems not to have rendered complete satisfaction; hence the division of his labors by the above appointment, and his subsequent dismissal; for in 1753. April, he was "notified that his services as schoolmaster would end in May, 1754." †

1755.—The Consistory, at this period, finding themselves unable to procure here the services of an individual possessed of those varied qualifications deemed by them essential in a voorleezer and schoolmaster, and being anxious of obtaining one capable of performing aright those important and responsible duties connected with the instruction of youth, especially where the cultivation of their moral faculties was to be appropriately considered, "*Resolved* (January 27) *to call a chorister, catechist and schoolmaster from Holland*." Articles were prepared, prescribing the duties required, and stipulating the salary, which were committed to the President, to prepare a letter to certain persons in Holland, to be forwarded by the first opportunity.

To Daniel Bratt, who had still been retained in the school, notwithstanding the notification of April, 1753, "notice was directed to be given, 'to look out for another place.'" ‡

The letter which was prepared and sent to Holland, as above directed, was as follows:

To MR. JOHN DREVES, *Cashier;* N. N. SCHOUTE, *Foresinger, of the South Church, Amsterdam;* and CHRISTIAN BORDING, *at Oostsaane:*

RESPECTED SIRS: The Consistory of the Dutch Reformed Church in the city of New York, encouraged by the recommendation of Mr. Cornelius Clopper, Jr., who is acquainted with you, take the liberty to send you this letter, requesting you, as being able and willing, to aid us in the matter proposed. Our congregation has for some time been destitute of a *capable* schoolmaster and chorister, to the evident injury of our youth and the cause of religion; the Consistory have finally resolved to incur the trouble and expense of procuring one from Holland; and for such beseech your most friendly help and support, and offer such emoluments as will be nearly double of what has been before enjoyed by any one in that capacity. This is the strongest evidence of our ardent desire to obtain a worthy person, who shall fulfill our expectations, and discharge the duties of his station to satisfaction.

The requisites which the Consistory desire in the person whom you may be so good as to procure for us, are:

First, That he be a person of suitable qualifications to officiate as *schoolmaster* and *chorister,* possessing a knowledge of *music,* a good voice, so as to be heard; an aptitude to teach others the science, and that he should be a good *reader, writer* and *arithmetician.*

Second, That he should be of the Reformed religion, *a member of the Church,* bringing with him testimonials of his Christian character and conduct.

* Con. Min., Lib. B. 137. † *Ibid.*, 144. ‡ *Ibid.*, 155.

Third, That, whether married or unmarried, he be not under twenty-five, nor over thirty-five.

The following are the *emoluments* which the Consistory promise and pledge to said person, for the required services, annually, so long as he seems capable of discharging his duties in the school and church, and so long as his Christian conduct is to the edification of the congregation:

First, *A free dwelling-house*, a new and commodious one, standing directly over [opposite] the church in which he is to officiate as chorister, not only twice, and sometimes three times on the Sabbath, but also every Wednesday. In this house, besides the large school-room, there is a small chamber, a kitchen, a cellar under the house, behind the house a fine kitchen-garden, a well, with a pump therein, and other conveniences besides, the annual rent of which would be valued at more than *twenty pounds* New York currency. While the sums mentioned are New York currency, we deem it necessary to state that one pound, New York currency, must be reckoned at six guilders and twelve stivers.

Second, For *leading the singing* at the times before stated annually, *fifteen pounds*.

Third, As the master shall be bound to instruct *twenty* poor children in *reading*, *writing* and *ciphering*, he shall receive annually *twenty-four pounds*, whether the whole number be filled up or not.

Fourth, *Firewood* for these children, *six pounds* annually.

Fifth, For *keeping the account-books* of receipts and expenditures of the church, neatly executed, *eight pounds*.

Sixth, For *entering baptisms* in the Church Register. This cannot be accurately defined, but will at least average *seven pounds*.

Seventh, Besides these, an *annual salary* of *twenty pounds*.

Total, *eighty pounds* ($200) and *dwelling*.

Upon this, gentlemen, the schoolmaster coming over may confide with certainty. To this may be added, *that the school is open for the children of all the citizens*, and from those who learn, whether *reading* alone, or *writing*, *singing* or *ciphering*, a considerable sum may be expected, as there is *no other suitable school of the Low Dutch* in the city. The master may, therefore, confidently expect that, with his zeal and industry, his income will increase, so that *forty pounds* more may at least be added. *Finally*, in order that nothing may be omitted in endeavors to attain this pious object, the Consistory (as the person selected cannot come here without expense) promise, on his arrival, to remunerate him to the amount of *fifteen* pounds. If you should seek to gain this object as speedily as practicable, so that the person selected may come over to us with Captain John Keteltas, a great service will be rendered to us and our church, and we shall feel ourselves obligated to acknowledge our gratitude.

We subscribe ourselves, with prayer for the blessings of grace upon your persons and families,

   Your servants, THE CONSISTORY OF NEW YORK.

      In their behalf, J. RITZEMA, PRES.

February 17, 1755.

N. B. This comprises, under the name of (Voorsanger) chorister, also that of (Voorleeser) leader in reading, whose duty it shall be, during the absence or sickness of the minister (as we are not provided with candidates), to read a sermon for the edification of the congregation.

P. S. The Consistory also requests that Captain John Keteltas may be consulted as to the qualifications of the person who may be selected.*

* Con. Min., Lib. B. 157.

No vessel having sailed, the following letter was written to accompany the above :

March 28, 1755.

Messrs. JAN DREVES, N. N. SCHOUTE, and CHRISTIAN BORDING.

Esteemed Sirs: *—Since Capt. John Keteltas does not now journey to Amsterdam and there is another shipmaster in his place, with whom we are not so well acquainted, I am requested to inform you that the matter of providing a suitable man is left entirely in your hands. Yet if you do not find a suitable person, the Consistory would rather no one came over than to receive one lacking the requisite qualifications. However, the Consistory does not at all mean by this to frighten you, as if they were so scrupulous that scarce any one would meet their views, but only intends to indicate their urgent need of a well-qualified person. Expecting that this postscript will be well received, I subscribe myself, in the name and authority of the Low Dutch Church Reformed Congregation of Jesus Christ at New York.

Your obedient servant,

J. RITZEMA, V. D. M.,

p. t. PRAESES.

This call happily provides us with the aspect of the school, and the standard of the schoolmaster's qualifications, *more than a century and a quarter ago ;* and it resulted in the procurement of a teacher from Holland, who served the school faithfully till called away by a messenger from God.

1755.—Mr. JOHN NICHOLAS WELP having arrived from Amsterdam as *chorister* and *reader* in the Old Church, and also as *schoolmaster*, delivered his testimonials, which were satisfactory to the Consistory. It was Resolved, that eight pounds be appropriated for the freight, etc., of his goods from New London, in addition to the fifteen pounds promised for the expenses of his voyage ; † and the following letter betokens the kind hearts and magnanimous spirits which constituted the Consistory of that day:

Letter from Consistory to Messrs. JOHN DREVES, N. N. SCHOUTE, *and* CHRISTIAN BORDING.

Mr. Cornelus Clopper, Jr., one of our members, has already made you acquainted with the course of correspondence and safe arrival here of Mr. John Nicholas Welp, with his wife and children, in good health. We, however, feel ourselves in the highest measure obliged to express unto you our obligations more particularly, and to acknowledge with cordial thankfulness the trouble and care taken for us, and feel ready to reciprocate in anything which can be done on our part. What respects the small expenses of which Mr. Bording makes mention, in his letter, we send accompanying this, with Captain Anthony Rutgers,‡ four Spanish pieces, with the charge to pay in our name anything further which may exist. You, gentlemen, doubtless, expect to learn from us whether the person of Mr. Welp satisfies our expectation. We can say, although all is yet new, that there is nothing which can lead us to apprehend that the Consistory will regret the *heavy* and *unusual* expenses

---

* Con. Min., Lib. B. 165. † *Ibid.*, 176.
‡ Memb. Com. Coun. for eleven years. Val. Man. 1850, 221 *et seq.*

incurred by obtaining a person from Holland for such a service. His testimonials are highly laudatory, and the proof of his work hitherto being satisfactory to the congregation, good hope is entertained that, by his example and labors, he will be very useful in our Church, if it should please the Lord to spare him for some years, which we also desire on his account. The Consistory have, according to their promise, paid the passage-money from Holland, and have also paid, besides this, the expenses from New London, which were a little more than eight pounds. *Also*, considering the loss which Mr. Welp suffered in the sale of his goods, on account of his removing from Amsterdam at a short notice, as was mentioned in the letter of Mr. Bording, the Consistory have *voluntarily* made up a present of twenty pounds, which was very gladly received by Mr. Welp. We thus trust that, diligently employed in his school labors, he will feel himself satisfied with his situation, and find matter for thankfulness to the providence of God which has brought him here, of which he already gives tokens of acknowledgment. This, we believe, gentlemen, will give you satisfaction in the work you have done. We pray the God of heaven to bless you and the land of your residence, that it may not prove a prey to ambitious tyranny, especially not to the anti-Christian king of France, whose irreligious cruelty many, especially on the borders of our neighboring provinces, experience by the murders and burnings committed by the barbarous heathen hired by money, and mated for this purpose.

We subscribe ourselves, with great respect and affectionate greetings to Jaffron Bording, respected and well-known, gentlemen, your obedient and obliged servants.

In the name of Consistory,*

J. RITZEMA.

Dec. 29, 1755.

November 16, 1755.—Mr. Welp was allowed to claim for his instruction of the children, per quarter, for reading only, five shillings, for reading and writing, eight shillings, and sixpence for pen and ink ; and ten shillings for ciphering, and six shillings for those who learn singing.

August 22, 1757.—Ten children taught by the late Mr. Van Dalsen were allowed to Mr. Welp provisionally.†

* Con. Min., Lib. B. 177. The closing paragraph alludes to the barbarities perpetrated by the savages on the frontier inhabitants during the French and Indian war, 1754 1763. On the surrender of Oswego, the terms which had been agreed to were shamefully violated. Several of the British officers and soldiers were insulted, robbed, and massacred by the Indians. Most of the sick were scalped in the hospitals, and the French general delivered twenty of the garrison to the savages, that being the number they had lost during the seige, and these were tortured and burnt. Subsequently, on the surrender of Fort William Henry, on Lake George, "it was expressly stipulated by Montcalm that the prisoners should be protected from the savages by a guard, and that the sick and wounded should be treated with humanity. But the next morning, a great number of Indians, having been permitted to enter the lines, began to plunder. They massacred the sick and wounded, and attacked the defenseless troops with fiend-like fury. The stipulated guard was denied. On every side savages were butchering and scalping their wretched victims. Their hideous yells, the groans of the dying, and the frantic shrieks of others, shrinking from the uplifted tomahawk, were heard by the French unmoved. The fury of the savages was permitted to rage without restraint, until a large number were killed or hurried captives into the Wilderness." *Hale*, 119. † Con. Min., Lib. B. 191.

July 29, 1765.—A proposition* was made by Mr. Jacobus Van Zandt to establish a Latin and English Grammar School under the direction of our Consistory, in which, together with the languages, the elements of our religion will be taught.

This was agreed to by a majority; and it was further agreed that for the building or hiring of such a school-house a voluntary collection should be made through our congregation.

It was reserved for further consideration what site would be the most suitable for it; whether on the Harpending grounds or those which lie along the Old Church.

August 1.—The heading of a subscription to build or hire a suitable school-house was presented, but for important reasons the going round with it was delayed till the beginning of September.

"Until a few years before the erection [1769] of the North Church, all the public religious services had been held in the Dutch language. But the increase of the English language among the people, and the proportionate decline of the Dutch, became too apparent to escape the notice of observing men; and it became more and more evident to reflecting minds that unless the English language was introduced, the younger people would attach themselves to churches where that language was used, and the Dutch churches would dwindle away. Long discussions were held on this subject, and no little excitement was produced by the resolution which was finally adopted by the Consistory of the Collegiate Church, to call a minister who should officiate in the English language, while the Dutch was still to be continued for a part of each Sabbath. The Rev. Dr. Laidlie was the person called, and he preached his *first sermon in English* in the *Middle Dutch Church* on the *afternoon* of the last Sabbath in *March*, 1764, from 2 Cor. v. 11: '*Knowing therefore the terror of the Lord, we persuade men.*' All the services were conducted in English except the singing, which was performed in Dutch, led by *Jacobus Van Antwerp* (Voorsanger), 'the fore-singer,' as the congregation were unacquainted with the English psalmody. The house was densely crowded; the aisles were filled, many climbed up in the windows, and many of the most respectable people stood through the whole exercise." †

This measure, as might naturally be expected, gave great offence to some individuals, and their opposition to it was manifested for a long time, until, finally, finding expostulation vain, they invoked the aid of the civil power.

On the 6th day of July, 1767, more than three years after the settlement of the "English preacher," a few members of the

---

* Con. Min., Lib. B. 277.   † Greenleaf's Hist. N. Y. Churches, 15.

Dutch Church, opposed to his appointment, presented a remonstrance to his Excellency, Sir Henry Moore, Bart., Governor of New York, in which they complain that the Consistory had impinged upon the Constitution of the Church by violating certain liberties and privileges originally conferred at the capitulation in 1664; confirmed and enlarged by William III.'s charter, 1696;* and still further established, confirmed and extended to the ministers, elders, deacons and members of said Church by George II., in 1755. The remonstrance was signed by *Abel Hardenbrook, Jacobus Stoutenburgh* and *Huybert Van Wagenen.*† It consists of ten grievances, bearing directly or indirectly upon the introduction into the pulpit of the English language in the person of Mr. Laidlie. The sixth article was as follows: "That the *catechising* in the *Dutch language* is forbidden by one of the elders, alleging *it was a detriment* to Mr. Leadly. And Mr. Leadly has forbidden Mr. Leydecker (who was qualified for that business) to catechise, and say'd that the Consistory did not approve of it." The seventh states "that the Dutch school is not taken care of by the Rulers, to the total Ruin of the Dutch Education."

The Rev. John Ritzema, in the name and by the order of Consistory, addressed to his Excellency an answer to the Remonstrance, in which he sets the whole matter before the Governor and Council in its true light, and ably vindicates the action of Consistory. The following extract disposes of the charges which refer to the school:

> The sixth article alleges that catechising in the Dutch language was forbid by one of the elders, as also by Mr. Laidlie; this is not true, and if it was, the complainants must know that no one member of our Consistory has a right to forbid anything. Mr. Leydecker never was appointed by the Consistory to catechise in our Congregation, and is therefore not qualified; though one *Adrian Van Dersman* ‡ was so appointed; but on finding him a man of very immoral behavior, having forged the hand-writing of the Rev. Mr. Ritzema and others; wrote and subscribed letters directed to the Synod of North Holland, recommending himself as a proper person for the Ministry, by which the Rev. Mr. Ritzema at that time suffered much in his character. On the discovery of this fact the Consistory thought proper to discharge him from that office, and immediately appointed another in his stead; since which he has been upheld and supported by Mr. Hardenbrook's Party.
>
> In answer to the seventh article, "That the Dutch School is not taken care of, to the Ruin of the Dutch Education," we say that we have at present, and for twelve years last past, have employed Mr. Welp, who was sent for to Holland as a schoolmaster and catechist; he keeps a school constantly open, *receives payment from us* for teaching the poor children of the congre-

---

* *Ante,* pp. 37.

† This last-named individual was he who was the schoolmaster from 1743 to 1749. This remonstrance having failed of its object, he withdrew and connected himself with the English Church.

‡ *Ante,* p. 48.

gation, to the number of *thirty*, which number never was completed. He is a person very well qualified to catechise and teach a school, and we pay him a very handsome salary for his service; insomuch that his place is coveted by others. It has been insinuated to some of our congregation that if Mr. Vandersman could be restored as a catechist, and Mr. Stoutenburgh have Mr. Welp's place, all would be well. The first cannot be done, from the character above given; the latter cannot in honor be agreed to, as Mr. Welp is, beyond all comparison, better qualified, and was encouraged to come from Holland by the then Ruling Consistory.

It is observed, moreover,

That the Protest was wrote by Mr. Stoutenburgh, and all the names subscribed in his own hand-writing, and some of the same persons twice mentioned. It never appeared to the Consistory that Mr. Stoutenburgh had any directions from the people whose names he put down, and some of them denied that they ever had given him any.

This answer was dated 23d September, and on November 11, it was read in Council, and an Order made *dismissing the Petition of the Remonstrants.**

Sept. 11, 1769.—The Deacons requested that the catechists in the Dutch and English languages, to wit, Welp and Van Antwerp be discharged, because they could not, without injury to the poor, raise the sum of £31 to pay them both:

Resolved—Both should continue; and, in case of need, application should be made to the Elders.

April 30, 1770.—Mr. Welp asks £10 for his wife, for the use of the room for the Consistory:

Resolved—That the Deacons pay this amount; also, that Mr. Welp's appointment for a time as Visitor of the Sick and Catechist, with an added salary of £16, cease, as he is not in a condition (owing to bodily infirmity) to bear the burden; and the more as the Consistory makes no use of him in these offices.

RITZEMA, PRAES.

April 27, 1772.—The Praeses (Lambertus De Ronde) had in hand a letter to the Consistory, signed by Messrs. Richard Bancker, Abram Brasher and Cornelius Low, in the name of some charitable members of our church, proffering to the Consistory a sum of 5 and 70£ eight shillings, as the beginning of a Fund for the erection and maintenance of a Public School to be set up by the Consistory.

This charity was received with thanksgiving, and it was—

Resolved—That the money should be applied to no other use, and that the Praeses and Dominie Laidlie should thank the donors in the name of the Consistory.

Further—That this sum be given to the Treasurer, Bancker, and be put at interest for the purpose stated.†

* *Vide* Remonstrance and Reply in full, Doc. Hist. N. Y., iii. 511, *et seq.*
† Con. Min., Lib. B. 382.

Jan. 21, 1773.—Mr. Welp having deceased, the Deacons ask Consistory if they should pay the salary of the *late* Mr. Welp up to this day :

Resolved—That, since his son has hitherto provided for the foresinging, the full sum of £6 10s. 9d. shall be given him.

2nd.—Whether the payment for the Consistory Chambers shall now continue :

Resolved—That, as Mr. Welp owes a note of £20—advanced to him by the Deacons, January 21, 1771, to be deducted from his salary when due—of which £5 are still due, which would be discharged by twice fifty shillings, ending with May, 1773, the note should be surrendered as paid, and henceforth no rent be paid for the Consistory Chamber.

3rd.—Deacons to pay expenses of his funeral.
4th.—Shall Anthony Welp continue in the service?

To continue until further notice, and receive, for each Sunday, four shillings ; and also have the recording of the children in the Old Church.
He shall give place if Dominie Ritzema wishes to try any one else in the exercise of his gifts.
The widow and family shall remain in the Church house until May, 1773, without charge.

May 24.—The widow of Mr. Nicholas Welp shall receive from Consistory £20 for her yearly support.

Sept. 16.—She requested that the support promised might be given, and to know from whom she should receive it.

Resolved—That it be paid to her every quarter, from May 1, by the Treasurer, Bancker.

J. RITZEMA, p. t. PRAES.*

1773.—The expectations created by the appointment of Mr. Welp were fully realized. For more than seventeen years his duties as schoolmaster and chorister were faithfully and satisfactorily performed, when, yielding to the mandate from on high, his labors of love and usefulness were closed.

The English language (introduced into the pulpit just nine years previously) having now become quite prevalent, regard was had to this in the selection of his successor.

March 19, a proposition was offered to the Consistory, relating to a new schoolmaster in the place of the deceased, Mr. Welp, which was taken into mature deliberation. This proposition was in the following words :

Inasmuch as Mr. Nicholas Welp, who was our *Free School* master, is deceased, and it is highly necessary that another schoolmaster should be appointed to instruct *thirty poor* children in *reading, writing, and arithmetic, as well as in both the English and Dutch languages*, and as in the meantime, after

* Con. Min. under date.

inquiry, a suitable person has been found in the person of Mr. PETER VAN STEENBURGH, who is qualified to teach in BOTH languages; and, as the present school-house and Consistory-chamber * is so far decayed that it cannot stand much longer, it is therefore submitted to the consideration of the Consistory whether it is not advisable to pull down the school-house now standing, and erect a new one, —— more feet in breadth and —— feet more in length than the present; and also to erect a second story above it for a Consistory-chamber, and a free room for catechising, and the new school-building to be under one roof with the dwelling-house, and to be a frame building with a brick front. This can be done before the schoolmaster be ready to enter upon his labors. If the Consistory should deem it necessary to call the above-named schoolmaster, it is then submitted to them whether the following will not prove an adequate salary.

Here follow the six articles of stipulation, which will be found in the call made to Mr. Van Steenburgh.

The Consistory immediately resolved to carry the above proposition into execution, "as being the best which, in present circumstances, can be devised."

It was further resolved that a committee be appointed to prepare a call, according to the above proposition, on Mr. Van Steenburgh for one. The President and the elders, *A. P. Lott, Brinckerhoff, Rapelye* and *Duryee*, were appointed said committee. The elders, *Brinckerhoff,* and *Duychingh,* and *Beekman,*† and the deacons, *Abeel*‡ and *Hoffman*, were appointed a committee for the building of a new school-house.§

CALL. ‖ *of the Consistory of the Dutch Reformed Church of New York on Mr. Peter Van Steenburgh, at present schoolmaster at Flatbush, on Long Island:*

On account of the death of Mr. Nicholas Welp, schoolmaster of the Dutch congregation at New York, the school is broken up, on which account the children of the poor of our Congregation are destitute of necessary instruction; and as daily experience teaches us that the English language in this land gains such prevalence, that the Low Dutch language is continually diminished, and grows out of use, the Consistory of New York have therefore deemed it proper to call a person who is qualified to instruct and educate the Children in the *English* as well as the *Dutch* language; thus opening the way to induce the children of the poor of our congregation to receive instruction in the language which they or their parents may choose. The Consistory, having heard many favorable testimonials of your gifts and qualifications, and also having seen some proofs thereof, have unanimously agreed that you were a proper person to whom a call should be presented; and, learning that you are favorably disposed to undertake the service of schoolmaster, if an adequate support should be given, they have resolved to make a call upon you; and they hereby call you to instruct the children of the poor of the congregation, hereafter named, both in the English and Dutch languages, as may be required to

* Erected, 1748.
† Member Com. Coun. for nine years. Val. Man. 1850, 225, *et seq.*
‡ Member Com. Coun. for six years. Val. Man. 1850, 222, *et seq.*
§ This *second* school-house was erected, 1773, on the site of the former one; but, being larger, its front was nearer the line of the street. It was built by Mr. Anthony Post, an elder in the Dutch Church.
‖ Con. Min., Lib. B. 393.

teach them *reading, writing*, and *arithmetic*, also the questions in the *Heidelbergh Catechism*, or *such other as is conformable to the doctrine of our Low Dutch Church*. The scholars are to be instructed and exercised therein at least once a week. The school is to be opened every morning, and also closed, with prayer, that all may be conducted with order and to edification, and prove a good example to all present. We promise to pay you, for the service thus rendered,

First.—For the instruction of *thirty* poor children in the Low Dutch or English language, as above stated, in reading, writing, and arithmetic, the fourth part of which shall be paid every three months, £60.

Second.—*Firewood* for one year, £8

Third.—Books, paper, ink, quills, etc., for one year, £5.

Fourth.—For taking care of and cleaning the Consistory and catechising chamber, and the making of fires and lighting when required, £8.

N. B. The wood and candles for the same shall be furnished by the deacons.

Fifth.—For your encouragement you shall have a *dwelling-house and garden free*, and also a good room for the school.

Sixth.—It shall be allowed to you to instruct as many other children as may offer themselves to you, but not beyond the number of *thirty*, and also *to keep an evening school*.

This, our agreement with you, shall, according to your request, be for one year, reckoning from the 1st day of June next. If, then, it shall not be agreeable to you to continue longer our schoolmaster, you shall be obligated to give notice to Consistory three months before the expiration of your labors, that they may during that time provide another teacher; and if, then, the Consistory should be satisfied with your instruction and service, and be desirous that you should longer continue our schoolmaster, further stipulations may then be made. We hope the above offer will meet with your approbation. Wishing you and your family all prosperity and blessing, we remain, with great respect,

In the name, and by the order, of the Consistory,

Your servants,

ARCH. LAIDLIE, p. t. Pres.
JACOB DURYEE,
GERRIT RAPELYE,*
ABRAHAM P. LOTT,†
DIRCK BRINCKERHOFF.‡

This call, which was accepted by Mr. Van Steenburgh, was dated March 20, 1773.

On the 6th of August following, the *newly built* school-house was ready for the reception of school-children, and Mr. Van Steenburgh entered upon his duties.

Nov. 27, 1773.—Consistory held, after calling on God's name.

The account was presented for the new school-house, with its dependencies, amounting to £856 15s. 1½d., on which already had been paid by the Treasurer, Bancker, £554 1s. 4½d., leaving a remainder of £302 13s. 9d.; and Mr. Bancker was ordered to take up for the Church so much money as should be required to pay off the workmen and other necessary claims.§

J. RITZEMA, p. t. Praeses.

* Member Com. Coun. for three years. Val. Man. 1850, 220.
† Member Com. Coun. for eight years. Val. Man. 1850, 221.
‡ Member Com. Coun. for five years. Val. Man. 1850, 220.
§ Con. Min., Lib. B. 403.

For three years, in the midst of intense public excitement, the school continued its operations under Mr. Van Steenburgh, when, by force of uncontrollable circumstances, it was obliged to disband.

Opposition to those measures which eventually led to a rupture with the mother-country was nowhere more strongly manifested than in New York. Here the Provincial Congress met (1765), and passed the famous Declaration of Rights. Here the stamped paper had been destroyed, and the Lieutenant-Governor hung in effigy (1765). The Assembly had refused to provide quarters and provisions for such troops as England wished to march into the colony (1767); and on the arrival of a cargo of tea (1773, the year of Van Steenburgh's appointment) the "Sons of Liberty," a formidable organization, destroyed it. These, and other like measures, when the crisis arrived, led to the early subjugation of the city, which, as the headquarters of the British army, was under martial law. Many of the citizens fled to neighboring places. All the churches and schools were closed, and naught was heard save the accidents of war.

RECAPITULATION.

The disseveration of the Dutch Church from the Colonial Government, the absence of Consistorial records, and there being no newspapers as yet established, the information respecting the school for several years after the capitulation is necessarily very limited; but, identified with the Dutch Church as an institution of long-cherished inheritance, she could not dispense with it, without the violation of principles and feelings totally incompatible with her constitution and aims. The testimony of its existence by the Roman Catholic, Dongan, and by some of the Episcopal governors, who strenuously promoted the extension of their own denominational peculiarities, so much so as to call for decided action on the part of Consistory, when attempts were made under the guise of authority, even in the face of chartered privileges, to suppress or control it, is not only strongly inferential, but of a decidedly positive character.

1661.—Evert Pietersen Keteltas appointed schoolmaster, clerk, chorister and visitor of the sick, was still teaching, although infirm, Dec. 16, 1686, and it is highly probable that he continued to teach until 1687—twenty-three years after the capitulation.

1705.—Upon the existence of a vacancy, Lord Cornbury claimed the right of appointing the schoolmaster, notwithstanding the clause in the incorporation-act of William III. (1696), reserving this right to the ministers and Consistory. This claim led to a meeting of the Great Consistory, who determined to preserve their chartered privileges inviolate.

January 1, 1726.—*Barent De Forest*, schoolmaster, until December, 1732.

June 1, 1733.—*Gerrit Van Wagenen*, foresinger, schoolmaster and visitor of the sick. School at the corner of Marketfield and Broad streets. Deceased 1743, and was succeeded by his son, *Huybert Van Wagenen*, who resigned April, 1749.

1743.—The population having extended "far uptown," the Deacons opened a School in Cortlandt Street, of which Abraham De Lanoy was appointed teacher. He commenced with *ten* scholars, receiving from Consistory, in quarterly payments, the amount of money and firewood which Mr. Huybert Van Wagenen received for the same number. This branch school was still in existence about 1763, and probably continued until the British took possession of the city in 1776. The catechetical instruction in the Garden Street Church was attended to by Mr. Huybert Van Wagenen, and in the Middle Church by Mr. De La Noy.

1748.—The first school and dwelling-house for the teacher were built in Garden Street, opposite the church.

April 1, 1749.—Daniel Bratt, schoolmaster and chorister in the Middle Church. He had twelve free scholars, six in reading and six in writing, for which he received £12 10s. and a load of wood for each scholar, annually, half nut and half oak. For his services as chorister, he received £12 10s. and fees for entering baptisms. Removed by Consistory in 1755.

1751.—Adrian Van Dersman, visitor of the sick and catechiser; removed by Consistory previous to 1767.

1755.—John Nicholas Welp was called from Holland as schoolmaster and chorister in the Old Church. He had twenty scholars and a salary of £80, and the use of dwelling-house. Deceased in 1773.

1767.—Complaint made to the Governor by certain parties respecting the management of the school, and the introduction therein of the English language; which complaint was dismissed.

June 1, 1773.—Peter Van Steenburgh, who had been schoolmaster at Flatbush since 1762, succeeds Mr. Nicholas Welp (whereupon Anthony Welp, who had assisted his father as foresinger, was appointed master of the school at Flatbush, where he continued until 1776). Reading, writing, and arithmetic taught in *both* languages. The school and dwelling-house rebuilt; the Consistory-chamber and catechising-room occupying the second floor. Number of pupils, *thirty*. Salary, same as Mr. Welp's. He had the privilege of receiving *thirty* pay scholars, and of teaching evening school. On the arrival of the British army, in 1776, the school disbanded. We have now lost sight of the Krank-besoecker, the Voorsanger, and the Voorleeser.

ADDITIONAL FACTS

CONNECTED WITH EDUCATION IN NEW-YORK, WHILE UNDER THE ADMINISTRATION OF THE ENGLISH.*

1673.—The Latin school, established by the Dutch in 1659, and which was so successful under the management of Ægidius Luyck, was sustained by the English authorities for eight years, when it was closed. In 1673 Luyck was appointed a Schepen.

1674.—*Matthew Hillyer* licensed to teach by "The Worshipfull the Mayor and Alldermen of this Citty of New Yorke."

August 25, 1676.—The privilege continued to Hillyer and a license granted to *Ebenezer Kirtland*.

1685.—Father *Henry Harrison*, S. J.; 1686-7, Father *Charles Gage*, S. J., teachers in a Latin School, set up during the administration of Governor Dongan.

About 1690-1.—*David Jamison*, from Scotland, taught a Latin School for a brief period.

1696-7.—*David Vilant*, by permission of the Mayor and Aldermen, kept a school in the publick Citty Hall.

1698.—*Alexander Paxton* and *Johannes Schanck* taught school.

1701.—*Robert Parkinson*.

1702.—An act passed by the Generall Assembly of this Province for the encouragement of a Free Grammar School, to be built on the King's farm. The first teacher thereof was *George Muirson*, who was appointed by Lord Cornbury, Aprill Twenty-ffifth, 1704.

Jan. 22, 1705.—*Andrew Clarke* was appointed to succeed him. The Records furnish no further information respecting the School.

1702.—*Peter Bontecon* and *John Selwood* private schoolmasters.

1703.—*John Stevens* and *Dan Twaites*, schoolmasters. *Andrew ffoucault* Impowered to teach an English and ffrench school, as alsoe ye art of Writeing, Arethmetick, &c.

1704.—*William Vesey*, Episcopal Missionary, opened a catechising school for blacks, with *Elias Neau* as catechist, from August 24, 1704.

August 29, 1705.—*Mr. Prudent De La Fayole* was licensed to keep a French school.

1706.—Lord Cornbury "authorized and Impowered Mr. *James Jeffray* to Keep and Teach School within the city of New York, and to Instruct all children with whom he Should be intrusted in the art of Writing and Arithmetick for and During his Pleasure."

* Culled mainly from New Amsterdam Records; MSS. Records in the office of the Secretary of State, Albany; History of Trinity Church, by Rev. William Berrian, D.D.; Valentine's Hist. N. Y. and Manual for 1863; Watson's Annals; and from advertisements in the newspapers of the last century.

1709.—The Society for the Propagation of the Gospel in Foreign Parts appointed *William Huddlestone* (clerk of Trinity Church) the first schoolmaster of the Episcopal Church School. Deceased 1723, and was succeeded in both offices by his son, *Thomas Huddlestone*. 1731–1741, *Thomas Noxon*. 1741–1777. *Thomas Hildreth*. 1777–1781, *Amos Bull*. Instruction in the Catechisms of the Church was statedly imparted to the pupils by persons well qualified to inculcate the principles of Divine Truth. The earliest Catechists were *Elias Neau*, 1709–1722; *Rev. James Wetmore*, 1724–1726; *Rev. Thomas Colgan*, 1726–1731; *Rev. Mr. Charlton*, 1731–1747; *Rev. Samuel Auchmuty*, 1747–1764.

This school has received from Trinity Church over $60,000 in money and in real estate, which is now very valuable. In 1800 it was endowed and placed in the hands of Trustees, who in 1806 received an act of Incorporation from the Legislature of New York.

It was known as the "Episcopal Charity School" from 1748 to 1826; subsequently, as the New York Protestant Episcopal Public School, and since 1845 as the Trinity School.

In 1748 the first School-house was built on Rector Street, west of Broadway.

In 1832 Trinity Church granted to the Trustees at a nominal rent a lease of five lots of ground on Canal, Varick, and Grand streets, on which was erected a commodious school-house.

Rev. William Morris, who was the Rector of the School for about a quarter of a century, resigned in 1857, and was succeeded by *Charles D'Urban Morris*, M. A., who was superseded in 1863 by the present Rector, *Rev. Robert Holden*. The School is located at present at No. 1517 Broadway.

1712.—*Allane Jarratt*, having applied for a "Lycence to teach Writing, Arithmetick, Navigation and other parts of the Mathematicks," his application was granted in due form, as follows:

By His Excellency Robert Hunter, Esq., etc.

To ALLANE JARRATT, GENTLEMAN, GREETING: Being assured of your experience and Knowledge in ye practice of ye art of Navigation and of all parts of the Mathematicks, I doe hereby authorize and Impower you to Teach writing, arithmetick, navigation, and other parts of mathematicks, to all such persons as shall be desirous to be Instructed therein within this City or province of New York for and during my pleasure.

Given under my hand and Seale at Fort Anne, in New York, ye flourth day of July, in ye Eleaventh yeare of ye reigne of our Soveraigne, Lady Anne, by ye grace of God of Great Brittaine, ffrance and Ireland, Queene, Defender of ye ffaith, &c. Annoque, D. M. 1712.

R. O. HUNTER.

By His Excellencie's command,

J. WILEMAN, D. Secretary.

1715.—*John Conrad Codwise*, private Schoolmaster.
1721.—*Geo. Browning* and *Wm. Glover*, do.
1723.—*John Walton*, do.
1724.—*Jonathan Sherer*, do.
1725.—*Peter Finch*, do.
1728.—*Edward Gatehouse*, Writing Master.

1730.—*James Lyde* commenced to teach "evening school at the Custom House in a room conveniently fitted up for the purpose."

1731.—*George Brownell*, near the Custom House, taught "Reading, Writing, Ciphering, Merchants' Accounts, Latin, Greek, &c.; also Dancing, Plain-work, Flourishing, Imbroidery, and various Sorts of Works."

1732.—The first free school was established by law for teaching the Latin and Greek, and practical branches of mathematics. *Mr. Alexander Malcolm*, of Aberdeen, was appointed Principal, at £40 per annum. At the end of seven years it was discontinued.

1732.—*William Thurston*, Schoolmaster, at the Corner-House by Koentie's Market, over against the Skotch Arms.

1735.—*Peter Stoutenburgh* and *Daniel Shatford*.
1736.—*John Cavelier*, private schoolmaster.
1737.—*Charles Henley*, do.
1739.—*Walter Hetherington*, do.
1740.—*Thomas Allen*, do.
1742.—*Edward Marriner*, do.

1744.—*Charles Johnston* advertised to teach Writing, Arithmetick and Latin.

1746.—*Malcolm Campbell*, ⎫
1747.—*Archibald McEwen*, ⎬ Private schoolmasters.
1748.—*Joseph Hildreth*, ⎭

1748.—*Cornelius Lynch* taught writing, arithmetic, vulgar and decimal fractions, navigation, gauging, surveying, dialling, mensuration, and merchants' accounts, in Stone Street.

George Gordon taught book-keeping, next the French Church.

1749.—*Benjamin Leigh*, Broad street, near the Long Bridge; *Thomas Evans*, shoemaker, near the new dock, reading, writing, and arithmetic.

1750.—By the Governor's permission, a benefit was given the Episcopal school, at the theatre in Nassau Street.

Charles Dutens, teacher of French, and jeweller, in a long advertisement, full of self-conceit and egotism, and bountifully interlarded with Latin phrases, proclaimed that he taught a school, "for the use of young ladies and gentlemen, whose love of learning might incline them to take lessons from him in French, at his house, on Broad Street, near the Long Bridge, where he also makes and vends finger and earrings, solitaires, stay-hooks and lockets, and sets diamonds, rubies, and other stones. Science and virtue are two sisters, which the most part of the New York ladies possess," &c.

1751.—*John Nathan Hutchins.*
1752.—*Thomas Allen*, near Alderman Cortlandt's.
Robert Leith, Wall street.

July 6, 40 boys and 12 girls, Episcopal charity scholars, were present at the consecration of St. George's Chapel.

1753.—*John Lewis*, Broad street, near Long Bridge, and *Garret Noel*.

1757.—*Richard R. Smith*, *Nicholas Barrington* and *Thomas Clark*, taught private schools in Maiden lane.

Edward Willetts, day and night school, Broadway.

First notice of charity sermon at Trinity Church. Collection taken to clothe the children, and suitable anthem sung.

1762.—*Thomas Jackson*, Latin and Greek, head of New Street, opposite Presbyterian Church.

William Clajon, teacher of French, Beaver street.

1765.—*Henry Peckwell.*
1768.—*John Young.*
1770.—*Stephen Van Voorhis* and *Jacob Tyler.*
1773.—*Thomas Byerly* opened an English grammar-school.
1774.—*James Gilleland.*

1777.—Charity sermon at St. George's Chapel. Fifty-six boys and thirty girls; reading, writing, and arithmetic taught, and needle-work to the girls. Mr. *Wood*, teacher.

1793.—Episcopal school-house, built near and for St. Paul's Church.

Vanbombeler was the last schoolmaster who taught in the Dutch language *exclusively*, about the year 1785.

CHAPTER IV.

HISTORY OF THE SCHOOL OF THE REFORMED DUTCH CHURCH, FROM 1783 TO THE PRESENT TIME.

During the Revolutionary War New York was the headquarters of the British power in America, and here the most important schemes for operations against the patriots were planned and put in motion. The municipal government was overthrown, martial law prevailed, and the business of the city degenerated almost into the narrow operations of suttling. Many of the residents left the city, and their deserted houses were taken possession of by the officers of the army and the refugee loyalists. Barracks and entrenchments were erected from Corlaer's Hook and on the line of Chambers Street to the North River. Five thousand American prisoners were confined in the jails, sugar-houses, and dissenting churches of the city. For about two months several hundred prisoners were huddled together in the Middle Dutch Church, when they were removed, and it was converted into a riding-school. The North Church contained eight hundred prisoners, it having been floored over from gallery to gallery. The mahogany pulpit was carefully removed, sent to London, and placed in a chapel there; the pews were used for fuel. A theatre was established; tennis-courts and other kinds of amusements were introduced, and for *seven years* the city remained a prey to the licentiousness of strong and idle detachments of a well-provided army. To add to these evils, in Sept., 1776, four hundred and ninety-three houses, located between Whitehall Slip and Cortlandt Street, and from the North to the East rivers, were consumed by fire—Trinity and the Lutheran Church falling a prey; and again, in August, 1778, three hundred houses were consumed in the neighborhood of Coenties Slip. "There were no public-moneyed or charitable institutions; no banks or insurance offices; all church services were suspended; education was entirely neglected, and the schools and college closed."* On the cessation of hostilities the scattered inhabitants gradually returned; but the evils of war were protracted long beyond its duration; and the impoverished inhabitants as well as the municipal government suffered for many years from the disastrous consequences of British occupation.

* Lossing's Field-Book of the Revolution, 835, 836, 865. Valentine's Man. Com. Coun., 1852, p. 435, *et seq.*

Yet, notwithstanding this sad and calamitous state of affairs, both public and private, on the re-organization of Consistory, while the interiors of the churches were still in a dilapidated condition, it was

Resolved, That Mr. Peter Van Steenburgh, who was the *public schoolmaster* of this congregation at the commencement of the war, and is again returned to this city, shall be considered as bound by his former call, and shall have permission to dwell in the school-house, and open his school in the large room built for that purpose.*

This resolution is dated September 7, 1783, but four days subsequent to the signing of the treaty of peace at Paris. Thus, while the British still remained in possession of the city, the school was re-organized; the evacuation not taking place till the 25th of November following.

March 22, 1784.—"It was ordered that the number of children to be educated by Mr. Van Steenburgh, as charity scholars, shall be restricted to *ten*." †

This is the first use of the term "charity." The school, from the date of its establishment up to the passage of the last resolution, was designated as the *Public, Free*, or *Low Dutch School*. Subsequent to the war, there being no public provision for the education of youth, schools were established in connection with the different religious denominations. These depended for their support upon the voluntary contributions of church members. The Episcopal Charity School, known as such since 1748, had received many valuable legacies from individuals in that communion, and was materially aided by the large annual collections of the Episcopal churches. These facts led to the adoption of the term "charity" by the various schools organized, as, in that day of general poverty, some such movement was necessary in order to work effectually on the sympathies of the people; but, like everything adopted upon the principle of availability, in the end it proved most disastrous to the well-being of those very institutions for whose pecuniary interests its use was originally introduced. The Episcopal school subsequently discarded the term, and became a chartered institution under a new and less repulsive title. Our own school, dearly loved and cherished from *principle*, though laboring for many years under the disadvantages arising from the use, under the sanction of custom, of the obnoxious term, still exists, though it cannot be denied that its usefulness, from this cause, in days that are past was seriously impaired.

The term charity may be as appropriately applied to Sabbath-schools or to our common schools as to church schools; yet who

---

* Consist. Rec., anno 1783, Lib. G. p. 3.
† *Ibid*, anno 1784, Lib. G. p. 16.

is there that would advocate the application of this term to them? No! It may answer for other latitudes; but there is that in it so repugnant to the republican spirit of our people and institutions, that where used injudiciously and unnecessarily in connection with any institution, it so wounds those fine and correct sensibilities of our nature that even the necessitous are led to keep aloof from it, lest they may be pointed at by the finger of derision.

The church schools that sprung into existence towards the close of the last century have long since ceased to exist.

The period succeeding protracted war has ever constituted the dark days of religion and literature; and such was the crippled condition of the Collegiate Church at this time, that it was with difficulty the school was sustained. As yet, no fund had been instituted for its support, nor had collections been made for it in the churches; and as Mr. Van Steenburgh was privileged to have *thirty* pay scholars, exclusive of those educated by the Church, a proposition was made for renting the school-house and attached dwelling to him, on condition that he would teach such children as the Consistory might send him, at the same rate per quarter for tuition as he received from his other scholars.

An arrangement to this effect was consequently entered into with Mr. Van Steenburgh, Consistory furnishing him with twelve scholars.* The result, however, was far from satisfactory.

The Church felt that she was not performing her full duty towards her children. This institution was her time-honored legacy; she had long realized the important blessings flowing from it, and she could not relinquish it, nor her jurisdiction over it, without coming short of imperative obligations to her youth.

Impelled by a recurring sense of her responsibilities to her youth, and actuated by a regard to her future interests, special efforts were made for a thorough re-organization of the school.

To effect this, a committee of Consistory, consisting of Messrs. John Stagg, William Hardenbrook, Elias Nexsen, Nicholas Anthony, and Leonard Bleecker, was appointed. This was in December, 1788. The arrangement with Mr. Van Steenburgh, which had been existing for three years, was revoked. A new engagement was entered into with him, to commence in May following, whereby he was to educate thirty free scholars, for which he was to receive from Consistory £35 per annum.†

In April, 1789, the above Committee reported to Consistory certain regulations respecting the school, which were unanimously adopted, "subject, however, to such alterations as the Consistory shall hereafter judge necessary to be made."

The first of these was, "That the *free* school shall always be considered as depending for its existence and support on the

* Con. Rec., Lib. G. 87.   † Con. Rec., Lib. G. 146, 147.

Consistory, and as such be subject to the direction and control of the whole Board."

The school, replaced under the jurisdiction of the Board of Deacons as a standing committee, was to be visited by the whole Consistory quarterly, viz.: in the first week after every administration of the Lord's Supper; and provision was made for the attendance of the children on divine service. The remaining regulations, relating mainly and specifically to the internal management of the school, were substantially the same as those now in force in the institution.*

In the fall of this year, so far as can be ascertained from the Church records, commenced the practice of providing each scholar with a full suit of clothing, collections being made in the Collegiate Church for that express purpose. The first sermon upon this subject was preached in the North Church, December 17, services commencing at 5½ P. M.† The sum contributed by the congregation amounted to $216.05, the most of which was expended by the deacons for the object contemplated.

The year following, 1790, collections were taken in the Old, New and North Churches, and "the Consistory rejoiced in finding themselves enabled, by the generous donations of the congregations, to increase the number of scholars, and resolved unanimously to admit twenty more children in the school on the 1st of February next."‡

For a number of years the liberality of the Collegiate Church in this cause was proverbial, the donations in one instance amounting to $753; but of late, from the operation of various causes, the collections have materially diminished. Notwithstanding this, the trustees of the institution, with an humble and firm reliance upon Divine Providence, have never yet been coerced to say to any of the necessitous committed to their charge, "Be ye clothed."

* Con. Rec., Lib. G. 154, *et seq.*

† A public journal of that day, in publishing the notice for this sermon, adds the following:

"Institutions of this kind, which afford to poor children the means of education, and prepare them for usefulness in Church or State, appear of all charities the most laudable. Several denominations of this city have accordingly turned their attention to them. The Reformed Dutch Church had, before the war, a charity school, which, during this year, they have been able to revive. They have at present thirty scholars, who are instructed in such branches of learning as will qualify them to be good members of society. The school is visited monthly by the deacons, and quarterly by Consistory; and whenever the scholars have made such proficiency as is judged necessary, their places are supplied by others. This church depend for the clothing and tuition of the children wholly upon charitable donations, and they trust that their endeavors will be countenanced by the public." *Vide New York Journal and Weekly Register*, December 17, 1789.

‡ Con. Rec., Lib. G. 197.

1791.—From the establishment of the school in 1633, the schoolmasters had, with but one or two exceptions, acted as choristers ; and, in order to preserve this peculiarity, Mr. Stanton Latham, who had been Clerk in the North Church from October, 1789, was appointed in January, 1790, to supersede Mr. Van Steenburgh ; but the change did not actually take place till May 1, 1791. On the 11th of January of this year, a committee, appointed to confer with Mr. Latham, made a report to Consistory, and produced a written proposal, signed by Mr. Latham, in which he offered to teach fifty scholars for seven shillings per quarter. After some deliberation, it was resolved to accept the offer ; and Mr. Latham was accordingly appointed to be the schoolmaster of the school under the patronage of this Consistory, and to commence in that duty 1st May next, on which day "he is to take possession of the house in which Mr. Van Steenburgh now lives, and occupy as much of the same as Mr. Van Steenburgh now occupies, which house, and the aforesaid sum of seven shillings per quarter for fifty scholars, shall be the whole of his salary as schoolmaster.

Resolved, further, that this Consistory have a high sense of the abilities, assiduity, and faithfulness which Mr. Van Steenburgh has for many years exerted in the school which has been under his care, and excepting for the particular reason which respected Mr. Latham as a singing-master in the congregation, would have been loth to part with him.

Resolved, further, that a copy of this minute be made and given to Mr. Van Steenburgh, which will be at the same time a notification that Mr. Latham is to take possession of the house in which Mr. Van Steenburgh now lives, 1st May next." *

November 27.—A collection was taken for the school in the Garden Street Church in the afternoon, and in the Middle Church in the evening, where the children were in attendance, and sung a hymn † suited to the occasion.

January 5, 1792.— Dr. Livingston, Messrs. Stoutenburgh, Oothout, Wilson, Gilbers and Sickels, were appointed a committee of Consistory to digest a plan for the most successful promotion of the interests of the school.

February 2.—The above committee reported as follows :

In order as far as possible to extend the benefit of this institution, and to secure to the boys admitted into the school the permanent advantages of the instruction there received, they conceive it proper that it be an indispensable condition of the admission of boys in future, that their parents or guardians

---

* Con. Rec., Lib. G. 199.

† This custom, which was discontinued, 1865, was borrowed from the Episcopal Church school, in which it had obtained as far back as the year 1757, and probably a few years earlier. The hymns used by the children of the Reformed Dutch school on these occasions have been prepared, from year to year, by the friends of the institution. A majority of these compositions, running back as far as the year 1813, are now in the possession of the present Principal.

do previously, by bond, engage themselves to bind them to some useful profession or employment at the expiration of their terms in school, or secure to Consistory the power of so doing.

This article was never carried out.

That, as far as the consent of the parents or guardians can be obtained, the same resolution be extended to the boys already admitted.

That *ten* boys be admitted into the school, in addition to the present number under the care of Mr. Latham.

That *ten* girls, at present under the tuition of Mr. Latham, be removed and be put under the care of a female instructor.*

MISS ELIZABETH TEN EYCK was accordingly engaged, and continued in this capacity until the year 1809, when, upon the introduction into the school of the Lancasterian system of education, "the Madam's school was dispensed with." She immediately opened a private school, to which, during a period of three years, the trustees occasionally sent some of their female pupils to receive instruction in sewing.† During Miss Ten Eyck's connection with the school, and for thirty years afterwards, she had the making of the girls' clothing; and, in whatever capacity she was engaged by the trustees, her duties were always performed in a satisfactory manner.

1795.—Mr. Latham, like his predecessor, enjoyed the privilege of having pay scholars; but the Consistory, impressed with the necessity of having the school composed exclusively of charity scholars, had an interview with him, and, on the 8th day of January, they "*Resolved*, that from and after the 1st February next, none but charity scholars shall be admitted into the school; and that the number of such shall remain unlimited, and depend from time to time upon the direction of Consistory." And, further, "*Resolved*, that from and after the said day, the Consistory will pay unto Mr. Latham £200 per annum, and that he shall continue to remain in the house, as hitherto, free of all rent." Also, "*Resolved*, to allow twelve loads of wood every year for the school; and it is expressly understood that, besides the usual education in literature, Mr. Latham shall teach the scholars psalmody, as is usual in all institutions of this nature."

"Mr. Latham being called, and these resolutions communicated to him, he acquiesced, and declared his willingness and gratitude for this arrangement; and it is now reciprocally understood that all former agreements are hereby superseded, and that this shall be the basis for the future services of Mr. Latham, and no alteration is to be made therein on either side under at least six months' notice; and that a copy of this minute be handed to Mr. Latham." ‡

* Con. Rec., Lib. G. 225-227. † Trus. Min. i. 26, 30, 32, 40, 67, 73.
‡ Con. Rec., Lib. H. 1.

June 17.—Dr. Linn reported he had received from Dr. Joshua Lathrop, of Norwich, Conn., a guinea for the benefit of the School.*

May 25, 1799.—By a resolution of Consistory, the number of children was restricted to fifty ; † probably in consequence of the withdrawal of the funds which, during the years 1796 and 1797, the school had received from the State.

1801.—The catechising of the scholars by the ministers was transferred to the North Church.

March 1, 1804.—The number of scholars under the care of the master was limited to *sixty;* and he was privileged to receive six pay scholars.‡ In addition to the studies already taught in the school, the boys, if time and circumstances admitted, were to be instructed in the principles of English grammar.

A committee was appointed to report upon the propriety of extending the benefits of the institution to such individual or individuals, of superior talents or acquirements, as might be calculated to fit them for future usefulness in Church or State.

1808.—For a period of one hundred and seventy-five years, commencing in 1633, the deacons had constituted the Standing Committee of Consistory for the management of the school ; but in the year 1808, May 5, the code of 1789 was amended so as to place the institution under the care of a "Board of Trustees," whose duty it should be "to advise with Consistory in all matters that may be deemed important, and in all things to be under their control." §

The original members of the Board were, Messrs. John Stoutenburgh, Richard Duryee, Isaac Heyer, Abraham Brinckerhoff, Anthony Dey, Jesse Baldwin, and John Nitchie, Jr. Their first meeting was held June 9, 1808, in the Consistory-chamber, Garden Street. John Stoutenburgh was chosen Chairman, and John Nitchie, Jr., Secretary.

The VIIth Article of their By-Laws provided for a committee of two of the Trustees, to be called the School Committee ; and at each stated meeting the "Chairman shall appoint one of the School Committee in succession from the Trustees, to supply the place of one whose term shall expire." This was amended in 1831, so that there is now but one member on the Visiting Committee.

January 1, 1809.—The school-room having been enlarged, the Lancasterian or monitorial system was introduced into the school, and the number of scholars was increased from seventy-two to one hundred.

* Con. Rec., Lib. II. 21. † *Ibid.*, 138. ‡ *Ibid.*, 326.
§ The Rules for the government of the Board of Trustees are contained in the "Standing Rules of the Consistory of the Collegiate R. P. D. Church," Art. xiii.,

February 27.—Thirteen girls each received a pair of scissors for their improvement in writing; and twelve boys each a pen-knife. These were presents from Richard Duryee, Esq. At subsequent dates, useful articles, the gifts of different individuals, were presented to the most meritorious children.

March 7.—The number of scholars having been increased, and Mr. Latham having relinquished the pay scholars granted him in 1804, his salary was advanced to six hundred dollars per annum, and his house-rent.

December 6.—Mr. Latham presented his resignation, to take effect the first of May following; and Joseph Hinds, who graduated from the school in 1808, was engaged as an assistant-teacher for a period of seven weeks.

December 7.—James Forrester was unanimously elected by Consistory, to supersede Mr. Latham. His competitors were Richard Witts and Paul J. Micheau.*

May 1, 1810.—Mr. Forrester entered upon his duties, and the school was divided, under the Lancasterian system, as follows:

In sand.
- First Class—A B C, and figures.
- Second Class—Monosyllables.
- Third Class—Words of two syllables, and writing same on slate.

On slate.
- Fourth Class—Words of more than two syllables, and irregular words.
- Fifth Class—Reading in Child's Instructor; Catechism.
- Sixth Class—Reading in New Testament; Heidelbergh Catechism.

Seventh Class—Reading in Old Testament, Murray's Grammar, and Penmanship.

All to study arithmetic, at the discretion of the teacher.

June 21.—In case the minister was absent, from sickness or otherwise, one of the elders was to conduct the catechetical exercise.

January 10, 1811.—The eight-day clock, which had hung for many years in the Garden Street Church, was cleansed and recased by M. Demilt, at an expense of twenty-five dollars. It was then put up in the school-room. What the bank or railway clock is to the adult, this, for many years, has been to anticipative youth; and though it cannot foretell, yet its indications have signalized the period for the resumption of study, or the desired release. Venerable by age, and faithful amidst all the changes of time, suspended on the walls of the present building, it still answers nobly the precise object for which it was made; and, were it gifted with speech, it could undoubtedly reveal more knowledge of mischievous frolic than ever fell under the cognizance of the teacher.

* Con. Rec., Lib. I. 107. Trus. Min. i. 24, 26, 36.

January 25, 1813.—Mr. Nitchie having resigned his situation as Secretary of the Board, a unanimous vote of thanks was passed to him by the trustees, for the diligent and able discharge of his duties for nearly five years ; and at the annual election of officers in 1814, Mr. Richard Duryee having been chosen chairman, it was on motion resolved, that the thanks of the Board be communicated to Mr. Stoutenburgh, for his faithful and punctual attendance as chairman for nearly six years.

1813.—"On the 2d of April, 1805 (the same year in which the Free School Society was founded), the Legislature passed an act providing that the net proceeds of 500,000 acres of the vacant and unappropriated lands of the people of this State, which should be first thereafter sold by the Surveyor-General, should be appropriated as a permanent fund for the support of common schools ; the avails to be safely invested until the interest should amount to $50,000, when an annual distribution of that amount should be made to the several school districts. This act laid the foundation of the present fund for the support of common schools."

" By the act to incorporate the Merchants' Bank in the city of New York, passed the same year, the State reserved the right to subscribe for three thousand shares of the capital stock of that institution, which, together with the accruing interest and dividends, were appropriated as a fund for the support of common schools, to be applied in such manner as the Legislature should from time to time direct."

" By acts passed March 13, 1807, and April 8, 1808, the Comptroller was authorized to invest such moneys, together with the funds arising from the proceeds of the lotteries authorized by the act of 1803, in the purchase of additional stock of the Merchants' Bank, and to loan the residue of the fund." *

On the 19th day of June, 1812, an act was passed for the establishment of common schools in this State, and provision was soon after made, in accordance with the act of 1805, for the distribution of the interest arising from the common school fund.† As there were several Societies in the city of New York at this time already engaged in the work of educating the poor, all of which had for many years been successfully and satisfactorily engaged in this laudable undertaking, a law was passed March 12, 1813, "directing that the portion of the school fund received by the city and County of New York shall be apportioned and paid to the trustees of the Free School Society of New York, the trustees or treasurers of the Orphan Asylum Society, the Society of the Economical School, the African free

* Common School System of the State of New York, by Samuel S. Randall, Dep. Sup. Com. Sch., p. 9.   † Rand. Com. Sch. Sys. S. N. Y., 13.

school, *and of such incorporated religious Societies in said city as supported or should establish charity schools*, who might apply for the same." Under the operation of this law, as the money to be received was to be in proportion to the number of scholars on register, it is natural to suppose that efforts would be made by each school sharing in the distribution of the fund to obtain as many scholars as possible. So far as the Dutch Church school was concerned, however, the limit of scholars fixed in 1809, four years previously, remained unaltered.

Impressed with the necessity and importance of imparting religious instruction to the youth under their charge, the trustees of the Free School Society, "on the suggestion, and to meet the wishes of numerous well-meaning individuals, yielded readily to a proposition that an Association of more than fifty ladies, of high respectability and of different religious denominations, who had volunteered for the purpose, should meet in the school-room one afternoon in each week, to give instruction to the pupils from such denominational catechisms as might be designated by their parents. At the same time, to meet their expressed wishes, monitors were appointed to lead them on the Sabbath to their appropriate places of worship."*

This movement was naturally calculated to affect the charity schools then existing in the city; and on receiving an assurance from the Free School Society that their children should enjoy the same privileges, literary and religious, which they had enjoyed among themselves, the trustees of the Presbyterian school relinquished the portion of the State fund to which they were entitled, and the school eventually disbanded; but the Dutch Church, adhering to her principles on this subject, and to the practice which for centuries had obtained with her, declined the overture; and the Consistory on the 14th of January resolved "that the children belonging to the Dutch Church who attended the New York free school, be presented each with a catechism, and be invited to attend a public catechising every Wednesday, at 3 P.M., in the North Church." †

One week later a communication was received by the Consistory, from the Free School Society, accompanied by a resolution of the trustees of that institution in the following words:

Resolved, That the afternoon of Tuesday (third day) in each week be appropriated for the instruction of the children of the New York free school in the principles of the Christian religion; and in order that they may be educated in the peculiar tenets of the denomination to which they respectively belong, the several churches with which they are connected be respectfully invited to send suitable persons to catechise and otherwise so to instruct them.

* *Vide* Sketch of the Rise and Progress Pub. Sch. Soc., xxxvii. An. Rep. 20.
† Con. Rec., Lib. I. 228.

Thereupon the Consistory

Resolved, That John Vanderbilt be appointed to instruct the children connected with the Dutch Church, attending the New York free school on the day designated, until further arrangement be made. *

The name of Mr. Vanderbilt does not occur again in this connection; and it is presumed that the catechising of the children connected with the Dutch Church and attending the free school, was left in the hands of the ladies associated for that purpose.†

* Con. Rec., Lib. I. 232. A communication and resolution of the same character were presented to the Vestry of Trinity Church, and "it was thereupon ordered that the Assistant-Rector and other Clergy of this church be requested to give the necessary attention to the said resolution, and that 200 Common Prayer books be appropriated to the use of the scholars who belong to the Episcopal Church, to be distributed under the direction of the Assistant-Rector." *Vide* Hist. Trin. Ch., p. 254.

† The following extracts from the Annual Reports of the Free School Society furnish, probably, all the information now to be had upon this subject.

In their Ninth Annual Report, bearing date May 2, 1814, over the signature of De Witt Clinton, President, after speaking of the progress of their pupils in intellectual attainments, the Report adds:

"While the Trustees have been thus engaged in communicating to the understandings of the children the elements of useful knowledge, they have not been unmindful of the importance of imbuing their minds also with a sense of moral and religious obligation.

"The afternoon of every Tuesday, or third day of the week, has been set apart for this purpose; and the children have been instructed in the catechisms of the churches to which they respectively belong. This pious office is performed by an Association of highly respectable females, who are in profession with the different religious denominations in the city. The number of children educated in the peculiar tenets of each religious community is, at the present time, as follows:

Presbyterians	271	Baptists	119
Episcopalians	186	Dutch Church	41
Methodists	172	Roman Catholic	9

"In the furtherance of the same interesting object, the children have been required to assemble at their respective schools on the morning of every Sabbath, and proceed under the care of a monitor, to such place of public worship as was designated by their parents or guardians. This requisition has been regularly attended to by many, but the want of suitable clothing has prevented others from complying with it. It is believed that this deficiency might be amply supplied by the appropriation to this purpose of the garments which are laid aside as useless, in the families of our wealthy fellow-citizens. And, surely, few acts of charity could be more truly benevolent and useful. It would not only contribute to the personal comfort of the children, but it would enable them to join in the public celebration of religious worship.

"In cases where an attendance at school previous to going to church is particularly inconvenient, liberty has been given for the children to attend public worship in company with their parents or guardians."

Extract from the Tenth Annual Report of May 1, 1815:

"The office of communicating religious instruction to the children, by teaching them the catechisms of their respective churches, is still performed by

The difference between the number of children attending these schools from the Presbyterian and Dutch churches, the former being 34 per cent. and the latter only 5 per cent., may be accounted for by the discontinuance of the Presbyterian charity school, as above stated, while the Dutch Church continued to sustain her institution, and the weekly catechetical expositions to her children.

In the year 1815, in order to give more efficiency to these exercises, the Consistory resolved that each of the ministers ought to have separate classes of the children and youth, and on different days, so as not to interfere with each other; and the ministers were directed to carry this out. Two months subsequently, on the request of the Rev. Dr. Milledoler, Elders Wilson and Duryee were appointed to assist him in catechising the children,* Mr. Forrester's scholars, in common with the other children connected with the Dutch Church, assembling as usual in a body for that purpose.

March 12, 1818.—The Teacher's Annual Report to Consistory sets forth the attainments of the children at this time, and presents the school in a very favorable aspect. He says: "The school consists of 100 scholars, viz., 76 boys and 24 girls. Of these, 24 boys and 8 girls read in the Old Testament, and 17 boys

the Association of benevolent females who so zealously engaged in it. Their kindness has also prompted them to furnish many of the scholars with comfortable clothing during the late inclement season.

"The children at present under the care of the Society are said to belong to the different religious denominations as follows:

Presbyterians	365	Baptists	144
Methodists	175	Roman Catholics	57
Episcopalians	159	Dutch Church	33."

Extract from the Eleventh Annual Report, May 6, 1816:

"The children continue to receive the advantages of religious instruction communicated to them from the catechisms used in the respective churches to which they belong, in the manner mentioned in the Report of last year."

The wide extension of the free schools, and the establishment this year of Sunday-schools, "to which excellent institutions they thereafter commended their pupils," led to a discontinuance of this measure.

The free schools in operation at this time were No. 1, opened in 1806, in Bancker Street (now Madison), near Pearl; and No. 2, opened in 1811, in Henry Street. The original object of this Society was "the education of children who do not belong to, and are not provided for by any religious society;" but, in 1808, they received "authority to educate all children who were proper objects of gratuitous instruction." Clothing donated for the purpose was at times distributed to the necessitous. For the use of the Reports from which the above extracts were taken, the author is indebted to the kindness of Samuel W. Seton, an individual who has rendered incalculable service to the cause of education in this city.

* Con. Rec., Lib. I. 340, 350.

and 11 girls, in the New Testament ; the remaining 15 boys and 5 girls write on sand-tables, and read in the Child's Instructor, and Spelling Book ; 48 boys and 12 girls are in arithmetic ; 5 of the boys have been through Vulgar and Decimal Fractions, and are now in Interest. The second class consists of 10 in the Rule of Three. The third class, of 10 in Reduction. The fourth class, of 19 in Compound Addition ; 7 of the girls have been through Practice, and 6 more are in Compound Addition ; 43 boys and 12 girls recite a new section of the Heidelbergh Catechism every week ; 31 boys and 10 girls study the Shorter Catechism, and every week commit a portion thereof to memory, according to their several capacities ; 24 of the children can recite the Heidelbergh Catechism throughout."

The Annual Report of the Trustees, accompanying that of the teacher, closes with the following commendatory language, which shows the high estimation in which his services were regarded : "The Board rejoices in being able to say that they are satisfied with the zeal, ability and attention of the teacher, and particularly with the parental care with which he watches over the religious and moral condition of those committed to his charge."

December 24.—Commenced the custom of closing the school between Christmas and New Year's.

December 28.—Hereafter the school was kept from nine o'clock to three, from the 15th of November to the 15th of March.

March 4, 1819.—A committee of Consistory having determined that the state of the funds warranted an increase of scholars, the number was extended from one hundred to one hundred and ten.

April 26.—Bell's system of instruction was introduced into the school.

December 27.—The parents were required to furnish certificates of the baptism of children hereafter admitted.

May 29, 1820.—From this date the school sessions have been between the hours of nine and three, throughout the year.

1825.—During the years 1796, 1797, and 1801, this school, in connection with the other charity schools of this city, received from the State certain appropriations, and enjoyed for a number of years, in common with the Free School Society, and other educational institutions, the privileges granted by the law of 1813 ; but, in the year 1820, the Bethel Baptist Church organized a free school in the basement of the church, corner of Delancey and Chrystie streets ; and subsequently, in 1822 and 1823, by the permission of the Legislature, two others, from the surplus money which they had in hand : thus they enjoyed privileges equal to those of the Free School Society, the Trustees of which, apprehensive that the buildings thus erected for the Bethel free school "becoming church property, might also be appropriated to other purposes than exclusively for the education of the poor," memorialized, with the sanction and co-operation of the Common Council, the State Legislature for a repeal of the law enacted in favor of the Baptists, and for an amendment to the law relative to the distribution of the school-fund in this city, so as "to prevent any religious society, entitled to a participation in the fund, from drawing for any other than the poor children of their respective congregations." "For," say they, "the Bethel free schools have taken away many scholars from the Society's schools, and thereby diminished the amount of attendance upon them, and, consequently, their revenue derived from the Common-school Fund."

The Trustees of the Free School Society thought, also, that they had "discovered a manifestation of a disposition on the part of some other religious societies, to follow the example of the Bethel Baptist Church to the extent of enlarging their schools so as to receive for instruction poor children generally, without restricting themselves, as heretofore, to those of their own particular congregations. A school of this description has been opened in Grace Church, under the pastoral care of the Rev. Mr. Wainwright; another, for the education of female children, by the Congregational Church in Chambers Street; and a third will soon be opened by the Dutch Church, in the large rooms in Harmony Hall, at the corner of William and Duane streets;" "and when it [the Dutch Church School] shall get in full operation, the Trustees have little doubt that they shall be under the necessity of discontinuing Free School No. 1."

So far as the location of the Dutch Church School and the intention of its Trustees were concerned, the knowledge of a few facts would have materially allayed the fears of the Trustees of the Free School Society. Since the year 1809, when the six pay-scholars allowed the teacher were removed, and at that date (1824), the school consisted *exclusively* of children whose parents were either *members* or *habitual attendants of the Dutch Church*, the Trustees had *never* entertained the idea of "conferring a gratuitous education upon poor children without distinction of sect," which was the peculiar province of the Free School Society.

Again, the erection of *additional* school-houses was never contemplated by the Dutch Church. For seventy-six years the school had been held in Garden Street; and the general occupation of this section of the city at this period by mercantile warehouses, and the consequent removal of the most of the children from the neighborhood of the school, rendered its *removal* to a more convenient locality a work of absolute necessity. And, when the school was opened in Duane Street, the premises in Garden Street were leased for a number of years, and occupied for other purposes; and the fear expressed that the four hundred and sixty-six children attending Free School No. 1 would be withdrawn from it, to attend the Dutch Church School, was groundless, as accommodations were provided in Duane Street for no more scholars than the Trustees were restricted by Consistory to receive, which at that period and up to 1850 was 110.

The strenuous opposition of Rev. Johnson Chase, the principal opponent to the revision of the law, as proposed by the Free School Society, was of little avail, as in the November session of 1824 the Legislature passed "an act by which that portion of the common school fund, drawn for the city of New York, was left to the disposal of the Common Council, who were directed by it to designate to whom such distribution should from time to time be made." The Committee of the Common Council, to whom the subject was referred to hear and report upon the claims of the respective parties applying under this act for a share of the fund, deeming "that the school fund of the State was purely of a civil character, designed for civil purposes; and that the intrusting of it to religious or ecclesiastical bodies was a violation of an elementary principle in the politics of the State and country," "reported against distributing any portion of the fund to the schools of religious societies;" and, in 1825, introduced an ordinance, which was *unanimously* adopted, directing the distribution to be made to the "Free School Society," "Mechanics' Society," the "Orphan Asylum Society," and the "Trustees of the African Schools." *

1831.—During Mr. Forrester's connection with the school, it had no female teacher, consequently the girls were not instructed in needlework.† To meet this want, Miss Eliza Duryee informed the Board, November, 1831, that an Association had been formed by several ladies for the purpose of teaching the children the ordinary branches of sewing and needlework; and it was resolved that this facility should be afforded to the girls two afternoons in the week; this regulation existed for some time.

September 8, 1835.—The death of their late President having been announced to the Board, they unanimously

Resolved—That in the decease of our beloved and lamented friend, Richard Duryee, we have been deprived of an able counselor, a warm-hearted friend, and an active, useful member of this Board.

---

* For the details of this whole subject, *vide* xx. An. Rep. N. Y. P. S. Soc., 1825.
† With the exception stated *ante* p. 69.

Resolved—That the charity children of this church have sustained an irreparable loss, in his fervent prayers, affectionate admonition, and Christian example.

Resolved—That we recognize the hand of our covenant God in taking him to his eternal rest, and bow with submission to His holy will, believing that our loss is his gain.

Resolved—That we tender to his bereaved widow and afflicted family our sincere and warm sympathies under this painful stroke of Divine Providence, and commend them to the guidance, support and protection of Him who hath said, "Leave thy fatherless children; I will preserve them alive; and let thy widows trust in me."

Resolved—That a copy of the above resolutions be presented by the Secretary to his widow.

1840.— The increase of our denomination in the city, and the growing demand for a more extended course of study than that pursued in the school, had long impressed the Trustees with the necessity of endeavoring to procure an edifice for the express accommodation of the school, and of devising such ways and means for increasing its income, that its benefits might be more greatly extended.

After mature deliberation, a communication,* prepared by the Secretary, fully expressing the unanimous views of the Board upon these subjects, was presented to Consistory.

1842.— Mr. Forrester, the Principal of the school, was now approaching the allotted period of threescore and ten.

For more than forty-five years, the last thirty-two of which he had spent in this school, he had been engaged in performing the arduous and responsible duties which devolve upon an instructor of youth, and the Trustees felt that he "ought to be relieved in a great measure from the bustle and noise with which he had so long been surrounded, and be suffered to enjoy his advancing age with more peace and quietness than could be expected if required to continue in his present station." They therefore recommended a division of the labors of the school, by the employment of a younger person for the general education of the children while Mr. Forrester should be retained as catechist. In doing this, the Trustees cheerfully bore their testimony to the faithfulness of Mr. Forrester, and of their confidence in his desire to promote the welfare of the children. Those whom he had instructed in the year 1810, the first year of his connection with the school, if still living, had now attained to middle age. During this period, in the commencement of which the schools of this country were in their infancy, rapid advances had been made in the system of instruction; many new text-books had come into use, and studies had been introduced into the schools, which at an earlier period would have been deemed superfluous;

---

* *Vide* Trus. Min. iii. 116 *et seq.*

and it was with the view of enabling the school to enjoy the advantages of these improvements that the Trustees proposed the above change. Consistory having taken action upon the subject, the object which the Trustees had in view was consummated in 1842 by the appointment of the present Principal. Mr. Forrester was retained as catechist, the duties pertaining to which office he faithfully performed for twelve months, when his connection with the school ceased altogether.*

Thirty-three years! One generation had passed away, and another had taken its place on the stage of existence.

Forty-eight years of joy and sorrow, of labor and reward! Eternity alone can reveal the nature and importance of those influences which it is the duty and privilege of a teacher to exert, for so many years, over the hearts and minds of young immortal beings.

Many are they, now members of the body of Christ, whose religious feelings and exercises were called forth and strengthened while under his instruction; and to him it was ever a source of grateful acknowledgement, that he had been the instrument, under God's hand, of leading so many to walk in the ways of truth.

Mr. Forrester, in withdrawing from the charge which he had so long sustained, retired in the enjoyment of the "confidence and esteem of the Trustees in his moral and Christian character, and in his desire to promote the well-being of the numerous children which had been intrusted to his care."

Heretofore, the children of both sexes had been classified together for the purpose of receiving instruction; but on the re-organization of the school in 1842, the girls were segregated, and placed under the supervision and care of Miss Frances Campbell. This was an important advantage secured to the school, the need of which had been long felt.

It is ever a subject of regret when any institution is deprived of the counsels, labors and prayers of an efficient officer, through

* Mr. Forrester was born in the environs of the city of Edinburgh, February 25, 1774, and was baptized in the West Kirk by Sir Harry Moncrief. In the year 1794, he set sail for America. Before reaching port, he, with a number of others, was impressed and placed on the British man-of-war, the "Africa." Subsequently, for some reason unknown to him, he was placed on board the ship "Fanny," and landed October 16, at the Fly Market. He shortly afterwards located in Tappan. In the year 1795, at the age of twenty-one years, he commenced teaching school at Closter. Here he remained three years and a half, when he returned to the "Liberty Pole," six miles nearer to this city. Here he taught for eight years, when he was offered the charge of the school in Nassau street, opposite the Middle Dutch Church, then under the care of the Presbyterian Church. Having spent three years in this connection, he was appointed, in the year 1810, as the master of the Dutch Reformed Church School. Deceased March 26, 1865, aged 91 years and one month.

SCHOOLMASTER
1810 to 1842

whose instrumentality its advantages have been secured and its best interests advanced.

Such a deprivation this school was called to experience in 1848, in the decease of Noah Wetmore, Esq. For the thirteen years that he had been a member of the Board of Trustees (a period longer than any of his predecessors in office had served), he had been its presiding officer.

Hon. *Thomas Jeremiah*, Secretary of this Board from February, 1846, to February, 1852, and its presiding officer from February, 1857, to February, 1872, having died the 2d inst., at the age of 79 years, 7 months and 3 days, the accompanying preamble and resolutions were unanimously adopted by the Board of Trustees, November 5, 1872:

WHEREAS, It has pleased Almighty God, in His all-wise Providence, to call from earthly labors to his heavenly rest, although at a ripe old age, yet in the day of usefulness, our venerable and esteemed friend, Hon. *Thomas Jeremiah*, who for twenty-one years has been an officer of this Board, and its President for the past fifteen years ; and,

WHEREAS, It is fitting that this Board express its feelings in regard to this sad dispensation ; therefore, be it

Resolved, That in his decease the School of the Collegiate Dutch Church, and the pupils therein, have sustained a loss that will be long felt in the departure of a warm-hearted sympathizer, and that, while we shall deeply feel his absence from the counsels of this Board, yet we bow in submission to the Divine will, and are sincerely grateful to our Heavenly Father that he was so long permitted to remain among us, to aid us by his advice, his fervent prayers, affectionate admonitions and Christian liberality and example.

Resolved, That we do most sincerely and affectionately sympathize with his bereaved family in this dispensation of Providence, which has deprived them of a father loving and beloved, the State of an honest and honorable citizen, this Board of a wise and prudent counselor, the Church of a steadfast supporter and faithful witness.

Resolved, That in testimony of our attachment to his memory and respect to his worth, this Board and the school under its care attend his funeral in a body, and that the rooms of the school be draped in mourning for thirty days.

Resolved, That these resolutions be published in the *Christian Intelligencer* and *New York Observer*, and communicated to the family of deceased.

JOHN C. CALHOUN, *Chairman*.
HENRY SNYDER, *Secretary*.

November 27, 1874.—At a special meeting of the Board of Trustees, the following resolutions in regard to the death of Mr. *John C. Calhoun* were adopted and ordered to be entered upon the minutes :

WHEREAS, God in His Providence has been pleased to remove from our midst *John C. Calhoun*, who has been a member of this Board for thirteen years, and for the past three years its Chairman ; and,

WHEREAS, He has ever been faithful in his discharge of the duties committed to his trust, seeking by his efforts and prayers to promote the welfare of this school of the Church ; therefore,

Resolved, That by his death this Board has lost a most useful member and an efficient presiding officer; that we regret the loss of his prayers, his zeal and his wise and judicious counsels, and that the school, by this Providence, is deprived of the aid of one who manifested an abiding interest in its prosperity, who cherished it as an object dear to his Christian heart, and who, in his intercourse with the scholars, was ever so kind and genial, that it may be said, all the children loved him.

Resolved, That we deeply and sincerely sympathize with his family in this sad bereavement, which deprived them of an affectionate husband and a kind and loving father.

Resolved, That out of respect to his memory and worth, the school-room be draped in mourning for a period of thirty days; that the members of this Board attend his funeral in a body; and that the school be closed until Tuesday, December 1st, in order to afford the teachers and scholars an opportunity to attend his funeral.

Resolved, That a copy of these resolutions, signed by the officers of the Board, be sent to the family of the deceased, and be published in the *Christian Intelligencer* and the *Sower and Gospel Field.*

    HENRY W. BOOKSTAVER, *Chairman, pro tem.*
    ALEXIS A. JULIEN, *Secretary.*

APPENDIX.

ATTENDANCE OF THE CHILDREN ON THE SABBATH.

In conformity with a prominent feature of this institution, which happily combines religious with intellectual education, its pupils, independent of instruction in the principles of Divine truth received through the week, have ever been required to attend divine service on the Sabbath. Subsequent to the Revolutionary War, the children assembled every Sabbath at the school-room in Garden Street, in ample time to proceed with their teacher to the seats provided for them in the "Old Church."

After Sabbath Schools were established in the city, they attended the one held in the Consistory building, at the corner of Nassau and Ann streets, till the year 1829, when a school was organized in the New or Middle Church, Nassau Street; and here, under Sabbath School instruction and the teachings of the sacred desk, they remained till the year 1840, when they occupied the gallery of the North Church, attending at the same time the Sabbath School in the Consistory building, at the corner of Ann and Nassau streets. In September, 1841, a majority of the children having been found to reside north of Grand Street, Consistory directed them to attend the Sabbath School and church in Ninth Street, between Broadway and the Fourth Avenue.

This institution being the only one of the kind connected with the Dutch Church, and being composed of children whose parents resided in the vicinity of the churches which they respectively attended, it became an onerous duty for the scholars to attend twice on the Sabbath, from distances ranging from Dey Street to Twenty-third Street, and from the North to the East River. Many communications on the subject having been addressed to the Trustees by the parents, the Consistory, in January, 1847, granted the Board the privilege of permitting the children to attend Sabbath School and church at those churches with which their parents were connected, and near which they resided.

This privilege was then generally enjoyed by the children, under the following regulations, which accompanied each certificate :

Resolved, That in all cases in which any pupil of the school is permitted to attend Sabbath School and church elsewhere than at Ninth Street, it shall be the duty of such child to produce a monthly certificate from his Superintendent that he regularly attends the Sabbath School and church with which he is connected, and it shall be the duty of the Principal of the school to report all cases of omission to this Board, accompanied with explanations of the cause.

Resolved, That a copy of these resolutions be communicated by the Principal to parents, guardians and Superintendents who are interested in the same.

As one great object of the school is religious instruction, the above resolutions have been adopted, that the Trustees may be assured that the Sabbath is not violated by any of the pupils of the school, but that they are in the enjoyment of religious instruction in the Sabbath School and under the preaching of the Gospel.

January 25, 1847.
THOMAS JEREMIAH, *Secretary*.

This same privilege is now conceded to all the scholars, residing, as many of them do, at a considerable distance from the school.

REVENUE OF THE SCHOOL.

During the first thirty years of the existence of the school, its teachers, appointed by the Dutch West India Company, in connection with the Classis of Amsterdam, were remunerated from the treasury of the Colonial Government.

While the city was under the jurisdiction of the English, the support of the school devolved entirely upon Consistory. Whether its expenses, which were not very great, were defrayed by annual collections in the churches, or by a resort to such limited sources of revenue as the Church may have possessed, cannot be definitely ascertained.

On the re-organization of the school, subsequent to the Revolutionary War, commencing in 1789, collections were annually made in the three branches of the Collegiate Church. The money thus obtained was expended in clothing the children : the teacher's salary, and other expenses of the school, were defrayed from the general fund of the Church.

Subsequently (1792) a legacy, amounting to seven hundred and fifty dollars, was bequeathed by Elias Brevoort to Consistory for the benefit of the school. This gave rise to an effort "to secure an independent revenue for the future advancement of the seminary ;" and it was *Resolved*, "That measures be taken for establishing a fund to be put at interest." "That, in addition to testamentary and other donations which have been or may be given for the support of the school, the overplus of all moneys annually collected, after the payment of all charges, be added to the fund." "That all money received and collected for the use of the school shall be received by the Treasurer, and paid by him, on the warrants of Consistory." In the year 1808, this was amended so as to read, "on the audit and order of the Board of Trustees only, and not otherwise." And it was further *Resolved* (1792),

"That the Treasurer shall hereafter keep a separate and distinct account of all moneys received on account of this fund, and of their appropriation : and that both principal and interest of said moneys shall be applied invariably to the maintenance of this charity, and the promotion of its interests." The Treasurer, in his Annual Report to Consistory, renders an account of the receipts and expenditures of this fund, which report is audited by a Committee of Consistory appointed for the purpose.

As the combined result of four different legacies,* and annual collections in the Collegiate Church, the fund of the school, in 1826, amounted to eleven thousand and twenty-seven dollars and ninety-two cents ($11,027.92).

This was subsequently increased by annual collections in the Collegiate Church, so that, in 1847, the fund amounted to sixteen thousand two hundred and eighteen dollars and eight cents ($16,218.08).

The purchase of the lots on Fourth Street, and the erection of the school-house, exhausted $9,260.70 of this, which, with subsequent outlays upon the building, amounting to $561.79, left in the Treasurer's hands $6,395.59.

The salaries of the teachers, the clothing of the children, fuel, books and stationery amounted, for the year 1852, according to the Treasurer's Annual Report, to $2,412.72.

The income from the different sources of revenue for the same year amounted to $1,121.74; leaving a deficit of $1,290.98, which was met by Consistory.

Is there not sufficient of the spirit of our godly ancestors, who founded and sustained the school for so many generations, to induce its friends, in view of the incalculable good which the institution has accomplished in days that are past; in view of its present acknowledged usefulness to the children of our Church, to make an effort to secure for it an independent fund, fully adequate to its support? We believe that there is.

Locality of the School.

For more than a hundred years after its establishment the school was kept at various places in the vicinity of the Bowling-Green, apartments being hired for that purpose. Prior to 1748 it was at the corner of Marketfield and Broad streets. At this date the first school-house was erected in Garden Street, where it remained for a period of seventy-six years; but as the congregation removed from the lower extremity of the city, the North Church became its centre; and under these circumstances the prop-

---

* Elias Brevoort's, 1792, $750; Sarah De Peyster's, 1802, $5,392.78; Isaac Slidell's, 1804, $831.37; Mary Bassett's, 1807, $1,500.

erty, No. 9 Duane Street, near William Street, was leased ; and after undergoing some necessary alterations the school was removed thither, 1824 ; and a dwelling-house for the teacher (in lieu of the one vacated in Garden Street) was erected in William Street, east of Duane Street. The Newsboys' Lodging House, formerly the Shakspeare Hotel, now occupies the space formerly intervening between the school-house and the teacher's residence. Here the school remained till 1835, when it removed to No. 106 Elm Street, south-west corner of Canal Street, and the teacher resided No. 25 Carmine Street.

From 1836 to 1841 it occupied the basement of the church corner of Broome and Greene streets, removing thence to the basement of the church on the corner of Greene and Houston streets, where it remained for one year, removing, in 1842, to the premises No. 91 Mercer Streeet. Here it continued for five years, when a temporary provision was made for it in the basement of the Ninth Street Church, pending the erection of the school edifice at No. 183 Fourth Street.

In the beginning of the year 1840 the Trustees, impelled by a sense of duty towards the children under their care, prepared and presented a communication to Consistory, in which their attention was drawn to the necessity of providing a suitable and permanent locality for the school, as previously mentioned, and of adopting such other reformatory measures as would be calculated to increase the efficiency of the institution over which they presided. This was the commencement of a series of efforts which secured to the school, from time to time, important advantages, and which, after a period of seven years, resulted in the purchase of the ground in Fourth Street, west of the Sixth Avenue. Immediate measures were taken to erect thereon an edifice suitable for school purposes, Messrs. PETER R. WARNER, MORTIMER DE MOTTE, and THOMAS JEREMIAH constituting the Building Committee.

The building, No. 183 Fourth Street, erected for the express accommodation of the school, was a substantial brick edifice, forty feet front by forty-five feet deep.

The main room on the first floor was occupied by the Boys' Department ; adjacent to which were two class-rooms, and a wardrobe for their accommodation.

The second floor was occupied by the Girls' Department. It consisted of one large room and four class-rooms. In one of these the Trustees held their stated meetings ; and its walls were occupied with specimens of drawings and ornamental needlework executed and presented by the graduates of the institution ; and also with frames containing their daguerreotypes, from the establishment of ABRAHAM BOGARDUS, photographer.

The rooms on the third floor were appropriated to exercises in sewing, drawing, etc.

Outline maps were delineated on the walls of the schoolrooms, and each department was supplied with the Croton water.

The Trustees of the institution, desirous of providing for the children the means of enriching their minds with profitable reading, and of cultivating among them a taste for literary pursuits, induced a number of its friends to contribute funds sufficient to procure not only a list of miscellaneous works adequate at that time (1847) to the wants of the school, but also some astronomical apparatus. The number of volumes in the library has since been augmented by some valuable works donated by Hon. *James W. Beekman*, and in March, 1856, *fifty-one* volumes were added, the gift of *Peter R. Warner, Esq.*, of the Board of Trustees, and again, in 1864, for all which a vote of thanks was presented to him by the Board.

Ground was broken in July, 1847, and the building was so far completed that the anniversary exercises were held therein, October 28th, in the presence of a crowded audience. The Order of Exercises was as follows :

1. PRAYER, by *Rev. John Knox, D.D.*
2. HYMN, *by the Scholars*, "Jerusalem, my happy home."
3. DECLAMATION, "The President".......... *Alexander H. Layman*
4. EXAMINATION IN ARITHMETIC.
5. SINGING, "Come, come, come."
6. DECLAMATION, "Our School"................. *Charles F. Conant*
7. ROUND, *by Twenty-one Young Ladies*—

   "Esto perpetua,
   With the heavenly blessing,
   May each one wish for 'Our School'
   Esto perpetua."

8. CLASS of Young Ladies in ASTRONOMY.
9. DECLAMATION, "A General Description of the Solar System"
   Miss Rachel A. Mickens
10. CHORUS, "When up the Mountains climbing."
11. EXAMINATION IN GEOGRAPHY.
12. READING, "I would not live alway".. *Miss Catharine W. Edmonds*
13. THIRD CATECHISM CLASS................. *Miss Sarah C. Mickens*
14. CHORUS, "Long Live America."
15. DIALOGUE, "Singing for the Million" } PEACEFUL...*Chas F. Conant*
    { MR. SOLO..*John Marseilles*
16. CLASS IN READING.......................... *John H. Magonigle*
17. READING, "Moses in the bulrushes"............. *Miss Sophia See*
18. SINGING, *by a Class of Young Ladies*—

    "Daughter of Zion awake from thy sadness,
    Awake, for thy foes shall oppress thee no more.
    Bright o'er the hills dawns the day-star of gladness,
    Arise, for the night of thy sorrow is o'er." etc.

19. DIALOGUE, "The Mother," *by Misses Isabella W. Gray, Mary E. Banker, Agnes L. Gray, Louisa J. Ayres, Ann Augusta Ayres, Edgar Ayres, and James Lamberson.*

20. SENIOR CATECHISM CLASS.
21. CHORUS, "Starlight is streaming".... .*By a Class of Young Ladies*
22. DISTRIBUTION OF PREMIUMS, and Presentation of the "Honors" of the School to the graduates.
23. TRIO, "Oft in the Stilly Night,"*Misses Ann E. Myers, Elizabeth A. Mickens and Hannah T. Gray.*
24. VALEDICTORY.................. ....*Joseph Banvard Ayres*
25. PARTING SONG BY THE GRADUATES.
  " Then take the hand that now is warm,
    Within a hand of thine
   No distant day shall lose the grasp
    Of auld lang syne," etc.
26. CHORUS, *accompanied with motions*—
  " We are all noddin', nid, nid, noddin'
   We are all noddin' and dropping off to sleep—
   Our parents, too, are waiting—Oh, we hope they will not scold,
   Our teachers, too, are tired, therefore, good night, young and old."
27. DOXOLOGY AND BENEDICTION.

November 10.—The building having been properly furnished with desks, etc., the school was removed from the Ninth Street Church, where the sessions had been held while the school-house was being built, and *Noah Wetmore, Esq.*, who was then and had been for many years the presiding officer of the Board of Trustees, conducted the opening exercises, and commended the school in all its interests to the favor of the Almighty.

A Mission Sabbath School, of which Mr. Richard Amerman was Superintendent, had been sustained for some years by the Collegiate Church, 29th Street and 5th Avenue. It had been held in hired halls, which were occupied during the week for other purposes.

Notwithstanding this serious inconvenience the school increased in numbers and became so successful that an effort was made to secure for it a permanent home. Some objection having been made to this on account of the expense, the friends of the Mission School proposed to Consistory to dispose of the property in Fourth Street and to erect a building in West 29th Street, No. 160, in which the Mission School could be held and Divine services introduced under a regularly appointed pastor.

The second and third stories were to be constructed with the view of accommodating the day school.

This proposition was approved by the Consistory; the present school edifice, now known as the De Witt Chapel, was finished and the school removed thither from Fourth Street, November 14, 1861.

The building is 50 feet front, 84 feet deep, and 63 feet in height.

The hallway is 25 feet by 19 feet 6 inches, and contains two flights of stairs, 4 feet wide.

On the first floor is the Chapel, used for Divine worship and for Sabbath School purposes ; also, the Pastor's Study.

The second floor consists of the assembly room for the day-school, 55 by 35, and two recitation rooms, each 21 by 12. On the walls of these three rooms are suspended the photographs of the Trustees and of the Graduates ; delineations of the Grecian orders of architecture, used in the lectures given on that subject ; and specimens of worsted work, maps and drawings, executed by the scholars. This room is also furnished with a piano and a cabinet organ.

On the third floor are two recitation rooms, each 23 by 17 ; two others, each 21 by 12 ; a Library room, 14 by 12, and another of the same dimensions containing astronomical and philosophical apparatus.

All of the rooms have high ceilings, are thoroughly ventilated and well lighted. The play ground extends beneath the entire building with the exception of the furnace rooms.

The 228th Anniversary of the School and the Inauguration of this building, erected for its accommodation by the Consistory of the Collegiate Church, took place on the evening of November 14, 1861.

"The large room and all the approaches to it, wherever standing room could be procured, were filled with the friends of the institution and the pupils. The Addresses were interspersed with Exercises by the Scholars, which were in every way creditable to them and to their Teachers."

1. The DEDICATORY ADDRESS and Prayer were by *Rev. James M. Mathews, D.D.*,* Chancellor of the New York University.
2. CHANTING OF THE LORD'S PRAYER, *by the Pupils*.
3. ADDRESS, *by Rev. Thomas De Witt, D.D.*, in which he alluded to the origin of the School and its distinctive feature of religious instruction.
4. DEDICATION SONG, *by the Pupils*.
5. "OUR GUIDING STAR" (Composed for the occasion by Mr. Thomas G. Williamson), *by James S. Huyler*.
6. ADDRESS, *by Rev. Talbot W. Chambers, D.D.*
7. SOLO, "Annie Lisle"........................*Miss Mary E. Worth*
8. A DIALOGUE, *by Alfred P. Vredenburgh, Frederick H. Crum, and Edward P. Tracy*, in which Governor PETRUS STUYVESANT (personated *by John D. Giffing*) revisits the school after a lapse of two centuries.
9. DUET, "Sister spirit stay not here" .... { *Miss Emma Morrell* / *Miss Henrietta H. Huyler* }
10. DECLAMATION, " Washington "............*Robert H. Van Deusen*
11.   "   " The American Flag "........*L. C. Levin Jordan*
12. CHORUS, " Song of Liberty."

* Dr. Mathews was also Pastor of the South Church in Garden Street from 1813 to 1835, and of the Church on Washington Square from 1837 to 1842.

13. PRESENTATION OF PREMIUMS *by Hon. Thomas Jeremiah and Mr. Richard Amerman*, the Committee for the month.
14. ADDRESS, *by John D. Giffing*, and PRESENTATION TO THE TRUSTEES, on behalf of the members of the Prayer Meeting, of a 4to BIBLE, for the lectern of the School.
15. RESPONSE by the Chairman, *Hon. Thomas Jeremiah*.
16. PRESENTATION of the " Honors " of the School to the Graduates—

    Sarah C. Mott.   *Peter I. Ackerman.*
    Mary F. Huyler.   *Charles P. Arkills.*
    Wilhelmina Steinhaus.   *James Oliver Bogert.*
    Jacob Hahn.   *Thomas Tully.*
        Samuel D. Van Saun.

17. ADDRESS to the Graduates, *by Rev. Peter Stryker*.
18. ADDRESS, *by Elder Samuel B. Schieffelin*.
19. A ROUND, *by the Pupils*, " Esto Perpetua."
20. PRAYER, *by Rev. T. W. Chambers, D.D.*
21. DOXOLOGY—" Praise God, from whom all blessings flow."

THE SCHOOL,

Its Present Condition, Qualifications for Admission, Course of Study, Etc.

Number of Scholars.—Previous to the Revolutionary War the greatest number of children in the school at any one period was thirty. Subsequently (1783), when the ravages of war had unsettled everything relating to educational affairs, and the resources of the Church were limited, the school re-organized with ten scholars.

In 1786 the number of pupils was limited to twelve.
" 1789 " " " thirty.
" 1791 " " " fifty.
" 1800 " " " seventy.
" 1808 " " " seventy-two.
" 1809 " " " one hundred.

Up to this date, as a general thing, the Principal had enjoyed the privilege of having *pay*-scholars, in addition to the numbers above given; but none of that class have been received since.

In 1819 the limit was extended to one hundred and ten; which number, however, was not complete till the year 1842. Subsequently the number of applicants for admission greatly increased. This fact, coupled with the earnest desire of the Trustees to extend the peculiar privileges of the school to as many pupils as the building would accommodate, led, in the beginning of 1850, to the simultaneous admission of forty new scholars: thus extending the limit to *one hundred and fifty*.

In January, 1862, shortly after taking possession of the present school building, so great was the number of applicants for admission that the limit was extended to *two hundred*, and the fifty additional scholars were immediately admitted.

Qualifications for Admission into the School.—During the greater part of the first one hundred and seventy-five years of the existence of the school, its doors were open to all the citizens who wished to have their children educated therein. But as our denomination increased in the city, by the formation of different congregations issuing from the Collegiate Church, it was found necessary to confine the privileges of the school to those whose ancestors had been its liberal supporters; and the common schools having sprung into existence, those precluded were not left destitute of the means of education. The school was, therefore, from necessity, maintained exclusively for the children of those persons who were either communing members, or habitual attendants, of some church in our denomination ; a certificate to that effect, signed by the pastor, being required from the applicant.

April, 1869, Consistory "authorized the Trustees to receive into the school children from churches of other denominations, provided they do not prevent the reception of children from our own churches," thus, virtually, throwing open its doors to the public.

COURSE OF STUDY.

Algebra.
Arithmetic.
Astronomy.
Book-keeping.
Catechism.
Composition.
Drawing — map, freehand and mechanical.
Elocution.
Geography.
Geometry.

Grammar and Etymology.
History of United States.
Natural Philosophy.
Penmanship.
Reading.
Spelling and Definitions.
Universal History, with occasional lectures on Moral Philosophy, Conchology, Architecture, Botany, Physiology, etc.

The scholars are examined annually by the Trustees, and at the Anniversary or Commencement premiums and prizes are presented to those pupils who have distinguished themselves by diligence in their studies and correct deportment ; and the "Honors" of the school are bestowed upon the graduates. These consist of a Bible, a Psalm Book, containing the Catechism, and liturgy of our Church ; the history of the School, and a Diploma * signed by the Board of Trustees and the Principal.

The extent and thoroughness of the instruction imparted, the correct habits induced, and the integrity of their moral character, have acquired for the children a worthy reputation. Of late years the demand for clerks and apprentices, from merchants and others, has exceeded the ability to supply them. Many scholars have thus obtained desirable situations with individuals in whose employ no fear is entertained of the corruption of their moral principles ; and of the whole number of those who have graduated within the past ten years, and entered upon the active duties of life, not one, so far as is known, has failed to sustain a reputation for intelligence, ability and moral worth. And it is a

* These testimonials, originally written, were first presented in 1792. In 1827 they were printed from a copperplate engraved expressly for the purpose. The Bible was added in 1809, and the psalm-book in 1812. Many individuals who hold these honors are now mantaining, by their integrity and usefulness, a high rank as merchants, artisans, and members of the learned professions ; among whom may be found the names of a few in the ministerial calling. Books were first distributed as premiums in 1810.

happiness to know that a majority of them, under the influences of the Holy Spirit, have embraced the truth inculcated and early impressed, and are now wielding their influence for the advancement of their Saviour's cause.

Thus fruit abounds to the praise of Him who has watched over and guided this institution amidst all the vicissitudes of changing time, till it now stands a venerable monument of the past, yet possessed of pristine vigor to meet the claims of the future; contemplating, as the true idea of education, the simultaneous and harmonious development of the moral, intellectual and physical powers; co-operating in rendering efficiency to the instructions of home and the sanctuary; preparing the future citizen for usefulness and happiness here and hereafter, and imparting light to the future saint, whose influence shall be on the side of truth, and whose fervent prayer will go up to the God of love and grace, for the hastening of the day when "*wisdom and knowledge shall be stability of the times*," and for the fulfillment to His Church of the promise of the covenant-keeping God: "*All thy children shall be taught of the Lord.*"

OFFICERS OF THE SCHOOL.

1642—1883.

From 1633 to 1808 the school was under the supervision of the *Board of Deacons*, each of whom served at least *two* years. Many were re-elected several terms. The dates prefixed to their names indicate when the term of service commenced.

1642.—Joachim Pietersen Kuyter (*Merchant*). *Schepen*, 1654. Records lacking.

Appointed.
1668.—Boole Roelofszen.
    Mr. Gerrit Van Fricht.
    Jacobus de Kay, *Ald. Out Ward*, 1702 to 1705.
1669.—Hendrick Cutrier.
1670.—Pieter Jacobus Marius (*Merchant*), *Ald.*, 1677 to 1682.
    Mr. Jacob Leixsler.
1671.—Hieronymus Ebbing, *Schepen*, 1659, '61, '73.
    Pieter Stoutenberg.
1672.—Nicolaes Bayard, *Asst.-Ald. Out Ward*, 1743 to 1753. *Ald.*, 1785 to 1796.
    Stephanus Cortlandt.
1673.—Balthazar Bayard, *Asst.-Ald. West Ward*, 1686–87. *Ald.*, 1691.
1674.—Isaac van Kleeck.
1675.—Reynier Wilhemszen.
1676.—Adolf Pieterszen.
    Pieter de Riemer.
1677.—Thomas Laurenszen.
    Pieter de la Noy.
1678.—John Darvall.
    Petrus Bayard (*Merchant*), *Asst.-Ald. West Ward*, 1706–07.
1681.—Dr. Johanness Kerfbyl.
1682.—Jan Harberding.
1683.—Brandt Schuyler (*Merchant*), *Ald. South Ward*, 1691 to 1699.
    Hendrick Wessels.
1684.—Johannes Kip (*Merchant*), *Asst.-Ald.*, 1684. *Ald.*, 1685. *North Ward*, 1687, '91, '92, '96.
1685.—Jacob Boelen (*Merchant*), *Ald. North Ward*, 1695–97–98, 1701.
1686.—Theunis de Kay, *Asst.-Ald. North Ward*, 1685 to 1687. 1691–92.

1687.—Carlton Luerson.
Jacobus Kip, Jr.
1688.—Jan Spratt (*Merchant*), *Ald. Dock Ward*, 1688-89.
1689.—Isaac de Freest, *Schepen*, 1658.

Records Lacking.

1693.—Jacobus van Cortlandt (*Merchant*), *Ald.*, 1686. *Dock Ward*, 1694 to 1703. *Mayor*, 1710, 1719.
1694.—Johannes de Peyster (*Merchant*), *Asst.-Ald. Dock Ward*, 1694-95. *Mayor*, 1698. *Ald. East Ward*, 1700-01, 1710.
1695.—Isaac de Riemer (*Merchant*), *Asst.-Ald. South Ward*, 1696-97. *Ald. West Ward*, 1699. *Mayor*, 1700. *Ald.*, 1702, '07 ; 1714 to 1717.
1696.—Dirck ten Eyck.
Isaacq de Peyster (*Merchant*), *Asst.-Ald. South Ward*, 1730 to 1733.
1697.—Nicolas Roosevelt, *Ald. South Ward*, 1700-01.
Isaacq Kip.
1698.—Johannes van Giessen.
David Provost, Jr. (*Merchant*), *Ald. Dock Ward*, 1697. *Mayor*, 1699. *Ald.*, 1700-01-02-08.
1699.—Alburtis Ringo.
Jacobus Goelet.
1700.—Mr. Samuel Staats.
1701.—Gerrit Duiken.
Leendert Huigen.
1702.—Gysbert van Imburg.
Jan Wanshaar.
1703.—Johannes Hardenbroek, *Asst.-Ald. North Ward*, 1695-96. *Ald. Montgomerie Ward*, 1731-32-33.
Jacobus van der Spiegel.
1704.—Olphert Syoerts (*Mason*), *Asst.-Ald. West Ward*, 1704-05-07.
Andries Maerschalk, *Asst.-Ald. North Ward*, 1714 to 1727.
1705.—Jan Narbury.
Pieter van Tilburg.
1706.—Benjamin Wynkoop.
1708.—Johannes Kruger.
Andries Abrahamze.
1709.—Capt. Cornelius de Peyster (*Merchant*), *Asst.-Ald. South Ward*, 1703 to 1705—1710 to 1718.
Barend Reynders, *Ald. East Ward*, 1705-06.
Isaac Stoutenburg, *Asst.-Ald. North Ward*, 1740 to 1747.
1710.—Gerrit van Hoorn.

1711.—Antony Rutgers (*Baker*), *Asst.-Ald. North Ward*, 1710 to 1712. *Ald.*, 1727 to 1734.
1712.—Samuel Bayard (*Merchant*), *Asst.-Ald. Dock Ward*, 1698-99, 1700.
1713.—Adriaan Man.
Mr. Jacobus Kip (*Merchant*), *Ald. North Ward*, 1709 to 1726.
1714.—Mr. Philip Schuyler (*Merchant*), *Asst.-Ald. South Ward*, 1719 to 1722.
1715.—Capt. Joan van Hoorn.
Philip van Cortlandt, *Asst.-Ald. East Ward*, 1714 to 1716. *Ald.*, 1717 to 1729.
1716.—Willem Provost.
Olivier Teller (*Merchant*), *Asst.-Ald. Dock Ward*, 1715 to 1729.
1717.—Johannes van der Heul.
Dr. Jacob Moene.
1718.—Abraham Keteltas, *Asst.-Ald. North Ward*, 1703 to 1706. *Asst. East Ward*, 1708-09.
1719.—Jacob Ten Eyck.
Cornelius Louw.
1721.—Jan Roosevelt (*Merchant*), *Asst.-Ald. East Ward*, 1717 to 1729. *Ald.*, 1730 to 1733.
1722.—Hermanus van Gelder (*Merchant*), *Asst.-Ald. West Ward*, 1714. *Ald.*, 1715 to 1733.
Christoffel Banker, *Ald. North Ward*, 1738 to 1742; 1755.
1723.—Abraham van Horne.
Willem Roseboom.
1724.—Charles Le Roux (*Goldsmith*), *Asst.-Ald. East Ward*, 1735 to 1738.
Abraham Boelen.
1725.—Gerrit Keteltas.
Abraham Lefferts.
1726.—Hendrick van der Spiegel.
Abraham van Vleck.
1728.—Paul Richard (*Merchant*), *Mayor*, 1735 to 1739 ; *and from 1743 until his death, Dec. 1756, he represented the City of New York in the General Assembly.*
Frederick van Courtland.
1729.—Harmanus Rutgers.
1730.—Hendrick Cuyler (*Merchant*), *Ald. Dock Ward*, 1758-59.
Jacobus Roseveldt.
Abraham van Wyk.
Gerardus Beekman (*Merchant*), *Asst.-Ald. Montgomerie Ward*, 1731. *Dock Ward*, 1736-37.

1731.—Gerrit Roos (*Merchant*), *Asst.-Ald. North Ward*, 1731 to 1734.
    Philip French (*Merchant*), *Asst.-Ald. Dock Ward*, 1696. *Ald.*, 1701. *Mayor*, 1702.
    Matthew Clarkson.
1732.—Wynant Van Zandt.
    Henry Coerten.
    Coenraadt Ten Eyck.
1733.—Gerrit Harsen, *Asst.-Ald. Dock Ward*, 1790. *Asst.-Ald. Second Ward*, 1792 to 1797.
    Jacobus Goelet.
1734.—Johannes Maerschalk.
    Nicolaus Bayard, *Asst.-Ald. Out Ward*, 1743 to 1753. *Ald.*, 1785 to 1796.
1735.—Ide Myer, *Asst.-Ald. South Ward*, 1734 to 1744.
    Johannes Graat.
1736.—Johannes Groesbeck.
    Jan Bogert.
    Petrus Rutgers (*Brewer*), *Asst.-Ald. East Ward*, 1730 to 1733.
1737.—Evert Byvank, *Ald. Montgomerie Ward*, 1754.
    David Abeel.
    Gulian Ver Plank.
    Robert Livingston, Jr.
1738.—Gerardus Duyckink.
    Abraham Lynsen.
    Francois Maerschalk.
1739.—Joris Brinckerhoff.
    Abel Hardenbroek, *Asst.-Ald. Montgomerie Ward*, 1732-33.
    Petrus Van Ranst, *Ald. Montgomerie Ward*, 1737 to 1739.
1740.—Cornelius Van Horne, Gerviter.
    Harmanus Rutgers, Jr.
    Cornelis Turck.
1742.—Andries Breestede.
    Pieter Maerschalk.
    Abraham Ten Eyck.
1743.—Adriaen Bancker.
    Elbert Herring, *Asst.-Ald. Out Ward*, 1754 to 1758.
    Pieter Low.
    Hendrick Reyke.
1745.—Jacob Abrahamse.
    Robert Benson, *Asst.-Ald. Montgomerie Ward*, 1740 to 1749. *Ald.*, 1750 to 1753. *Asst.*, 1766-67.
    Gerardus Stuyvesant, *Ald. Out Ward*, 1722 to 1753.

OFFICERS OF THE SCHOOL.

1748.—Cornelius Bogert, *Alderman*.
    C. Van Ranst.
    Theodore Van Wyck, *Asst.-Ald. Dock Ward*, 1756. *Ald.* 1764.
1749.—Philip Livingston (*Merchant*), *Ald. East Ward*, 1754 to 1762.
1750.—Leonard Lispenard, *Asst.-Ald. North Ward*, 1750 to 1755. *Ald.*, 1756 to 1762.
    Pieter Clopper, *Asst.-Ald. East Ward*, 1751 to 1762.
    J. Turk.
    John Brevoort.
1752.—Hendrick Bogert, *Asst.-Ald. West Ward*, 1734 to 1749.
    Dirck Lefferts.
    Cornelius Clopper, Jr.
    Evert Bancker.
    John Livingston.
1753.—Albert Tiebout.
1755.—Willem De Peyster, *Asst.-Ald. Montgomerie Ward*, 1750 to 1753.
    Richard Ray.
1756.—Pieter Keteltas.
    Anthony Ten Eyck.
1757.—John G. Lansing, *Asst.-Ald. Dock Ward*, 1760–61–62.

Records lacking.

1763.—Gerrit Rapelye, *Asst.-Ald. East Ward*, 1763–64–65.
    Dirck Brinckerhoff, *Asst.-Ald. Dock Ward*, 1763–64. *Ald.*, 1765–66–67.
    John Hardenbrook, *Asst.-Ald. Out Ward*, 1771–72–73.
    Teunis Tiebout.
    Isaac Roosevelt.
    Theodore Roosevelt, Jr.
1764.—Fac. Bogert.
1766.—Henry Kip.
    Gerrit Abeel.
    Nicholas Bogert.
    Adrian Bancker, Jr.
    Jakob Duryè.
1767.— —— Maerschalk.
1769.—James Beekman.
    Isaac Stoutenberg (*Merchant*), *Ald. West Ward*, 1789 to 1794.
    Jeremiah Brouwer.
1771.—William W. Gilbert (*Silversmith*), *Ald. West Ward*, 1783 to 1788. *Asst. Seventh Ward*, 1801. *Ald. Eighth Ward*, 1804.

1771.—John Stagg, *President of the General Society of Mechanics and Tradesmen*, 1790 and 1794; *Sheriff*, 1801 to 1803.
Baltus Van Kleeck.
1773.—David Abeel.
—— Hoffman.
1774.—Nicholas N. Anthony.
Thomas Andrew Hoog.
Tobias Van Zandt (*Chocolate Manufacturer*), *Asst.-Ald. Montgomerie Ward*, 1786 to 1793.
John Forbes, *Secretary and Librarian of N. Y. Society Library*, 1794 to 1824.
William Heyer.
1775.—Henry Romer.
Philip Minthorne.
John Anthony.

In 1783 a majority of the Consistory having returned to the city, they re-organized and *Resolved*, "That the same persons who were Elders and Deacons on the 15th of July, 1776, when the city was taken by the troops of Great Britain, and the congregation became dispersed, shall be now considered as being still the Elders and Deacons of the Reformed Protestant Dutch Church of the City of New York, as if no time had elapsed, and the same shall form (together with the Minister, who is also returned) the Consistory of the said Church.*

The following named Deacons then resumed their office:

John Anthony.   John Forbes.
William W. Gilbert. Gerrit Harsen.
        William Heyer.

1784.—William J. Elsworth, *Asst.-Ald. West Ward*, 1789-90-91.
William Hardenbrook.
Francis Basset.
Elias Nexsen (*Merchant*), *Ald. Second Ward*, 1805.
Robert Manley.
Isaac Johnson.
1785.—William De Peyster.
Coenrad W. Ham.
Ahasuerus Turk.
John Brouwer.
George Janeway (*Brewer*), *Asst.-Ald. North Ward*, 1784 to 1795. *Ald. Sixth Ward*, 1803-04.
John J. Roosevelt.
1786.—John Sickels.

* Con. Min., Lib. G. 1.

1786.—Anthony Post (*Builder*), *President of the General Society of Mechanics and Tradesmen*, 1789 and 1793. *Asst.-Ald. Fourth Ward*, 1792 to 1796. *Ald. Fourth Ward*, 1797.
  Anthony Abramse.
  John H. Kip.
  Abraham Van Gelder, *Asst.-Ald. West Ward*, 1783 to 1788.
  Thomas Storm (*Merchant*), *Asst.-Ald. First Ward*, 1796-97-98.
1787.—Leonard Bleecker.
  Charles Dickinson, *Ald. Third Ward*, 1808 to 1813.
  George Harsen.
  John Van Dycke (*Chocolate Manufacturer*), *Asst.-Ald. South Ward*, 1785 '86 '89 '90.
1788.—Stephen Van Cortlandt.
  James Van Antwerp.
  Abraham Kip.
  William G. Forbes.
  John T. Elsworth.
1789.—Frederick Steymets (*Baker*), *Asst.-Ald. First Ward*, 1792 to 1795.
  Andrew Hopper.
  Jacobus Brown.
1790.—John Crolius (*Potter*), *Asst.-Ald. Sixth Ward*, 1799.
  John Stryker.
1791.—Jacob J. Lansing.
  Thomas Le Foy.
  William Van Dolsem.
  Simon Van Antwerp (*Merchant*), *Asst.-Ald. Third Ward*, 1804-5-7.
  Peter Cole.
1792.—Peter De Reimer.
  Abraham Polhemus.
  Jacob Abramse.
  Stephen Smith.
1793.—Nicholas Van Antwerp.
  Charles Duryee.
  James Teller.
1794.—Jacob Harsen, *Ald. Ninth Ward*, 1803.
  Henry M. Solinger.
  John Elting.
  John Nitchie, *Asst.-Ald. First Ward*, 1799, 1800-1, 1812-13.
1795.—Charles Dickenson.
  John Crolius, Jr.

1795.—Garrit Waldegrove.
   John New Kirck.
   James Roosevelt (*Merchant*), *Ald. Fourth Ward*, 1809.
   John Waldron.
1796.—John Varick.
   Peter H. Wendover (*Sailmaker*), *Asst.-Ald. Fourth Ward*, 1801; *Ald. Eighth Ward*, 1811-12-13; *President of the General Society of Mechanics and Tradesmen*, 1819; *Sheriff*, 1822 to 1826.
   Garrit Hopper.
1797.—Alexander Phœnix Waldron.
   Abraham Labagh, *President of the General Society of Mechanics and Tradesmen*, 1802.
   Peter Amerman.
   John V. B. Varick.
1798.—Joseph Demaray.
   Daniel Hitchcock, *President of the General Society of Mechanics and Tradesmen*, 1800.
   John Stagg, Jr.
1799.—Abraham Childs.
   Garrit De Bow.
   William King.
   James H. Kip.
1801.—Samuel Doughty.
   Frederick Maybee.
   Lawrence Proudfoot.
   Cornelius P. Wyckoff.
1802.—Abraham Brouwer, Jr., *M.D.*
   Nicholas Evertson.
   Isaac Sebring.
   John L. Van Kleek.
   John Van Orden.
   John Westervelt.
   James J. Westervelt.
1803.—Isaac L. Kip.
   John Manly.
   John Stoutenburgh.
1804.—Seba Brinckerhoff.
   Peter Dumont, *M.D.*
   Wandle Ham.
   James Van Dyck.
   John Wright.
1805.—Samuel Delamater.
   Richard Duryea.
   John Vanderbilt, Jr. (*Merchant*), *Ald. Second Ward*, 1812.
   Thomas B. Whitlock.

1806.—Thomas Boyd, *M. D.*
    Cornelius Heyer.
    Guysbert Bogert Vroom.
1807.—Benjamin S. Knapp.
    John I. Labagh (*Stone Yard*), *President of the General Society of Mechanics and Tradesmen,* 1811 ; *Asst.- Ald. First Ward,* 1831-2-3-40 ; *Ald.* 1834-5.
    Abraham Van Nest (*Hardware*), *President of the General Society of Mechanics and Tradesmen,* 1815. *Alderman Ninth Ward,* 1833.
1808.—Jesse Baldwin.
    Abraham Bogert.
    Matthias Bruen.
    Richard Duryee.
    John W. Hinton, *President of the General Society of Mechanics and Tradesmen,* 1823.

In 1808 the Consistory appointed a *Board of Trustees,* consisting of seven persons, four of whom, at least, must be members in full communion of the Collegiate Church. The said Trustees are arranged in three classes ; one class is elected annually for *three* years. The first and second classes consist of two members each, and the third class of three members.

They direct the management of the school and carry into effect the rules and regulations of Consistory respecting the same. They meet monthly to receive the report of the Principal ; for the admission and withdrawal of pupils ; and to transact such other business pertaining to the School as may come before them.

The Members of the Board serve monthly, in rotation, as the Visiting Committee of the School.

Names of the Members of the Board of Trustees,

From the year 1808 to the present time.

When Appointed.	
June 2, 1808.	John Stoutenburgh, *Chairman*. Term expired, Dec. 31, 1814.
June 2, 1808.	John Nitchie, Jr., *Secretary*, resigned, Jan., 1813.
June 2, 1808.	Richard Duryee, *Chairman* from Jan. 1, 1814, to Jan., 1815, when his term expired. Re-elected as *Trustee* and *Chairman*, Oct., 1831. Deceased, Sept., 1835.
June 2, 1808.	Isaac Heyer, *Chairman* from Jan., 1815, to the time of his decease, April, 1827.
June 2, 1808.	Abraham Brinckerhoff, Jr., resigned, Jan., 1813.
June 2, 1808.	Anthony Dey. Resigned, Feb., 1810.
June 2, 1808.	Jesse Baldwin. Resigned, March, 1812.
Feb., 1810.	Huybert Van Wagenen, *Secretary* from Jan., 1813, to Jan., 1815. Term expired, Dec. 31, 1817.
March, 1812.	Henry J. Wyckoff. Term expired, Feb., 1818.
Feb., 1813.	John D. Keese. do. Jan., 1819.
Feb., 1813.	John V. B. Varick, *Secretary* from Jan., 1815, to Jan., 1820, when his time expired.
Jan., 1814.	John Kane. Resigned, Jan., 1818.
Jan., 1815.	Michael Schoonmaker. Removed from the city, Oct., 1823.
Jan., 1817.	John Clarke, *M. D.* Resigned, July, 1824.
Jan., 1818.	William Hardenbrook, Jr. Removed to Harlem, April, 1827.
Feb., 1818.	John Van Vechten. Deceased, Oct. 13, 1821.
Jan., 1819.	Jeromius Johnson, *Secretary*, Jan., 1820. Resigned, July, 1824.
March, 1820.	Peter I. Nevius. Resigned, Sept., 1821.
Sept., 1821.	John A. Lent. Deceased, Oct. 13, 1821.
Nov., 1821.	Timothy Hutton. Resigned, July, 1824.
Nov., 1821.	Obadiah Holmes. do. do.
Oct., 1823.	Abraham Van Nest. do. March, 1826.
July, 1824.	Abraham Bloodgood. Resigned, March, 1826.
July, 1824.	James C. Roosevelt, *Chairman*, April, 1827. Resigned, July, 1831.
July, 1824.	John Nexsen. Resigned, July, 1831.
July, 1824.	Isaac Young, *Secretary*, July, 1824. Resigned, July, 1831.

BOARD OF TRUSTEES, FROM THE

When Appointed.

March, 1826.	John I. Labagh. Resigned, July, 1831.
March, 1826.	Stephen Van Brunt. Deceased, Feb., 1828.
May, 1827.	Peter Stagg. Resigned, July, 1831.
May, 1827.	Theophilus Anthony. Resigned, July, 1831.
April, 1828.	John Oothout. Resigned, July, 1831.
Oct. 6, 1831.	John Clark. Resigned, Dec., 1834.
Oct. 6, 1831.	John Limberger. Resigned, Nov., 1836.
Oct. 6, 1831.	James V. H. Lawrence, *Secretary*, Oct., 1831. Resigned, July, 1836.
Oct. 6, 1831.	James Ward. Term expired, Feb., 1844.
Oct. 6, 1831.	James Van Antwerp. Resigned, Jan., 1834.
Feb., 1834.	Reuben Van Pelt. Resigned, March, 1839.
Jan., 1835.	David L. Haight. Resigned, Feb., 1839.
Feb., 1835.	Noah Wetmore, *Chairman* from Sept., 1835, to his decease, July 12, 1848.
Oct., 1835.	James Suydam. Resigned, July, 1836.
Sept., 1836.	Joseph V. Varick. Removed from the city, Oct., 1838.
Sept., 1836.	James Simmons, *Secretary*, Sept., 1836. Removed from the city, Aug., 1839.
Dec., 1836.	Peter R. Warner, *Secretary*, Sept., 1839. Resigned, on account of protracted illness, Oct., 1843. Re-elected to the Board, Feb., 1844. *Secretary* from Feb., 1845, to Feb., 1846. Resigned, Feb., 1848. Re-elected to the Board, Oct., 1852, and elected *Chairman*, Feb., 1853, to Feb., 1857, when his term expired. Re-elected to the Board, Feb., 1867, to Feb., 1870.
Nov., 1838.	John I. Brower. Term expired, Feb., 1846. Re-elected, Dec., 1849, to Feb., 1868.
Feb., 1839.	Valentine Van De Water. Term expired, Feb., 1845.
Sept., 1839.	Charles Devoe, *Chairman*, July, 1848, removed to Michigan, 1850.
Sept., 1839.	John I. De Foreest. Resigned, Jan., 1842.
Jan., 1842.	James D. Oliver. Term expired, Feb., 1846.
Oct., 1843.	John Ackerman, *Secretary* from Dec., 1843, to Feb., 1845. Resigned, April, 1849.
Feb., 1845.	Mortimer de Motte. Term expired, Feb., 1851.
Feb., 1846.	Thomas Jeremiah, *Secretary* from March, 1846, till his term expired, Feb., 1852. Re-elected to the Board, Feb., 1857, and served as *Chairman* until Feb., 1872, when his term expired.

Feb., 1846.	Edward L. Beadle, *M. D.*, *Chairman*, from Nov., 1850, to Feb., 1853. Continued a member of the Board until he resigned, June 2, 1859. Re-elected to the Board, Feb., 1861, to Feb., 1864.
April, 1848.	John Van Nest. Resigned, March 26, 1855.
Feb., 1849.	Huybert Van Wagenen, Jr. Deceased, Sept. 10, 1850.
April, 1849.	George Zabriskie. Deceased, Aug., 1849.
Oct., 1850.	George S. Stitt, *Secretary* from March, 1852, to Feb., 1853, and from Feb., 1854, to Feb., 1859. Re-elected to the Board, Feb., 1861, to Feb., 1867.
Oct., 1850.	Charles S. Little. Resigned, Sept., 1855.
April, 1851.	Henry Oothout. Resigned, Sept., 1852.
Feb., 1852.	Gamaliel G. Smith, *Secretary*, Feb., 1853, to Feb., 1854. Continued in the Board until Feb., 1861. Re-elected, Feb., 1866, to Feb., 1869.
April, 1855.	James Van Benschoten. Term expired, 1862.
Oct., 1855.	Charles F. Hunter, *Secretary* from Feb., 1859, until his term expired, Feb., 1863.
Feb., 1859.	William H. Dunning. Resigned, April 24, 1860.
June, 1859.	John C. Calhoun, to Feb., 1861. Re-elected, Feb., 1864, and was *Chairman* from Feb., 1872, until his decease, Nov. 26, 1874.
April, 1860.	Richard Amerman. Term expired, Feb., 1862.
Feb., 1862.	Calvin F. Knox, to Feb., 1871. *Secretary* from Feb., 1863, to March, 1870.
Mar. 6, 1862.	William Wood. Resigned, Jan., 1872.
Feb., 1863.	Abraham V. W. Van Vechten,* to 1866. Re-elected, Feb., 1876. *Secretary* from Feb., 1881, to Feb., 1882.
Feb., 1868.	Henry Snyder, to 1874. *Secretary* from March, 1870, until Feb., 1874, when his term expired. Re-elected to the Board, Feb., 1877, to Feb., 1880.
Feb., 1869.	Frederick T. Locke. Term expired, Feb., 1876.
Feb., 1871.	Abraham Bogardus to Feb., 1874, and from Feb., 1875 to Feb., 1876.
Feb., 1872.	Henry W. Bookstaver,* *Chairman* from Nov., 1874, to the present time.
Feb., 1872.	Robert Buck, to Feb., 1874.

* Present members of the Board of Trustees.

Feb., 1872.	Alexis A. Julien, *Secretary* from March, 1874, to Feb., 1881, when his term expired.
Feb., 1874.	Robert Schell.*
Feb., 1874.	Cornelius V. Clarkson, *M.D.* Term expired, Feb., 1877.
Feb., 1874.	John Adriance. Deceased, Nov. 3, 1874.
Feb., 1875.	Wm. Wheeler Smith, to Feb., 1877.
Feb., 1876.	Henry E. Knox, to Feb., 1879.
Feb., 1877.	James Anderson, *M.D.**
Feb., 1879.	Ralph N. Perlee.*
Feb., 1880.	Augustus S. Whiton.*
Feb., 1881.	Frederic R. Hutton,* *Secretary* from Feb., 1881, to the present time.

* Present members of the Board of Trustees.

ANCIENT AND MODERN NAMES OF STREETS.

The following Table is inserted to enable streets in the *old* records to be identified by those familiar only with the *modern* names of New York streets.

Old Name.	Present Name.
Almshouse	South side Chambers St., site of New Court House.
Augustus	City Hall Place.
Back of Jail	Chambers Street, near Centre.
Bancker	Madison, from Pearl to Oliver.
Barley	Duane.
Barracks	City Hall Park, South side of Chambers.
Batavia Lane	Batavia Street.
Bear Market	Greenwich, between Fulton and Vesey.
Bedlow	Madison, from Oliver to Grand.
Bowery Lane	Bowery, to 6th Street; Fourth Avenue to 14th St.
Bridewell	Broadway, opposite Murray.
Budd	Vandam.
Near Burke's	Spring, near Hudson.
Bunker Hill.	Grand, from Mott to Broadway.
Chapel	West Broadway.
Col. Burr's	Richmond Hill, S. E. corner Varick & Charlton.
Col. Varick's	....
The Collect	Centre Street, between Pearl and Hester.
Crolius's	North side Chatham, between Pearl and Duane.
Cross	Park Street.
Dock	Pearl, from Whitehall to Hanover Square.
East George	Market Street.
Factory	Waverly Place, north of Christopher.
Fair	Fulton, from Broadway to Cliff.
Fayette	Oliver, from Chatham Square to Madison.
Federal Hall	N. E. cor. Wall and Nassau; now the Sub-Treasury.
Fifth	Orchard.
First	Chrystie.
Fisher	Bayard, east of the Bowery.
Fly Market	Foot of Maiden Lane, East River.
Fourth	Allen.
Garden	Exchange Place.
George	Spruce.
Gould	Gold.
Gr. Furnace	....
Harman	East Broadway.
Laurens	West Fifth Avenue.
Lispenard's	West of Hudson Street, betw. Desbrosses and Watts.
Little Catharine	Catharine Lane.
Little Chapel	College Place.

ANCIENT AND MODERN NAMES OF STREETS—*continued.*

Old Name.	Present Name.
Lombard } Lombardy }	Monroe.
Lower Robinson	Robinson, from College Place to North River.
Lumber	New Church.
Magazine	Pearl, from Broadway to Chatham.
Mary	{ Baxter, from Bayard to Prince. { Changed to Orange, 1807.
N. R. Furnace	Foot of Hubert Street.
Orange	Baxter.
Partition	Fulton, west of Broadway.
Princess	Beaver, from Broad to William.
Provost	Franklin, from West Broadway to North River.
Pump	Canal, east of Centre.
Robinson } Robertson }	Park Place, from Broadway to Church.
Rynders	Centre.
St. John Street	St. John's Lane, from Beach to Laight.
Second	Forsyth.
Sixth	Ludlow.
Sloat	S. of Wall, from Will. to Hanov. Sq., now obliterated.
Spring, near Tyler's ..	....
Sperry	Spring? or Perry?
Sugar Loaf	Franklin, from Broadway to West Broadway.
Third	Eldridge.
Union Furnace	Southeast corner Broadway and Howard.
Vauxhall	Broadway and Bowery, from 4th St. to Astor Place.
Wine } Winne } .... Wynne }	Mott.

CATALOGUE OF SCHOLARS.

INTRODUCTION.

The following pages contain the names of the scholars for the past ninety-four years. The record of scholars previous to the American Revolution has not been preserved, which is to be regretted, for our ancestors on this island were so attached to their language and their Church polity, that it is reasonable to infer that they would cause their children, from generation to generation, to be instructed in those elements of Divine truth and of secular knowledge, which would foster attachment to the Mother Church and prepare them for usefulness in the Church and in the world. Two names, at least, have been preserved.

Abram Brower, who at the time of his death, in 1832, was aged 80, states (*vide* Watson's Annals, N. Y., p. 172), that when a lad "he went to the Dutch School, to his grandfather, Abraham Delanoye (a French Huguenot, *via* Holland), whose school was in Cortlandt Street."

This was undoubtedly the branch school established by Consistory in 1743, for the convenience of those children attending the Middle Church, Nassau Street, who resided too far up-town to attend the Main School, near the Garden Street Church, of which Gerrit and Huybert Van Wagenen were the schoolmasters from 1733 to 1749; *vide* History of the School, and its Locality.

The late Judge Egbert Benson (in an address read by him before the N. Y. Historical Society, Dec. 31, 1816), states that "in his early youth he attended school at the corner of *Marketfield* and *Broad Streets, where he learned the Dutch Catechism.* They used in the Dutch churches," he adds, "an *hour-glass* near the clerk, to ascertain the length of the sermon, which was always limited to one hour. They made the collections in a bag with a *bell*, to give notice of the approach of the deacons (gatherers)." *

1765, May 21.—Egbert Benson graduated from King's (now Columbia) College.
 1775.—Was a Deputy to the Provincial Congress.
 1777.—Attorney-General, State of N. Y.
 1777-8.—Member of the Council of Safety.
 1778-81.—Member of Assembly.

* *Vide* the address in Historical Society publications and Watson's Annals, p. 191.

1780.—Appointed Commissioner to the Federal Constitutional Convention.

1781-4.—Delegate to Continental Congress.

1784.—One of the Commissioners for settling the boundary between New York and Massachusetts.

1790.—One of the Commissioners for settling the boundary between New York and Connecticut.

1782 to 1802.—Regent of the University.

1786.—Commissioner to a Convention for promoting a uniform system of commercial intercourse between the several States.

1789-93.—Member of First and Second Congress.

1813-15.—Member of Thirteenth Congress.

1794.—Justice of New York State Court.

1801.—Judge United States Circuit Court.

1803 to 1815.—Trustee of the New York Society Library.

Was one of the founders of the New York Historical Society, and was elected its first President, serving from 1805 to 1816.

The dates of admission and withdrawal in the following catalogue refer to the days when the Board of Trustees met, and the names came before them.

In those instances where a scholar *re-entered* the school after a brief interval, the dates of the *original entry* and *final withdrawal* only are given.

Where the interval was a year or over, all the dates are inserted.

In this catalogue will be found the names of many who have filled offices of honor and trust in the community.

The Records of the Teachers previous to 1842 are occasionally incomplete, and, as neither of them is now living, it is possible that the name of some former scholar may not be found in the catalogue, or he may have failed to receive the special notice to which he is justly entitled for public services rendered.

It is requested that information respecting such names or services be forwarded to the Principal, or to any member of the Board of Trustees.

CATALOGUE OF SCHOLARS.

No.	Pupil.	Age	Admitted.	Withdrawn.	Parent.	Residence.	Graduated.
1	Degraw, Aaron						
2	Romine, Isaac						
3	Shepherd, Charles						
4	Couenhoven, Chr.						
5	Dempsey, William						
6	Kiersted, Luke						
7	Vanlewater, Henry						
8	Anderson, Nicholas						
9	Vandervort, James						
10	Anderson, Walter						
11	Kip, Hubert						
12	Bania, Peter						
13	McDougal, Duncan						
14	Ackerman, Abraham						
15	Warner, Daniel						
16	Miller, Isaac						
17	Hopper, Matthew						
18	Bogert, Gilbert						
19	Helms, Peter						
20	Stymets, Abraham						
21	Waldron, John						
22	Pullis, William						
23	Phister, George						
24	Shepherd, James						
25	Hurborow, Mary						
26	Devoe, Sarah						
27	Fardon, Elizabeth						
28	Rogers, Cornelia						
29	Taylor, Mary						
30	Stanton, Catherine *						

* The Entry Register contains the following memorandum: "The first thirty children were delivered to Stanton Latham by Peter Van Steenburg, May 4, 1791." No further records relating to them have been found. Some of them may have been in the school one, two, three or more years.

CATALOGUE OF SCHOLARS—Continued.

No.	Pupil.	Age	Admitted.	Withdrawn.	Parent.	Residence.	Graduated.
31	Ferris, Margaret						
32	Amerman, Mary			Dec. 30, 1795			Dec. 30, 1795
33	Myers, David						
34	Hays, Cornelia						
35	Vandewater, Ann						
36	Chardevoyne, Ann						
37	Hardenbrook, Wm.						
38	Low, Jane						
39	Romine, Andrew						
40	Valentine, Jacob						
41	Rosier, John						
42	Storm, Jemima		May 4, 1792				
43	Anderson, Elizabeth		do.				
44	Brower, Nicholas		do.				
45	Armstrong, Elizabeth		May 12, 1792	, 1796			
46	Grant, John		June 10, 1792				
47	Myers, Elizabeth		June 29, 1792				
48	Martling, Henry		July 25, 1792				
49	Leonard, Jacob		August 19, 1792	May 15, 1795			
50	Myers, Cornelia		Oct. 22, 1792				
51	Hopper, Martha		Nov. 3, 1792				
52	Deacon, James		Nov. 5, 1792	May 18, 1795			
53	Wentworth, John		do.	Feb. 4, 1795			
54	Forbes, Alexander		Nov. 7, 1792				
55	Skinner, David		Nov. 8, 1792				
56	Taylor, Abraham		do.	June 8, 1795			
57	Wheeler, Abraham		do.	July 3, 1796			
58	Storm, Rulef		do.	April 7, 1795			
59	Earle, Morris		do.	Dec. 30, 1795			April 7, 1795
60	King, Gilbert		do.	April 7, 1795			Dec. 30, 1795
61	Couenhoven, Nicholas		do.	January 5, 1798	James	Magazine	April 7, 1795
62	Grant, John		do.	June 8, 1795			Jan. 5, 1798
63	Rykeman, James		do.	Feb. 12, 1794	James	Byard's	
64	Romine, Ob.		do.	July 10, 1796	Casper	Bowery	
65	Vonck, Catherine		do.	Feb. 1, 1796	Peter	Warren	
66	Wheeler, Andrew		do.	July 3, 1796			
67	King, Harman		do.	Oct. 16, 1795	Widow King	Thomas	Oct. 16, 1795
68	Benschoten, Cornelius		do.	April 1, 1796	Elias	Wine	

CATALOGUE OF SCHOLARS—Continued.

No.	Pupil.	Age	Admitted.	Withdrawn.	Parent.	Residence.	Graduated.
69	McKinney, George		Nov. 8, 1792.	September, 1795.			
70	Sigmets, Benjamin		do.	May 27, 1796.			
71	Hulett, Phebe		do.	May, 1796.			
72	Roome, Ann		do.	December, 1795.	Widow Roome	Fair	Dec., 1795
73	Taylor, Susan		do.	April, 1795.			April, 1795
74	Van Evour, Ed.		do.	May, 1797.			May, 1797
75	Roberts, James		do.	July, 1797.			July, 1797
76	Christie, James		Dec. 4, 1792.	June, 1795.			
77	Adams, James		do.	October, 1794.	Alexander Stevens	92 Gold	
78	Forbes, Tobias		March, 1793.	do.	William A	L. Chapel	
79	Van Den Bergh, John		May 29, 1793.	Jan. 5, 1798.	John	Barley	Jan. 5, 1798
80	Tremper, Harman		do.	February, 1797.			
81	Anderson, Elias		May 4, 1793.	March, 1795.	Widow Anderson	5 Rector	March, 1795
82	Lewis, Leonard		June 19, 1793.	May, 1795.	Widow Lewis	95 Fair	
83	Bogart, James		August 27, 1793.	June 5, 1799.	Widow Bogart	73 Princess	
84	Waldron, Wm		Oct. 16, 1793.	April 7, 1795.			
85	Morris, Rachel		Oct. 17, 1793.	July, 1795.			
86	Graham, John		Nov. 25, 1793.	Jan. 5, 1798.	Jacob	6 Harley	Jan. 5, 1798
87	Anderson, John		Dec. 5, 1793.	Jan. 19, 1798.	Isaac Monday	Lumber	Jan. 19, 1798
88	Osborne, Benjamin		Dec. 16, 1793.	April 3, 1795.	Nicholas	44 Little Chapel	
89	Darborow, Joseph		Dec. 16, 1793.	Jan. 5, 1798.	Joseph	Vesey	Jan. 5, 1798
90	Lyon, Michael		Dec. 16, 1793.	July 8, 1797.	Widow Lyon	10 Liberty	July 8, 1797
91	Robertson, John		Dec. 18, 1793.	Sept. 7, 1796.	Widow	Ann	Sept. 7, 1796
92	Myers, Edward		Jan. 12, 1794.	July 8, 1797.	Isaac	Harley	July 8, 1797
93	Stagg, John		April 14, 1794.	April 15, 1796.	Isaac	46 Harley	
94	Bogart, Daniel		May 9, 1794.	March 1, 1797.	Widow		
95	Terbose, Luke		May 19, 1794.	March 15, 1796.			
96	Hopper, Jacob		June 16, 1794.	August 2, 1795.			
97	Salter (or Selseer), John		July 18, 1794.	August 12, 1799.	Widow		
98	Ackerman, Lawrence		August 4, 1794.	June 4, 1799.	Abraham	99 Chambers	June 4, 1799
99	Fenton, David		Sept. 18, 1794.	Feb. 18, 1795.			
100	Decker, John		do.	do.			
101	Colbart, John		Oct. 8, 1794.	Jan. 2, 1797.	Samuel Ellsworth	Beale	Jan. 2, 1797
102	Verveelen, Margery		do.	March 16, 1798.	Cornelius	Greenwich	March 16, 1798
103	Myers, James		Jan. 12, 1795.	July 10, 1798.		54 Vesey	
104	Vinson, John		Jan. 23, 1795.	August 1, 1796.	Widow	Prince	
105	Morris, Susan		Jan. 28, 1795.	—, 1797.	Jacob	6 Harley	
106	Collard, Archer		Jan. 29, 1795.	March 16, 1796.	Jacob	Murray	

CATALOGUE OF SCHOLARS—Continued.

No.	Pupil.	Age	Admitted.	Withdrawn.	Parent.	Residence.	Graduated.
107	Waldron, Tunis		Feb. 2, 1795	Oct. 10, 1796			
108	Huett, Francis R		do.	Sept. 1, 1795			
109	Kykeman, Mary		do.	June 4, 1798	James	Mulberry	
110	Holloway, Isabella		do.	March 16, 1798	Widow	Reade	
111	Mabee, Ann		do.	Sept., 1795			
112	Emmet, George		{ Feb. 1, 1795, { July 10, 1797	Sept. 20, 1795, April 6, 1802	James	15 William	
113	Van Tassel, Tunis		Feb. 3, 1795	Jan. 18, 1801			July 1, 1797
114	Waldron, Ann		Feb. 4, 1795	July 1, 1797	Joshua	Dutch	—, 1798
115	Slidell, Nicholas		do.	—, 1798	Samuel	Bowery	
116	Romine, Samuel		do.	—, 1796	Mrs. Crown	Pump	
117	Howsey, Elizabeth		do.	July 10, 1795			
118	Serine, Elisha		do.	—, 1797			
119	Skaats, Harman		Feb. 5, 1795	Jan. 19, 1798	Bartholomew	Federal Hall	Jan. 19, 1798
120	Bania, John		do.	Sept. 1, 1795			Sept. 1, 1795
121	Wandell, Catherine		do.	Sept. 2, 1795	James	80 Beekman	
122	Wandell, Mary		do.	March 16, 1798	James	do.	Mar. 16, 1798
123	Valentine, John		Feb. 8, 1795	June 4, 1799			June 4, 1799
124	Miller, William		Feb. 18, 1795	June 10, 1795			
125	Koame, Rachel		Feb. 20, 1795	Jan., 1798	Widow	5 Dey	
126	Earle, John		Feb. 28, 1795	Dec., 1798		Fair	
127	Smith, Edward		do.	Jan. 14, 1797	Widow Kip	6 Ferry	
128	Acker, Laney		do.	April 17, 1796	Ann Fash	7 Division	
129	Rykeman, Isaac		do.	June 22, 1795	John	Reade	
130	Ayres, Tobias		do.	July 7, 1796	Thomas	Gr. Furnace	
131	Penny, John		Feb. 3, 1795	April 1, 1797	Charles	Collect	
132	Lane, Daniel		Feb. 5, 1795	Sept. 1, 1795	Daniel	Near Crolius's	
133	Dodge, Jacob		March 9, 1795	June, 1795			
134	Hill, George		do.	Sept., 1801	William Hillman	Back of Jail	
135	Huestis, Hannah		March 16, 1795	April 19, 1798	Peter Elting	Dock	April 19, 1798
136	Acker, Rachel		May 18, 1795	March 4, 1797	Ann Fash	Division	
137	King, Jacob		May 19, 1795	June 17, 1796	Walter	Behind the Bridewell	
138	Wortendyke, R		May 20, 1795	May 21, 1796	Frederick	43 Partition	May 21, 1796
139	Kiersted, James		do.	May 13, 1797	James	Behind the Barrak	
140	Leaycraft, John		June 8, 1795	March 7, 1796	Eliza	12 Frankfort	
141	McNeal, John		June 9, 1795	July, 1798	Mary	8 Fair	
142	Mead, John		June 17, 1795	March 1, 1801	Nicholas	6 Harley	Mar. 1, 1801
143	Amerman, Isaac	9	June 17, 1795	June 4, 1799	Albert	Vandewater	June 4, 1799

CATALOGUE OF SCHOLARS—Continued.

No.	Pupil.	Age	Admitted.	Withdrawn.	Parent.	Residence.	Graduated.
144	Banner, John	8	July 13, 1795	Jan. 1, 1796	James	5 Ann	....
145	Salter (or Selser), Abraham	5	July 15, 1795	Oct. 20, 1800	Widow	Pump	....
146	Nicholas, Henry	9	July 27, 1795	July 1, 1799	Henry	56 Stone	....
147	Switzer, Martin	9	August 27, 1795	March 15, 1800	Peter	N. R. Furnace	Jan. 19, 1798
148	Phillips, Thomas	9	do.	Jan. 10, 1798	John	Almshouse	....
149	Van Dyke, Charles	9	Sept. 1, 1795	Aug. 9, 1798	Charles	Dey	....
150	Dekive, Peggy	11	Sept. 21, 1795	March 15, 1796	Leonard	24 Garden	Nov., 1797
151	Devoe, Laney	9	do.	Nov., 1797	James	32 Lower Chapel	Jan. 2, 1797
152	Garrison, Simon	11	Oct. 25, 1795	Jan. 2, 1797	John	74 Reade	....
153	Hays, Maria		Dec. 6, 1795	April 12, 1796	Sarah	28 Warren	....
154	Miner, James	8	Jan. 3, 1796	April 12, 1799	John	36 Robertson	....
155	Ackerman, John	10	Jan. 12, 1796	Sept. 13, 1797	Morris	Greenwich	June 4, 1799
156	Verralen, Andrew	9	Jan. 12, 1796	June 4, 1799	Cornelius	12 Vesey	....
157	Earl, Thomas	7	Feb. 1, 1796	July, 1798	Widow	6 Barley	Mar. 1, 1801
158	Mead, Mary	8	Feb. 14, 1796	March 1, 1801	Nicholas	Gr. Furnace	May 13, 1802
159	Ayres, Daniel (*Vide Notes*)	6	March 14, 1796	May 13, 1802	Thomas	....	May 25, 1802
160	Post, Jacob	7	April 17, 1796	May 25, 1801	Widow	....	Mar. 20, 1801
161	Sibdell, Joshua	7	May 17, 1796	March 20, 1801	Joshua	....	....
162	Symets, John	13	May 27, 1796	, 1798	John Apple	Barclay	....
163	Garrison, Maria	8	May 31, 1796	June 4, 1799	John	93 Partition	....
164	Devoe, Daniel	8	June 5, 1796	July 5, 1799	John	Harman	Oct. 14, 1801
165	Demarest, James	10	June 12, 1796	Oct. 14, 1801	Frederick	47 Chapel	....
166	Wortendyke, Martha	10	June 15, 1796	, 1798	George	43 Partition	....
167	Becknam, Henry	10	June 15, 1796	June 4, 1799		9 Reade	....
168	Barnet, Jane			Aug. 3, 1798			
169	Hugert, Polly			do.			
170	Cole, John	7	July 14, 1796	June 4, 1799	Edward Lansdown	Cliff	....
171	Meshet, Frederick	6	do.	July 5, 1798	Jane Warner	103 Reade	....
172	Seaman, Sarah	9	August 31, 1796	April 3, 1801	Peter	70 Reade	April 3, 1801
173	Holloway, John		Sept. 2, 1796	March 2, 1798	Thomas	Reade	....
174	Helms, Cornelia	12	Sept. 20, 1796	April 20, 1797	Samuel	Little Catharine	....
175	Purdy, Luke	12	do.	April 14, 1799	John	71 Chatham	....
176	Amerman, Hannah	13	Sept. 22, 1796	April 15, 1797	Albert	2 Harraks	....
177	Colegrove, William	8	Sept. 23, 1796	June 4, 1799	Fran.	39 Liberty	....
178	Myers, James	8	Sept. 26, 1796	August, 1798	Elizabeth	11 Barley	April 20, 1803
179	Morris, Eleanor	6	do.	August, 1797	Isaac	17 Thames	....
180	Askins, James	9	Oct. 3, 1796	April 20, 1803	John	9 Reade	....
181	Beckman, Catherine	11	Oct. 4, 1796	July 23, 1797	George		....

CATALOGUE OF SCHOLARS—Continued.

No.	Pupil.	Age	Admitted.	Withdrawn.	Parent.	Residence.	Graduated.
182	Britton, Nicholas	12	Oct. 7, 1796	Feb., 1797	Nicholas	44 Reade	
183	Tom, Peter	6	Oct. 19, 1796	April 7, 1802	Peter	40 Reade	
184	Devoe, Daniel S.	7	Oct. 31, 1796	Feb. 10, 1803	Catharine	48 Gold	Feb. 10, 1803
185	Warner, James	10	Nov. 8, 1796	Aug. 1, 1798	Thomas	Fayette	
186	Westerveit, Abraham	10	Nov. 14, 1796	April 3, 1800	Peter	Barclay	April 3, 1800
187	Van Aulen, Cornelius		Jan. 6, 1797	June 4, 1799	Cornelius	Barclay	
188	Brower, John	12	Jan. 22, 1797	March 16, 1800	Widow	16 Barclay	Mar. 16, 1800
189	Wessels, Wm.	6	do	June 4, 1799	Widow	10 Beaver	
190	Demorest, Catherine	9	do	May 8, 1800	Cornelius	Barley	May 8, 1800
191	Heyer, Sophia	12		, 1798	William	Magazine	
192	Brower, Thomas		Jan. 23, 1797	May 4, 1799	Widow	Barclay	May 4, 1799
193	Osborne, Charles	12	Jan. 25, 1797	Aug. 2, 1798	Charles	Frankfort	
194	Demilt, Frederick	10	Jan. 29, 1797	Aug. 4, 1799	Isaac	14 Murray	
195	Acker, Stephen	9	Feb. 21, 1797	April 20, 1802	Catharine	20 Cherry	April 20, 1802
196	Gordon, Jane		Feb. 6, 1797	April 20, 1797			
197	Lane, Elijah	9	April 20, 1797	March 2, 1798	Daniel	113 Reade	
198	Mattass, Robert	9	do	July, 1797	John	George	
199	Burtsell, Edward D.		April 21, 1797	Aug., 1798	John Annesley	57 Dock	
200	Fraunces, George W.	9	April 24, 1797	Oct. 20, 1801	Andrew G.	73 Liberty	
201	Reburgh, Mar'l	7	do	May 1, 1798		Heckman	
202	Demorest, Maria		May 22, 1797	, 1792	Daniel	73 Reade	
203	Devoe, William		June 14, 1797	April 5, 1802	Joseph	74 Garden	April 5, 1802
204	Dunn, William	9	June 26, 1797	June 4, 1799	Rachel	Broadway	
205	Demarest, Elizabeth	8	July 5, 1797	, 1799	David	Church	
206	Remmy, John	12	July 10, 1797	March 12, 1798	William	198 Broadway	
207	Van Alst, John	10	do	Jan. 3, 1800	John	175 William	Jan. 3, 1800
208	Skaats, John	9	do	April 20, 1802	Elizabeth	Greenwich	April 20, 1802
209	Ackerman, John	10	July 30, 1797	April 3, 1801	Abraham	47 Robertson	April 3, 1801
210	Phillips, James	8	Oct. 4, 1797	Jan. 1798	John		
211	Martling, Robert	9	do	Aug. 17, 1798	Widow	60 Broad	
212	Devoe, Abbey		do	June, 1801	Joseph	24 Garden	June, 1801
213	Wilks, George	11	Jan. 8, 1798	April 10, 1800	George	52 Warren	April 10, 1800
214	Demarest, Sarah		Jan. 9, 1798	do	David	Church	do
215	Helmes, Charles	8	do	Feb. 10, 1803	Charles	87 Warren	Feb. 10, 1803
216	Rogert, John	8	Jan. 16, 1798	March, 1798	Peggy	Rose	
217	Delamater, Jane	10	Jan. 31, 1798	April 26, 1802	Sarah	Chambers	
218	Skaats, William	9	Feb. 12, 1798	Dec. 28, 1801	Jacob	Vesey	Dec. 28, 1801

CATALOGUE OF SCHOLARS—Continued.

No.	Pupil.	Age	Admitted.	Withdrawn.	Parent.	Residence.	Graduated.
219	Retan, John	9	Feb. 13, 1798	Feb. 11, 1803	Henry	18 Augustus	Feb. 11, 1803
220	Vandewater, William	11	do.	Aug. 1, 1798	C. Crolius		
221	Couenhoven, William	9	Feb. 16, 1798	Nov. 20, 1801	James	Magazine	
222	Fothergill, George	11	March 9, 1798	Dec. 2, 1798	Hannah Crips	29 George	
223	Mowcson, Mary	11	March 21, 1798	June, 1798	Nathaniel	40 Harley	
224	Nicholas, John	9	March 22, 1798	April, 1801	Henry	11 Robinson	
225	Askins, Sarah	11	March 25, 1798	July 1, 1800	John	Sloat	July 1, 1800
226	Jacobus, Rachel	14	March 7, 1798	March 20, 1799	Rulef	Warren	
227	Washington, George Francis			Aug. 27, 1800			
228	Ackerman, John	12	May 28, 1798	June 4, 1799	Sarah	35 Reade	
229	Miller, George	10	May 30, 1798	April 5, 1799	Mrs. Wills	26 Frankfort	
230	Van Den Bergh, Samuel	8	July 13, 1798	Feb. 11, 1803	John	Barley	Feb. 11, 1803
231	Snider, Rachel	9	July 14, 1798	July 15, 1799	Widow	10 Cross	
232	Demarest, Stephen	7	do.	March 4, 1802	John	47 L. Chapel	
233	Van Horne, Ann		Aug. 3, 1798				
234	Lewis, Elias	12	Aug. 8, 1798	Jan. 1, 1801	Rachel	14 Barclay	
235	Pettinger, Phillip	13	Aug. 26, 1798	Oct. 20, 1800	Richard	19 Rose	Oct. 20, 1800
236	Canterman, John	8	Nov. 22, 1798	Feb. 1, 1803	Widow	Pump	Feb. 11, 1803
237	Phillips, Esther	11	Nov. 23, 1798	May 1, 1800	John	Greenwich	
238	Colegrove, Catherine	8	March 16, 1799	May, 1800	Francis	Union Furnace	
239	Colbart, Sarah	7	March 21, 1799	April 3, 1801	Juliana	Reade	
240	Garrison, Jane		April 11, 1799	May 8, 1800			
241	Vanderbeek, Catherine	13	July 1, 1799	Aug. 1801	David	Bear Market	
242	Heyer, Hannah	12	do.	May 1, 1801	William	5 Magazine	
243	Shepherd, Thomas	8	do.	April 1, 1805	John	12 Lower Chapel	
244	Smith, Henry M	9	July 8, 1799	Jan. 7, 1800	William	13 Chambers	
245	Sneiden, Robert	8	Nov. 7, 1799	Feb. 11, 1803	Jacoba	9 Rector	Feb. 11, 1803
246	Shelden, George	12	Nov. 11, 1799	July 6, 1800	George	Nassau	
247	Graven, James	12	do.	June 10, 1801	Widow	62 Warren	June 10, 1801
248	Skaats, Kinier	8	Nov. 14, 1799	April 3, 1805	Thomas	Reade	April 3, 1805
249	Knifflin, Hannah	13	Nov. 22, 1799	April 3, 1801	Amos	Reade	April 3, 1801
250	Waldron, Sarah	10	Dec. 2, 1799	May 1, 1801	Widow of Charles	Second	
251	Demorest, Eleanor	7	Jan. 20, 1800	Feb. 4, 1804	David	36 Thomas	Feb. 4, 1804
252	Young, Isaac (Vide Notes)	9	Jan. 22, 1840	July 19, 1804	Catharine	57 Chapel	July 19, 1804
253	Vandewater, John	9	do.	March 20, 1801	Mary	215 Greenwich	
254	Conckling, Esther	10	Jan. 23, 1800	Aug. 10, 1800	Mary	25 Reade	
255	Stymets, Francis	7	Jan. 26, 1800	May 1, 1800	Ann	24 Pine	

CATALOGUE OF SCHOLARS—Continued.

No.	Pupil.	Age	Admitted.	Withdrawn.	Parent.	Residence.	Graduated.
256	Ackerman, Hannah	6	Feb. 6, 1800	June, 1800	Elizabeth	32 Harley	
			Feb. 8, 1803	July 10, 1804	do.	Catharine	
257	Sherman, William	10	Feb. 7, 1800	Dec. 26, 1800	Widow	82 Liberty	
258	Montanye, Isaac	8	Feb. 10, 1800		Mary	Thomas	
259	Sigrison, James	7	Feb. 14, 1800	Sept. 10, 1802	John	40 Gold	
260	Sneden, Elsie	10	March 1, 1800	May 14, 1802	Jacoba	9 Rector	
261	Westervelt, Samuel	8	March 12, 1800	April 16, 1807	Cornelius	Thomas	April 16, 1807
262	Lent, Jane	12	March 24, 1800	April 4, 1801	John Degrove	Catharine	
263	Demarest, Peter	11	April 15, 1800	May, 1803	David	15 Thomas	Mar. 1803
264	Verralen, James	8	April 21, 1800	July 30, 1803	Cornelius	Greenwich	
265	Bogart, John	9	April 24, 1800	Oct. 1801	Margaret	37 Rose	
266	McGwyer, Fanny	9	May 12, 1800	Feb. 11, 1803	Elizabeth	49 Little Chapel	Feb. 11, 1803
267	Barr, Catherine	11	June 9, 1800	May 19, 1802	Henry	6 Little Chapel	
268	Brooks, Isaac	7	do.	Feb. 1, 1805	Samuel Delamater	18 Dey	Feb. 1, 1805
269	Alyea, James	9	July 9, 1800	Deceased	Isaac Guerney	Pump	
270	Durborow, Wm. H	8	July 10, 1800	March 29, 1804	Joseph	Fisher	Mar. 29, 1804
271	Post, Alexander	8	do.	Feb. 4, 1804	Widow	Cedar	
272	Couenhoven, Jacob	13	July 11, 1800	March 29, 1804	Benjamin	18 Division	
273	Retan, Mary	12	July 15, 1800	April 26, 1802	Henry	87 Keale	
274	Salter (or Selser), Elizabeth	9	July 28, 1800	March 1803	Widow	Theatre Alley	
275	Johnston, Samuel	10	Sept. 29, 1800	March 29, 1804	John N.	Magazine	Mar. 29, 1804
276	Waldron, Benjamin	5	Oct. 6, 1800	May 23, 1805	Widow	Second	
277	Canterman, Ann	10	Oct. 28, 1800	May, 1801	Widow	70 Liberty	
278	Bertholf, William	3	Nov. 3, 1800	Feb. 4, 1804	Guilliam	Duane	
279	Westervelt, H. (Vide Notes)	10	Nov. 11, 1800	Feb. 11, 1803	Peter	208 L. Chapel	Feb. 11, 1803
280	Ackerman, John	9	Nov. 27, 1800	Aug. 6, 1802	John	L. Chapel	
281	Morris, Eleanor	12	Feb. 2, 1801	April 1, 1801	Elizabeth Anderson	20 L. Chapel	
282	Young, Margaret L		March 5, 1801	May, 1801	Edward	Jacob	
283	Demorest, Maria	12	March 15, 1801	April 16, 1802	Daniel	39 Chambers	
284	Seaman, Phebe	9	March 25, 1801	Aug. 1, 1804	Peter	71 Reade	Aug. 1, 1804
285	Valentine, Cornelius	11	April 11, 1801	June 3, 1803	Evert	Barley	
286	Pettinger, Richard	9	April 13, 1801	Nov. 1803	Richard	19 Rose	
287	Mead, Peter	9	April 23, 1801	Feb. 1, 1805	Jacob	Near Vauxhall	Feb. 1, 1805
288	Jones, Catharine	8	June 14, 1801	Aug. 1, 1804	Thomas Black	15 Keale	Aug. 1, 1804
289	Kniffin, Robert	11	June 8, 1801	Dec. 26, 1805	Amos	44 Harley	
290	Bertholf, George	10	June 4, 1801	Feb. 4, 1804	Guilliam	71 Chambers	
291	Leach, George	9	June 15, 1804	June 3, 1803	Elizabeth	31 Chambers	
292	Kelly, Sarah	11	July 13, 1801	Sept. 1803	Thomas	32 Chambers	

CATALOGUE OF SCHOLARS—Continued.

No.	Pupil.	Age	Admitted.	Withdrawn.	Parent.	Residence.	Graduated.
293	McGwyer, John	8	July 15, 1801	Aug. 29, 1808	Elizabeth	Harrison	Aug. 29, 1808
294	Forshea, Elizabeth	10	July 30, 1801	Nov. 1801	Matthew	72 Chambers	
295	Van Aulen, Sarah	10	Oct. 5, 1801	March 29, 1804	Char.	76 Reade	Mar. 29, 1804
296	Heyer, William	7	Oct. 12, 1801	Jan. 27, 1807	William	Between Reade and Harley	
297	Skaats, Abraham	9	Oct. 28, 1801	March, 1805	Widow M	69 Church	
298	Craven, Jacob	12	Nov. 2, 1801	April, 1803	Mercy	83 Warren	
299	Van Evour, Isaac	9	Nov. 9, 1801	April 19, 1806	Eve	10 Roosevelt	
300	Van Wart, Samuel	10	do.	March 28, 1805	William	37 Robertson	
301	Couenhaven, James	8	Nov. 20, 1801	Sept. 30, 1807	James	Magazine	
302	Kitchel, Eliza	9	Jan. 15, 1802	May, 1806	Isaac	8 Warren	
303	Van Alst, Magdalen	12	Jan. 18, 1802	Oct. 5, 1802	Widow	175 William	
304	Van Harcum, Edward	9	Jan. 19, 1802	May, 1806	David	34 Barley	
305	Fisher, Henry	10	April 13, 1802	June 3, 1803	Widow	14 Augustus	
306	Heckman, John	10	May 11, 1802	Feb. 27, 1805	George	9 Reade	
307	Demarest, John	10	do.		David	15 Thomas	
308	Acker, Eliza	8	May 24, 1802	June 20, 1805	Catharine	6 Cherry	June 20, 1805
309	Van Tassel, William	9	do.	Aug. 6, 1802	Catharine	Hester	
310	Fash, William	9	May 25, 1802	March 17, 1808	Jeff. Leonard, guardian	78 Church	
311	Fash, Isaac	9	do.	Sept. 21, 1804	do.	do.	
312	Vanderlake, Thomas		do.	March 29, 1804	David	Lispenard	
313	Post, Henry	11	June 11, 1802	Dec. , 1802	Abraham	L. Chapel	
314	Smith, Thomas	11	July 19, 1802	March 29, 1804	Moris	Reade	
315	Losey, Sarah	10	do.	Dec. , 1803	William	70 Reade	
316	Collins, Elizabeth	11	July 20, 1802	June 20, 1805	William	83 Chambers	June 20, 1805
317	Ayres, Sarah (Vide Notes)	11	Aug. 3, 1802	April 3, 1805	Thomas	Ferry	April 3, 1805
318	Chardavoyne, T. C. Vide Note	8	Aug. 26, 1802	1807	Isaac	John	—, 1807
319	Skaats, Mary	10	Sept. 30, 1802	April 16, 1807	Elizabeth	Church	April 16, 1807
320	Van Alst, Catherine	11	Oct. 5, 1802	May 23, 1805	Widow	William	
321	Van Harcomb, Hannah	10	Nov. 23, 1802	May 12, 1806	Sarah Taylor	Reade	
322	Russel, William	10	Feb. 8, 1803	March 29, 1804	Catharine	87 Greenwich	
323	Helmes, Elizabeth	10	do.	June, 1805	Charles	312 Broadway	June, 1805
324	Ackerman, Helen	11	do.	Sept., 1803	Abraham	32 Greenwich	
325	Blank, Ephraim	12	do.	March 29, 1804	Abigail	17 Batavia Lane	
326	Whitlock, James	12	do.	May 23, 1805	Samuel	50 Maiden Lane	
327	Quackenbush, Lawrence	10	do.	May, 1806	John	Marketfield	
328	Slote, James	10	April 25, 1803	June 20, 1805	Auty Lamb	29 Reade	June 20, 1805
329	Ridabach, Hester	12	do.	do.	Hester	18 Reade	
330	Rutan, Letty	12	do.	Nov. 8, 1804	Widow	46 Barley	

CATALOGUE OF SCHOLARS—Continued.

No.	Pupil	Age	Admitted.	Withdrawn.	Parent.	Residence.	Graduated.
331	Barr, Frederick	9	April 25, 1803	Sept. 5, 1806	Henry	47 Little Robinson	May, 1806
332	Westervelt, James	10	May 23, 1803	May, 1806	Peter	74 Little Chapel	
333	Ryckman, Richard	10	June 3, 1803	June 12, 1806	John		
334	King, Rachel	6	do.	May 25, 1812	Eve	Lispenard	May 25, 1812
335	Blauvelt, John	10	June 14, 1803	May, 1806	John	18 Thomas	May, 1806
336	Hilliger, Christianna	10	July 1, 1803	do.	John	Greenwich	do.
337	Van Alst, Aletta	10	Aug. 12, 1803	July 15, 1804	Widow	175 William	
338	Crygier, Sarah	12	Nov. 29, 1803	May 24, 1804	John	6 Chambers	
339	Nack, Mary	8	Dec. 8, 1803	Aug. 29, 1808	Matthias		Aug. 29, 1808
340	Kortright, Nicholas	9	Dec. 9, 1803	Sept. 5, 1806	Daniel Warner	51 Broad	
341	Thurston, John	9	Dec. 12, 1803	May 24, 1804	Jacob	Robertson	
342	Kelly, John	9	Jan. 9, 1804	Oct. 29, 1807	Thomas	15 Thomas	
343	Sneiden, Mary	12	Feb. 4, 1804	July, 1805	Robert	116 Chambers	
344	Burger, Rebecca	12	do.	April 16, 1807	Gerardus	Chambers	April 16, 1807
345	Adams, Joseph P.	11	do.	Aug. 7, 1806	Thomas	45 Henry	Aug. 7, 1806
346	Blauvelt, Isaac	10	do.	Nov. 8, 1804	Daniel	18 Thomas	
347	Beekman, Eliza		do.	May 25, 1805	George		
348	Bogert, Peter	10	do.	April 16, 1807	Albert	16 Thomas	
349	Sebring, Cornelius	8	Feb. 4, 1804	Feb. 27, 1809	Ann	171 Greenwich	Feb. 27, 1809
350	Van Alst, Maria	10	March 29, 1804	May, 1806	Widow	75 Rose	May, 1806
351	Ayres, Hester	10	do.	do.	Thomas	1 Dutch	do.
352	Pettinger, James	12	April 26, 1804	March 28, 1805	Richard	Cliff	
353	Smith, John R	11	do.	May 27, 1805	Widow	72 Chambers	
354	Demarest, Jacob	11	do.	Feb. 27, 1805	Widow Smith	Greenwich	
355	Quackenbush, Samuel	12	do.	May, 1806	Abraham	Chapel	May, 1806
356	Duthurrow, Walter	10	do.	July 9, 1807		5 Fisher	
357	Collins, Samuel	11	do.	May, 1806	Widow	82 Chambers	
358	Shaver, Susan	8	July 19, 1804	April 30, 1810	John	Murray	
359	Jones, Isaac	8	July 21, 1804	Feb. 27, 1809	Mary Jones	13 Roosevelt	Feb. 27, 1809
360	Collard, James	9	do.	do.	Jeremiah	16 Reade	do.
361	Ackerman, Albert	9	Aug. 16, 1804	Feb. 27, 1805	Abraham	Near Lispenard's	
362	Kiersted, H. T. (Vide Notes)	12	do.	Jan. 7, 1808	James	Barley	Jan. 7, 1808
363	Ward, Uzal		do.	May, 1806	Widow Magee	Barley	
364	Van Harcum, Elizabeth		Nov. 8, 1804				
365	Kint, Nathaniel	12	do.	May, 1806	James	Bayard	
366	Burger, Daniel	9	do.	July 31, 1809	Widow	42 Chambers	July 31, 1809
367	Hulett, Phebe	12	do.	May, 1805	Daniel	Mary	
368	Van Alst, Eliza	10	do.	Oct. 29, 1807	Widow	175 William	

CATALOGUE OF SCHOLARS—Continued.

No.	Pupil.	Age	Admitted.	Withdrawn.	Parent.	Residence.	Graduated.
369	Beekman, Ann	12	Jan. 31, 1805	Nov., 1806	Richard	Bunker Hill	
370	Mead, John	9	Feb. 11, 1805	Feb. 18, 1808	Jacob		
371	Rikeman, Ann	11	do.	Oct. 29, 1807	Mrs. John Rikeman		
372	Kitchell, Andrew	10	March 4, 1805	June, 1808	Isaac	8 Warren	
373	Van Tassel, David	8	do.	May 14, 1807	Widow	Barclay	
374	Peterson, Sarah	8	March 12, 1805	July 18, 1805	Jane	Bowery	
375	Harper, Robert	11	March 20, 1805	do.	Lucretia	50 Gold	
376	Shepherd, Thomas	13	April 15, 1805	Aug. 29, 1808	John	27 Church	
377	Tom, Abraham	9	April 23, 1805	Jan., 1807	Peter	Robertson	
378	Lewis, Leonard	9	do.		Levi		
379	Rikeman, Albert	—	April 25, 1805	Oct. 30, 1809	Mary	69 Church	
380	Skaats, Isaac	9	April 29, 1805	Sept., 1805	David Ridgeway	1 Hague	
381	Annely, Eliza	10	May 27, 1805	March 17, 1808	Eliza	65 Church	
382	Skaats, Elsie	11	do.		Jacob	9 Lumber	
383	Snedeker, Jane	11	do.	June, 1808	Hester	44 Little Chapel	
384	Ridaback, Lenah	10	do.	March 17, 1808	Peter	57 Cedar	
385	Bogart, Eliza	6	do.	March 28, 1809	Charles	15 Barclay	
386	Helmes, John	8	do.		Theodosia		
387	Banta, Hannah	11	May 28, 1805	July 30, 1810	do.		
388	Snedeker, Rinier	8	June 20, 1805		Widow	Cor. Rector and Lumber	
389	Dolly, Mary	10	do.		Phillip	Division	
390	Gaston, Susan	11	do.		Mary	Leonard, near the Sugar House	
391	Gaskin, Susannah	8	July 1, 1805	Feb. 27, 1809	William	Leonard	Feb. 27, 1809
392	Witzel, John C.	11	July 18, 1805	March 17, 1808	Eliza Witzel and William Castle	Rector and Lumber	Mar. 17, 1808
393	Ridabock, Ann	9	do.	June 27, 1812	Hester	44 Little Chapel	June 27, 1812
394	Ridabock, Nancy	12	do.	do.	do.	do.	
395	Westervelt, James	11	do.	June 27, 1812	Cornelius	25 Thames	June 27, 1812
396	Stadwell, John	12	do.	July 9, 1807	Bart. Deklyn	Greenwich	
397	Burger, Gerardus C.	7	do.	Sept. 28, 1812	Elinor	76 Chapel	Sept. 28, 1812
398	Van Tassel, Isaac	8	do.		Isaac	Budd, 2d door from Hudson	
399	Gordon, Alexander	8	Dec. 1, 1805	Aug. 28, 1809	Henry Rich	William	
400	Gordon, Henry	7	do.	May, 1806	do.	do.	
401	Haynes, Annett	11	Dec. 2, 1805	April 14, 1808	Widow	do.	
402	Stanton, William	8	Feb. 11, 1806	Aug. 29, 1809	John	Leonard	

CATALOGUE OF SCHOLARS—Continued.

No.	Pupil	Age	Admitted	Withdrawn	Parent	Residence	Graduated
404	Sebring, Edw'd (Vide Notes)	6½	Feb. 20, 1806	Nov. 28, 1813	Widow	Greenwich	Nov. 28, 1813
405	Quackenbush, John	12	April 4, 1806	Oct. 29, 1807	Abraham	132 Bedlow	....
406	Quackenbush, James	9	do.	May 12, 1808	do.	do.	....
407	Skaats, George	7	April 10, 1806	....	Elinor	8 Reade	....
408	Collins, Jane	7	do.	March 29, 1813	Jane	37 Little Chapel	Mar. 29, 1813
409	Wilkes, Sarah	12	do.	April 24, 1809	William Losey	Walker	April 16, 1807
410	Rikeman, Eliza	14	May 1, 1806	April 16, 1807	Mary	20 Augustus	Jan. 28, 1811
411	Van Alst, Edward	9	May 15, 1806	Jan. 28, 1811	Matthias	Washington	
412	Nack, Eleanor	9	do.		Widow	86 Chambers	
413	King, Hannah	10	do.	May 29, 1809	Benjamin	167 Washington	Mar. 11, 1811
414	Beaumont, Mary Ann	9	May 29, 1806	March 11, 1811	Widow	173 William	
415	Van Alst, Isaac	7	do.	June 26, 1809	Mary	54 Pump	June 27, 1808
416	Van Alst, James	11	do.	June 27, 1808	Hannah	75 Chapel	
417	Hinds, Joseph	8	do.	Oct. 30, 1809	Isaac	Church	Mar. 17, 1808
418	Van Tassel, Abraham	10	do.	March 17, 1808	Widow	68 Warren	Feb. 27, 1809
419	McGuire, Philip	9	do.	Feb. 26, 1810	Isaac	Warren	
420	Kitchell, Isaac	9	do.	Feb. 27, 1809	Abraham	Leonard	
421	Banker, Rachel	4	do.	July 9, 1807	Jeff Leonard, G'n.	13 Harley	
422	Fash, John	8	June 12, 1806	April 14, 1808	Francis A.	42 Harman	
423	Marschalk, Francis A.	6	do.		A.	42 William	
424	Gordon, Matilda	6	Aug. 7, 1806	March 26, 1810	Samuel	87 Gold	Feb. 27, 1809
425	Whitlock, Samuel	8	Sept. 4, 1806	May 29, 1809	Hannah	83 Chamber	
426	Harr, Henry	8	Oct. 7, 1806	Nov. 27, 1809	V. Valentine	12 Barley	
427	Valentine, Jacob	10	do.	Jan. 30, 1809	Ian'h	189 Greenwich	
428	Hilliker, William	11	do.	Feb. 27, 1809	Widow	76 Reade	
429	Edwards, Gitty	11	Oct. 21, 1806	June 19, 1810	Thomas Chapman	95 Beekman	June 25, 1810
430	Braird, Eliza		Oct. 30, 1806	June 25, 1810	William	36 Leonard	April 29, 1811
431	Gaskin, John		do.	April 26, 1811	Abraham Bancker	Leonard	
432	Kortright, Daniel	7	Nov. 4, 1806	April 26, 1809	John	22 Heury	Feb. 25, 1811
433	Bennet, Andrew H.	10	March 19, 1807	Feb. 25, 1811	Richard	175 William	June 26, 1809
434	Ten Eyck, Peter S.	9	do.	June 26, 1809	Margaret Warner	Moore	
435	Kortright, Ellen	10	do.	July 30, 1810	Mary	13 Roosevelt	
436	Jones, Ann	9	April 16, 1807	Sept. 1807	Walter	Chapel	
437	King, Jane	13	do.	March 9, 1812	Mary	102 Church	Mar. 9, 1812
438	Van Hoaten, Mary	9	do.	June 29, 1812	John	94 Chambers	June 29, 1812
440	Montanye, William	10	do.	April 24, 1809	Mary	Elizabeth	April 24, 1809
441	Van Alst, Leah	10	May 14, 1807	June 14, 1811	Garrit	16 Warren	
	Benson, John	9	do.				

CATALOGUE OF SCHOLARS—Continued.

No.	Pupil.	Age	Admitted.	Withdrawn.	Parent.	Residence.	Graduated.
442	Cozine, Mary	10	May 14, 1807	July 29, 1809	Garrit	Washington	July 29, 1809
443	Cozine, Garrit	10	July 9, 1807	Feb. 27, 1809	Garrit do.	do.	Feb. 27, 1809
444	Roomer, Barnet	10	do.	May 12, 1808	Jacob	53 Anthony	
445	Bogert, Margaret	8	do.	do.	Andrew	North Moore	
446	Van Houten, James	6	do.	June 28, 1813	Mary	102 Church	June 28, 1813
447	King, Abraham	8	Aug. 5, 1807	April 30, 1810	Aaron	63 Church	
448	Bancker, Sophia	8	Sept. 30, 1807	March 9, 1812	Abraham	Leonard	Mar. 9, 1812
449	Van Houten, John	10	do.	Aug. 11, 1810	Peter	103 Church	Aug. 11, 1810
450	Weldon, Eliza Ann	6	do.	Jan. 25, 1809	Widow	Water	
451	Witzel, Sophia	8	do.	April 26, 1812	do.	Lombard	April 26, 1812
452	Rikabock, Jacob II	7	do.	Oct. 10, 1814	Hester	Keade	Oct. 10, 1814
453	Acker, Jacob (Vide Notes)	12	Oct. 29, 1807	Aug. 29, 1808	Jacob	Mercer	
454	Losey, William	12	do.	May 29, 1809	William	Cannon	
455	Freeland, Peggy	8	do.	June 29, 1812	Simeon	Leonard	Jan. 29, 1812
456	Van Aulen, Peter	8	do.	Feb. 6, 1812	Staats	do.	
457	Blauvelt, Catharine	10	Jan. 20, 1808	Aug. 26, 1811	Martha	18 Thomas	
458	Resseque, Abraham	9	Feb. 18, 1808	Feb. 27, 1809	Abraham	26 Thomas	
459	Myers, Cornelius	10	March 17, 1808	Feb. 24, 1812	Thomas	12 Harley	
460	Van Orden, John	10	do.	April 30, 1811	Widow	5 Thomas	April 30, 1811
461	Whitlock, Daniel	9	do.	May 25, 1812	Thomas B.	Lispenard	May 25, 1812
462	Hendrickson, John	9	do.	April 30, 1810	Jacob	57 Reade	
463	Kikeman, Rachel	10	May 12, 1808	June 27, 1808	Mary	13 Barclay	
464	Kelly, James	11	do.	Sept. 10, 1810	Ann Hughes	77 Hedlow	
465	Couenhoven, Sarah	10	do.	June 24, 1811	Eliz.	40 Mulberry	
466	Smith, Lidia	.6	do.	Oct. 10, 1815	John L.	9 Little Chapel	Oct. 10, 1815
467	Witzel, Mary	8	do.	March 30, 1812	Widow	18 Rector	
468	Whitlock, James	10	do.	Feb. 27, 1809	Thomas B.	Rose	
469	Holloway, John	10	June 9, 1808	Sept. 26, 1808	John	Grand	
470	Bicker, Victor	11	June 27, 1808	Jan. 29, 1810	Catharine	31 Elm	
471	Collins, Jemimah	11	do.	March 25, 1811	Mrs.	37 Little Chapel	Mar. 25, 1811
472	Doremus, John	9	do.	March 28, 1809	Mary	59 Church	
473	King, Andrew	10	do.	June 24, 1811	Jacob	Greenwich	
474	Mills, Luther	12	do.	Feb. 6, 1812	Jacob	Harley	
475	Illnois, Thomas	9	July 25, 1808	Oct. 29, 1810	David	76 Chapel	Oct. 29, 1810
476	Cortelyou, Elizabeth	9	Aug. 29, 1808	July 30, 1810	Elizabeth	13 Roosevelt	
477	McGwier, Sally	9	do.	Oct. 31, 1808	Elizabeth Chambers	Rynders	
478	Bogert, Peter	9	do.	Jan. 29, 1810	James	Desbrosses	
479	Kills, Polly	12	do.		Mary Gearicourt	Orange	

CATALOGUE OF SCHOLARS—Continued.

No.	Pupil.	Age	Admitted.	Withdrawn.	Parent.	Residence.	Graduated.
480	Flock, Maria or Mary	9	Aug. 29, 1808	Oct. 29, 1810	John	Murray and Little Chapel	Mar. 26, 1810
481	Van Beuren, Jane	12	Sept. 26, 1808	March 26, 1810	Samuel	76 Hudson	....
482	Blanchard, James	12	Dec. 27, 1808	do.	Francis	Near Col. Varick	....
483	Blanchard, Nicholas	10	do.	Sept. 30, 1811	do.	do.	Mar. 9, 1812
484	Van Norden, Alice	8	do.	March 9, 1812	do.	7 Thomas	June 8, 1812
485	Hilliker, Fanny	7	do.	June 28, 1811	Widow	389 Greenwich	....
486	Wilkes, Mary	13	do.	Feb. 25, 1811	Widow	Canal	Mar. 29, 1813
487	Collard, Maria	9	do.	March 29, 1813	Jane Losey	18 Reade	Mar. 30, 1812
488	Warner, Elizabeth	8	do.	March 30, 1812	Widow	Broad	July 25, 1814
489	Everitt, Benjamin	7	do.	July 25, 1814	John	25 Thames	....
490	Bennett, Sally F.	7	do.	July 30, 1810	Catharine	57 Pump	....
491	Nack, Catherine	11	do.	April 29, 1811	John	Washington, near Jay	April 29, 1811
492	Fenton, Thomas	6	do.	June 28, 1811	Matthias	44 Reade	....
493	Emery, Elizabeth	10	do.	Jan. 28, 1811	Peter	5 Water	....
494	Conklin, David	11	Jan. 4, 1809	April 29, 1811	David	Canal	April 29, 1811
495	Layman, Alexander	8	do.	Nov. 27, 1809	Mary Matts	do.	....
496	Volk, Garret	9	do.	Feb. 6, 1812	John	Second	....
497	Day, John I.	6	do.	Aug. 26, 1811	Thomas	101 Reade	....
498	Gibson, Nancy	9	do.	Oct. 29, 1810	Abraham	5 Canal	....
499	De Graw, Catharine	9	do.	May 28, 1810	Rachel Ramp	53 Reade	....
500	'' Sally	..	do.	April 27, 1812	do.	do.	April 29, 1811
501	Herring, Frederick	10	do.	April 29, 1811	Catharine	282 Greenwich	....
502	Sexton, Henry	11	do.	Oct. 30, 1809	Martha	Beach and Chapel	June 29, 1812
503	Zabriskie, John	9	do.	June 29, 1812	Albert	Canal	....
504	Heyer, Catharine	8	do.	Aug. 26, 1811	Patrick Niblow	43 Augustus	Mar. 28, 1814
505	Freeland, Reuben	7	do.	March 28, 1814	Simeon	38 Leonard	....
506	Demarest, Isaac	10	do.	July 29, 1811	James Hall	4 Chapel	June 29, 1812
507	Cortelyou, Peter C.	8	Jan. 17, 1809	June 29, 1812	Elizabeth	13 Roosevelt	....
508	Wade, Phebe	9	do.	Jan. 27, 1812	Laush Smart	7 Oliver	....
509	'' Andrew	8	do.	Sept. 28, 1811	do.	do.	April 29, 1811
510	Van Norden, John M	12	do.	April 29, 1811	Matthew	69 Church	....
511	Case, Maria	11	do.	June 26, 1809	John	Broome	....
512	Fenton, Susan	11	Jan. 30, 1809	March 26, 1810	Peter	44 Reade	....
513	Hauvelt, Maria	7	Feb. 27, 1809	Sept. 28, 1812	Martha	18 Thomas	July 27, 1812
514	Gordon, Henry	10	do.	Aug. 28, 1809	Mr. Latham, guardian	Mrs. Warner, Broad St	....
515	Demarest, Henry	7	March 7, 1809	July 27, 1812	Albert	Canal, near Broadway	....
516	'' James	10	do.	March 30, 1812	do.	do.	....
517	Kniffen, Jane	8	do.	May 31, 1813	Jane	11 Fayette	May 31, 1813

125

CATALOGUE OF SCHOLARS—Continued.

No.	Pupil.	Age	Admitted.	Withdrawn.	Parent.	Residence.	Graduated.
518	Acker, Mary	10	March 7, 1809	June 25, 1800	Jacob	Crosby	Mar. 28, 1814
519	Parker, Margaret	7	do.	March 28, 1814	Jacob	10 Broadway	
520	Cawood, Phebe	9	do.	July 30, 1810	Gersham	Canal	
521	Smith, Hannah	...	do.	March 9, 1812	John I.	9 Little Chapel	Mar. 9, 1812
522	Place, John	10	March 27, 1809	April 30, 1810	Judith	Mr. Stoutenburgh's	
523	Van Tassel, David	9	April 24, 1809	April 29, 1811	Robert Kirk	Hudson	
524	Forbus, Isaac B.	11	do.	Nov. 27, 1809	J. L. Van Kleeck	155 Washington	April 29, 1811
525	Van Norden, William	9	May 29, 1809	April 29, 1811	Abraham	Sullivan	Mar. 26, 1810
526	Rosencrantz, Sally	15	do.	March 26, 1810	Phœbe	Near Colonel Burr's	Mar. 28, 1814
527	Locke, Frederick	8	do.	March 28, 1814	Henry	P. L. Vandervoort's	
528	Place, Jane	7	do.	July 30, 1810	Judith	Mr. Stoutenburgh's	
529	Westervelt, Anne	11	June 26, 1809	May 27, 1811	Cornelius	25 Thames	May 27, 1811
530	Rogert, Margaret	10	do.	April 29, 1811	Andrew	121 Reade	
531	Van Allen, James	10	do.	Jan. 28, 1811	John	159 Broadway	Jan. 28, 1811
532	Wyckoff, Samuel	12	do.	Oct. 21, 1811	Cornelius	Broome and Suffolk	Mar. 30, 1812
533	Dorcmus, Margaret	8	do.	March 30, 1812	Mary	Provoost	July 25, 1814
534	Cozine, George	8	July 29, 1809	July 25, 1814	Garrit	167 Washington	
535	Van Alst, Letitia	3	do.	May 27, 1811	Margaret	Elizabeth	
536	Helms, Maria	6	do.	Oct. 21, 1811	Hester	47 Greenwich	
537	Anderson, John	10	Aug. 28, 1809	Jan. 28, 1811	Barnet	6th St. bet Hester & Grand	
538	Anderson, Phebe	9	do.	do.	do.	do. do.	
539	Gardner, John	13	Oct. 30, 1809	May 27, 1811	Sarah	Desbrosses	Jan. 29, 1816
540	Lawrence, Abraham	8	do.	Jan. 29, 1816	Abraham	32 Beaver	
541	Sturms, Ezekiel	7	Nov. 9, 1809	Jan. 28, 1811	Isaac	2 Leonard	
542	Vanderlocke, David	10	do.	Feb. 28, 1814	James	Spring	Feb. 28, 1814
543	Kint, Jeremiah	9	do.	April 26, 1813	Catharine	Orange near Broome	April 26, 1813
544	Van Tassel, Jacob	8	Nov. 27, 1809	March 28, 1814	David Matts	15 Pine	
545	Wyckoff, Cornelius	9	do.	Sept. 28, 1812	Cornelius	Broome and Suffolk	
546	Coitus, Sarah Ann	7	Jan. 29, 1810	April 25, 1814	Jane	Duane	April 25, 1814
547	Glover, Eliza	8	do.	May 30, 1814	Thomas	114 Broad	May 30, 1814
548	Devew, James	11	Feb. 26, 1810	April 27, 1812	Nicholas	Near Tyler's	Jan. 28, 1811
549	Rosencrantz, Mary	14	March 26, 1810	Jan. 28, 1811	Phebe	Near Col. Burr's	
550	Duryca, Richard	12	do.	Aug. 26, 1811	Samuel	Spring, near Tyler's	
551	Corbett, William	7	do.	Oct. 30, 1810	Catharine	292 Bowery	Feb. 28, 1815
552	Gurnee, Samuel	8	do.	Feb. 28, 1815	do.	At Simeon Freeland's	
553	Collard, John	10	do.	Feb. 6, 1812	Abraham	Chapel, near Sugar-Loaf	Mar. 9, 1812
554	Blauvelt, Christiana	...	April 30, 1810	March 9, 1812	Mary	20 Leonard	Mar. 28, 1814
555	Greenham, Joseph	9	do.	March 28, 1814	Anne Devoe	46 Thomas	

CATALOGUE OF SCHOLARS—Continued.

No.	Pupil.	Age	Admitted.	Withdrawn.	Parent.	Residence.	Graduated.
556	Barr, Garret	9	April 30, 1810	April 26, 1813	Hannah	80 Chambers	May 27, 1816
557	Van Beuren, James	9	May 28, 1810	May 27, 1816	Camina	Budd and Varick	May 31, 1813
558	Gaskin, William	10	June 25, 1810	May 31, 1813	William	34 Leonard	April 25, 1815
559	Van Allen, William	8	Sept. 10, 1810	April 25, 1815	Mary	75 Maiden Lane	Oct. 21, 1814
560	Myers, Cornelius C.	6	do.	Oct. 31, 1814	Cornelius C.	175 Duane	April 24, 1820
561	Myers, Andrew H.	6	do.	April 24, 1820		do.	
562	Durand, Nancy	7	do.	June 29, 1817	Elizabeth	At John Suydam's	
563	Teunure, Ab'm (Vide Notes)	9	do.	July 25, 1814	Lawrence	139 Reade	July 25, 1814
564	Emmett, Sarah	7	do.	Jan. 30, 1815	Abraham	166 Pearl	Jan. 30, 1815
565	Montanye, Ab'm (Vide Notes)	10	do.	March 28, 1814	John	67 Warren	Mar. 28, 1814
566	Lawrence, Jane	6	do.	March 27, 1815	Catharine	32 Beaver	Mar. 27, 1815
567	Consenhoven, John L.	10	do.	April 25, 1814	Elizabeth	100 Magazine	April 25, 1814
568	Onderdonk, Asa	11	Sept. 24, 1810	Sept. 30, 1811	Rebecca	25 Budd	
569	Badgley, Isaac	11	Oct. 29, 1810	April 25, 1814	Eve Wardale	Reade and Greenwich	April 25, 1814
570	Rosencrantz, Susan	9	do.	June 28, 1813	Phebe	Near Col. Burr's	June 28, 1813
571	Higgins, Charles	10	do.	Jan. 25, 1813	Rachel	Robinson and Greenwich	
572	Fawcel, Lanah	10	do.	March 27, 1815	Mary	11 Fair	Mar. 27, 1815
573	Butler, John	10	Jan. 28, 1811	May 27, 1811	Mrs. Van Houten	58 Vesey	
574	Embree, John	7	do.	March 31, 1817	Hannah	At John Suydam's	Mar. 31, 1817
575	Rosencrantz, Ann	13	do.	Sept. 28, 1812	Phebe	Near Mrs. Glover's	
576	Adams, John W	8	Feb. 12, 1811	March 31, 1817	Sem'r	85 Henry	Mar. 31, 1817
577	Westervelt, John	10	Feb. 25, 1811	Nov. 25, 1811	Catharine	109 Mott	
578	Heyer, Maria	12	do.	April 26, 1813	Daniel	71 Chatham	April 26, 1813
579	Devoe, Joseph	11	March 25, 1811	June 28, 1813	Joseph	Greene, N. of Grand	
580	Warner, Thos. V. W	7	do.	Feb. 26, 1816	Daniel	53 Broad	Feb. 26, 1816
581	Van Horne, Eliza	7	do.	Jan. 29, 1816	Garret	76 Chapel	Jan. 29, 1816
582	Herring, Eliza	9	do.	July 25, 1814	Catharine	282 Greenwich	July 25, 1814
583	Van Orden, Samuel	13	April 29, 1811	April 29, 1812	Matthew	69 Church	
584	Rogert, Catharine	10	do.	July 27, 1812	Andrew	121 Reade	
585	Conklin, Elleanor	12	do.	March 9, 1812	David Matts	139 Reade	Mar. 9, 1812
586	Gardner, Thomas	8	do.	Oct. 21, 1811	Sarah	Desbrosses	
587	Van Blarcom, George	11	do.	May 25, 1812	Jacob	Orange	
588	Brower, Sarah	9	do.	June 28, 1813	Jane	Lispenard	June 28, 1813
589	Rutan, Rachel	8	do.	Oct. 31, 1814	Matthias	71 Thomas	
590	Nack, Runer	12	do.	July 27, 1812	Thomas	Harrison	
591	Volk, Catharine	10	May 27, 1811	May 25, 1812	Staats	Second	July 27, 1812
592	Van Aulen, Thomas	10	do.	Sept. 23, 1813	John C.	Beach	
593	Smith, Eliza	7	June 24, 1811	May 25, 1812		9 Chapel	

CATALOGUE OF SCHOLARS—Continued.

No.	Pupil.	Age	Admitted.	Withdrawn.	Parent.	Residence.	Graduated.
594	Ackerson, Charles	10	June 24, 1811	Oct. 21, 1814	Jacob	Near 25 Budd	
595	Hogger, Andrew	11	July 29, 1811	March 1, 1813	Garret	Watts	
596	Wyckoff, Eliza	8	do.	May 29, 1813	Cornelius	Broome	May 29, 1815
597	Locke, Thos. H. (of Vide Notes)	7	Aug. 26, 1811	April 27, 1818	Henry	P. L. Vandervoort's	April 27, 1818
598	Day, Catharine	7	do.	April 25, 1814	Abraham	167 Duane	
599	Van Benthuysen, Catharine	10	Sept. 30, 1811	Oct. 10, 1815	William	36 Cedar	Oct. 10, 1815
600	Blanchard, George	8	do.	March 30, 1812	Francis	Cor. Grand and Greene	
601	Van Bussum, Peter	11	do.	June 28, 1813	Sophia	Mulberry	
602	Skillman, Ann	10	do.	July 27, 1812	Chr. Stegle	Third	
603	Post, Albert	8	Oct. 21, 1811	July 1, 1814	Mary	Spring	July 3, 1815
604	Bogert, Lavina	9	do.	March 27, 1815	Isaac	143 Reade	Mar. 27, 1815
605	Hatfield, William	11	do.	Oct. 10, 1814	Mary	139 Reade	Oct. 10, 1814
606	Vanderbeek, Abraham	9	do.	June 29, 1812	James	Spring	June 29, 1812
607	King, Guty	13	Oct. 28, 1811	March 28, 1813	Magdalen	Church and Walker	
608	Storms, Jacob	9	Nov. 25, 1811	May 30, 1814	Henry	Beach, near Greenwich	
609	Heyer, Catharine	10	Jan. 27, 1812	June 26, 1815	Mrs. Niblow	43 Augustus	June 26, 1815
610	Storms, Abraham	8	do.	May 25, 1812	Isaac	Reade	May 25, 1812
611	Blauvelt, Catharine	13	Feb. 6, 1812	March 27, 1815	John Johnson	Uncertain	Mar. 27, 1815
612	Collard, Jacob	10	do.	Oct. 30, 1815	Abraham	Little Chapel	
613	Burgess, Aaron		do.	May 31, 1813	Daniel	Rusid and Varick	
614	Bogert, Jane	10	Feb. 24, 1812	April 28, 1817	Wert	Crosby	April 28, 1817
615	Dubaum, Peter	8	March 30, 1812	Oct. 5, 1812	Albert	Near Burke's	
616	Van Bussum, Agnes	7	do.	April 26, 1813	Sophia	Mulberry	
617	Helms, Archibald McC.	7	do.	May 31, 1813	Esther	47 Greenwich	
618	Duff, Mary	7	do.	Oct. 31, 1814	Donald Bradley	77 Warren	
619	Doremus, Abraham	8	do.	Dec. 14, 1813	Mary Van Houten	Hester	
620	Blauvelt, Anne	9	do.	Jan. 26, 1818	J. Betham	20 Leonard	
621	Beck, Louisa	9	do.	Sept. 28, 1813	Catharine	16 Warren	
622	Carlock, Christian	9	do.	March 26, 1816	Coenradt	Vestry	
623	Hedden, Anne	8	do.	Oct. 25, 1819	William	Greenwich	Oct. 25, 1819
624	Van Tassel, Eliza Ann	7	do.	Sept. 28, 1819	Robert Kirk	110 Reade	
625	Gallow, James	8	do.	March 27, 1815	Stephen	8 Orange	
626	Forshay, Maria	10	April 27, 1812	Aug. 24, 1816	Garret	71 Chatham	
627	Heyer, Hannah	8	do.	Oct. 7, 1816	Daniel	Watts	
628	Anderson, David	7	May 25, 1812	April 24, 1815	Daniel Demarest	Lispenard	
629	King, Aaron	7	do.	Feb. 3, 1816	Effice	Clark	Mar. 27, 1815
630	Dobbs, William	9	do.		Thomas		
631	Volk, Rachel	8	do.		Thomas	Norfolk	

CATALOGUE OF SCHOLARS—Continued.

No.	Pupil.	Age	Admitted.	Withdrawn.	Parent.	Residence.	Graduated.
632	Blauvelt, Catharine	10	May 25, 1812	March 27, 1815	John Betham	20 Leonard	Mar. 27, 1815
633	Bogert, Jacob	9	do.	July 29, 1814	Stephen	Thompson	
634	Blauvelt, James	7	do.	Sept. 28, 1812	Garrit	18 Thomas	
635	Fox, Maria	12	June 22, 1812	April 26, 1813	John	111 Mulberry	April 26, 1813
636	Fox, Catharine	9	do.		John		
637	Post, John	7	do.		Rachel		
638	Vandervoort, Lucy Ann	9	June 29, 1812	June 28, 1813	Jacob	Duane, near West	Feb. 26, 1816
639	Duryee, John	9	do.	Feb. 26, 1816	Daniel	96 Chambers	Feb. 23, 1818
640	Bayard, Ann	9	do.	Jan. 30, 1815	Elizabeth	Broome	Jan. 30, 1815
641	Marinus, John	11	do.	March 29, 1813	Adrian	43 Anthony	
642	Devoe, John	10	do.	March 31, 1817	Joseph, Grandfather	30 Anthony	Mar. 31, 1817
643	McBride, Walter	8	July 1, 1812	April 26, 1819	Charlotte Carr	Greene	April 26, 1819
644	Zabriskie, Garrit	6	July 27, 1812	Jan. 12, 1819	Albert	Reade	
645	Losey, James	7	do.	Feb. 3, 1816	William	Hudson	
646	Vandervoort, Jacob	7	do.	Sept. 28, 1818	Jacob	98 Leonard	Sept. 28, 1818
647	Herring, Edward	8	do.	March 12, 1817	Hester	96 Chambers	Mar. 12, 1817
648	Day, Abraham A.	7	do.	Oct. 7, 1816	Abraham		
649	Sip, Adrian	8	Sept. 27, 1812	May 31, 1815	Cornelius	167 Duane	Jan. 30, 1815
650	Wyckoff, Hannah	10	do.	Jan. 30, 1815	Nancy	Mulberry	Mar. 27, 1815
651	Brazier, James H.	10	do.	March 27, 1815	Andrew	72 Second	Jan. 30, 1814
652	Bogert, Sally	8	Oct. 5, 1812	Jan. 30, 1815	John	Alms-house	May 30, 1814
653	Ramp, Henry	9	do.	May 30, 1814	Mary	Spring	Mar. 27, 1815
654	Pawpel, Hannah	9	do.	March 27, 1815	John	16 Thomas	
655	Rutan, David S.	14	Jan. 25, 1813	Oct. 31, 1814	Jane	11 Fair	Feb. 23, 1818
656	Delamater, Abraham	9	March 1, 1813	Feb. 23, 1818	Abraham	21 Thomas	
657	Ackerson, Edward	11	March 29, 1813	Aug. 2, 1813	Garrit	45 Lower Robinson	
658	Hudson, John	7	do.	May 26, 1817	John	Budd	May 26, 1817
659	Tucker, Thomas F.	8	do.	June 29, 1818	Hannah	Mrs. Glover's	June 29, 1818
660	Van Horne, Susan	6	do.	March 12, 1817	Garrit	28 Barclay	Mar. 12, 1817
661	Westervelt, Peter	9	do.	April 24, 1815	Garrit	45 L. Robinson	April 24, 1815
662	Fox, Hannah	8	April 26, 1813	April 28, 1817	John	164 Duane	April 28, 1817
663	Acker, William	9	do.	Aug. 12, 1813	William	111 Mulberry	
664	Warts, Peter B	9	do.	April 29, 1816	Henry	199 Church	April 29, 1816
665	Bennett, Sarah F.	11	do.	Oct. 25, 1813	John	23 Budd	
666	Miller, Joseph	9	do.	Oct. 10, 1814	Aaron	Second	
667	Koers, Polly	10	do.	March 12, 1817	Cornelius	Fourth	Mar. 12, 1817
668	Tom, Maria	11	do.	June 28, 1813	Thietta	112 Chambers	
669	Gaskin, Sally Ann	8	May 31, 1813	June 24, 1816	William	At Mr. Stoutenburgh's. 60 Leonard	June 24, 1816

CATALOGUE OF SCHOLARS—Continued.

No.	Pupil	Age	Admitted	Withdrawn	Parent	Residence	Graduated
670	Van Marcom, David	11	May 31, 1813	April 28, 1817	Peter	66 North Moore	April 28, 1817
671	King, Susan	6	do.	Jan. 5, 1818	Eve	Corner White and Church	
672	Harris, Peggy	12	do.	April 25, 1814	Margaret	76 Chapel	
673	Hilliker, Stephen	9	June 28, 1813	Sept. 22, 1817	Ellen	Warren	
674	Rosencrantz, Eliza	13	do.	May 30, 1814	Phœbe	Near Burr's Place	May 29, 1814
675	Blanchard, Maria	11	do.	April 26, 1819	Francis	Near Lispenard's Meadow	April 26, 1819
676	Buck, John	9	do.	Dec. 13, 1814	Catharine	Spring	
677	Brower, Martin	10	do.	Jan. 26, 1816	Jacob	Spring	Jan. 26, 1816
678	Martinus, Henry	10	do.	March 25, 1816	Adrian	2 Catharine Lane	Mar. 25, 1816
679	Bogert, Ann	9	do.	Sept. 28, 1813	Weart	38 Crosby	
680	Demarest, Sally	9	do.	March 31, 1817	Daniel	Watts	
681	Evans, George	7	Aug. 2, 1813	Nov. 29, 1813	George	224 William	
682	Baldwin, Justus	8	do.	April 24, 1815	Margaret Low	25 Hudd	
683	Emmet, Nathaniel	9	Sept. 28, 1813	Sept. 22, 1817	Abraham	166 Pearl	
684	Hyer, John F.	9	do.	Feb. 28, 1818	Daniel	17 Cliff	Feb. 28, 1818
685	Bayard, Peter	13	do.	April 25, 1814	Elizabeth	36 Anthony	
686	Brower, Abraham D.	12	Oct. 25, 1813	May 29, 1815	Ann	94 Reade	May 29, 1815
687	Scott, Andrew	7	do.	Feb. 22, 1817	Andrew	Thompson	
688	Scott, William	8	do.	June 30, 1817	Gitty	Spring	
689	Devoe, Henry	9	do.	March 12, 1817	Joseph	Greene	
690	Duryee, Maria	8	do.	May 26, 1817	Daniel	Broome, near Varick	May 26, 1817
691	Finney, David	7	Nov. 29, 1813	Jan. 30, 1815	Mary	89 William	
692	Litchholt, Catharine	11	do.	Oct. 10, 1814	Margaret	507 Greenwich	
693	Gardiner, Margaret	10	Dec. 14, 1813	April 25, 1814	Margaret Tennure	45 Robinson	
694	Westervelt, Peter	10	do.	Aug. 26, 1816	Nancy	Desbrosses	Aug. 26, 1816
695	Van Derbeeck, Stephen	11	Feb. 28, 1814	March 30, 1818	James	89 Crosby, near Prince	Mar. 30, 1818
696	Parker, Garrit	7	March 28, 1814	June 24, 1816	Ann	1 Broadway	
697	Van Varick, Peter	7	do.	Oct. 25, 1819	Catherine	Hudd	Oct. 25, 1819
698	Greenham, William	12	do.	May 29, 1815	Anne Devoe, G'd'm'r		May 29, 1815
699	Myers, Harriet	9	do.	May 27, 1816	Thomas	Greenwich	May 27, 1816
700	Latham, Francis S.	6	do.	Aug. 29, 1817	Stanton Latham	Washington and Warren	
701	Freeland, Jacob B.	7	do.	April 24, 1820	Simeon	Barclay	April 24, 1820
702	Layman, Sophia	11	do.	July 3, 1817	John	68 North Moore	
703	Myers, David	10	April 25, 1814	Sept. 28, 1818	Cornelius	Pitt	Sept. 28, 1818
704	Heilden, William	7	do.	do.	Josiah	3 Beach	
705	Heilden, Ann	9	do.	Oct. 9, 1815	Ann	8 Beach	
706	Lewis, John M	7	do.	Sick	Hannah	42 Little Chapel	
	do. do.		May 25, 1818	Feb. 28, 1821		Vesey	Feb. 28, 1821

CATALOGUE OF SCHOLARS—Continued.

No.	Pupil.	Age	Admitted.	Withdrawn.	Parent.	Residence.	Graduated.
707	White, James	7	April 25, 1814	April 28, 1817	Thomas Powers	12 Spring	April 28, 1817
708	Skinner, Amos	8	do.	April 24, 1815	Richard	16 Warren	June 30, 1817
709	Ennis, James	11	do.	June 30, 1817	James	Thompson	
710	Ramp, Robert T.	10	May 30, 1814	July 3, 1814	John	Church	
711	Glover, Thomas	11	do.	April 27, 1818	Thomas	163 Bowery	April 27, 1819
712	Pullis, Abraham	11	do.	June 26, 1819	Abraham	Broome	
713	Blauvelt, Ann P.	9	do.	May 27, 1816	Mary	Leonard	May 27, 1816
714	Evertson, Jane	10	July 25, 1814	Dec. 19, 1814	Elizabeth	Thompson	
715	Kint, Catharine	11	July 26, 1814	Aug. 1, 1815	Catharine	Budd	
716	Riley, George	10	July 29, 1814	May 29, 1815	do.	Chapel	May 29, 1815
717	Vanderbeck, Eliza	10	Oct. 10, 1814	March 31, 1817	James	89 Crosby, near Prince	Mar. 31, 1817
718	Doremus, Caty	11	do.	April 29, 1816	Cornelius	Christopher	April 29, 1816
719	Bogert, Washington	11	do.	April 25, 1822	Weart	38 Crosby	April 29, 1822
720	McBride, Abraham	12	do.	April 29, 1815	Jane	172 Duane	April 29, 1815
721	Van Beuren, Maria	10	do.	Aug. 1, 1815	Kammener	Hudd	
722	Koeirs, William	14	do.	Oct. 31, 1815	Cornelius	112 Chambers	Oct. 31, 1815
723	Koeirs, Eliza	7	Oct. 31, 1814	Oct. 27, 1817	do.	do.	
724	Quackenbush, Maria	7	do.	March 25, 1816	Jane	Partition	
725	Letts, Eleanor	11	Nov. 26, 1814	May 27, 1816	Ann	46 Leonard	
726	Bogert, Simon J.	7	Nov. 28, 1814	March 25, 1822	Peter	81 Greene	Mar. 25, 1822
727	Van Rantz, Nicholas	11	do.	March 27, 1815	Ann Pitman	8 George	
728	Layman, Susannah	10	Dec. 19, 1814	July 3, 1815	John	North Moore	
729	Smith, Harvey	8	Jan. 30, 1815	May 29, 1820	Catharine	9 Chapel	
730	Snelien, Samuel	9	do.	May 25, 1818	Robert	17 Budd	
731	Emmet, William T.	7	do.	June 26, 1821	Abraham	Lispenard	June 26, 1821
732	Bogart, Lanah Ann	7	do.	April 27, 1818	Andrew	Thompson, near Spring	April 27, 1818
733	Demarest, Rachel	13	do.	March 12, 1817	Simon	34 Lower Robinson	
734	Smith, James H.	8	Feb. 1, 1815	April 24, 1821	Catharine	46 Robinson	April 24, 1821
735	Callow, Ann	8	Feb. 28, 1815	do.	Alice Burger	110 Reade	do.
736	Hicks, Thomas	7	March 27, 1815	June 25, 1821	Mary	Orange, near Broome	June 25, 1821
737	Doremus, James	9	do.	April 26, 1819	Mary	5 Warren	April 26, 1819
738	Fawpell, Maria	9	do.	March 27, 1820	Maria	11 Rector	Mar. 27, 1820
739	Lawrence, Mary	7	do.	do.	Catharine	20 Leonard	do.
740	Blauvelt, Herman	8	do.	April 30, 1821	Mary	19 Cliff	April 30, 1821
741	Heyer, Henry	8	do.	Feb. 26, 1821	Daniel	Greene	Feb. 26, 1821
742	Devoe, Aletta	9	do.	March 12, 1817	Joseph	44 Leonard	Mar. 12, 1817
743	Bogert, Stephen	9	do.	April 20, 1826	Rachel	32 Lispenard	April 20, 1826
744	Westervelt, Isaac	10	do.	Aug. 26, 1816	Garrit		Aug. 26, 1816

CATALOGUE OF SCHOLARS—Continued.

No.	Pupil.	Age	Admitted	Withdrawn	Parent.	Residence.	Graduated.
745	Anderson, George	11	April 24, 1815	June 24, 1816	Andrew	43 Nassau	
746	Nack, Experience P.	10	do.	April 28, 1817	Matthias	Jay and Washington	April 28, 1817
747	Thomas, Eliza	10	May 29, 1815	Aug. 1, 1815		11 Thomas	
748	Hrower, William	7	do.	July 30, 1821	Margaret	P. Vandervoort's	July 30, 1821
749	Duryee, Catharine	11	do.	March 31, 1817	John L.	Greenwich	Mar. 31, 1817
750	Duryee, John	9	do.	April 29, 1822	do.	do.	April 29, 1622
751	Cortelyou, Eleanor	12	do.	May 27, 1816	Elizabeth	61 Ann	
752	Duremus, Noah	8	July 10, 1815	May 28, 1821	Cornelius	Perry	May 28, 1821
753	Demarest, Simeon	9	Aug. 1, 1815	Aug. 29, 1817	do.	7 Beach	
754	Brinkerhoff, Christian	5	do.	Sept. 22, 1817	Eve	Desbrosses	
755	Dobbs, John	3	do.	March 29, 1819	John	Dominick	
756	Hogert, Susannah	9	do.	June 29, 1818	Rachel	54 Leonard	
757	Hrower, Jeremiah	10	Oct. 9, 1815	Oct. 7, 1816	Jacob	5 Thomas	June 29, 1818
758	Marinus, Maria	7	do.	Oct. 10, 1816	Adrian	52 Canal, corner Church	
759	Hudson, Mary Ann	7	do.	March 30, 1818	John	Varick and Clarke	
760	Cortelyou, John	10	do.	Sept. 28, 1818	Elizabeth	61 Ann	
761	Ouderdonk, Garrit	7	do.	do.	Rebecca	46 Crosby	
762	Van Tassel, Amy	13	do.	March 25, 1816	Robert Kirk	60 Leonard	
763	Anderson, Mary	10	Oct. 30, 1815	April 28, 1817	Andrew	43 Nassau	
764	Ackerman, Jane	10	do.	June 29, 1818	Letty Payne	90 Chapel	June 29, 1818
765	Van Winkle, Henry	12	Jan. 28, 1816	April 27, 1818	Jacob	25 Garden	April 27, 1818
766	Wood, Catharine	10	March 5, 1816	March 31, 1817	John	Vandam and Spring	
767	McCreery, William	9	do.	June 25, 1821	Phoebe	103 Church	June 25, 1821
768	Burgess, James	10	do.	Sept. 28, 1818	Daniel	Clarke	Sept. 28, 1818
769	Hrower, Rebecca	9	do.	April 28, 1817	Jacob	32 Spring	
770	Valentine, Henry	9	March 25, 1816	May 31, 1819	Evert	Second	
771	Trout, Eliza	10	do.	Jan. 25, 1819	John	401 Greenwich, cor. Laight	
772	Duryee, Peter C.	15	do.	April 28, 1817	Samuel	Thompson	April 28, 1847
773	Hedden, John	7	do.	May 27, 1816	Elizabeth	20 North Moore	
774	Doremus, Betsy	11	April 29, 1816	Oct. 7, 1816	Cornelius	Christopher, near Bedford	
775	McBride, Irving	8	do.	April 29, 1822	Jane	172 Duane	April 29, 1822
776	Van Norden, Abraham	9	do.	July 31, 1820	Abraham	Vandam	
777	Hogert, Peter	9	May 27, 1816	May 28, 1821	Elizabeth	14 Thomas	May 28, 1821
778	Van Heuren, Adeline	8	do.	Jan. 26, 1818	Kammener	66 North Moore	
779	Myers, Martin	9	do.	April 29, 1822	Thomas	Spring and Laurens	April 29, 1822
780	Mead, John	8	do.	Oct. 26, 1818	Henry	36 Crosby	
781	Seaman, John	10	do.	May 28, 1821	Maria	Charles	May 28, 1821
782	Debaun, Joseph	7	do.	March 11, 1822	Albert	4 Chapel	

CATALOGUE OF SCHOLARS—Continued.

No.	Pupil.	Age	Admitted.	Withdrawn.	Parent.	Residence.	Graduated.
783	Gaskin, Maria	10	June 24, 1816	April 24, 1820	William	60 Leonard	April 24, 1820
784	Blauvelt, John	10	do.	Feb. 23, 1818	John	7 Leonard	
785	Dickson, Sam'l (*Vide Notes*)	14	do.	June 30, 1817	William	48 Beaver	June 30, 1817
786	Hogert, Jane	11	do.		Peter	Greene	
787	Vanderbilt, Cornelius	9	Aug. 26, 1816	July 31, 1820	John C	Green'h, b Ham'd & Perry	July 31, 1820
788	Devoe, Abraham	11	do.	Feb. 26, 1821	Isaac	132 Mulberry, near Hester	
789	Simmons, William R	11	do.	April 26, 1819	Elizabeth	20 Beekman	April 26, 1819
790	Hrower, Henry	9	Oct. 10, 1816	April 27, 1818	Catharine	134 Mulberry	April 27, 1818
791	Doremus, Betsy G	8	do.	March 29, 1819	Mary	46 Crosby	Mar. 29, 1819
792	Pullis, Tunis	10	do.	Jan. 29, 1822	Abraham	Walker and Chapel	Jan. 29, 1822
793	Stewart, Charles	10	do.	March 29, 1819	William	70 Murray	
794	Marinus, Ann	11	do.		Adrian	54 Leonard	
795	Van Norden, Abraham	10	Oct. 28, 1816	June 29, 1818	Matthew	Near St. John's	
796	Jersey, Hannah	11	Feb. 3, 1817	April 27, 1818	James	Sullivan	April 27, 1818
797	Dickson, Jas. (*Vide Notes*)	10	do.	June 28, 1819	do.	43 Beaver	
798	Nevius, Simeon H	9	March 12, 1817	June 30, 1817	Mary	18 Thomas	
799	Ashley, Margaret	8	do.	March 25, 1822	David	Sullivan, near Prince	Mar. 25, 1822
800	Hogert, William	10	do.	July 30, 1821	Rulef	72 Cedar	July 30, 1821
801	Degroot, Jacob	12	do.	May 25, 1818	Eleanor	60 Anthony	May 25, 1818
802	Vanderbeck, Mimyan	11	March 31, 1817	April 26, 1819	James	89 Crosby, near Prince	April 26, 1819
803	Duryee, Henry H	9	do.	Jan. 31, 1825	John L	Greenwich	
804	Embree, Samuel	11	do.	April 27, 1818	Hannah	M J. Suydam's	
805	Demarest, Peter	10	do.	March 29, 1819	Daniel	36 Sullivan	
806	Ramsay, George	8	do.	Jan. 5, 1818	John	Sullivan	
807	Losey, Thomas	8	do.	March 30, 1818	William	270 Canal	
808	Marinus, Thomas	10	do.	Jan. 29, 1822	Adrian	54 Leonard	Jan. 29, 1822
809	La Forge, John A	7	April 16, 1817	Aug. 13, 1821	Hester	Broome	Aug. 13, 1821
810	Fox, Margaret	8	April 28, 1817	March 27, 1822	John	66 North Moore	Mar. 27, 1822
811	Van Blarcom, Bernard	10	do.	March 11, 1822	Peter	Jay and Washington	Mar. 11, 1822
812	Nack, James M. (*Vide Notes*)	8	do.	May 25, 1818	Matthias	4 Chapel	
813	Freeland, John M	7	do.	March 11, 1822	Simeon	3 Spring St. Glue Factory	Mar. 11, 1822
814	Vanderhoof, Henry V L	9	do.	March 29, 1819	James	Broome, near Varick	
815	Verbryck, Mary Ann	8	do.	June 30, 1817	Henry	163 Fly Market	
816	Simmons, James D	8	do.	Feb. 23, 1824	Jane	Greenwich	Feb. 23, 1824
817	Paulisson, Paul	10	April 28, 1817	Sept. 10, 1821	Peggy	Thompson	Sept. 10, 1821
818	Duryee, Garrit	10	May 26, 1817	Aug. 16, 1818	Samuel	Thompson	
819	Ramsay, Maria	10	do.	Oct. 27, 1817	Martin	199 Church	
820	Ennis, Mary	12	June 30, 1817	April 26, 1819	James	Thompson, near Spring	April 26, 1819

CATALOGUE OF SCHOLARS—Continued.

No.	Pupil	Age	Admitted	Withdrawn	Parent	Residence	Graduated
821	Dixon, Mary	8	June 30, 1817	Jan. 29, 1822	William	4 Front	Mar. 29, 1819
822	Degroot, Abraham	8	do.	Oct. 29, 1817	Abraham	Provoost	
823	Requa, Mary W.	9	do.	April 30, 1821	Mary	Cornelius Ray's, 56 B'way	
824	Brower, Augustus	10	do.	March 30, 1818	Mary	68 Chapel	
825	Doreman, Betsey	12	do.	March 29, 1819	Cornelius	Sullivan, near Spring	Mar. 29, 1819
826	Brower, Elias	8	July 29, 1817	July 29, 1822	Jacob	Near St. John's	July 29, 1822
827	Beaumont, Benjamin	11	Sept. 22, 1817	April 29, 1822	Catharine	Church, near Sugarhouse	April 29, 1822
828	Mead, Henry	9	do.	June 25, 1821	Henry	36 Crosby	June 25, 1821
829	Devoe, Isaac	9	do.	March, 1823	Isaac	132 Mulberry	
830	Blanchard, Christian B.	8	do.	Oct. 11, 1824	Francis	Spring and Thompson	
831	Zabriskie, Eliza	8	do.	March 29, 1819	Albert	Prince	Mar. 29, 1819
832	Degroot, Michael F.	9	Oct. 27, 1817	March 25, 1822	Eleanor	60 Anthony	Mar. 25, 1822
833	Degroot, Rachel	8	do.	April 27, 1818	Abraham	Provoost, n. Washington	
834	Quereau, Philip	9	Jan. 5, 1818	March 26, 1821	William	89 Front	
835	Debevoise, Courtlandt	12	Jan. 26, 1818	April 27, 1822	Courtlandt	54 Leonard	
836	Esler, Eleanor	10	Jan. 27, 1818	March 29, 1819	Henry	35 Spring	
837	Packer, Jane	12	Feb. 23, 1818	Jan. 12, 1819	Sarah	2 Beach	
838	Van Pelt, Peter	7	do.	May 19, 1824	Mary	45 Eldridge	May 19, 1824
839	Wartz, Henry A.	7	do.	April 28, 1823	Zipporah	Crosby, near Spring	April 28, 1823
840	Duryee, James	9	do.	Sept. 28, 1818	Daniel	Broome and Sullivan	
841	Robinson, John	7	do.	May 26, 1822	James	187 Church	May 26, 1822
842	Vanderbeck, Maria	10	March 30, 1818	Feb. 26, 1821	James	89 Crosby, near Prince	Feb. 26, 1821
843	McDonald, Mary	6	do.	Feb. 23, 1824	William	Thompson, next Church	Feb. 23, 1824
844	Stanton, Henry	12	do.	Sept. 10, 1821	Jane	Lispenard, next Church	Sept. 10, 1821
845	Van Winkle, John	13	April 27, 1818	Feb. 28, 1820	Jacob	251 William	Feb. 28, 1820
846	Voorhees, John C.	10	do.	Nov. 11, 1822	Henry	Orange and Prince	Nov. 11, 1822
847	Glover, Hester	11	do.	April 29, 1822	Catharine	156 Bowery	April 29, 1822
848	Brinckerhoff, Henry	12	do.	July 31, 1821	Abraham	82 Catharine	July 31, 1821
849	Ropert, Maria	7	do.	May 28, 1821	Ann	Thompson, near Spring	May 28, 1821
850	Ackerman, Garrit G.	11	do.	June 29, 1818	Garrit	3 Vestry	
851	Blauvelt, Eliza	10	do.	Feb. 22, 1819	Elizabeth	Clarke, near Spring	
852	Beach, Mary	8	do.	May 31, 1819	William	do.	
853	Starr, Jane	11	do.	May 25, 1818	Abraham	4 Vestry	
854	Hammond, Caroline	12	do.	Oct. 25, 1824	Henry	Greenwich and Amos	Oct. 25, 1824
855	Hammond, Washington	8	May 25, 1818	June 26, 1821	Henry	do. do.	June 26, 1821
856	Brower, Rebecca	11	do.	May 29, 1823	Sarah	Spring and Mott	
857	Vanderbilt, J'b (Vide Notes)	9	do.	Oct. 27, 1823	John C.	Green'h. b. Ham'd & Perry	Oct. 27, 1823
858	Debaun, John	7	June 29, 1818		Martha	72 Warren	

133

CATALOGUE OF SCHOLARS—Continued.

No.	Pupil.	Age	Admitted.	Withdrawn.	Parent.	Residence.	Graduated.
859	Simmons, Ab'm A.	8	June 29, 1818	July 30, 1820	Elizabeth	4 Liberty	Feb. 27, 1821
860	Dob, Neilson	9	do.	Feb. 27, 1821	John	Dominick	
861	Vanderhoof, James B.	8	do.	May 31, 1819	James	140 Spring	
862	Beaumont, Peter S.	10	do.	May 29, 1821	Catharine	Church	May 27, 1821
863	Emmet, James W.	9	do.	Aug. 4th, 1824	Abraham	21 Catharine Lane, n. Elm	Aug. 30, 1824
864	Dickson, Eliza	11	Sept. 17, 1818	May 28, 1821	Andrew	15 Water	
865	Freeman, Alex'r	8	do.	April 28, 1823	Marshall	28 Stone	April 28, 1823
866	Walkington, Ann	8	do.	March 11, 1822	Sarah	83 Stone	Mar. 11, 1822
867	Miller, John	9	Sept. 30, 1818	Dec. 27, 1819	Aaron	Allen, bet. Broome and Delancy	
868	Evertson, Benj'n	9	do.	June 26, 1821	Elizabeth	Thompson, near Spring	
869	Conklin, Abm.	10	Oct. 26, 1818	July 30, 1821	Isaac	Thompson and Spring	July 30, 1821
870	Combes, Mary	8	do.	do.	Nathaniel	28 Stone	
871	Platt, Richard	12	Jan. 25, 1819	Sept. 10, 1821	Richard	23 Norfolk	Sept. 10, 1821
872	Wilbur, Francis H.	12	do.	April 26, 1819	James	55 Dey	
873	Shields, Eliza Ann	8	do.	April 24, 1821	Martha	Church and Reade	April 24, 1821
874	Appleby, Chas.	9	Feb. 22, 1819	March 26, 1821	James	15 Water	Mar. 26, 1821
875	Dickson, James A.	8	do.	May 28, 1821	Andrew	do.	May 28, 1821
876	Esler, Henry	8	March 29, 1819	Feb. 26, 1821	Henry	35 Spring	Feb. 26, 1821
877	Degroot, Peter	8	do.	Sept. 5, 1825	Eleanor	41 Anthony	Sept. 5, 1825
878	Platt, Ab'm	13	do.	Sept. 10, 1821	Richard	23 Norfolk	Sept. 10, 1821
879	Freeman, Eliza A.	6	do.	April 27, 1824	Martha	28 Stone	April 27, 1824
880	Doremus, Mary Ann	7	do.	May 28, 1821	Cornelius	Sullivan, near Spring	May 28, 1821
881	Hicks, Catharine	8	do.	Feb. 23, 1824	Catharine	110 Reade	Feb. 23, 1824
882	Marsh, John A.	12	do.	Oct. 25, 1819	N.	Batavia and James	
883	Vanderbeck, James	9	April 26, 1819	Feb. 26, 1825	James	80 Crosby, near Prince	Feb. 26, 1825
884	Ennis, Eliza	12	do.	June 28, 1819	do.	do.	
885	Blanchard, Susan	7	do.	Feb. 27, 1826	Francis	Thompson and Spring	
886	Van Horne, Andrew	7	do.	Feb. 26, 1821	Joanna	15 Harman	Feb. 26, 1821
887	Day, Jacob E.	7	do.	April 25, 1825	Jane	Hester	April 25, 1825
888	Valentine, John	10	do.	May 31, 1819	Orphan	Crosby	
889	Stanton, Matilda	8	do.	Jan. 31, 1825	Jane	Lispenard, near Church	Jan. 31, 1825
890	Van Orden, Henry	9	do.	Sept. 5, 1825	Abraham	Broome, near Varick	Sept. 5, 1825
891	Peiham, Sarah	7	May 31, 1819	Jan. 29, 1823	William	Sullivan	
892	De Camp, George	10	do.	Sept. 10, 1821	Charity	21 Catharine Lane	Jan. 31, 1825
893	Collins, Eliz'h	6	do.	Jan. 31, 1825	Stephen	35 Thomas	
894							
895	Collins, Mary Ann	8	June 28, 1819	April 30, 1824	do.	69 Gold	May 26, 1822

CATALOGUE OF SCHOLARS—Continued.

No.	Pupil.	Age	Admitted.	Withdrawn.	Parent.	Residence.	Graduated.
896	Smith, Maria	11	June 28, 1819	April 24, 1821	Lewis	Christopher	April 24, 1821
897	Sproulis, Sam'l E. (Vide Note)	8	do.	April 20, 1824	Margaret	35 Chapel	April 20, 1824
898	Combes, Catharine	.	July 26, 1819	July 30, 1821	Nathaniel	Water	July 30, 1821
899	Robinson, Margaret	9	do.	do.	Sarah	187 Church	do.
900	Dickson, Samuel	10	Oct. 25, 1819	June 24, 1822	Andrew	15 Water	June 24, 1822
901	Enris, William	11	do.	June 26, 1821	James	Thompson, near Spring	June 26, 1821
902	Day, William	8	do.	Oct. 11, 1824	Catharine	409 Broadway	Oct. 11, 1824
903	Meyers, John F.	8	do.	May 29, 1826	George	18 Leonard	May 29, 1826
904	Earl, Peter	10	Dec. 2, 1819	March 29, 1823	Albert	Church and Canal	
905	Hill, Mary	11	Feb. 8, 1820	June 25, 1821	John	75 Nassau	June 25, 1821
906	Day, Mary	8	March 27, 1820	Jan. 29, 1822	Charles	100 Chapel	Jan. 29, 1822
907	Betham, Peter P.	9	do.	April 29, 1826	Mary	18 Leonard	April 20, 1826
908	Marinus, Jane	6	do.	March 7, 1822	Adrian	54 Leonard	
909	Combes, John	6	do.	Nov. 27, 1822	Nathaniel	28 Stone	
910	Appleby, Amelia	6	April 24, 1820	May 29, 1820	James	Front	
911	Bogert, James	11	do.	June 28, 1824	Rulef	38 Crosby, near Broome	June 28, 1824
912	Hill, Sally	9	do.	April 20, 1824	John	75 Nassau	
913	Kocirs, John	7	do.	June 26, 1820	Cornelius	76 Franklin	
914	Seaman, Ann	7	do.	Sept. 5, 1825	Maria	Charles, betw'n Hudson and Greenwich	
915	Wessells, John H	11	do.	April, 1822	John	165 Washington	
916	Beaumont, Catharine Susan	7	May 29, 1820	April 29, 1823	Catharine	Franklin and the Collect	
917	Tice, Henry	7	do.	May 29, 1823	John Van Riper	64 Mott	
918	Ashley, Conrad	10	June 26, 1820	Sept. 29, 1823	David	155 Hudson	Sept. 29, 1823
919	Bogert, John	9	do.	April 25, 1823	Peter	81 Greene	
920	Freeland, Aaron M	8	do.	June 26, 1826	Simeon	21 Anthony	June 26, 1826
921	Heyer, Margaret	11	do.	March 31, 1823	Daniel	30 Ann	
922	Moore, Sophia	8	do.	April 29, 1823	Abigail	Canal	
923	Bureau, John	8	do.	March 26, 1821	William	Beaver	
924	Van Riarcom, John	7	do.	March 5, 1823	Peter	2 King	
925	Van Nostrand, Garrit	11	do.	July 30, 1820	Matthew	Hudson and Perry	
926	Van Orden, Abraham M	13	do.	June 24, 1822	Henry	Orchard and Broome	June 24, 1822
927	Voorhees, Isaac	9	do.	Jan. 31, 1825	Jane	Hester	Jan. 31, 1825
928	Day, Rebecca	10	July 31, 1820	May 28, 1821	John C.	8 Beach	
929	Vanderbilt, John V.	6	do.	April 28, 1828	John C.	89 Mulberry	
930	Wessells, Albert A.	8	Sept. 25, 1820	June 26, 1826	Stephen	21 Thomas	April 28, 1824
931	De Camp, James	11	Sept. 26, 1820	March 5, 1823	Stephen	21 Thomas	Mar. 5, 1823
932	Gaskin, Abby	9	do.	Feb. 23, 1824	Mary	58 Leonard	Feb. 23, 1824

CATALOGUE OF SCHOLARS—Continued.

No.	Pupil.	Age	Admitted.	Withdrawn.	Parent.	Residence.	Graduated.
933	Navin, Jane	10	Sept. 26, 1820	Jan. 29, 1822	Mitchel	77 Thomas	
934	Navin, James	10	May 28, 1821		do.	do.	
935	Perkins, Joseph	11	Sept. 26, 1821	March 25, 1822	John Cregier, guard'n	Greenwich and Reade	
936	Myers, Edward	11	do.	May 26, 1822	Edward	549 Pearl	
937	Decker, Lewis	12	Oct. 30, 1820	July 29, 1822	Elizabeth	90 Chapel	
938	Lee, Letitia	8	do.	Sept. 10, 1824	William	17 William	Sept. 10, 1824
939	Remmey, Joshua	9	do.	Dec. 31, 1824	Mary	14 Liberty	
940	Sproulls, Harriet	9	do.	March 28, 1825	Margaret	35 Chapel	Mar. 28, 1825
941	Conklin, Henry	6	do.	May 28, 1827	Mary	34 Chapel	May 28, 1827
942	Huxley, Maria	11	Feb. 26, 1821	June 24, 1822	Ann	41 Hudson	
943	Heach, William	8	Feb. 27, 1821	March 28, 1825	Thomas	25 Thomas	Mar. 28, 1825
944	Demarest, Jacob D	7	do.	May 19, 1824	David P	14 Leonard	
945	Devoe, Jacob	10	do.	Oct. 26, 1826	Isaac	133 Mulberry	Oct. 26, 1826
946	Debevoise, James	12	March 26, 1821	May 26, 1823	Courtland	52 Leonard	
947	Emmet, Eliza Ann	7	do.	April 28, 1828	Abraham	Thompson and Prince	April 28, 1828
948	Goodrich, Wm. B	7	do.	March 5, 1823	Catharine	68 Vesey	
949	Loveland, John	7	do.	Sept. 10, 1824	Abigail	166 Mulberry	Sept. 10, 1824
950	Sembler, Andrew	8	do.	Jan. 29, 1822	Abigail Loveland, grandmother	139 Mulberry	
951	Vanderbeck, John V. N	9	do.	Oct. 26, 1826	James	89 Crosby	Oct. 26, 1826
952	Van Orden, James G	7	April 30, 1821	June 28, 1822	Abraham	38 Sullivan	
953	Dami, John	12	May 28, 1821	March 31, 1823	Helenor	34 Essex	Mar. 31, 1823
954	Dami, Edward	9	do.	Aug. 30, 1824	do.	do.	Aug. 30, 1824
955	Simmons, Matilda	14	do.	June 24, 1822	Elizabeth	33 Liberty	June 24, 1822
956	Bogert, Henry	11	do.	May 29, 1823	Weart	38 Crosby	
957	Huxley, Louisa	7	June 25, 1821	April 26, 1826	Ann	40 Hudson	
958	Simmons, Mary Ann	10	July 30, 1821	April 27, 1824	Elizabeth	33 Liberty	
959	Ashley, John	8	Sept. 10, 1821	March 28, 1825	David	Spring and Thompson	
960	Bogert, Stephen B	7	do.	April 20, 1826	Rulef	38 Crosby	April 20, 1826
961	Day, Maria	7	do.	Oct. 31, 1825	Jane	Hester	
962	Earle, Sally	8	do.	Sept. 29, 1823	do.	24 Lawrence	
963	Glover, William	8	do.	July 30, 1827	Catharine	119 Forsyth	July 30, 1827
964	Prierea, Emanuel J	11	do.	April 20, 1824	do.	Forsyth	April 20, 1824
965	Prierea, Mary Ann	8	do.	May 30, 1825	do.	do.	May 30, 1825
966	Van Harcom, James	12	do.	April 20, 1824	Peter	66 North Moore	April 20, 1824
967	Van Houten, Thomas	9	do.	July 12, 1824	Catharine	Greenwich and Varick	
968	Walkington, Melvena	7	do.	May 26, 1827	Sarah	72 Front	
969	White, Jane	7	do.	March 28, 1825	Elizabeth	Chapel and Duane	Mar. 28, 1825

136

CATALOGUE OF SCHOLARS—Continued.

No.	Pupil.	Age	Admitted.	Withdrawn.	Parent.	Residence.	Graduated.
970	Ayers, Albert	11	Oct. 29, 1821	May 26, 1822	Elihu	17 White	
971	Dickson, Easter	8	Jan. 29, 1822	May 19, 1824	William	Stone and Broad	
972	Day, Jacob	9	do.	April 30, 1827	John	Dominick and Varick	April 30, 1827
973	McDonald, William	8	do.	Sept. 5, 1825	William	7 Chapel	
974	Van Orden, William	8	do.	May 26, 1828	Matthew	Orchard and Broome	May 26, 1824
975	Verhoff, John	7	do.	May 31, 1830	Anthony	7 Water	May 31, 1830
976	Degroot, Jno. M	8	March 25, 1822	March 27, 1826	Eleanor	59 Anthony	
977	Freeman, Joseph	7	do.	June 26, 1826	Sarah	62 William	June 26, 1826
978	Hicks, Elsie	7	do.	April 29, 1823	Catharine	26 Frankfort	
979	Marinus, Deborah	7	do.	April 29, 1827	Adrian	98 Chapel	
980	Marselis, Amelia	12	do.	June 30, 1823	Elizabeth	59 Warren	
981	Meeker, Kitty C	8	do.	Jan. 31, 1825	do.	95 Broad	
982	Bogert, James W	10	April 29, 1822	May 28, 1827	John	Near Greenwich	
983	Duryee, Peter V	10	do.	March 28, 1825	William	Hammond, near Fourth	March 28, 1825
984	Dickson, McCauley	11	do.	July 28, 1827	Bennet	87 Broad	
985	Knickerbocker, Bennet	8	do.	July 28, 1823	Catharine	McDougal and Vandam	
986	Glover, Catharine	12	do.	March 28, 1825	Jane Grady	119 Forsyth	April 28, 1823
987	McBride, Sally A		do.	Feb. 26, 1825	Mary	172 Duane	March 28, 1825
988	Passman, Francis	7	do.	Sept. 28, 1829	Thomas	23 New	
989	Robinson, Thomas	7	do.	Feb. 26, 1835	Jane	25 New	Feb. 26, 1825
990	Simmons, Rachel	8	do.	June 26, 1829	Elizabeth	250 William	
991	White, Mary E	6	do.	March 29, 1825	Josiah	Lispenard	
992	Wines, Alexander	11	May 27, 1822	Oct. 29, 1827	Stephen	95 Chapel	March 28, 1827
993	Collins, Susan	6	do.	July 31, 1826	Elbert	17 Rose	July 31, 1826
994	Conover, Daniel	8	do.	June 28, 1824	do.	8 Pelham	June 28, 1824
995	Conover, Elisha	14	do.	April 30, 1827	do.	do.	April 30, 1827
996	Conover, Geo. S. / Vide Notes	7	do.	do.	Henry	Greenwich, near Perry	do.
997	Hammond, Henry	13	do.	Feb. 26, 1825	Sarah	189 Church	
998	Robinson, Leonard	6	do.	Sept. 29, 1823	John Van Riper	4 Beach	
999	Tice, Jacob	9	do.	Oct. 29, 1827	Elizabeth	172 Duane	Oct. 29, 1827
1000	Van Pelt, Jane Ann	7	do.	May 26, 1827	John	Leonard	
1001	Brown, Mary Ann	8	June 24, 1822	April 20, 1826	Matilda	155 Plymarket	April 20, 1826
1002	Dorset, John	9	do.	Aug. 25, 1828	do.	do.	Aug. 25, 1828
1003	Dorset, James	7	do.	Nov. 27, 1822	Andrew	Pearl	
1004	Dickson, Mary	9	do.	Sept. 29, 1823	John	Ludlow and Broome	
1005	Earle, Cornelius	7	do.	May 19, 1824	Jane Ann	8 Pump	May 19, 1824
1006	Wessels, Gertrude A	11	do.	Jan. 28, 1824	Wm. Ironside	20 Fulton	
1007	Anderson, John W	8	July 29, 1822				

CATALOGUE OF SCHOLARS—Continued.

No.	Pupil.	Age	Admitted.	Withdrawn.	Parent.	Residence.	Graduated.
1008	Hopper, Clarissa	10	July 29, 1822	March 28, 1825	Mary	90 Fulton	Mar. 28, 1825
1009	Hopper, Edward	7	do.	April 28, 1828	do.	do.	......
1010	Huxley, William	7	Nov. 27, 1822	Sept. 5, 1825	Ann	29 Desbrosses	......
1011	Romain, Abraham C.	12	do.	April 29, 1823	Sally	Kenwick, near Spring	......
1012	Voorhees, Elizabeth	10	do.	March 28, 1825	Henry	Prince and Orange	Mar. 28, 1825
1013	Carman, Ruth	10	do.	May 19, 1824	Patience	15 Stone	May 19, 1824
1014	Carman, Peter	8	do.	Oct. 31, 1825	do.	do.	......
1015	Week, Gilbert D.	8	Jan. 29, 1823	April 25, 1825	Alpheus	7 Water	......
1016	Beach, Edward	7	do.	April 29, 1826	William	30 Water	April 29, 1826
1017	Rundle, Elizabeth	11	do.	May 29, 1826	Michael	30 Thomas	May 29, 1826
1018	Rundle, Christian	8	do.	May 30, 1825	do.	do.	......
1019	Frost, Theodore (Vide Note)	10	March 5, 1823	June 25, 1827	Ann Maria Van Orden	142 Ludlow	June 25, 1827
1020	Buckley, Lucy Ann	6	March 31, 1823	May 30, 1825	Catharine	52 Vesey	......
1021	Frost, Sally Ann	9	April 29, 1823	Feb. 27, 1826	Ann Maria Van Orden	142 Ludlow	......
1022	Romain, Ann	9	do.	April 27, 1829	Sally	Greenwich, near Spring	......
1023	Chappel, James	8	May 26, 1823	Sept. 29, 1826	Helenor	Greenwich and Robinson	Sept. 29, 1823
1024	Danu, William	8	do.	March 29, 1830	Courtlandt	123 Division	......
1025	De Revoise, Washington	8	do.	July 16, 1824	Hannah	52 Leonard	......
1026	Styers, Alfred	6	do.	April 26, 1824	John C.	114 Washington	......
1027	Vanderbilt, Sally Ann	6	do.	Sept. 28, 1829	Matthew	8 Beach	Sept. 28, 1829
1028	Van Orden, Eliza	11	do.	Feb. 27, 1830	Phebe	Orchard	......
1029	Blauchard, Margaret Ann	7	June 30, 1823	July 28, 1828	Catharine	88 Harman	......
1030	Wilmot, Theodore	12	July 28, 1823	March 26, 1827	Maria	28 Charlton	......
1031	Ashley, Clarisa	8	Sept. 29, 1823	April 29, 1826	William	32 Lumber	......
1032	Black, Garrit C.	8	do.	April 26, 1824	Jane	28 Thomas	......
1033	Demarest, Peter	7	do.	April 26, 1824	Ann Stymets, guard'n	28 Pine	......
1034	Lynch, Adaline	10	do.	Oct. 26, 1826	do.	do.	......
1035	Lynch, Maria	8	do.	May 29, 1826	Patience	15 Stone	......
1036	Carman, Benjamin	7	Jan. 28, 1824	Nov. 29, 1830	Anthony	2 Water	......
1037	Verhoff, Anthony	7	do.	June 26, 1826	James King	243 Mulberry	......
1038	Bogart, John W.	8	Feb. 23, 1824	Sept. 5, 1825	Isaac	Greenwich Village	Sept. 5, 1825
1039	See, Isaac	11	do.	do.	do.	do.	do.
1040	See, Abraham	12	March 29, 1824	Jan. 26, 1829	Peter	118 William	......
1041	Bogert, Peter B.	9	do.	April 10, 1827	Charles	164 Greene	......
1042	Jeroleman, James O.	11	do.	July 26, 1824	John	27 Desbrosses	......
1043	Van De Linda, Hetty	8	do.	Oct. 26, 1826	John C.	8 Beach	Oct. 26, 1826
1044	Vanderbilt, Margaret	11	do.	Jan. 11, 1825	Catharine	104 Chrystie	......
1045	Day, Rebecca Jane	7	April 26, 1824				

CATALOGUE OF SCHOLARS—Continued.

No.	Pupil.	Age	Admitted.	Withdrawn.	Parent.	Residence.	Graduated.
1046	Wines, Henrit	10	April 20, 1824	Jan. 31, 1825	Josiah	18 Anthony	
1047	Hill, John	8	April 20, 1824	March 23, 1828	John	Charles and Hudson	
1048	Hilliker, Sally Ann	13	do.	Feb. 26, 1825	William	60 Watts	
1049	Hunter, Ann	11	do.	July 30, 1827	Maria	30 Gold	April 30, 1827
1050	Hunter, Fanny	7	do.	July 27, 1829	do.	do.	July 27, 1829
1051	Van Orden, James G. M.	8	do.	April 28, 1828	Matthew	Orchard	April 28, 1828
1052	Bissett, Hannah	6	May 10, 1824	April 27, 1829	Hannah	114 Washington	
1053	Van Pelt, Maria	11	May 20, 1824	April 30, 1827	Elizabeth	27 Oak	April 30, 1827
1054	Devoe, George I.	7	June 28, 1824	June 29, 1829	Sarah Lysg.	93 Chapel	
1055	Rutan, John	14	July 12, 1824	July 26, 1824	John	223 Orange	
1056	Rutan, Susan	9	Oct. 11, 1824	April 30, 1827	do.	Hester, near Bowery	
1057	King, Herman B.	9	July 26, 1824	April 30, 1827	John A	Lombardy, near Walnut	
1058	Simmons, Peter	18	do.	Sept. 5, 1825	Jane	89 Henry	
1059	Arents, Stephen	13	Aug. 30, 1824	Jan. 31, 1825	Elizabeth	Greenwich and Amos	
1060	White, Eli	7	do.	June 29, 1826	do.	114 Elizabeth	
1061	Button, Thomas	13	Oct. 11, 1824	July 31, 1826	John	8 Grand	July 31, 1826
1062	Bogert, Gilbert	10	do.	April 27, 1829	David	57 Sullivan	April 27, 1829
1063	Hammond, Latourette	9	Oct. 25, 1824	June 28, 1830	Henry	Charlton and Hudson	
1064	Bogert, William	7	Jan. 31, 1825	May 25, 1829	David	57 Sullivan	May 25, 1829
1065	Conklin, Margaret	8	do.	April 28, 1828	Mary	54 Anthony	April 28, 1828
1066	Devoe, Gilbert	6	do.	Sept. 24, 1827	Isaac	132 Mulberry	
1067	Emmet, Jane Ann	7	do.	April 27, 1829	Abraham	64 Spring	April 27, 1829
1068	Hone, John V. A.	3	do.	April 25, 1825	Maria	28 Frankfort	
1069	Jones, James N.	7	do.	April 30, 1827	James N.	49 Sullivan	
1070	Jones, Peter	12	March 12, 1825	do.	do.	do.	
1071	King, William	7	Jan. 31, 1825	Sept. 27, 1830	John A	Lombardy, near Walnut	
1072	Wessels, Helen Maria	9	do.	May 28, 1827	John	81 Pump	May 28, 1827
1073	Lyon, Aaron G.	9	do.	April 25, 1831	Effy	171 Duane	April 25, 1831
1074	Lyon, Rachel D.	7	Feb. 26, 1825	do.	do.	do.	do.
1075	Lyon, David D.	11	June 27, 1825	April 28, 1828	do.	60 Thompson	April 28, 1828
1076	Packer, Ann W.	8	Feb. 26, 1825	March 28, 1825	Isaac	358 Greenwich	
1077	See, Leah	20	do.	June 27, 1825	Mary	Greenwich Village	
1078	Taylor, Ann	7	April 25, 1825	May 30, 1825	do.	123 Greenwich Village	
1079	Taylor, Richard	8	March 28, 1825	Sept. 5, 1825	Garrit	do.	
1080	Van Horn, John	8	March 28, 1825	June 30, 1828	do.	19 Thomas	
1081	Day, John	9	do.	Sept. 27, 1830	Charles	45 Watts	Sept. 27, 1830
1082	Jeroleman, Wm. H.	9	do.	June 29, 1829	Charles	164 Greene	
1083	Machett, Chas. E.	12	do.	Sept. 5, 1825	Clarissa Collard	16 New	

CATALOGUE OF SCHOLARS—Continued.

No.	Pupil.	Age	Admitted.	Withdrawn.	Parent.	Residence.	Graduated.
1084	Morris, Samuel	9	March 28, 1825	May 25, 1829	Jacob	41 Chapel	
1085	Morris, Francis	6	Sept. 5, 1825	June 27, 1831	do.	do.	
1086	Munson, George	12	March 28, 1825	Feb. 27, 1826	Daniel	Beason (now Barrow)	
1087	Reed, Ephraim	7	do.	May 26, 1828	Elizabeth	88 Harman	
1088	Reed, Ann	9	April 25, 1825	do.	do.	do.	
1089	Van Iderstein, Isaac	9	March 28, 1825	Oct. 26, 1826	John	74 Sullivan	
1090	Van Iderstein, James	7	April 25, 1825	July 27, 1829	do.	do.	
1091	Voorhees, Clarissa C.	8	March 28, 1825	March 30, 1829	Henry	244 Orange	
1092	Biermann, Jacob H	8	April 25, 1825	Sept. 5, 1825	Thomas	Beach and Chapel	
1093	Cook, James	7	do.	do.	Elizabeth	71 Murray	
1094	Day, William	8	do.	March 29, 1830	Jane	372 Washington	Mar. 26, 1830
1095	Miller, Isaac	10	do.	March 26, 1827	Aaron	40 Delancey	
1096	Miller, Sarah	7	Sept. 5, 1825	do.	do.	do.	
1097	Stephens, Horatio	9	April 25, 1825	Aug. 25, 1828	Abraham	7 Chapel	
1098	Wilmot, Cornelia	12	do.	April 30, 1827	Catharine	88 Harman	April 30, 1827
1099	Ten Broeck, William H	10	May 30, 1825	June 27, 1825	John A	Elizabeth and Broome	
1100	Holly, Samuel	8	June 27, 1825	May 25, 1829	Letitia	Eldridge and Delancey	
1101	Holly, William	7	do.	Aug. 29, 1831	do.	do.	
1102	Kneringer, Matthias	10	do.	April 27, 1829	Elizabeth	45 Greene	April 27, 1829
1103	Robinson, William	6	do.	May 28, 1832	Thomas	12 Lumber	May 28, 1832
1104	Deshays, Charles	12	Sept. 5, 1825	June 25, 1827	David	72 Orange	
1105	Deshays, David	10	do.	do.	do.	do.	
1106	Forshay, Henry	11	do.	May 29, 1826	Thomas Ball	235 Elizabeth	
1107	Forshay, Garrit	9	do.	March 28, 1831	do.	do.	
1108	Giraud, George	6	do.	July 30, 1827	George	15 Anthony	
1109	Huxley, Charles C.	7	do.	April 26, 1826	James	131 Greene	
1110	Powles, John	11	do.	Jan. 26, 1829	{ Peter Traphagen, Stepfather }	358 Greenwich	Jan. 26, 1829
1111	Glover, Charles	11	Oct. 10, 1825	April 25, 1831	Catharine	119 Forsyth	
1112	Harper, Angeline	10	Oct. 31, 1825	May 28, 1827	William	137 Church	
1113	Bogert, Rulef	14	Feb. 27, 1826	April 28, 1828	Gertrude	14 Thames	
1114	Bogert, James W	10	do.	April 29, 1827	Rulef	41 Wooster	
1115	Hill, William	14	do.	May 28, 1827	John	Hamersley	
1116	Lyman, Christian R.	7	do.	Oct. 26, 1826	Matthew	13 Thames	
1117	Lyman, John H. L.	7	do.	do.	do.	do.	
1118	Rand, Jane	7	do.	July 21, 1826	Stephen Collins	114 Washington	
1119	Zabriskie, Albert G. H	9	do.	April 30, 1827	Henry G	557 Broome	
1120	Bruce, George W	11	March 27, 1826	May 25, 1829	Mary	36 Augustus	May 26, 1832

CATALOGUE OF SCHOLARS—Continued.

No.	Pupil.	Age	Admitted.	Withdrawn.	Parent.	Residence.	Graduated.
1121	Collins, Stephen	11	March 27, 1826	May 8, 1827	Stephen	114 Washington	
1122	Francisco, Cornelius	11	do.	April 28, 1828	Thomas Kikeman	Bowery	April 28, 1828
1123	Fentonburgh, John	8	April 20, 1826	June 6, 1826	Mrs. Kuetinger	Broome	
1124	Forshay, James	7	May 29, 1826	July 31, 1826	Margaret Ball	69 Harman	
1125	King, Peter Wilson	11	May 29, 1826	May 25, 1829	Ann	241 Delancey	
1126	Smith, Isaac	12	do.	April 25, 1831	Samuel	83 Washington	April 25, 1831
1127	Smith, John	9	do.	April 28, 1834	do.	do.	April 28, 1834
1128	Stuyvesant, Peter J. D.	12	do.	April 25, 1831	Peter	29 Elm	April 25, 1831
1129	Harper, John	7	June 26, 1826	April 29, 1833	William	137 Mott	
1130	Harper, William	10	do.	April 25, 1831	do.	do.	April 25, 1831
1131	Bissett, Eliza	7	July 31, 1826	April 27, 1829	Samuel	114 Washington	
1132	Chadwick, Thomas	10	do.	do.	John	74 Liberty	
1133	Chadwick, Daniel	6	do.	June 25, 1827	do.	do.	
1134	Voorhees, Esther Ann	6	do.	April 25, 1831	Henry	241 Orange	April 25, 1831
1135	Bennet, Nancy	11	Oct. 26, 1826	March 26, 1827	William Herper	Mulberry	
1136	Bauvelt, Cornelius I.	8	do.	June 27, 1831	Abraham J.	Varick, near Dominick	June 27, 1831
1137	Cloyd, Ann Maria	9	do.	May 25, 1829	Margaret	115 Washington	May 25, 1829
1138	Cloyd, Peter	7	do.	Sept. 24, 1832	do.	do.	
1139	King, James L.	13	do.	May 28, 1827	John A.	Lombardy, near Walnut	
1140	Morris, Isaac	6	do.	March 26, 1832	Jacob	41 Chapel	
1141	Park, John	8	do.	Nov. 29, 1830	David	13 Stone	
1142	Ryer, Abraham	7	do.	Dec. 24, 1827	Michael	8 Dominick	
1143	Stuyvesant, Benton H.	8	do.	April 29, 1833	Peter	29 Elm	April 29, 1833
1144	Vanderbilt, Martha	8	do.	do.	John C.	48 Beach	
1145	Van Iderstein, Ann E.	7	do.	April 30, 1832	Mrs. M. E.	Hudson	
1146	Westervelt, John	9	do.	April 30, 1827	John	do.	
1147	Foster, Isaac	10	Jan. 29, 1827	Jan. 28, 1828			
1148	Knapp, Jonathan	9	March 26, 1827	March 26, 1827	Jacob P.	Greenwich, near Spring	
1149	Demarest, Sarah	7	do.		do.	do.	
1150	Kelly, John	8	do.	Oct. 29, 1827	William	318 Broadway	
1152	Low, John J.	9	do.	June 25, 1827	Benjamin	62 Vandam	
1153	Baxter, Elizabeth	11	April 30, 1827	Oct. 26, 1849	Henry	282 Grand	
1154	Baxter, Samuel	10	do.	do.	do.	do.	
1155	Collard, Jeremiah	9	do.	June 27, 1831	James	66 North Moore	
1156	Cook, John	8	do.	July 28, 1828	Elizabeth	40 North Moore	
1157	Kip, James	12	do.	May 28, 1827	Albert	75 Sullivan	
1158	Kuetinger, Elizabeth	9	do.	June 28, 1830	Elizabeth	21 Minetta	June 28, 1830

CATALOGUE OF SCHOLARS—Continued.

No.	Pupil.	Age	Admitted.	Withdrawn.	Parent.	Residence.	Graduated.
159	Day, Henry	7	May 28, 1827	Sept. 30, 1833	John	33 Watts	Sept. 30, 1833
160	Anderson, Wm. (*Vide Notes*)	12	June 25, 1827	April 25, 1831	Jane	53 Liberty	April 25, 1831
161	Hunter, John	16	do.	July 30, 1827	John	Broadway	
162	Beach, Jane	9	Sept. 24, 1827		William	9 Clarke	
163	Hill, Neilson	5	do.	Nov. 29, 1830	John	51 Carmine	
164	Westervelt, Catharine A	10	do.	Sept. 27, 1830	James	Harrison	
165	Lake, William H	11	Oct. 29, 1827	June 28, 1831	William	94 Perry	
166	Miller, Peter	9	Dec. 24, 1827	June 25, 1832	Phebe	53 Warren	
167	Miller, Sarah Ann	7	do.	do.	do.	do.	
168	Cook, Peter V. H	7	Jan. 28, 1828	Sept. 24, 1832	Elizabeth	181 Varick	
169	Hardie, Susan		do.	Jan. 26, 1829	*Orphan*		
170	Lawrence, Robert B	11	do.	June 27, 1831	John		June 27, 1831
171	Lawrence, John	9	do.	April 29, 1833	do.		April 29, 1833
172	Lake, John H	6	Feb. 25, 1828	Sept. 24, 1833	William	94 Perry	
173	Waugh, John De Witt	8	do.	June 28, 1830	David	Houston and Mercer	
174	Bennet, George A. H	9	April 28, 1828	Jan. 30, 1832			Jan. 30, 1832
175	Cowsen, Emma	10	do.	April 29, 1833	Lucy	118 Bedford	April 29, 1833
176	Coisen, Samuel	8	do.	Sept. 30, 1834	do.	do.	
177	Harper, Catharine	7	do.	May 25, 1835	William	137 Mott	May 25, 1835
178	King, Nicholas	8	do.	Nov. 28, 1831	John A.	Lombardy, near Walnut	
179	Norbury, Samuel	8	do.	Sept. 24, 1832	*Orphan*		
180	Stuyvesant, Charles S.	8	do.	Sept. 30, 1834	Peter	29 Elm	
181	Tisdale, John	9	do.	Nov. 29, 1830	Sarah	Elm	
182	Tisdale, William	7	do.	do.	do.	do.	
183	Trapbagen, James	12	do.	June 29, 1829	Peter	114 Hammond	
184	Trapbagen, Peter	10	do.	do.	do.	do.	
185	Vanderbilt, Peter	7	do.	Oct. 8, 1833	John C	48 Beach	Oct. 8, 1833
186	Westercelt, Mary Jane	7	do.	June 25, 1832	James	do.	
187	Blauvelt, Eliza Ann	8	June 30, 1828	April 29, 1833	Abraham J	85 Sullivan	April 29, 1833
188	Erskine, Magdalene	9	do.	April 28, 1834	James N.	64 Water	April 28, 1834
189	Anderson, Euphemia	10	Sept. 29, 1828	June 28, 1830	Jane	53 Liberty	
190	Doremus, Isaac	10	Jan. 26, 1829	Oct. 31, 1831	John	41 Chapel	
191	Doremus, Nicholas	8	do.	Nov. 28, 1831	do.	do.	
192	Morris, Mary Ann	8	do.	May 25, 1835	Jacob	do.	May 25, 1835
193	Kneringer, Julia A.	9	May 25, 1829	June 27, 1831	Elizabeth	13 York	
194	Morris, Jane E.	7	do.	May 30, 1836	Jacob	284 Greenwich	May 30, 1836
195	Van Wart, Alexander	12	do.	April 25, 1831	Samuel	92 Barrow	April 25, 1831
196	Van Wart, William	9	do.	Sept. 28, 1835	do.	do.	Sept. 28, 1835

CATALOGUE OF SCHOLARS—Continued.

143

No.	Pupil	Age	Admitted	Withdrawn	Parent	Residence	Graduated
197	Cook, Thomas M.	6	June 29, 1829	Sept. 28, 1829	Elizabeth		
198	Erskine, Harriet	6	do.	June 30, 1834	James		
199	Jerdeman, Charles	11	do.	March 28, 1831	Charles		
200	Terhune, Henry	11	July 27, 1829	May 30, 1831	Stephen	64 Water	
201	Collard, George W.	7	Sept. 28, 1829	Jan. 25, 1836	James	58 Sullivan	
202	Junior, Patience	7	Oct. 26, 1829	Dec. 27, 1840		62 Caroline	
203	Van Iderstein, John Z.	7	do.	June 30, 1838	Elizabeth Mexcey	41 Chapel	
204	Van Wart, Ann	13	do.		Henry	98 Barrow	June 27, 1831
205	Van Wart, James		do.	June 27, 1831	do.	do.	
206	Gringer, Thomas	14	Nov. 30, 1829	April 6, 1831	Sarah Pettigrass	Bayard	April 25, 1836
207	Lyon, Eleanor S.	8	do.	April 25, 1836			
208	Storms, Henry	10	do.	April 29, 1833	John	47 Robinson	
209	Storms, John	8	do.	Nov. 25, 1833	do.	do.	
210	Stuyvesant, Theodore	5	do.	May 30, 1836	Peter	29 Elm	
211	Harper, Jesse	6	Jan. 25, 1830	April 27, 1840	William	137 Mott	
212	Kip, Harriet	11	March 29, 1830	April 30, 1832	Albert	556 Broome	
213	Kip, Nicholas	11	do.	Sept. 30, 1834	do.	do.	April 30, 1832
214	Vanderbeck, Richard	11	do.	April 30, 1832	Abraham	47 Wooster	April 29, 1833
215	Parsel, Edwin		April 26, 1830	June 28, 1830			Oct. 27, 1834
216	Chambers, John H. (C. Note)	12	Sept. 27, 1830	April 29, 1833	Willi'm	5 Duane	
217	Chambers, Ann Maria	12	do.	Oct. 27, 1834	do.	do.	
218	Chambers, William	9	do.	Jan. 4, 1836	do.	do.	
219	Chambers, Hannah	6	do.	July 25, 1831	do.	do.	
220	Forshay, Margaret Ann	6	do.	May 25, 1835	Margaret Ball	49 Anthony	
221	Jeffers, Charles D.	7	do.	July, 1831	Juliana		
222	Jeffers, Emeline	8	do.	Sept. 1831	do.		
223	Jeffers, Harriet	6	do.	May, 1831	do.		
224	Jeffers, Mary E.	11	do.	Sept. 1831	do.		
225	Knettinger, Sarah	8	do.	June 27, 1831	Elizabeth	13 York	
226	Hammond, Sarah	12	Oct. 25, 1830	April 30, 1832	Henry	19 Grove	
227	Lyon, Robert S.	7	do.	April 25, 1836	Eleanor Henry	112 Franklin	April 25, 1836
228	Rocherey, Rachel	8	do.	May 25, 1835	Rachel	112 Orange	May 25, 1835
229	Rocherey, William	11	do.	March 30, 1835	do.	do.	Mar. 30, 1835
230	Voorhees, Phebe M	7	April 25, 1831	Oct. 20, 1831	Phebe	5 Hester	
231	Morris, Jacob	7	June 27, 1831	Feb. 29, 1836	Jacob	41 Chapel	
232	Blauvelt, Margaret		July 25, 1831	Nov. 27, 1837			
233	Eaton, Mary J		do.	June 25, 1832	Mrs. John Eaton	46 Christie	
234	Eaton, Thomas	11	do.	June 27, 1836	do.	do.	

CATALOGUE OF SCHOLARS—Continued.

No.	Pupil.	Age	Admitted.	Withdrawn.	Parent.	Residence.	Graduated.
1235	Russell, Mary	7	July 25, 1831	March 31, 1834	James	48 Vandam	May 28, 1836
1236	Collard, Eliza	10	Oct. 10, 1831	May 28, 1833	Cynthia	16 Church	
1237	Hammond, William	12	do.	April 29, 1833	Cynthia, (Grandmother)	do.	
1238	Hilliard, James	7	do.	July 29, 1833	John	138 Varick	
1239	Hill, Thomas	9	do.	April 29, 1833	Sally		
1240	Dodge, Cornelius B.	11	Oct. 31, 1831	Sept. 4, 1833	John	Vandam	
1241	Doremus, Jacob	9	do.	April 30, 1834	James	1 Vandam	
1242	Dunlap, James	12	do.	March 31, 1834	Mrs. John	21 Lispenard	
1243	Eaton, James	10	do.	Sept. 30, 1834	David	117 Chapel	
1244	Shannon, William	9	do.	Jan. 26, 1835	Isaac	98 Barrow	
1245	Van Wart, Alexander	12	do.	Jan. 3, 1834	do.	do.	
1246	Van Wart, Lawrence	9	do.	do.	do.	do.	
1247	Mitchell, Mary	8	Nov. 28, 1831	Sept. 1832	With Jos. C. Ashley	43 Cortlandt	
1248	Woolley, Charles	13	do.	Jan. 29, 1833	Henry	118 Bedford	
1249	Shay, William	10	Jan. 30, 1832	Sept. 28, 1835	Widow	10 Thompson	Jan. 30, 1835
1250	Shay, John	7	do.	Jan. 26, 1833	do.	do.	
1251	Smith, Garret	9	do.	Jan. 28, 1834	Samuel	73 Washington	
1252	Bowman, Daniel	7	Feb. 27, 1832	Oct. 30, 1837	Peter	106 Hudson	
1253	Robinson, Henry	8	do.	April 25, 1836	Jno. Mathews, Nephew	12 Lumber	April 25, 1836
1254	Robinson, Margaret	10	March 26, 1832	July 29, 1833	do.	do.	
1255	McPherson, John D.	10	do.	May 27, 1833	John	119 Washington	
1256	Post, Sarah Ann	8	do.	May 25, 1835	Margaret Lawrence	Carlisle, near the Dock	
1257	Spears, Francis	8	April 30, 1832	June 24, 1839	Peter Van Varick	42 Leonard	June 4, 1837
1258	Boardman, William J.	6	do.	May 25, 1835	William	28 King	
1259	Chambers, Henry	5	do.	do.	do.	5 Duane	
1260	Woolley, Simon F.	6	May 28, 1832	Sept. 30, 1834	Henry	118 Bedford	
1261	Ellenwood, Clarissa	4	do.	July 25, 1836	Mary McPherson	William	
1262	Erskine, Edward	7	do.	June 29, 1835	James	16 Marketfield	
1263	Hammond, Ann Amelia	7	do.	March 31, 1834	Mrs.	141 Amos	
1264	Penson, Henry H.	11	do.	April 29, 1833	Isabella	30 Hammersley	
1265	Murray, William	10	June 25, 1832	April 28, 1834	Mary H.	59 North Moore	
1266	Storms, Robert	9	do.	Nov. 25, 1833	John	47 Robinson	
1267	Billings, Elizabeth	7	Sept. 24, 1832	June 27, 1836	Henry Dunningberg	366 Water	
1268	Hawkins, Zeeariah	12	do.	Jan. 27, 1835	do.	do.	
1269	Morris, William N.	11	do.	Jan. 26, 1835	Jacob	40 Barrow	
1270	Morris, John J.	8	do.	do.	do.	do.	
1271	Post, Gideon	6	do.	April 27, 1835	Alice Verhott	166 Water	
1272	Rich, Noah Wetmore	10	do.	April 29, 1833	Jacob	14 Thomas	

CATALOGUE OF SCHOLARS—Continued.

No.	Pupil	Age	Admitted	Withdrawn	Parent	Residence	Graduated.
1273	Riell, Evert	8	Sept. 24, 1832	April 29, 1833	Jacob	14 Thomas	April 27, 1835
1274	Van Saun, John	12	do.	April 27, 1835	Helen	99 Bedford	do.
1275	Van Winkle, Cornelius V. R.	11	do.	do.	Peter	554 Broome	
1276	Van Winkle, Theo. V. R.	6	do.	do.	do.	do.	
1277	Verhoff, Escaba	8	do.	April 24, 1837	Anthony	166 Water	
1278	Verhoff, William	6	do.	do.	do.	do.	
1279	Wood, Elizabeth Ann	9	do.	May 27, 1833	Hannah, G'dmother	5 Duane	
1280	Barr, Garrit	12	Oct. 29, 1832	April 28, 1834	Lydian Brooks	40 Thompson	
1281	Brooks, Wm. H.	9	do.	do.	do.	do.	
1282	Clements, Caroline	12	do.	April 29, 1833	Hannah Barr	do.	
1283	Ellis, Mary	11	do.	May 25, 1835	Mary	14 Orchard	May 25, 1833
1284	Ellis, Theodore	9	do.	May 27, 1833	do.	do.	
1285	Garns, Henrietta	5	do.	May 12, 1841	Henry	63 Provost	May 12, 1841
1286	Myers, Isaac H.	11	do.	March 3, 1835	Edward	74 Greene	Mar. 3, 1835
1287	Post, John	11	do.	Jan. 26, 1835	Abraham	Jersey City	
1288	Stewart, Maria L.	10	do.	May 26, 1834	William	167 Essex	
1289	Stewart, William Henry	9	do.	Feb. 22, 1834	do.	do.	
1290	Way, Henry	9	Nov. 26, 1832	April 29, 1833	Mary Forsyth	156 William	
1291	Shay, James F.	6	Jan. 28, 1833	Sept. 30, 1833	Lucretia	12 Thompson	
1292	Berdan, Albert	7	Feb. 25, 1833	Feb. 23, 1835	Isaac	352 Broome	
1293	Bruce, Jane	15	do.	July 29, 1833	Alexander	Harrison and Staple	
1294	Bruce, Catharine	12	do.	Sept. 30, 1834	do.	do.	
1295	Bruce, Alexander	9	do.	Aug. 5, 1834	do.	do.	
1296	Romeyn, Peter	9	do.	Nov. 30, 1835	John	100 Bedford	April 27, 1835
1297	Price, Reuben	11	March 25, 1833	April 27, 1835	Samuel	279 William	
1298	Price, Samuel	10	do.	Feb. 22, 1831	do.	do.	
1299	Stuyvesant, Elizabeth A.	4	do.	May 30, 1830	Peter	12 Thomas	
1300	Worden, Mary Ann	9	do.	May 26, 1834	Alfred	106 Monroe	
1301	Worden, Sidney	6	do.	June 30, 1831	do.	do.	
1302	Coppinger, Deborah		April 29, 1833	June 24, 1833	John C.	3 Anthony	June 24, 1835
1303	Coppinger, Adriana		do.	April 25, 1836	do.	do.	April 25, 1836
1304	Coppinger, Charles		do.	March 27, 1843	do.	do.	
1305	Myers, John	9	do.	May 28, 1833	Edward	74 Greene	May 28, 1833
1306	Myers, Cornelius P.	7	do.	March 25, 1839	do.	do.	Mar. 25, 1839
1307	Myers, Andrew W.	5	do.	Nov. 30, 184..	d.	do.	
1308	Anderson, John	9	May 27, 1833	June 29, 1835	Robert	35 Clinton	
1309	Bryant, William	8	do.	May 26, 1834	Joseph	167 Essex	
1310	Bryant, Reuben	6	do.	do.	do.	do.	

CATALOGUE OF SCHOLARS—Continued.

No.	Pupil.	Age	Admitted.	Withdrawn.	Parent.	Residence.	Graduated.
1311	Ellis, Robert	5	May 27, 1833	Nov. 26, 1838	Mary	141 East Broadway	Nov. 26, 1838
1312	Myers, Lavinia	10	do.	Oct. 28, 1833	Lydia	Hudson	
1313	Myers, Cornelius F.	8	do.	Jan. 31, 1842	Cornelius	45 Crosby	Jan. 31, 1842
1314	Phelps, Augustus E.	8	do.	Oct. 31, 1836	Asa H.	165 Essex	
1315	Shepherd, Joseph	7	do.	June 25, 1838	Cath. Battell	31 Watts	
1316	Frazier, Jane Ann	8	July 29, 1833	Feb. 24, 1840	Rebecca	22 Hamersley	June 25, 1838
1317	Frazier, George W.	6	do.	June 29, 1843	do.	do.	Feb. 20, 1840
1318	Besher, John H.	9	Sept. 3, 1833	March 28, 1836	Ann	41 Oak	
1319	Besher, Ann M.	8	do.	do.	do.	do.	
1320	Eldridge, Simeon	5	do.	Oct. 26, 1835	Richard	54 Anthony	
1321	Eldridge, Edgar	7	do.	Jan. 26, 1835	do.	do.	
1322	Harrington, Washington	10	do.	Sept. 30, 1834	Sarah	113 Elizabeth	
1323	Jones, Aaron	12	do.	Jan. 26, 1835	James N.	122 Spring	
1324	Jones, William	7	do.	May 30, 1836	do.	do.	
1325	Morris, John	6	do.	Jan. 25, 1841	Jacob	41 Chapel	
1326	Ripley, Sarah J.	6	do.	June 30, 1834	Eden	152 Cherry	
1327	Smith, Maria	7	do.	Sept. 30, 1834	Henrietta Snell	187 Spring	
1328	Ware, Harriet	6	do.	May 26, 1834	Samuel Ripley	152 Cherry	
1329	Collard, James	7	Oct. 28, 1833	June 24, 1839	James	639 Washington	
1330	Mansfield, Matthew	10	do.	Sept. 28, 1835	Matthew Van Orden	118 Bedford	
1331	Schiener, Lewis	8	do.	Sept. 27, 1841	Lewis Olmsted	148 Elizabeth	
1332	Olmsted, James H.	5	do.	May 16, 1842	Lewis	do.	
1333	Olmsted, John	7	Nov. 25, 1833	Sept. 27, 1841	do.	do.	Sept. 27, 1841
1334	Wartz, Samuel T.	7	Jan. 28, 1834	May 28, 1838	Peter	Broadway and Walker	
1335	Brown, Wm. A. P.	4	Feb. 22, 1834	May 26, 1834	Mary	67 Cedar	
1336	Burtas, Wm. H. (Vide Notes)	8	April 28, 1834	Nov. 1, 1841	Francis	199 Church	Nov. 1, 1841
1337	Dougherty, George	6	do.	Oct. 30, 1837	Sarah	Mulberry	
1338	Bragaw, Francis	10	May 26, 1834	Nov. 27, 1837	Isaac	31 Essex	Nov. 27, 1837
1339	Bragaw, Isaac	8	do.	July 30, 1838	do.	do.	July 30, 1838
1340	Cooper, Robert J.	6	do.	April 25, 1836	Joseph T.	25 Rose	
1341	Filberg, John	7	do.	June 25, 1838	Mrs. Winckelmann, (Gdm.)	47 Leonard	
1342	Winckelmann, John	11	do.	April 27, 1837	John	do.	
1343	Winckelmann, Catharine	10	do.	June 25, 1838	do.	do.	
1344	Winckelmann, Rachel A.	7	do.	March 25, 1839	do.	do.	
1345	Brown, John	7	June 30, 1834	May 29, 1837	Elizabeth	706 Greenwich	
1346	Brown, Amanda	10	Aug. 5, 1834	June 29, 1835	do.	do.	
1347	Ackerman, William	12	do.	April 25, 1836	Jno. E. Burkbee	143 Amos	

147

CATALOGUE OF SCHOLARS—Continued.

No.	Pupil.	Age	Admitted.	Withdrawn.	Parent.	Residence.	Graduated.
348	Baker, Isaac B	11	Sept. 30, 1834	May 3, 1836	Jane Thorn, G'dm'r	183 South	
349	Baker, Benjamin F	7	do.	do.	do. do.	do.	
350	Devoe, George	8	do.	Sept. 30, 1839	Margaret	165 Reade	Sept. 30, 1839
351	Morris, Catharine	5	do.	April 26, 1841	Ann	Hudson and Franklin	
352	Boyce, Catharine K.	7	Oct. 27, 1834	July 25, 1836	Hannah Barr	197 Washington	
353	Doremus, Jacob	7	do.	June 29, 1835	John	41 Chapel	
354	Doremus, Sarah	7	do.	Jan. 26, 1835	do.	do.	
355	Heyer, Sarah M.	12	do.	July 27, 1835	William	192 Rivington	
356	Heyer, William G.	11	do.	Oct. 30, 1837	do.	do.	
357	Heyer, Catharine M	7	do.	do.	do.	do.	Sept. 28, 1840
358	Mooney, Manoah		do.	Sept. 28, 1840			
359	Mooney, Frederick		do.	June 23, 1838			
360	Shannon, Margaret	7	do.	June 29, 1835	David	172 Chapel	
361	Smith, Archibald	7	do.	April 27, 1835	Harriet	44 Roosevelt	
362	Smith, Harriet	7	do.	Sept. 28, 1835	do.	do.	
363	Van Wart, Mason	8	do.	April 26, 1841	Samuel	80 Christopher	April 26, 1841
364	Hell, William H.	11	Jan. 26, 1835	Nov. 30, 1835	Mrs.	241 Hudson	
365	Romeyn, Isaac	9	do.	Nov. 26, 1838	John	103 Troy	
366	Sanberg, Joshua	12	March 30, 1835	Sept. 28, 1835	Nicholas	680 Greenwich	
367	Sanberg, Emily	10	do.	do.	do.	do.	
368	Sanberg, Peter	8	do.	do.	do.	do.	
369	Sanberg, Nicholas	6	do.	do.	do.	do.	
370	Collard, William	7	May 25, 1835	May 26, 1843	Rachel	639 Washington	
371	Hyde, Henry	6	do.	Sept. 26, 1842	Eliz'h Keyser, G'dm'r	628 Washington	
372	Keyser, Henry	9	do.	June 29, 1839	Elizabeth	do.	
373	Vanderbeck, James	8	do.	Sept. 28, 1835	Maria, Grandmother	166 Essex	
374	Vanderbeck, Abraham	6	do.	Sept. 26, 1842	do.	do.	Oct. 31, 1842
375	Bragaw, Lewis	9	April 27, 1835	July 30, 1838	Isaac	31 Essex	
376	Ackerman, Mary	10	June 29, 1835	Nov. 30, 1835	Jane Vosburgh	Fourth St. and Sixth Ave.	
377	Brown, William	10	do.	July 25, 1836	Sarah	227 Mulberry	
378	Cregier, Joseph	9	do.	March 28, 1836	John	44 6th Ave. cor. 4th St	
379	Myers, Mary F.	8	do.	July 30, 1838	Lucretia Day	37 Watts	
380	Sullivan, Jeremiah W	9	do.	Sept. 28, 1835	Jane	15 Thompson	
381	Olmsted, Mary M.	4	do.	Sept. 26, 1842	Mary Ann	148 Elizabeth	
382	Romeyn, James H	6	do.	April 26, 1841	John	103 Troy	
383	Barry, Catharine J.	4	Sept. 28, 1835	Feb. 24, 1840	Elinor S.	179½ Pearl	
384	Penson, Abraham	7	do.	Sept. 24, 1838	Isabella	Christopher	
385	Williams, Peter	11	do.		Robert	79 Hamersley	

CATALOGUE OF SCHOLARS—Continued.

No.	Pupil.	Age	Admitted.	Withdrawn.	Parent.	Residence.	Graduated.
1386	Williams, Samuel	7	Sept. 28, 1835	July 31, 1837	Robert	79 Hamersley	
1387	Christie, John	6	Oct. 26, 1835	June 24, 1839	Elizabeth	57 Laurens, cor. Broome	
1388	Meeker, Uzal	7	do.	Oct. 30, 1838	Michael	Hamersley	
1389	Danningberg, Lucinda	5	Nov. 30, 1835	June 27, 1836	Henry	2 Monroe	
1390	Powles, John	13	do.	Sept. 24, 1838	Martin	204 Mott	Sept. 24, 1838
1391	Vanderbeck, Maria	11	do.	April 25, 1836	Eliza	164 Broome	
1392	Van Wart, Daniel	11	do.	May 30, 1842	Daniel	80 Christopher	
1393	Titus, William		Jan. 25, 1836	April 25, 1836			
1394	Ackerman, John	11	April 25, 1836	July 31, 1837	Peter	3 King	
1395	Filberg, Catharine A.	6	do.	May 25, 1840	Mrs.	25 Park Place	
1396	Walmsley, Stephen B.	7	do.	May 12, 1843	Harriet	40 Crosby	May 12, 1843
1397	Dugan, William	10	May 30, 1836	Sept. 24, 1838	Mary Ann	60 Greene	Sept. 24, 1838
1398	Sec. Maria	10	do.	July 31, 1837	Eunice	178 Thompson	
1399	Traphagen, William	13	do.	Oct. 30, 1837	Peter	57 Jane	Oct. 30, 1837
1400	Waldron, John R	7	do.	April 26, 1837	Richard	73 Sullivan	
1401	Bovee, Alfred	8	June 27, 1836	Sept. 26, 1842	Jacob	53 Greene	
1402	Bovee, Joseph	9	do.	Sept. 25, 1837	do.	do.	
1403	Dyckman, Peter B.	9	do.	Oct. 30, 1839	John	13 Dominick	
1404	} Pettiner, Daniel	7	do.	June 24, 1839	John S.	24 Thomas	
	} do.	14	Feb. 27, 1843	Sept. 25, 1843	do.	181 Varick	
1405	{ Pettiner, James	5	June 27, 1836	June 24, 1839	do.	25 Thomas	
	{ do.	11	Oct. 31, 1842	April 29, 1844	do.	181 Varick	Oct. 28, 1844
1406	{ Pettiner, John	9	June 27, 1836	June 24, 1839	do.	25 Thomas	
	{ do.	12	Nov. 25, 1839	April 27, 1840	do.	105th Street	June 24, 1839
1407	Vanderbeck, Eliza A.	11	June 27, 1836	May 28, 1838	David	166 Essex	
1408	Collard, Richard	6	Sept. 26, 1836	April 29, 1844	Rachel	659 Washington	Oct. 28, 1844
1409	Boardman, Mary E.	9	Oct. 31, 1836	March 27, 1843	William	144 Sullivan	
1410	Coleman, Charles	11	do.	Feb. 27, 1837	Nathaniel	713 Greenwich	
1411	Riker, Jacob	11	do.	June 25, 1838	Elizabeth	623 Washington	
1412	Riker, Abraham	8	do.	do.	do.	do.	
1413	Foster, Enos	7	Nov. 28, 1836	July 29, 1844	Lydia	Greenwich Lane	
1414	Foster, John	5	do.	Nov. 28, 1842	do.	do.	
1415	Pettiner, William H	14	do.	July 30, 1838	John S.	25 Thomas	July 30, 1838
1416	Concklin, Jacob	12	Dec. 22, 1836	May 29, 1837	Jacob		
1417	Concklin, Henry	9	do.	do.	do.		
1418	Mount, Sarah M.	12	do.	do.	Isaac	120 Warren	
1419	Willse, Peter	10	do.	do.	do.	171 Eighth Avenue	
1420	Willse, George W	8	do.	do.	do.	do.	

CATALOGUE OF SCHOLARS—Continued.

No.	Pupil.	Age	Admitted.	Withdrawn.	Parent.	Residence.	Graduated.
1421	Baird, William A	4	Jan. 30, 1837	March 25, 1840	David A	70 Greene	
1422	Clute, Cecilia H	6	Feb. 27, 1837	Oct. 30, 1837	Henry	388 Broome	
1423	Love, Alexander	9	do.	Sept. 26, 1842		Jersey City	
1424	Moffat, Isaac L	9	March 27, 1837	Sept. 28, 1843	John	38 Bowery	
1425	Moss, James R	12	April 22, 1837	March 20, 1841	Hannah Smith	146 Christopher	
1426	Vanderbeek, Harriet	6	do.	April 20, 1841	David	166 Essex	
1427	Earle, John S	8	May 29, 1837	March 20, 1841	William H	39 Bowery	
1428	Freeland, Ann	12	do.	Sept. 24, 1838	Samuel	34 Grand	
1429	Freeland, Mary	7	do.	do.	do.	do.	
1430	Freeland, John	5	do.	do.	do.	do.	
1431	Payne, Samuel	9	June 26, 1837	June 24, 1839	Jesse	201 Church	
1432	Peskyn, Harriet	12	July 31, 1837	Sept. 25, 1837	Mrs.	72 Thompson	
1433	Boardman, Sarah J	7	Sept. 25, 1837	May 27, 1844	William	144 Sullivan	
1434	Boyce, John	7	do.	May 12, 1843	Jacob	53 Greene	
1435	Coppinger, Eliza J	6	do.	May 25, 1846	John C	241 Broome	
1436	Kaylor, Isaac	12	do.	June 25, 1838	Mrs.	36 Watts	
1437	Trumper, Emily A	10	do.	Nov. 27, 1837	Peter	76 Greene	
1438	Trumper, Henry	5	do.	do.	do.	do.	
1439	Ouereau, Abigail	12	do.	July 30, 1838	William	103 Greene	
1440	Ouereau, Hannah W	6	do.	do.	do.	do.	
1441	Denecham, Bernard	7	Oct. 30, 1837	June 27, 1842	Mrs. Michael	141 Spring	
1442	Eilberg, Charles P	11	do.	Sept. 24, 1838	Mrs.	57 Eldridge	
1443	Maconnicle, Charles E	10	do.	Jan. 25, 1841	John	41 Renwick	
1444	Maconnicle, John Henry (Twin Sister)	7	do.	April 3, 1848	do.	do.	April 26, 1848
1445	Meers, John J	7	do.	Sept. 25, 1843	Andrew	119 Christopher	Oct. 30, 1843
1446	Pine, Samuel	8	do.	April 27, 1844	Elizabeth	1-2 Spring	
1447	Clark, Eliza	9	Nov. 27, 1837	July 30, 1838	Mrs.	28 Grand	
1448	Hill, William H	12	do.	Sept. 24, 1841	Mrs.	241 Hudson	
1449	Whitlock, James A	5	do.	March 25, 1839	Mrs.	229 Church	
1450	Whittle, Maria A	7	do.	March 27, 1843	Peter	28 Grand	
1451	Whittle, Samuel R	11	do.	Sept. 30, 1839	do.	do.	
1452	Buckley, Benjamin	6	Dec. 26, 1837	June 25, 1839		158 Hammond	
1453	Corson, Christina	9	do.	May 28, 1838		do.	
1454	Frazier, Rebecca	8	Jan. 29, 1838	March 25, 1844	Rebecca	22 Hammersley	
1455	Sayres, Aeneas H	5	Feb. 25, 1838	Dec. 30, 1845	Nathan	14 Thompson	
1456	Stewart, Charles	5	do.	April 26, 1844	Catharine Flack	31 Watts	April 26, 1844
1457	Stewart, Catharine	7	April 30, 1838	June 28, 1841	do.	Varick and Watts	

CATALOGUE OF SCHOLARS—Continued.

No.	Pupil.	Age	Admitted.	Withdrawn.	Parent.	Residence.	Graduated.
1458	Earle, Martha J.	11	May 28, 1836	Sept. 30, 1839	William H	426 Bowery	
1459	Moffat, Lucy G.	5	do.	Nov. 25, 1844	John	65 Leonard	
1460	Dawsson, Samuel B	10	June 25, 1836	Sept. 30, 1839	Rachel H.	69 Greene	
1461	Gray, William H	8	do.	May 26, 1845	James	146 Sixth Ave.	Oct. 29, 1845
1462	Griffith, Joseph	12	do.	Sept. 28, 1840	Rachel	2d Ave., bet. 24th & 25th	
1463	Mead, Peter.	13	do.	April 26, 1841	William	170 Christopher	April 26, 1841
1464	Mead, David V. N	7	do.	April 29, 1844	do.	do.	
1465	Mead, Abraham R	5	do.	May 26, 1840	do.	do.	
1466	Moffat, Mary	8	do.	June 29, 1840	John H	49 Carmine	
1467	Galatian, Samuel W	4	July 30, 1838	July 29, 1844	John	209 Elm	
1468	Galatian, William	11	do.	June 24, 1839	do.	do.	
1469	Ackerman, Jacob W	11	Sept. 24, 1838	April 26, 1841	do.	174 12th, n. University Pl.	April 26, 1841
1470	Cregier, Eliza J.	7	do.	Feb. 23, 1846	Michael V.	43 Christopher	
1471	Degroot, Eleanor A	10	do.	March 27, 1843	do.	Varick and Downing	
1472	Degroot, Mary J.	7	do.	June 29, 1840	Joseph	do.	
1473	Hill, John M.	5	do.	Nov. 29, 1847	John	41 Grand	
1474	Romaine, Caroline	6	do.	June 29, 1845	Peter.	83 Eleventh	
1475	Whittle, Abraham	11	do.	Oct. 3, 1843	Mrs.	41 Grand	
1476	Hillyer, John	6	Oct. 31, 1838	Sept. 30, 1839	Henry.	107 Spring	
1477	Schenck, Robert.	12	do.	do.	George W	do.	
1478	Van Beuren, Rachel	7	do.	March 29, 1841	Mrs. Hawes.	107 Christopher	
1479	Van Beuren, Maria.	11	do.	April 29, 1841	Mrs. Clark, Gr'm'y	do.	
1480	Post, Richard.	5	Nov. 29, 1838	June 24, 1839	Christina.	552 Houston	Oct. 28, 1844
1481	Clark, Thomas.	7	Dec. 21, 1838	July 25, 1842	do.	do.	
1482	Earle, George	9	do.	Sept. 30, 1844	Mrs. Vanderhoff.	168 Christopher	
1483	Earle, Henry	10	do.	Sept. 26, 1842	William, Grandfather	Jersey City	
1484	Sillick, Abraham A	11	Feb. 25, 1839	April 27, 1841	Hannah	98 Barrow	
1485	Love, Charles	11	March 25, 1839	Sept. 29, 1842	Rebecca	120 Greenwich Lane	
1486	Van Wart, William.	8	April 29, 1839	May 30, 1842	Christina	22 Hamersley	
1487	Rowman, Jane	8	June 24, 1839	Feb. 26, 1842	Catharine Ackerman	558 Houston	
1488	Frazier, John W.	5	do.	May 26, 1845	Samuel.	37 Renwick	
1489	Earle, John	9	July 29, 1839	March 4, 1847	Christopher	109 Christopher	
1490	Hadden, Thomas.	6	Sept. 2, 1839	March 27, 1843	do.	114 Pitt	April 26, 1844
1491	Van Wart, Henry.	10	do.	June 27, 1842	do.	do.	
1492	Childs, Christopher	12	Sept. 30, 1839	March 27, 1843	Jane.	do.	
1493	Childs, Deborah J	8	do.	April 29, 1844		17 Christopher	Oct. 30, 1843
1494	Childs, Elizabeth	11	do.	April 27, 1846			
1495	Logan, Anna		do.	Sept. 25, 1843			

CATALOGUE OF SCHOLARS—Continued.

No.	Pupil	Age	Admitted	Withdrawn	Parent	Residence	Graduated
1496	Logan, Sarah	6	Sept. 30, 1839	Jan. 27, 1845	Jane	17 Christopher	
1497	Moore, Samuel	12	Oct. 28, 1839	Nov. 30, 1840	Mrs. Stones	221 Sullivan	
1498	Quereau, William	7	do.	do.	Catharine	138 Thompson	
1499	Quereau, John	5	do.	do.	do.	do.	
1500	Springsteen, Abraham	8	do.	Sept. 30, 1844	Lydia	671 Washington	
1501	Springsteen, Richard H.	8	do.	Feb. 26, 1844	do.	do.	
1502	Van Seiver, Mary	6	do.	March 26, 1844	Peter	91 Christopher	
1503	Van Seiver, Peter	8	do.	Oct. 31, 1842	do.	do.	
1504	Evans, Issac	9	Nov. 25, 1839	April 29, 1844	James G.	71 Watts	
1505	Olmsted, Ann Maria	7	do.	Jan. 30, 1843	Lewis	148 Elizabeth	
1506	Ashby, William H.	10	Feb. 24, 1840	Sept. 26, 1842	Catharine	264 Bleecker	
1507	Moffat, Elijah	6	do.	June 29, 1840	John H.	49 Carmine	
1508	Moffat, Janet	4	do.	do.	do.	do.	
1509	Moffat, Margaret	5	do.	do.	do.	do.	
1510	Stewart, Mary E.	13	May 25, 1840	April 27, 1840	Catharine Flack	147½ Franklin	
1511	Frazier, Sarah	7	June 29, 1840	April 3, 1848	Rebecca	109½ Charlton	
1512	West, Elijah	9	do.	July 26, 1841	Daniel	87 Perry	Oct. 29, 1845
1513	Norris, Agnes	10	July 27, 1840	May 26, 1845	do.	19 Christopher	April 26, 1844
1514	Norris, Margaret	12	do.	Jan. 22, 1844	do.	do.	
1515	Pine, William T.	6	do.	Oct. 3, 1843	Elizabeth	133 Amity	
1516	Ryard, Mary	4	Sept. 28, 1840	June 28, 1841	David	87 Perry	
1517	Herring, Catharine	9	do.	May 30, 1845	Eliza Garns, Aunt	85 Charlton	Oct. 29, 1845
1518	Porter, Julia	4	do.	do.	Thomas	29 Christopher	
1519	Porter, Elizabeth	7	do.	Feb. 23, 1846	do.	do.	
1520	Post, Ann B.	7	do.	June 28, 1841	David Ryard	87 Perry	
1521	Van Beuren, Emeline	7	do.	April 28, 1845	George W.	84 Hammersley	
1522	Dawson, Jacob H.	6	Oct. 7, 1840	Dec. 27, 1847	George	40 North Moore	
1523	Dawson, States	4	do.	Nov. 24, 1845	do.	do.	
1524	Hill, Jefferson	9	do.	Sept. 26, 1842	do.	Greenwich and King	
1525	Woolley, Ezra	9	do.	May 30, 1842	John	do. do.	
1526	Parsons, John H.	6	Oct. 26, 1840	May 31, 1841	John, Grandfather	110 Greenwich Lane	
1527	Parsons, Margaret A.	12	do.	do.	William	do. do.	
1528	Parsons, Peter N.	12	do.	do.	do.	do. do.	
1529	Manleville, Elizabeth	10	Nov. 30, 1840	May 12, 1843	Elizabeth	5 Weehawken	
1530	Manleville, Hannah A.	11	do.	April 29, 1844	do.	do.	
1531	Norris, Elizabeth	4	do.	Feb. 23, 1846	Daniel	19 Christopher	
1532	Vandenburgh, Samuel	4	Dec. 28, 1840	Feb. 25, 1847	Oliver	Sixth Ave., near Twelfth	
1533	Vandenburgh, Thomas	6	do.	May 30, 1846	do.	do.	

CATALOGUE OF SCHOLARS—Continued.

No.	Pupil.	Age	Admitted.	Withdrawn.	Parent.	Residence.	Graduated.
1534	Kettleman, John J.	7	May 31, 1841	April 26, 1847	Peter	28 Cornelia	Oct. 28, 1847
1535	Springsteen, Josiah	5	do.	Dec. 29, 1845	Lydia	84 Eleventh	
1536	Chambers, Mary	12	June 28, 1841	Feb. 28, 1842	Hannah Wood, G'dm'r	527 Greenwich	
1537	Chambers, Solomon	10	do.	May 30, 1842	do.	do.	
1538	Banker, Catharine A.	9	Sept. 27, 1841	Feb. 23, 1846	Benjamin	125 Goerck	
1539	Banker, John	12	do.	April 28, 1845	do.	do.	April 28, 1845
1540	Banker, Thomas A.	7	do.	April 25, 1849	do.	do.	Oct. 31, 1860
1541	Crezier, Josephine	6	do.	March 30, 1846	George	12 Gay	
1542	Davis, Mary J.	13	do.	Sept. 26, 1842	Martin Fenn	51 Ridge	
1543	Downs, Cornelius T. (Vide Notes)	6		Sept. 23, 1843	Cornelius H.	76 Sullivan	
1544	Downs, John S. (Vide Notes)	12	do.	do.	do.	do.	
1545	Downs, Sabrina	9	do.	do.	do.	do.	
1546	Fenn, Adaline	7	do.	Sept. 26, 1842	Martin	51 Ridge	
1547	Fenn, Julia Ann	9	do.	do.	do.	do.	
1548	Goldsmith, Sarah	9	do.	April 28, 1845	John Senbebi	171 Christopher	
1549	Hopper, Rachel J.	11	do.	May 1, 1842	Albert	9th Ave. and 17th St.	
1550	Hopper, Sarah C.	8	do.	do.	do.	do.	
1551	Layman, Alexander	7	do.	Dec. 27, 1847	Henry	1 Gay	
1552	Layman, Harriet J.	10	do.	May 26, 1845	do.	do.	Oct. 29, 1845
1553	Moore, Ellen	9	do.	June 30, 1843	Joseph	820 Broadway	
1554	Olmsted, Jane E.	5	do.	Jan. 30, 1843	Lewis	79 Mercer	
1555	Romaine, Sarah	6	do.	June 30, 1845	John	31 Barrow, cor. 6th Ave.	
1556	Post, Elizabeth	9	Oct. 25, 1841	Dec. 27, 1841	John A.	8c Charlton	
1557	Russell, Columbia	4	do.	Jan. 31, 1842	Eliza Garns, G't Aunt	Houston	
1558	Fisher, Catharine	13	Nov. 1, 1841	Sept. 26, 1842	Mary Atkinson	87 Perry	
1559	Haulenbeck, William H.	7	do.	June 29, 1843	Garrit, Uncle	21 Bedford	
1560	Harris, James		Nov. 29, 1841	July 25, 1841	John A.	1 Gay	
1561	Post, Adrian	12	do.	Dec. 29, 1841	John A.	1 Gay	
1562	Volk, Thomas E.	8	Dec. 27, 1841	Nov. 27, 1843	Edward	92 Broome	
1563	Springsteen, Letty J.	5	Jan. 31, 1842	April 27, 1846	Letty	84 Eleventh	
1564	Springsteen, Rachel	13	do.	March 27, 1843	do.	do.	
1565	Volk, Abby E.	11	do.	Oct. 31, 1842	Edward	92 Broome	
1566	Volk, Catharine A.	6	do.	Nov. 27, 1843	do.	do.	
1567	Vail, Eleanor	11	March 28, 1842	March 26, 1844	William	63 Goerck	April 26, 1844
1568	York, Andrew J.	6	do.	May 26, 1845	Sarah	83 Perry	
1569	Haulenbeck, Almira	8	April 25, 1842	April 24, 1848	Tunis	Greenwich Lane	

CATALOGUE OF SCHOLARS—Continued.

No.	Pupil.	Age	Admitted.	Withdrawn.	Parent.	Residence.	Graduated.
1570	Mickens, Elizabeth A	11	April 25, 1842	April 26, 1847	Tunis Haulenbeck, Stepfather	Greenwich Lane	Oct. 28, 1847
1571	Mickens, George T	15	do.	Dec. 30, 1844	do.	do.	April 28, 1845
1572	Mickens, Rachel A. (Vide Notes)	7	do.	Feb. 25, 1850	do.	do.	Feb. 20, 1850
1573	Mickens, Sarah C. (Vide Notes)	9	do.	do.	do.	do.	do.
1574	Ranker, Mary E	6	June 27, 1842	April 28, 1852	Benjamin	152 Stanton	
1575	Helms, Charles	8	do.	July 29, 1844	Peter	16 Clark	
1576	Helms, Emily	10	do.	Jan. 27, 1845	do.	do.	
1577	Lamberson, Cornelius V	7	do.	Feb. 28, 1848	David	12 King	
1578	Lamberson, David W	9	do.	Feb. 23, 1846	do.	do.	
1579	Mandeville, Sophronia E. F.	6	do.	May 31, 1847	Elizabeth	69 Fourth	
1580	Storrs, George	8	do.	Nov. 24, 1845	Sarah	do.	
1581	Storrs, John J	10	do.	do.	do.	do.	
1582	Storrs, Wm. H. (Vide Notes)	12	do.	May 31, 1847	do.	do.	April 29, 1846
1583	Vandenburgh, Louisa	6	do.	Feb. 25, 1847	Oliver	114 Perry	
1584	Wilson, Catharine J	6	do.	Nov. 28, 1842	John	14 King	
1585	Wilson, George	9	do.	June 29, 1843	do.	do.	
1589	Bowers, Mary C	11	Sept. 26, 1842	Feb. 23, 1846	Mrs.	87 Greenwich Lane	
1587	Clendenin, Wm	6	do.	Feb. 28, 1848	George	354 Houston	
1588	Cullard, Stephen D	10	do.	March 30, 1846	Rachel	645 Washington	
1589	Gray, Hannah T	11	do.	Jan. 25, 1847	James	109 Barrow	Oct. 28, 1847
1590	Gray, Isabella W	7	do.	May 26, 1851	do.	do.	Oct. 27, 1852
1591	Layman William	7	do.	Jan. 29, 1849	Henry	1 Gay	
1592	Myers, Ann Eliza	11	do.	April 26, 1847	Andrew	105 Hamersley	
1593	Galatian, Magdalen	11	Oct. 31, 1842	May 27, 1844	John B.	43 Sullivan	
1594	Porter, John	7	do.	Nov. 30, 1847	Thomas	29 Christopher	
1595	Barber, Silas	8	Nov. 28, 1842	May 27, 1844	John Shepherd, Gdfr	155 Chapel	
1596	Davis, John	9	do.	Sept. 29, 1845	Benjamin	Great Kiln Road	
1597	Freeland, John	12	do.	April 29, 1844	Mrs.	18 Leonard	Oct. 28, 1844
1598	Lippincott, Ebenezer W	11	do.	April 28, 1845	Henry	56 Greene	
1599	Lippincott, Edward E	13	do.	April 29, 1844	do.	do.	Oct. 28, 1844
1600	Lippincott, Henry	9	do.	April 27, 1846	do.	do.	
1601	Myers, Andrew	14	do.	May 29, 1844	Andrew	105 Hamersley	
1602	Myers, Edward S	7	do.	May 29, 1848	do.	do.	
1603	Warner, Leonard W	8	do.	Feb. 29, 1848	Ann	189 Mulberry	
1604	Parkinson, Randolph	11	Dec. 29, 1842	May 12, 1841	Sarah	140 Amos	

CATALOGUE OF SCHOLARS—Continued.

No.	Pupil.	Age	Admitted.	Withdrawn.	Parent.	Residence.	Graduated.
1605	Burns, Mary J.	12	Feb. 27, 1843	April 28, 1845	Mary	828 Broadway	Oct. 27, 1858
1606	Gray, Agnes J.	7	do.	May 18, 1852	James	109 Barrow	
1607	Mansleville, Wm.	9	March 27, 1843	Feb. 23, 1846	John	3 Weehawken	
1608	Verlander, Eliza Ann	9	do.	April 26, 1847	Margaret	5th Ave. and 13th St.	
1609	Marseilles, John	9	April 25, 1843	Dec. 18, 1848	John	547 Broome	
1610	Acker, Mary E.	10	May 12, 1843	Jan. 22, 1844	Mrs.	153 Perry	
1611	Boardman, Rachel	8	do.	May 27, 1850	William	680 Greenwich	
1612	Capewell, Susan A.	7	May 29, 1843	do.	Mrs. Varick	69 King	
1613	Purdy, Catharine W.	6	June 29, 1843	Nov. 30, 1847	Abraham B.	250 Hudson	Oct. 29, 1845
1614	Purdy, Jas. W. (Vide Notes)	11	do.	May 26, 1845	do.	do.	Oct. 31, 1860
1615	Kelly, Charles Jerome	9	July 24, 1843	Nov. 25, 1840	Luke.	235½ Spring	
1616	Van Houten, Henry	8	do.	Sept 26, 1847	Jacob	15 Cornelia	Oct. 31, 1865
1617	Van Houten, Mary E.	12	do.	May 27, 1844	do.	do.	
1618	Van Houten, Sarah J.	10	do.	do.	do.	do.	
1619	Herdan, Peter	6	Sept. 25, 1843	Feb. 23, 1846	John	110 Barrow	Oct. 27, 1857
1620	Bogert, Wm. C.	6	do.	May 12, 1852	James	40 Crosby	Oct. 28, 1844
1621	Childs, Rebecca	6	do.	May 27, 1850	Christopher	123 Pitt	
1622	Somerindyke, William	13	do.	June 24, 1844	George	275 Spring	
1623	Verlander, Theodore	6	do.	April 26, 1847	Margaret	151 Waverley Place	
1624	Callow, Catharine A.	9	Oct. 3, 1843	Feb. 24, 1845	Rheula	250 West 18th	
1625	Colfax, Mary Jane	10	do.	June 30, 1845	Mrs. Haulenbeck, Sister	3 Troy	
1626	Brady, Abner S.	7	Nov. 27, 1843	April 3, 1848	Archibald C.	335 Fourth	
1627	Chapin, Henry A.	9	do.	Sept. 28, 1846	Augustus	11 Cornelia	
1628	Tinslay, Caroline	13	do.	Sept. 16, 1845	Thomas P.	105 Franklin	
1629	Varick, Joseph	9	do.	Nov. 1, 1844	Joseph, Grandfather	46 Amity	
1630	York, Jacob S.	10	do.	April 29, 1844	Sarah	138 Barrow	
1631	Higgins, William	8	Jan. 22, 1844	Oct. 31, 1844	Abraham Spader	47 Perry	
1632	Pullis, Sarah E.	11	do.	April 28, 1845	Nicholas	64 Grove	
1633	Magonigle, Mary	11	March 26, 1844	Sept. 29, 1845	John	47 Wooster	
1634	Noline, Mary Ann	8	do.	Feb. 24, 1845	Mrs. Pullis	64 Carmine	Oct. 31, 1860
1635	Banks, Ann Amelia	10	April 29, 1844	Feb. 23, 1846	Ann Eliza	10 Carmine	do.
1636	Banks, Obadiah	8	do.	Jan. 29, 1849	do.	do.	
1637	Chapin, James F.	7	do.	April 3, 1848	Augustus	11 Cornelia	
1638	Cromner, Joseph	10	do.	July 29, 1844	Albert	86 Sixteenth	
1639	Haulenbeck, James B.	7	do.	June 24, 1844	Mrs.	87 Perry	
1640	Kelly, Anna	7	do.	Nov. 30, 1846	Luke	225½ Spring	
1641	Kettleman, Maria	7	do.	Feb. 24, 1851	Elizabeth	31 Charles	

CATALOGUE OF SCHOLARS—Continued.

No.	Pupil.	Age	Admitted.	Withdrawn.	Parent.	Residence.	Graduated.
1642	Myers, Wm. Henry	11	April 29, 1844	May 25, 1846	Julia	261 Washington	Oct. 30, 1850
1643	Roe, Nathaniel	11	do.	July 29, 1844	Mrs. Joseph Varick	83 Amity	
1644	Stoll, George	12	do.	Oct. 26, 1846	George	183 Seventh	
1645	Tinslay, Hephzibah	8	do.	Feb. 25, 1847	Thomas P.	105 Franklin	
1646	Voorhis, Peter	7	do.	May 27, 1850	Richard	do.	Oct. 30, 1850
1647	Voorhis, Samuel	5	do.	July 25, 1844	do.	do.	
1648	Cregier, Ann Maria	6	May 27, 1844	March 30, 1846	Mrs. George C.	103 Eleventh	
1649	Mandeville, Elmira	10	do.	do.	Nicholas H.	71 Perry	
1650	Van Houten, Martha	6	do.	July 22, 1850	Jacob	15 Cornelia	Oct. 31, 1860
1651	Lefferts, Edward E.	11	June 24, 1844	May 27, 1851	William	154 Perry	
1652	Lefferts, William H.	13	do.	June 29, 1840	do.	do.	
1653	Lynch, Peter	8	July 29, 1844	May 29, 1848	Sophia	12 Gay	
1654	Ackerman, Frederick	13	Sept. 30, 1844	July 28, 1845	Mrs. Lefferts	5 Factory	Oct. 31, 1860
1655	Banks, William O.	13	do.	April 28, 1845	Ann Eliza	10 Carmine	Oct. 29, 1851
1656	Pettinger, Mat'w (Vide Notes)	13	do.	March 31, 1851	John	181 Varick	
1657	Vanderbilt, John J.	10	do.	June 30, 1845	Ann	31 Bethune	
1658	Vanderbilt, Peter J.	16	do.	May 26, 1845	do.	do.	
1659	Van Houghten, Alfred	9	do.	Feb. 26, 1846	Jacob	15 Cornelia	
1660	Van Houghten, John R.	11	do.	Oct. 28, 1846	Sarah	177 Amos	
1661	Mandeville, Edward	7	Nov. 1, 1844	April 27, 1846	Elizabeth	69 Fourth	
1662	Tinslay, William E.	7	do.	April 27, 1847	Thomas P.	105 Franklin	
1663	Van Ness, Benjamin H.	9	do.	May 26, 1845	Simon S.	168 West Seventeenth	
1664	Cadmus, Harrison F.	9	Nov. 25, 1844	Sept. 3, 1849	John K.	Bleecker and Barrow	Feb. 20, 1850
1665	Mandeville, David H.	9	Dec. 30, 1844	March 30, 1846	Nicholas H.	71 Perry	
1666	Stoll, Margaret	10	do.	June 29, 1846	George	183 Seventh	
1667	Conover, Ann Elizabeth	10	Jan. 27, 1845	April 25, 1849	Peter	66 Essex	
1668	Mandeville, Ellen	12	do.	March 30, 1846	Nicholas H.	71 Perry	
1669	Conover, Mary S.	6	Feb. 24, 1845	July 22, 1850	Peter	66 Essex	Feb. 20, 1850
1670	Lefferts, Mary	10	do.	Sept. 28, 1846	John H.	5 Factory	
1671	Van Ness, Sarah E.	10	do.	May 26, 1845	Simon S.	168 West Seventeenth	
1672	Conover, Cath. A.	8	April 28, 1845	July 22, 1850	Peter	66 Essex	Oct. 30, 1850
1673	Lyons, Jefferson W.	12	do.	May 25, 1846	Eleanor	Washington and Charles	
1674	McKibbin, Charlotte	9	do.	Nov. 30, 1846	Frances	Spring and Laurens	
1675	McKibbin, John	11	do.	Oct. 27, 1845	do.	do.	
1676	Moffat, John	7	do.	May 26, 1845	John	194 West Broadway	
1677	Van Houten, Maria J.	13	do.	March 29, 1847	Sarah	177 Amos	
1678	Van Ness, Maria	14	do.	May 26, 1845	Simon S.	168 West Seventeenth	
1679	Brady, Charles E.	7	May 26, 1845	Dec. 18, 1845	Archibald C.	335 East Fourth	

155

CATALOGUE OF SCHOLARS—Continued.

No.	Pupil.	Age	Admitted.	Withdrawn.	Parent.	Residence.	Graduated.
1680	Brady, James H.	7	May 26, 1845	Dec. 18, 1848	Archibald C.	335 East Fourth	Oct. 29, 1851
1681	Devoe, Edwin F.	7	do.	Sept. 29, 1851	Daniel	739 Washington, n. Troy	Oct. 27, 1852
1682	Devoe, Margaret Ann	8	do.	May 18, 1852	do.	do.	Oct. 27, 1852
1683	Lyons, Sarah W.	8	do.	May 27, 1850	Eleanor	Washington and Charles	Oct. 30, 1850
1684	Marselles, Adrian	9	do.	do.	John	547 Broome	
1685	Stoll, Catharine	7	do.	June 29, 1846	George	91 Ridge	
1686	Westervelt, William	10	do.	June 26, 1847	John	549 Broome	
1687	Herring, Charles E.	7	June 30, 1845	May 18, 1852	Eliza Cairns	85 Charlton	Oct. 27, 1852
1688	Banker, Susan J.	6	Sept. 16, 1845	April 28, 1851	Benjamin	15 East Thirteenth	
1689	Grascal, George	9	do.	Jan. 29, 1849	Frederick	145 Monroe	
1690	Grascal, Louisa	10	do.	May 31, 1847	do.	do.	
1691	Lippincott, Alfred B.	7	do.	Dec. 27, 1847	Henry	56 Greene	
1692	Mandeville, Mary C.	7	do.	March 30, 1846	Nicholas H.	345 Bleecker	
1693	McKibbin, George A.	7	do.	Sept. 26, 1847	Frances	4 Sixth Avenue	
1694	Roth, Jacob	7	do.	Feb. 28, 1853	William	317 Houston	
1695	Tinslay, Theodosia M.	6	do.	Nov. 29, 1847	Thomas P.	76 Greene	
1696	Birdsall, Constant	14	Sept. 29, 1845	March 30, 1846		240 Mercer	
1697	Capewell, Richard	7	Oct. 27, 1845	Nov. 29, 1852	Mrs. Varick, & ndm r	107 Greene	Oct. 27, 1852
1698	Hunneumunder, Mary	11	do.	June 29, 1846	Catharine	171 Allen	
1699	Heardman, Charles H.	8	Nov. 12, 1845	Oct. 26, 1846	William	630 Washington	
1700	Ratz, Dorotha	9	Nov. 24, 1845	Oct. 30, 1848	Maria	161 Christie	Oct. 25, 1848
1701	Roth, William G.	7	do.	May 24, 1852	George	77½ Norfolk	Oct. 27, 1852
1702	Elbert, Catharine E.	10	Dec. 29, 1845	Oct. 30, 1848	Henry	49½ Allen	
1703	Metnich, Henry	8	March 30, 1846	April 27, 1846	Jacob	204 Walker	
1704	Metnich, Jacob	9	do.	do.	do.	do.	
1705	Powles, Jacob (Vide Notes)	9	do.	March 25, 1850	Paul M.	148 Thompson	Oct. 29, 1851
1706	Voorhis, Calvin M.	9	do.	March 28, 1853	Richard	9 Cornelia	Oct. 31, 1865
1707	Wenz, Christian	11	do.	Feb. 25, 1847	Christian	94 Essex	Oct. 27, 1858
1708	Wenz, William	8	do.	Oct. 25, 1852	do.	do.	
1709	Ayers, Edgar	8	April 27, 1846	April 25, 1849	Daniel	177 Laurens	Oct. 28, 1847
1710	Ayers, Joseph B.	15	do.	June 28, 1847	do.	do.	
1711	Van Orden, Charles	8	do.	Feb. 26, 1849	Jane	183 Perry	
1713	Clendenin, Geo. (Vide Note)	7	June 29, 1846	June 28, 1847	Charlotte	23 Christopher	Oct. 29, 1851
1714	Conant, Charles F.	10	do.	March 31, 1851	Erastus D.	214 Seventh	
1715	Kyle, David	12	do.	June 28, 1847	W. F. Van Wagenen	Nineteenth	
	Nicholson, Elsie J. (Vide Notes)	8	do.	Oct. 31, 1853	E. S. Burras	199 Church	Oct. 26, 1853
1716	Bogert, Orrin S.	7	Sept. 28, 1846	April 24, 1855	James	40 Crosby	Oct. 31, 1855

CATALOGUE OF SCHOLARS—Continued.

No.	Pupil	Age	Admitted	Withdrawn	Parent	Residence	Graduated
1717	Lambertson, James M.	7	Sept. 28, 1846	June 28, 1852	David	14 King	......
1718	Maverick, Wm. H. (*Vide* Notes)	8	do.	do.	Mary	45½ Carmine	......
1719	Fowles, Henry	7	do.	March 25, 1850	Paul M.	148 Thompson	Oct. 31, 1860
1720	Wiseburn, Harriet S.	14	do.	April 26, 1847	Lawrence	do.	Oct. 30, 1859
1721	Wiseburn, Margaret	11	do.	July 22, 1850	do.	do.	Oct. 26, 1859
1722	Wenz, Augustus	7	do.	April 26, 1854	Christian	34 Essex	......
1723	Devoe, Frederick	7	Oct. 26, 1846	May 12, 1852	Rachel	151 Hammond	......
1724	Ketteman, George W.	7	do.	do.	Peter	1 Morton	......
1725	Ayers, Ann Augusta	8	Nov. 30, 1846	Nov. 21, 1848	Daniel	177 Laurens	......
1726	Ayers, Louiza J.	6	do.	do.	do.	do.	......
1727	Hoiskampfer, Direk	20	do.	March 29, 1847	John	35 Hammersly	......
1728	Lawson, Ann Elizabeth	8	do.	Sept. 27, 1847	do.	147 Laurens	......
1729	Lawson, Charlotte	6	do.	Nov. 29, 1847	do.	do.	......
1730	Lawson, Lydia	7	do.	do.	do.	do.	......
1731	Marshall, Jesse D. W.	11	Jan. 25, 1847	April 24, 1848	Henry V.	Avenue B and Fifth	Oct. 27, 1852
1732	Hoagland, William H.	9	Feb. 25, 1847	Nov. 25, 1849	Jacob	133 Mulberry	......
1733	Van Houten, John	7		Dec. 28, 1851		687 Greenwich	......
1734	Jelliffe, Samuel G. (*Vide* Notes)	9	March 29, 1847	May 12, 1852	William B.	34 Troy	......
1735	Melcin, Frederick	8	do.	Sept. 4, 1849	Solomon	96 Greene	......
1736	Melcin, Mortimer	10	do.	Jan. 10, 1849	do.	do.	......
1737	Spader, Marin	12	April 26, 1847	Nov. 29, 1847	Jonathan	83 Perry	Oct. 26, 1853
1738	Arkills, Mary E.	9	May 31, 1847	Oct. 31, 1853	Peter E.	589½ East Fourth	......
1739	Button, John	7	do.	Jan. 27, 1851	John, *Grandfather*	256 Ninth	......
1740	Clapon, Charles	7	do.	May 27, 1850	Augustus	151 Cornelia	Oct. 25, 1854
1741	Tallman, Dowah D.	11	do.	April 3, 1848	Peter	110 Bank	......
1742	Tallman, John H.	12	do.	do.	do.	do.	......
1743	Tinsley, Susannah	12	do.	Nov. 29, 1847	Thomas P.	105½ Greene	......
1744	Cadmus, Charles C.	9	June 28, 1847	May 29, 1848	John K.	48 Avenue D.	Oct. 27, 1852
1745	Dickhuoit, Catharine	9	do.	Nov. 29, 1852	Conrad	214 East Seventh	Oct. 25, 1848
1746	Edmonds, Catharine W.	12	do.	Oct. 25, 1848	Erastus D. Conant	318 Bleecker	......
1747	Hunt, Abigail	9	do.	Sept. 1, 1851	Eliza	634 Washington	Oct. 27, 1852
1748	See, Charles H.	8	do.	May 1, 1852	Joseph	39 Christopher	Oct. 25, 1848
1749	See, Margaret Ann	13	do.	Oct. 25, 1848	Cornelius	do.	......
1750	See, Mary E.	6	do.	do.	do.	do.	Oct. 25, 1848
1751	See, Sophia	12	do.	do.	do.	do.	Oct. 25, 1848
1752	See, William I.	10	do.	Nov. 21, 1851	do.	do.	

CATALOGUE OF SCHOLARS—Continued.

No.	Pupil.	Age	Admitted.	Withdrawn.	Parent.	Residence.	Graduated.
1753	Duckhout, Henry	8	Sept. 26, 1847	May 12, 1852	Conrad	48 Avenue D	Feb. 29, 1850
1754	Jones, Wm. D. (Vide Not. s)	13	do.	Jan. 28, 1850	Charles J	84 West Twentieth	do.
1755	McAdoo, Elizabeth R	12	do.	Oct. 16, 1849	Sarah	68 West Washington Place	
1756	McAdoo, Margaret A	9	do.	March 26, 1853	do.	do. do.	
1757	McAdoo, Sarah J	6	do.	Oct. 30, 1854	do.	do. do.	
1758	Neal, Wilhelmina	13	do.	Oct. 31, 1850	Jane, Sister	14 Orchard	Oct. 30, 1850
1759	Brady, Catharine Ann	5	Oct. 26, 1847	Nov. 21, 1848	Archibald C	449 East Fourth	
1760	Ciemleuin, Eliza	6	do.	Feb. 28, 1848	George	20 Factory	
1761	Gray, Maria T	8	do.	April 24, 1853	James	109 Barrow	Oct. 27, 1858
1762	Jones, Mary L	11	do.	Feb. 25, 1851	Charles J	84 West Twentieth	Oct. 29, 1851
1763	Jones, Sarah K	8	do.	Oct. 31, 1853	do.	do.	Oct. 26, 1853
1764	Knight, John L	17	do.	Feb. 28, 1848	Daniel	362 East Tenth	
1765	Blauvelt, Julia F	8	do.	July 28, 1851	Hartenbergh, StepF'r	143 Sixteenth	
1766	Butler, Emma	6	do.	July 24, 1848	Daniel	84 West Twentieth	
1767	Butler, Julia	8	do.	do.	do.	do.	
1768	Collins, Jesse	9	do.	May 28, 1849	Helen	Houston and Cottage Place	
1769	Collins, John P	5	do.	do.	do.	do.	
1770	Hulick, Lemmey	6	do.	April 28, 1851	Henry	15 Cornelia	
1771	Marshall, Hester Ann	10	do.	May 29, 1848	Margaret	Avenue B and Fifth	
1772	Myers, Sarah J	11	Nov. 29, 1847	April 3, 1848	Jane Ann	259½ Bleecker	
1773	Nicholson, Thomas D. W	7	do.	June 29, 1849	Eliza	199 Church	
1774	Reger, Nancy J	7	do.	May 31, 1858	Joseph	19 Burton	Oct. 27, 1858
1775	Maverick, Samuel	7	Dec. 27, 1847	Sept. 1, 1851	Mary	453½ Carmine	
1776	Overshultz, Mary	6	do.	May 28, 1855	Francis	24 Cornelia	
1777	Overshultz, Rebecca	10	do.	Sept. 30, 1850	do.	do.	
1778	Schilling, Herman	8	do.	May 28, 1849	Herman	7 Cornelia	
1779	Slingerland, Henry T	7	do.	Nov. 26, 1849	John V	83 Perry	
1780	Clark, William H	13	Feb. 28, 1848	May 29, 1848	Margaret Randolph	24 Wooster	Oct. 29, 1851
1781	Consklin, Mary E	10	do.	Jan. 27, 1851	Eliza, Grandmother	101 Charles	
1782	Mandeville, Thomas	13	do.	April 3, 1848	Leah	111 Perry	
1783	Myers, William E	9	do.	do.	John J	146 Sullivan	
1784	Rowland, William H	8	do.	do.	Tunis	29 Jane	
1785	Verbryck, Caroline	8	April 3, 1848	Oct. 27, 1851	Peter A	16 Morton	Oct. 29, 1856
1786	Arkills, James E	7	do.	Oct. 29, 1856	Peter E	387 East Fourth	
1787	Conant, George H	7	do.	April 24, 1854	Erastus D	214 East Seventh	
1788	Lefferts, Lydia Ann	9	do.	May 27, 1850	John B	5 Factory	
1789	Lyon, John H	7	do.	June 25, 1849	Alvin	14 Morton	
1790	Vehslage, Henry (Vide Note)	11	do.	Sept. 26, 1848	Henry	59 Houston	Oct. 27, 1858

CATALOGUE OF SCHOLARS—Continued.

No.	Pupil.	Age	Admitted.	Withdrawn.	Parent.	Residence.	Graduated.
1791	Westervelt, Garret H	13	April 3, 1848	May 12, 1852	Benjamin	31 Burton	Oct. 27, 1852
1792	Westervelt, Maria E	9	do.	Oct. 31, 1853	do.	do.	Oct. 26, 1853
1793	Anderson, Jacob	11	April 24, 1848	April 28, 1854	Albert	16 Morton	Oct. 29, 1851
1794	Mabie, Andrew E	7	do.	May 26, 1856	Peter	1 Bethune	Oct. 29, 1856
1795	Mabie, Cornelius	10	do.	Jan. 30, 1854	do.	do.	Oct. 25, 1854
1796	Vereance, Cath. L. E. (Vide Notes)	9	do.	Nov. 2, 1853	Richard	44 Downing	Oct. 26, 1853
1797	Clark, Aletta	7	May 29, 1848	Feb. 24, 1851	Margaret Jane	14 Commerce	
1798	Clark, Cornelia	9	do.	March 31, 1851	do.	do.	
1799	Haring, Henry	7	do.	Sept. 30, 1850	John	128 Hammond	
1800	He-keith, Joseph H	7	do.	Sept. 25, 1848	Joseph	739 Washington	
1801	Horton, Antoinette	8	do.	Sept. 24, 1849	James P.	12 Sixth Avenue	
1802	Moore, David	6	do.	Sept. 30, 1850	James	413 Hudson	
1803	Reger, Harriet A	7	do.	May 31, 1858	Joseph	81 Harrow	Oct. 27, 1858
1804	Voorhis, James	9	do.	Feb. 25, 1856	Richard	220 West Twenty-seventh	Oct. 29, 1856
1805	Webb, Charles E	12	June 26, 1848	Oct. 29, 1849	Jane A. Myers	3 Morton	
1806	Hoagland, Catharine W	8	July 24, 1848	May 26, 1851	Henry V.	133 Mulberry	
1807	Moore, Letitia	10	do.	Nov. 29, 1849	James	413 Hudson	
1808	McCain, John	8	Sept. 28, 1848	Dec. 19, 1853	Mary	83 Charlton	
1809	Porter, Mary	10	do.	Jan. 27, 1851	Thomas	29 Christopher	
1810	Anderson, Lavinia	6	Oct. 30, 1848	April 25, 1853	Albert	16 Morton	Oct. 31, 1860
1811	Brinckerhoff, John J	7	do.	Dec. 26, 1851	Henry V.	741 Greenwich	
1812	Lefferts, Lydia Ann	11	do.	Jan. 27, 1852	William	158 Perry	
1813	Lefferts, Sarah M	9	do.	Feb. 28, 1853	do.	do.	
1814	Lowe, Margaret	12	do.	May 27, 1850	Lawrence	6 Varick	
1815	Rothe, Henry E	8	do.	Oct. 29, 1855	George	77½ Norfolk	Oct. 27, 1858
1816	Weiler, Jacob	12	do.	July 22, 1850	Frederick	66 Avenue A	
1817	Haring, Ann	13	Nov. 27, 1848	Sept. 24, 1849	William	128 Hammond	
1818	Gallagher, Theodore H	9	Dec. 18, 1848	March 28, 1853	Leah Dyckman, 2^d du y		
1819	Baker, Edgar	11	Jan. 29, 1849	April 28, 1851	Dowling E.	154 Perry	Oct. 27, 1852
1820	Raymond, Charles	10	do.	June 25, 1849	Wm. A	17 Fourth	
1821	Bogert, David	12	Feb. 26, 1849	July 23, 1849	Caroline	40 McDougal	
1822	Bogert, Eugenia A	10	do.	Sept. 24, 1849	do.	do.	
1823	Demarest, Hannah J	10	do.	Oct. 31, 1853	Benjamin P.	15 Jones	
1824	Haring, Eliza	11	do.	April 30, 1851	William	128 Hammond	Oct. 29, 1851
1825	Mason, Sarah	10	do.	April 28, 1851	Jane Brown	87 Perry	Oct. 27, 1852
1826	Ruston, Charles (Vide Notes)	10	do.	Dec. 28, 1854	John G.	19 Bedford	Oct. 31, 1855
1827	Ruston, George	8	do.	Oct. 29, 1855	do.	do.	

CATALOGUE OF SCHOLARS—Continued.

No.	Pupil.	Age	Admitted.	Withdrawn.	Parent.	Residence.	Graduated.
1828	Sprouil, Henry S. (Vide Nota).	7	Feb. 26, 1849	Jan. 27, 1851	George V.	16 Cornelia	
1829	Jones, John J.	13	March 26, 1849	Oct. 29, 1849	Nicholas	131 Hammond	Oct. 25, 1854
1830	Jones, Stephen	9	do.	Jan. 30, 1851	do.	do.	do.
1831	Rabb, Ellen V.	11	April 25, 1849	March 26, 1855	William G.	581 Hudson	Oct. 28, 1857
1832	Rabb, Thomas Earle (Vide Note).	8	do.	March 26, 1856	do.	do.	Oct. 29, 1856
1833	Dufois, James	9	do.	Nov. 28, 1853	Grant	267 Seventh	Oct. 29, 1851
1834	Dufois, William L.	11	do.	Dec. 19, 1853	do.	do.	Oct. 25, 1854
1835	Ferdon, Garret	9	do.	May 29, 1854	Henry	86 Bedford	Oct. 27, 1852
1836	Jones, Emma G.	12	do.	Nov. 29, 1852	Nicholas	131 Hammond	Oct. 27, 1858
1837	McCain, Mary	6	do.	Jan. 26, 1857	Mary	11 East Thirteenth	Oct. 27, 1852
1838	Rabb, George F.	12	May 28, 1849	Feb. 23, 1852	William G.	581 Hudson	do.
1839	Bogert, Sarah J.	10	do.	May 12, 1852	Peter	11 Le Roy	
1840	Hall, Charles H.	10	do.	Feb. 25, 1850	Huldah	138 West Sixteenth	
1841	Hall, Huldah	8	do.	Oct. 30, 1851	do.	do.	
1842	Hall, Sarah F.	6	do.	do.	do.	do.	
1843	Jones, Lucinda	0	do.	Oct. 29, 1855	Charles J.	332 Bleecker	Oct. 31, 1855
1844	Steins, Frederick W.	12	do.	June 24, 1850	Rev. Frederick	122 Broome	Oct. 31, 1860
1845	Steins, Gustavus	9	do.	May 26, 1851	do.	do.	
1846	Steins, Herman C.	13	do.	May 27, 1850	do.	do.	Oct. 31, 1860
1847	Childs, Andrew	7	June 25, 1849	May 26, 1856	Mary	685 East Fourth	
1848	Hickok, Cordelia N.	6	do.	Jan. 27, 1851	Preston	10 Greenwich Avenue	
1849	Hickok, Sarah A.	13	do.	July 28, 1851	do.	do.	Oct. 29, 1851
1850	Kieler, Charles	11	July 23, 1849	March 31, 1851	Elizabeth	297 Division	
1851	See, Ann Margaret	9	do.	Feb. 25, 1850	Isaac	332 Bleecker	
1852	Mauri, Julia C. M.	9	Sept. 30, 1849	Oct. 23, 1849	Louis	21 Cornelia	
1853	Bogarden, James	13	Nov. 26, 1849	Nov. 29, 1852	Richard	115 Bedford	
1854	Decker, William	11	do.	May 28, 1853	Eliza	25 Bethune	
1855	McCain, Elizabeth	11	do.	Nov. 28, 1853	Mary	11 East Thirteenth	
1856	Pettiner, Joseph (Vide Note).	7	do.	May 25, 1857	John	354 Hudson	Oct. 28, 1857
1857	Ackerman, Jacob D.	8	Jan. 28, 1850	Oct. 29, 1856	David	5 Morton	Oct. 29, 1856
1858	Ackerson, Almira	12	do.	July 22, 1850	John	49 Anthony	
1859	Ackerson, Charles P.	8	do.	May 27, 1850	do.	do.	
1860	Anderson, Daniel A.	10	do.	Nov. 29, 1852	Albert	16 Morton	Oct. 27, 1852
1861	Annin, Sarah L.	7	do.	do.	Catharine E.	127 Christopher	
1862	Archer, Catharine	10	do.	July 22, 1850	Floyd D.	69 Morton	
1863	Archer, Mary	7	do.	do.	do.	do.	

CATALOGUE OF SCHOLARS—*Continued.*

No.	Pupil	Age	Admitted	Withdrawn	Parent	Residence	Graduated
1864	Bogert, Garret	8	Jan. 28, 1850	Jan. 31, 1853	Peter	11 Le Roy	
1865	Devoe, Mary M	7	do.	Feb. 27, 1854	Daniel	84 Hammond	
1866	Ferdon, James H	7	do.	Oct. 29, 1853	Henry	86 Bedford	
1867	Ferdon, John	12	do.	May 30, 1853	do.	do.	Oct. 26, 1853
1868	Heppe, Otto	11	do.	May 26, 1851	Lisette	39 Norfolk	
1869	Hickok, Benjamin	11	do.	Oct. 25, 1857	Preston	10 Greenwich Avenue	
1870	Hulick, Anna L.	6	do.	Dec. 19, 1853	Henry	16 James	
1871	Johnson, Amelia	7	do.	Dec. 23, 1850	William	43½ Carmine	
1872	Johnson, Martha	13	do.	Sept. 30, 1850	do.	do.	
1873	Kettleman, Catharine	8	do.	March 26, 1855	Peter	138 West Sixteenth	
1874	Lefferts, John B.	8	do.	March 25, 1850	John B.	5 Factory	
1875	Metzgar, John V.	10	do.	Dec. 27, 1850	Christiana	201 Seventh	
1876	Newbrunner, Wm	11	do.	Jan. 26, 1852	Christian	48 First Avenue	
1877	Ryerson, Cornelius	8	do.	May 27, 1850	Abigail	105 Grove	
1878	Ryerson, George	8	do.	Sept. 12, 1853	do.	do.	
1879	Smith, Charles	8	do.	Sept. 30, 1850	Anna	38 Perry	
1880	Tamson, Sarah	8	do.	June 24, 1852	Hardenbrook, *Step*	69 Sixth Avenue	
1881	Tamson, Wardell	7	do.	Feb. 23, 1852	do.	do.	
1882	Tamson, William	13	do.	Feb. 24, 1851	do.	do.	
1883	Velsdage, William	10	do.	Nov. 29, 1852	Henry	207 Fifth, cor. Avenue B	Oct. 27, 1858
1884	Westervelt, Catherine D	12	do.		James P.	727 Greenwich	Oct. 27, 1852
1885	Westervelt, David	9	do.	March 27, 1854	do.	do.	
1886	Westervelt, James	7	do.	Oct. 25, 1854	David	5 Morton	
1887	Ackerman, Rachel J	6	Feb. 25, 1850	Nov. 29, 1858	Conrad	613 Fourth	Oct. 27, 1858
1888	Beekman, Magdalen	8	do.	Nov. 29, 1852	John	48 First Avenue	Oct. 27, 1852
1889	Bogert, Christian	7	do.	May 12, 1852		do.	
1890	Lateshar, Mary	12	do.	Jan. 3, 1854	Catharine	457 Sixth Avenue	Oct. 27, 1851
1891	Munson, Chas. R. (*Vide Note*)	9	do.	May 29, 1854	do.	do.	
1892	Munson, George V.	6	do.	Oct. 29, 1855	Alfred	117 Perry	
1893	Rice, Emma	8	do.	June 28, 1852	do.	do.	
1894	Rice, Theodore	10	do.	Sept. 12, 1853	William	48 First Avenue	
1895	Roth, Hannah	9	March 25, 1850	Oct. 17, 1856	Peter E.	675 Fourth	Oct. 29, 1856
1896	Atkills, Lydia A. (*Vide Note*)	9	do.	Nov. 28, 1853	Philip	18 Jane	
1897	Brackerhoff, John W.	11	do.	April 27, 1857	Benjamin	15 Jones	Oct. 28, 1857
1898	Demarest, Cornelius V. R.	7	do.	March 29, 1858	Jacob C.	129 Hammond	Oct. 29, 1856
1899	Haring, Dan'l J. (*Vide Note*)	8	do.	Oct. 29, 1856	Jane	22 Le Roy	
1900	Palmer, John H		do.	Oct. 30, 1851	Christian	236 Stanton	
1901	Schaver, Frederica	11	do.				

M

CATALOGUE OF SCHOLARS—Continued.

No.	Pupil.	Age	Admitted.	Withdrawn.	Parent.	Residence.	Graduated.
1902	Clark, William W	10	April 22, 1850	Feb. 24, 1851	Stephen	28 Amos	
1903	{ Dombaski, Charles	8	do.	July 28, 1851	Mary	75 Avenue A	
	do. do.	11	Dec. 18, 1854	April 24, 1855	Philip S	164 Attorney	
1904	Haulenbeck, Mary F	7	April 22, 1850	April 28, 1851	Tunis	30 Troy	
1905	Valentine, Henry M	9	do.	do.	Henry M	155 Laurens	
1906	Allen, James	7	May 27, 1850	March 31, 1851	Mary	McDougal	
1907	Black, Eliza Jane	10	do.	Oct. 31, 1853	Eliza	48 Avenue D	Oct. 26, 1853
1908	Clark, Priscilla	6	do.	March 31, 1851	James M	14 Commerce	
1909	Ross, James	12	do.	Jan. 27, 1851	Nancy	96 Ridge	
1910	Ryerson, Eliza J	6	do.	June 29, 1857	Abigail	10½ Grove	
1911	Ferdon, James A	9	June 24, 1850	Oct. 29, 1855	John	101 Varick	
1912	Ferdon, Sarah C	10	do.	do.	do.	do.	Oct. 27, 1858
1913	Smith, Charles E	13	do.	May 12, 1852	John A	638 Washington	Oct. 31, 1855
1914	Williamson, Henry V	11	do.	April 28, 1851	John	300 Mott	Oct. 27, 1852
1915	Ferdon, David	7	July 24, 1850	April 24, 1855	Jacob B	87 West Twenty-eighth	
1916	Ferdon, James S	12	do.	May 30, 1853	do.	do.	Oct. 26, 1853
1917	Ferdon, Margaret	10	do.	Dec. 19, 1853	do.	do.	
1918	Oethermann, Augustus	10	do.	Sept. 1, 1851	Peter	104 Attorney	
1919	Steins, Victor H	6	do.	Oct. 1, 1850	Rev. Frederick	122 Broome	
1920	Kelsey, Sarah M	8	Sept. 1, 1850	April 28, 1851	Job	282½ Fifth	
1921	Roth, Elizabeth	7	do.	May 26, 1856	George	77½ Norfolk	
1922	Bakewell, George W	10	Oct. 1, 1850	Feb. 27, 1854	Joseph	59 Fourth	
1923	Bakewell, Milton	7	do.	Nov. 27, 1854	do.	do.	
1924	Barth, Mary Elizabeth	12	do.	Sept. 29, 1851	Charles	157 Second	
1925	Clark, Abraham	9	do.	Dec. 28, 1851	Daniel D	78 Jane	
1926	Clark, Peter	10	do.	Oct. 30, 1850	do.	do.	
1927	Larkins, Ellen M	13	do.	Sept. 12, 1853	Daniel Colyer	23 Christopher	
1928	{ Sproull, William O	11	Feb. 26, 1855	Jan. 27, 1851	George V	16 Cornelia	
	do. do.	7	Oct. 1, 1850	May 26, 1856	do.	661 Greenwich	
1929	Talman, Martin	10	do.	July 28, 1851	Rachel	29 Le Roy	
1930	Van Orden, Edward	8	do.	May 30, 1853	Jane	31 Downing	
1931	Williamson, George H	7	do.	March 28, 1853	John	300 Mott	
1932	Anderson, Maria A	6	Nov. 1, 1850	Nov. 27, 1860	Albert	16 Morton	Oct. 31, 1860
1933	Palmer, Peter (Vide Notes)	12	do.	May 30, 1853	Jane	22 Le Roy	Oct. 26, 1853
1934	Van Dyk, Francis C	13	do.	Nov. 29, 1852	Maria F	93½ Fourth Avenue	Oct. 27, 1852
1935	Hahn, Elizabeth	8	Dec. 27, 1850	May 26, 1856	Christian	48 First Avenue	Oct. 29, 1856
1936	Cook, Francis W	10	Jan. 27, 1851	May 25, 1857	Jacob	234 West Eighteenth	Oct. 28, 1857
1937	Cook, Peter A	7	do.	May 31, 1858	do.	do.	Oct. 27, 1858

CATALOGUE OF SCHOLARS—Continued.

No.	Pupil.	Age	Admitted.	Withdrawn.	Parent.	Residence.	Graduated.
1938	Demarest, John K. (*Vide Note*)	7	Jan. 27, 1851	Nov. 30, 1858	Jasper	550 Broome	Oct. 28, 1857
1939	McKay, Francis J.	7	do.	Sept. 1, 1852	Hester J.	81 Hanersley	....
1940	Colgrove, Ann E.	10	Feb. 24, 1851	April 24, 1854	William	330 Bleecker	....
1941	McPherson, Ann M.	11	do.	Oct. 27, 1851	Alexander	450 Twelfth	....
1942	McPherson, Donald	13	do.	May 17, 1852	do.	do.	....
1943	McPherson, John	13	do.	Sept. 1, 1851	do.	do.	....
1944	Reichmann, Chas	12	do.	do.	Henry	139 Third	....
1945	Roberts, Ellen L.	10	do.	May 26, 1851	Pattillow	337 Bleecker	Oct. 29, 1856
1946	Vanderbilt, Mary C., *Vide Note*	9	do.	Oct. 27, 1856	Cornelius	15 Cornelia	Oct. 26, 1853
1947	Vanderbilt, Sarah L., *Vide Note*	12	do.	Nov. 28, 1853	do.	do.	Oct. 26, 1859
1948	Wenz, Elizabeth	6	do.	May 31, 1859	Christian	63 Norfolk	Oct. 31, 1860
1949	Wenz, Maria L.	9	do.	May 26, 1856	do.	do.	Nov. 14, 1861
1950	Bogert, James O.	8	March 31, 1851	May 29, 1860	James	40 Crosby	Oct. 26, 1859
1951	Hrant, Mary W.	10	do.	Oct. 30, 1854	John C.	53 Troy	do.
1952	Hrant, Sophia E.	8	do.		do.	do.	....
1953	Lefferts, Harriet	10	do.	Oct. 27, 1851	Harmon	9 Commerce	....
1954	Cook, Rachel E.	6	April 28, 1851	May 31, 1859	Jacob	234 West Eighteenth	Oct. 27, 1858
1955	Eagleson, Fanny	10	do.	Oct. 29, 1855	William Alexander	730 Broadway	do.
1956	Eagleson, James H.	8	do.	Nov. 30, 1858	do.	do.	Oct. 31, 1860
1957	Eagleson, Mary E.	11	do.	Dec. 18, 1854	do.	do.	Oct. 27, 1858
1958	See, John Jacob	8	do.	Jan. 27, 1854	George	198 West Twenty-first	Oct. 28, 1857
1959	Van Orden, Sarah A., *Vide Note*	8	do.	Nov. 30, 1857	Jane	31 Downing	....
1960	Williamson, Albert V.	10	do.	March 28, 1853	John	300 Mott	....
1961	Barth, Caroline	11	May 26, 1851	Sept. 29, 1851	Charles	157 Second	....
1962	Eagleson, Sarah J.	7	do.	Nov. 24, 1856	William Alexander	730 Broadway	Oct. 31, 1860
1963	Langdon, Cornelia	13	do.	Oct. 27, 1851	William R.	120 Hammond	....
1964	Loromer, Cornelia	12	do.	Jan. 26, 1852	James A.	Greenwich & Hammond	....
1965	Loromer, John	7	do.	do.	do.	do.	....
1966	Stoller, John J.	8	July 28, 1851	Nov. 24, 1851	John J.	49½ Allen	....
1967	Bogert, Euphemia	11	do.	Dec. 19, 1853	Mary	170 West Twenty-sixth	Oct. 25, 1854
1968	Ferdon, Andrew T.	7	do.	May 26, 1856	Henry	86 Bedford	....
1969	Koeker, Louisa	12	do.	Oct. 27, 1851	William	134 Third	....
1970	Mabie, Henry P.	8	do.	Feb. 22, 1858	Peter	1 Bethune	Oct. 27, 1858
1971	Altenhain, Charles	9	Sept. 1, 1851	May 29, 1854	John	289 Sixth Avenue	Oct. 25, 1854
1972	Giffing, Isaac A.	8	do.	Oct. 29, 1856	Isaac H.	53 Bank	Oct. 29, 1856
1973	Giffing, William C.	7	do.	May 31, 1858	do.	do.	Oct. 27, 1858
1974	Keller, Antoinette	8	do.	April 24, 1854	John W.	551 Fourth	Oct. 29, 1856
1975	Kircheis, Alex't F. (*Vide Note*)	10	do.	Oct. 29, 1856	Frederick	483 Sixth Avenue	

CATALOGUE OF SCHOLARS—Continued.

No.	Pupil.	Age	Admitted.	Withdrawn.	Parent.	Residence.	Graduated.
1976	Kircheis, Chas. A. (*Vide Notes*)	8	Sept. 1, 1851	April 27, 1857	Frederick	483 Sixth Avenue	Oct. 28, 1857
1977	Kircheis, Wm. H. (*Vide Notes*)	10	do.	Oct. 29, 1856	do.	do.	Oct. 29, 1856
1978	Koeker, William	10	do.	Oct. 27, 1851	William	134 Third	
1979	Rott, Jacob	10	do.	May 29, 1854	Martin	613 Fourth	
1980	Van Dyk, Henry M.	15	do.	Nov. 29, 1852	Maria E.	95½ Fourth Avenue	Oct. 25, 1854
1981	Smith, Margaret Ellen	11	Sept. 29, 1851	Jan. 30, 1854	John A.	638 Washington	
1982	Bakewell, Louisa	13	Oct. 27, 1851	May 29, 1854	Joseph	59 Fourth	
1983	Bogardus, Julia E.	6	do.	April 27, 1857	Richard	115 Bedford	
1984	Clendenin, Thomas	13	do.	Nov. 29, 1852	Adam	188 Seventh	
1985	Van Der Weyde, Peter H.	13	do.	do.	Peter H.	N. Y. University	
1986	Hasie, Charles	7	Nov. 24, 1851	May 12, 1852	Mark N.	579 Grand	
1987	Hasie, Montague	10	do.	do.	do.	do.	
1988	Keller, Louis	10	do.	May 29, 1854	John W.	551 Fourth	
1989	Kline, Elizabeth W.	11	do.	Oct. 27, 1856	Jacob	51 Le Roy	Oct. 29, 1856
1990	Kline, Margaretta	8	do.	April 24, 1854	do.	do.	
1991	Thorburn, Bithiah B.	13	do.	do.	James R.	81 West Eleventh	Oct. 25, 1854
1992	Thorburn, Isabella G.	11	do.	do.	do.	do.	Oct. 27, 1858
1993	Wichelhouse, Chas.	10	do.	Oct. 30, 1854	Charles	140 Greenwich Avenue	
1994	Van Der Weyde, John J.	12	Dec. 29, 1851	Sept. 26, 1853	Peter H.	N. Y. University	
1995	Blauvelt, Helen M.	13	Jan. 26, 1852	Nov. 29, 1854	David	735 Greenwich	Oct. 25, 1854
1996	Bogert, Samuel P.	7	do.	April 30, 1854	Mary	170 Twenty-sixth	
1997	Merritt, Julia F.	7	do.	May 31, 1853	Frederick	128 Sixth Avenue	
1998	Del Noy, Virginia	7	March 29, 1852	July, 1853	John M.	214 Bleecker	
1999	Kip, Araminta	12	do.	June 28, 1852	Rachel	151 West Twenty-sixth	
2000	Berry, John M.	10	May 12, 1852	Nov. 30, 1857	John	109 Christopher	Oct. 31, 1860
2001	Blauvelt, John D.	9	do.	May 26, 1856	David D.	735 Greenwich	
2002	Bogert, N. I. Marseius (*Vide Notes*)	9	do.	Sept. 27, 1852	William	82 Charles	
2003	Brant, John C.	7	do.	Oct. 29, 1855	John C.	49 Troy	
2004	Demarest, Ann Maria	12	do.	Nov. 29, 1852	Samuel	640 Washington	Oct. 28, 1857
2005	Demarest, Cath. Amanda	8	do.	Nov. 30, 1857	Cornelius	122 Amos	
2006	Demarest, Samuel E.	10	do.	Nov. 29, 1856	Abraham	124 Amos	
2007	Devoe, John	8	do.	Dec. 19, 1853	Daniel W.	84 Hammond	
2008	Disbrow, Emily J.	12	do.	April 24, 1855	Thomas R.	651 Greenwich	Oct. 27, 1858
2009	Disbrow, Stephen L.	7	do.	Oct. 29, 1855	do.	do.	
2010	Jones, Charles H.	7	do.	Feb. 25, 1856	Charles	332 Bleecker	Oct. 31, 1860
2011	Kircheis, Louis P. (*Vide Notes*)	7	do.	Nov. 30, 1857	Frederick	306 Eighth Avenue	Oct. 28, 1857
2012	Stryker, James V. W.	7	do.	Nov. 28, 1853	Peter J.	54 Sixth Avenue	

164

CATALOGUE OF SCHOLARS—Continued.

No.	Pupil.	Age	Admitted.	Withdrawn.	Parent.	Residence.	Graduated.
2013	Van Der Weyde, Jos. J.	6	May 12, 1852	Nov. 29, 1852	Peter H.	N. Y. University, 33 W. Washington Pl.	
2014	do.	7	Jan. 30, 1854	March 27, 1854	do.	do.	
2014	Ellerman, Mary A	12	June 26, 1852	Sept. 12, 1853	Adam Lutz	334 Houston	
2015	Sexton, Abraham	8	do.	May 30, 1853	William	1 Minetta Place	
2016	Demarest, Ephraim H.	11	Sept. 13, 1852	March 29, 1858	David S.	345 West Twenty-fourth	Oct. 28, 1857
2017	Demarest, Marg't Ann	8	do.	Nov. 30, 1858	do.	do.	Oct. 27, 1858
2018	Waugh, James	12	do.	May 30, 1853	James L.	112 Franklin	
2019	Clark, Catalina C	11	Sept. 27, 1852	Dec. 24, 1855	Cornelia	32 Perry	Oct. 28, 1857
2020	Perrine, Frances	10	do.	Nov. 30, 1857	Jane	352 Bleecker	Oct. 31, 1860
2021	Perrine, Julia	8	do.	Nov. 27, 1860	do.	do.	
2022	Reynolds, Irwin	12	Oct. 25, 1852	July 25, 1853	G. G. Smith, *Guard'n*	76 Tenth	
2023	Hodaling, Harriet A	6	Nov. 1, 1852	do.	Samuel, *Guardian*.	127 Amity	
2024	Martin, Eliza J	10	do.	Sept. 12, 1853	Margaret	304 Ninth	
2025	Martin, Ellen	7	do.	do.	do.	do.	
2026	Atkinson, Elizabeth	14	Nov. 29, 1852	Oct. 25, 1854	Wilhelmina	322 Bowery	Oct. 25, 1854
2027	Christie, Gamaliel	11	do.	do.	Christian W	1 King	
2028	Croitus, Josephine	12	do.	Nov. 30, 1858	John	32 Perry	Oct. 27, 1858
2029	Hahn, John	9	do.	Oct. 25, 1859	Christian	48 First Avenue	Oct. 26, 1859
2030	Christie, Maria E	7	Dec. 27, 1852	Nov. 30, 1858	Christian W	1 King	Oct. 27, 1858
2031	Gurnee, Ellen	11	do.	Jan. 30, 1854	Francis W	650 Washington	
2032	Vanderbilt, Cornelius	8	Jan. 31, 1853	May 25, 1857	Cornelius	15 Cornelia	Oct. 26, 1859
2033	Gallagher, Benjamin D.	7	do.	March 28, 1853	Martha	192 Grand	
2034	Gallagher, Wm. E	8	do.	do.	do.	do.	
2035	Waugh, Henry M	13	Feb. 28, 1853	May 30, 1853	James L.	112 Franklin	
2036	Lanier, Charles	7	March 28, 1853	do.	Charles, *Uncle*	267 Seventh	
2037	Beeker, Herman R	7	do.	Jan. 25, 1858	Henriette	20 Seventeenth	
2038	Demarest, James Henry		do.	Nov. 30, 1858	Cornelius	122 Amos	Oct. 31, 1860
2039	McKee, Thos. W (*vide Notes*)	7	April 25, 1853	May 31, 1858	Beulah Atkinson	322 Bowery	Oct. 27, 1858
2040	Bogardus, Alfred M	11	do.	Feb. 25, 1856	Cornelius	18 Commerce	
2041	Bogardus, Cornelius	9	do.	do.	do.	do.	
2042	Bogardus, E. Webster	13	do.	Sept. 12, 1853	do.	do.	
2043	Duffois, Catharine	8	do.	May 26, 1856	Catharine	214 Seventh	Oct. 21, 1863
2044	Duffois, Gertrude	10	do.	do.	do.	do.	Oct. 29, 1856
2045	Ottignon, Alice	8	do.	May 31, 1859	Lucy	13 Cornelia	do.
2046	Ottignon, Claudius	12	do.	Oct. 29, 1855	do.	do.	
2047	Ottignon, Mary F	10	do.	April 27, 1857	do.	do.	
2048	Beach, Anna C	9	May 30, 1853	Nov. 30, 1858	David	80 Fourth	Oct. 27, 1858

CATALOGUE OF SCHOLARS—Continued.

No.	Pupil.	Age	Admitted.	Withdrawn.	Parent.	Residence.	Graduated.
2049	Niemann, Mary	7	May 30, 1853	Nov. 30, 1858	Henry W	620 Greenwich	Oct. 27, 1858
2050	Ruston, John F	7	do.	May 26, 1856	John D	87 Jane	
2051	Wilson, John	10	June 29, 1853	Nov. 29, 1856	William	5 La Fayette Place	
2052	Wilsem, Margaret	12	do.	Oct. 29, 1856	do.	do.	
2053	Diehl, John Jacob (*Vide Notes*)	7	Sept. 12, 1853	May 25, 1857	Jacob	133 Essex	
2054	Dolde, Elizabeth	9	do.	May 29, 1860	John	Avenue B and Sixth	Oct. 31, 1860
2055	Ferdon, Frances	7	do.	May 26, 1859	Henry	86 Bedford	Oct. 26, 1859
2056	Ferdon, Stephen L	7	do.	Jan. 31, 1860	John	7 Bethune	Oct. 26, 1859
2057	Gerhauser, Margaret	9	do.	May 26, 1850	do.	172 Second	
2058	Gerhauser, Mary A	7	do.	do.	do.	do.	
2059	Kemp, Wm. M. (*Vide Notes*)	7	do.	Oct. 29, 1855	William	Avenue B and Fifth	
2060	Nebsiage, Mary	7	do.	May 25, 1857	Henry	Avenue B and Fifth	Oct. 26, 1859
2061	Westervelt, Charles	10	do.	Oct. 30, 1854	John	64 Twenty-ninth	
2062	Powell, Emily B	10	Sept. 26, 1853	Nov. 30, 1857	Elisha	5 Hammond	
2063	Ackerson, Eunice A	9	Oct. 31, 1853	Nov. 27, 1854	Eunice	33 Fourth	Oct. 28, 1857
2064	Ackerson, James T	7	do.	do.	do.	do.	
2065	Black, Robert	11	do.	June 26, 1854	Elizabeth	41 Avenue D	
2066	Cowing, Charles J	11	do.	Dec. 19, 1853	Henry Hulick	116 Christopher	
2067	Lewis, Gertrude D. B	10	do.	May 28, 1855	Abraham	367 Eighth	
2068	Vanderbilt, Richard	13	do.	April 24, 1854	John H	130 Barrow	
2069	Vanderbilt, William	8	do.	do.	do.	do.	
2070	Dilloway, Georgine	17	Nov. 28, 1853	May 29, 1854	George W	461 Eighth Avenue	
2071	Galsberg, Wm. C	12	do.	Oct. 30, 1854	Charles	Ridge	
2072	Wemlover, Olivia (*Vide Notes*)	16	do.		Peter P	99 Christopher	
2073	Bedford, Augustus	9	Dec. 29, 1853	Oct. 29, 1856	Augustus	72 Fourth	Oct. 25, 1854
2074	Wilson, Joseph	9	do.	Jan. 25, 1858	John T	113 Bank	Oct. 26, 1859
2075	Cooke, Leah M	10	Jan. 30, 1854	Nov. 27, 1860	Jacob	35 Eighth Avenue	
2076	Wilsey, Louisa	11	do.	Nov. 16, 1858	Henry P	279 Bleecker	Oct. 31, 1860
2077	Wilsey, Mary C	9	do.	May 25, 1857	do.	do.	Oct. 28, 1857
2078	Wilsey, Sarah J	9	do.	May 31, 1858	do.	do.	Oct. 31, 1860
2079	Hammond, Theodore A	12	Feb. 27, 1854	April 26, 1854	Joseph	115 Bank	
2080	Roth, Julia	8	do.	May 29, 1860	George	77½ Norfolk	
2081	Westervelt, Cornelius A	7	do.	Oct. 25, 1854	James P	727 Greenwich	
2082	Ferdon, Abraham	7	March 27, 1854	Oct. 29, 1855	Jacob B	132 Perry	
2083	Giffing, John Ferguson	7	do.	Nov. 27, 1860	Isaac H	53 Bank	
2084	Mabie, Richard	8	do.	Feb. 25, 1856	Abraham	134 Perry	Oct. 31, 1860
2085	Sunter, Theodore	11	do.	April 26, 1854	James Glass	234 Bleecker	

CATALOGUE OF SCHOLARS—Continued.

No.	Pupil.	Age	Admitted.	Withdrawn.	Parent.	Residence.	Graduated.
2086	Ashenfelder, Anna B.	9	April 24, 1854	May 26, 1856	Philip.	105 First.	......
2087	Bemarest, Jane	6	do.	March 27, 1860	Jasper.	556 Broome.	......
2088	Hahn, Jacob.	7	do.	April 30, 1861	Christian.	91 First.	Nov. 14, 1861
2089	Green, Catharine	11	May 29, 1854	Oct. 29, 1855	Ellen Harrington.	673 Greenwich.	......
2090	Hartman, Henry	11	June 26, 1854	May 26, 1856	Margaret.	285 Bowery.	......
2091	Baker, William F.	14	Sept. 25, 1854	April 23, 1855	John R.	123 Sheriff.	......
2092	Blauvelt, Kate M.	9	do.	Nov. 29, 1859	Harriet.	95 McDougal.	Oct. 31, 1860
2093	Brown, Wm. H.	7	do.	Nov. 30, 1857	John G.	456 Sixth Avenue.	......
2094	Butz, Henry	8	do.	Nov. 29, 1859	Frederick.	249 Sullivan.	Oct. 26, 1859
2095	Frost, Georgiana	15	do.	Oct. 29, 1855	Abraham, G'd father.	94 Seventh.	Oct. 27, 1858
2096	Howland, Wm. W.	7	do.	Sept. 24, 1855	William.	15 Bethune.	......
2097	Huyler, Henrietta	6	do.	Oct. 27, 1863	James.	235 Sullivan.	Oct. 21, 1863
2098	Huyler, Mary F.	13	do.	Jan. 28, 1862	do.	do.	Nov. 14, 1861
2099	Pray, George.	10	do.	Nov. 27, 1854	Henry.	38 Hammond.	......
2100	Veholage, Charles	9	do.	May 25, 1857	do.	Avenue B and Fifth.	Oct. 26, 1859
2101	Wheeler, Albert	12	do.	Dec. 18, 1854	Edward, Grandfather.	46 Bedford.	......
2102	Wheeler, Charles	10	do.		do.	do.	......
2103	Wheeler, Sarah	7	do.	March 26, 1855	do.	do.	......
2104	Arkills, Charles F.	12	Oct. 30, 1854	Feb. 25, 1862	Peter E.	674 Fourth.	Nov. 14, 1861
2105	Genin, Louis E. (Vide Notes)	7	do.	March 27, 1860	Erastus.	22 Greene.	Oct. 31, 1860
2106	Nick, Jacob.	13	do.	April 23, 1855	Bernhard.	57 Pearl.	......
2107	Bedford, John S.	8	Nov. 27, 1854	Nov. 9, 1856	Augustus.	99 Amos.	......
2108	Case, Julia D.	9	do.	May 26, 1856	Orrin.	324 Bowery.	......
2109	Lange, Anna	11	do.		Charles W.	263 Bleecker.	......
2110	Lange, Clara	7	do.	Nov. 24, 1856	do.	do.	......
2111	Lange, Ida	9	do.		do.	do.	......
2112	Ware, Jane	9	do.	May 25, 1857	{ Rev. N. J. Marselus, Guardian. }	46 Hammond.	......
2113	Dilloway, Godfrey	12	Dec. 18, 1854	Sept. 24, 1855	George W.	464 Eighth Avenue.	......
2114	Bartholf, Leah Jane	9	Jan. 29, 1855	May 31, 1859	Lettice.	285 Bleecker.	Oct. 27, 1858
2115	Brant, Abraham	7	do.	Oct. 29, 1855	John C.	49 Troy.	......
2116	Dilloway, Catharine	14	do.	Sept. 24, 1855	George W.	464 Eighth Avenue.	......
2117	Dilloway, Elizabeth	14	do.	do.	do.	do.	......
2118	Elbert, Caroline	9	do.	April 23, 1855	Catharine.	318 Ninth.	......
2119	Elbert, Wm. H.	7	do.	do.	do.	do.	......
2120	Wenzel, George	11	do.	Nov. 29, 1856	John H.	134 Attorney.	......
2121	Brown, Charles E.	13	Feb. 26, 1855	Oct. 29, 1855	Matthias.	89 Cannon.	......
2122	Van Wagenen, Cornelia	15	do.	Nov. 30, 1857	Catharine.	229 Ninth.	Oct. 28, 1857

CATALOGUE OF SCHOLARS—Continued.

No.	Pupil.	Age	Admitted.	Withdrawn.	Parent.	Residence.	Graduated.
2123	Walser, Emil (Vide Notes)	16	Feb. 26, 1855	Oct. 29, 1855	Edward	Staten Island	Oct. 31, 1860
2124	Berdan, Abby L	8	March 26, 1855	April 27, 1857	James	748 Washington	
2125	Berdan, Mary E	6	do.	do.	do.	do.	
2126	Harman, Margaret	9	do.	March 27, 1860	Margaret	285 Bowery	Oct. 31, 1860
2127	Hitchcock, James R. (Vide Notes)	14	do.	May 26, 1856	Daniel R	Staten Island	Oct. 26, 1859
2128	Bogardus, Mary	6	April 24, 1855	April 27, 1857	Richard	102 Bedford	
2129	Horaceman, Francis	10	do.	Nov. 28, 1857	Amelia	561 Fourth	
2130	Crolius, James W	7	do.	Nov. 27, 1860	John	32 Perry	Oct. 30, 1860
2131	Hopper, Calvin	7	do.	May 29, 1856	Garret J	103 Amos	
2132	Parker, Henrietta	11	do.	May 26, 1856	Rev. Charles	West Hoboken	
2133	Parker, Julia M	13	do.	do.	do.	do.	
2134	McArdle, Catharine	7	May 28, 1855	Nov. 27, 1860	Christiana	Cor. Hammersley and Greenwich	
2135	McArdle, Mary	9	do.	Nov. 29, 1859	do.		
2136	McGregor, Cara L	8	do.	May 26, 1856	Rev. Edwin R	203 W. Twenty-seventh	
2137	Roth, Charles (Vide Notes)	7	do.	April 30, 1861	George	77½ Norfolk	Oct. 21, 1863
2138	Powles, Euphemia (Vide Notes)	7	June 25, 1855	Oct. 27, 1863	John H	11 Cornelia	Oct. 31, 1863
2139	Powles, James E	9	do.	April 24, 1860	do.	do.	
2140	Presler, Charles	7	do.	May 26, 1856	George	112 Sixth	
2141	Bedford, Harriet A	7	Sept. 24, 1855	Nov. 29, 1856	Augustus	99 Amos	
2142	Clarke, Walter S	8	do.	do.	Henry	141 Christopher	
2143	Demarest, Francis Eugene	7	do.	June 24, 1862	David S	345 W. Twenty-fourth	
2144	Letman, Emma	10	do.	May 29, 1860	Henry	115 Union Place, Hoboken	Oct. 26, 1859
2145	Letman, George W	11	do.	May 31, 1858	Henry	do.	Oct. 27, 1858
2146	Crum, Emma F	6	Oct. 29, 1855	Nov. 25, 1864	Henrietta	348 Hudson	Nov. 25, 1864
2147	Crum, Frederick H	8	do.	Sept. 30, 1862	do.	do.	Nov. 29, 1862
2148	Ginnn, Nancy E	6	do.	April 29, 1862	Erastus	22 Greene	Nov. 2, 1864
2149	Parker, Frank	8	do.	May 26, 1856	Rev. Charles	West Hoboken	
2150	Parker, Laura	7	do.	do.	do.	do.	
2151	Blanche, Emma A	10	Nov. 26, 1855	Nov. 29, 1859	John H	644 Hudson	Oct. 26, 1859
2152	Garretson, Charity	11	do.	Nov. 24, 1856	Abraham	153 Perry	
2153	Dearing, James	8	Dec. 24, 1855	May 26, 1856	Catharine	284 W. Twenty-sixth	
2154	Ostrom, Julia (Vide Notes)	16	do.	Nov. 30, 1857	Ann, Sister	101 Sixth Avenue	Oct. 28, 1857
2155	Wenzel, Albert F	7	do.	Jan. 28, 1862	Henry	134 Attorney	Oct. 29, 1862
2156	Wenzel, Herman	10	do.	May 31, 1859	do.	do.	
2157	Dewitt, Joseph C. H	14	Feb. 25, 1856	May 26, 1856	Gasherie	125 Sixteenth	
2158	Roth, Catharine	12	March 31, 1856	Nov. 24, 1856	William	Houston Street Church	
2159	James, Cath. E. (Vide Notes)	14	May 26, 1856	Nov. 30, 1857	Levi Onderdonk	95 Bank	Oct. 28, 1857

CATALOGUE OF SCHOLARS—Continued.

No.	Pupil.	Age	Admitted.	Withdrawn.	Parent.	Residence.	Graduated.
2260	Goodrich, Sarah A	14	June 30, 1856	May 31, 1859	Sarah	169 East Seventeenth	
2261	Hopper, Cornelius A	8	do.	Nov. 30, 1857	Abraham C	93 Charles	
2262	Mabie, Ann E. (*Vide Notes*)	9	do.	Feb. 23, 1864	Peter	7 Hethune	Oct. 21, 1863
2263	Ferdon, Abraham	7	Sept. 27, 1856	Jan. 31, 1860	John	do.	
2264	Hyne, Frances	12	Nov. 25, 1862	May 26, 1865	do.	226 S. First, Jersey City.	
2265	Hyne, Mary	6	Sept. 27, 1856	Dec. 19, 1859	Joseph W	6 King	
2266	Letsnan, Robert L	8	do.	Nov. 29, 1859	do.	do.	
2267	Leipold, Robt. H. T. (*Vide Notes*).	14	do.	Sept. 29, 1864	Henry	15 Union Pl., Hoboken.	
2268	Mott, Emma J	8	do.	Nov. 30, 1857	Charles Wm	211 Fifth	
2269	Mott, Sarah C. (*Vide Notes*)	10	do.	Oct. 27, 1863	Israel A	62 Amos	Oct. 21, 1863
2270	Colwell, Charles G	10	Oct. 6, 1856	April 29, 1862	do.	do.	Nov. 14, 1864
			Jan. 31, 1860	Jan. 25, 1858	Lewis	307 West Twenty-fourth	
2271	Lefferts, Anna	13	Oct. 29, 1856	March 27, 1860	do.	do.	
2272	Veen, Adrian	9	do.	Feb. 25, 1862	William	158 Perry	Oct. 29, 1862
2273	Veen, Cornelia	7	do.	Sept. 24, 1861	Dirck Jan	163 Christie	
2274	Vredenburgh, Alfred P	10	do.	March 27, 1860	do.	do.	Oct. 31, 1860
2275	Bartholf, Lydia Ann	8	do.	Nov. 27, 1860	do.	do.	do.
2276	Colwell, Warren A	6	Jan. 26, 1857	June 24, 1862	Alfred	673 Houston	Oct. 29, 1862
2277	Dean, Lemuel P	14	do.	Jan. 28, 1862	Jno. Haywood, *Siefy'y*	278 Bleecker	
2278		7	do.	April 27, 1857	Lewis	307 West Twenty-fourth	Oct. 26, 1859
2279	Wilsey, Elizabeth A	6	Oct. 2, 1860	May 26, 1858	John H	18 Cornelia	Oct. 21, 1863
		9	Feb. 23, 1857	May 31, 1858	Henry P	279 Bleecker	
2280	Moir, Archibald S	10	March 30, 1857	Jan. 28, 1862	William	do.	
2281	Anderson, Lorena	8	do.	May 27, 1862	Albert	23 Minetta	May 30, 1866
2282	Carpenter, Robert L	10	do.	May 31, 1866	Henry	6 Ninth Avenue	
2283	Clarkson, John S	16	do.	Nov. 30, 1857	Charles	29 Harrison.	
2284	Cottrell, Israel A	7	do.	May 31, 1859	Israel A. Mott	Staten Island	Oct. 27, 1858
2285	Mead, John W	11	do.	March 31, 1864	John H	62 Amos	
2286	Baker, Oscar	9	April 27, 1857	Dec. 19, 1859	Mary	7 Jones	
2287	Lippold, Henry F. (*Vide Note*)	12	do.	April 30, 1861	Augustus F	148 Perry	
2288	Stager, Ann Amelia		do.	April 24, 1860	Abraham	42½ Norfolk	Oct. 31, 1860
2289	Veen, William V	7	do.	Nov. 30, 1858	Dirck Jan	387 Ninth Avenue	Oct. 27, 1858
2290	Voorhis, Sarah J	8	do.	Sept. 28, 1865	Nicholas K	167 Christie	
2291	Acker, Laura G	15	May 25, 1857	May 31, 1859	John H	78 Horatio	
			Sept. 29, 1864	June 24, 1862	do.	4 Vandam	
2292	Beckar, Louisa	8	May 25, 1857	Nov. 30, 1865	William	do.	
				Nov. 29, 1859		105 Wooster	

CATALOGUE OF SCHOLARS—Continued.

No.	Pupil.	Age	Admitted.	Withdrawn.	Parent.	Residence.	Graduated.
2193	Blanche, Chas. A.	9	May 25, 1857	Sept. 29, 1863	John H.	236 West Seventeenth	Oct. 21, 1863
2194	Hauuquet, Charles	12	do.	Nov. 30, 1857	Louisa	273 West Thirty-seventh	......
2195	Hauuquet, Louisa	10	do.	do.	do.	do. do.	......
2196	Hauuquet, Virginia	9	do.	do.	do.	do. do.	......
2197	Lehmkuhl, Geo. H. (Vide Note)	9	do.	May 31, 1859	John H.	188 Seventh	Oct. 31, 1860
2198	{ Reger, Louisa	6	do.	Nov. 30, 1857	Joseph.	918 Broadway	......
			Oct. 2, 1860	Nov. 22, 1866	do.	55 West Twenty-first.	
2199	Roth, Caroline	10	May 25, 1857	Sept. 24, 1861	George	77¼ Norfolk	......
2200	Vreilenburgh, Frank	6	do.	May 26, 1863	Alfred	673 Houston	......
2201	Wurster, Louisa	7	do.	Nov. 30, 1857	William	21 Greenwich Avenue	......
2202	Gayler, Ellen H.	13	do.	May 26, 1864	Sarah	116 Christopher	......
2203	Gayler, Jessie	8	do.	Nov. 25, 1864	do.	do.	Nov. 2, 1864
2204	Hahn, William	8	do.	Sept. 28, 1865	Christian	91 First	......
2205	Ackerman, Peter D.	7	July 27, 1857	Nov. 25, 1863	David	177 Christopher	......
2206	Cleverley, Wm. (Vide Notes)	15	do.	Nov. 30, 1858	Thomas	240 West Forty-second	Oct. 27, 1858
2207	Myers, Gabriel D.	7	do.	Sept. 29, 1863	John J.	24½ Christopher	......
2208	{ Acker, Frances	13	Sept. 28, 1857	Nov. 29, 1859	John B.	4 Vandam	......
		17	Sept. 28, 1861	Jan. 28, 1862	do.	209 Bleecker	Oct. 31, 1860
2209	Anderson, Jessie	11	do.	May 28, 1861	John	21 Clark	......
2210	Anderson, Martha	7	do.	Nov. 29, 1849	do.	do.	......
2211	Dunshee, James	8	do.	Jan. 31, 1860	James	235 Sullivan	Nov. 2, 1864
2212	Huyler, James S.	7	do.	Feb. 25, 1862	do.	21 Minetta Lane	......
2213	Jeffrey, Mary J.	10	do.	Nov. 30, 1858	William	21 Hammond	......
2214	Marrener, James H	10	do.	Oct. 30, 1860	David J.	71 Eighth Avenue	......
2215	Van Dyke, Wm. L. (Vide Note)	8	Oct. 30, 1857	Sept. 29, 1863	Peter	102 West Twentieth	......
2216	Dunn, Sarah F.	13	Jan. 25, 1858	Nov. 30, 1858	Matthew S.	117 Christopher	Oct. 21, 1863
2217	Mason, Anna Melissa	9	do.	May 26, 1863	George	7 Bethune	......
2218	{ Ferdon, George W	7	Feb. 22, 1858	Jan. 31, 1860	John	226 S. First, Jersey City	......
		11	Nov. 25, 1862	May 26, 1863	do.	15½ Frankfort	......
2219	Steinhaus, Wilhelmina	10	Feb. 22, 1858	Nov. 30, 1858	Christine	46 S. Fifth, Williamsb'gh	Nov. 14, 1861
2220	Dunn, Henry	12	Oct. 2, 1860	Jan. 28, 1862	Nancy	27 Cornelia	......
2221	Haight, John E. B.	10	March 29, 1858	May 31, 1859	John E. B.	43 McDougal	Oct. 31, 1860
2222	Rose, Ann Eliza	9	do.	Nov. 30, 1858	Edwin S.	236 West Seventeenth	......
2223	Blanche, Ann Amelia	14	do.	Nov. 27, 1860	John H.	251 Seventh Avenue	Oct. 21, 1863
2224	Hornmann, Chas. G.	8	May 31, 1858	Nov. 25, 1864	Amelia	42 East Fourth	Oct. 29, 1862
2225	Duval, John E.	9	do.	Feb. 24, 1863	Rev. Richard Horton	53 Vandam	Nov. 2, 1864
2226	Little, Helen A. (Vide Notes)	7	do.	March 25, 1864	Thomas		

CATALOGUE OF SCHOLARS—Continued.

No.	Pupil.	Age	Admitted.	Withdrawn.	Parent.	Residence.	Graduated.
2227	Moore, Mary A.	11	May 31, 1858	Nov. 30, 1858	Myron K.	127 Sullivan	
2228	Moore, Willis L.	9	do.	do.	do.	do.	
2229	Scott, Amelia G.	9	do.	May 30, 1860	James	119 Sullivan	
2230	Van Saun, Samuel S.	9	do.	April 30, 1861	Samuel J.	119 Greenwich	Nov. 14, 1861
2231	Hall, Mary Ann	9	June 24, 1858	Nov. 30, 1858	Mary Ann	786 Greenwich	
2232	Martyn, Sarah A.	7	do.	May 26, 1863	Benjamin	202 Spring	
2233	{ Trins, Johanna	6	do.	Jan. 28, 1862	Joachim	151 Waverley Place	Nov. 2, 1864
				May 26, 1864	do.	86 Grove	
2234	Hoagland, Anna I.	11	July 1, 1863	Oct. 27, 1863	Catharine	56 Sixth Avenue	Oct. 21, 1865
2235	Mason, George II.	7	Sept. 28, 1858	May 26, 1863	George	117 Christopher	
2236	McKibben, Charles C.	7	do.	April 24, 1860	Frances	148 Wooster	Oct. 31, 1860
2237	Norris, Wm. C.	12	do.	Nov. 29, 1859	Daniel S.	17 Christopher	
2238	Oram, Jane A.	13	do.	Oct. 27, 1863	James D.	158 Mott	Oct. 21, 1863
2239	Pine, Charles II	13	do.	Oct. 30, 1860	Charles II	156 Wooster	
2240	Roof, Mary Anna	12	do.	Dec. 19, 1859	Jane A.	192 Bleecker	
2241	Thorne, Elizabeth II	7	do.	Sept. 24, 1861	Richard	78 Horatio	
2242	Voorhis, George W.	7	do.	May 30, 1867	John R	222 W. Twenty-seventh	May 23, 1867
2243	Wilson, Eliza F.	8	do.	Nov. 27, 1860	William T	9 Morton	
2244	Wood, Lula	8	do.	Oct. 27, 1863	John II.	14 McDougal	Oct. 21, 1863
2245	Hyne, Charles II	7	Oct. 26, 1858	May 29, 1860	Charles II.	37 King	
2246	Pitman, James M	10	do.	Nov. 27, 1860	William E.	190 Hudson	
2247	Trusdell, Samuel	7	do.	May 27, 1870	Samuel	122 Hamersley	
2248	Norris, Julia P.	11	Nov. 30, 1858	May 28, 1861	Daniel S.	17 Christopher	
2249	Quackenbush, James N.	8	do.	Jan. 26, 1864	James J.	749 Washington	
2250	Norris, Sarah M	15	Dec. 21, 1858	Nov. 27, 1860	Daniel S.	17 Christopher	
2251	Johnson, Maggie II	7	Jan. 25, 1859	do.	Elizabeth II	Sixth Avenue	
2252	Krechting, John P. (Vide Note)	20	do.	May 31, 1859	Jeremiah Lanphier	Tammany Hall	Oct. 31, 1860
2253	Marrener, Edward	14	do.	Dec. 19, 1859	David J.	21 Hammond	
2254	Wenzel, Adolph C.	7	do.	March 30, 1865	Henry	59 Attorney	May 30, 1866
2255	Wilson, Wm. T.	11	do.	March 25, 1862	Margaret Hughes	7 Cherry	Oct. 29, 1862
2256	Allen, Frances A	11	Feb. 22, 1859	Oct. 27, 1863	Henry A.	233 Sullivan	Oct. 21, 1863
2257	{ Allen, Kate.	8	do.	Nov. 25, 1864	do.	do.	
				May 30, 1867	do.	do.	May 23, 1867
2258	Worth, Mary E.	14	Sept. 28, 1865	March 30, 1865	Marian	150 W. Forty-seventh	
2259	Worth, Sydney B.	11	Feb. 25, 1859	do.	do.	191 West Fourth	
2260	Campbell, Adolphus W.	8	do.	March 26, 1860	Theo. F. Pruden	do.	Oct. 31, 1860
2261	Jordan, Wm. B. M.	14	April 30, 1859	Nov. 25, 1862	Philip	208 W'hington, Hobok'n	Oct. 29, 1862
2262	Jordan, Louis C. Levin	10	do.	Oct. 27, 1863	do.	148 West Thirty-third	Oct. 21, 1863

CATALOGUE OF SCHOLARS—Continued.

No.	Pupil.	Age	Admitted.	Withdrawn.	Parent.	Residence.	Graduated.
2263	Marshall, Delia	9	April 30, 1859	Sept. 24, 1861	Elvin F	742 Washington	....
2264	Patterson, Robert I	9	do.	Dec. 19, 1859	Caroline	31 Christopher	....
2265	Patterson, Augustus F	8	do.	do.	do.	do.	....
2266	{ Soper, Julia F	8	do.	Sept. 30, 1862	Charles	do.	....
2267	Acker, Josephine C	15	Sept. 28, 1865	June 24, 1862	do.	27 Barrow	....
2268	Baldwin, Harris J	7	May 31, 1859	Nov. 22, 1866	John B	41 Harrow	Oct. 21, 1863
2269	Baldwin, Lucy E	8	do.	Sept. 29, 1863	Andrew H	4 Vandam	Nov. 2, 1864
2270	Brady, William H	12	do.	Nov. 25, 1864	do.	4 Warren Place	....
2271	Corwin, Mary E	8	do.	Jan. 30, 1865	John H	136 Amity	....
2272	Fergusson, Thomas	14	do.	Nov. 27, 1860	John B	43 McDougal	Oct. 31, 1860
2273	Giffing, Anna M	11	do.	May 29, 1860	Robert	6 Walker	....
2274	Giffing, John D	13	do.	Feb. 23, 1864	William H	151 West Seventeenth	Oct. 29, 1862
2275	Haight, Julia	11	do.	May 27, 1862	do.	do. do.	....
2276	Lawson, Miller	7	do.	March 27, 1860	John W	81 Hudson	....
2277	Lownds, Cornelius V. C.	12	do.	Jan. 28, 1862	James M	107 Hammond	....
2278	Mayereau, Louisa	10	do.	May 29, 1860	Jacob	44 Charlton	Nov. 2, 1864
2279	Tracy, Edward P	12	do.	Nov. 25, 1864	Bernard A	254 Hudson	Oct. 29, 1862
2280	Tracy, John N	10	do.	April 28, 1862	Caleb C	103 Greenwich Avenue	do.
2281	Tracy, William H	7	do.	Feb 26, 1865	do.	do.	....
2282	Hanshe, Grace	7	June 28, 1859	Jan. 28, 1862	John	16 Christopher	....
2283	Styles, Harriet H	13	do.	Dec. 19, 1859	James	567 Broome	....
2284	Wendover, Thomas P	7	do.	Oct. 29, 1861	Thomas P	8 Jones	Nov. 14, 1861
2285	Ackerman, Peter I. (Vide Note.)	13	Sept. 27, 1859	do.	John H	Washington St., Hoboken	....
2286	Beach, Emma	11	do.	Nov. 29, 1860	David	80 West Fourth	....
2287	Bedford, Eleanor	6	do.	Oct. 29, 1861	Harriet	99 West Tenth	May 30, 1866
2288	Root, P. Edward	6	do.	Jan. 25, 1866	Peter	332 West Sixteenth	....
2289	Ferguson, William L	11	do.	Oct. 27, 1863	Robert	6 Walker	....
2290	Haight, Georgiana	7	do.	March 27, 1860	John W	81 Hudson	....
2291	Leifman, Amelia	9	do.	Oct. 27, 1864	Henry	15 Union Place, Hobok'n	....
2292	Runk, William B	6	do.	Oct. 29, 1860	William T	36 Seventh Avenue	....
2293	Scott, Mary Isabella	13	do.	May 29, 1860	James J	119 Sullivan	....
2294	Tully, John	6	Oct. 25, 1859	June 24, 1861	Alexander	124 Bank	Oct. 29, 1862
2295	Bogert, Alice	6	do.	May 30, 1867	Stephen	53 West Fourth	May 23, 1867
2296	Moir, Elizabeth	6	do.	April 29, 1862	William	21 Minetta	....
2297	Murvihill, Fanny	15	do.	Sept. 29, 1863	Marcella	177½ West Fourth	....
2298	Tully, Thomas	12	Nov. 29, 1859	Nov. 27, 1860	Alexander	124 Bank	Nov. 14, 1861
2299	Carrer, Alida			do.	Charles T. Bogert	86 Bedford	....

CATALOGUE OF SCHOLARS—Continued.

No.	Pupil.	Age	Admitted.	Withdrawn.	Parent.	Residence.	Graduated.
2300	Dusenberry, Henry K.	10	Nov. 29, 1859	Sept. 29, 1864	William H.	32 Morton.	
2301	Homan, Charles A.	10	do.	March 27, 1860	Thomas.	156 Hammond.	
2302	Homan, Marsalons.	8	do.	do.	do.	do.	
2303	Martin, William V.	7	do.	Feb. 25, 1862	John S.	10 Carroll Place.	
2304	Morris, Louis C. L.	10	do.	Sept. 24, 1861	John H.	280 West Thirty-third.	
2305	Dexter, Emma	7	Dec. 22, 1859	Jan. 28, 1862	Esther C.	16 Sixth Avenue.	
2306	Morris, Florence V.	11	do.	Oct. 29, 1861	John H.	280 West Thirty-third.	
2307	Ward, Frances.	12	do.	May 28, 1861	Thomas P. Wemlover.	8 Jones.	
2308	Heacock, William C. B.	6	Feb. 28, 1860	Nov. 27, 1860	Spencer.	200 Prince.	
2309	Hopper, James F. F.	9	do.	Oct. 30, 1862	Garret J.	103 Amos.	
2310	Voorhees, Annie I.	9	do.	Sept. 29, 1864	Edward M.	157 Laurens.	Oct. 29, 1862
2311	Unkel, Otto.	11	March 27, 1860	Jan. 28, 1862	Charles.	39 Avenue A.	May 30, 1866
2312	Anderson, Alfred.	7	April 24, 1860	Sept. 28, 1865	Albert.	74 Horatio.	
2313	Tompkins, Marietta.	12	do.	Sept. 30, 1865	John.	776 Washington.	
2314	Wood, Evelyn.	7	do.	March 29, 1866	Thomas.	72 Hammond.	
2315	Wood, Juliana L.	6	do.	Nov. 24, 1864	John H.	14 McDougal.	
2316	Doremus, Sarah	10	May 29, 1860	Sept. 29, 1863	Daniel.	76 Horatio.	
2317	Jones, Emeline	11	do.	June 24, 1862	John.	721 Houston.	
2318	Jones, Mary L.	10	do.	do.	do.	do.	
2319	Jordan, Eleanor N.	7	do.	Sept. 28, 1865	Philip.	282 W. Twenty-second	
2320	Pitman, Lucy A.	10	do.	Nov. 27, 1860	William E.	Bleecker.	
2321	Zulauf, John H.	11	do.	Oct. 27, 1863	John.	112 Greenwich	Oct. 21, 1863
2322	Ackerman, John A.	8	June 26, 1860	May 25, 1865	Henry.	8 Irving Pl., Hoboken	
2323	Ackerman, Christie.	7	Oct. 2, 1860	do.	do.	do.	
2324	Clark, Mary E.	13	do.	May 27, 1861	Anna T.	233 Bleecker.	Oct. 29, 1862
2325	Dusenberry, William P.	7	do.	Oct. 24, 1864	William H.	32 Morton.	
2326	Kidd, Charles W.	8	do.	Oct. 31, 1867	William.	84 Grove.	April 30, 1868
2327	Lowry, Sarah F.	14	do.	May 27, 1862	Charles.	65½ Greenwich.	
2328	Morris, Robert S.	6	do.	Sept. 29, 1864	Helen.	63 East Fourth.	
2329	Morris, William.	7	do.	Oct. 29, 1861	John H.	35th St. and Broadway.	
2330	Okie, Phebe	12	do.	Jan. 28, 1862	Martin.	100 Barrow.	
2331	Reger, Alisla.	7	do.	Dec. 23, 1869	Joseph.	55 West Twenty-first.	
2332	Thorne, George.	10	do.	Nov. 27, 1860	Sarah.	703 Washington.	
2333	Veen, Eva Marie.	8	do.	Jan. 26, 1865	Dirck Jan.	42 Delancey.	
2334	Berry Mandeville.	8	Oct. 30, 1860	April 26, 1865	John S.	321 W. Twenty-fourth.	
2335	Gessner, Angeline S.	6	do.	March 25, 1862	Matilda.	58 Grove.	
2336	Hyde, Emma J.	7	do.	Sept. 24, 1861	Henry P.	9 Barrow	
2337	Van Deusen, Lydia	11	do.	Dec. 21, 1863	Robert D.	76 Christopher.	

CATALOGUE OF SCHOLARS—Continued.

No.	Pupil.	Age	Admitted.	Withdrawn.	Parent.	Residence.	Graduated.
2338	Van Deusen, Robert H	14	Oct. 30, 1860	April 29, 1862	Robert D	76 Christopher	Oct. 29, 1862
2339	Van Deusen, William F	7	do.	Oct. 27, 1864	do.	do.	Nov. 2, 1864
2340	White, Catharine E	12	do.	Nov. 25, 1864	Catharine W	18 Vandam	
2341	Armstrong, Charles O	10	Nov. 27, 1860	Jan. 28, 1862	William W. Hedges	180 Fourth	
2342	Brown, Alice Knox	7	do.	May 28, 1861	Anna M	160 West Twelfth	
2343	Minor, Jacob	16	Dec. 18, 1860	April 30, 1861	Elizabeth	94 West Twentieth	
2344	Wood, Henrietta L	11	do.	Jan. 28, 1862	Jacob B	14 McDougal	Oct. 21, 1863
2345	Van Thof, Isaac	23	Jan. 29, 1861	Sept. 30, 1862	Self	415 Ninth Avenue	
2346	Blauvelt, Elizabeth L	11	Feb. 26, 1861	May 26, 1864	John P	64 Grove	
2347	Blauvelt, Rachel C	10	do.	Feb. 22, 1866	Mary	do.	May 30, 1866
2348	Morrell, Emma	14	do.	April 29, 1862	do.	East Fifty-third	Oct. 29, 1862
2349	Morrell, Robert N	11	do.	do.	do.	do.	
2350	Giffing, Sarah Emily	7	March 26, 1861	Feb. 23, 1864	William H	151 West Seventeenth	
2351	Lehnkuhl, Margaret C	11	do.	Jan. 28, 1862	John H	339 East Ninth	
2352	Mandeville, Emeline	10	do.	Dec. 21, 1865	Samuel	258 West Thirty-third	
2353	Mandeville, James B	14	do.	Nov. 25, 1862	do.	do.	
2354	Mandeville, Millard	8	do.	Dec. 21, 1865	do.	do.	Oct. 21, 1863
2355	Martin, Charles	7	do.	Feb. 25, 1862	John S	107 Waverley Place	
2356	Post, Josephine	9	do.	June 25, 1868	Aaron	258 West Thirty-third	
2357	Rogers, Ph. Smith	13	do.	March 25, 1862	Nicholas	260 West Thirty-third	
2358	Stager, Abraham	7	do.	Nov. 24, 1863	Abraham	do.	
2359	Stager, George A	12	do.	Nov. 25, 1862	do.	do.	Oct. 29, 1862
2360	Adams, Charles F	11	April 30, 1861	Feb. 25, 1863	Charles	157 West Thirty-third	
2361	Brower, John L	7	do.	Nov. 25, 1864	William H	425 8th Ave., cor. W. 32d	
2362	Dusenberry, Susan A	15	do.	Nov. 25, 1862	William H	32 Morton	Oct. 29, 1862
2363	Genin, Thaddeus	8	do.	April 29, 1862	Erasmus	325 West Fifteenth	
2364	Knight, Charles P	10	do.	May 26, 1864	Daniel	72 West Thirty-seventh	
2365	Van Voorhis, Aaron	8	do.	May 25, 1865	John L	247 West Thirty-second	
2366	Willard, John E. (Vide Notes)	8	do.	May 30, 1867	John W	21 Cornelia	May 23, 1867
2367	Zulauf, Charles F	8	do.	Jan. 28, 1862	John	112 Greenwich	
2368	Huyler, Abraham L	7	May 28, 1861	Feb. 23, 1863	James S	235 Sullivan	
2369	Lefferts, Benjamin	7	do.	May 26, 1864	William	158 Perry	
2370	Voorhis, Charles W	14	do.	Sept. 30, 1869	John K	222 W. Twenty-seventh	
2371	Blauvelt, Isaac M	6	June 25, 1861	March 25, 1862	John P	64 Grove	
2372	Derr, Hester	11	do.	Oct. 31, 1867	John C	194 Seventh Avenue	
2373	Derr, Hobart	8	do.	April 28, 1863	do.	do.	
2374	Green, Charles E	10	do.	March 29, 1866	Jonathan	282 West Forty-second	
2375	Green, Ella J	10	do.	Feb. 23, 1865	do.	do.	

CATALOGUE OF SCHOLARS—Continued.

No.	Pupil.	Age	Admitted.	Withdrawn.	Parent.	Residence.	Graduated.
2376	Porter, Esther G.	7	June 25, 1861	March 31, 1863	Alexander M.	453 Hudson	Oct. 21, 1863
2377	Porter, Mary E.	12	do.	do.	do.	do.	
2378	Demarest, Ebenezer	9	Sept. 28, 1861	Nov. 25, 1862	David S.	95 Ninth Avenue	
2379	Ennis, Geraldine	6	do.	May 30, 1867	John J.	84 West Twenty-ninth	
2380	Lehmkuhl, John W.	8	do.	Jan. 28, 1862	John H.	339 Ninth	
2381	Lowry, Charles	11	do.	May 27, 1862	Charles	651 Greenwich	
2382	Menges, Josephane	13	do.	Nov. 25, 1862	Magdaleene	256 West Thirty-fifth	
2383	Menges, Julia	15	do.	April 29, 1862	do.	do.	
2384	Morris, Helen D.	6	do.	May 31, 1866	Helen	63 Fourth	
2385	Powles, Margaretta	10	do.	Sept. 30, 1862	John H.	11 Cornelia	
2386	Ulmer, Traugott	10	do.	March 30, 1865	Dorah	103 West Thirty-first	
2387	White, Benjamin F.	10	do.	April 28, 1864	William Moir	21 Minetta Lane	
2388	Wood, Jane E.	13	do.	Sept. 29, 1863	Isaac	121 West Twenty-fourth	
2389	Ramsen, Henry C.	7	Oct. 28, 1861	May 30, 1867	Isaac E.	143 West Thirtieth	May 20, 1869
2390	Stephens, Anna H.	9	do.	May 27, 1869	James	158 West Thirty-fifth	
2391	Stephens, Thomas G.	7	do.	Sept. 30, 1869	do.	do.	
2392	Voorhees, Elizabeth C. B.	15	do.	Nov. 25, 1864	Edward M	68 West Forty-eighth	Oct. 29, 1862
2393	Baldwin, Addie	9	Nov. 26, 1861	Jan. 30, 1863	Albina	153 West Thirty-third	
2394	Baldwin, Annie	6	do.	Nov. 25, 1864	do.	do.	
2395	Baldwin, Phebe J.	10	do.	do.	do.	do.	
2396	Barkley, Ella	9	do.	do.	John C.	208 West Thirtieth	
2397	Barkley, Sarah	8	do.	do.	do.	do.	
2398	Bennet, Sarah Elizabeth	9	do.	Sept. 29, 1863	Sarah R.	58 West Twenty-ninth	
2399	Clinton, Isabella	12	do.	June 30, 1864	Elizabeth McEvoy	350 West Thirty-fifth	
2400	Darr, Christina	9	do.	April 26, 1865	George	557 First Avenue	May 30, 1866
2401	Fox, Lewis	7	do.	Nov. 25, 1864	David	152 West Thirty-first	
2402	Fox, Edward	5	do.	March 31, 1863	do.	do.	
2403	Hues, Alice	8	do.	Sept. 29, 1864	Alexander	368 West Thirty-fifth	
2404	Hues, Henry L.	13	do.	Sept. 29, 1863	do.	do.	Oct. 21, 1863
2405	Hoffman, Anna	12	Nov. 26, 1861	Sept. 28, 1865	John G	98 West Twenty-fourth	Nov. 2, 1864
2406	Hoffman, George C.	11	do.	Nov. 25, 1864	do.	do.	
2407	Jordan, Mary H. S.	10	do.	Sept. 28, 1865	Philip	186 West Twenty-fifth	
2408	Kuntz, Jacob	10	do.	Jan. 30, 1863	Jacob	247 West Thirty-fifth	
2409	Kuntz, Barbara	10	do.	do.	do.	do.	
2410	Lowry, George E.	13	do.	May 27, 1862	Charles	651 Greenwich	
2411	Raquet, Katharine	8	do.	Dec. 20, 1866	Frederick	155 West Thirty-second	
2412	Scott, Gilbert C.	15	do.	Sept. 30, 1862	Margaret M.	156 West Thirty-fourth	
2413	Smith, John Boyce	10	do.	Oct. 27, 1863	Thomas H	307 West Twelfth	

CATALOGUE OF SCHOLARS—Continued.

No.	Pupil.	Age	Admitted.	Withdrawn.	Parent.	Residence.	Graduated.
2414	Steinhaus, Henrietta	16	Nov. 26, 1861	June 24, 1862	Christine	155 Frankfort	
2415	{ Van Voorhis, Rachel A. } (Vide Notes)	16	do.	Nov. 25, 1862	John A	247 West Thirty-second	Oct. 29, 1862
2416	Williamson, W. Alex	9	do.	Sept. 29, 1863	Cornelius T	116 West Twenty-eighth	
2417	Williamson, Frederick	7	do.	do.	do.	do.	
2418	Williams, Peter R	8	do.	do.	Edward	118 West Twenty-eighth	
2419	West, Magdelina	14	do.	Sept. 30, 1862	Henrietta	98 West Twenty-ninth	
2420	Brooks, George A	11	Jan. 28, 1862	do.	Thomas S	101 West Forty-fifth	
2421	Brown, James H	15	do.	June 25, 1862	James H	249 Eighth Avenue	
2422	Cabana, Hannah R	8	do.	Nov. 30, 1865	Charles	91 West Thirty-third	
2423	Cowie, Alexander G	11	do.	May 26, 1863	David	323 Ninth Avenue	
2424	Dick, Delia	8	do.	May 25, 1865	William	2 Pacific Place	
2425	Eyre, Mary Ann	10	do.	Sept. 29, 1864	Anna Lowe, G'adm'r	3 Pacific Place	
2426	Eichler, Christian H	10	do.	June 24, 1862	Christian H	248 West Thirty-fifth	
2427	Farr, George	8	do.	Jan. 30, 1863	James	293 West Thirty-third	
2428	Farr, Thomas	10	do.	Feb. 24, 1863	do.	do.	
2429	Hoffstaetter, Frederick	7	do.	May 27, 1869	Ernst	557 First Avenue	May 20, 1869
2430	Hoppert, Albert	9	do.	Jan. 30, 1863	Charles	138 West Thirtieth	
2431	Hoppert, Pauline	8	do.	do.	do.	do.	
2432	Houseman, Rosanna	10	do.	Nov. 28, 1862	George	West Twenty-ninth	
2433	Howe, Robert R	8	do.	Dec. 24, 1868	Benjamin F	6 Pacific Place	
2434	Hustell, Eulalie	14	do.	March 25, 1862	John A	139 West Twenty-ninth	
2435	Hurrell, John A	9	do.	Sept. 29, 1863	do.	do.	
2436	Kidd, Isabella	15	do.	Nov. 25, 1862	James W	117 West Thirty-third	
2437	Kidd, Peter E	11	do.	Feb. 23, 1864	do.	do.	
2438	Knight, George	8	do.	Sept. 28, 1865	Daniel	72 West Thirty-seventh	
2439	{ Kuntz, Louisa }	11	May 25, 1865	Nov. 24, 1863	Jacob	247 West Thirty-fifth	
2440	Lawson, George W	14	Jan. 28, 1862	March 30, 1867	do.	128 East Fortieth	
2441	Le Blanc, Louis	14	do.	Sept. 29, 1865	Samuel L	104 West Twenty-fourth	Oct. 21, 1863
2442	{ Locke, Lavinia }	10	do.	May 26, 1864	William	74 West Thirty-fourth	
2443	Locke, Mary C	15	Feb. 22, 1866	May 31, 1866	Henry Louis	791 Sixth Avenue	
2444	{ McKinney, Margaret A }	7	Jan. 28, 1862	Jan. 30, 1863	do.	272 West Thirty-first	
2445	Miller, Martin	8	do.	May 24, 1864	Frederick T	38 East Thirtieth	
2446	Peek, Emily	12	Nov. 30, 1865	May 30, 1867	David	255 West Thirty-second	
2447	Peek, George W	7	Jan. 28, 1862	Jan. 26, 1864	do.	214 West Thirty-fifth	
		14	do.	June 30, 1864	Vincent	313 Seventh Avenue	
			do.	April 28, 1863	David T	651 Sixth Avenue	Oct. 21, 1863
					do.	do.	

CATALOGUE OF SCHOLARS—Continued.

No.	Pupil.	Age	Admitted.	Withdrawn.	Parent.	Residence.	Graduated.
2448	Peek, Margaretta	9	Jan. 28, 1862	June 30, 1864	David T	651 Sixth Avenue	
2449	Possoen, Charles	9	do.	May 26, 1863	Charles	507 Second Avenue	
2450	Simons, Ella M	6	do.	Oct. 27, 1864	Charles H	264 West Thirty-first	
2451	Simons, Ida C	8	do.	do.	do.	do.	
2452	Simons, Margaretta	10	do.	do.	do.	do.	
2453	Smith, Margaretta	13	do.	Feb. 24, 1863	Theodore E	115 West Thirty-third	
2454	Smith, Susan Amelia	10	do.	May 31, 1866	do.	do.	
2455	Van Hennick, Anna	8	do.	Sept. 30, 1862	John	402 Seventh Avenue	
2456	Van Hennick, Sebastian	12	do.	June 24, 1862	do.	do.	
2457	Van Horsen, Lewis K	14	do.	Sept. 30, 1862	John M	169 West Thirty-eighth	
2458	Campbell, William	9	Feb. 25, 1862	Nov. 25, 1862	Robert	405 East Fortieth	
2459	Cowie, Annie	15	do.	April 28, 1863	David	323 Ninth Avenue	
2460	Burns, Georgiana	11	do.	Feb. 23, 1864	Jane	287 Tenth Avenue	
2461	Burns, Margaret C	9	do.	do.	do.	do.	
2462	Robbins, Wm. B	9	do.	Oct. 27, 1863	Browning Wm.	241 West Thirty-fourth	
2463	Stoutenburgh, John H. (Vide Notes)	8	do.	Sept. 26, 1865	William T	66 West Thirty-second	
2464	Weaver, Edward	8	do.	Sept. 29, 1863	Benjamin	408 Ninth Avenue	
2465	Weaver, Mary A	12	do.	Nov. 24, 1863	do.	do.	
2466	Danner, Hannah	9	March 25, 1862	do.	Lewis	131 West Twenty-ninth	
2467	Danner, Jacob	11	do.	Jan. 30, 1863	do.	do.	
2468	Kline, Lewis A	11	do.	April 28, 1863	Jacob P	251 So. 2d, Jersey City	
2469	Van Thof, Henry	20	do.	Sept. 30, 1862	Isaac	415 Ninth Avenue	
2470	Bogert, Ella	9	April 29, 1862	May 26, 1864	Peter	76 Horatio	
2471	Jollie, Elizabeth P	8	do.	do.	Edward	331 Tenth Avenue	
2472	Mount, Kate M	8	do.	Jan. 30, 1863	John	225 West Forty-eighth	
2473	Mount, Margaret A	10	do.	do.	do.	do.	
2474	Steele, John A. (Vide Notes)	8	do.	April 28, 1864	James	160 West Twenty-sixth	Nov. 2, 1864
2475	Austin, Wm. A. F. P	9	May 27, 1862	Sept. 30, 1862	John E	436 Seventh Avenue	
2476	Fisher, Peter	13	do.	do.	do.	do.	
2477	Lawson, Caspar N	14	do.	Oct. 27, 1863	Nicholas	3rd Street and 6th Ave.	
2478	Lawson, Edward W	11	do.	Jan. 26, 1865	Caspar N	139 Christopher	
2479	Lowry, Mary F	13	do.	do.	do.	do.	
2480	McCarthy, Annetta	9	do.	Sept. 30, 1862	Charles	651 Greenwich	
2481	Smith, Daniel H. (Vide Notes)	11	do.	Nov. 25, 1862	Lydia K	74 West Thirty-third	
2482	Steinbach, Charles	10	do.	Jan. 30, 1863	Henry J	362 Ninth Avenue	
2483		8	do.	Nov. 24, 1863	Abraham C	165 West Thirty-second	
2484	Hardesch, Jacob	7	June 24, 1862	Nov. 25, 1862	Christopher	121 West Twenty-eighth	

CATALOGUE OF SCHOLARS—Continued.

No.	Pupil.	Age	Admitted.	Withdrawn.	Parent.	Residence.	Graduated.
2485	Dominick, Harriet P	9	June 24, 1862	May 30, 1865	Henry	317 Ninth Avenue	
2486	Greene, Sarah Louise	6	do.	Dec. 24, 1868	Jonathan	282 West Forty-second	
2487	Jackson, Harriet E	13	do.	Nov. 25, 1864	James	1141 Bloomfield St., Hoboken	Nov. 2, 1864
2488	Jackson, Henry S	8	do.	May 25, 1865	do.	15 Union Pl., Hoboken	
2489	Letman, Albert	7	do.	Oct. 27, 1864	John Harley	53 Vandam	
2490	Little, Lucy J	6	do.	Sept. 29, 1865	Thomas	South Third, Jersey City	
2491	Ludlam, George	12	do.	May 30, 1867	John	115 West Thirty-third	
2492	Smith, Charles L	6	do.	May 26, 1864	Theodore	121 West Twenty-fourth	
2493	Wood, Cath. Coe		Jan. 27, 1870	March 31, 1870	Isaac	63 West Sixty-fourth	
2494	Ackerman, Anna	13	Sept. 30, 1862	Oct. 27, 1871	Jane	153 West Eighteenth	June 8, 1871
2495	Boor, Margaretta	7	do.	May 31, 1866	Jacob W	32 West Sixteenth	
2496	Dick, Ida	7	do.	May 25, 1865	Peter	2 Pacific Place	
2497	Fisher, Nicholas	8	do.	Oct. 27, 1863	William	52d St. and 6th Ave	
2498	Franz, Jacobine	10	do.	May 26, 1864	Nicholas	167 West Thirty-second	
2499	Ladd, Abraham Wilson	12	do.	Sept. 28, 1865	Frederick	17 West Eleventh	May 30, 1866
2500	Miles, Stephen E	11	do.	Oct. 27, 1863	George	260 West Forty-fourth	Oct. 21, 1863
2501	Myers, Eva	7	do.	Sept. 28, 1865	Stephen E	249 West Fifteenth	
2502	Riebe, Louise	9	do.	do.	John J	534 Sixth Avenue	
2503	Riebe, Theodore	6	do.	June 27, 1871	Theodore	do.	June 8, 1871
2504	Stephens, Mary Adelaide	9	do.	May 31, 1866	James	1184 Broadway	
2505	Williams, Elizabeth M	6	do.	Sept. 28, 1865	Edward	118 West Twenty-eighth	
2506	Coleman, David E	9	Nov. 25, 1862	March 30, 1865	Henry	367 Ninth Avenue	
2507	Coleman, Marianna	7	do.	do.	do.	do.	
2508	Cramer, Augustus H		Oct. 2, 1866	Dec. 23, 1869	William S	364 Eighth Avenue	May 20, 1869
2509	Hughes, Ella I	9	Nov. 25, 1862	May 27, 1869	Mary	173 West Twenty-fourth	
2510	Hughes, Mary A	9	do.	Sept. 29, 1863	do.	7 Cherry	
2511	Jackson, Lewis F	12	do.	do.	do.	do.	
2512	Janes, Josephine A	13	do.	May 26, 1864	Hiram B	13 Henderson Pl., J. C	
2513	Knight, John	7	do.	Sept. 28, 1865	Rev. Frederick	1248 Broadway	
2514	Lamoureau, Delia	14	do.	do.	Daniel	72 West Thirty-seventh	
2515	Mount, Lydia	10	do.	Feb. 25, 1864	Margaret	475 Eighth Avenue	Nov. 2, 1864
2516	Mount, Robert W	14	do.	Nov. 25, 1864	Reuben B	E. 120th St., betw. 3d and 4th Aves	
2517	St. Lee, Anna	17	do.	May 25, 1865	do.	58 West Twenty-ninth	
2518	Stootenburgh, Adeline	11	do.	April 28, 1865	Jas. O. Bennet	87 West Forty-seventh	May 23, 1867
2519	Stootenburgh, Mary F	14	do.	Oct. 27, 1863	Alfred	66 West Thirty-second	Oct. 21, 1863
2520	Wheeler, John J	8	do.	Nov. 27, 1866	William T	149 West Forty-sixth	

CATALOGUE OF SCHOLARS—Continued.

No.	Pupil.	Age	Admitted.	Withdrawn.	Parent.	Residence.	Graduated.
2521	Wood, Benjamin F.	10	Nov. 25, 1862	May 26, 1864	Jacob B.	Staten Island	
2522	Cole, Ferdinand S.	14	Jan. 30, 1863	Jan. 26, 1864	Stephen H.	24 Cornelia	May 30, 1866
2523	Cole, Samuel A.	11	do.	do.	do.	do.	
2524	Littell, Bloomfield (Vide Note)	14	March 30, 1865	March 29, 1866	Julia E.	177 East Forty-first	May 30, 1866
	Locke, Henry Louis	12	Jan. 30, 1863	May 26, 1864	Henry Louis	35 Washington Square	
2525	Locke, Henry Louis			do.	do.	792 Sixth Avenue	
2526	McEvoy, Mary E.	12	Feb. 22, 1866	Sept. 26, 1867	John	772 West Thirty-first	
2527	Martine, Charles		Jan. 30, 1863	Sept. 29, 1863	Mary	473 Eighth Avenue	
2528	Spence, Mary A.	7	do.	May 30, 1867	Robert	294 West Forty-ninth	
2529	Van Tine, Francis	10	do.	Feb. 22, 1866	Charles	757 West Thirty-second	
2530	Lowe, Mary (Vide Notes)	8	do.	Jan. 28, 1869	Andrew	141 West Thirty-eighth	
2531	Quin, Robert F.	15	Feb. 24, 1863	Nov. 25, 1864	Mary	129 East Houston	Nov. 2, 1864
2532	Brinckerhoff, Ransford W.	13	do.	May 26, 1863	James J.	Sailor Snug Harbor, S. I.	
2533	Cabana, Charles I.	10	March 31, 1863	Oct. 2, 1866	Catharine	56 Garden St., Hoboken	
2534	Cragin, Ida E.	7	do.	May 30, 1867	Eliza J.	91 West Thirty-third	
2535	Cragin, James W.	8	do.	Sept. 28, 1865		146 West Thirty-third	
2536	Frühingstradt, John	11	do.			do.	
2537	Lawson, Clementine	10	do.	May 31, 1866	Fred'k A.	123 West Twenty-ninth	
	Van Emburgh, Walter	8	do.	March 30, 1865	Caspar	139 Christopher	
2538	(Vide Notes).	7	do.	May 27, 1869	John	467½ Eighth Avenue	May 20, 1869
2539	Clark, James Clifford	13	April 28, 1863	May 26, 1864	Henry E.	141 Christopher	
2540	Dealing, Charles E.	7	do.	June 26, 1866	Michael	425 Eighth Avenue	
2541	Dealing, Oberlin	10	do.	Feb. 22, 1866	do.	do.	
2542	Bogert, Warren	7	May 26, 1863	Sept. 24, 1868	Stephen	320 West Twelfth	
2543	Cole, Charles S.	8	do.	Jan. 26, 1864	Stephen H.	348 West Thirty-ninth	
2544	Dealing, Micheletta	11	May 25, 1863	May 27, 1869	Michael	177 East Forty-first	May 20, 1869
2545	McCulloch, Lewis R. (Vide Notes).	12	May 26, 1863	June 26, 1866	James	425 Eighth Avenue	
2546	Silliman, Chauncey H.	12	do.	Jan. 31, 1867	Joseph	56 Newark St., Hoboken	May 23, 1867
2547	Bopp, Matilda	7	Dec. 20, 1866	Nov. 25, 1864	do.	249 West Thirty-second	
2548	Bopp, Sophia	10	July 1, 1863	Sept. 24, 1868	Charles	130 West Twenty-eighth	
2549	Klauberg, Frances M.	9	do.	Feb. 25, 1869	do.	103 West Thirty-first	
2550	Klauberg, Frederick L.	14	do.	May 31, 1866	Karl	do.	
2551	Mickens, George W.	7	do.	Feb. 23, 1864	do.	6 Pacific Place	
	Peek, Henry	10	do.	Sept. 29, 1864	Thomas	198 Hudson St., Hob'k'n	
2552	Peek, Henry	7	do.	Nov. 25, 1864	David T.	625 Sixth Avenue	

CATALOGUE OF SCHOLARS—Continued.

No.	Pupil.	Age	Admitted.	Withdrawn.	Parent.	Residence.	Graduated.
2553	Perkins, Maria E.	14	July 1, 1863	Nov. 24, 1863	George	135 West Thirty-fifth	......
2554	Barney, Augustus W.	15	Sept. 29, 1863	Nov. 25, 1864	Daniel J.	315 West Twenty-fourth	......
2555	Barney, Daniel	10	do.	Feb. 23, 1865	do.	do.	......
2556	Brennan, Agnes A. (Vide Note).	13	do.	May 31, 1866	Cornelia D. Marsh	10 Third	April 30, 1868
2557	Hill, Emma	16	Sept. 26, 1867	Feb. 25, 1869	George	do.	May 23, 1867
2558	Hill, J. Edmund	12	Sept. 29, 1863	May 30, 1867	do.	813 Sixth Avenue	May 20, 1869
2559	Hill, Kate	9	do.	May 27, 1869	do.	do.	do.
2560	Hoffacker, Bernard	8	do.	Dec. 21, 1865	Louisa	291 Seventh Avenue	......
2561	Hoffacker, Mary	11	do.	do. do.	do.	do.	......
2562	Kennar, Charles	7	do.	Feb. 28, 1868	George	110 West Thirty-second	......
2563	Kennar, Kate	9	do.	do.	do.	do.	......
2564	Kircheis, Emma L	9	do.	Nov. 23, 1870	Frederick	108 Fifth	......
2565	Kircheis, Mary M	12	do.	Nov. 25, 1864	do.	do.	Nov. 2, 1864
2566	Mount, Andrew	6	do.	Oct. 26, 1865	Reuben B.	East 120th Street	......
2567	Post, Mary Adelaide	8	do.	May 31, 1866	Aaron	258 West Thirty-third	......
2568	Van Tine, Henrietta	12	do.	Oct. 29, 1868	Charles	141 West Thirty-eighth	......
2569	Wolff, William	12	do.	Sept. 28, 1865	Rev. Wm.	116 Seventh	......
2570	Zipp, Jacob F.	12	Oct. 27, 1863	Nov. 25, 1864	Jacob	104 Seventh	Nov. 2, 1864
2571	Denizot, Agnes	9	do.	Oct. 25, 1865	John	225 West Forty-third	......
2572	Denizot, Ellen J.	13	do.	do.	do.	do.	......
2573	Jackson, Peter A. H	8	do.	Oct. 2, 1866	Peter A. H	93 East Twenty-seventh	......
2574	Mills, George V	12	do.	May 30, 1867	Samuel H	205 South Fifth, B'klyn	May 23, 1867
2575	Odell, Wm. M.	8	do.	Sept. 28, 1865	William H	464 Eighth Avenue	......
2576	Thornall, Edw'd V. (Vide Note	12	May 28, 1868	March 25, 1869	Benjamin	152 West Forty-eighth	......
2577	Tittrington, Sophronia A	7	Oct. 27, 1863	Oct. 2, 1866	do.	do.	......
2578	Tittrington, Whitfield	9	do.	May 25, 1865	do.	126 West Thirty-seventh	......
2579	White, George B	10	do.	Jan. 26, 1865	do.	do.	......
2580	Haywood, Eleanor V. D	11	do.	April 28, 1864	Jane	Thirty-second Street	......
2581	Howell, Hannah L	7	Nov. 24, 1863	Nov. 22, 1866	George M	54 Irving Place	May 30, 1866
2582	Howell, Sarah	14	do.	Oct. 26, 1865	George C.	81 West Twenty-seventh	......
2583	Janes, Wm. A.	7	do.	Sept. 28, 1865	Rev. Frederick	do.	......
2584	Butler, William B.	15	Jan. 3, 1872	Oct. 1, 1872	do.	1,248 Broadway	......
2585	Dixon, Amanda	13	Jan. 26, 1864	Sept. 28, 1865	Henry	27 West Thirty-first	......
2586	Dunlap, Frank P.	12	do.	Nov. 25, 1864	Maria	414 West Twenty-third	......
2587	Hoffman, Chas. J.	7	do.	Sept. 28, 1865	Thomas	116 W. Twenty-seventh	......
					Charles	211 West Thirty-first	......
						229 West Twenty-eighth	......

CATALOGUE OF SCHOLARS—Continued.

No.	Pupil.	Age	Admitted.	Withdrawn.	Parent.	Residence.	Graduated.
2588	Jackson, Esther H.	6	Jan. 26, 1864	June 1, 1874	Peter A. H.	93 East Twenty-seventh	May 26, 1874
2589	McAleese, Kate	12	do.	Feb. 28, 1868	Sarah	77 West Twenty-eighth	
2590	Steinbring, Charles	9	do.	Jan. 26, 1865	Christine	131 West Twenty-ninth	
2591	Wilson, John D.	12	Jan. 25, 1866	Sept. 26, 1867	do.	123 West Twenty-ninth	
2592	Wolff, Julius H. (Vide Notes)	7	Jan. 26, 1864	May 27, 1869	Martha	118 W. Twenty-seventh	
2593	Wolff, Theodore	9	do.	Sept. 28, 1865	Rev. Wm.	116 Seventh	
2594	Dean, Henry F.	11	Feb. 23, 1864	Nov. 25, 1864	Harriet H.	18 Cornelia	
2595	Lutz, Philip	11	May 30, 1867	Nov. 27, 1867	do.	39 West Twenty-first	
2596	Mabie, Samuel H. (Vide Notes)	9	Feb. 23, 1864	Nov. 25, 1864	Nicholas	6 Clinton	
2597	Mabie, Sarah	11	do.	March 25, 1869	Abraham	165 West Twenty-eighth	May 23, 1872
			do.	Jan. 25, 1866	do.	do.	
2598	Mabie, Wm. H.	7	do.	Nov. 23, 1870	do.	do.	
2599	Regen, Henry F.	13	Oct. 3, 1871	Oct. 31, 1871	Henrietta	358 West Forty-fourth	
2600	Regen, Louis C.	9	Feb. 23, 1864	May 31, 1866	do.	1st Franklin Avenue, Greenpoint	
2601	Soutenburgh, Frank	11	do.	do.	Alfred	133 West Forty-seventh	
2602	Brower, Wm. J.	9	do.	Jan. 30, 1868	Wm. H.	425 Eighth Avenue	
2603	Clark, Ada N.	7	March 31, 1864	Nov. 25, 1864	Theodore	141 East Fifty-first	
2604	Gruenewald, Charles	8	do.	Sept. 28, 1865	William	362 Seventh Avenue	
2605	Oyms, Henry	7	do.	Feb. 28, 1868	Nicholas	224 William	
2606	Dolph, Clarence	15	April 28, 1864	May 26, 1864	Cath. J.	206 West Thirty-eighth	
2607	Fuhrmann, Henry G.	7	do.	March 29, 1866	John J.	111 Second	
2608	Van Emburgh, Clara	6	do.	Nov. 25, 1864	John	467½ Eighth Avenue	
2609	Becker, Helen C.	8	May 26, 1864	May 27, 1869	Henry C.	152 West Thirty-first	
2610	Demarest, Francis L. (Vide Notes)	7	do.	Sept. 28, 1865	John G.	241 W. Twenty-seventh	May 29, 1873
2611	Streubel, Edward	9	do.	Oct. 1, 1872	Fred'k	174 West Thirty-first	
2612	Ackermann, Mary	10	June 30, 1864	Sept. 24, 1868	Peter	222 West Thirty-seventh	
2613	Danehee, William P.	13	do.	March 28, 1867	Henry W.	36 West Tenth	May 30, 1866
2614	McAleese, Wm.	9	do.	Oct. 2, 1866	Sarah	77 West Twenty-eighth	
2615	Barthey, Katharine	7	Sept. 29, 1864	Nov. 25, 1864	Gottfried	110 West Thirty-second	
2616	Blauvelt, Cornelius	9	do.	Oct. 28, 1869	John P.	85 Christopher	
			May 25, 1865	Sept. 28, 1865	do.	do.	
2617	Brampton, Francis	12	May 17, 1869	Sept. 29, 1870	do.	do.	
2618	Brown, Frank	11	Sept. 29, 1864	March 29, 1866	John	348 W. Twenty-second	
2619	Cabana, Mary M.	6	do.	Sept. 28, 1865	James H.	249 Eighth Avenue	
			do.	May 30, 1867	Katharine	259 West Forty-ninth	

CATALOGUE OF SCHOLARS—Continued.

No.	Pupil.	Age	Admitted.	Withdrawn.	Parent.	Residence.	Graduated.
2620	Crocheron, Charlotte E.	14	Sept. 29, 1864	March 29, 1866	Edmond S.	5 Pacific Place	
2621	Gravsal, Henry	11	do.	Sept. 28, 1865	Frederick	181 Henry	
2622	Harbeck, Anna	9	do.	Oct. 31, 1867	Charles	212 East Thirty-third	
2623	Hinman, Amanda M. II	7	do.	Sept. 28, 1865	Samuel S.	1,246 Broadway	
2624	Hinman, Wm. H.	11	do.	do.	do.	do.	
2625	Howe, Anna F. U.	6	do.	Oct. 28, 1869	Benjamin F.	5 Pacific Place	
2626	Jordan, Caroline E.	7	do.	Sept. 28, 1865	Philip	186 West Twenty-fifth	
2627	McAleese, Daniel	7	do.	Nov. 5, 1872	Sarah	77 West Twenty-eighth	
2628	Mayer, John W.	8	do.	May 31, 1866	John M.	521 Sixth Avenue	
2629	Page, Eugenia	7	do.	Sept. 28, 1865	Charles B.	271 Seventh Avenue	
2630	Paterson, Edward W.	11	Sept. 30, 1869	Oct. 3, 1871	Robert	449 Ninth Avenue	
2631	Paterson, Matilda	9	Sept. 29, 1864	May 31, 1866	do.	259 West Fifty-fourth	
2632	Paterson, Robert A.	13	do.	Oct. 26, 1865	do.	do. do.	
2633	Radcliff, Anna E.	16	do.	Nov. 31, 1865	Isaac	300 Ninth Avenue	
2634	Byers, John	11	do.	Oct. 29, 1868	do.	525 West Fifty-first	
2635	Byers, Moses	8	Feb. 24, 1870	Dec. 22, 1870	John	89 West Twenty-eighth	
2636	Edwards, Charles	10	Oct. 27, 1864	May 30, 1867	do.	do.	
2637	Gardner, Walter	8	do.	Nov. 22, 1865	do.	311 Ninth Avenue	
2638	Garretson, John	9	do.	May 31, 1866	John W.	293 W. 43d St., c. 8th Av.	
2639	Gruenewald, Cecilia	6	do.	Nov. 22, 1865	Stephen E.	Richmond, S. I.	May 30, 1866
2640	Mayer, Sophia J.	6	do.	May 31, 1866	Jacob C.	362 Seventh Avenue	
2641	Brown, Alexander F.	6	Nov. 25, 1864	Feb. 28, 1868	Magdalen	521 Sixth Avenue	
2642	Ennis, Adelaide	8	do.	May 31, 1866	John M.	114 West Fifteenth	
2643	Weeks, Cornelia	12	do.	Dec. 20, 1865	Rev. Isaac S. Hartley	84 West Twenty-ninth	
2644	Blauvelt, Henry C.	9	Dec. 15, 1864	Dec. 24, 1867	John J.	440 Eighth Avenue	
2645	Churchwell, Mary E.	13	do.	Sept. 28, 1865	Hiram	20 Charles	
2646	Coleman, John L.	14	do.	Nov. 22, 1866	David I.	1,143 Broadway	
2647	Franz, Catharine	10	do.	Jan. 25, 1866	Mary E.	354 Eighth Avenue	
2648	White, Robert	7	do.	Nov. 22, 1866	Henry	137 West Thirty-fourth	
2649	Gibson, Robert II	10	Jan. 26, 1865	March 25, 1869	Frederick	77 West Twenty-eighth	
2650	Coleman, Charles E.	7	March 30, 1865	May 25, 1865	Thomas	440 Sixth Avenue	
2651	Feldmuth, Barbara	9	do.	May 31, 1866	Cornelia	364 Eighth Avenue	
2652	Gardner, Oscar K.	14	do.	May 30, 1867	Henry	121 West Twenty-ninth	
2653	Hoffstaedter, George	9	do.	Sept. 5, 1871	Barbara	293 W. 43d St., c. 8th Av.	
2654	Hyatt, Fanny	13	do.	May 30, 1867	Stephen E.	462 Sixth Avenue	
2655	McKee, Nathaniel	16	do.	Sept. 28, 1865	Ernst	121 West Thirty-third	
					John S.	369 Ninth Avenue	
					Nathaniel		

CATALOGUE OF SCHOLARS—Continued.

No.	Pupil.	Age	Admitted.	Withdrawn.	Parent.	Residence.	Graduated.
2656	Mills, Samuel H	12	March 30, 1865	Sept. 28, 1865	Samuel H	205 South Fifth, B'klyn.	
2657	Morris, William	13	Sept. 26, 1865	May 27, 1869	John	99 First Place, Brooklyn	May 20, 1869
2658		11	March 30, 1865	May 31, 1866	William	63 West Twenty-second	
2659	Nollman, Annie	10	do.	Oct. 26, 1865	William	406 Ninth Avenue	
2660	Nollman, Charles	12	Oct. 31, 1867	May 27, 1869	do.	1,244 Third Avenue	
2661	Nollman, William	8	March 30, 1865	Oct. 26, 1865	do.	406 Ninth Avenue	
2662	Paterson, Frank	13	Oct. 31, 1867	Oct. 3, 1871	do.	1,244 Third Avenue	
2663	Pitman, William J	7	March 30, 1865	Oct. 26, 1865	do.	406 Ninth Avenue	
2664	Shay, Charles C	9	do.	May 31, 1866	Robert	259 West Fifty-fourth	
2665	Twisker, Emma I	12	do.	Sept. 30, 1869	William	351 Eighth Avenue	
2666	Hill, Sarah F	7	do.	Jan. 27, 1870	William E	91 West Twenty-ninth	
2667	Hyatt, Emma	7	April 26, 1865	May 31, 1866	Hannah	85 West Thirty-third	
2668	McKee, Mary	14	do.	do.	John M	79 West Thirty-third	
2669			do.	May 30, 1867	John S	121 West Thirty-third	
2670	Stacker, Josephine	8	June 25, 1868	Oct. 29, 1868	Nathaniel	366 Ninth Avenue	
2671				Nov. 12, 1866	William	123 West Twenty-ninth	
2672	Stacker, Theresa	8	April 26, 1865	Jan. 27, 1870	do.	304 Eleventh Avenue	
2673	Cote, Georgiana	15	May 25, 1865	Nov. 22, 1866	do.	123 West Twenty-ninth	
2674	Goetschius, Howard H	8	Jan. 3, 1872	June 3, 1873	Stephen H	177 East Forty-first	May 29, 1873
2675	Raquet, Emelina	7	May 25, 1865	Sept. 28, 1865	Joseph	Hoboken	
2676	Ackerman, Martha J	10	Sept. 28, 1865	Sept. 24, 1868	Frederick	539 Ninth Avenue	
2677	Becker, Bertha	8	do.	Oct. 3, 1871	Jacob W	126 East Fortieth	
2678	Becker, Mary	13	do.	May 30, 1867	Jacob	91 West Twenty-eighth	
2679	Byers, William	16	do.	do.	do.	123 West Twenty-ninth	
2680	Demarest, Ella V. R	7	do.	Nov. 22, 1866	John	89 West Twenty-eighth	
2681	Earle, Margaret A	8	do.	Feb. 28, 1867	Emma	West Thirty-second	
2682	Ernst, Elizabeth	11	do.	Nov. 25, 1868	John	93 West Twenty-ninth	
2683	Ernst, Paulina	14	do.	Nov. 22, 1866	do.	356 Seventh Avenue	
2684	Friedel, Ida	9	do.	do.	do.	do.	
2685	Friedel, Selma	7	do.	May 28, 1866	Rev. Henry A	127 Norfolk	
2686	Friedel, Theophilus	11	do.	do.	do.	do.	
2687	Gackstatter, Evaline	7	do.	do.	do.	do.	
2688	Graf, Ernst	7	do.	Nov. 22, 1866	Michael	123 West Twenty-ninth	
2689	Greene, Anna M	7	do.	May 31, 1866	Louisa	127 Bleecker	
2690	Hammel, George	12	do.	Dec. 24, 1868	Jonathan	442 Sixth Avenue	
2691	Herbst, Frank C	12	do.	May 31, 1869	John	286 Third	
2692			do.	May 28, 1868	Frank	288 Third	May 20, 1869

CATALOGUE OF SCHOLARS—Continued.

No.	Pupil.	Age	Admitted.	Withdrawn.	Parent.	Residence.	Graduated.
2689	Hill, Sophia	7	Sept. 28, 1865	Oct. 27, 1870	George A.	837 Sixth Avenue	
2690	McKee, Samuel B.	10	do.	May 27, 1869	Nathaniel	309 Ninth Avenue	
2691	McKee, Susan	12	do.	Oct. 3, 1871	do.	do. do.	May 23, 1872
2692	McKinney, Anna	13	do.	Oct. 29, 1868	John	84 West Thirty-third	
2693	McKinney, George E.	18	do.	May 26, 1870	do.	do. do.	
2694	McKinney, Helen	11	do.	do.	do.	do. do.	
2695	Oertter, Samuel J. (Vide Notes)	8	do.	June 27, 1871	Rev. John H.	143 West Thirty-first	June 8, 1871
2696	Pitman, Frances J.	6	do.	do.	William	297 Ninth Avenue	
2697	Rogers, David T.	8	do.	Oct. 2, 1866	do.	434 West Thirty-second	
2698	} Stacker, Caroline	9	June 25, 1868	Nov. 22, 1866	do.	123 West Twenty-ninth	
		12	Oct. 31, 1871	Sept. 29, 1870	do.	102 East Houston	
2699	Stephens, Helen C.	6	Sept. 28, 1865	June 4, 1872	James	304 Eleventh Avenue	
2700	Trimble, Starr	9	do.	June 3, 1873	James N.	3 Pacific Place	May 29, 1873
2701	Atz, Frederick	9	Oct. 26, 1865	Oct. 3, 1871	Adam	128 East Twenty-eighth	
2702	Atz, George A. C.	8	do.	May 26, 1870	do.	47 Avenue B	
2703	Boyden, James S.	7	do.	Oct. 1, 1872	Elias W.	96 Morton	
2704	Boyden, William H.	6	do.	do.	do.	do.	
2705	Clearman, William H.	10	do.	May 30, 1867	John	48 King	
2706	Kirchner, Amelo	8	do.	Sept. 26, 1867	August	103 West Twenty-eighth	
2707	Kirchner, Henry	7	do.	do.	do.	do.	
2708	Munn, Regina V.	8	do.	Oct. 2, 1875	Samuel E.	65 West Twenty-seventh	
2709	Allason, Clarissa (Vide Notes)	7	Nov. 30, 1865	June 22, 1866	William	122 West Twenty-fourth	May 29, 1873
2710	Blair, William A.	13	do.	Jan. 25, 1866	do.	1303 Broadway	
2711	Coe, Samuel I.	9	do.	Feb. 25, 1869	Samuel L.	104 West Twenty-eighth	
2712	Howe, William	6	do.	May 30, 1867	Benjamin F.	71 Tenth Avenue	
2713	Keyser, Catharine	8	do.	do.	Michael	105 West Thirty-first	
2714	McKinney, Alpheus	15	do.	Oct. 31, 1867	David	214 West Thirty-fifth	
2715	Peters, Anthony J.	11	do.	Sept. 30, 1869	John A.	163 S. Fourth St., Bklyn.	May 23, 1867
2716	Radcliff, Andrew A.	6	do.	May 29, 1875	Isaac	300 Ninth Avenue	
2717	Tiers, Anna A.	7	do.	May 30, 1867	George W.	117 West Twenty-ninth	
2718	Warren, Emma J.	14	do.	May 27, 1869	Andrew J.	144 West Twenty-ninth	
2719	Zabriskie, Peter J.	14	do.	May 30, 1867	James P.	{ Whiton St., La Fay-ette, New Jersey }	May 23, 1867
2720	Conover, Clementine G.	15	Dec. 21, 1865	May 27, 1869	Peter	227 West Forty-third	May 20, 1869
2721	Crygier, John U. (Vide Notes)	7	do.	Oct. 1, 1872	John J.	307 West Twenty-fifth	May 29, 1873
2722	Lippert, George	10	do.	May 27, 1869	John	219 East Fourth	May 20, 1869
2723	Robbins, Leonora	8	do.	Sept. 29, 1870	Sabina	50 West Thirty-first	

CATALOGUE OF SCHOLARS—Continued.

No.	Pupil.	Age	Admitted.	Withdrawn.	Parent.	Residence.	Graduated.
2724	Conklin, Francis M	7	Jan. 25, 1866	Oct. 31, 1867	Stephen A	174 West Thirty-seventh	
2725	Schoonmaker, Mary G	7	do.	May 31, 1866	William J	65 West Forty-ninth	
2726	Littlepage, Urania	7	Feb. 22, 1866	Oct. 2, 1866	William H	260 West Thirty-second	
2727	McCarty, Chas. R	10	do.	June 3, 1873	Peter Conover, *G'd'n*	27 West Forty-third	May 29, 1873
2728	Miles, Robert J	12	do.	Sept. 24, 1868	Frances E	116 Christopher	May 20, 1869
2729	Purdy, Isaac T	7	do.	May 27, 1869	Isaac	176 West Thirty-seventh	
2730	Risht, John	10	do.	May 30, 1867	John	317 Broome	
2731	Van Emburgh, Lizzie	14	Jan. 27, 1870	Nov. 23, 1870	do.	135 East Houston	
2732	Bell, Thomas J	6	Feb. 22, 1866	May 27, 1869	John H	467½ Eighth Avenue	
2733	Campbell, John C	9	March 29, 1866	Nov. 22, 1866	Thomas J	77 West Thirty-third	
2734	Campbell, Phebe M	10	do.	Oct. 31, 1867	Cecilia M	340 West Thirty-sixth	
2735	Hamm, Charles	9	do.	June 27, 1871	Charles	do.	June 8, 1871
2736	Hamm, Louisa	11	do.	Sept. 26, 1867	do.	151 East Eleventh	
2737	Sacks, Augustus	9	do.	May 27, 1867	Justus	do.	
2738	Sacks, Mary	11	do.	May 31, 1866	do.	49 Norfolk	
2739	Van Biarcum, Thomas	13	do.	Dec. 24, 1867	Charles R	278 West Twenty-ninth	
2740	Linder, Kate	10	April 26, 1866	May 27, 1869	Frank	240 West Thirty-second	
2741	Wroeger, Hermann P	12	May 31, 1866	June 4, 1872	William	211 Avenue A	May 30, 1869
2742	Allason, Martha W., *VideNote*	6	do.	March 26, 1868	Robert S	102 West Twenty-fourth	May 29, 1873
2743	Allen, Mary E	10	do.	Feb. 4, 1873	John J	152 West Forty-eighth	
2744	Crygier, Kate V	6	do.	June 27, 1871	Henry W	307 West Twenty-fifth	
2745	Dunshee, Mary P	9	do.	Oct. 29, 1868	Elizabeth	142 West Tenth	June 8, 1871
2746	Jenzer, Arnold	9	do.	Oct. 3, 1871	Heinrich	1,250 Third Avenue	
2747	Nollman, George	11	do.	May 30, 1867	do.	do.	April 30, 1868
2748	Nollman, William	13	do.	Sept. 24, 1868	Philip	163 West Thirty-third	
2749	Carr, George G	9	June 26, 1866	Oct. 29, 1868	do.	do.	
2750	Carr, Sarah L	8	do.	March 31, 1870	Augustus F	42½ Norfolk	May 23, 1872
2751	Lippold, Frederick A	9	do.	Dec. 3, 1872	Nathaniel	369 Ninth Avenue	
2752	McKee, Gertrude	9	do.	May 30, 1867	George	453 East Houston	
2753	Miller, George	12	do.	do.	Charles	160 East Eleventh	
2754	Tush, George	11	do.	do.	John	117 Sixth	
2755	Utz, Louis	10	do.	Sept. 24, 1868	Anna E. Hardley	217 West Thirty-sixth	
2756	Boarden, Emily R	6	Oct. 2, 1866	June 24, 1869	William A	214 West Thirty-sixth	
2757	Byrnes, Corrinne A	10	do.	Oct. 31, 1867	do.	do.	
2758	Campbell, Elizabeth A	13	do.	Feb. 4, 1873	Charles	165 West Thirty-third	
2759	Campbell, Jane E	7	do.	Oct. 31, 1867	William A	New Brighton, S. I.	
2760	Collins, William A	15	do.				

CATALOGUE OF SCHOLARS—Continued.

No.	Pupil.	Age	Admitted.	Withdrawn.	Parent.	Residence.	Graduated.
2761	Ehlert, Mary J.	13	Oct. 2, 1866	April 25, 1867	Sophia	115 West Thirty-third	
2762	Fichtel, Charles G.	7	do.	Oct. 1, 1872	Charles	115 Eighth	May 29, 1873
2763	Hall, Mary Ann	8	do.	June 3, 1873	Margaret	141 West Twenty-ninth	do.
2764	Laver, Henry	11	do.	Oct. 29, 1868	Katharine	146 East Fourth	
2766	Nollman, Mary	11	do.	Sept. 24, 1868	Frank	282 Henry	
2767	Ramsen, Franklin E.	7	do.	May 30, 1867	Isaac E.	157 West Thirtieth	
2768	Scherz, Wilhelmina	9	do.	do.	Augustus	214 West Thirty-fifth	
2769	Waldmayer, Julius	9	do.		Francis J.	143 West Thirty-first	
2770	Hay, John T.	7	Nov. 22, 1866	Sept. 26, 1867	Jane	158 West Thirty-first	
2771	Jackson, Abigail H.	6	do.	Nov. 27, 1875	Peter A. H.	93 East Twenty-seventh	
2772	Jackson, Harry	8	do.	Oct. 1, 1872	Henry	126 West Thirty-sixth	
2773	Laverty, Agnes	11	do.	May 26, 1870	John	291 Seventh Avenue	
2774	Laverty, Elizabeth	6	do.	Jan. 3, 1872	do.	do.	
2774	Logan, Ida	9	do.	April 30, 1867	Mary	192 W. Twenty-seventh	
2775	McGregor, Malcolm	11	Jan. 27, 1870	Oct. 31, 1867	Peter Van Beuren, M. D.	214 West Twenty-second	
		14	Dec. 3, 1872	Sept. 29, 1870		do. do.	
2776	McLaren, Agnes J.	17		Sept. 30, 1873	do.	do.	
2777	Radcliff, Charles E. D	8	Nov. 22, 1866	May 30, 1867	John	158 West Thirty-first	
		8		Oct. 29, 1868	Isaac	571 West Fifty-second	
2778	Radcliff, Isaac	11	Feb. 24, 1870	Dec. 27, 1870	do.	525 West Fifty-first	
		7	Nov. 22, 1866	Oct. 29, 1868	do.	571 West Fifty-second	
2779	Stryker, Peter	9	Feb. 24, 1870	Dec. 22, 1870	do.	525 West Fifty-first	
2780	Van Beuren, Harold S.	8	Nov. 22, 1866	May 30, 1867	John P.	841 Sixth Avenue	
2781	Van Voorhis, Abraham	10	do.		Gen. Thomas B.	4 West Twenty-ninth	
2782	Wroeger, Matilda	13	do.	May 27, 1869	Henry	121 Barrow, Jersey City	May 20, 1869
2783	Hoehm, David	8	Dec. 20, 1866	Feb. 25, 1867	Louisa	211 Avenue A	
2784	Silliman, Anna	8	do.	Sept. 30, 1869	Margaret	325 West Thirty-ninth	
2785	Van Biarcum, William	9	do.	Dec. 28, 1869	Joseph	130 West Twenty-eighth	
2786	Van Wagenen, Walter	7	do.	Dec. 24, 1867	Charles R.	278 West Twenty-ninth	
2787	Friedenreich, Wallgoth R.	10	Jan. 31, 1867	Sept. 26, 1867	Charles	249 Ninth Avenue	
2788	Laverty, John	14	do.	May 30, 1867	Charlotte	310 West Thirty-sixth	
2789	Lloyd, Joseph F.	12	do.	Sept. 20, 1867	John	291 Seventh Avenue	
2790	Tapper, Sarah E.	7	do.	do.	Joseph F.	248 West Thirty-seventh	
2791	Tapper, William	10	do.	May 27, 1869	William	4 Pacific Place	
2792	Clark, Margaret	7	Feb. 28, 1867	Dec. 22, 1870	do.	do.	
2793	Clark, Martha	10	do.	Dec. 23, 1870	John	141 West Twenty-ninth	
2794	Normann, Lyllian E.	10	do.	Oct. 31, 1867	David H	182 Seventh Avenue	

CATALOGUE OF SCHOLARS—Continued.

No.	Pupil.	Age	Admitted.	Withdrawn.	Parent.	Residence.	Graduated.
2795	Pitman, Samuel	12	Feb. 28, 1867	Sept. 24, 1868	William	297 Ninth Avenue	......
2796	Coleman, Joseph V. D.	7	March 28, 1867	May 26, 1870	Henry	364 Eighth Avenue	......
2797	Earle, Ella	6	do.	Nov. 25, 1868	John	91 West Twenty-ninth	......
2798	Kockler, Margaret	10	do.	May 27, 1869	Margaret	250 West Thirty-second	......
2799	Linder, Anna	7	do.	Dec. 25, 1867	Frank	240 West Thirty-second	......
2800	Wolf, Max	7	do.	Jan. 30, 1868	Frederick	268 West Thirty-sixth	......
2801	Allen, Kate ()	7	April 25, 1867	March 26, 1868	Robert S.	152 West Forty-eighth	......
2802	Van Roulen, Henry E	7	do.	Feb. 3, 1874	Cornelius	13 West Forty-eighth	......
2803	Van Roden, Susan	9	do.	Oct. 2, 1875	do.	do. do.	......
2804	Brown, Harry	10	May 30, 1867	Sept. 30, 1873	Jane	490 Sixth Avenue	May 29, 1873
2805	Dunn, Catharine F	9	do.	June 3, 1873	Matthew S.	156 Seventh Avenue	May 25, 1875
2806	Dunn, Mary E.	7	do.	June 26, 1873	do.	do. do.	......
2807	Frühlingstradt, August	9	do.	Oct. 29, 1868	Frederick A.	143 West Thirtieth	......
2808	Jones, Mary Ann	11	do.	Nov. 27, 1867	Harriet H. Dean	39 West Twenty-first	......
2809	Pertback, Ferdinand	9	do.	Sept. 24, 1868	Adolph	282 Henry	......
2810	Trimble, Sarah A.	14	Jan. 30, 1875	Feb. 28, 1871	James N.	220 East Twenty-eighth	......
2811	Van Keuren, Matthew	9	May 30, 1867	June 2, 1877	Isaiah Clearwater	do. do.	......
2812	Dudge, Carrie L.	7	June 27, 1867	Oct. 31, 1867	Amos	7 Pacific Place	......
2813	Hoffstaetter, Jacob	8	do.	Sept. 24, 1868	Ernst	208 West Thirty-sixth	......
2814	Miller, Christina H.	11	do.	Oct. 1, 1872	Margaret	470 Sixth Avenue	......
2815	Gerdes, Caroline	9	Sept. 26, 1867	May 26, 1870	Albert	139 West Nineteenth	......
2816	Gerdes, Elizabeth	11	do.	Oct. 3, 1871	do.	531 West Twenty-ninth	......
2817	Gerdes, Sophia	7	do.	Oct. 3, 1871	do.	do. do.	......
2818	Jackson, Edward	6	do.	Oct. 1, 1872	Henry	126 West Thirty-sixth	......
2819	Laverty, Joseph	9	do.	Sept. 29, 1870	John	291 Seventh Avenue	......
2820	McKinney, John A	8	do.	May 26, 1870	do.	114 West Thirty-third	......
2821	Meyer, Clara	10	do.	May 28, 1868	Adolph	282 Henry	......
2822	Shepard, George E	16	do.	May 27, 1869	Thomas	Communipaw St., South Bergen	May 20, 1869
2823	Hammel, Mary	10	Oct. 31, 1867	do.	John	115 Eighth	......
2824	Perkins, Emma W	10	do.	May 28, 1868	George	430 Fourth Avenue	......
2825	Purdy, Charles	7	do.	March 28, 1871	Isaac	42d St. and Eighth Ave.	......
2826	Schmidt, George H	11	do.	Jan. 26, 1871	Frederick	341 W. Twenty-seventh	......
2827	Smyth, Adam	14	do.	May 27, 1869	Joseph	298 Eighth Avenue	......
2828	Smyth, Archibald	13	do.	June 4, 1872	do.	do.	......
2829	Smyth, Margaret	11	do.	Oct. 3, 1871	do.	do.	......
2830	Sonnemann, Amedeus H.	10	do.	Feb. 28, 1868	John	6 Clinton	......

CATALOGUE OF SCHOLARS—Continued.

No.	Pupil.	Age	Admitted.	Withdrawn.	Parent.	Residence.	Graduated.
2831	Stoetzel, Henry	14	Oct. 31, 1867	Feb. 25, 1869	Theodore	315 West Thirty-eighth	
2832	Van Wagenen, Charles F.	14	do.	May 27, 1869	Anna, Aunt	11 East Forty-ninth	
2833	Atz, Adolph	7	Nov. 27, 1867	Sept. 5, 1871	Adam	47 Avenue B	
2834	Bingenheimer, Christopher	12	do.	May 28, 1868	Jacob	6 Clinton	
2835	Turner, William C.	7	do.	do.	John	422 Seventh Avenue	
2836	Hewlett, George B.	7	Dec. 24, 1867	Sept. 28, 1874	Joseph	299 Seventh Avenue	May 26, 1874
2837	McGowan, Anna	10	do.	Nov. 23, 1870	John	157 West Thirty-first	
2838	McGowan, Benjamin F.	12	do.	Jan. 26, 1871	do.	do. do.	
2839	Muir, James P.	9	do.	June 2, 1874	James	27 Greenwich Avenue	May 26, 1874
2840	Perlback, Adolph	8	Jan. 30, 1868	Sept. 24, 1868	Adolph	282 Henry	
2841	Wood, Joseph	8	do.	Oct. 27, 1870	Joseph	367 Seventh Avenue	
2842	Wood, Marion	11	do.	Nov. 23, 1870	do.	do.	
2843	Stokesherry, Catharine	7	Feb. 28, 1868	June 25, 1868	John	490 Sixth Avenue	
2844	Stokesherry, Margaret	9	do.	do.	do.	do.	
2845	Stokesherry, Mary A.	11	do.	do.	do.	do.	
2846	McGowan, Edward	8	March 26, 1868	Nov. 23, 1870	do.	157 West Thirty-first	
2847	Hill, George A.	7	April 30, 1868	Oct. 27, 1870	George A.	837 Sixth Avenue	
2848	Hopper, Peter F.	7	Dec. 24, 1872	Dec. 2, 1873	Abraham D.	149 East 127th	
2849	Simons, Charles C.	9	April 30, 1868	Sept. 30, 1869	Charles H.	235 Bleecker	
2850	Swann, James H.	7	do.	Nov. 5, 1872	James H.	244 West Thirty-first	
2851	Friaul, George	11	May 28, 1868	Oct. 31, 1871	Jacob	160 West Twenty-ninth	
2852	Friaul, Justine	8	do.	Sept. 30, 1869	do.	178 Ludlow	
2853	Segrist, Bertha	11	do.	do.	Rudolph	220 West Thirty-sixth	
2854	Segrist, Julius	9	do.	do.	do.	do.	
2855	Serrine, Henry E.	7	do.	Dec. 5, 1871	Gertrude	442 West Fifty-fourth	
2856	Simons, Carrie S.	7	do.	Sept. 30, 1869	Charles H.	244 West Thirty-first	
2857	Stanwood, Carrie	14	do.	Oct. 31, 1871	Nancy	322 W. Twenty-seventh	
2858	Odell, Emma L.	7	June 25, 1868	May 27, 1869	William H.	464 Eighth Avenue	
2859	Ryerson, Edward	7	do.	Oct. 1, 1872	John	368 West Eleventh	
2860	Ryerson, George M.	10	do.	do.	do.	do.	
2861	Borst, Jane	8	Sept. 24, 1868	Oct. 28, 1869	Leonard	221 Tenth Avenue	
2862	Borst, William	10	Sept. 5, 1871	Sept. 30, 1873	do.	219 West Thirty-first	
2863	Crocheron, Edward	12	Sept. 24, 1868	Feb. 25, 1869	do.	221 Tenth Avenue	
2864	Fichtel, Henry	14	do.	Sept. 30, 1869	Charlotte D.	17 Chariton	
2865	Hall, Joseph H.	7	do.	Oct. 24, 1872	Charles	361 Bleecker	May 20, 1869
2866	Henshaw, Augustus	11	do.	Oct. 30, 1875	Margaret	225 West Twenty-ninth	
				June 4, 1872	William	26 Seventh Avenue	

CATALOGUE OF SCHOLARS—Continued.

No.	Pupil.	Age	Admitted.	Withdrawn.	Parent.	Residence.	Graduated.
2867	Henshaw, Vanderbilt	10	Sept. 24, 1868	April 29, 1873	William	26 Seventh Avenue	
2868	Knowd, Sarah A	9	do.	Sept. 29, 1870	Mary J	213 West Twenty-ninth	
2869	Pierce, Arthur W	14	do.	April 28, 1870	Elizabeth A	Eng. Neighbor'd, N.J.	April 25, 1870
2870	Prince, Benjamin	10	do.	Sept. 30, 1869	Christopher	22 West Thirtieth	
2871	Styles, Walter R. (Vide Notes)		do.	Sept. 30, 1876	Charles H	110 West Thirtieth	May 18, 1876
2872	Wheaton, James W	11	do.	June 27, 1871	Ann Watson, Gr'dm'r	47 Beach	June 8, 1871
2873	Horst, Corstiaan	16	Oct. 29, 1868	Nov. 25, 1868	Leonard	221 Tenth Avenue	
2874	Hoyd, Abraham A	12	do.	June 27, 1871	Moore	Tompkinsville, S. I.	June 8, 1871
2875	Conrad, Emily	9	do.	Feb. 25, 1869	Wm. Schmidt	150 Nassau	
2876	De Groff, Edward	8	do.	Oct. 31, 1871	John	11 Warren Place	
2877	Van Cott, George F	12	do.	May 27, 1869	Myer	426 Eighth Avenue	
2878	Batcheldes, Louis		Nov. 25, 1868	April 29, 1869	Louis	212 West Twenty-ninth	
2879	Danforth, Anna	17	do.	March 25, 1869	Joseph Silliman	222 West Twenty-eighth	
2880	Griggs, Mary J	8	do.	May 26, 1870	Henry Coleman	420 West Thirty-first	
2881	Schwickert, Adolph	9	do.	May 27, 1869	William	157 West Thirty-first	
2882	Teutscher, Mary	11	Dec. 24, 1868	May 26, 1870	Charles	226 West Thirty-first	
2883	Carr, William	7	do.	Sept. 29, 1870	Benjamin	449 Eighth Avenue	
2884	Cramer, William J. C. P.	8	do.	do.	William J. C. P.	42 Ninth	
2885	Franz, John Frederick	9	do.	Feb. 24, 1870	Jacobine	356 West Thirty-fifth	
2886	Knight, Josephine E	9	do.	Sept. 29, 1877	Daniel	1,166 Broadway	May 24, 1877
2887	{ Lord, David S	10	Feb. 24, 1870	Jan. 28, 1869	Margaret	1,373 Broadway	
			Dec. 24, 1868	Dec. 22, 1870	do.	do.	
2888	{ Lord, William H	8	Feb. 24, 1870	June 24, 1869	do.	do.	
			Jan. 28, 1869	Dec. 22, 1870	do.	do.	
2889	Allason, Anna	9	do.	April 25, 1871	William, Uncle	132 West Twenty-fourth	
2890	Byrnes, George A	7	do.	June 2, 1877	William A	227 West Thirty-fifth	June 26, 1878
2891	Cleverley, Thomas H	7	do.	Sept. 29, 1877	John	454 Eighth Avenue	May 24, 1877
2892	Flint, George	12	do.	Oct. 28, 1869	Edward	369 Ninth Avenue	
2893	Heunisch, Emma	9	do.	Feb. 25, 1869	Frank	434 West Thirty-first	
2894	Heunisch, Lena	11	do.	do.	do.	do.	
2895	Heunisch, Louisa	7	do.	May 27, 1869	do.	do.	
2896	Knowd, Charles	8	do.	Sept. 29, 1870	Mary J	213 West Twenty-ninth	
2897	Miner, Luella	12	do.	Oct. 3, 1871	Henry	220 West Thirty-fifth	
2898	Perkins, Emma J	19	do.	May 26, 1870	Catharine A	124 West Eleventh	
2899	Tait, Peter	7	do.	Sept. 29, 1870	Otis A	50 West Twenty-eighth	
2900	Tait, Theodore	9	do.	do.	do.	do.	
2901	Ehrhart, Louisa		Feb. 25, 1869	Sept. 30, 1873	Ferdinand	1,034 Third Avenue	
2902	Lehmkuhl, Araminta B	13	do.	Oct. 28, 1869	Henry	30 Norfolk	

CATALOGUE OF SCHOLARS—Continued.

No.	Pupil.	Age	Admitted.	Withdrawn.	Parent.	Residence.	Graduated.
2903	Lehmkuhl, Charles E. C.	10	Feb. 25, 1869	Oct. 28, 1869	Henry	30 Norfolk	
2904	Lord, Francis	7	do.	March 26, 1871	Margaret	1,373 Broadway	
2905	Urlacher, Philip	10	do.	Sept. 30, 1869	John	361 Bleecker	
2906	Demarest, Kate	9	March 25, 1869	Dec. 13, 1878	Margaret	405 W. Twenty-seventh	
2907	Free, Caroline	13	do.	Oct. 28, 1869	Joseph Gegenhimer	725 Sixth	
2908	Hausin, William	8	do.	April 29, 1869	Gottfried	256 West Thirty-fifth	
2909	Stoll, Frederica	12	do.	May 27, 1869	Barbara	741 Sixth	
2910	Antz, Francis B	8	April 29, 1869	Sept. 30, 1869	Francis B	412 West Thirty-first	
2911	Basnar, William	10	do.	Oct. 1, 1872	Peter Nestrom, Step/r	410 Greenwich	
2912	Friauf, Charlotte	10	do.	Oct. 31, 1871	Jacob	178 Ludlow	
2913	Gambel, Frederick	11	do.	Sept. 30, 1869	Henry	310 Fourth	
2914	Henshaw, Adele	9	do.	April 1, 1873	William	26 Seventh Avenue	
2915	Henshaw, Viola	7	do.	do.	do.	do.	
2916	Knapp, August	12	do.	Sept. 30, 1869	Charles	1,248 Third Avenue	
2917	Knapp, William	9	do.	do.	do.	do.	
2918	Miller, John	13	do.	June 24, 1869	John	1,244 Third Avenue	
2919	Miner, Andrew	8	do.	Oct. 1, 1872	Henry	220 West Thirty-fifth	
2920	Richardson, Sarah A	16	do.	Sept. 30, 1869	Joseph	414 West Thirty-first	May 26, 1874
2921	Conrey, John D	10	May 27, 1869	Sept. 28, 1874	John F.	318 West Twenty-fifth	
2922	Van Derzee, Gordon D.	15	do.	May 26, 1870	Martha	Quarantine, S. I	
2923	Wingassen, Charles W.	12	do.	Sept. 30, 1869	George H	341 Hammond	
2924	Alcorn, Emma L.	11	June 24, 1869	do.	David	423 West Thirtieth	
2925	Bochmer, August	11	do.	do.	Henry	162 Seventh	
2926	Brown, Gertrude	12	do.	Oct. 1, 1872	William	226 West Twenty-ninth	
2927	Miner, Morton F	10	do.	Oct. 28, 1869	Henry	220 West Thirty-fifth	
2928	Rogers, Amanda S.	11	do.	June 30, 1870	Catharine Ganier	724 Sixth	
2929	Schaefer, John	12	do.	June 4, 1872	Jacob	332 Broome	
2930	Shepard, Frances E.	13	do.	Oct. 28, 1869	Thomas	8 Grove Terrace, J. C	
2931	Wagner, George F.	12	do.	Sept. 30, 1869	Peter	216 Second	
2932	Angus, William	9	Sept. 30, 1869	June 3, 1873	David	426 W. Twenty-eighth	
2933	Bascom, William B.	7	do.	April 2, 1872	Henry C	2 Pacific Place	
2934	Bates, Robert	10	do.	Oct. 3, 1871	Robert	219 West Thirty-second	
2935	Heatson, William	10	Dec. 3, 1872	Sept. 30, 1873	do.	162 West Twenty-sixth	
2936	Beggs, Ada	9	Sept. 30, 1869	Sept. 29, 1870	Andrew	307 Ninth Avenue	
2937	Chapman, Wm. R. (Vide Note)	14	do.	Oct. 27, 1870	John W	208 West Forty-ninth	
2938	Dolde, George	9	do.	April 25, 1871	Wm. J. Valentine	Fordham	
2939	Dunham, Catharine	9	do.	June 4, 1872	John	361 Bleecker	
				Oct. 27, 1870	Sarah C	246 West Thirtieth	

CATALOGUE OF SCHOLARS—Continued.

No.	Pupil.	Age	Admitted.	Withdrawn.	Parent.	Residence.	Graduated.
2940	Gierdes, Dora	7	Sept. 30, 1869	Oct. 3, 1871	Albert	531 West Twenty-ninth	
2941	Graham, Augusta	8	do.	April 25, 1871	Amanda	213 W. Twenty-eighth	
2942	Griffen, Phebe	12	do.	May 26, 1870	Anna C	4 West Twenty-ninth	
2943	Griffen, Sabina F	15	do.	do.	do.	do.	June 8, 1871
2944	Losee, Mary F. (Vide Notes)	13	do.	June 27, 1871	Willett G	936 Eighth Avenue	May 26, 1874
2945	Millis, Charles L	10	do.	June 1, 1874	Samuel H	203 S. Fifth, Brooklyn	
2946	Page, Clara	9	do.	Oct. 3, 1871	Charles B	449 Ninth Avenue	
2947	Peabody, Ella	10	do.	April 29, 1873	William H	201 W. Twenty-seventh	
2948	Spader, Electa	6	do.	Oct. 2, 1875	Jesse B	121 West Thirty-third	
2949	Stage, Harriet E	11	do.	March 5, 1872	Stephen	382 Ninth Avenue	
2950	Stewart, William	12	do.	Dec. 23, 1869	Elias Watson	399 Ninth Avenue	
2951	Terry, Walstein T. (Vide Notes)	14	Sept. 5, 1871	June 4, 1872		47 Beach	
2952	Townsend, Henry M	17	Sept. 30, 1869	do.	Thomas	Marlboro, Ulster Co	
2953	Townsend, Thomas	13	do.		do.	Eng. Neighborh'd, N. J.	
		12				do.	
						Fairview, N. J.	
2954	Wicks, George P	15	Dec. 3, 1871	Dec. 2, 1873	Oscar	435 West Twenty-fifth	
2955	Wicks, Mary E.	11	Sept. 30, 1869	Oct. 1, 1872	do.	244 West Thirty-third	
2956	Willis, Walton P.	15	Dec. 2, 1873	June 1, 1874	do.	435 West Thirty-fifth	
		9	Sept. 30, 1869	Nov. 2, 1875		417 W. Twenty-eighth	
2957	Brownlee, J. Harrison (Vide Notes)	13	Oct. 28, 1869	April 2, 1872	James		
				Oct. 3, 1871	Thomas	161 West Thirty-first	May 23, 1872
2958	Burton, Minnie H	10	do.	June 27, 1871	Amos	216 West Thirty-first	
2959	Connelley, Jennie	8	do.	Sept. 28, 1874	Rebecca	226 West Thirty-first	
2960	Libby, William H	17	do.	Dec. 23, 1869	John	Brighton Heights, S. I.	
2961	Lounsberry, Josephine	11	do.	Dec. 5, 1871	Alexander	229 West Thirty-fourth	
2962	Turquand, Victoria	13	do.	March 31, 1870	Sarah E	245 West Twenty-first	
2963	McEown, Joseph T.	7	Nov. 25, 1869	Oct. 3, 1871	Susan	162 W. Twenty-eighth	
2964	Smith, Ida	13	do.	Jan. 27, 1870	Frances	236 W. Thirty-seventh	
2965	Voorhis, Albert E	9	do.	Jan. 29, 1876	Albert	442 West Thirty-fourth	
2966	Willis, Christina	15	do.	Nov. 23, 1870	Isabella Handwerk	82 Frankfort	
2967	Carss, John B	9	Dec. 23, 1869	Sept. 28, 1874	John	261 West Thirtieth	May 26, 1874
2968	Fiske, Susie J	11	do.	Jan. 27, 1870	Matilda	870 Broadway	
2969	Knauber, John	8	do.	March 31, 1870	John	85 Division	
2970	Ryerson, Edward J	8	do.	Feb. 26, 1876	George N	556 West Forty-second	
2971	Ayers, Martha J. (Vide Notes)	7	Jan. 27, 1870	May 29, 1875	Joseph B	5 Pacific Place	
2972	De La Mater, C. H. (Vide Note)	15	Jan. 27, 1877	Sept. 29, 1877	do.	435 Eighth Avenue	
		10	Jan. 27, 1870	April 1, 1873	Benjamin	519 West Twenty-third	

CATALOGUE OF SCHOLARS—Continued.

No.	Pupil.	Age	Admitted.	Withdrawn.	Parent.	Residence.	Graduated.
2973	De La Mater, Du Bois	12	Jan. 27, 1870	April 1, 1873	Benjamin	519 West Twenty-third	
2974	Homan, Jessie A	11	do.	Dec. 2, 1873	Isaac	400 West Twenty-fourth	
2975	Knickmyer, Frederick W	10	do.	May 26, 1870	Frederica	352 East Tenth	
2976	{ Lammers, Elizabeth	7	do.	June 25, 1872	Frederick II	423 West Twenty-fifth	
2977	Lammers, Emma	11	Sept. 28, 1874	Oct. 2, 1875	do.	do. do.	
2978	McMekin, Jane	11	Jan. 27, 1870	Sept. 30, 1873	do.	do. do.	
2979	McMekin, William J	9	do.	June 4, 1872	Samuel	342 Eighth Avenue	
2980	Nelson, Mary E	11	do.	June 30, 1870	do.	do. do.	
2981	Heatson, George	9	do.	May 26, 1870	Maria	50 West Thirty-first	
2982	Huchanan, Sarah J	10	do.	Sept. 29, 1870	Andrew	307 Ninth Avenue	
2983	Dakin, Isabella	8	Feb. 24, 1870	Sept. 30, 1870	Edward	304 West Thirty-eighth	
2984	Dakin, John	10	do.	June 4, 1872	William	410 West Twenty-sixth	
2985	Leonard, Charles	11	do.	Dec. 5, 1871	do.	do. do.	
2986	Pringle, Isabella	6	do.	Oct. 27, 1870	Harriet Williamson	425 Ninth Avenue	
2987	Radcliff, William W	7	do.	Oct. 1, 1872	James	159 West Thirty-first	
2988	Stewart, Emily	10	do.	Dec. 22, 1870	Isaac	525 West Fifty-first	
2989	Stewart, Mary	7	do.	Sept. 31, 1873	Samuel	307 Ninth Avenue	
2990	Dixon, Ella R	7	March 31, 1870	March 5, 1872	Rebecca	do. do.	
2991	Dixon, James E	10	do.	do.	do.	161 West Thirty-first	
2992	Dixon, Samuel S	6	do.	do.	do.	do. do.	
2993	Ferris, Joseph	10	do.	Nov. 23, 1870	John A	do. do.	
2994	Nebol, Louis	13	do.	Jan. 26, 1871	Michael	309 Seventh Avenue	
2995	Oliver, Sarah A	17	do.	May 30, 1871	James	162 Houston	
2996	Oliver, Ida	8	do.	Sept. 29, 1870	Frances A	313 West Fifty-first	
2997	Osterlay, Charles	11	do.	do.	Henry	33 W. Twenty-seventh	
2998	{ Brownlee, Archibald G. (Vide Notes)	12	April 28, 1870	Oct. 3, 1871	Thomas	631 Eleventh	May 23, 1872
2999	Campbell, William J	9	do.	Feb. 25, 1875	Charles	161 West Thirty-first	
3000	Crane, John	10	do.	Sept. 29, 1870	John	241 West Thirty-first	
3001	Edwards, Oliver C	7	do.	do.	Jesse	157 W. Twenty-seventh	
3002	Franz, Sophia	12	do.	Dec. 22, 1870	John	508 West Thirty-third	
3003	Grosheim, Bernard	8	do.	Sept. 28, 1874	Frederick	744 Ninth Avenue	
3004	Henderson, Thomas	7	do.	Oct. 1, 1872	William	244 West Thirty-second	
3005	Holstein, Fritz	11	do.	Sept. 29, 1870	Frederick	291 Seventh Avenue	
3006	Mandeville, Henrietta E	7	do.	do.	John L	248 West Thirty-second	
3007	Meal, Anne G	8	do.	Nov. 23, 1870	Henry V	331 West Twenty-ninth	
3008	Smyth, Matthew	7	do.	Oct. 3, 1871	Joseph	342 Eighth Avenue	

CATALOGUE OF SCHOLARS—Continued.

No.	Pupil.	Age	Admitted.	Withdrawn.	Parent.	Residence.	Graduated.
3009	Bechthold, Julius E. J.	7	May 26, 1870	Sept. 23, 1874	Rev. A. H.	245 West Twentieth	
3010	Clancy, Georgiana	14	do.	March 28, 1871	Wm. T. Stoutenburgh	110 West Thirty-second	
3011	Drumgold, Henry	8	do.	Sept. 28, 1874	Henry	729 Eleventh Avenue	
3012	Edwards, Alice	12	do.	Sept. 29, 1870	Jesse	508 West Thirty-third	
3013	Fay, Georgiana	6	do.	June 29, 1871	Julius	151 West Thirty-eighth	
3014	Hose, Henry	9	do.	Sept. 29, 1870	Henry	695 East Eleventh	
3015	Houston, Henry L.	9	do.	Oct. 27, 1870	Letitia	212 West Thirty-first	
3016	Lindsey, John W.	9	do.	do.	Catharine	353 West Thirty-ninth	
3017	McClenachan, Lillian P.	14	do.		Charles F.	203 W. Twenty-second	
3018	Officer, Letitia	13	do.	June 4, 1872	James	313 West Fifty-first	
3019	Barclay, Kate	11	do.	June 1, 1874	Catharine	211 West Twenty-ninth	May 26, 1874
3020	De La Croix, Andrew	7	June 30, 1870	Sept. 29, 1870	Matilda	144 West Twenty-ninth	
3021	De La Croix, Matilda C. (*Vide Notes*).	11	Sept. 30, 1873	Nov. 23, 1870	do.	144 Fourth Avenue	
3022	Myers, Henry	9	Sept. 30, 1873	Nov. 23, 1870	do.	144 West Twenty-ninth	
3023	O'Shea, Francis A. K.	12	Sept. 30, 1873	June 26, 1875	do.	439 Fourth Avenue	May 25, 1875
3024	Page, Sarah E.	7	June 30, 1870	Oct. 27, 1870	Anna	253 W. Twenty-seventh	
3025	Troutman, Ida	8	do.	March 4, 1873	Thomas	117 West Thirtieth	
3026	Young, Adaline	11	do.	Oct. 3, 1871	Charles B.	495 Ninth Avenue	
3027	Young, John R.	9	do.	Sept. 30, 1870	Peter	138 West Twenty-ninth	May 18, 1876
				Sept. 27, 1878	James	West and India, Gr'np't	
3028	Young, Mary E.	17	Nov. 21, 1879	Jan. 27, 1880	do.	do. do.	
3029	Angus, James	7	June 30, 1870	June 1, 1874	do.	130 Java, Greenpoint	May 26, 1874
				May 4, 1874	David	West and India, Gr'np't	
3030	Ayers, Minnie I.	12	Sept. 29, 1870	May 29, 1875	Joseph H.	426 W. Twenty-eighth	
				Sept. 27, 1878		135 West Twenty-sixth	June 26, 1878
3031	Bates, Jane	7	Jan. 27, 1877	Oct. 3, 1871	Robert	435 Eighth Avenue	
3032	Brandon, George	10	Sept. 29, 1870	June 27, 1871	Alexander	333 West Thirty-second	
3033	Brown, Isabella I.	6	do.	June 4, 1871	William	220 West Thirty-third	
3034	Brown, Louis G.	12	do.	Oct. 3, 1871	Elijah T.	226 West Twenty-ninth	
3035	Butt, John	13	do.	June 4, 1872	George	72½ Irving Place	
3036	Carey, John	11	do.	Nov. 5, 1872	John Tonilear	329 Seventh Avenue	
3037	Clark, Frank W.	7	do.	May 30, 1871	Charles W.	333 West Thirty-second	
3038	Collins, James Ross	8	do.	June 4, 1872	James R.	133 West Twenty-ninth	
3039	Dorn, John	11	do.	Oct. 31, 1871	John	135 West Twenty-sixth	
3040	Dow, Mary	10	do.	Sept. 5, 1871	William	219 East Fourth	
3041	Lippett, Elizabeth	10	do.	Oct. 31, 1871	John	270 West Thirty-fourth	
3042	Marsh, Charles B	11	do.	Jan. 26, 1871	Samuel	219 East Fourth	
						10 Third	

CATALOGUE OF SCHOLARS—Continued.

No.	Pupil.	Age	Admitted.	Withdrawn.	Parent.	Residence.	Graduated.
3043	Marun, Alexander H.	10	Sept. 29, 1870	Oct. 2, 1875	John T. Seymour	225 East Thirty-first	
3044	McArthur, Martha	12	do.	Nov. 23, 1870	Mary	73 West Fifty-third	
3045	Morley, Fredwood	8	do.	Sept. 28, 1874	Lawrence	259 West Forty-first	
3046	Munn, Emma P.	6	do.	Oct. 28, 1876	Samuel E.	121 West Twenty-third	
3047	Smith, Ira G.	15	do.	Nov. 23, 1870	Allen R.	323 West Twenty-eighth	
3048	Thompson, Eugene	13	do.	Dec. 24, 1872	George W.	463 West Thirty-fourth	
3049	Traver, Leah C.	13	do.	Sept. 28, 1874	Henry E.	182 Seventh Avenue	
3050	Van Koden, Catharine J.	6	do.	do.	Cornelius	840 Sixth Avenue	
3051	Vaubel, William	13	do.	April 30, 1872	Conrad	145 East Houston	May 23, 1872
3052	Warley, Susan V.	14	do.	June 27, 1871	Emma	702 Seventh Avenue	
3053	Whelan, William	11	do.	April 25, 1871	James	316 West Twenty-eighth	
3054	Wright, Walter L.	9	do.	Sept. 29, 1877	Henry F.	409 W. Twenty-seventh	
3055	Veury, Frank	9	do.	June 2, 1877	John S.	361 West Eleventh	May 24, 1877
3056	Adams, Frances	14	Oct. 27, 1870	Sept. 28, 1874	Samuel	254 W. Twenty-second	do.
3057	Drysdale, Anna	6	do.	Oct. 3, 1871	Matthew	262 Seventh Avenue	
3058	Engle, Charles	15	do.	June 4, 1872	Andrew	Eng. Neighborh'd, N. J.	
3059	McCabe, William	10	do.	April 29, 1873	Mary Ann	225 West Twenty-ninth	
3060	McClenachan, Emily	14	Nov. 27, 1874	Feb. 27, 1875	Charles F.	323 West Twenty-first	
3061	McCrum, Ruth C.	9	Oct. 27, 1870	June 27, 1871	Elizabeth	207 W. Twenty-second	
3062	Mortimer, Fredrick	7	do.	Sept. 19, 1879	Peter F.	5 Pacific Place	June 26, 1879
3063	Sedgwick, Russell	9	do.	Feb. 28, 1871	Ann Hall	142 West Twenty-ninth	
3064	Van Houten, Ida	12	do.	May 30, 1871	Edward	427 West Thirty-second	
		15	March 3, 1874	June 4, 1872		58 West Thirty-first	
3065	Watson, Florence	13	Oct. 27, 1870	Oct. 2, 1875	George	do.	
3066	Byrnes, Ann Eola	6	Nov. 23, 1870	Feb. 4, 1873	William A.	592 Sixth Avenue	
3067	Danziger, Esther	10	do.	Sept. 19, 1879	Hermann	227 West Thirty-fifth	June 26, 1879
3068	Howle, William	9	do.	Oct. 3, 1871	John	1,259 Broadway	
3069	Jones, Howard	11	do.	Dec. 22, 1870	Abraham L.	435 West Twenty-sixth	
3070	Kesselem, Catharine	12	do.	June 4, 1872	Frederick	411 W. Twenty-seventh	
3071	Lyster, Georgia	6	do.	Dec. 22, 1870	Mary A. Charles	535 West Twenty-ninth	
3072	McDonald, Jeremiah	8	do.	Feb. 28, 1871	Thomas	211 West Thirty-sixth	
3073	McNeil, Emma	17	do.	April 25, 1871	Edward	Eng. Neighborh'd, N. J.	
3074	McNeil, Frances	11	do.	Nov. 27, 1874	do.	157 West Twenty-eighth	
3075	Merritt, Edward	12	do.	Oct. 2, 1875	Mary C.	do.	
3076	Simmons, May	6	do.	March 28, 1871	Jeffray	53 East Twenty-sixth	
3077	Stossel, Albert	11	do.	April 25, 1871	Ferdinand	207 W. Twenty-second	
3078	Watson, Josephine L.		do.	Oct. 2, 1875	Anna	235 West Twenty-sixth	May 25, 1875
						1,166 Broadway	

CATALOGUE OF SCHOLARS—Continued.

No.	Pupil.	Age	Admitted.	Withdrawn.	Parent.	Residence.	Graduated.
3079	Whitemore, Francisco	11	Nov. 23, 1870	Oct. 3, 1871	Francisco	64 West Forty-eighth	....
3080	Whitemore, Theodore	13	do.	do.	do.	do. do.	....
3081	Brown, Benjamin W	16	Dec. 22, 1870	May 30, 1871	Henry	{ Guttenburg, New Jersey.	....
3082	Hoyt, Samuel A	12	do.	April 25, 1871	Samuel W	436 W. Twenty-eighth	....
3083	Kruse, Henrietta	12	do.	Oct. 3, 1871	Henry	225 West Twenty-ninth	....
3084	Linkroum, Courtlandt	12	do.	March 5, 1872	James A	261 West Thirtieth	....
3085	Thompson, Mary G	9	do.	Dec. 5, 1871	Theron	769 Sixth Avenue	....
3086	Tracy, William H	11	do.	Oct. 31, 1871	William	109 West Thirty-third	....
3087	Ballerman, Annie	12	Jan. 26, 1871	Sept. 30, 1873	Charles	477 Ninth Avenue	....
3088	Blauvelt, John M	16	do.	Feb. 28, 1871	Blauvelt A	115 West Thirtieth	....
3089	Thompson, George R	13	do.	June 4, 1872	Theron	769 Sixth Avenue	....
3090	Tracy, Elizabeth	10	do.	April 1, 1873	William	109 West Thirty-third	....
3091	{ Tracy, Rebecca	7	}	Nov. 2, 1874	do.	do. do.	....
		12		Nov. 27, 1875	do.	do. do.	
3092	Carss, Joseph	12	Oct. 2, 1875	Oct. 2, 1875	John	261 West Thirtieth	....
3093	Grau, Michael	9	Feb. 28, 1871	Oct. 3, 1871	do.	426 West Twenty-sixth	....
3094	McCracken, Anna	8	do.	Nov. 5, 1872	Ellen	419 West Thirty-second	....
3095	Ahmuty, Matthew	10	March 28, 1871	April 2, 1872	Albert	123 West Thirty-third	....
3096	{ Gerdes, William	7	}	Oct. 3, 1871	Mary	531 West Twenty-ninth	....
		11		Oct. 28, 1876		537 West Twenty-ninth	
3097	Goetchius, Clifford L	11	Nov. 27, 1875	Jan. 3, 1872	William L	263 West Thirty-ninth	....
3098	Henderson, Samuel	13	March 28, 1871	April 2, 1872	William	331 Seventh Avenue	....
3099	Hoffman, Schuyler V. V	7	do.	Oct. 31, 1871	Charles	31 Madison Avenue	....
3100	Seiss, Augusta	9	do.	do.	Herman	440 W. Twenty-eighth	....
3101	Seiss, Gustave	8	do.		do.	do.	....
3102	Thompson, Margaret C	8	do.	Oct. 3, 1871	John	209 West Twenty-sixth	....
3103	Hartine, Jenny	7	April 25, 1871	do.	Louisa	115 West Thirtieth	....
3104	Eagleson, Agnes	8	do.	June 27, 1871	Thomas	112 West Thirtieth	....
3105	Elsie, Frances	14	do.	May 30, 1871	Fanny	1,251 Broadway	....
3106	Evans, Jennie	11	do.	June 4, 1872	John J	340 Ninth Avenue	....
3107	Monfort, Samuel S	10	do.	Oct. 3, 1871	John H	407 W. Twenty-seventh	....
3108	Sefton, Ida	12	do.	May 30, 1872	Joseph	112 West Thirtieth	....
3109	Slaight, Annie M	12	do.	March 30, 1872	John	426 West Thirty-second	....
3110	Smith, John B	12	do.	Jan. 30, 1872	Joseph	261 West Thirtieth	....
3111	Sykes, Mary	7	do.	June 27, 1871	Edward	490 Sixth Avenue	....
3112	Gordon, Luanna	8	May 30, 1871	Oct. 3, 1871	Stephen	412 West Thirty-third	....
3113	McIlvaine, Elizabeth J	7	do.	Oct. 2, 1875	George	321 Seventh Avenue	....

CATALOGUE OF SCHOLARS—Continued.

No.	Pupil.	Age	Admitted.	Withdrawn.	Parent.	Residence.	Graduated.
3114	Munn, Edward F	12	May 30, 1871	Oct. 31, 1871	Stephen H	405 West Thirty-third	
3115	Schooonmaker, Selah	13	Dec. 3, 1872	Sept. 30, 1873	do.	523 West Twenty-ninth	
3116	Shute, George W	9	May 30, 1871	June 4, 1872	John	801 Washington	
3117	Tyler, Cora	12	do.	April 1, 1873	William H	261 West Thirtieth	
3118	White, Emma F	7	do.	Oct. 3, 1871	John Day	245 West Twenty-ninth	
3119	Wright, Joseph A	16	June 27, 1871	do.	Hiram	407 Ninth Avenue	
3120	Wright, William	12	do.	do.	Joseph	444 West Thirty-first	
3121	Anderson, Richard C	7	do.	do.		do.	
3122	Baisden, Hannah J	17	Sept. 5, 1871	June 4, 1872	Lydia J	Cresskill, New Jersey	
3123	Busch, Adeline	14	do.	April 29, 1873	John J	110 West Thirtieth	
3124	Busch, Margaret	10	do.	Oct. 2, 1875	Henry	271 Ninth Avenue	
3125	Dangler, Adolphus E	8	do.	Sept. 30, 1876	do.	do.	
3126	Hewkett, James L	7	do.	Sept. 28, 1874	Augusta	261 West Thirtieth	
3127	Howells, Elizabeth	13	do.	April, 1878	Joseph	343 Seventh Avenue	June 26, 1878
3128	Howells, Martha	7	do.	Nov. 5, 1872	John	203 West Twentieth	
3129	Howells, Rhoda	11	do.	do.	do.	do.	
3130	Lammers, Edward	7	do.	Oct. 2, 1875	do.	do.	
3131	Schultz, Nicholas	10	do.	Jan. 29, 1876	Frederick H	423 West Twenty-fifth	
3132	Schultz, William	10	do.	Oct. 2, 1875	Nicholas	153 East Houston	
3133	Shute, Charles H	7	Sept. 30, 1876	Jan. 30, 1875	do.	do.	
3134	Signa, Ella	10	Sept. 5, 1871	Sept. 27, 1878	William H	261 West Thirtieth	
3135	Vere, Henry	7	do.	April 2, 1872	Elizabeth	414 Eighth Avenue	
3136	Ahmaty, Elizabeth	9	Oct. 3, 1871	June 4, 1872	Henry	207 West Twentieth	
3137	Ahrens, Alfred	9	do.	March 5, 1872	Maria	46 West Thirtieth	
3138	Armstrong, Emeline W	15	do.	Sept. 30, 1873	William	123 West Thirty-third	
3139	Corbett, Elizabeth	12	do.	June 1, 1874	do.	335 Seventh Avenue	May 26, 1874
3140	Corbett, Julia B	10	do.	Dec. 24, 1872	Robert C	140 West Twenty-sixth	
3141	Crane, Everett F	8	do.	do.	Robert H	118 West Forty-second	
3142	Crane, Lemuel F	5	do.	June 4, 1872	Lemuel P	do.	
3143	Crossingham, Caroline	6	do.	do.	Daniel	228 West Forty-second	
3144	De Host, Alwyn	7	do.	Oct. 31, 1871	Augustus B	356 West Twenty-sixth	
3145	De Host, Leon	11	do.	do.	do.	200 West Forty-fifth	
3146	De Host, Marie Louise	10	do.	do.	do.	do.	
3147	De Turk, Herbert	14	do.	Dec. 5, 1871	Eliza	309 West Twenty-first	
3148	Dunlap, Edwin J	14	do.	Oct. 1, 1872	James	401 West Thirty-third	
3149	Evans, William	8	do.	Nov. 4, 1873	William	236 W. Twenty-seventh	

CATALOGUE OF SCHOLARS—Continued.

No.	Pupil.	Age	Admitted.	Withdrawn.	Parent.	Residence.	Graduated.
3150	Farrell, Florence H.	11	Oct. 3, 1871	May, 1878	Mitchell	211 West Twentieth	June 26, 1878
3151	Forrest, Anna M.	9	do.	Oct. 1, 1872	Thomas	415 West Twenty-fifth	......
3152	Halsey, Edwin B.	12	do.	Feb. 27, 1875	James E.	34 Grove	......
3153	Halsey, Josephine R.	8	do.	Oct. 2, 1875	do.	do.	......
		13	Oct. 28, 1876	Sept. 29, 1877		Cherry Hill, N. J.	
3154	Hamilton, Isabella	15	Oct. 3, 1871	March 3, 1874	Isabella	817 Sixth Avenue	......
3155	Henderson, Sarah	7	do.	Oct. 1, 1872	William	144 Seventh Avenue	......
3156	Henderson, William	16	do.	April 2, 1872		do.	......
3157	Jacobs, Sarah	16	do.	Oct. 31, 1871	William H.	404 West Thirty-third	......
3158	Just, James	13	do.	Jan. 3, 1872	Alexander	Fairview, N. J.	......
3159	Kuhn, Amelia	9	do.	Nov. 5, 1872	Charles	213 W. Twenty-seventh	May 24, 1877
3160	Kuhn, Charles	11	do.	Sept. 29, 1877	do.	do.	......
3161	Kuhn, Louisa	7	do.	Nov. 27, 1874	do.	do.	......
3162	Kuhn, William	11	do.	Jan. 24, 1879	do.	do.	......
3163	Linder, Johanna	8	do.	March 5, 1872	Frank	240 West Thirty-second	......
3164	Linder, Rosina	13	Sept. 28, 1874	March 4, 1873	do.	do.	......
				May 29, 1875		do.	
3165	Owens, Benjamin	13	Oct. 3, 1871	June 25, 1872	Benjamin	421 West Thirtieth	......
3166	Owens, Mary L.	10	do.	April 29, 1873	do.	do.	......
3167	Ryerson, Harriet	7	do.	Oct. 1, 1872	John	632 Greenwich	......
3168	Snyder, Alfred L.	11	do.	Feb. 3, 1874	Henry	104 West Forty-ninth	......
3169	Snyder, Frederick G.	13	do.	do.	do.	do.	June 26, 1879
3170	Styles, Charles H.	7	do.	Sept. 19, 1879	Charles H.	110 West Thirtieth	......
3171	White, Mark Henry	11	do.	March 5, 1872	Mary L.	248 West Forty-second	......
3172	Whitehead, Gertrude	11	do.	Oct. 31, 1871	John	415 West Thirtieth	......
3173	Wilcox, Margaret	13	do.	March 5, 1872	Edward	333 Seventh Avenue	......
3174	Abernethy, Mary A.	6	Oct. 31, 1871	June 4, 1872	William	440 West Twenty-eighth	......
3175	Ahmuty, William	7	do.	March 5, 1874	do.	123 West Thirty-third	......
3176	Armstrong, Charles	9	do.	Nov. 2, 1874	Robert C.	140 West Twenty-sixth	......
3177	Burns, Arthur	7	do.	June 1, 1874	William	306 West Twenty-eighth	......
3178	Burns, Grace	14	do.	Sept. 30, 1873	do.	do.	......
3179	Burns, William J.	11	do.	June 1, 1874	do.	do.	......
3180	Carman, Melissa C.	12	do.	Sept. 30, 1876	Samuel	1 and Wash'gt'n, Gr'np't	May 28, 1876
3181	Corbett, Charlotte	15	do.	Dec. 24, 1872	Robert H.	118 West Forty-second	......
3182	De Haun, Edward	10	do.	June 4, 1872	Housmann	351 W. Thirty-fourth	......
3183	Doolittle, Washington	7	do.	Jan. 30, 1872	Sarah	213 W. Twenty-seventh	......
3184	Hopper, Margaret	10	do.	June 4, 1872	James A.	113 West Twenty-ninth	......
3185	Hopper, Mary	12	do.	do.	do.	do.	......

CATALOGUE OF SCHOLARS—Continued.

No.	Pupil.	Age	Admitted.	Withdrawn.	Parent.	Residence.	Graduated.
3186	Kolb, Elizabeth	9	Oct. 31, 1871	Sept. 28, 1874	Philip	304 Eleventh Avenue	
3187	Kolb, Samuel	11	do.	Sept. 30, 1873	do.	do.	
3188	McDougal, Matilda J.	11	do.	Nov. 4, 1873	Hugh	236 W. Twenty-seventh.	
3189	Porter, Georgiana	14	Sept. 28, 1874	Oct. 2, 1875	do.	89 Ninth Avenue	May 25, 1875
3190	Simmons, Edward	6	Oct. 31, 1871	June 4, 1872	Elizabeth	342 Eighth Avenue	
3191	Stacker, Elizabeth	6	do.	Dec. 5, 1871	John	149 West Thirty-third	
3192	Van Haughton, Kate	13	do.	June 5, 1872	William	304 Eleventh Avenue	
3193	Warner, Margaret A.	11	do.	do.	Maria L.	3 Pacific Place	
3194	Cossum, Caroline	6	do.	do.	Leonard	161 West Twelfth	
3195	Cossum, William H.	8	do.	do.	Charles	421 West Thirtieth	
3196	Gross, John Frederick	12	do.	Sept. 30, 1873	Frederick	do.	
3197	Huchton, Viola	14	do.	Nov. 5, 1872	Julia	304 Eleventh Avenue	
3198	McCluskey, Esther	8	do.	June 4, 1872	Edward	110 West Thirtieth	
3199	Marks, Amelia	8	do.	do.	Abraham	247 West Thirtieth	
						134 West Thirtieth	
3200	Moore, John T.	7	do.	Oct. 1, 1872	Margaret	325 Seventh Avenue	
3201	Moore, Mary E.	6	Feb. 27, 1875	Oct. 2, 1875	Abigail Adair	415 West Thirty-third	
3202	Pfeffer, Catharine	9	Dec. 5, 1871	Oct. 1, 1872	Margaret	325 Seventh Avenue	
3203	Ruding, Duncan	12	Feb. 27, 1875	Oct. 2, 1875	Abigail Adair, Aunt.	415 West Thirty-third	
3204	Travis, Alice	13	Dec. 5, 1871	Jan. 3, 1872	Frederick	304 Eleventh Avenue	
3205	Yoost, Bertha	11	do.	Nov. 5, 1877	Walter	202 Jersey Avenue, J. C.	
3206	Yoost, Charles	7	do.	June 3, 1873	William H.	233 West Thirty-first	
3207	Bullene, John J.	13	Jan. 3, 1872	Feb. 2, 1878	Claus	242 West Thirtieth	
3208	Chamberlain, Perry	14	do.	June 4, 1872	do.	do.	
3209	Engel, Peter	8	do.	Jan. 30, 1872	John	151 West Twelfth	
3210	Francis, Marion	15	do.	June 4, 1872	George W.	Englewood, N. J.	
3211	Peabody, Alfred	8	do.	Nov. 4, 1873	Peter	328 West Twenty-ninth	May 29, 1873
3212	Schultz, Michael S.	12	do.	Sept. 30, 1873	Isaac	242 Garden, Hoboken	
3213	Wade, William H.	7	do.	Nov. 5, 1872	William H.	239 West Twenty-sixth	
3214	Crosson, Mary M.	10	Jan. 30, 1872	March 5, 1872	Michael S.	52 Eighth	
3215	Crosson, William	15	do.	do.	Harrison	325 Seventh Avenue	
3216	Holgate, Ella H.	7	do.	Sept. 24, 1880	Uriah	248 West Thirtieth	
3217	Norberg, Lily	13	do.	April 2, 1872	Thomas H., M. D.	217 West Twelfth	May 27, 1880
3218	Oman, Mary	14	do.	Sept. 30, 1873	Mary	224 West Thirty-second	
3219	Wagner, Charles	12	do.	April 2, 1872	Thomas H.	147 Sixth Avenue	
3220	Adina, Elizabeth	8	March 5, 1872	Nov. 5, 1872	Charles	202 West Twenty-first	
					Francis	459 Sixth Avenue	

199

CATALOGUE OF SCHOLARS—Continued.

No.	Pupil.	Age	Admitted.	Withdrawn.	Parent.	Residence.	Graduated.
3221	Beach, Clarence W	11	March 5, 1872	Sept. 30, 1873	John, M. D.	111 West Forty-fifth	....
3222	Beach, Willard Parker (Vide Notes)	12	do.	do.	do.	do.	....
3223	Connolly, Jessie	11	do.	do.	Robert	213 W. Twenty-seventh	....
3224	Craddick, Emma	10	do.	Nov. 5, 1872	Sarah	405 West Thirty-third	....
3225	Decker, William	13	do.	Dec. 3, 1872	Richard	Norwood, New Jersey	....
3226	Grigg, Emma	10	do.	June 4, 1872	Louisa	429 West Thirtieth	....
3227	Grosheim, Louisa G	8	do.	Nov. 27, 1874	Frederick	244 West Thirty-second	....
3228	Gross, George	10	do.	do.	do.	304 Eleventh Avenue	....
3229	Maxwell, William	8	do.	Feb. 4, 1873	Arabella	201 West Thirty-fourth	....
3229	Maxwell, William	8	do.	May 1, 1875	do.	454 Eighth Avenue	....
3230	Prins, Joachim M	12	Nov. 27, 1874	Sept. 30, 1873	Joachim	86 Grove	....
3231	Seawaid, William	12	March 5, 1872	Dec. 24, 1872	Robert Wilson	415 West Thirtieth	....
3232	Van Emmerick, Bertha	10	do.	Nov. 5, 1872	Garret	511 West Forty-third	....
3233	Allen, Mary	9	April 2, 1872	Dec. 3, 1872	Lewis J.	357 West Twenty-ninth	....
3234	Dunn, Esther A	6	do.	Oct. 2, 1875	Matthew S	215 West Nineteenth	....
3235	Gross, Emma	7	do.	May 1, 1875	Frederick	304 Eleventh Avenue	....
3236	Haight, Willis D.	8	do.	Dec. 2, 1873	Edward	263 West Thirtieth	....
3237	Jagels, Cathalina	9	do.	April 29, 1873	Henry	249 West Twenty-ninth	....
3238	Reed, Ida	8	do.	Nov. 4, 1873	Henry C	311 W. Twenty-eighth	....
3238	Reed, Ida	8	do.	Jan. 30, 1875	do.	773 Eighth Avenue	....
3239	Clegg, Margaret J	7	Sept. 28, 1874	Nov. 5, 1872	Robert	138 West Twenty-fifth	....
3240	Evensen, Isabelle	10	April 30, 1872	Oct. 1, 1872	Henry, Jr.	245 West Thirteenth	....
3241	Inslee, Elizabeth	12	do.	Feb. 3, 1874	Matilda	414 Eighth Avenue	....
3242	Johnson, George	11	do.	Dec. 3, 1872	Maria	555 West Twenty-ninth	....
3243	Kahl, Martin	12	do.	do.	Martin	539 West Twenty-ninth	....
3244	Knight, Leola	13	do.	Sept. 30, 1873	William	128 West Forty-first	....
3245	Sweeney, Alexander	11	do.	March 4, 1873	Sarah	413 Ninth Avenue	....
3246	Ward, Emma C	14	do.	June 1, 1874	John Jones	450 West Thirty-fourth	....
3247	Albrecht, Charles	9	June 4, 1872	Nov. 30, 1872	John	253 West Twenty-ninth	....
3248	Bell, James	13	do.	do.	do.	256 W. Twenty-seventh	....
3249	Clark, Alexander A	11	do.	Feb. 27, 1875	Asa	411 West Twenty-fifth	....
3250	Cocks, Louis A	15	do.	Oct. 1, 1872	Albert H.	Classon's Point, N. Y.	....
3251	Coey, Elizabeth	10	do.	June 1, 1874	Mary	239 West Twenty-sixth	....
3252	Connelley, John H	8	do.	Nov. 2, 1874	Rebecca	226 West Thirty-first	....
3253	Eckert, Louis V	11	do.	Dec. 3, 1872	John J	523 West Twenty-ninth	....
3254	Hagelman, Lizzie B	8	do.	Nov. 5, 1872	Louis	359 West Twenty-ninth	....
3255	Horner, Annie M	6	do.	Feb. 24, 1877	Joseph W	503 Sixth Avenue	....

CATALOGUE OF SCHOLARS—Continued.

No.	Pupil.	Age	Admitted.	Withdrawn.	Parent.	Residence.	Graduated.
3256	Lutz, George	9	June 4, 1872	Dec. 3, 1872	George	251 West Twenty-ninth	
3257	Newkirk, George W.	14	do.	June 26, 1875	Frederick	528 West Twenty-ninth	May 25, 1875
3258	Ohlandt, Christian	8	do.	April 1, 1873	Christian	563 West Twenty-ninth	
3259	Peterson, Edward	12	do.	Dec. 24, 1872	William	32 India, Greenpoint	
3260	Rollins, Ella	13	do.	Jan. 29, 1876	Hugh	236 W. Twenty-seventh	
3261	Rollins, James	10	do.	Sept. 30, 1873	do.	do. do.	
3262	Rollins, Margaret	10	do.	Sept. 29, 1877	do.	do. do.	
3263	Rollins, William	7	do.	June 1, 1874	do.	do. do.	
3264	Schmidt, Emma	11	do.	Sept. 29, 1877	Philip	251 West Twenty-ninth	
3265	Shute, Alice	7	do.	Nov. 27, 1874	William H	261 West Thirtieth	
3266	Tobin, Angelo	12	do.	Nov. 5, 1872	Louisa	468 Eighth Avenue	
3267	Young, Grace	7	do.	Sept. 29, 1877	James	32 India, Greenpoint	
3268	Dinkelman, Herman	8	June 25, 1872	Nov. 5, 1872	Henry	277 Seventh Avenue	
3269	Wheaton, Anna	13	do.	do.	William H	235 West Thirty-third	
3270	Anderson, Annie	12	Sept. 3, 1872	March 30, 1874	John	494 Ninth Avenue	
3271	Angus, Mary F.	11	do.	May 4, 1874	David	426 W. Twenty-eighth	
3272	Armstrong, Cora A.	7	Dec. 16, 1876	Sept. 27, 1878	do.	402 West Thirty-second	
3272		6	Sept. 3, 1872	Sept. 29, 1875	Samuel B	134 West Thirty-second	
3273	Bell, George H	10	Oct. 28, 1876	Sept. 29, 1877	do.	204 West Thirty-second	May 25, 1875
3273		14	Sept. 3, 1872	May 1, 1875	do.	86 Second, Hoboken	
3274	Carman, Ella L.	8	do.	Sept. 28, 1874	Susan	1 & Washington, G'np't	
3274		12	Sept. 30, 1876	Oct. 27, 1877	Samuel	666 Lorimer, Greenpoint	May 25, 1882
3275	Carss, Henry K.	15	May 28, 1880	Sept. 29, 1882	do.	do.	
3275		7	Sept. 3, 1872	Oct. 2, 1875	John	261 West Thirtieth	
3276	Eldershaw, Fanny	8	do.	April 29, 1873	Thomas	{30½ West Thirty- first.	
3277	Grint, Emma	15	do.	Oct. 1, 1872	James	213 First, Jersey City	
3278	Grint, Louisa	13	do.	do.	do.	do. do.	
3279	Lockwood, Emma F.	11	do.	Sept. 30, 1876	Nathaniel	34 India, Greenpoint	May 18, 1876
3280	Mason, George	7	do.	Sept. 19, 1879	John	261 West Thirtieth	
3281	O'Shea, Mary	12	do.	March 4, 1873	Thomas	122 West Thirty-third	
3282	Quick, Julia	6	do.	Sept. 28, 1874	Smith	40 India, Greenpoint	
3283	Spader, Maria	11	Oct. 1, 1872	Sept. 30, 1875	Georgiana	259 West Forty-third	
3284	Bell, John E	14	do.	Sept. 30, 1873	Samuel	358 West Twenty-fifth	
3285	Corner, Margaret	11	do.	April 1, 1876	John	Claremont, N. Y.	
3286	Corner, Mary	12	do.	do.	do.	do.	
3287	Daniels, Nellie	11	do.	Nov. 4, 1873	William	348 West Thirty-sixth	
3288	Davis, Sarah	11	do.	April 1, 1876	John	316 West Fifty-third	

CATALOGUE OF SCHOLARS—Continued.

No.	Pupil.	Age	Admitted.	Withdrawn.	Parent.	Residence.	Graduated.
3289	Drumgold, Charles G.	7	Oct. 1, 1872	Sept. 30, 1876	Henry	313 W. Twenty-seventh.	......
3290	Dunn, Maria	12	Feb. 2, 1873	April, 1878	do.	do.	......
3291	McLeod, D. Adrian	17	Oct. 1, 1872	April 29, 1873	Walter	215 West Nineteenth.	......
3292	Preusser, John E. R.	15	do.	Sept. 28, 1874	David	High Bridge, N. Y.	May 26, 1874
3293	Purdy, John	9	do.	June 1, 1874	Richard E.	541 West Twenty-ninth.	......
3294	Purdy, William	12	do.	Nov. 2, 1874	William	400 West Twenty-sixth.	......
3295	Scott, James H.	13	do.	do.	do.	do.	......
3296	Stetler, George	10	do.	Dec. 3, 1872	Catharine E.	21 Morton.	......
3297	Stetler, Henry I.	12	do.	March 4, 1873	Frederick M.	Fairview, New Jersey.	......
3298	Walton, John A.	14	do.	June 1, 1874	do.	do.	May 26, 1874
3299	Whiteside, Mary J.	9	do.	Feb. 3, 1874	John.	400 West Twenty-sixth.	......
				May 1, 1875	Margaret J. Stewart	230 West Thirtieth.	......
3300	Adams, Jennie	15	Nov. 5, 1872	Feb. 2, 1878	Samuel M.	719 Seventh Avenue.	......
3301	Armstrong, John G.	15	May 23, 1879	Nov. 29, 1879	do.	96 East 15th.	......
3302	Bates, Louis	13	Nov. 5, 1872	Dec. 23, 1873	Robert C.	140 West Twenty-sixth.	......
3303	Ewing, Jane	8	do.	Nov. 2, 1874	Charles L.	Fairview, New Jersey.	......
3304	Finner, Emma S.	8	do.	Sept. 28, 1873	Elizabeth	331 Seventh Avenue.	......
3305	Finner, Lizzie L.	8	do.	Sept. 28, 1874	Louis.	208 W. Twenty-seventh.	......
3306	Hanks, Annie D. W.	9	do.	May 27, 1876	do.	do.	May 18, 1876
3307	Jackson, Adrian	4	do.	Nov. 27, 1874	Edwin J.	74 West Fifty-third.	......
3308	Jackson, Henry	7	do.	Sept. 30, 1873	Peter A. H.	93 East Twenty-seventh	......
3309	Jagels, Anna	6	do.	Nov. 27, 1874	do.	do.	......
3310	Knight, William	11	do.	Sept. 30, 1873	Henry	249 West Twenty-ninth.	......
3311	Lehman, Albert D.	12	do.	Dec. 24, 1872	William.	377 Bleecker.	......
3312	Lockwood, Alonzo	13	do.	Feb. 4, 1873	Nathaniel.	379 Bleecker	......
3313	Potts, Benjamin E.	10	do.	Sept. 30, 1873	Agnes.	31 India, Greenpoint.	......
3314	Scully, Jessie	13	do.	do.	Henry.	231 West Twenty-sixth	......
3315	Van Roden, William	7	do.	June 1, 1874	Cornelius.	135 West Twenty-sixth	......
3316	Hamilton, Elizabeth	8	Dec. 3, 1872	do.	Isabella.	840 Sixth Avenue.	......
3317	Jagels, Henry	12	do.	Jan. 30, 1875	Henry.	753 Sixth Avenue.	......
3318	Widmayer, George	12	do.	Oct. 2, 1875	George.	249 West Twenty-ninth.	......
3319	Widmayer, Hannah	9	do.	Feb. 24, 1877	do.	217 Seventh Avenue.	......
3320	Inslee, Hannah A.	7	Dec. 24, 1872	Feb. 27, 1875	Sarah.	do.	......
3321	Purdy, Josephine	14	do.	Sept. 30, 1873	Johnson	257 West Thirty-third.	......
3322	Wilks, Seaman	7	do.	June 3, 1873	Charles P.	235 Ninth Avenue.	......
3323	Wilks, Seth	9	do.	do.	do.	311 W. Twenty-seventh.	......
3324	Ballard, Asa B.	11	Feb. 4, 1873	June 1, 1874	Thomas Moffat.	441 Ninth Avenue.	......

CATALOGUE OF SCHOLARS—Continued.

No.	Pupil.	Age	Admitted.	Withdrawn.	Parent.	Residence.	Graduated.
3325	Barthey, Gustave	10	Feb. 4, 1873	Sept. 30, 1873	Godfrey	214 West Thirty-first	
3326	Barthey, Lena	8	do.	do.	do.	do.	May 18, 1876
3327	Bartholomae, Augusta C	12	do.	Sept. 30, 1876	Augusta	352 West Fifty-first	
3328	Kohl, Augusta	13	do.	Sept. 30, 1873	August	452 Eighth Avenue	
3329	Quick, Isabella	15	do.	Sept. 28, 1871	Smith	40 India, Greenpoint	
3330	Seymour, Jeannette	11	do.	Nov. 27, 1875	Allen	160 West Twenty-sixth	
3331	Anderson, Peter	11	March 4, 1873	Dec. 2, 1873	John	216 W. Twenty-seventh	
3332	Collins, Jeannette	13	do.	April 29, 1873	Thomas	65 West Twenty-fourth	
3333	Hatton, Amelia	12	do.	Sept. 30, 1873	Margaret Castello	West Twenty-seventh	
3334	McCabe, Anna E	8	do.	do.	James	190 Seventh Avenue	
3335	Purdy, Caroline	12	Jan. 27, 1877	Dec. 1, 1877	Mary Ann	65 West Twenty-fifth	
3336	Apgar, Charles	10	March 4, 1873	May 1, 1875	William	400 West Twenty-sixth	
3337	Bell, George	8	April 1, 1873	April 29, 1873	Wilbur	202 W. Twenty-seventh	
3338	Exner, Edmund	10	do.	Dec. 2, 1873	Samuel	358 West Twenty-fifth	
3339	Hogenbruin, John	11	do.	Dec. 21, 1874	Edmund	561 West Twenty-ninth	
		8	do.	May 1, 1875	William	36th Street and 8th Ave	
3340	Coward, Charles	8	April 29, 1873	Nov. 4, 1873	Jonathan	121 West Thirty-third	
		9	Sept. 28, 1874	Nov. 27, 1874	do.	do.	
3341	Coward, George	10	April 29, 1873	Nov. 4, 1873	do.	do.	
			Sept. 28, 1874	Nov. 27, 1874	do.	do.	
3342	Peery, Elizabeth	9	April 29, 1873	Nov. 4, 1873	Mary	472 Sixth Avenue	
3343	Hasclrot, Frederick	12	do.	May 29, 1875	Frederick	422 West Forty-first	
3344	Leith, Nicholas	7	do.	June 1, 1874	John D	402 Eighth Avenue	
3345	McIlvaine, George	7	do.	Oct. 2, 1875	George	321 Seventh Avenue	
3346	Stadter, Elizabeth	14	do.	Sept. 30, 1873	do.	242 West Thirtieth	
3347	Stadter, Mary	12	do.	do.	do.	do.	
3348	Corson, Frank	12	June 3, 1873	May 1, 1875	Samuel D	422 West Twenty-ninth	
3349	Hall, John W	7	do.	Sept. 30, 1873	John	156 West Twenty-eighth	
3350	Kloepfer, Christine	11	do.	do.	Matthew	537 West Twenty-ninth	
3351	Kloepfer, Louisa	13	do.	do.	do.	do.	
3352	Busch, Andrew	7	Sept. 30, 1873	Sept. 29, 1877	Henry	271 Ninth Avenue	
3353	Corson, George H	15	do.	Nov. 4, 1873	Samuel B	422 West Twenty-ninth	
3354	Dangler, Ella A	5	do.	Oct. 2, 1875	Augusta	261 West Thirtieth	
3355	Dunn, Alexandra M	9	do.		David	361 West Fifty-second	
3356	Finkenaur, Josephine	14	do.	June 7, 1877	Eliza	377 West Thirty-first	
3357	Hedden, J. Adele	10	do.	Sept. 19, 1879	Charles B	219 West Fourth	June 26, 1879
3358	Hill, Sarah	13	do.	Feb. 27, 1875	Mary Ann	435 West Thirty-third	
3359	Hinn, Henry	9	do.	Dec. 23, 1873	John	304 Eleventh Avenue	

CATALOGUE OF SCHOLARS—Continued.

No.	Pupil.	Age	Admitted.	Withdrawn.	Parent.	Residence.	Graduated.
3360	Leonard, Frederick F.	7	Sept. 30, 1873	Jan. 30, 1875	Caleb R.	327 West Thirty-first	
3361	Lester, Andrew	12	do.	March 3, 1874	Joseph S.	524 West Forty-second	
3362	Lucken, Henry	9	do.	March 27, 1875	John	416 West Twenty-ninth	
3363	Lucken, Rebecca	11	do.	do.	do.	do.	
3364	McNeil, Harriet L.	6	do.	Oct. 2, 1875	Edward	157 W. Twenty-eighth	
3365	Miller, Fanny	9	do.	do.	Frank	226 West Twenty-ninth	
3366	Outwater, William	12	do.	Nov. 2, 1874	Thomas	8 W. Hamilton Pl., J. C.	
3367	Pasco, George R.	7	do.	Oct. 27, 1877	George E.	66 West Thirty-third	
3368	Pasco, Marion L.	11	do.	Feb. 24, 1877	George	430 West Thirty-first	
3369	Plate, Caroline	7	do.	Jan. 27, 1877	Henry	258 West Thirty-seventh	
3370	Reichel, George V.	10	do.	Sept. 27, 1878	Eliza	217 Broome	June 26, 1878
3371	Stoppani, Charles F.	7	do.	Oct. 2, 1875	Charles F.	114 West Twenty-ninth	
3372	Stoppani, Eliza J.	11	do.	March 31, 1877	do.	do.	
3373	Colwell, Frederick L.	8	Nov. 4, 1873	June 1, 1874	Lewis	336 W. Twenty-eighth	
3374	Comstock, Anna	11	do.	Sept. 28, 1874	Abigail	301 West Thirty-first	
3375	Dale, Alexander R.	10	do.	June 1, 1874	Mary Foster	131 W. Twenty-eighth	
3376	Fowler, Elizabeth	13	do.	May 29, 1875	Lydia	717 Seventh Avenue	
3377	Jackson, Charles	11	do.	Feb. 3, 1874	Mary J.	434 Seventh Avenue	
3378	Jackson, Laura	9	do.	June 1, 1874	do.	do.	
3379	Nickerson, Frank	13	do.	do.	Prince William	398 Ninth Avenue	
3380	Nickerson, Prince William	9	do.	Sept. 28, 1874	do.	do.	
3381	Russell, Adele	11	do.	Sept. 30, 1876	Lucius D.	404 W. Twenty-eighth	
3382	Secor, Richard J.	8	do.	June 1, 1874	James D.	405 W. Twenty-eighth	
3383	Tier, William S.	12	Oct. 27, 1877	Sept. 29, 1882	do.	333 West Thirty-first	May 25, 1882
3384	Hemler, George P.	7	Nov. 4, 1873	Jan. 29, 1876	William B.	236 West Twenty-ninth	
3385	Enholm, Ivar	7	Dec. 2, 1873	Oct. 2, 1875	George C.	236 W. Twenty-seventh	
3386	Enholm, Oscar	12	do.	June 1, 1874	Axile H.	390 Eighth Avenue	
3387	Kuhn, Emil	7	do.	do.	Charles	do.	
3388	Meadon, Ada	16	do.	Sept. 25, 1880	Thomas J.	213 W. Twenty-seventh	
3389	Park, Margaret	16	do.	Feb. 3, 1874	Margaret	115½ India, Greenpoint	
3390	Philp, Frederick	12	do.	June 1, 1874	William	231 East Twentieth	
3391	Walter, Henry	14	do.	Nov. 2, 1874	Mary	363 West Forty-first	
3392	Whittier, Lizzie	15	do.	March 3, 1874	Jason H.	244 West Thirty-third	
3393	Nyam, Andrew J.	11	do.	Nov. 2, 1874	Martha A. Sears	100½ Dupont, Greenp't.	
3394	Demarest, Charlotte	9	Dec. 23, 1873	May 29, 1875	Ephraim B.	50 Newark St., Hoboken	
3395	Hebron, George	9	do.	Sept. 30, 1876	Thomas	359 West Fifty-second	
3396	Purdy, Ella	11	do.	Sept. 28, 1874	Francis	233 West Twenty-sixth	
				June 1, 1874		131 West Thirty-fifth	

CATALOGUE OF SCHOLARS—Continued.

No.	Pupil.	Age	Admitted.	Withdrawn.	Parent.	Residence.	Graduated.
3397	Taylor, Isabella	14	Dec. 23, 1873	May 1, 1875	Henry F.	215 East Twenty-sixth	
3398	Allason, Laurence F.	8	Feb. 3, 1874	Sept. 30, 1876	William	227 Tenth Avenue	
3399	Bell, Hortense	10	do.	May 29, 1875	Thomas	203 West Thirty-third	
		14	June 2, 1877	April, 1878	do.	781 Sixth Avenue	
3400	Bell, Louis	7	Feb. 3, 1874	May 29, 1875	do.	203 West Thirty-third	
		10	June 2, 1877	Sept. 23, 1881	do.	781 Sixth Avenue	
3401	Fowler, Maria	9	Feb. 3, 1874	Nov. 27, 1875	Frances	325 Seventh Avenue	
3402	Rüdt, Charles	12	do.	Nov. 2, 1874	John	617 East Sixth	
3403	Taylor, Edward C.	10	do.	June 26, 1875	Henry F.	215 East Twenty-sixth	
3404	Taylor, Henry M.	8	do.	do.	do.	do. do.	
3405	Thomas, James E.	16	do.	June 1, 1874	David H.	High Bridge, N. Y.	
3406	Van Riper, Edward	12	do.	do.	Peter	Hackensack, N. J.	
3407	Watts, Walter	7	do.	do.	James	319 West Twenty-sixth	
3408	Widmayer, Louisa A.	6	do.	Oct. 2, 1875	William	249 Seventh Avenue	
3409	Woodruff, Gertrude	11	do.	May 1, 1875	Frederick Riker	343 Seventh Avenue	
3410	Forrest, Grace	9	do.	Sept. 27, 1878	William	26 W. Twenty-eighth	
3411	Gwinn, Happy H.	7	March 3, 1874	Oct. 27, 1877	George	7 Pacific Place	
3412	Stover, John H.	8	do.	Jan. 28, 1881	Antoine	45 West Eleventh	
3413	Stover, Marie	13	do.	Sept. 30, 1876	do.	do.	May 25, 1882
3414	Vreeland, Richard F.	11	do.	May 29, 1875	Francis	328 Ninth Avenue	
3415	Bensel, Fanny	9	March 30, 1874	Sept. 24, 1880	J. Warner	58 East Fourth	May 27, 1880
3416	Knight, Thomas	7	do.	Sept. 29, 1877	Daniel	1,166 Broadway	
3417	Kostar, William D	12	do.	Jan. 30, 1877	John	414 West Forty-fourth	
3418	Rosell, Abraham L.	10	do.	Nov. 2, 1874	Thomas	424 West Thirty-third	
3419	Cochard, August	9	May 4, 1874	March 27, 1875	Stephanie	54 W. Twenty-ninth	
3420	Great, William J.	7	do.	Nov. 27, 1878	Isabella	157 W. Twenty-eighth	
3421	Kirk, Samuel	9	Sept. 29, 1877	May 1, 1875	Richard	347 Seventh Avenue	
		12	May 4, 1874	Sept. 19, 1879	do.	492 Seventh Avenue	
3422	Morse, Martha	6	do.	May 1, 1875	Charles	229 West Thirty-first	
3423	Plate, Elizabeth	6	do.	Jan. 27, 1877	Henry	258 West Thirty-seventh	
3424	Swan, Henry	9	do.	June 2, 1877	James H.	160 West Twenty-ninth	
3425	Warner, William M.	7	do.	Dec. 21, 1874	Leonard W.	119 West Seventeenth	
3426	Hardie, William	14	June 1, 1874	Jan. 30, 1875	William	231 Bloomfield, Hobok'n	
3427	Ryerson, Nicholas A.	14	do.	Sept. 30, 1876	Abraham N.	11 West Forty-second	
3428	Schultz, Minnie E.	4	do.	May 1, 1875	James	209 Freeman, Greenp't	
3429	Allason, Mary Louise	7	Sept. 28, 1874	Sept. 30, 1876	William	227 Tenth Avenue	
3430	Bowden, Jennie	11	do.	May 1, 1875	Louis	113 West Thirty-third	
3431	Demarest, Llewellyn L.	7	do.	Oct. 29, 1880	Margaret	405 W. Twenty-seventh	

CATALOGUE OF SCHOLARS—Continued.

No.	Pupil.	Age	Admitted.	Withdrawn.	Parent.	Residence.	Graduated.
3432	De Wilde, Andrew	14	Sept. 28, 1874	May 29, 1875	Louis	443 West Forty-seventh	
3433	Dibel, Margaret	8	do.	Oct. 2, 1875	Paul	240 West Thirty-second	
3434	Heron, Daniel	9	do.	May 29, 1875	Sarah J.	347 Eighth Avenue	
3435	Hintze, Henry	11	do.	March 28, 1879	Henry C.	146 Hudson, Hoboken	
3436	Kroll, Charles G.	7	do.	Oct. 2, 1875	Conrad B.	315 W. Twenty-seventh	
3437	Lammers, William	7	do.	April 1, 1876	Frederick H.	423 West Twenty-fifth	
3438	Linsler, Elizabeth	7	do.	Sept. 29, 1877	Frank	240 West Thirty-second	
3439	McCrum, Howard	8	do.	May 24, 1878	Elizabeth	164 West Thirty-ninth	
3440	Mason, Hannah	12	do.	Jan. 29, 1876	John	261 West Thirtieth	
3441	Purdy, Elizabeth	7	do.	Oct. 2, 1875	William B.	357 West Twenty-fifth	
3442	Ralph, George W.	7	do.	May 29, 1875	George W.	226 West Twenty-ninth	
3443	Raymond, Ellen M.	6	do.	Oct. 2, 1875	James	135 West Twenty-sixth	
3444	Rockwell, Elizabeth	12	do.	May 1, 1875	Elizabeth J.	5 Spencer Place	
3445	Smith, Jennie	14	do.	Jan. 30, 1875	Jane Brown	81 West Forty-fifth	
3446	Tibbits, Charles E.	15	do.	Feb. 27, 1875	James E.	715 Sixth Avenue	
3447	Tracy, Samuel	7	do.	March 4, 1878	William	109 West Thirty-third	
3448	Washburn, Frank	7	do.	Oct. 2, 1875	George H.	313 W. Twenty-seventh	
3449	Winship, Carrie	8	do.	May 29, 1875	Miss S. Hutchinson	137 West Twenty-ninth	
3450	Witman, Biena	9	do.	Oct. 2, 1875	Karl	240 West Thirty-second	
3451	Cole, George A.	11	Nov. 2, 1874	Oct. 30, 1875	Catharine M.	431 West Thirty-fourth	
3452	Cole, John H.	8	do.	Sept. 30, 1876	do.	do.	
3453	Connell, Henry W.	11	April, 1878	Sept. 27, 1878	Henry	327 West Thirty-sixth	
3454	Connell, Regina	8	Nov. 29, 1874	Oct. 2, 1875	do.	163 West Twenty-ninth	
3455	Langdon, Charlotte	6	do.		Calvin	do.	
3456	Lucken, Christopher	12	do.	Jan. 29, 1876	John	261 West Thirtieth	
3457	Reed, Mary E.	7	do.	March 27, 1875	Godfrey R.	410 West Twenty-ninth	
3458	Riddle, Anna D.	8	do.	Sept. 30, 1876	John	1,372 Broadway	
3459	Rogers, William J.	17	do.	Nov. 27, 1875	William J.	215 West Twenty-first	
3460	Siebel, Emma	13	do.	Oct. 2, 1875	Rudolph	329 West Forty-first	
3461	Smith, Florine	7	do.	Jan. 30, 1875	J. Finlay S.	253 West Twenty-ninth	
3462	Smith, Lester	12	do.	Oct. 2, 1875	do.	333 West Twenty-eighth	
3463	Stagg, Frederick S.	12	do.	do.	Peter M.	do.	
3464	Stoppani, Joseph	7	do.	Dec. 8, 1877	Charles F.	418 West Twenty-sixth	
3465	Weber, William	11	do.	Sept. 30, 1876	Edward	114 West Twenty-ninth	
3466	Baxter, Kate E.	9	Nov. 27, 1874	May 1, 1875	Philip	134 West Twenty-eighth	
3467	Demarest, Francis W.	7	do.	Sept. 30, 1876	Ephraim B.	402 West Fifty-second	
		15	Nov. 24, 1882	Oct. 12, 1883	do.	350 West Fifty-second	
						451 West Fifty-third	

CATALOGUE OF SCHOLARS—Continued.

No.	Pupil.	Age	Admitted.	Withdrawn.	Parent.	Residence.	Graduated.
3468	Demarest, James E.	14	Nov. 27, 1874	May 29, 1875	James E.	27 West Washington Pl.	
3469	Dunbar, Esther	12	do.	Jan. 29, 1876	Peter Goodheart	749 Sixth Avenue	
3470	Griswold, Myrtilla	10	do.	May 29, 1875	Alfred D.	313 West Twenty-first	
3471	Peters, Anna	7	do.	Jan. 29, 1876	Herman	247 West Twenty-ninth	
3472	Kentz, August	9	do.	do.	John	258 West Twenty-ninth	
3473	Simpson, John A.	10	do.	April 1, 1876	Robert G.	466 Ninth Avenue	
3474	Kahrs, Henry	8	Dec. 21, 1874	Sept. 30, 1876	Heins Diederich	436 West Twenty-fifth	
3475	Pasco, Charles E.	7	do.	Dec. 1, 1877	George E.	649 Sixth Avenue	
3476	Cleverley, Abraham H.	7	Jan. 30, 1875	Jan. 29, 1877	John	434 West Forth-fifth	
3477	De Wilde, William M.	13	do.	May 29, 1875	Louis	103 West Fifty-fifth	
3478	Groff, Sebastian	12	do.	do.	Thomas	495 Ninth Avenue	
3479	Ward, Emily	13	do.	do.	Mary	343 West Twenty-first	
3480	Stauder, Charles	7	Feb. 27, 1875	Sept. 30, 1876	Georgiana	222 West Forty-third	
3481	Styles, Hattie	6	do.	Sept. 24, 1880	Charles H	600 Sixth Avenue	
3482	Swan, William	10	do.	Sept. 30, 1876	James H.	166 West Twenty-ninth	
3483	Finck, Otto	10	March 27, 1875	do.	Jacob	249 Ninth Avenue	
3484	Widmayer, Frank	9	do.	Oct. 2, 1875	George	217 Seventh Avenue	
3485	Huntze, Annie M.	10	May 1, 1875	Sept. 30, 1876	Henry C.	146 Hudson, Hoboken	
3486	Allason, Emma G.	6	May 29, 1875	do.	William	227 Tenth Avenue	
3487	Bird, Charles E.	9	do.	Dec. 19, 1879	Edgar J.	469 West Thirteenth	
3488	Edgarton, Gertrude	8	do.	May 27, 1876	Eliza McClenachan	150 West Thirty-fourth	
3489	Hill, William R.	7	do.	Oct. 27, 1877	William	235 West Thirtieth	
3490	Siccardi, Laura	6	do.	Sept. 29, 1877	John.	1,724 Broadway	
3491	Corn, Louisa	12	June 26, 1875	Oct. 2, 1875	Gustave	212 West Twenty-sixth	
3492	Jaynes, Charles H	9	do.	May 27, 1876	Rev. Frederick.	19 Great Jones	
3493	Linder, Frederica	6	Oct. 2, 1875	Sept. 29, 1877	Frank	240 West Thirty-second	
3494	Planten, Herman	17	do.	do.	Gerrit	Paterson, New Jersey	
3495	Riddle, Fanny D.	10	do.	Sept. 24, 1880	John.	215 West Twenty-first	
3496	Riddle, Lizzie A.	14	do.	Sept. 29, 1877	do.	do.	May 24, 1877
3497	Jones, Annie H.	16	Sept. 27, 1878	Sept. 29, 1879	do.	do.	May 24, 1877
3498	Smith, Susan.	14	Oct. 30, 1875	Jan. 24, 1879	Henry	10 West Twenty-fourth	June 26, 1879
3499	Hard, Emma I.	11	Nov. 29, 1875	Nov. 27, 1875	Patrick	238 West Thirty-second	
3500	Prybil, Pauline.	15	do.	Sept. 30, 1876	Cyrenus.	434 West Fifty-first	May 18, 1876
3501	Forrest, Mamie	14	Feb. 26, 1876	Jan. 29, 1876	Paul.	456 West Forty-ninth	
3502	Wright, Thomas.	15	do.	Jan. 27, 1877	Joseph.	183 Newell, Greenpoint	
3503	Geddes, William E	8	April 1, 1876	June 2, 1876	John.	1,166 Broadway	
3504	Hain, Benjamin F.	11	April 29, 1876	Oct. 28, 1876	John C.	36 Union Square.	
		12		June 2, 1877	Gilbert.	323 West Thirty-fifth.	

CATALOGUE OF SCHOLARS—Continued.

No.	Pupil.	Age	Admitted.	Withdrawn.	Parent.	Residence.	Graduated.
3505	Hall, Alfred	7	April 29, 1876	Oct. 27, 1877	William	235 West Thirtieth	
3506	Ball, Louisa M.	8	May 27, 1876	Sept. 29, 1877	William G.	211 West Twenty-ninth	
3507	Anderson, Eva C.	12	Sept. 30, 1876	Sept. 27, 1878	James A. Demarest	405 W. Twenty-seventh	
3508	Cleverley, Margaret A.	6	do.	Sept. 29, 1877	John	434 West Thirty-fifth	
3509	Cornelisse, Lena	12	do.	Jan. 27, 1877	do.	12 West Thirty-first	
3510	Lockwood, John	12	do.	do.	Nathaniel	34 India, Greenpoint	
3511	Planten, Peter	14	do.	Nov. 22, 1878	Gerrit	Paterson, N. J.	
3512	Sadler, James	11	do.	March 28, 1879	Thomas	419 West Thirty-fifth	
3513	Stone, Emma	12	do.	Oct. 28, 1876	Chester P.	431 West Thirty-fifth	
3514	Terrell, Ida	9	do.	Jan. 27, 1877	Isaac H.	370 Eighth Avenue	
3515	Tierney, Walter D.	9	do.	Sept. 29, 1877	George Call	229 West Thirty-fourth	
3516	Door, Ella J.	16	Oct. 28, 1876	March 22, 1878	Elizabeth	154 West Thirty-sixth	
3517	Elly, William	14	do.	June 2, 1877	William Townsend	318 West Twenty-ninth	
3518	Fleming, Robert W.	11	do.	Dec. 16, 1876	Charles Murthe	213 West Twenty-ninth	
3519	Jones, Charles Parker	8	do.	do.	Charles W.	69 Bedford	
3520	Lee, Horace	10	do.	Sept. 24, 1880	James	414 Eighth Avenue	
3521	Lee, Oliver	9	do.	Jan. 24, 1879	do.	do.	
3522	Reynolds, Lillian	10	do.	March 28, 1879	Abijah	251 West Thirty-fourth	
3523	Stone, Thomas E.	16	do.	Jan. 27, 1877	Chester P.	431 West Thirty-fifth	
3524	Donnelly, Robert	12	Dec. 16, 1876	Sept. 29, 1877	Robert Alexander	982 Sixth Avenue	
3525	Miller, George S.	13	do.	do.	William T.	140 West Thirty-first	
3526	Ayers, Isabella B.	10	Jan. 27, 1877	Sept. 27, 1878	Joseph B.	435 Eighth Avenue	
3527	Bullene, Frank Jay	9	Feb. 24, 1877	Dec. 1, 1877	John, Jr.	39 West Twenty-sixth	
3528	Griggs, Jennie May	10	do.	June 2, 1877	Jane Hawkins	60 West Thirty-third	
3529	Horton, Charles	9	do.	do.	E. B., Jr.	9 East Thirtieth	
3530	Horton, Lillie	6	do.	do.	do.	do.	
3531	La Forge, Fanny A.	12	do.	March 22, 1878	Henry	13 Warren Place	
3532	Dobbs, Howell	9	March 31, 1877	Nov. 25, 1881	Howell	137 West Thirty-second	
3533	Grant, Ella H.	12	do.	May 23, 1879	Elihu	357 Ninth Avenue	
3534	Knapp, David A.	10	do.	Sept. 29, 1877	David A.	449 West Thirty-third	
3535	Lyman, Joseph E.	12	do.	do.	Frances E. A.	do.	
3536	Walcutt, Agnes L.	15	April 28, 1877	do.	Rev. S. D. Burchard, D.D., G. d/r.	24 West Fortieth	
3537	Henshaw, Sarah L.	9	do.	Feb. 2, 1878	William A.	435 West Thirty-fourth	
3538	Knobloch, Anna	10	do.	Sept. 29, 1877	John	239 West Thirtieth	
3539	Knobloch, Washington	8	do.	do.	do.	do.	
3540	Kuhn, David	7	do.	March 31, 1883	Charles	213 W. Twenty-seventh	
3541	Sprague, Minor W.	14	do.	Sept. 29, 1877	Tunis Cooper	351 West Fiftieth	

CATALOGUE OF SCHOLARS—Continued.

No.	Pupil.	Age	Admitted.	Withdrawn.	Parent.	Residence.	Graduated.
3542	Stone, Henry	7	April 28, 1877	Nov. 22, 1878	William	138 West Thirty-second	....
3543	Dobbs, Marion	7	June 2, 1877	May 25, 1882	Howell	137 West Thirty-second	....
3544	Kerr, John C.	9	do.	Sept. 29, 1877	Charles H.	670 Sixth Avenue	....
3545	Kerr, Margaret S.	10	do.	do.	do.	do.	....
3546	Marchand, Julia	8	do.	April 25, 1879	Levi	340 Ninth Avenue	....
3547	Robinson, Freeman M.	9	Jan. 28, 1881	Sept. 23, 1881	do.	331 West Thirty-sixth	....
3548	Acton, Wilhelmina L.	11	June 2, 1877	Sept. 29, 1877	George F.	434 West Forty-fifth	....
3549	Berry, Maria J.	6	Sept. 29, 1877	May 23, 1879	Samuel G.	10 West Twenty-ninth	....
3550	Bodenheimer, Morris	10	do.	Nov. 25, 1881	William J. C.	7 West Twenty-ninth	....
3551	Demarest, William E.	12	do.	Feb. 2, 1878	Isaac	25 Gr'np't Ave., Gr'np't	....
3552	Livingston William A.	11	do.	March 28, 1879	William E.	401 West Thirty-fourth	....
3553	McCram, William S.	8	do.	Sept. 27, 1879	William	451 West Thirty-fourth	....
3554	Martyn, Egbert	7	do.	March 4, 1878	Elijah	164 West Twenty-ninth	....
3555	Martyn, Ferter	8	do.	June 21, 1878	Rev. William C.	449 West Thirty-fourth	....
3556	Paine, Asa H.	8	do.	do.	do.	do.	....
3557	Patten, Frank F.	11	do.	Sept. 19, 1879	James L.	332 West Thirty-first	....
3558	Reinders, Abramina	10	do.	Jan. 24, 1879	John P.	78 Franklin, Greenpoint	....
3559	Smith, John T.	11	do.	Dec. 1, 1877	John	456 West Thirty-fifth	....
3560	Tremain, Grace	10	do.	Feb. 27, 1880	Elizabeth, Aunt	125 Franklin, Greenpoint	....
3561	Van Houten, Margaret	11	do.	Oct. 28, 1881	Frank	464 Seventh Avenue	....
3562	Fackner, David	15	Oct. 27, 1877	May 27, 1881	John R.	451 West Thirty-third	....
3563	Sidman, Henry H.	12	do.	May 28, 1880	Henry	Port Richmond, S. I.	....
3564	Farnham, Florence	13	Dec. 1, 1877	Sept. 23, 1881	John E.	144 West Thirty-sixth	....
3565	Ford, Lillie	11	do.	Oct. 29, 1880	Frank	241 West Thirtieth	....
3566	Sprague, Sarah A.	7	Feb. 2, 1878	April 25, 1879	William Y.	411 West Twenty-fourth	....
3567	Butler, Ida	13	do.	Sept. 27, 1878	Charles	224 West Thirty-first	....
3568	Harrison, Walter	12	do.	March 22, 1878	William	165 W. Twenty-eighth	....
3569	Martyn, Paul	10	do.	May 24, 1878	Thomas J.	449 W. Twenty-seventh	....
3570	Swinnerton, James	10	do.	June 21, 1878	Rev. Wm. C.	439 West Thirty-fourth	....
3571	Lewis, Robert	13	March 4, 1878	Nov. 22, 1878	Samuel A.	102 Fourth Avenue	....
3572	Lennessey, John S.	14	do.	May 24, 1878	John	218 W. Twenty-seventh	....
3573	Miramla, George B.	7	do.	April 25, 1878	William H.	63 Zabriskie, J. C. Hghts	....
3574	Noice, Edward H.	14	do.	Dec. 19, 1879	Cornelia	445 West Thirty-fourth	....
3575	Bennet, Benjamin	8	March 22, 1878	April 22, 1881	Benjamin	309 West Nineteenth	....
3576	Swayze, Albert	12	do.	Sept. 27, 1878	Warren	Thirty-fifth St. & 7th Av	....
3577	Tremain, Frederick	9	do.	Sept. 23, 1881	Frank	241 West Thirtieth	....
3578	Carter, Agnes Maud	11	April 25, 1878	Jan. 23, 1880	George	208 W. Twenty-eighth	....

CATALOGUE OF SCHOLARS—Continued.

No.	Pupil.	Age	Admitted.	Withdrawn.	Parent.	Residence.	Graduated.
3579	De Garcia, Carrie V	9	April 25, 1878	Sept. 27, 1878	Carlos	232 West Thirtieth	
3580	Miller, Jennie B	10	do.	Oct. 25, 1878	William	327 West Thirty-first	
3581	Carpenter, William E	14	May 24, 1878	Nov. 21, 1879	Robert	79 Zabriskie, J. C. H'ghts	
3582	Mallon, John H	11	do.	March 28, 1879	Catharine	21 Pacific Place	
3583	Marsh, Lydia L	6	do.	Sept. 19, 1879	Martin	313 W. Twenty-seventh	
3584	Tremain, Frances A	6	June 21, 1878	Sept. 23, 1881	Frank	241 West Thirtieth	
3585	Brooks, Washington	11	Sept. 27, 1878	Feb. 14, 1879	Margaret	117 W. Twenty-seventh	
3586	Carpenter, Nellie	8	do.	Oct. 28, 1881	John H	126 East Twenty-fourth	
3587	Heeder, Henry	9	do.	Oct. 10, 1879	Louis	147 West Thirty-first	
3588	Huetze, Arthur B	11	do.	May 28, 1880	Henry C	146 Hudson, Hoboken	
3589	Kaufmann, Henry	13	do.	Sept. 24, 1880	August	14 Eldridge	
3590	Mc Michael, Carrie	15	do.	May 28, 1880	John	8 West Fifty first	
3591	Miranda, Robert R	7	do.	Sept. 19, 1879	Cornelia	63 Zabriskie, J. C. H'ghts	
3592	Peck, Eben M	12	do.	do.	David T	215 West Thirty-sixth	
3593	Prinulle, Sara L	16	do.	Sept. 24, 1880	George	Shady Side, N. J.	
3594	Howland, Francis	10	Oct. 25, 1878	Sept. 29, 1882	Horace	445 West Twenty-third	
3595	Kurz, Henry	12	do.	Dec. 13, 1878	Valentine	252 Seventh Avenue	
3596	Cortelyou, George S	10	Nov. 22, 1878	Sept. 24, 1880	Eugene A	409 West Twenty-second	
3597	Gabel, Jacob	10	do.	Feb. 14, 1879	Jacob	147 West Thirty-first	
3598	Mackey, Ella	8	do.	Sept. 24, 1880	Charles E	255 West Thirtieth	
3599	Meiers, Julia	7	do.	Sept. 19, 1879	Jacob	211 West Twenty-eighth	
3600	Morse, Jennie	8	do.	Jan. 24, 1879	Thos. W. *G'ndfather*	333 West Thirty-first	
3601	Soper, Jennie	14	do.	Oct. 28, 1881	Charles A	242 West Twenty-fourth	
3602	Elmendorff, John B	13	Feb. 14, 1879	May 23, 1879	John	203 East Thrtieenth	
3603	Smith, Ida	11	do.	May 27, 1881	Samuel	63 Franklin, Greenpoint	
3604	Archer, James R	13	March 28, 1879	April 22, 1880		208 Bloomfield, Hoboken	
3605	Gaunt, William	13	do.	do.	Charles W	274 Garden, Hoboken	
3606	Holmes, Annie H	15	do.	Sept. 25, 1880	George W	298 Washington, Hob'k'n	May 27, 1880
3607	Young, William	11	do.	March 31, 1883	James	130 Java, Greenpoint	
3608	Clandening, Clarence	13	April 29, 1879	April 22, 1880	William T	434 West Twenty-third	
3609	Giles, Jennie M	9	do.	do.	Charles A	200 Franklin, Greenpoint	
3610	Mengs, Catharine H	9	May 23, 1879	May 28, 1880	Robert	127 East Seventeenth	
3611	Benson, George E	7	Sept. 19, 1879	Sept. 24, 1880		236 W. Twenty-seventh	
3612	Benson, Sarah	8	do.	do.		do.	
3613	Hamje, Adeline	9	do.		Adeline	249 West Thirty-third	
3614	Herbst, William F	12	do.	Jan. 20, 1882	Frank	60 First Avenue	
3615	Holmes, Maggie A	10	do.	Sept. 29, 1882	George W	298 Washington, Hob'k'n	May 25, 1882
3616	Kuhn, Margaretta	6	do.		Margaretta	230 W. Twenty-seventh	

CATALOGUE OF SCHOLARS—Continued.

No.	Pupil.	Age	Admitted.	Withdrawn.	Parent.	Residence.	Graduated.
3617	Miller, Hattie	13	Sept. 19, 1879	Nov. 21, 1879	Benjamin	334 Ninth Avenue	
3618	Soper, William	7	do.	Sept. 29, 1882	Charles A.	242 West Twenty-fourth	
3619	Van Houten, Henrietta	8	do.		John R.	438 West Thirty-ninth	
3620	Connor, Harry F.	8	Oct. 10, 1879	Oct. 12, 1883	James E.	236 West Twenty-first	
3621	Fuhrer, Harry	13	do.	Oct. 29, 1880	Anton	432 West Fortieth	
3622	Hewlett, Nellie R.	7	do.		Joseph	363 West Thirty-sixth	
3623	Hitchcock, Wilbur K.	7	do.	Sept. 24, 1880	Mary E.	7 East Forty-sixth	
3624	Orton, Annie D.	14	do.		William H.	406 West Twenty-eighth	
3625	Pasco, Isabella E.	10	do.	May 23, 1880	George E.	628 Sixth Avenue	
3626	Thompson, James W.	10	do.	Jan. 29, 1881	Rev. Abraham	341 West Ninety-second	
3627	Winn, Robert S.	9	do.	May 25, 1882	Henry H.	do.	May 25, 1882
3628	Bowers, Daniel	11	Nov. 21, 1879	Sept. 24, 1880	George	141 East Houston	
3629	Carner, Alonzo L.	8	do.	Sept. 29, 1882	Alonzo P.	235 West Thirty-eighth	
3630	Chipman, Charles M	11	do.	Oct. 12, 1883	Horace W.	217 West Twenty-first	
3631	Conron, Lulu	15	do.	Oct. 28, 1881	Emma M.	220 Hudson, Hoboken	
3632	Emmons, Walter E.	12	do.	Sept. 24, 1880	John H.	245 West Twentieth	
3633	Emmons, William	7	do.	do.	do.	do.	
3634	Gunn, Agnes	11	do.	May 28, 1880	George F.	117 West Twenty-fourth	
3635	Young, Howard W.	9	Dec. 19, 1879	Sept. 23, 1881	George	255 West Twenty-first	
3636	Sinclair, Finlay	12	Jan. 23, 1880	May 28, 1881	Finlay	330 West Forty-second	
3637	{ Dana, Helen E.	11	March 34, 1883	Sept. 29, 1882	Samuel W., M. D.	313 West Thirty-third	
		14	Jan. 23, 1880		do.	do.	
3638	Dobbs, William D.	7	do.	May 25, 1882	Howell	137 West Thirty-second	
3639	Farnham, Frank H.	7	do.	Oct. 29, 1880	Frank	239 West Thirtieth	
3640	Holt, George H.	13	do.	May 28, 1880	Milton	54 Bloomfield, Hoboken	
3641	Waters, Madge	15	do.	May 27, 1881	John H.	424 W. Twenty-second	
3642	Briggs, Arthur E.	10	Feb. 27, 1880	Feb. 25, 1881	Mary E.	Fordham	
3643	Broad, John E.	15	do.	May 28, 1880	Henry R.	589 Lorimer, Greenpoint	
3644	Gray, Laura E.	16	do.		Henry Depew	211 West Twenty-ninth	
3645	Harrison, William	8	do.	Sept. 24, 1880	Chas. Schwart	414 West Thirty-first	
3646	Ingram, Jennie	12	do.	Jan. 28, 1881	Jane	249 W. Twenty-seventh	
3647	Morris, William	15	do.	Sept. 24, 1880	William C.	237 Bloomfield, Hoboken	
3648	Nelson, Catharine	9	do.	May 27, 1881	James	162 West Twenty-eighth	
3649	Nelson, Sophia	8	do.	do.	do.	do.	
3650	Pearce, George D.	10	do.	do.	George W.	256 West Twenty-first	
3651	Smyth, Ellen J	9	do.	Nov. 24, 1882	Rosanna	442 West Thirty-second	
3652	Smyth, Rosanna	12	do.	Jan. 28, 1881	do.	do.	
3653	Spratt, Bowman M	11	do.	Jan. 29, 1882	James K	424 W. Twenty-second	

CATALOGUE OF SCHOLARS—Continued.

No.	Pupil.	Age	Admitted.	Withdrawn.	Parent.	Residence.	Graduated.
3654	Taylor, Charles	7	Feb. 27, 1880	May 27, 1881	Charles	301 West Twenty-ninth	
3655	Taylor, Emma J	10	do.	Jan. 28, 1881	do.	do.	
3656	Taylor, Maggie	6	do.	May 27, 1881	do.	do.	
3657	Taylor, Thomas	11	do.	Jan. 28, 1881	do.	do.	
3658	Abernethy, Margaret	8	April 22, 1880	Oct. 29, 1880	William	504 West Twenty-sixth	
3659	Barnard, Charles	8	do.	Jan. 28, 1881	Edward	262 West Twenty-first	
3660	Breene, Carrie	9	do.	Oct. 29, 1880	John	211 West Twenty-sixth	
3661	Breene, Isabella	7	do.		do.	do.	
3662	Crowell, John	9	do.	Feb. 24, 1882	Martin L.	256 West Twenty-first	
3663	Hardy, William	7	do.	Nov. 25, 1881	William	226 W. Twenty-seventh	
3664	Newell, Charles A	8	do.	Sept. 29, 1882	Edward A	140 West Twenty-first	
3665	Smith, Rosa	10	do.	Oct. 27, 1882	Herman	158 West Twenty-sixth	
3666	Snook, Minton J	14	do.	Jan. 20, 1882	Jacob P.	352 E. Seventy-seventh	May 25, 1882
3667	Abrahams, Thomas F.	18	Jan. 19, 1883	May 25, 1883	do.	125 West Eleventh	
3668	Benson, Emily	11	May 28, 1880	Sept. 24, 1880	Elizabeth	238 West Thirty-first	
3669	Deveau, Franklin L.	6	do.	do.	Catharine	216 W. Twenty-seventh	
3670	Wood, Ella	10	do.		do.	87 East Tenth	
3671	Wood, Eva	10	do.	Sept. 29, 1882	Thomas	3 Pacific Place	
3672	Wood, Henrietta	9	do.	Jan. 19, 1883	do.	do.	
3673	Alberti, Annie	7	Sept. 24, 1880		do.	do.	
3674	Anderson, John	12	do.	May 27, 1881	Henry	208 West Twenty-eighth	
3675	Boyd, Charles E	7	do.	Nov. 19, 1880	James	145 West Twenty-ninth	
3676	Noice, Walter R.	10	do.	Sept. 23, 1881	Andrew A	396 Ninth Avenue	
3677	Olmstead, Louise B.	7	do.	Oct. 12, 1883	Edward H	259 West Twenty-first	
3678	Prins, Illigondas	15	do.	Jan. 20, 1882	Albert S. Beakes	Hawthorn, N. J.	
3679	Kaiser, Amelia	11	do.	Sept. 23, 1881	Johanna	23 West Thirty-ninth	
3680	Swan, Jennie E.	11	do.	Nov. 25, 1881	Andrew	248 West Twenty-eighth	
3681	Thomsen, Lillie	10	do.		James H	160 West Twenty-ninth	
3682	Baxter, John Thomas	8	do.	Oct. 12, 1883	Charles	206 W. Twenty-seventh	
3683	Hemmingway, Annie	11	Oct. 29, 1880	March 24, 1882	Philip	898 Eighth Avenue	
3684	Kimball, Mary	10	do.	Jan. 20, 1882	Frank V	410 West Twenty-ninth	
3685	Taylor, Mary C	13	do.	Feb. 25, 1881	George R.	304 West Fifty-fourth	
3686	Waters, Daisy	15	do.	Jan. 28, 1881	Charles E.	326 W. Twenty-seventh	
3687	Bartlett, Charles H	7	Nov. 19, 1880	Oct. 28, 1881	John H	451 West Twenty-first	
3688	Bartlett, William H. S.	9	do.		Henry	442 West Thirty-fourth	
3689	Fairchild, Louis	12	do.	Nov. 25, 1881	Rev. Elijah S.	do.	
3690	Fairchild, Meredith	7	do.	do.	do.	433 West Nineteenth	

CATALOGUE OF SCHOLARS—Continued.

No.	Pupil.	Age	Admitted.	Withdrawn.	Parent.	Residence.	Graduated.
3691	Geel, Cornelius	9	Nov. 19, 1880	Aug. 3, 1882	Cornelius	315 Ninth Avenue	
3692	Herbison, Jennie	12	do.	Jan. 28, 1881	Sarah	122 Seventh Avenue	
3693	Baker, Etta	13	Jan. 28, 1881	April 27, 1883	George	223 West Thirty-first	
3694	Love, Elmer	9	do.	Jan. 20, 1882	Samuel G.	234 West Twenty-first	
3695	Dana, Emma L.	7	Feb. 25, 1881		Samuel W., M. D.	313 West Thirty-third	
3696	Newell, Frank	7	do.	Sept. 29, 1882	Edward A.	140 West Twenty-first	
3697	Hartley, George W.	13	March 25, 1881	do.	David	92 Ninth Avenue	
3698	Mahrenholz, August	11	do.	Jan. 19, 1883	Henry	153 East Twenty-ninth	
3699	Elder, Edward D.	12	April 22, 1881	Sept. 23, 1881	George J. Morris	239 West Thirty-first	
3700	Giffin, Harry	7	do.		Harry	229 West Thirty-first	
3701	Giffin, Lily	5	do.		do.	do.	
3702	Hardy, Nellie	7	do.	Nov. 25, 1881	William	226 W. Twenty-seventh	
3703	Kaske, William	8	do.	Jan. 20, 1882	Gustave	109 West Twenty-fourth	
3704	Miller, Edith	8	do.	April 27, 1883	Thomas	251 West Twenty-third	
3705	Raisner, Andrew	8	do.	Sept. 29, 1882	Andrew	248 West Twenty-eighth	
3706	Raisner, Christopher	7	do.		do.	do.	
3707	Voskuyl, Mary	10	do.		Henry	301 West Thirty-first	
3708	Voskuyl, Sarah	7	do.		do.	do.	
3709	Cornelisse, Paulie W.	7	May 27, 1881	Oct. 12, 1883	John	229 West Thirty-first	
3710	Post, Frederick	7	do.	Oct. 27, 1882	Altred	223 West Thirty-third	
3711	Stanichut, Mary	10	do.	Jan. 20, 1882	Theodore	211 West Twenty-eighth	
3712	Connell, Annie R.	13	Sept. 23, 1881	Oct. 27, 1882	Henry	163 West Twenty-ninth	
3713	Hemmingway, Charles	12	do.	Jan. 20, 1882	Frank V.	454 West Twenty-ninth	
3714	Muir, Magrie I.	10	do.	Oct. 12, 1883	James	140 West Tenth	
3715	Muir, Thomas D. W.	15	do.	Sept. 29, 1882	do.	do.	
3716	Munroe, Sadie	8	do.	do.	William	32 West Thirty-first	
3717	Smith, Maud	16	do.	do.	Elizabeth	1,247 Lexington Avenue	
3718	Vissers, Henri G.	11	do.		Johan C.	265 Seventh Avenue	
3719	Vissers, Johan C.	7	do.		do.	do.	
3720	Voillard, Angeline	14	do.	May 25, 1882	August	280 Sixth Avenue	
3721	Wakeham, James	8	do.	Feb. 24, 1882	William	81 Sixth Avenue	
3722	Wood, Gussie	10	do.	Oct. 27, 1882	Alfred	301 West Thirty-first	
3723	Good, Catharine	6	Oct. 28, 1881	Sept. 29, 1882	William	309 Seventh Avenue	
3724	Good, Joseph	10	do.	do.	do.	do.	
3725	Good, Mary Ann	8	do.	do.	do.	do.	
3726	Lawrenz, Anna	8	do.	Jan. 20, 1882	Frederick	109 West Twenty-fourth	
3727	Lawrenz, Eliza	10	do.	do.	do.	do.	
3728	Mayer, William	9	do.	Jan. 19, 1883	John	410 West Thirty-sixth	

CATALOGUE OF SCHOLARS—Continued.

No.	Pupil.	Age	Admitted.	Withdrawn.	Parent.	Residence.	Graduated.
3729	Schultza, Sophia	12	Oct. 28, 1881	Jan. 20, 1882	Julius Rrickner	249 West Thirty-third	
3730	Clark, Ethel	7	Nov. 25, 1881	Jan. 20, 1882	Fanny E.	125 West Twenty-ninth	
3731	O'Neil, Lillian	14	do.		Thomas	139 West Twenty-ninth	
3732	Wendt, Frederick	9	do.		Charles	9 W. T Twenty-seventh	
3733	Lee, Ida A.	12	Jan. 20, 1882		James	232 East Forty-sixth	
3734	McCowan, Hannah	7	do.	March 31, 1883	John	312 West Thirtieth	
3735	Sanders, Emma	9	do.		Annie	236 West Thirty-fifth	
3736	Diedrich, Mary	8	Feb. 24, 1882	Oct. 27, 1882	Katharine	209 West Twenty-sixth	
3737	Ferguson, Samuel E.	13	do.	Nov. 24, 1882	Andrew	336 Ninth Avenue	
3738	Hancke, Katie	10	do.		Sumner R. Stone	106 East Thirty-seventh	
3739	Mustin, Herbert S.	9	do.	Sept. 29, 1882	John J. Ennis, Grndf'r	128 West Twenty-ninth	
3740	Strube, Adelaide	11	do.	Nov. 24, 1882	Gardner A.	249 West Thirty-first	
3741	Strube, Louisa	6	do.	do.	do.	do.	
3742	Dunn, Mabel V.	8	March 24, 1882	Jan. 19, 1883	James E.	414 West Twenty-ninth	
3743	Garey, William S.	12	do.		Joseph E.	126 Oak, Greenpoint	
3744	Rutherford, Isabella	12	do.	May 25, 1882	Henry Wolcott	258 West Thirty-seventh	
3745	Hroetzel, Minnie	9	April 28, 1882	Sept. 29, 1882	Frederick	141 West Twenty-eighth	
3746	Exner, Mary	10	do.	Dec. 14, 1883	Edmund	520 West Thirtieth	
3747	Exner, William	13	do.		do.	do.	
3748	Grosen, Elizabeth	9	do.	Jan. 19, 1883	Jacob	228 West Twenty-eighth	
3749	Grosen, John	7	do.	Sept. 29, 1882	do.	do.	
3750	Hildenbrand, Lilly	8	do.		Basil	230 West Thirty-second	
3751	Smith, Alice	9	do.	Oct. 27, 1882	Michael	334 West Twenty-eighth	
3752	Stoll, John H.	12	do.	May 25, 1882	Mary A.	304 West Thirtieth	
3753	Stoll, Laura	10	do.	Nov. 24, 1882	do.	do.	
3754	Strahan, Katie	9	do.		William G.	217 W. Twenty-seventh	
3755	Strahan, Lena	11	do.		do.	do.	
3756	Zauner, Anna	9	do.	Sept. 29, 1882	George J.	234 West Twenty-eighth	
3757	Giffing, Caroline	9	May 25, 1882		Isaac A.	63 Bank	
3758	Kronvall, Ida T.	7	do.	March 31, 1883	John	206 West Twenty-seventh	
3759	Abrams, Robert Russel	8	Sept. 29, 1882		James C	111 West Twenty-ninth	
3760	Adams, Addie	7	do.	Jan. 19, 1883	Isaac	141 West Twenty-eighth	
3761	Bergstraser, Anna	12	do.		Samuel	81 W. Third, L. I. City	
3762	Bergstraser, Elizabeth	14	do.		do.	do.	
3763	Frazee, Myrtie	12	do.		Alonzo	479 West Thirty-sixth	
3764	House, Lillie E.	14	do.		Rev. Isaac E.	338 Garden, Hoboken	
3765	McCowan, John	7	do.	March 31, 1883	John	261 West Sixteenth	
3766	McKinney, Claude	9	do.		Frank	East Third, L. I. City	

CATALOGUE OF SCHOLARS—Continued.

No.	Pupil.	Age	Admitted.	Withdrawn.	Parent.	Residence.	Graduated.
3767	Martin, Mazie	10	Sept. 29, 1882		George	367 West Thirty-sixth	
3768	Meeks, Charles	11	do.	Jan. 19, 1883	Charles	316 East 121st Street	
3769	Miller, Flora Helen	6	do.	April 27, 1883	Thomas	251 West Twenty-third	
3770	Overocker, Mary E.	11	do.		William	4th & Vernon Av., L. I. C.	
3771	Prinzensing, Catharine	7	do.		Joseph	249 West Thirty-third	
3772	Safford, Minnie M	14	do.		Silas S.	West Sixth, L. I. City	
3773	Stagg, Peter M	12	do.		Peter M	546 West Fifty-first	
3774	Strahan, Agnes	6	do.		William G.	309 Seventh Avenue	
3775	Vail, Carrie F.	15	do.	Oct. 12, 1883	James C. Abrams	111 West Forty-ninth	
3776	Wendt, Ernst C.	7	do.		Charles	211 West Twenty-sixth	
3777	Westervelt, Catharine	11	do.		Andrew	440 West Thirty-fifth	
3778	Allison, Harry	11	Oct. 27, 1882	Oct. 12, 1883	Mary. Grandmother	135 Bank	
3779	Cannon, Charlotte	6	do.	Jan. 19, 1883	Mary	206 W. Twenty-seventh	
3780	Cannon, Lillie	7	do.	do.	do.	do.	
3781	Halvorsen, Huldah	7	do.		Halver	221 West Twenty-eighth	
3782	Lockwood, Charles	12	do.		Nathaniel	144 Java, Greenpoint	
3783	Overocker, Helen L	9	do.	Oct. 12, 1883	William	4th & Vernon Av. L. I. C.	
3784	Roberts, Edgar G	13	Nov. 24, 1882		Griffith J	157 Kent, Greenpoint	
3785	Thomas, Harriet E	10	do.	Oct. 12, 1883	William M	146 West Thirty-first	
3786	Abrams, Harold B	7	Jan. 19, 1883		James C	111 West Forty-ninth	
3787	Bocheim, Eugene	12	do.	Oct. 12, 1883	Max	465 Sixth Avenue	
3788	Coiley, William	12	do.		Alexander	178 Kent, Greenpoint	
3789	Eichorn, Azile	13	do.		Joseph	56 Jackson Ave. L. I. C.	
3790	Habenstein, Wilhelmina	10	do.		Charles	209 West Twenty-ninth	
3791	Hardel, Louisa	6	do.		Frank	204 West Thirtieth	
3792	Buchta, Gottlieb	7	Feb. 23, 1883	Oct. 12, 1883	Gottlieb	217 West Thirty-first	
3793	Dickinson, Mary	13	do.		Susan	771 Sixth, L. I City	
3794	Habenstein, Charles	9	do.		Charles	209 West Twenty-ninth	
3795	Knox, Margaret	10	do.	Oct. 12, 1883	Thomas	243 West Twenty-ninth	
3796	Knox, Samuel	8	do.	do.	do.	do.	
3797	Kracke, Frederick H	14	do.		Henry	93 East Eighth	
3798	Simpson, Sarah J	7	do.		George W	244 West Twenty-ninth	
3799	Welter, Hannah	9	do.		Henry	251 West Twenty-ninth	
3800	Welter, Mary	6	do.		do.	do.	
3801	Burns, Howard M	13	March 31, 1883		Dr. William	424 West Forty-third	
3802	Decker, Katie	13	do.	Oct. 12, 1883	William H	33 East Third, L. I. City	
3803	Kirke, Alexander	11	do.	Dec. 14, 1883	Edwin	254 West Thirtieth	
3804	Martin, Doretta	6	do.		Charles	253 West Twenty-ninth	

CATALOGUE OF SCHOLARS—Continued.

No.	Pupil.	Age	Admitted.	Withdrawn.	Parent.	Residence.	Graduated.
3805	Martin, Emma	10	March 31, 1883		Charles	253 West Twenty-ninth	
3806	Ranges, Anna	7	do.		Herman	316 W. Twenty-seventh	
3807	Burns, Emmet C.	12	April 27, 1883		Dr. William	424 West Forty-third	
3808	Cassiday, Elizabeth	10	do.		Mary	206 West Twenty-eighth	
3809	Ivers, May M.	16	do.	Oct. 12, 1883	William H.	48 India, Greenpoint	
3810	Lyon, Bertha E.	14	do.		Sylvester	119 Kent, Greenpoint	
3811	Pasco, Ruth	8	May 25, 1883		William	253 West Thirty-fifth	
3812	Wilson, Isaac C.	13	do.	Oct. 12, 1883	Emma	105 East 121st Street	
3813	Wood, Henry	7	do.		Thomas	303 Seventh Avenue	
3814	Wood, William	8	do.		do.	do.	
3815	Burgher, Nellie May	14	Oct. 12, 1883		George W.	146 Milton, Greenpoint	
3816	Burns, Eva	10	do.		William, M. D.	424 West Forty-third	
3817	Burns, Wesley	8	do.		do.	do.	
3818	Deeley, Mary	7	do.		Joseph	437 West Thirty-fourth	
3819	Dimelow, Irving	7	do.		Roland	448 West Thirty-seventh	
3820	Dimelow, Roland	12	do.		do.	do.	
3821	Dimelow, Stephen	8	do.		do.	do.	
3822	Hahner, Edward	7	do.		Christian	410 West Twenty-ninth	
3823	Hahner, Elizabeth	10	do.		do.	do.	
3824	Halsey, Stephen A.	15	do.		John J.	Perrott Avenue, Astoria	
3825	Halvorsen, Charles	7	do.		Charles	221 West Twenty-eighth	
3826	Hildenbrand, Samuel	7	do.		Basil	230 West Thirty-second	
3827	Hudson, Anna	13	do.		William H.	169 E. Twelfth, L. I. City	
3828	Johnston, Edward	9	do.		William	251 W. Twenty-seventh	
3829	Ketchum, John Winslow	15	do.	Nov. 9, 1883	Mary W.	244 Sixth Avenue	
3830	Knuchel, Bertha	6	do.		Edward	48 West Twenty-eighth	
3831	Lang, Clara	7	do.		William	243 West Twenty-ninth	
3832	Lang, Lena	8	do.		do.	do.	
3833	Lang, Matilda	11	do.		do.	do.	
3834	Powis, Craig	8	do.		Jennie M.	140 West Twenty-sixth	
3835	Smith, Cora	9	do.		Herman	253 W. Twenty-seventh	
3836	Speer, Eva	11	do.		Christiana	253 West Twenty-ninth	
3837	Thompson, Catharine	11	do.		Elizabeth	406 Seventh Avenue	
3838	Thompson, Wayne Hubert	8	do.		Rev. Abraham	303 West Twenty-ninth	
3839	Thompson, John Henry	10	do.		do.	do.	
3840	Walch, Ida	6	do.		Charles	205 West Twenty-ninth	
3841	Wohlfarth, Anna	6	do.		Bernard	do.	
3842	Wohlfarth, Lizzie	8	do.		do.	do.	

CATALOGUE OF SCHOLARS—Continued.

No.	Pupil.	Age	Admitted.	Withdrawn.	Parent.	Residence.	Graduated.
3843	Harrison, Horace Moore	7	Nov. 9, 1883		Mary	111 East 117th Street	
3844	King, Gertrude	13	do.		James A.	15 Third, L. I. City	
3845	Montrose, Elizabeth	10	do.		Abraham	do. do.	
3846	Sterner, Lucetta F.	10	do.		Jacob G.	92 W. Third, L. I. City	
3847	Woolruff, Anna F.	8	do.		John H.	Third Street, L. I. City	
3848	Ingraham, Archibald	11	Dec. 14, 1883		Jane	249 West Forty-seventh	
3849	McIntire, Jesse Annan	14	do.		Henry E.	New Lots, L. I.	
3850	Nielson, Frederick H. R.	11	do.		Anson	234 West Twenty-eighth	
3851	Nielson, Ludwig	9	do.		do.	do. do.	
3852	Nielson, Martha	8	do.		do.	do. do.	
3853	Romain, Conrad B.	10	do.		Joseph	Long Island City	
3854	Weed, Wm. Wallace	14	do.		Vitruvious	10 Java, Greenpoint	

The preceding CATALOGUE terminates at the close of the 250th year of the existence of the School—*1883*.

To facilitate reference to any particular scholar, the names in the preceding CATALOGUE—arranged in ALPHABETICAL ORDER—will be found in the following pages.

NAMES OF THE SCHOLARS IN ALPHABETICAL ORDER.

The Number opposite each Name indicates its Place in the Preceding Catalogue.

Name.	No.	Name.	No.	Name.	No.
Abrahams, Thomas F.	3667	Adma, Elizabeth	3220	Angus, William	2932
Abrams, Harold B.	3786	Ahmuty, Elizabeth	3136	Annely, Eliza	381
Abrams, Rob't Russell.	3759	Ahmuty, Matthew	3095	Annin, Sarah L.	1861
Aburnethy, Margaret	3658	Ahmuty, William	3175	Antz, Francis B.	2910
Aburnethy, Mary A.	3174	Ahrens, Alfred	3137	Apgar, Charles	3336
Acker, Eliza	308	Alberti, Annie	3673	Appleby, Amelia	910
Acker, Frances	2208	Albrecht, Charles	3247	Appleby, Charles	874
Acker, Jacob	453	Alcorn, Emma L.	2924	Archer, Catharine	1862
Acker, Josephine C.	2267	Allason, Anna	2889	Archer, James R.	3604
Acker, Laney	128	Allason, Clarissa	2709	Archer, Mary	1863
Acker, Laura G.	2191	Allason, Emma G.	3486	Arents, Stephen	1059
Acker, Mary	518	Allason, Laurence F.	3398	Arkills, Charles P.	2104
Acker, Mary E.	1610	Allason, Martha W.	2742	Arkills, James E.	1786
Acker, Rachel	136	Allason, Mary Louise.	3429	Arkills, Lydia A	1896
Acker, Stephen	195	Allen, Frances A	2256	Arkills, Mary E.	1738
Acker, William	663	Allen, James	1906	Armstrong, Charles,	3176
Ackerman, Abraham	14	Allen, Kate	2257	Armstrong, Charles O.	2341
Ackerman, Albert	361	Allen, Kate D	2801	Armstrong, Cora A	3272
Ackerman, Anna	2494	Allen, Mary	3233	Armstrong, Eliz.	45
Ackerman, Christie.	2323	Allen, Mary E	2743	Armstrong, Emeline W.	3138
Ackerman, Frederick	1654	Allison, Harry	3778	Armstrong, John G.	3301
Ackerman, Garrit G.	850	Altenhain, Charles	1971	Ashby, William H.	1506
Ackerman, Hannah,	256	Alyea, James	269	Ashenfelter, Anna B.	2086
Ackerman, Helen	324	Amerman, Hannah	176	Askins, James	180
Ackerman, Jacob D.	1857	Amerman, Isaac	143	Askins, Sarah	225
Ackerman, Jacob W.	1469	Amerman, Mary	32	Ashley, Clarian	1031
Ackerman, Jane	764	Anderson, Alfred	2312	Ashley, Conrad	918
Ackerman, John	155	Anderson, Annie	3270	Ashley, John	939
Ackerman, John	209	Anderson, Daniel A	1860	Ashley, Margaret	799
Ackerman, John	228	Anderson, David	628	Atkinson, Elizabeth	2026
Ackerman, John	280	Anderson, Elias	81	Atz, Adolph	2833
Ackerman, John	1394	Anderson, Elizabeth	43	Atz, Frederick	2701
Ackerman, John A.	2322	Anderson, Euphemia	1189	Atz, George A. C.	2702
Ackerman, Lawrence	98	Anderson, Eva C.	3507	Austin, John E.	2475
Ackerman, Martha J.	2673	Anderson, George.	745	Austin, William A. F. P.	2476
Ackerman, Mary	1376	Anderson, Jacob	1793	Avers, Ann Augusta	1725
Ackerman, Mary	2612	Anderson, Jessie	2209	Ayers, Edgar	1709
Ackerman, Peter D.	2295	Anderson, John	87	Ayers, Isabella B.	3526
Ackerman, Peter J.	2285	Anderson, John	537	Ayers, Joseph B.	1710
Ackerman, Rachel J.	1887	Anderson, John	1308	Ayers, Louisa J.	1726
Ackerman, William.	1347	Anderson, John	3674	Ayers, Martha J	2971
Arkerson, Almira	1858	Anderson, John W.	1007	Avers, Minnie L.	3030
Ackerson, Charles	394	Anderson, Lavinia	1810	Ayres, Albert	970
Ackerson, Charles P.	1859	Anderson, Lorena	2181	Ayres, Daniel	159
Ackerson, Edward	657	Anderson, Maria A.	1932	Ayres, Hester.	351
Ackerson, Eunice A.	2063	Anderson, Martha	2210	Ayres, Sarah	317
Ackerson, James T.	2264	Anderson, Mary	763	Ayres, Tobias	130
Acton, Wilhelmina L.	3548	Anderson, Nicholaus	8		
Adams, Addie	3765	Anderson, Peter	3331	Babb, Ellen V	1831
Adams, Charles F.	2360	Anderson, Phebe	538	Babb, George F.	1838
Adams, Frances	3056	Anderson, Richard C.	3121	Babb, Thomas E.	1832
Adams, James	77	Anderson, Walter	10	Badgley, Isaac	569
Adams, Jennie	3300	Anderson, William	1160	Bain, Benjamin F.	3504
Adams, John W.	576	Angus, James	3029	Baird, William A	1421
Adams, Joseph P.	345	Angus, Mary F.	3271	Baisden, Hannah J.	3122

NAMES OF THE SCHOLARS

Name.	No.	Name.	No.	Name.	No.
Baker, Benjamin F.	1349	Bayard, Ann	640	Bierman, Jacob H.	1092
Baker, Edgar	1819	Bayard, Peter	685	Billings, Elizabeth	1267
Baker, Etta	3693	Beach, Anna C.	2048	Bingenheimer, Christoph	2834
Baker, Isaac B.	1348	Beach, Clarence W.	3221	Bird, Charles E	3487
Baker, Oscar	2186	Beach, Edward	1016	Birdsall, Constant	1696
Baker, William F.	2091	Beach, Emma	2286	Bissett, Eliza	1131
Bakewell, George W.	1922	Beach, Jane	1162	Bisset, Hannah	1052
Bakewell, Louisa	1982	Beach, Mary	852	Black, Eliza Jane	1907
Bakewell, Milton	1923	Beach, Sarah	891	Black, Garrit C.	1032
Baldwin, Addie	2393	Beach, Willard Parker	3222	Black, Robert	2065
Baldwin, Annie	2394	Beach, William	943	Blair, William A	2710
Baldwin, Harris J.	2268	Beatson, George	2981	Blanchard, Christian B.	830
Baldwin, Justus.	682	Beatson, William	2935	Blanchard, George	600
Baldwin, Lucy E.	2269	Beaumont, Benjamin	827	Blanchard, James	482
Baldwin, Phebe J.	2305	Beaumont, Cath. Susan	916	Blanchard, Marg't Ann.	1029
Ball Louisa M.	3506	Beaumont, Mary Ann	414	Blanchard, Maria	675
Ballard, Asa B.	3324	Beaumont, Peter S.	862	Blanchard, Nicholas	483
Ballerman, Annie	3087	Bechthold, Julius E. J.	3009	Blanchard, Susan	885
Bancker, Sophia	448	Becker, Helen C.	2609	Blanche, Ann Amelia	2223
Banker, Catherine A.	1538	Becker, Louisa	2192	Blanche, Charles A	2193
Banker, John	1539	Becker, Bertha	2674	Blanche, Emma A	2151
Banker, Mary E.	1574	Becker, Mary	2675	Blank, Ephraim	325
Banker, Rachel	421	Bedford, Augustus	2073	Blauvelt, Ann P	713
Banker, Susan J.	1688	Bedford, Eleanor	2287	Blauvelt, Anne	620
Banker, Thomas A.	1540	Bedford, Harriet A.	2141	Blauvelt, Catharine	457
Banks, Ann Amelia	1635	Bedford, John S.	2107	Blauvelt, Catharine	611
Banks, Obadiah	1636	Beeker, Herman R.	2037	Blauvelt, Catharine	632
Banks, William O.	1655	Beekman, Ann	369	Blauvelt, Christiana	354
Banner, John	144	Beekman, Catharine	181	Blauvelt, Cornelius	2616
Banta, John	120	Beekman, Eliza	347	Blauvelt, Cornelius L.	1136
Banta, Hannah.	387	Beekman, Henry	167	Blauvelt, Eliza	851
Banta, Mary	388	Beekman, John	306	Blauvelt, Eliza Ann.	1187
Banta, Peter	12	Beggs, Ada	2936	Blauvelt, Elizabeth L.	2346
Barber, Silas	1595	Bell, George	3337	Blauvelt, Herman	740
Barclay, Kate	3019	Bell, George H.	3273	Blauvelt, Helen M.	1995
Bardusch, Jacob	2484	Bell, Hortense	3399	Blauvelt, Henry C.	2644
Barkley, Ella	2396	Bell, James	3248	Blauvelt, Isaac	346
Barkley, Sarah	2397	Bell, John E.	3284	Blauvelt, Isaac M	2371
Barnard, Charles	3659	Bell, Louis	3400	Blauvelt, James	634
Barnet, Jane	168	Bell, Thomas J.	2732	Blauvelt, John	335
Barney, Augustus W.	2554	Bell, William H.	1364	Blauvelt, John	784
Barney, Daniel	2555	Bender, George P.	3384	Blauvelt, John D	2001
Barr, Catharine	267	Bennet, Andrew H	433	Blauvelt, John M.	3088
Barr, Frederick	331	Bennet, Sarah Elizabeth.	2308	Blauvelt, Julia F.	1765
Barr, Garret	556	Bennett, Benjamin	3573	Blauvelt, Kate M	2692
Barr, Garrit	1280	Bennett, George A. H	1174	Blauvelt, Margaret	1232
Barr, Henry	426	Bennett, Nancy	1135	Blauvelt, Maria	513
Barry, Catharine J	1383	Bennett, Sally F.	490	Blauvelt, Rachel C.	2347
Barth, Caroline	1961	Bennett, Sarah F.	665	Boarden, Emily R	2756
Barth, Mary Elizabeth.	1924	Benschoten, Cornelius.	68	Boardman, Charles H.	1699
Barthey, Gustave	3325	Bensel, Fanny	3415	Boardman, Mary E.	1409
Barthey, Katharine.	2615	Benson, Emily	3668	Boardman, Rachel	1611
Barthey, Lena	3326	Benson, George E	3611	Boardman, Sarah J.	1433
Bartholf, Leah Jane	2114	Benson, John	441	Boardman, William J.	1258
Bartholf, Lydia Ann	2176	Benson, Sarah	3612	Bodenheimer, Morris	3550
Bartholomae, Aug'ta C.	3327	Berdan, Abby L.	2124	Boeheim, Eugene	3787
Bartine, Jenny	3103	Berdan, Albert	1292	Boehm, David	2783
Bartlett, Charles B.	3687	Berdan, Mary E.	2125	Boehmer, August	2925
Bartlett, William H. S.	3688	Berdan, Peter	1619	Bogardus, Alfred M.	2040
Bartley, George W.	3697	Bergstraser, Anna	3761	Bogardus, Cornelius	2041
Bascom, William B.	2933	Bergstraser, Elizabeth	3762	Bogardus, Edward W.	2042
Basmar, William	2911	Berry, John M.	2000	Bogardus, James	1853
Bates, Jane	3031	Berry, Mandeville	2334	Bogardus, Julia E.	1983
Bates, Louis	3302	Berry, Maria J.	3549	Bogardus, Mary	2128
Bates, Robert	2934	Bertholf, George	290	Bogart, Daniel	94
Bartheldes, Louis	2878	Bertholf, William	278	Bogart, Eliza	385
Baxter, Elizabeth	1153	Besher, Ann M.	1319	Bogart, Ella	2470
Baxter, John Thomas	3682	Hesher, John H.	1318	Bogart, James	83
Baxter, Kate E.	3466	Betham, Peter P.	907	Bogart, John	265
Baxter, Samuel	1154	Bicker, Victor	470	Bogart, John W.	1038

IN ALPHABETICAL ORDER—continued.

Name.	No.	Name.	No.	Name.	No.
Bogart, Lanah Ann	732	Brady, James H	1680	Buchta, Gottlieb	3792
Bogert, Alice	2295	Brady, William H	2270	Buck, John	676
Bogert, Ann	679	Bragaw, Francis	1338	Buck, Louisa	621
Bogert, Andrew	687	Bragaw, Isaac	1339	Buckbee, Benjamin	1452
Bogert, Catharine	584	Bragaw, Lewis	1375	Buckley, Lucy Ann	1020
Bogert, David	1821	Braird, Eliza	430	Bullene, Frank Jay	3527
Bogert, Eugenia A.	1822	Brampton, Francis	2617	Bullene, John J	3207
Bogert, Euphemia	1967	Brandon, George	3032	Bundle, Christian	1018
Bogert, Garret	1864	Brant, Abraham	2115	Bundle, Elizabeth	1017
Bogert, Gilbert	18	Brant, John C	2003	Burger, Daniel	366
Bogert, Gilbert	1062	Brant, Mary W	1951	Burger, Gerardus C.	398
Bogert, Henry	956	Brant, Sophia E	1952	Burger, Rebecca	344
Bogert, Jacob	633	Brazier, James H	651	Burgess, Aaron	613
Bogert, James	911	Breene, Carrie	3660	Burgess, James	768
Bogert, James O	1950	Breene, Isabella	3661	Burgher, Nellie May	3815
Bogert, James W	982	Brennan, Agnes A	2556	Burns, Arthur	3177
Bogert, James W	1114	Brett, Francis R	108	Burns, Emmett C	3807
Bogert, Jane	614	Briggs, Arthur E	3642	Burns, Eva	3816
Bogert, Jane	786	Brinckerhoff, Henry	848	Burns, Georgiana	2460
Bogert, John	216	Brinckerhoff, John J	1811	Burns, Grace	3178
Bogert, John	919	Brinckerhoff, John W	1897	Burns, Howard M	3801
Bogert, Lavinia	604	Brinckerhoff, Ransf'd W.	2532	Burns, Margaret C	2461
Bogert, Margaret	445	Brinkerhoff, Christian	754	Burns, Mary A	1605
Bogert, Margaret	530	Britton, Nicholas	182	Burns, Wesley	3817
Bogert, Maria	849	Broad, John E	3643	Burns, William J	3179
Bogert, N. I Marselus	2002	Broetzell, Minnie	3745	Burras, William H	1336
Bogert, Orrin S	1716	Brooks, George A	2420	Burton, Minnie H	2958
Bogert, Peter	348	Brooks, Issac	268	Burtsell, Edward D	199
Bogert, Peter	478	Brooks, Washington	3585	Busch, Adeline	3123
Bogert, Peter	777	Brooks, William H	1281	Busch, Andrew	3352
Bogert, Peter B	1041	Brower, Abraham D	686	Busch, Margaret	3124
Bogert, Polly	169	Brower, Augustus	824	Butler, Emma	1766
Bogert, Rulef	1113	Brower, Elias	826	Butler, Ida	3567
Bogert, Sally	652	Brower, Henry	790	Butler, John	573
Bogert, Samuel P	1996	Brower, Jeremiah	757	Butler, Julia	1667
Bogert, Sarah Jane	1830	Brower, John	188	Butler, William B	2584
Bogert, Simon J	726	Brower, John L	2361	Butt, John	3035
Bogert, Stephen	743	Brower, Martin	677	Button, John	1739
Bogert, Stephen B	960	Brower, Nicholas	44	Button, Thomas	1061
Bogert, Susannah	756	Brower, Rebecca	769	Butz, Henry	2094
Bogert, Warren	2542	Brower, Rebecca	856	Byam, Andrew J	3393
Bogert, Washington	719	Brower, Sarah	588	Byard, Mary	1316
Bogert, William	800	Brower, Thomas	192	Byers, John	2634
Bogert, William	1064	Brower, William	748	Byers, Moses	2635
Bogert, William C	1620	Brower, William J	2602	Byers, William	2676
Boor, Margaretta	2495	Brown, Alexander F	2641	Byrnes, Ann Eola	3066
Boor, Peter Edward	2288	Brown, Alice Knox	2342	Byrnes, Corrinne A	2757
Bopp, Matilda	2547	Brown, Amanda	1346	Byrnes, Elizabeth A	2758
Bopp, Sophia	2548	Brown, Benjamin W	3081	Byrnes, George A	2890
Bornmann, Charles G.	2224	Brown, Charles E	2121		
Bornmann, Francis	2129	Brown, Frank	2618	Cabana, Charles I	2533
Horst, Corstiaan	2873	Brown, Gertrude	2926	Cabana, Hannah R	2422
Borst, Jane	2861	Brown, Harry	2804	Cabana, Mary M	2619
Horst, William	2862	Brown, Isabella L	3033	Cadmus, Charles C	1744
Bovee, Alfred	1401	Brown, James H	2421	Cadmus, Hartson P	1664
Bovee, John	1434	Brown, John	1345	Callow, Ann	735
Bovee, Joseph	1402	Brown, Louis G	3034	Callow, Catharine A	1624
Bowden, Jennie	3410	Brown, Mary Ann	1001	Callow, James	625
Bowers, Daniel	3628	Brown, William	1377	Campbell, Adolphus W.	2260
Bowers, Mary C	1586	Brown, William A. P	1335	Campbell, Jane E	2759
Bowman, Daniel	1252	Brown, William H	2093	Campbell, John C	2733
Bowman, Jane	1487	Brownlee, Archibald G.	2998	Campbell, Phœbe M	2734
Boyce, Catharine E	1352	Brownlee, J. Harrison	2957	Campbell, William	2458
Boyd, Abraham A	2874	Bruce, Alexander	1295	Campbell, William J	2999
Boyd, Charles E	3675	Bruce, Catharine	1294	Cannon, Charlotte	3779
Boyden, James S	2703	Bruce, George W	1120	Cannon, Lillie	3780
Boyden, William H	2704	Bruce, Jane	1293	Canterman, Ann	277
Brady, Abner S	1626	Bryant, Reuben	1310	Canterman, John	236
Brady, Catharine Ann	1759	Bryant, William	1309	Capewell, Richard	1697
Brady, Charles E	1679	Buchanan, Sarah J	2982	Capewell, Susan A	1612

Name.	No.	Name.	No.	Name.	No.
Carey, John	3036	Clark, William W.	1902	Colwell, Warren A.	2177
Carlock, Christian	622	Clarke, Walter S.	2142	Combes, Catharine	898
Carman, Benjamin	1636	Clarkson, J. Schurem'n.	2183	Combes, John	909
Carman, Ella L.	3274	Clearman, William H.	2705	Combes, Mary	870
Carman, Melissa C.	3180	Clegg, Margaret J.	3239	Comstock, Anna	3374
Carman, Peter	1014	Clements, Caroline	1282	Conant, Charles F.	1713
Carman, Ruth	1013	Clendenin, Eliza	1760	Conant, George H.	1787
Carner, Alonzo L.	3629	Clendenin, George	1712	Concklin, Henry	1417
Carpenter, Nellie	3586	Clendenin, Thomas	1984	Concklin, Jacob	1416
Carpenter, Robert L.	2182	Clendenin, William	1587	Concklin, Mary E.	1781
Carpenter, William E.	3581	Cleverley, Abraham H.	3476	Conckling, Esther	254
Carr, George G.	2749	Cleverley, Margaret A.	3508	Conklin, Abraham	869
Carr, Sarah L.	2750	Cleverley, Thomas H.	2891	Conklin, David	494
Carr, William	2883	Cleverley, William	2206	Conklin, Eleanor	385
Carss, Henry R.	3275	Clinton, Isabella	2399	Conklin, Francis M.	2724
Carss, John B.	2967	Cloyd, Ann Maria	1137	Conklin, Henry	941
Carss, Joseph	3092	Cloyd, Peter	1138	Conklin, Margaret	1065
Carter, Agnes Maud	3578	Clute, Cecelia H.	1422	Connell, Annie R.	3712
Carter, Alida	2299	Cochard, August	3419	Connell, Henry W.	3453
Case, Julia D.	2108	Cocks, Louis A.	3250	Connell, Regina	3454
Case, Maria	511	Coe, Samuel L.	2711	Connelley, Jennie	2959
Cassiday, Elizabeth	3808	Coey, Elizabeth	3251	Connelley, John H.	3252
Cawood, Phebe	520	Coiley, William	3788	Connolly, Jessie	3223
Chadwick, Daniel	1133	Colbart, John	101	Connor, Harry F.	3620
Chadwick, Thomas	1132	Colbart, Sarah	239	Conover, Ann Elizab'h.	1667
Chamberlain, Perry	3208	Cole, Charles S.	2543	Conover, Catharine A.	1672
Chambers, Ann Maria.	1217	Cole, Ferdinand S.	2522	Conover, Clementine G.	2720
Chambers, Hannah	1219	Cole, George A.	3451	Conover, Daniel	994
Chambers, John H.	1216	Cole, Georgiana	2670	Conover, Elisha	995
Chambers, Mary	1259	Cole, John	170	Conover, George S.	996
Chambers, Mary	1536	Cole, John H.	3452	Conover, Mary S.	1669
Chambers, Solomon	1537	Cole, Samuel A.	2523	Conrad, Emily	2875
Chambers, William	1218	Colegrove, Catharine	238	Conrey, John D.	2921
Chapin, Charles	1740	Colegrove, William	177	Conron, Lulu	3631
Chapin, Henry A.	1627	Coleman, Charles	1410	Cook, James	1093
Chapin, James F.	1637	Coleman, Charles E.	2650	Cook, John	1156
Chapman, William R.	2937	Coleman, David B.	2506	Cook, Peter V. H.	1168
Chappel, James	1023	Coleman, John L.	2646	Cook, Thomas M.	1197
Chardevoyne, Ann.	36	Coleman, Joseph V. D.	2796	Cooke, Francis W.	1936
Chardevoyne, Thos. C.	318	Coleman, Marianna	2507	Cooke, Leah M.	2075
Childs, Andrew	1847	Colfax, Mary Jane	1625	Cooke, Peter A.	1937
Childs, Christopher	1492	Colgrove, Ann E.	1940	Cooke, Rachel E.	1934
Childs, Deborah J.	1493	Collard, Archer	106	Cooper, Robert J.	1340
Childs, Elizabeth	1494	Collard, Eliza	1236	Coppinger, Adriana	1303
Childs, Rebecca	1621	Collard, George W.	1201	Coppinger, Charles	1304
Chipman, Charles M.	3630	Collard, Jacob	612	Coppinger, Deborah	1302
Christie, Gamaliel	2027	Collard, James	360	Coppinger, Eliza J.	1435
Christie, James	76	Collard, James	1329	Corbett, Charlotte	3181
Christie, John	1387	Collard, Jeremiah	1155	Corbett, Elizabeth	3139
Christie, Maria E.	2030	Collard, John	553	Corbett, Julia B.	3140
Churchwell, Mary E.	2645	Collard, Maria	487	Corbett, William	551
Clancy, Georgiana	3010	Collard, Richard	1408	Corn, Louisa	3491
Clandening, Clarence	3608	Collard, Stephen D.	1588	Cornelisse, Lena	3509
Clark, Abraham	1923	Collard, William	1370	Cornelisse, Paulie W.	3709
Clark, Ada A.	2603	Collins, Elizabeth	316	Corner, Margaret	3285
Clark, Alexander A.	3249	Collins, Elizabeth	894	Corner, Mary	3286
Clark, Allena	1797	Collins, James Ross	3038	Corson, Christina	1453
Clark, Catalina C.	2019	Collins, Jane	408	Corson, Emma	1175
Clark, Cornelia	1798	Collins, Jeannette	3332	Corson, Frank	3348
Clark, Eliza	1447	Collins, Jemima	471	Corson, George H.	3353
Clark, Ethel	3730	Collins, Jesse	1768	Corson, Samuel	1176
Clark, Frank W.	3037	Collins, John P.	1769	Cortelyou, Eleanor	751
Clark, James Clifford	2539	Collins, Mary Ann	895	Cortelyou, Elizabeth	476
Clark, Margaret	2792	Collins, Samuel	357	Cortelyou, George S.	3596
Clark, Martha	2793	Collins, Sarah Ann	546	Cortelyou, John	760
Clark, Mary E.	2324	Collins, Stephen	1121	Cortelyou, Peter C.	507
Clark, Peter	1926	Collins, Susan	993	Corwin, Mary E.	2271
Clark, Priscilla	1908	Collins, William A.	2760	Cossum, Caroline	3194
Clark, Thomas	1481	Colwell, Charles G.	2170	Cossum, William H.	3195
Clark, William H.	1780	Colwell, Frederick L.	3373	Cottrell, Israel A.	2184

IN ALPHABETICAL ORDER—continued.

Name.	No.	Name.	No.	Name.	No.
Couenhoven, Chr......	4	Day, Catharine	598	Demarest, Francis W...	3467
Couenhoven, Jacob....	272	Day, Henry	1159	Demarest, Francis Z....	2610
Couenhoven, James....	301	Day, Jacob	972	Demarest, Hannah J....	1823
Couenhoven, John L...	567	Day, Jacob E..........	887	Demarest, Henry......	515
Couenhoven, Nicholas..	61	Day, John.............	1081	Demarest, Isaac.......	506
Couenhoven, Sarah,...	465	Day, John I...........	497	Demarest, Jacob	354
Couenhoven, William .	221	Day, Maria............	961	Demarest, Jacob D.....	944
Coward, Charles..... ..	3340	Day, Mary............	906	Demarest, James......	165
Coward, George.......	3341	Day, Rebecca.........	928	Demarest, James	516
Cowie, Alexander G...	2423	Day, Rebecca Jane....	1045	Demarest, James E....	3468
Cowie, Annie..........	2459	Day, William..........	902	Demarest, James Henry.	2038
Cowing, Charles J.....	2066	Day, William..........	1094	Demarest, Jane.......	2087
Cozine, Garret........	443	Deacon, James,.... ...	52	Demarest, John.. ...	307
Cozine, George.......	534	Dealing, Charles E	2540	Demarest, John K.....	1938
Cozine, Mary...	442	Dealing, Micheletta ...	2544	Demarest, Kate........	2906
Craddick, Emma.......	3224	Dealing, Oberlin	2541	Demarest, Llewellyn L.	3431
Cragin, Ida E.........	2534	Dean, Henry F.......	2594	Demarest, Marg't Ann .	2017
Cragin, James W......	2535	Dean, Lemuel P	2178	Demarest, Peter.......	263
Cramer, Augustus H ..	2508	Dearing, James.......	2153	Demarest, Peter.......	805
Cramer, Wm. J. C. P...	2884	Debaun, Edward	3182	Demarest, Peter	1033
Crane, Everett I.......	3141	Debaun, John	858	Demarest, Peter.......	1149
Crane, John	3000	Debaun, Joseph	782	Demarest, Rachel.....	733
Crane, Lemuel F......	3142	Debaun, Peter	615	Demarest, Sally.......	680
Craven, Jacob	298	De Bevoise, Courtlandt.	835	Demarest, Samuel E...	2006
Craven, James........	247	Debevoise, James......	946	Demarest, Sarah	214
Cregier, Ann Maria....	1648	Debevoise, Washington,	1025	Demarest, Sarah......	1150
Cregier, Eliza J.......	1470	Debost, Alwyn	3144	Demarest, Simon	753
Cregier, Joseph.......	1378	Debost, Leon.........	3145	Demarest, Stephen....	232
Cregier, Josephine....	1541	Debost, Marie Louise..	3146	Demarest, William E...	3551
Crocheron, Charlotte E.	2620	De Camp, George......	893	Demill, Frederick	194
Crocheron, Edward....	2863	De Camp, James......	931	Demorest, Catharine ..	190
Crolius, James W......	2130	Decker, John	100	Demorest, Eleanor.....	251
Crolius, Josephine.....	2028	Decker, Katie...	3802	Demorest, Maria	202
Crossingham, Caroline .	3143	Decker, Lewis........	937	Demorest, Maria......	283
Crosson, Mary M.....	3214	Decker, William.......	1854	Dempsey, William	5
Crosson, William	3215	Decker, William	3225	Denizot, Agnes	2571
Crouter, Joseph	1638	Deely, Mary..........	3818	Denizot, Ellen J.......	2572
Crowell, John........	3062	De Garcia, Carrie V...	3579	Derr, Hester..........	2372
Cruger, Thomas.......	1206	De Graw, Aaron.	1	Derr, Hobart..........	2373
Crum, Emma F.	2146	De Graw, Catharine...	499	Deshays, Charles......	1104
Crum, Frederick H....	2147	De Graw, Sally.......	500	Deshays, David........	1105
Crygier, John U......	2721	De Groff, Edward.....	2876	De Turk, Herbert.....	3147
Crygier, Kate V.......	2744	De Groot, Abraham ...	822	De Veau, Franklin L...	3669
Crygier, Sarah........	338	De Groot, Eleanor A...	1471	Devew, James.........	548
		De Groot, Jacob	801	Devoe, Abby..........	212
DAKIN, Isabella	2983	De Groot, John M.....	976	Devoe, Abraham	788
Dakin, John	2984	De Groot, Mary J.....	1472	Devoe, Aletta	742
Dale, Alexander R.....	3375	De Groot, Michael F...	832	Devoe, Daniel........	164
Dally, Mary	390	De Groot, Peter	877	Devoe, Daniel S......	184
Dami, Edward....... .	934	De Groot, Rachel......	833	Devoe, Edwin F......	1681
Dami, John........ ..	953	De Klyn, Barnet.......	1432	Devoe, Frederick......	1723
Dami, William.........	1024	De Klyn, Peggy.......	150	Devoe, George	1350
Dana, Emma L........	3695	De La Croix, Andrew..	3020	Devoe, George L......	1054
Dana, Helen E........	3637	De La Croix, Matilda C..	3021	Devoe, Gilbert........	1066
Danforth, Anna.......	2879	Delamater, Abraham ..	656	Devoe, Henry.........	689
Dangler, Adolphus E...	3125	De Lamater, Charles H.	2972	Devoe, Isaac	829
Dangler, Ella A........	3354	De Lamater, Du Bois..	2973	Devoe, Jacob.........	945
Daniels, Nelly........	3287	De Lamater, Jane.....	217	Devoe, John..........	642
Danner, Hannah......	2466	De Lamater, Jno. (Vide (		Devoe, John..........	2107
Danner, Jacob.........	2467	Note No. 2791). ...)	...	Devoe, Joseph........	579
Danningberg, Lucinda..	1389	Del Noy, Virginia.....	1998	Devoe, Laney	151
Danziger, Esther......	3667	Demarest, Ann Maria,.	2004	Devoe, Margaret Ann..	1682
Darr, Christina	2400	Demarest, Cath. Am'nda	2005	Devoe, Mary M.......	1865
Davis, John	1596	Demarest, Charlotte...	3394	Devoe, Sarah	26
Davis, Mary J........	1542	Demarest, Cornel. V. R.	1898	Devoe, William	203
Davis, Sarah	3283	Demarest, Ebenezer...	2378	De Wilde, Ebenezer...	3432
Dawson, Jacob H......	1522	Demarest, Elizabeth...	205	De Wilde, William M...	3477
Dawson, Samuel B.....	1460	Demarest, Ella V. R...	2677	De Witt, Joseph C. H..	2157
Dawson, States	1523	Demarest, Ephraim B...	2016	Dexter, Emma........	2305
Day, Abraham A.......	648	Demarest, Francis Eug.	2143	Dibel, Margaret.......	3433

NAMES OF THE SCHOLARS

Name.	No.	Name.	No.	Name.	No.
Dick, Delia	2424	Downs, Cornelius T.	1543	Eaton, Thomas	1234
Dick, Ida	2496	Downs, John S.	1544	Eckert, Louis V.	3253
Dickhout, Catharine	1745	Downs, Sabrina	1545	Edgarton, Gertrude	3488
Dickhout, Henry	1753	Drumgold, Charles G.	3289	Edmonds, Catharine W.	1746
Dickhout, Magdalen	1888	Drumgold, Henry	3011	Edwards, Alice	3012
Dickinson, Mary	3793	Drysdale, Anna	3057	Edwards, Charles	2636
Dickson, Easter	971	Du Bois, Catharine	2043	Edwards, Gitty	429
Dickson, Eliza	864	Du Bois, Gertrude	2044	Edwards, Oliver C.	3001
Dickson, James	797	Du Bois, James	1833	Ehlert, Mary J.	2761
Dickson, James A.	875	Du Bois, William L.	1834	Ehrhart, Louisa	2901
Dickson, McCauley	984	Duff, Mary	618	Eichler, Christian H., Jr.	2426
Dickson, Mary	1004	Dugan, William	1397	Eichorn, Azile	3789
Dickson, Samuel	785	Dunbar, Esther	3469	Elbert, Caroline	2118
Dickson, Samuel	900	Dunham, Catharine	2939	Elbert, Catharine E.	1702
Diederich, Mary	3736	Dunlap, Edwin J.	3148	Elbert, William H.	2119
Diehl, John Jacob	2053	Dunlap, Frank P.	2586	Elder, Edward D.	3699
Dilloway, Catharine	2116	Dunlap, James	1242	Eldershaw, Fanny	3276
Dilloway, Elizabeth	2117	Dunn, Alexandra M.	3355	Eldridge, Edgar	1321
Dilloway, Georgine	2070	Dunn, Catharine F.	2805	Eldridge, Simeon	1320
Dilloway, Godfrey	2113	Dunn, Esther A.	3234	Ellenwood, Clarissa	1261
Dimelow, Irving	3819	Dunn, Henry	2220	Ellerman, Mary A.	2014
Dimelow, Rowland	3820	Dunn, Mabel V.	3742	Ellis, Mary	1283
Dimelow, Stephen	3821	Dunn, Maria	3290	Ellis, Robert	1311
Dinkelman, Herman	3268	Dunn, Mary E.	2806	Ellis, Theodore	1284
Disbrow, Emily J.	2008	Dunn, Sarah F.	2216	Elly, William	3517
Disbrow, Stephen L.	2009	Dunn, William	204	Elmendorf, John B.	3602
Dixon, Amanda	2585	Dunshee, James	2211	Elsie, Frances	3105
Dixon, Ella R.	2990	Dunshee, Mary P.	2745	Embree, John	574
Dixon, James E.	2991	Dunshee, William P.	2613	Embree, Samuel	804
Dixon, Mary	821	Durand, Nancy	562	Emmet, Eliza Ann	947
Dixon, Samuel S.	2992	Durborow, Joseph	89	Emmet, George	112
Dob, Neilson	860	Durborow, Mary	25	Emmet, Jane Ann	1067
Dobbs, Howell	3532	Durborow, William H.	270	Emmet, James W.	863
Dobbs, John	755	Durburrow, Walter	356	Emmet, Nathaniel	683
Dobbs, Marion	3543	Duryea, Richard	550	Emmet, Sarah	564
Dobbs, William	630	Duryee, Catharine	749	Emmet, William T.	731
Dobbs, William D.	3638	Duryee, Garrit	818	Emmons, Walter E.	3632
Dodds, Jacob	133	Duryee, Henry B.	803	Emmons, William	3633
Dodge, Carrie L.	2812	Duryee, James	840	Engel, Peter	3209
Dodge, Cornelius B.	1240	Duryee, John	639	Engle, Charles	3058
Dolde, Elizabeth	2054	Duryee, John	750	Enholm, Ivar	3385
Dolde, George	2938	Duryee, Maria	690	Enholm, Oscar	3386
Dolph, Clarence	2606	Duryee, Peter C.	772	Enney, David	691
Dombaski, Charles	1903	Duryee, Peter V.	983	Enney, Elizabeth	493
Dominick, Harriet P.	2485	Dusenberry, Henry K.	2300	Ennis, Adelaide	2642
Doneghan, Bernard	1441	Dusenberry, Susan A.	2362	Ennis, Eliza	884
Donnelly, Robert	3524	Dusenberry, William P.	2325	Ennis, Geraldine	2379
Doolittle, Washington	3183	Duval, John E.	2225	Ennis, James	709
Door, Ella J.	3516	Dyckman, Peter B.	1403	Ennis, Mary	820
Doremus, Abraham	619			Ennis, William	901
Doremus, Betsey	774	EAGLESON, Agnes	3104	Ernst, Elizabeth	2679
Doremus, Betsey	825	Eagleson, Fanny	1955	Ernst, Paulina	2680
Doremus, Betsey G.	791	Eagleson, James H.	1956	Erskine, Edward	1262
Doremus, Caty	718	Eagleson, Mary E.	1957	Erskine, Harriet	1198
Doremus, Isaac	1190	Eagleson, Sarah J.	1962	Erskine, Magdaline	1188
Doremus, Jacob	1241	Earl, Peter	904	Esler, Eleanor	836
Doremus, Jacob	1353	Earl, Thomas	157	Esler, Henry	876
Doremus, James	737	Earle, Cornelius	1005	Evans, George	681
Doremus, John	472	Earle, Ella	2797	Evans, Jennie	3106
Doremus, Margaret	533	Earle, George	1482	Evans, William	3149
Doremus, Mary Ann	880	Earle, Henry	1483	Evans, Isaac	1504
Doremus, Nicholas	1191	Earle, John	126	Everitt, Benjamin	489
Doremus, Noah	752	Earle, John	1489	Evertson, Benjamin	868
Doremus, Sarah	1354	Earle, John S.	1427	Evertson, Jane	714
Doremus, Sarah	2316	Earle, Margaret A.	2678	Evesson, Isabelle	3240
Dorn, John	3039	Earle, Martha J.	1458	Ewing, Jane	3303
Dorset, James	1003	Earle, Morris	59	Exner, Edmund	3338
Dorset, John	1002	Earle, Sally	962	Exner, Mary	3746
Dougherty, George	1337	Eaton, James	1243	Exner, William	3747
Dow, Mary	3040	Eaton, Mary J.	1233	Eyre, Mary Ann	2425

IN ALPHABETICAL ORDER—*continued.*

Name.	No.	Name.	No.	Name.	No.
Faekner, David	3562	Forshay, Margaret Ann.	1220	Gardner, Walter	2637
Fairchild, Louis	3689	Forshay, Maria	626	Garns, Henrietta	1285
Fairchild, Meredith	3690	Forshea, Elizabeth	294	Garretson, Charity	2152
Fardon, Elizabeth	27	Foster, Enos	1413	Garretson, John	2638
Farnham, Florence	3564	Foster, Isaac	1147	Garrison, Jane	240
Farnham, Frank H	3639	Foster, John	1414	Garrison, Maria	163
Farr, George	2427	Fothergill, George	222	Garrison, Simon	152
Farr, Thomas	2428	Fowler, Elizabeth	3376	Gaskin, Abby	932
Farrell, Florence H	3150	Fowler, Maria	3401	Gaskin, John	431
Fash, Isaac	311	Fox, Catharine	636	Gaskin, Maria	783
Fash, John	422	Fox, Edward	2402	Gaskin, Sally Ann	669
Fash, William	310	Fox, Hannah	662	Gaskin, Susannah	392
Fawpel, Hannah	654	Fox, Lewis	2401	Gaskin, William	558
Fawpel, Lanah	572	Fox, Margaret	810	Gaston, Susan	391
Fawpell, Maria	738	Fox, Maria	635	Gaunt, William	3605
Fay, Georgiana	3013	Francis, Marion	3210	Gavey, William S	3743
Feery, Elizabeth	3342	Francisco, Cornelius	1122	Gayler, Ellen H	2202
Feldmuth, Barbara	2651	Franz, Catharine	2647	Gayler, Jessie	2203
Fenn, Adaline	1546	Franz, Jacobine	2498	Geddes, William E	3503
Fenn, Julia Ann	1547	Franz, John Frederick	2885	Geel, Cornelius	3691
Fenton, David	99	Franz, Sophia	3002	Genin, Louis E	2105
Fenton, Susan	512	Fraunces, George W	200	Genin, Nancy E	2148
Fenton, Thomas	492	Frazee, Myrtie	3763	Genin, Thaddeus	2363
Fentonburgh, John	1123	Frazier, George W	1317	Gerdes, Caroline	2815
Ferdon, Abraham	2082	Frazier, Jane Ann	1316	Gerdes, Dora	2940
Ferdon, Abraham	2163	Frazier, John W	1488	Gerdes, Elizabeth	2816
Ferdon, Andrew T	1968	Frazier, Rebecca	1454	Gerdes, Sophia	2817
Ferdon, David	1915	Frazier, Sarah	1511	Gerdes, William	3096
Ferdon, Frances	2055	Free, Caroline	2907	Gerhauser, Margaret	2057
Ferdon, Garret	1835	Freeland, Aaron M	920	Gerhauser, Mary A	2058
Ferdon, George W	2218	Freeland, Ann	1428	Gessner, Angeline S	2335
Ferdon, James A	1911	Freeland, Jacob B	701	Gibson, Nancy	498
Ferdon, James H	1866	Freeland, John	1430	Gibson, Robert H	2649
Ferdon, James S	1916	Freeland, John	1597	Giffin, Harry	3700
Ferdon, John	1867	Freeland, John M	813	Giffin, Lillie	3701
Ferdon, Margaret	1917	Freeland, Mary	1429	Giffing, Anna M	2273
Ferdon, Sarah C	1912	Freeland, Peggy	435	Giffing, Caroline	3757
Ferdon, Stephen L	2056	Freeland, Reuben	505	Giffing, Isaac A	1972
Ferguson, Samuel E	3737	Freeman, Alexander	865	Giffing, John Ferguson	2083
Ferguson, Thomas	2272	Freeman, Eliza A	879	Giffing, John D	2274
Ferguson, William L	2289	Freeman, Joseph	977	Giffing, Sarah Emily	2350
Ferris, Joseph	2993	Friedel, Ida	2181	Giffing, William C	1973
Ferris, Margaret	31	Friedel, Selma	2682	Giles, Jennie M	3609
Fichtel, Charles G	2762	Friedel, Theophilus	2683	Giraud, George	1108
Fichtel, Henry	2864	Friedenfelt, Wallg'th R.	2787	Glover, Catharine	986
Filberg, Catharine A	1395	Frost, Georgiana	2095	Glover, Charles	1111
Filberg, Charles P	1442	Frost, Theodore	1010	Glover, Eliza	547
Filberg, John	1341	Frost, Sally Ann	1021	Glover, Hester	847
Finck, Otto	3483	Frülingstradt, August	2807	Glover, Thomas	711
Finkenaur, Josephine	3356	Frülingstradt, John	2536	Glover, William	963
Finner, Emma S	3304	Früauf, Charlotte	2912	Goetchius, Clifford L	3097
Finner, Lizzie L	3305	Früauf, George	2851	Goetchius, Howard B	2671
Fisher, Catharine	1558	Früauf, Justine	2852	Goldsmith, Sarah	1548
Fisher, Harry	305	Fuhrer, Harry	3621	Good, Catharine	3723
Fisher, Nicholas	2497	Fuhrmann, Henry G	2607	Good, Joseph	3724
Fisher, Peter	2477			Good, Mary Ann	3725
Fiske, Susie J	2968	Gabel, Jacob	3597	Goodrich, Sarah A	2160
Fleming, Robert W	3518	Gackstadter, Evaline	2684	Goodrich, William B	948
Flint, George	2892	Gaisberg, William C	2071	Gordon, Alexander	400
Flock, Mary	480	Galatian, Magdalen	1593	Gordon, Henry	401
Forbes, Alexander	54	Galatian, Samuel W	1467	Gordon, Henry	514
Forbes, Tobias	78	Galatian, William W	1468	Gordon, Jane	196
Forhoss, Isaac B	524	Gallagher, Benjamin D.	2033	Gordon, Luanna	3112
Ford, Lillie	3565	Gallagher, Theodore H.	1818	Gordon, Matilda	424
Forrest, Grace	3410	Gallagher, William E	2034	Graf, Ernst	2685
Forrest, Mamie	3501	Gambel, Frederick	2913	Graham, Augusta	2941
Forrest, Anna M	3151	Gardinier, Margaret	603	Graham, John	86
Forshay, Garrit	1107	Gardner, John	539	Grant, Ella B	3533
Forshay, Henry	1106	Gardner, Oscar K	2652	Grant, John	46
Forshay, James	1124	Gardner, Thomas	586	Grant, John	62

Name.	No.	Name.	No.	Name.	No.
Grassal, George	1689	Hamje, Adeline	3613	Helmes, Elizabeth	3231
Grassal, Henry	2521	Hamm, Charles	2735	Helmes, John	386
Grassal, Louisa	1690	Hamm, Louisa	2736	Helms, Archibald M'C.	617
Grau, Michael	3093	Hammel, George	2687	Helms, Charles	1575
Gray, Agnes L.	1603	Hammel, Mary	2823	Helms, Cornelia	174
Gray, Hannah T.	1589	Hammond, Ann Amelia.	1263	Helms, Emily	1576
Gray, Isabella W.	1590	Hammond, Caroline	854	Helms, Maria	536
Gray, Laura E.	3644	Hammond, Henry	997	Helms, Peter	19
Gray, Maria T.	1761	Hammond, Latourette	1063	Hemmingway, Annie	3683
Gray, William H.	1461	Hammond, Sarah	1225	Hemmingway, Charles.	3713
Grear, William J.	3420	Hammond, Theod. A.	2079	Henderson, Sarah	3155
Green, Catharine	2089	Hammond, William	1237	Henderson, Samuel	3098
Greene, Anna M.	2686	Hammond, Washington.	855	Henderson, Thomas	3004
Greene, Charles E.	2374	Hancke, Katie	3738	Henderson, William	3156
Greene, Ella J.	2375	Haniquet, Charles	2194	Hendrickson, John	462
Greene, Sarah Louisa.	2486	Haniquet, Louisa	2193	Hennessey, John S.	3571
Greenham, Joseph	555	Haniquet, Virginia	2196	Henshaw, Adele	2914
Greenham, William	698	Hanks, Annie D. W.	3326	Henshaw, Augustus	2866
Griffen, Phebe	2942	Hanshe, Grace	2282	Henshaw, Sarah L.	3537
Griffen, Sabina F.	2943	Harbeck, Anna	2622	Henshaw, Vanderbilt.	2867
Griffith, Joseph	1462	Hard, Emma L.	3499	Henshaw, Viola	2915
Griggs, Emma	3226	Hardel, Louisa	3791	Heppe, Otto	1868
Griggs, Jennie May	3528	Hardenbrook, William.	37	Herbison, Jennie	3692
Griggs, Mary J.	2880	Hardie, Susan	1169	Herbst, Frank C.	2688
Grint, Emma	3277	Hardie, William	3426	Herbst, William F.	3614
Grint, Louisa	3278	Hardy, Nellie	3702	Heron, Daniel	3434
Griswold, Myrtilla	3470	Hardy, William	3663	Herring, Catharine	1517
Groff, Sebastian	3178	Haring, Ann	1817	Herring, Charles E.	1687
Grosen, Elizabeth	3748	Haring, Daniel John	1899	Herring, Edward	647
Grosen, John	3749	Haring, Eliza	1824	Herring, Eliza	582
Grosheim, Bernard	3003	Haring, Henry	1799	Herring, Frederick	501
Grosheim, Louisa G	3227	Harman, Henry	2090	Hesketh, Joseph H.	1800
Gross, Emma	3235	Harman, Margaret	2126	Heunisch, Emma	2893
Gross, George	3228	Harper, Angeline	1112	Heunisch, Lena	2894
Gross, John F.	3196	Harper, Catharine	1177	Heunisch, Louisa	2895
Gruenewald, Cecilia	2639	Harper, Jesse	1211	Hewlett, George B.	2836
Gruenewald, Charles	2604	Harper, John	1129	Hewlett, James L.	3126
Gunn, Agnes	3634	Harper, Robert	375	Hewlett, Nellie B.	3622
Gurnee, Ellen	2031	Harper, William	1130	Heyer, Catharine	504
Gurnee, Samuel	552	Harrington, Washington	1322	Heyer, Catharine M	609
Gwynn, Happy H.	3411	Harris, James	1560	Heyer, Catharine M	1357
		Harris, Peggy	672	Heyer, Hannah	242
Habenstein, Charles	3794	Harrison, Horace Moore	3843	Heyer, Hannah	627
Habenstein, Wilhelm'a	3790	Harrison, Walter	3518	Heyer, Henry	741
Hadden, Thomas	1490	Harrison, William	3645	Heyer, Margaret	921
Hagelman, Lizzie B.	3254	Haselrot, Frederick	3313	Hever, Maria	578
Hahn, Elizabeth	1935	Hasie, Charles	1986	Heyer, Sarah M.	1355
Hahn, Jacob	2088	Hasie, Montague	1987	Heyer, Sophia	191
Hahn, John	2029	Hatfield, William	603	Heyer, William	296
Hahn, William	2204	Hatton, Amelia	3333	Heyer, William G.	1356
Hahner, Edward	3822	Haulenbeck, Almira	1569	Hickok, Benjamin	1869
Hahner, Elizabeth	3823	Haulenbeck, James B.	1639	Hickok, Cordelia A.	1848
Haight, Georgiana	2290	Haulenbeck, Mary F.	1904	Hickok, Sarah A	1849
Haight, John E. B.	2221	Haulenbeck, William H.	1559	Hicks, Catharine	881
Haight, Julia	2275	Hausin, William	2908	Hicks, Elsie	978
Haght, Willis D.	3236	Hawkins, Zechariah	1268	Hicks, Thomas	736
Hall, Charles H.	1840	Hay, John T.	2769	Higgins, Charles	571
Hall, Huldah	1841	Haynes, Annett	402	Higgins, William	1631
Hall, John W	3349	Hays, Cornelia	34	Hildenbrand, Lilly	3750
Hall, Joseph H.	2865	Hays, Maria	153	Hildenbrand, Samuel	3826
Hall, Mary Ann	2231	Haywood, Eleanor V.D.	2580	Hill, Alfred	3505
Hall, Mary Anna	2763	Heacock, William C. B.	2308	Hill, Emma	2557
Hall, Sarah E.	1842	Hebron, George	3395	Hill, George	134
Halsey, Edwin B.	3152	Hedden, Ann	705	Hill, George A	2847
Halsey, Josephine R.	3153	Hedden, Anne	623	Hill, Jefferson	1524
Halsey, Stephen A	3824	Hedden, Jennie Adèle	3337	Hill, John	1047
Halvorsen, Charles	3825	Hedden, John	773	Hill, John Edmund	2558
Halvorsen, Huldah	3781	Hedden, William	704	Hill, John M	1473
Hamilton, Elizabeth	3316	Heeder, Henry	3587	Hill, Kate	2559
Hamilton, Isabella	3154	Helmes, Charles	215	Hill, Mary	905

IN ALPHABETICAL ORDER—*continued*.

Name.	No.	Name.	No.	Name.	No.
Hill, Neilson	1163	Horner, Annie M.	3255	Jackson, Harriet E.	2487
Hill, Sally	912	Horton, Antoinette	1811	Jackson, Harry	2771
Hill, Sarah	3358	Horton, Charles	3529	Jackson, Henry	3338
Hill, Sarah F.	2665	Horton, Lillie	3530	Jackson, Henry S.	2488
Hill, Sophia	2689	Hose, Henry	3014	Jackson, Laura	3178
Hill, Thomas	1239	Hotaling, Harriet A.	2023	Jackson, Lewis F.	2511
Hill, William	1115	House, Lillie E	3764	Jackson, Peter A. H.	2573
Hill, William H.	1448	Houseman, Rosanna	2432	Jacobs, Sarah	3157
Hill, William R	3489	Houston, Henry I.	3015	Jacobus, Rachel	226
Hilliard, James	1238	Howe, Anna F. U	2625	Jagels, Anna	3309
Hilliger, Christiana	336	Howe, Robert B	2433	Jagels, Cathalina	3237
Hilliker, Fanny	485	Howe, William	2712	Jagels, Henry	3317
Hilliker, Sally Ann	1048	Howell, Hannah L.	2581	Janes, Charles H.	3492
Hilliker, Stephen	673	Howell, Sarah	2582	Janes, Josephine A	2512
Hilliker, William	428	Howells, Elizabeth	3127	Janes, William A	2583
Hillyer, John	1476	Howells, Martha	3128	Jeffers, Charles D.	1221
Hinds, Joseph	417	Howells, Rhoda	3129	Jeffers, Emeline	1222
Hinds, Thomas	475	Howie, William	3068	Jeffers, Harriet	1223
Hinman, Amanda M. H	2623	Howland, Francis H	3594	Jeffers, Mary E	1274
Hinman, William H.	2624	Howland, William W.	2096	Jeffrey, Mary J	2213
Hinn, Henry	3350	Howsey, Elizabeth	117	Jelliffe, Samuel G	1734
Hintze, Annie M	3485	Hoyt, Samuel A	3082	Jenzer, Arnold	2746
Hintze, Arthur B.	3588	Hudson, Anna	3827	Jeroleman, Charles	1193
Hintze, Henry	3435	Hudson, John	658	Jeroleman, James O	1042
Hitchcock, James R.	2127	Hudson, Mary Ann	759	Jeroleman, William H	1182
Hitchcock, Wilbur K.	3623	Hues, Alice.	2403	Jersey, Hannah	796
Hoagland, Anna L.	2234	Hues, Henry L.	2424	Johnson, Amelia	1871
Hoagland, Catharine W.	1806	Huestis, Hannah	135	Johnson, George	3742
Hoagland, William H.	1732	Hughes, Ella L	2509	Johnson, Maggie H.	2251
Hoffacker, Bernard	2560	Hughes, Mary A	2510	Johnson, Martha	1872
Hoffacker, Mary	2561	Hughton, Viola	3107	Johnston, Edward	3828
Hoffman, Anna	2405	Hulett, Phebe	71	Johnston, Samuel	273
Hoffman, Charles J.	2587	Hulett, Phebe	367	Jollie, Elizabeth P.	2471
Hoffman, George C.	2406	Hulick, Anna L.	1870	Jones, Aaron	1323
Hoffman, Schuyler, V.V	3390	Hulick, Lemmey	1770	Jones, Ann	436
Hoffstaetter, Frederick	2429	Hunnenmurder, Mary	1698	Jones, Annie H.	3497
Hoffstaetter, George	2653	Hunt, Abigail	1747	Jones, Catharine	288
Hoffstaetter, Jacob	2813	Hunter, Ann	1049	Jones, Catharine E	2159
Hogenbruin, John	3339	Hunter, Fanny	1050	Jones, Charles H	2010
Holgate, Ella H.	3216	Hunter, John	1161	Jones, Charles Parker	3519
Holloway, Isabella	110	Hurrell, Eulalie	2434	Jones, Emeline	2317
Holloway, John	173	Hurrell, John A.	2435	Jones, Emma G	1836
Holloway, John	469	Huxley, Charles C.	1109	Jones, Howard	3069
Holly, Samuel	1100	Huxley, Louisa	957	Jones, Isaac	339
Holly, William	1101	Huxley, Maria	942	Jones, James N	1050
Holmes, Annie H	3606	Huxley, William	1010	Jones, John J	1829
Holmes, Maggie A	3613	Huyler, Abraham L	2368	Jones, Lucinda	1843
Holskampfer, Dirck	1727	Huyler, Henrietta H	2297	Jones, Mary Ann	2808
Holstein, Fritz	3205	Huyler, James S	2212	Jones, Mary L.	1762
Holt, George E.	3640	Huyler, Mary F.	2098	Jones, Mary L	2318
Homan, Charles A.	2301	Hyatt, Emma	2666	Jones, Peter	1030
Homan, Jessie A.	2974	Hyatt, Fanny	2654	Jones, Sarah K	1763
Homan, Marsalous	2302	Hyde, Emma J	2336	Jones, Stephen	1830
Hone, John V. A.	1068	Hyde, Henry	1371	Jones, William	1324
Hopper, Andrew	595	Hyer, John F	684	Jones, William D	1754
Hopper, Calvin	2131	Hyne, Charles H	2245	Jordan, Caroline E	2626
Hopper, Clarissa	1008	Hyne, Frances	2164	Jordan, Eleanor N	2319
Hopper, Cornelius A	2161	Hyne, Mary	2165	Jordan, Louis C. Levin	2262
Hopper, Edward	1009			Jordan, Mary H. S.	2407
Hopper, Jacob	96	Ingraham, Archibald	3848	Jordan, William B. M.	2261
Hopper, James F.	2309	Ingram, Jennie	3646	Junior, Patience	1202
Hopper, Margaret	3184	Inslee, Elizabeth	3241	Just, James	3158
Hopper, Martha	51	Inslee, Hannah A.	3320		
Hopper, Mary	3185	Ivers, May M.	3809	Kahl, Martin	3243
Hopper, Matthew	17			Kahrs, Henry	3474
Hopper, Peter F.	2848	Jackson, Abigail H.	2770	Kaske, William	3703
Hopper, Rachel J	1540	Jackson, Adrian	3307	Kaufmann, Henry	3186
Hopper, Sarah C.	1550	Jackson, Charles	3377	Kaylor, Isaac	1437
Hoppert, Albert	2430	Jackson, Edward	2818	Keily, John A	1151
Hoppert, Pauline	2431	Jackson, Esther H	2588	Keller, Antoinette	1974

Q

NAMES OF THE SCHOLARS

Name.	No.	Name.	No.	Name.	No.
Keller, Louis.	1988	Kline, Lewis A.	2468	Lamberson, Cornel's V.	1577
Kelly, Anna	1640	Kline, Margaretta	1990	Lamberson, David W.	1578
Kelly, Charles J.	1615	Kloepfer, Christine	3350	Lamberson, James M.	1717
Kelly, James.	464	Kloepfer, Louisa	3351	Lammers, Edward	3130
Kelly, John.	342	Knapp, August	2916	Lammers, Elizabeth	2976
Kelly, Sarah.	292	Knapp, David A.	3534	Lammers, Emma	2977
Kelsey, Sarah M.	1940	Knapp, Jonathan	1148	Lammers, William.	3437
Kemp, William M.	2959	Knapp, William	2917	Lamoureau, Delia	2514
Kennar, Charles.	2562	Knauber, John	2969	Lander, Charles	2036
Kennar, Kate.	2563	Kneringer, Elizabeth.	1158	Lane, Daniel.	132
Kerr, John C.	3544	Kneringer, Julia A.	1193	Lane, Elijah	197
Kerr, Margaret S.	3545	Kneringer, Matthias	1102	Lang, Clara.	3831
Kesselem, Catharine.	3070	Kneringer, Sarah	1225	Lang, Lena	3832
Ketchum, Jno. Winslow	3829	Knickerbocker, Benner.	985	Lang, Matilda	3833
Kettleman, Catharine.	1873	Knickmyer, Fred'k W.	2975	Langdon, Charlotte.	3455
Kettleman, George W.	1724	Kniffen, Hannah.	249	Langdon, Cornelia.	1963
Kettleman, John J.	1534	Kniffen, Jane	517	Lange, Anna	2109
Kettleman, Maria.	1641	Kniffen, Robert.	289	Lange, Clara.	2110
Keyser, Catharine.	2713	Knight, Charles P.	2314	Lange, Ida	2111
Keyser, Henry	1372	Knight, George.	2438	Larkins, Ellen M.	1927
Kidd, Charles W.	2326	Knight, John	2513	Latham, Francis S	700
Kidd, Isabella	2436	Knight, John I.	1714	Latschar, Christian.	1889
Kidd, Peter E.	2437	Knight, Josephine E.	2886	Latschar, Mary.	1890
Kiefer, Charles.	1850	Knight, Leola	3244	Laver, Henry	2764
Kiersted, Henry T.	362	Knight, Thomas	3416	Laverty, Agnes.	2772
Kiersted, James	139	Knight, William	3310	Laverty, Elizabeth	2773
Kiersted, Luke	6	Knobloch, Anna	3538	Laverty, John.	2788
Kills, Polly	472	Knobloch, Washington.	3539	Laverty, Joseph	2810
Kimball, Mary	3684	Knowd, Charles.	2896	Lawrence, Abraham	540
King, Aaron	670	Knowd, Sarah A.	2868	Lawrence, Jane.	566
King, Abraham	447	Knox, Margaret	3795	Lawrence, John.	1171
King, Andrew	473	Knox, Samuel	3796	Lawrence, Mary.	739
King, Gertrude.	3844	Knuchel, Bertha	3830	Lawrence, Robert H.	1170
King, Gilbert	60	Kockler, Margaret.	2798	Lawrenz, Anna	3726
King, Gitty.	607	Koeirs, Eliza	723	Lawrenz, Eliza	3727
King, Hannah.	413	Koeirs, John.	913	Lawson, Ann Elizabeth.	1228
King, Harman	67	Koeirs, Polly.	667	Lawson, Caspar N.	2478
King, Herman B.	1057	Koeirs, William.	722	Lawson, Charlotte.	1729
King, Jacob.	137	Koeker, Louisa.	1969	Lawson, Clementine.	2537
King, James L.	1139	Koeker, William.	1978	Lawson, Edward W.	2479
King, Jane.	437	Kohl, Augusta.	3328	Lawson, George W.	2440
King, Nicholas.	1178	Kolb, Elizabeth.	3186	Lawson, Lydia	1730
King, Peter Wilson.	1125	Kolb, Samuel	3187	Lawson, Miller	2276
King, Rachel.	314	Kortright, Daniel.	432	Layman, Alexander.	495
King, Susan	671	Kortright, Ellen	435	Layman, Alexander	1551
King, William	1071	Kortright, Nicholas.	340	Layman, Harriet L.	1552
Kint, Catharine	715	Kostar, William D.	3417	Layman, Sophia	702
Kint, Jeremiah	543	Kracke, Frederick H.	3797	Layman, Susannah	728
Kint, Nathaniel	365	Krechting, John P.	2252	Layman, William	1591
Kip, Araminta	1999	Kroll, Charles G	3436	Leach, George.	291
Kip, Harriet	1212	Krouvall, Ida T.	3758	Laycraft, John	140
Kip, Hubert	11	Kruse, Henrietta	3083	Le Blanc, Louis.	2441
Kip, James	1157	Kuhn, Amelia	3159	Lee, Horace	3520
Kip, Nicholas.	1213	Kuhn, Charles	3160	Lee, Ida A	3733
Kircheis, Alexander F.	1975	Kuhn, David	3540	Lee, Letitia	938
Kircheis, Charles A	1976	Kuhn, Emil.	3387	Lee, Oliver.	3521
Kircheis, Emma L.	2364	Kuhn, Louisa.	3161	Lefferts, Anna	2171
Kircheis, Louis P.	2011	Kuhn, Margaretta	3616	Lefferts, Benjamin.	2369
Kircheis, Mary M.	2565	Kuhn, William	3162	Lefferts, Edward E.	1651
Kircheis, William H.	1977	Kuntz, Barbara	2409	Lefferts, John B.	1874
Kirchner, Ameao	2706	Kuntz, Jacob	2408	Lefferts, Lydia Ann	1788
Kirchner, Henry.	2707	Kuntz, Louisa	2439	Lefferts, Lydia Ann	1812
Kirk, Samuel	3421	Kurz, Henry.	3595	Lefferts, Harriet.	1953
Kirke, Alexander O.	3803	Kyle, David.	1714	Lefferts, Mary.	1670
Kitchell, Andrew	372			Lefferts, Sarah M.	1813
Kitchell, Eliza	302	Ladd, Abraham Wilson	2499	Lefferts, William H.	1652
Kitchell, Isaac	420	La Forge, Fanny A.	3531	Lefman, Albert	2489
Klauberg, Frances M	2549	La Forge, John A.	809	Lefman, Amelia.	2291
Klauberg, Frederick L.	2550	Lake, John B.	1172	Lefman, Emma	2144
Kline, Elizabeth W.	1989	Lake, William H.	1165	Lefman, George W.	2145

IN ALPHABETICAL ORDER—*continued.* 227

Name.	No.	Name.	No.	Name.	No.
Lefman, Robert L...	2166	Love, Elmer...	3694	McDougal, Matilda J...	3188
Lehman, Albert D...	3311	Loveland, John...	949	McEown, Joseph T...	2963
Lehmkuhl, Araminth B..	2902	Low, Jane...	38	McEvoy, Mary E...	2526
Lehmkuhl, Chas. E. C...	2903	Low, John J...	1152	McGowan, Anna...	2837
Lehmkuhl, George H...	2197	Lowe, Margaret...	1814	McGowan, Benjamin F.	2838
Lehmkuhl, John W...	2380	Lowe, Mary...	2530	McGowan, Edward...	2846
Lehmkuhl, Margaret C.	2351	Lownds, Cornelius V. C.	2277	McGregor, Cara I...	2136
Leipold, Robert H. T...	2167	Lowry, Charles...	2381	McGregor, Malcolm...	2775
Leith, Nicholas...	3344	Lowry, George E...	2410	McGuire, Philip...	419
Lent, Jane...	262	Lowry, Mary F...	2480	McGwyer, Fanny...	266
Leonard, Charles...	2985	Lowry, Sarah E...	2327	McGwyer, John...	293
Leonard, Frederick F.	3360	Lucken, Christopher...	3356	McGwier, Sally...	477
Leonard, Jacob...	49	Lucken, Henry...	3362	McIlvaine, Elizabeth J..	3113
Lester, Andrew...	3361	Lucken, Rebecca...	3363	McIlvaine, George...	3345
Letts, Eleanor...	725	Ludlam, George...	2491	McIntire, Jesse Annan..	3849
Lewis, Elias...	234	Lutz, George...	3236	McKay, Francis A...	1939
Lewis, Gertrude D. B...	2067	Lutz, Philip...	2595	McKee, Gertrude...	2752
Lewis, John M...	706	Lyman, Christian B...	1116	McKee, Mary...	2467
Lewis, Leonard...	82	Lyman, John H. L...	1117	McKee, Nathaniel...	2655
Lewis, Leonard...	378	Lyman, Joseph E...	3535	McKee, Samuel B...	2690
Lewis, Robert...	3572	Lynch, Adaline...	1034	McKee, Susan...	2691
Libby, William H...	2960	Lynch, Maria...	1035	McKee, Thomas W...	2039
Linder, Anna...	2799	Lynch, Peter...	1653	McKibbin, Charles C...	2236
Linder, Elizabeth...	3438	Lyon, Aaron G...	1073	McKibbin, Charlotte...	1674
Linder, Frederica...	3493	Lyon, Bertha E...	3810	McKibbin, George A...	1693
Linder, Johanna...	3163	Lyon, David D...	1075	McKibbin, John...	1675
Linder, Kate...	2740	Lyon, Eleanor S...	1207	McKinney, Alpheus...	2714
Linder, Rosina...	3164	Lyon, John H...	1789	McKinney, Anna...	2692
Lindsey, John W...	3016	Lyon, Michael...	90	McKinney, Claude...	3766
Linkroum, Courtlandt..	3084	Lyon, Rachel D...	1074	McKinney, George...	69
Lipfert, Elizabeth...	3041	Lyon, Robert S...	1227	McKinney, George E...	2693
Lipfert, George...	2722	Lyons, Jefferson W...	1673	McKinney, Helen J...	2694
Lippincott, Alfred B...	1691	Lyons, Sarah W...	1683	McKinney, John A...	2820
Lippincott, Ebenezer W.	1598	Lyster, Georgia...	3071	McKinney, Margaret A.	2444
Lippincott, Edward E..	1599			McLaren, Agnes J...	2776
Lippincott, Henry...	1600	McAdoo, Elizabeth R..	1755	McLeod, David Adrian.	3291
Lippold, Frederick A...	2751	McAdoo, Margaret A...	1756	McMekin, Jane...	2978
Lippold, Henry F...	2187	McAdoo, Sarah J...	1757	McMekin, William J...	2979
Litchhult, Catharine...	692	McAleese, Daniel...	2627	McMichael, Carrie...	3590
Littell, Bloomfield...	2524	McAleese, Kate...	2589	McNeal, John...	141
Little, Helen A...	2226	McAleese, William...	2614	McNeil, Emma...	3073
Little, Lucy J...	2400	McArdle, Catharine...	2134	McNeil, Frances...	3074
Littlepage, Urania...	2726	McArdle, Mary...	2135	McNeil, Harriet L...	3364
Livingston, William A..	3552	McArthur, Martha...	3044	McPherson, Anna M...	1941
Lloyd, Joseph F...	2789	McBride, Abraham...	720	McPherson, Donald...	1942
Locke, Frederick...	527	McBride, Irving...	775	McPherson, John...	1943
Locke, Henry Louis...	2525	McBride, Sally A...	987	McPherson, John D...	1255
Locke, Thomas H...	597	McBride, Walter...	643	Mabee, Ann...	111
Locke, Lavinia...	2442	McCabe, Anna E...	3334	Mabie, Andrew E...	1794
Locke, Mary C...	2443	McCabe, William...	3059	Mabie, Ann E...	2162
Lockwood, Alonzo...	3312	McCain, Elizabeth..	1855	Mabie, Cornelius...	1795
Lockwood, Charles...	3782	McCain, John...	1808	Mabie, Henry P...	1970
Lockwood, Emma E...	3279	McCain, Mary...	1837	Mabie, Richard...	2084
Lockwood, John...	3510	McCarthy, Annetta...	2481	Mabie, Samuel H...	2596
Logan, Anna...	1495	McCarty, Charles R...	2727	Mabie, Sarah...	2597
Logan, Ida...	2774	McClenachan, Emily...	3060	Mabie, William H...	2598
Logan, Sarah...	1496	McClenachan, Lilian P.	3017	Machett, Charles E...	1083
Lord, David S...	2887	McCluskey, Esther...	3198	Mackey, Ella...	3598
Lord, Francis...	2904	McCowan, Hannah...	3734	Magonigle, Charles E...	1443
Lord, William H...	2888	McCowan, John...	3765	Magonigle, John Henry	1444
Loromer, Cornelia...	1904	McCracken, Anna...	3094	Magonigle, Mary...	1633
Loromer, John...	1905	McCreery, William...	717	Mahrenholz, August...	3608
Losee, Mary Frances...	2944	McCrum, Howard...	3439	Mallon, John H...	3582
Losey, James...	645	McCrum, Ruth C...	3061	Mandeville, David H...	1665
Losey, Sarah...	315	McCrum, William S...	3553	Mandeville, Edward...	1661
Losey, Thomas...	817	McCulloch, Lewis R...	2559	Mandeville, Elizabeth...	1529
Losey, William...	454	McDonald, Jeremiah...	3072	Mandeville, Ellen...	1668
Lounsberry, Josephine.	2961	McDonald, Mary...	841	Mandeville, Elmira...	1649
Love, Alexander...	1423	McDonald, William...	973	Mandeville, Emeline...	2352
Love, Charles...	1485	McDougal, Duncan...	13	Mandeville, Hannah A..	1530

Name.	No.	Name.	No.	Name.	No.
Mandeville, Henr'tta E.	3006	Meadon, Ada	3388	Mooney, Manoah	1358
Mandeville, James B.	2353	Meeker, Kitty C	981	Moore, David	1802
Mandeville, Mary C	1692	Meeker, Uzal	1388	Moore, Ellen	1553
Mandeville, Millard	2354	Meeks, Charles	3768	Moore, John T.	3200
Mandeville, Sophronia E. F.	1579	Meiers, Julia	3599	Moore, Letitia	1807
		Meigs, Catharine H	3610	Moore, Mary A	2227
Mandeville, Thomas	1782	Melvin, Frederick	1735	Moore, Mary E.	3201
Mandeville, William	1607	Melvin, Mortimer	1736	Moore, Samuel	1497
Mansfield, Matthew	1330	Menges, Josephine	2382	Moore, Sophia	922
Marchand, Julia	3546	Menges, Julia	2383	Moore, Willis L	2228
Marinus, Ann	794	Merritt, Edward	3075	Morley, Fredwood	3045
Marinus, Deborah	979	Merritt, Julia E	1997	Morrell, Emma	2348
Marinus, Henry	678	Meshet, Frederick	171	Morrell, Robert N	2349
Marinus, Jane	908	Metnich, Henry	1703	Morris, Catharine	1351
Marinus, John	641	Metnich, Jacob	1704	Morris, Eleanor	179
Marinus, Maria	758	Metzgar, John V	1875	Morris, Eleanor	281
Marinus, Thomas	808	Meyer, Clara	2821	Morris, Florence V.	2306
Marks, Amelia	3199	Mickens, Elizabeth A	1570	Morris, Francis	1085
Marrenner, Edward	2253	Mickens, George T	1371	Morris, Helen D	2384
Marrenner, James H	2214	Mickens, George W	2551	Morris, Isaac	1140
Marschalk, Francis A.	423	Mickens, Rachel A	1572	Morris, Jacob	1231
Marseilles, Adrian	1684	Mickens, Sarah C	1573	Morris, Jane E	1194
Marseilles, John	1009	Miles, Robert J	2728	Morris, John	1325
Marselis, Amelia	980	Miles, Stephen E.	2500	Morris, John J	1270
Marsh, Charles B	3042	Miller, Christina B.	2814	Morris, Louis C. L.	2304
Marsh, John A.	882	Miller, Edith	3704	Morris, Mary Ann	1192
Marsh, Lydia L	3583	Miller, Fanny	3365	Morris, Rachel	85
Marshall, Delia	2263	Miller, Flora Helen	3769	Morris, Robert S.	2328
Marshall, Jesse D. W.	1731	Miller, George	229	Morris, Samuel	1084
Marshall, Hester Ann.	1771	Miller, George	2753	Morris, Susan	105
Martin, Alexander H	3043	Miller, George S	3525	Morris, William	2329
Martin, Charles	2355	Miller, Hattie	3617	Morris, William	2657
Martin, Doretta	3804	Miller, Isaac	16	Morris, William	3647
Martin, Eliza J	2024	Miller, Isaac	1095	Morris, William N	1269
Martin, Ellen	2025	Miller, Jennie B.	3580	Morse, Jennie	3600
Martin, Emma	3805	Miller, John	867	Morse, Martha	3422
Martin, Mazie	3767	Miller, John	2918	Mortimer, Frederick.	3062
Martin, William V	2303	Miller, Joseph	666	Moss, James R.	1425
Martine, Charles	2527	Miller, Martin	2445	Mott, Emma J	2168
Martling, Henry	48	Miller, Peter	1166	Mott, Sarah C	2169
Martling Robert	211	Miller, Sarah	1096	Mount, Andrew	2566
Martyn, Egbert	3554	Miller, Sarah Ann	1167	Mount, Kate M	2472
Martyn, Ferrer	3555	Miller, William	124	Mount, Lydia	2515
Martyn, Paul	3569	Mills, Charles I	2945	Mount, Margaret A	2473
Martyn, Sarah A.	2232	Mills, George V	2574	Mount, Robert W	2516
Mason, Anna Melissa	2217	Mills, Luther	474	Mount, Sarah M	1418
Mason, George	3281	Mills, Samuel H.	2656	Moweson, Mary	223
Mason, George H	2235	Miner, Andrew	2919	Muir, James P.	2839
Mason, Hannah	3440	Miner, James	154	Muir, Maggie J	3714
Mason, Sarah	1825	Miner, Luella	2897	Muir, Thomas D. W	3715
Mattass, Robert	198	Miner, Morton F	2927	Munn, Edward F	3114
Mauri, Julia C. M	1852	Minor, Jacob	2343	Munn, Emma P	3046
Maverick, Samuel	1775	Miranda, George B.	3573	Munn, Regina V	2708
Maverick, William H.	1718	Miranda, Robert R.	3591	Munroe, Sadie	3716
Maxwell, William	3229	Mitchell, Mary	1247	Munson, Charles R.	1891
Mayer, John W	2628	Moffat, Elijah	1507	Munson, George	1086
Mayer, Sophia J	2640	Moffat, Isaac L	1424	Munson, George E	1892
Mayer, William	3728	Moffat, Janet	1508	Murray, William	1205
Maverean, Louisa A	2278	Moffat, John	1676	Murvihill, Fanny	2297
Mead, Abraham R	1465	Moffat, Lucy G	1459	Mustin, Herbert S.	3739
Mead, Anna G.	3007	Moffat, Margaret	1509	Myers, Andrew	1601
Mead, David V. N.	1464	Moffat, Mary	1466	Myers, Andrew H	561
Mead, Henry	828	Moir, Archibald S.	2180	Myers, Andrew W	1307
Mead, John	142	Moir, Elizabeth	2296	Myers, Ann Eliza	1592
Mead, John	370	Monfort, Samuel S	3107	Myers, Cornelia	50
Mead, John	780	Montague, Abraham	565	Myers, Cornelius	459
Mead, John W	2185	Montanye, Isaac	258	Myers, Cornelius C	560
Mead, Mary	158	Montanye, William	439	Myers, Cornelius F	1313
Mead, Peter	287	Montrose, Elizabeth	3845	Myers, Cornelius P	1306
Mead, Peter.	1463	Mooney, Frederick	1359	Myers, David	33

IN ALPHABETICAL ORDER—*continued.* 229

Name.	No.	Name.	No.	Name.	No.
Myers, David	703	Odell, Emma I.	2858	Patterson, Augustus F.	2265
Myers, Edward	92	Odell, William M.	2575	Patterson, Robert I.	2264
Myers, Edward	936	Oelbermann, Augustus	1918	Patten, Frank E.	3557
Myers, Edward S.	1602	Oerter, Samuel J.	2695	Paulison, Paul	817
Myers, Elizabeth	47	Officer, Letitia	3018	Payne, Samuel	1431
Myers, Eva	2501	Officer, Sarah A.	2995	Peabody, Alfred	3211
Myers, Gabriel D.	2207	Ohlandt, Christian	3258	Peabody, Ella	2947
Myers, Harriet	699	Okie, Phebe	2330	Pearce, George D.	3630
Myers, Henry	3022	Oliver, Ida	2996	Peek, Eben M.	3592
Myers, Isaac H.	1286	Olmstead, Louise B.	3677	Peek, Emily	2446
Myers, James	103	Olmsted, Ann Maria	1505	Peek, George W.	2447
Myers, James	178	Olmsted, Jane E.	1554	Peek, Henry	2552
Myers, John	1305	Olmsted, James H.	1332	Peek, Margaretta	2448
Myers, John F.	903	Olmsted, John	1333	Pelham, Alfred	892
Myers, John J.	1445	Olmsted, Mary M.	1381	Penny, John	131
Myers, Lavinia	1312	Oman, Mary	3218	Penson, Abraham	1384
Myers, Martin	779	Onderdonk, Asa	568	Penson, Henry H.	1264
Myers, Mary F.	1379	Onderdonk, Garrit	761	Perkins, Emma J.	2898
Myers, Sarah J.	1772	O'Neil, Lillian	3731	Perkins, Emma W.	2824
Myers, William E.	1783	Ooms, Henry	2605	Perkins, Joseph	935
Myers, William H.	1642	Oram, Jane A.	2238	Perkins, Maria E.	2553
		Orton, Annie D.	3624	Perlback, Adolph.	2840
Nack, Catharine	491	Osborne, Benjamin	88	Perlback, Ferdinand	2809
Nack, Eleanor	412	Osborne, Charles	193	Perrine, Frances	2020
Nack, Experience F.	746	O'Shea, Francis A. K.	3023	Perrine, Julia	2021
Nack, James M.	812	O'Shea, Mary	3281	Peters, Anna	3471
Nack, Mary	339	Osterday, Charles	2997	Peters, Anthony J.	2715
Nack, Rinier	590	Ostrom, Julia	2154	Peterson, Edward	3259
Navin, James	934	Ottignon, Alice	2045	Peterson, Sarah	374
Navin, Jane	933	Ottignon, Claudius	2046	Pettiner, Daniel	1404
Neal, Wilhelmina	1758	Ottignon, Mary F.	2047	Pettiner, James	1405
Nebel, Louis	2994	Outwater, William	3366	Pettiner, John	1406
Nelson, Catharine	3648	Overocker, Helen L.	3783	Pettiner, Joseph	1836
Nelson, Mary E.	2980	Overocker, Mary E.	3770	Pettiner, Matthew	1656
Nelson, Sophia	3649	Overschultz, Mary	1776	Pettiner, William H.	1415
Nevius, Simeon H.	798	Overschultz, Rebecca	1777	Pettinger, James	352
Newbrunner, William	1876	Owens, Benjamin	3165	Pettinger, Phillip	235
Newell, Charles A.	3664	Owens, Mary L.	3166	Pettinger, Richard	286
Newell, Frank	3695			Pfeffer, Catharine	3202
Newkirk, George W.	3257	Packer, Ann W.	1076	Phelps, Augustus E.	1314
Nicholas, Henry	146	Packer, Jane	837	Phillips, Esther	237
Nicholas, John	224	Page, Clara	296	Phillips, James	210
Nicholson, Elsie J.	1715	Page, Eugenia	2629	Phillips, Thomas	148
Nicholson, Thomas D. W.	1773	Page, Sarah E.	3024	Philp, Frederick	3330
		Paine, Asa H.	3556	Phister, George	23
Nick, Jacob	2106	Palmer, John H.	1900	Pierce, Arthur W.	2869
Nickerson, Frank	3379	Palmer, Peter	1933	Pine, Charles H.	2239
Nickerson, Prince Wm.	3380	Park, John	1141	Pine, Samuel	1446
Nielson, Fred'k B. R.	3850	Park, Margaret	3389	Pine, William T.	1515
Nielson, Ludwig	3851	Parker, Frank	2149	Pitman, Frances J.	2196
Nielson, Martha	3852	Parker, Garrit	696	Pitman, James M.	2246
Niemann, Mary	2049	Parker, Henrietta	2132	Pitman, Lucy A.	2320
Nodine, Mary Ann	1634	Parker, Julia M.	2133	Pitman, Samuel	2795
Noice, Edward H.	3574	Parker, Laura	2150	Pitman, William J.	2662
Noice, Walter R.	3676	Parker, Margaret	519	Place, Jane	528
Nollman, Annie	2658	Parkinson, Randolph	1604	Place, John	522
Nollman, Charles	2659	Parsel, Edwin	1215	Planten, Herman	3494
Nollman, George	2747	Parsons, John H.	1526	Planten, Peter	3511
Nollman, Mary	2765	Parsons, Margaret A.	1527	Plate, Caroline	3369
Nollman, William	2660	Parsons, Peter N.	1528	Plate, Elizabeth	3423
Nollman, William	2748	Pasco, Charles E.	3475	Platt, Abraham	878
Norbery, Lily	3217	Pasco, George R.	3367	Platt, Richard	871
Norbury, Samuel	1179	Pasco, Isabella E.	3625	Porter, Elizabeth	1519
Norman, Lyllian E.	2794	Pasco, Marion L.	3368	Porter, Esther G.	2376
Norris, Agnes	1513	Pasco, Ruth	3811	Porter, Georgiana	3189
Norris, Elizabeth	1531	Pasman, Francis	988	Porter, John	1594
Norris, Julia P.	2248	Paterson, Edward W.	263	Porter, Julia	1518
Norris, Margaret	1514	Paterson, Frank	2661	Porter, Mary	1819
Norris, Sarah M.	2250	Paterson, Matilda	2631	Porter, Mary E.	2377
Norris, William C.	2237	Paterson, Robert A.	2632	Possien, Charles	2449

NAMES OF THE SCHOLARS

Name.	No.	Name.	No.	Name.	No.
Post, Adrian	1561	Quick, Julia	3282	Robbins, William B	2462
Post, Albert	603	Quin, Robert F	2531	Roberts, Edgar G	3784
Post, Alexander	271			Roberts, Ellen L	1945
Post, Ann B	1520	RADCLIFF, Andrew A	2716	Roberts, James	75
Post, Elizabeth	1556	Radcliff, Anna E	2633	Robertson, John	91
Post, Frederick	3710	Radcliff, Charles E. D	2777	Robinson, Freeman M	3547
Post, Gideon	1271	Radcliff, Isaac	2778	Robinson, Henry	1253
Post, Henry	313	Radcliff, William W	2987	Robinson, John	841
Post, Jacob	160	Raisner, Amelia	3679	Robinson, Leonard	998
Post, John	637	Raisner, Andrew	3705	Robinson, Margaret	899
Post, John	1287	Raisner, Christopher	3706	Robinson, Margaret	1254
Post, Josephine	2356	Ralph, George W	3442	Robinson, Thomas	989
Post, Mary Adelaide	2567	Ramp, Henry	653	Robinson, William	1103
Post, Richard	1480	Ramp, Robert T	710	Rockwell, Elizabeth	3444
Post, Sarah Ann	1236	Ramsay, George	806	Roe, Nathaniel	1643
Potts, Benjamin E	3313	Ramsay, Maria	819	Rogers, Amanda S	2928
Powell, Emily B	2062	Ramsen, Franklin E	2766	Rogers, Cornelia	28
Powis, Craig	3834	Ramsen, Henry C	2389	Rogers, David T	2697
Powles, Euphemia	2138	Rand Jane	1118	Rogers, Philip Smith	2357
Powles, Henry	1719	Ranges, Anna	3806	Rogers, William J	3459
Powles, Jacob	1705	Raquet, Emelina	2672	Rollins, Ella	3260
Powles, James E	2139	Raquet, Katharine	2411	Rollins, James	3261
Powles, John	1110	Ratz, Dorotha	1700	Rollins, Margaret	3262
Powles, John	1390	Raymond, Charles	1820	Rollins, William	3263
Powles, Margaretta	2385	Raymond, Ellen M	3443	Romain, Abraham C	1011
Pray, George	2099	Reburgh, Margaret	201	Romain, Ann	1022
Presler, Charles	2140	Reed, Ann	1088	Romain, Conrad B	3853
Preusser, John E. R	3292	Reed, Ephraim	1087	Romaine, Caroline	1474
Price, Reuben	1297	Reed, Ida	3238	Romaine, Sarah	1555
Price, Samuel	1298	Reed, Mary E	3457	Romeyn, Isaac	1365
Prierea, Emanuel J	964	Reger, Alida	2331	Romeyn, James H	1382
Prierea, Mary Ann	965	Reger, Harriet A	1803	Romeyn, Peter	1296
Prince, Benjamin	2870	Reger, Louisa	2198	Romine, Andrew	39
Prinzensing, Catharine	3771	Reger, Nancy J	1774	Romine, Isaac	2
Prindle, Sara L	3593	Reichel, George V	3370	Romine, Ob	64
Pringle, Isabella	2986	Reichmann, Charles	1944	Romine, Samuel	116
Prins, Hillgondas	3678	Reinders, Abramina	3558	Roof, Mary Anna	2240
Prins, Joachin M	3230	Remmey, Joshua	939	Roome, Ann	72
Prins, Johanna	2233	Remmy, John	206	Roome, Rachel	125
Pryibil, Pauline	3500	Rentz, August	3472	Roomer, Barnet	444
Pullis, Abraham	712	Requa, Mary W	823	Rose, Ann Eliza	2222
Pullis, Sarah E	1632	Ressegue, Abraham	458	Rosencrantz, Ann	575
Pullis, Tunis	792	Retan, John	219	Rosencrantz, Eliza	674
Pullis, William	22	Retan, Mary	273	Rosencrantz, Mary	549
Purdy, Caroline	3335	Reynolds, Irwin	2022	Rosencrantz, Sally	526
Purdy, Catharine W	1613	Reynolds, Lillian	3522	Rosencrantz, Susan	570
Purdy, Charles	2825	Rice, Emma	1893	Rosier, John	41
Purdy, Elizabeth	3441	Rice, Theodore	1894	Ross, James	1909
Purdy, Ella	3396	Richardson, Sarah A	2920	Rossell, Abraham I	3418
Purdy, Isaac T	2729	Ridabock, Ann	394	Roth, Caroline	2199
Purdy, James W	1614	Ridabock, Hester	329	Roth, Catharine	2158
Purdy, John	3293	Ridabock, Jacob H	452	Roth, Charles	2137
Purdy, Josephine	3321	Ridabock, Lenah	384	Roth, Elizabeth	1921
Purdy, Luke	175	Ridabock, Nancy	395	Roth, Hannah	1895
Purdy, William	3294	Riddle, Anna D	3458	Roth, Henry E	1815
		Riddle, Fanny D	3495	Roth, Jacob	1694
QUACKENBUSH, James	406	Riddle, Lizzie A	3496	Roth, Julia	2080
Quackenbush, James N	2249	Riebe, Louise	2502	Roth, William G	1701
Quackenbush, John	405	Riebe, Theodore	2503	Rotherey, Rachel	1328
Quackenbush, Law-rence	327	Riell, Evert	1273	Rotherey, William	1229
		Riell, Noah Wetmore	1272	Rott, Jacob	1979
Quackenbush, Maria	724	Rikeman, Albert	379	Rowland, William H	1784
Quackenbush, Samuel	355	Rikeman, Ann	371	Ruding, Duncan	3203
Quereau, Abigail J	1439	Rikeman, Eliza	410	Rüdt, Charles	3402
Quereau, Hannah W	1440	Rikeman, Rachel	463	Rüdt, John	2730
Quereau, John	923	Riker, Abraham	1412	Rugen, Henry F	2599
Quereau, John	1499	Riker, Jacob	1411	Rugen, Louis C	2600
Quereau, Philip	834	Riley, George	716	Runk, William B	2292
Quereau, William	1498	Ripley, Sarah J	1326	Russell, Adele	3381
Quick, Isabella	3329	Robbins, Leonora	2723	Russell, Columbia	1557

IN ALPHABETICAL ORDER—continued. 231

Name.	No.	Name.	No.	Name.	No.
Russell, Mary	1235	See, John Jacob	1958	Skaats, John	208
Russell, William	322	See, Leah	1077	Skaats, Mary	319
Ruston, Charles	1826	See, Margaret Ann	1749	Skaats, Rinier	248
Ruston, George	1827	See, Maria	1398	Skaats, William	218
Ruston, John E	2050	See, Mary E	1750	Skillman, Ann	602
Rutan, David S	655	See, Sophia	1751	Skinner, Amos	708
Rutan, John	1055	See, William L	1752	Skinner, David	55
Rutan, Letty	330	Sefton, Ida	3108	Slaight, Annie M	3109
Rutan, Rachel	589	Segrist, Bertha	2853	Slidell, Joshua	161
Rutan, Susan	1056	Segrist, Julius	2854	Slidell, Nicholas	115
Rutherford, Isabella	3744	Seiss, Augusta	3100	Slingerland, Henry T	1779
Ryckman, Richard	333	Seiss, Gustave	3101	Slote, James	328
Ryer, Abraham	1142	Sembler, Andrew	950	Smith, Alice	3751
Ryerson, Cornelius	1877	Serine, Elisha	118	Smith, Archibald	1361
Ryerson, Edward	2859	Serrine, Henry E	2855	Smith, Charles	1879
Ryerson, Edward J	2970	Sexton, Abraham	2013	Smith, Charles E	1913
Ryerson, Eliza J	1910	Sexton, Henry	502	Smith, Charles I	2492
Ryerson, George	1878	Seymour, Jeannette	3330	Smith, Cora	3835
Ryerson, George M	2860	Shadwell, John	307	Smith, Daniel H	2482
Ryerson, Harriet	3167	Shannon, Margaret	1360	Smith, Edward	127
Ryerson, Nicholas A	3427	Shannon, William	1244	Smith, Eliza	593
Rykeman, Isaac	129	Shaver, Susan	358	Smith, Florine	3461
Rykeman, James	63	Shay, Charles C	2663	Smith, Garrit	1751
Rykeman, Mary	109	Shay, James F	1291	Smith, Hannah	521
		Shay, John	1250	Smith, Harriet	1362
Sacks, Augustus	2737	Shay, William	1249	Smith, Harvey	729
Sacks, Mary	2738	Shelden, George	246	Smith, Henry M	244
Sadler, James	3512	Shepard, Frances E	2930	Smith, Ida	2964
Safford, Minnie M	3772	Shepard, George E	2822	Smith, Ida	3603
St. Lee, Anna	2317	Shepherd, Charles	3	Smith, Ira G	3047
Salter, Abraham	145	Shepherd, James	24	Smith, Isaac	1126
Salter, Elizabeth	274	Shepherd, Joseph	1315	Smith, James H	734
Salter, John	97	Shepherd, Thomas	243	Smith, Jennie	3445
Sanders, Emma	3735	Shepherd, Thomas	376	Smith, John	1127
Sayres, Zenas H	1455	Sherman, William	257	Smith, John B	3110
Schaefer, John	2919	Shields, Eliza Ann	873	Smith, John Boyce	2413
Schafer, Frederica	1901	Shute, Alice	3265	Smith, John R	353
Schenck, Robert	1477	Shute, Charles H	3131	Smith, John T	3539
Scherz, Wilhelmina	2767	Shute, George W	3116	Smith, Lester	3462
Schiener, Lewis	1331	Siccardi, Laura	3490	Smith, Lidia	466
Schilling, Herman	1778	Sidman, Henry H	3563	Smith, Margaretta	2453
Schmidt, Emma	3264	Siebel, Emma	3460	Smith, Margaret Ellen	1981
Schmidt, George H	2826	Sigison, James	259	Smith, Maria	896
Schoonmaker, Mary G	2725	Signa, Ella	3134	Smith, Maria	1327
Schoonmaker, Selah	3115	Sillick, Abraham A	1484	Smith, Maud	3717
Schultz, Michael S	3212	Silliman, Anna	2784	Smith, Rosa	3665
Schultz, Minnie E	3428	Silliman, Chauncy H	2546	Smith, Susan	3498
Schultz, Nicholas	3131	Simmons, Abraham A	859	Smith, Susan Amelia	2454
Schultz, William	3132	Simmons, Edward	3190	Smith, Thomas	314
Schultza, Sophia	3729	Simmons, James D	816	Smyth, Adam	2827
Schwickert, Adolph	2831	Simmons, Mary Ann	958	Smyth, Archibald	2828
Scott, Amelia G	2229	Simmons, Matilda	955	Smyth, Ellen J	3651
Scott, Gilbert C	2412	Simmons, May	3076	Smyth, Margaret	2829
Scott, James H	3295	Simmons, Peter	1058	Smyth, Matthew	3008
Scott, Mary Isabella	2293	Simmons, Rachel	990	Smyth, Rosanna	3652
Scott, William	688	Simmons, William R	789	Sneden, Elsie	260
Scully, Jessie	3314	Simons, Carrie S	2856	Sneden, Jane	383
Seaman, Ann	914	Simons, Charles C	2849	Sneden, Mary	343
Seaman, John	781	Simons, Ella M	2450	Sneden, Robert	245
Seaman, Phebe	284	Simons, Ida C	2451	Sneden, Samuel	730
Seaman, Sarah	172	Simons, Margaretta	2452	Sneeden, Rinier	389
Seaward, William	3231	Simpson, John A	3473	Snider, Rachel	231
Sebring, Cornelius	349	Simpson, Sarah J	3798	Snook, Minton J	3666
Sebring, Edward	404	Sinclair, Finlay	3636	Snyder, Alfred L	3168
Secor, Richard J	3382	Sip, Adrian	649	Snyder, Frederick G	3169
Sedgwick, Russell	3063	Skaats, Abraham	297	Somerindyke, William	1622
See, Abraham	1040	Skaats, Elsie	382	Sonnemann, Amedeus H	2830
See, Ann Margaret	1851	Skaats, George	407	Soper, Jennie	3601
See, Charles H	1748	Skaats, Harman	119	Soper, Julia P	2266
See, Isaac	1039	Skaats, Isaac	380	Soper, William	3618

NAMES OF THE SCHOLARS

Name	No.	Name	No.	Name	No.
Spader, Charles	3480	Stoll, George	1644	Tallman, Dowah D	1741
Spader, Electa	2948	Stoll, John H	3752	Tallman, John H	1742
Spader, Maria	1737	Stoll, Laura	3753	Talman, Martin	1929
Spader, Maria	3283	Stoll, Margaret	1666	Tapper, Sarah E	2790
Spears, Francis	1257	Stoller, John J	19 6	Tapper, William	2791
Speer, Eva	3836	Stone, Emma	3513	Taylor, Abraham	56
Spence, Mary A	2528	Stone, Henry	3542	Taylor, Ann	1078
Sprague, Minor W	3541	Stone, Thomas E	1573	Taylor, Charles	3654
Sprague, Sarah A	3566	Stoppani, Charles F	3371	Taylor, Edward C	3403
Spratt, Bowman M	3653	Stoppani, Eliza J	3372	Taylor, Emma J	3655
Springsteen, Abraham	1500	Stoppani, Joseph	3464	Taylor, Henry M	3404
Springsteen, Josiah	1535	Storm, Jemima	42	Taylor, Isabella	3397
Springsteen, Letty J	1563	Storm, Rulef	58	Taylor, Maggie	3656
Springsteen, Rachel	1364	Storms, Abraham	610	Taylor, Mary	29
Springsteen, Richard H	1301	Storms, Ezekiel	541	Taylor, Mary C	3685
Sproull, Henry S	1828	Storms, Henry	1208	Taylor, Richard	1079
Sproull, William O	1928	Storms, Jacob	6 8	Taylor, Susan	73
Sproulls, Harriet	940	Storms, John	1209	Taylor, Thomas	3657
Sproulls, Samuel E	897	Storms, Robert	1276	Ten Broeck, William H	1099
Stacker, Caroline	2798	Storrs, George L	1580	Ten Eyck, Peter S	434
Stacker, Elizabeth	3191	Storrs, John J	1581	Tennure, Abraham	563
Stacker, Josephine	2668	Storrs, William H	1582	Terboss, Luke	95
Stacker, Theresa	2669	Stossel, Albert	3077	Terhune, Henry	1200
Stadter, Elizabeth	3346	Stoutenburgh, Adeline	2518	Terrell, Ida	3514
Stadter, Mary	3347	Stoutenburgh, Frank	2601	Terry, Walstein T	2951
Stage, Harriet E	2949	Stoutenburgh, John H	2463	Teutscher, Mary	2882
Stager, Abraham	2338	Stoutenburgh, Mary E	2519	Thomas, Eliza	747
Stager, Ann Amelia	2188	Stover, John H	3412	Thomas, Harriet E	3785
Stager, George A	2359	Stover, Marie	3413	Thomas, James E	3405
Stagg, Frederick S	3463	Strahan, Agnes	3774	Thompson, Catharine	3837
Stagg, John	93	Strahan, Katie	3754	Thompson, Eugene	3048
Stagg, Peter M	3773	Strahan, Lena	3755	Thompson, George R	3089
Stanichit, Mary	3711	Streubel, Edward	2611	Thompson, James W	3626
Stanton, Catharine	30	Strube, Adelaide	3740	Thompson, John Henry	3839
Stanton, Henry	844	Strube, Louisa	3741	Thompson, Margaret C	3102
Stanton, Matilda	889	Stryker, James V. W	2012	Thompson, Mary G	3085
Stanton, William	403	Stryker, Peter	2779	Thompson, Wayne H	3838
Stanwood, Carrie	2857	Sturr, Jane	853	Thomsen, Lillie	3681
Steele, John A	2474	Stuyvesant, Benton H	1143	Thorburn, Bithiah B	1991
Steinbach, Charles	2483	Stuyvesant, Charles S	1180	Thorburn, Isabella G	1992
Steinbring, Charles	2590	Stuyvesant, Elizabeth A	1299	Thorne, Elizabeth H	2241
Steinhaus, Henrietta	2414	Stuyvesant, Peter J. D	1128	Thorne, George	2332
Steinhaus, Wilhelmina	2219	Stuyvesant, Theodore	1210	Thornall, Edward V	2576
Steins, Frederick W	1844	Styers, Alfred	1026	Thurston, John	341
Steins, Gustavus	1845	Styles, Charles H., Jr	3170	Tibbits, Charles E	3446
Steins, Hermann C	1846	Styles, Harriet B	2283	Tice, Henry	917
Steins, Victor H	1919	Styles, Hattie	3481	Tice, Jacob	999
Stephens, Anna H	2390	Styles, Walter B	2871	Tier, William S	3383
Stephens, Helen C	2699	Stymets, Abraham	20	Tierney, Walter D	3515
Stephens, Horatio	1097	Stymets, Benjamin	70	Tiers, Anna A	2717
Stephens, Mary Adel'de	2504	Stymets, Francis	255	Tinslay, Caroline	1628
Stephens, Thomas G	2391	Stymets, John	162	Tinslay, Hephzibah	1645
Sterner, Lucetta E	3846	Sullivan, Jeremiah W	1380	Tinslay, Susannah	1743
Stetler, George	3296	Sunberg, Emily	1367	Tinslay, Theodosia M	1695
Stetler, Henry I	3297	Sunberg, John	1366	Tinslay, William E	1662
Stewart, Catharine	1457	Sunberg, Nicholas	1369	Tisdale, John	1181
Stewart, Charles	793	Sunberg, Peter	1368	Tisdale, William	1182
Stewart, Charles	1456	Sunter, Theodore	2085	Tittrington, Sophronia A	2377
Stewart, Emily	2988	Swan, Henry	3424	Tittrington, Whitfield	2578
Stewart, Maria L	1288	Swan, James H	2850	Titus, William	1393
Stewart, Mary	2989	Swan, Jennie E	3680	Tobin, Angelo	3266
Stewart, Mary E	1510	Swan, William	3482	Tom, Abraham	377
Stewart, William	2950	Swayze, Albert	3576	Tom, Maria	668
Stewart, William H	1289	Sweeney, Alexander	3245	Tom, Peter	183
Stoetzel Henry	2831	Swinnerton, James	3570	Tompkins, Marietta	2313
Stokesberry, Catharine	2843	Switzer, Martin	147	Tooker, Emma L	2664
Stokesberry, Margaret	2844	Sykes, Mary	3111	Townsend, Henry M	2952
Stokesberry, Mary A	2845			Townsend, Thomas	2953
Stoll, Catharine	1685	Taft, Peter	2899	Tracy, Edward P	2279
Stoll, Frederica	2909	Tait, Theodore	2900	Tracy, Elizabeth	3090

IN ALPHABETICAL ORDER—*continued.* 233

Name.	No.	Name.	No.	Name.	No.
Tracy, John N.	2280	Van Heuren, Maria	1479	Van Dyke, William L.	2215
Tracy, Rebecca	3091	Van Heuren, Rachel	1478	Van Emburg, Clara	2608
Tracy, Samuel	3447	Van Blarcom, Bernard	811	Van Emburg, Lizzie	2731
Tracy, William H.	2281	Van Blarcum, David	670	Van Emburg, Walter	2538
Tracy, William H.	3085	Van Blarcom, Elizabeth	364	Van Emmerick, Bertha	3232
Traphagen, James	1183	Van Blarcom, George	987	Van Evour, Edward	74
Traphagen, Peter	1184	Van Blarcom, Hannah	321	Van Evour, Isaac	299
Traphagen, William	1399	Van Blarcom, James	966	Van Haughton, Kate	3192
Traver, Leah C.	3049	Van Blarcom, John	924	Van Hennick, Anna	2455
Travis, Alice	3204	Van Blarcum, Edward	304	Van Heunick, Sebastian	2456
Tremain, Frances A.	3584	Van Blarcum, Thomas	2739	Van Horn, John	1080
Tremain, Frederick	3577	Van Blarcum, William	2785	Van Horne, Andrew	886
Tremain, Grace	3560	Van Bussum, Agnes	616	Van Horne, Ann	233
Tremper, Harman	80	Van Bussum, Peter	601	Van Horne, Eliza	581
Trimble, Sarah A.	2810	Vancott, George F.	2877	Van Horne, Susan	665
Trimble, Starr	2700	Van De Linda, Hetty	1043	Van Horsen, Lewis K.	2457
Trout, Eliza	771	Van Den Bergh, John	79	Van Houten, Alfred	1659
Troutman, Ida	3025	Van Den Bergh, Samuel	230	Van Houten, Henrietta	3619
Trumper, Emily A.	1437	Vandenburgh, Louisa	1583	Van Houten, Henry	1616
Trumper, Henry	1438	Vandenburgh, Samuel	1532	Van Houten, Ida	3064
Trusdell, Samuel	2247	Vandenburgh, Thomas	1533	Van Houten, James	446
Tucker, Thomas E.	659	Vanderbake, Harriet	1246	Van Houten, John	440
Tully, John	2294	Vanderbake, Thomas	312	Van Houten, John	1733
Tully, Thomas	2298	Vanderbeck, Abraham	606	Van Houten, John R.	1660
Tunison, Sarah	1880	Vanderbeck, Abraham	1374	Van Houten, Margaret	3561
Tunison, Wardell	1881	Vanderbeck, David	542	Van Houten, Maria J.	1677
Tunison, William	1882	Vanderbeck, Eliza	717	Van Houten, Martha	1650
Turner, William C.	2835	Vanderbeck, Eliza Ann	1407	Van Houten, Mary	438
Turquand, Victoria	2962	Vanderbeck, James	883	Van Houten, Mary E.	1617
Tush, George	2754	Vanderbeck, James	1373	Van Houten, Sarah J.	1618
Tyler, Cora	3117	Vanderbeck, John V. N.	951	Van Houten, Thomas	967
		Vanderbeck, Maria	842	Van Iderstein, Ann E.	1145
Ulmer, Trougood	2386	Vanderbeck, Maria	1391	Van Iderstein, John	1089
Unkel, Otto	2311	Vanderbeck, Mimyan	802	Van Iderstein, James	1091
Urlacher, Philip	2905	Vanderbeck, Stephen	695	Van Iderstein, John	1203
Utz, Louis	2755	Vanderbeek, Catharine	741	Van Keuren, Matthew	2811
		Vanderbeek, Richard	1214	Van Ness, Benjamin H.	1663
Vail, Carrie F.	3775	Vanderbilt, Cornelius	787	Van Ness, Maria	1678
Vail, Eleanor	1567	Vanderbilt, Cornelius	2032	Van Ness, Sarah E.	1671
Valentine, Cornelius	285	Vanderbilt, Jacob	857	Van Norden, Abraham	776
Valentine, Henry	770	Vanderbilt, John J.	1657	Van Norden, Abraham	795
Valentine, Henry M.	1905	Vanderbilt, John V.	929	Van Norden, Abra'm M.	926
Valentine, Jacob	40	Vanderbilt, Margaret	1044	Van Norden, Alice	484
Valentine, Jacob	427	Vanderbilt, Martha	1144	Van Norden, John M.	510
Valentine, John	123	Vanderbilt, Mary C.	1946	Van Norden, William	525
Valentine, John	888	Vanderbilt, Peter	1185	Van Nostrand, Garrett	925
Van Allen, James	531	Vanderbilt, Peter J.	1658	Van Orden, Charles	1711
Van Allen, William	559	Vanderbilt, Richard	2068	Van Orden, Edward	1930
Van Alst, Aletta	337	Vanderbilt, Sally Ann	1027	Van Orden, Eliza	1078
Van Alst, Catharine	320	Vanderbilt, Sarah L.	1947	Van Orden, Henry	891
Van Alst, Edward	411	Vanderbilt, William	2069	Van Orden, James G.	952
Van Alst, Eliza	368	Vanderhof, Henry V. L.	814	Van Orden, James G. M.	1051
Van Alst, Isaac	415	Vanderhoof, James B.	361	Van Orden, John	461
Van Alst, James	416	Vandervoort, Jacob	646	Van Orden, Samuel	583
Van Alst, John	207	Vandervoort, Lucy Ann	638	Van Orden, Sarah A.	1917
Van Alst, Levi	440	Vandervort, James	9	Van Orden, William	971
Van Alst, Letitia	535	Vanderweyde, John J.	1994	Van Pelt, Jane Ann	1000
Van Alst, Magdalen	303	Vanderweyde, Joseph J.	2013	Van Pelt, Maria	1052
Van Alst, Maria	350	Vanderweyde, Peter H.	1985	Van Pelt, Peter	833
Van Aulen, Cornelius	187	Vanderzee, Gordon D.	2922	Van Rantz, Nicholas	727
Van Aulen, Peter	456	Vanleusen, Lydia	2137	Van Riper, Edward	3406
Van Aulen, Sarah	295	Vanleusen, Robert H.	2138	Van Roden, Catharine J.	3150
Van Aulen, Thomas	592	Vanleusen, William F.	2330	Van Roden, Henry E.	2802
Van Benthuysen, Cath.	599	Vandewater, Ann	35	Van Roden, Susan	2803
Van Beuren, Adeline	778	Vandewater, Henry	7	Van Roden, William	3315
Van Beuren, Emeline	1521	Vandewater, John	251	Van Saun, John	1271
Van Beuren, Harold S.	2781	Vandewater, William	220	Van Saun, Samuel S.	2230
Van Beuren, James	557	Van Dyk, Francis C.	1934	Van Sciver, Mary	1502
Van Beuren, Jane	481	Van Dyk, Henry M.	1980	Van Sciver, Peter	1503
Van Beuren, Maria	721	Van Dyke, Charles	149	Van Tassel, Abraham	418

Q 2

NAMES OF THE SCHOLARS

Name.	No.	Name.	No.	Name.	No.
Van Tassel, Amy	762	Voorhees, Clarissa C.	1091	Waugh, Henry M.	2035
Van Tassel, David	373	Voorhees, Elizabeth	1012	Waugh, James	2018
Van Tassel, David	523	Voorhees, Elizab'h C. B.	2392	Waugh, John De Witt.	1173
Van Tassel, Eliza Ann	624	Voorhees, Esther Ann	1134	Way, Henry	1290
Van Tassel, Isaac	399	Voorhees, Isaac	927	Weaver, Edward	2464
Van Tassel, Jacob	544	Voorhees, John	846	Weaver, Mary A	2465
Van Tassel, Tunis	113	Voorhees, Phebe M	1230	Webb, Charles E	1805
Van Tassel, William	309	Voorhis, Albert E	2965	Weber, William	3465
Van Thof, Henry	2409	Voorhis, Calvin M	1706	Weed, William Wallace	3854
Van Thof, Isaac	2345	Voorhis, Charles W	2370	Week, Gilbert D	1015
Van Tine, Francis	2529	Voorhis, George W	2242	Weeks, Cornelia	2643
Van Tine, Henrietta	2568	Voorhis, James	1804	Weiler, Jacob	1816
Van Varick, Peter	697	Voorhis, Peter	1646	Weldon, Eliza Ann	450
Van Voorhis, Aaron	2365	Voorhis, Samuel	1647	Welter, Hannah	3799
Van Voorhis, Abraham	2781	Voorhis, Sarah J	2190	Welter, Mary	3800
Van Voorhis, Rachel A	2415	Voskuyl, Mary	3707	Wendover, Olivia	2072
Van Wagenen, Chas. F.	2832	Voskuyl, Sarah	3708	Wendover, Thomas P.	2284
Van Wagenen, Cornelia	2122	Vredenburgh, Alfred P.	2175	Wendt, Ernst C	3776
Van Wagenen, Walter	2786	Vredenburgh, Frank	2200	Wendt, Frederick	3732
Van Wart, Alexander	1195	Vreeland, Richard F.	3414	Wentworth, John	53
Van Wart, Alexander	1245			Wenz, Augustus	1722
Van Wart, Ann	1204	Wade, Andrew	509	Wenz, Christian	1707
Van Wart, Daniel	1392	Wade, Phebe	508	Wenz, Elizabeth	1948
Van Wart, James	1205	Wade, William H.	3213	Wenz, Maria I	1949
Van Wart, Henry	1491	Wagner, Charles	3219	Wenz, William	1708
Van Wart, Lawrence	1246	Wagner, George F.	2931	Wenzel, Adolph C	2254
Van Wart, Mason	1363	Wakeman, James	3721	Wenzel, Albert F	2155
Van Wart, Samuel	300	Walch, Ida	3840	Wenzel, George	2120
Van Wart, William	1196	Walcutt, Agnes L	3536	Wenzel, Herman	2156
Van Wart, William	1486	Waldmayer, Julius	2768	Wessells, Albert A	930
Van Winkle, Cornelius C. R.	1275	Waldron, Ann	114	Wessells, Gertrude A	1006
		Waldron, Benjamin	270	Wessels, Helen Maria	1072
Van Winkle, Henry	765	Waldron, John	21	Wessels, John H	915
Van Winkle, John	843	Waldron, John R	1400	Wessels, William	189
Van Winkle, Thos. V. R.	1276	Waldron, Sarah	250	West, Elijah	1512
Varick, Joseph	1629	Waldron, Tunis	107	Westervelt, Abraham	186
Vaubel, William	3051	Waldron, William	84	Westervelt, Anne	529
Veen, Adrian	2172	Walkington, Ann	866	Westervelt, Catharine	3777
Veen, Cornelia	2173	Walkington, Melvena	968	Westervelt, Cath. A	1164
Veen, Eva Marie	2333	Walmsley, Stephen B.	1396	Westervelt, Cath. D	1884
Veen, John D	2174	Walser, Emil	123	Westervelt, Charles	2061
Veen, William V	2189	Walter, Henry	3391	Westervelt, Cornel's A	2081
Vehslage Charles	2100	Walton, John A	3298	Westervelt, David	1885
Vehslage, Henry	1790	Wandell, Catharine	121	Westervelt, Garret H	1791
Vehslage, Mary	2060	Wandell, Mary	122	Westervelt, Harmon	279
Vehslage, William	1883	Ward, Emily	3479	Westervelt, Isaac	744
Verbryck, Caroline	1785	Ward, Emma C	3246	Westervelt, James	332
Verbryck, Mary Ann	815	Ward, Frances	2307	Westervelt, James	396
Vere, Henry	3135	Ward, Uzal	363	Westervelt, James	1886
Verhoff, Anthony	1037	Ware, Harriet	1328	Westervelt, John	577
Verhoff, Essaba	1277	Ware, Jane	2112	Westervelt, John	1146
Verhoff, John	975	Warley, Susan V	3052	Westervelt, Maria E	1792
Verhoff, William	1278	Warner, Daniel	15	Westervelt, Mary Jane	1186
Verlander, Eliza Ann	1608	Warner, Elizabeth	488	Westervelt, Peter	661
Verlander, Theodore	1623	Warner, James	185	Westervelt, Peter	694
Vervalen, Andrew	150	Warner, Leonard W	1613	Westervelt, Samuel	261
Vervalen, James	264	Warner, Margaret A	3193	Westervelt, William	1686
Verveelen, Marg'y	102	Warner, Thomas V. W.	580	Wheaton, Anna	3209
Vinson, John	1	Warner, William M	3425	Wheaton, James W	2872
Vissers, Henry G	3718	Warren, Emma J	2718	Wheeler, Abraham	57
Vissers, Johan C	3719	Warts, Peter B	164	Wheeler, Albert	2101
Voillard, Angeline	1720	Wartz, Henry A	839	Wheeler, Andrew	66
Volk, Abby E	1565	Wattz, Samuel T	1334	Wheeler, Charles	2102
Volk, Cathrine	501	Washburn, Frank	3448	Wheeler, John J	2520
Volk, Catharine A	1566	Washington, George F.	227	Wheeler, Sarah	2103
Volk, Garrit	491	Waters, Daisy	3686	Whelan, William	3053
Volk, Rachel	631	Waters, Madge	3641	White, Benjamin F	2387
Volk, Thomas F	152	Watson, Florence	3065	White, Catharine E	2340
Vonck, Catharine	65	Watson, Josephine L	3078	White, Eli	1060
Voorhees, Annie I	2310	Watts, Walter	3407	White, Emma F	3118

IN ALPHABETICAL ORDER—*continued*. 235

Name.	No.	Name.	No.	Name.	No.
White, George H.	2579	Wilsey, Elizabeth A	2179	Wood, William	3814
White, James	707	Wilsey, Louisa	2076	Woodruff, Anna F.	3847
White, Jane	969	Wilsey, Mary C.	2077	Woodruff, Gertrude	3409
White, Mark Henry	3171	Wilsey, Sarah J.	2078	Woolley, Charles	1248
White, Mary E	991	Wilson, Catharine J.	1584	Woolley, Ezra	1525
White, Robert	2648	Wilson, Eliza F.	2243	Woolley, Simon F	1260
Whitehead, Gertrude	3172	Wilson, George	1585	Worden, Ashley	1301
Whiteside, Mary J.	3299	Wilson, Isaac C.	3812	Worden, Mary Ann	1300
Whitlock, Daniel	461	Wilson, John	2051	Wortendyke, Martha	166
Whitlock, James	326	Wilson, John D.	2591	Wortendyke, R.	138
Whitlock, James	468	Wilson, Joseph	2074	Worth, Mary E.	2258
Whitlock, James A	1449	Wilson, Margaret	2052	Worth, Sydney B.	2259
Whitlock, Samuel	425	Wilson, William T.	2255	Wright, Joseph A	3119
Whittemore, Francisco	3079	Winckelmann, Cath.	1343	Wright, Thomas	3502
Whittemore, Theodore	3080	Winckelmann, John	1342	Wright, Walter L.	3054
Whittier, Lizzie	3392	Winckelmann, Rachel A	1344	Wright, William	3120
Whittle, Abraham	1475	Wines, Alexander	992	Wroeger, Herman P.	2741
Whittle, Maria A	1450	Wines, Henritt	1046	Wroeger, Matilda	2782
Whittle, Samuel R	1451	Wingassen, Charles W.	2923	Wurster, Louisa	2201
Wichelhouse, Charles	1993	Winn, Robert S.	3627	Wust, Magdelina	2419
Wicks, George P.	2954	Winship, Carrie	3449	Wyckoff, Cornelius	545
Wicks, Mary E.	2955	Wiseburn, Harriet S.	1720	Wyckoff, Eliza	596
Widmayer, Frank	3484	Wiseburn, Margaret	1721	Wyckoff, Hannah	650
Widmayer, George	3318	Witman, Biena	3450	Wyckoff, Samuel	532
Widmayer, Hannah	3319	Witzel, John C.	393		
Widmayer, Louisa A	3408	Witzel, Mary	467	YERRANCE, Cath. L. E.	1796
Wilbur, Francis H	872	Witzel, Sophia	451	Yeury, Frank	3055
Wilcox, Margaret	3173	Wohlfarth, Anna	3841	Yoost, Bertha	3205
Wilkes, Mary	486	Wohlfarth, Lizzie	3842	Yoost, Charles	3206
Wilkes, Sarah	409	Wolf, Max	2800	York, Andrew J.	1568
Wilks, George	213	Wolff, Julius H.	2592	York, Jacob S.	1630
Wilks, Seaman	3322	Wolff, Theodore	2593	Young, Adaline	3026
Wilks, Seth	3323	Wolff, William	2569	Young, Grace	3267
Willard, John E.	2566	Wood, Benjamin F.	2521	Young, Howard W.	3635
Williams, Elizabeth M.	2505	Wood, Catharine	766	Young, Isaac	252
Williams, Peter	1385	Wood, Catharine Coe.	2493	Young, John R.	3027
Williams, Peter R	2418	Wood, Elizabeth Ann	1279	Young, Margaret I.	282
Williams, Samuel	1386	Wood, Ella	3670	Young, Mary E.	3028
Williamson, Albert V.	1960	Wood, Eva	3671	Young, William	3607
Williamson, Frederick	2417	Wood, Evelyna	2314		
Williamson, George H.	1931	Wood, Gussie	3722	ZABRISKIE, Albert G. H.	1119
Williamson, Henry V.	1914	Wood, Henrietta	3672	Zabriskie, Eliza	831
Williamson, Wm. Alex	2416	Wood, Henrietta L.	2344	Zabriskie, Garrit	644
Willis, Walton P.	2936	Wood, Henry	3813	Zabriskie, John	503
Wills, Christina	2966	Wood, Jane E	2388	Zabriskie, Peter J.	2719
Willse, George W	1420	Wood, Joseph	2841	Zauner, Anna	3756
Willse, Peter	1419	Wood, Juliana I.	2315	Zipp, Jacob F.	2570
Wilmot, Cornelia	1098	Wood, Lula	2244	Zulauf, Charles F.	2367
Wilmot, Theodore	1030	Wood, Marion	2842	Zulauf, John H.	2321

Names of the Assistant Teachers Since 1842.

May 1, 1842 .. . .Miss Frances Campbell ....To May 1, 1844
May 1, 1844.........Miss Henrietta Garns*........ .... " Nov. 1, 1846
Feb. 1, 1845 ....John H. Magonigle*... .... " May 1, 1852
Nov. 1, 1846 ....Miss Harriet Parker.............. " May 1, 1854
Nov. 1, 1847..... ...Miss Sarah C. Mickens*.. ...." Aug. 1, 1851
    do.   Miss Rachel A. Mickens*..... .... " May 1, 1851
Sept., 1849..........Charles F. Conant*.......... .... " Nov. 1, 1850
Nov. 1, 1850   ...Miss Wilhelmina Neal*..... ...." Sept. 1, 1851
Aug. 1, 1851 .... Miss Margaret McAdoo*............ " Aug. 1, 1852
    do.   .... Miss Elsie J. Nicholson* .... " June 1, 1859
Oct. 1, 1851   ...Miss Josephine Rogers.....   " June 1, 1853
May 20, 1852 ....Philander Reed.............. .... " Aug. 1, 1852
Oct. 1, 1852.........William H. Oram.................. " May 30, 1853
March 1, 1853 ...... Miss Sarah L. Vanderbilt*...... " Dec. 1, 1856
May 1, 1853........ ...William T. Graff .... " Jan. 1, 1855
Dec. 1, 1853.... .....Miss Catharine E. Yereance*..... " Nov. 1, 1863
June 1, 1854........ ....Miss Phebe E. Niven............. " Dec. 1, 1865
March 1, 1855........George N. Pratt .... " Dec. 1, 1855
April 6, 1856 ....William M. McLaury............ " Jan. 1, 1860
Dec. 1, 1856..........Miss Olivia Wendover*......... " Oct. 1, 1864
Feb. 1, 1860 ....Thomas G. Williamson .... " Oct. 15, 1866
Nov. 1, 1863 .... Miss Ann E. Mabie*........ .... " Dec. 1, 1864
Nov. 1, 1864........ Miss Mary Lowe*.... .... " Nov. 1, 1870
Dec. 1, 1864........ Miss Henrietta C. Burke........... " April 1, 1880
    do.   .... Miss Euphemia Powles*........... " April 1, 1867
Dec. 1, 1865 ....Miss Rachel A. Van Voorhis*....... " Sept. 1, 1875
Feb. 1, 1867 ....Crines H. DuBois................. " July 1, 1868
Sept. 16, 1867........Miss Carrie Allason .... " July 30, 1868
Sept. 1, 1868.........Sylvanus B. Husted............ " Sept. 1, 1872
    do.   .... Miss Margaret A. Stephens........ " Nov. 1, 1868
Nov. 16, 1868 ....Miss Lizzie Genet.................. " Nov. 10, 1869
Jan. 15, 1870........Miss Sarah C. Mott*
Oct. 1, 1870........Miss Mary M. Bryan............ " May 1, 1871
Sept. 1, 1871........,Miss Mary Frances Losee*......... " Sept. 1, 1875
Oct. 17, 1872........Charles R. Burke................. " Sept. 1, 1879
Dec. 1, 1879 ....Miss Mary P. Dunshee.*
Sept. 1, 1880.........Miss Jessie Bloomfield.

* Graduate of the School.

NOTES.

The Numbers and Dates preceding the Names correspond with those in the Catalogue of Scholars—pages 111 to 216.

No. 159.—*March*, 1796. Daniel Ayres, upon graduating, in May, 1802, entered the counting-house of Blackwell & McFarlane, Iron Merchants, in Coenties Slip. In 1830 the firm became McFarlane & Ayres. They purchased a tract of land among the iron mountains of New Jersey, erected forges, foundries, a bank, etc., and thus founded Dover, a few miles from Morristown. In 1833, after the death of Henry McFarlane, Mr. Ayres became associated with Boorman, Johnston & Co., 119 Greenwich Street, and in 1835 the firm became Boorman, Johnston, Ayres & Co., which continued until 1844, when Mr. Ayres retired from business with a large fortune. He was a Director in the North River Bank, and also in the Long Island Bank; and at the time of his decease, and for twenty-five years previous, was Vice-President of the Brooklyn Savings Bank, and a Director in the Long Island and Phœnix Insurance Companies. At the age of 15 (1805) he united with the Methodist Episcopal Church in John Street, New York, where he was Chorister for thirty years, from 1808 to 1838. He subsequently removed to Brooklyn Heights and held the offices of Trustee and Class-leader until his demise, September 26, 1873, in his 83d year.

No. 252. *January*, 1800. Isaac Young, Member of the Consistory of the Collegiate Dutch Church from 1827 to 1837. Treasurer of Consistory from March 2, 1837, until December 4, 1856. Treasurer of General Synod from June 6, 1827, to June 2, 1858—twenty-one years. Trustee of the School and Secretary of the Board from July, 1824, until July, 1831.

No. 279.—*November*, 1800. Harmon Westervelt, Counselor-at-Law, and Organist for many years of the Middle Dutch Church, Nassau Street.

No. 479½.—1800? John De Lamater. After the Catalogue of the Scholars had been printed—page 111—the following minute was accidentally discovered in the Book for Visitors in use at the school:

September 25, 1867. Visited this School this morning for the first time since I left it, a pupil, some sixty-two years ago. Was very much pleased with the perfect order and the singing of the children. At the time I was a member of the School it was in Garden Street, opposite the Old South Church, under the supervision of Mr. Latham. Well do I remember many incidents that occurred at that time, which appears but yesterday. I now look in vain for many of my then classmates.
JOHN DE LAMATER.

This would fix the date of his withdrawal about the year 1805, at which time his father, Samuel De Lamater, who resided from 1799 to 1802 at No. 18 Dey Street, was one of the school officers. The probability is that his son entered about the year 1800, when he was eight years of age. Prior to 1808, when the school was placed under the care of a Special Board of Trustees, it was managed by the Deacons, and the records were kept in a very incomplete manner. The Minutes found in their records usually states that the School Committee had admitted so many scholars to fill vacancies, without specifying any names. This was especially the case about the beginning of the present century, and may account for the fact that the name of John De Lamater is not to be found among the list of scholars. Other names may yet be brought to light which were omitted under the same circumstances. Mrs. McFarran (*Vide* Note 317), who left in 1805, well remembers him as a schoolmate. Mr. De Lamater, a Builder by trade, was a Trustee of the Northern Dispensary from 1829 until 1840. Treasurer of the Board, 1831 to 1836. 1830, Incorporator of the Greenwich Bank (State), and a Director until 1855—twenty-five years. 1832 to 1838, Trustee of the New York Public School Society. 1842, 1852, 1853, 1855, Commissioner of Common Schools, New York. 1850 to 1853, 1856, 1857, 1859 to 1879, School Trustee of the Sixteenth Ward. April 24, 1833, Incorporator of the Greenwich Savings Bank, and a Trustee thereof until 1854 twenty-one years. 1834, Assistant-Alderman of the Ninth Ward. 1835, Alderman. 1835, Incorporator of the Greenwich Fire Insurance Company, and a member of the Board of Directors until 1860—twenty-five years. March 4, 1835, became a member of the General Society of Mechanics and Tradesmen until his death, December 21, 1877 forty-two years. 1850 to 1854, Commissioner of Taxes and Assessments. Member of the Consistory of the Franklin Street Church, 1833 to 1835. Elder in the Reformed Dutch Church, West Twenty-first Street, from 1838 until it disbanded.

No. 317. - *August*, 1802. Sarah Ayres, sister of Daniel Ayres, still survives, in her 92d year, and is the oldest living graduate of the school.

No. 318. *August*, 1802. Thomas C. Chardavoyne, Member of the General Society of Mechanics and Tradesmen of the City of New York, and its President in 1846; and also a Director in the Mechanics' (State and National) Bank of this city.

No. 362. *August*, 1804. Henry T. Kiersted, a great-great grandson of Dr. Hans Kiersted (who came to New Amsterdam from Holland in 1636), and Sarah Roeloff, daughter of Annake Jans. The day after receiving his diploma entered the Drug store of John P. Fisher, Broadway and Pine Street. In 1814 commenced business in Murray Street, near Broadway, moved thence to Hudson and Anthony (now Worth), and in 1820 located on the southwest corner of Spring Street and Broadway. In 1853 moved to the Prescott House, on the northwest corner, and in 1860 to Forty-sixth Street and Broadway. In 1838, '39 and '40 was elected Collector of Taxes for the Eighth Ward; was subsequently, August 14, 1843, appointed Receiver of Taxes for the City— being the first incumbent of that office. May 27, 1845, resigned and was made Cashier of the Customs by Cornelius W. Lawrence, Collector of the Port, which office he retained four years. His military career commenced in 1814, when he was stationed where the old Powder House still stands, in the Park. While there, was appointed Orderly Sergeant; 1814, Third Corporal 75th Regiment, N. Y. S. M. (Infantry); 1815, Fourth Sergeant and Sergeant-Major; 1816, Ensign; 1817, Lieutenant; 1819, Captain; 1825, Lieutenant-Colonel; 1826, Colonel; 1836, Brigadier General, Sixty-third Brigade; 1844, Major-General, Third Division. He organized two regiments for the Mexican War. 1863, Commissioner of Drafting in New York. One of the founders of the College of Pharmacy, for some time its President. President of the Pharmaceutical Association of the United States. Member of the St. Nicholas Society. Vestryman and Treasurer of Christ Church, Episcopal.

No. 404. *February*, 1806. Edward Sebring, Wealthy Merchant and President of the State Bank, Charleston, S. C.

No. 453. -*October*, 1807. Jacob Acker, Alderman of the Seventeenth Ward, 1837. Sheriff of New York from January, 1838, to 1841.

No. 563.—*September*, 1810. Abraham Tennure, Pilot, New York.

No. 565.—*September*, 1810. Abraham Montanye, Merchant, New Orleans.

No. 597.—*July*, 1811. Thomas H. Locke, Justice of the Peace for many years, Penn Yan, Yates Co., N. Y.

No. 785. *June*, 1816. Samuel Dickson, Merchant, Charleston, S. C.

No. 797.—*February*, 1817. James Dickson, Merchant, Charleston, S. C.

No. 812.—*April*, 1817. James N. Nack, in County Clerk's office from 1830 to 1864. Possessed poetical talent of a high order. See his *Memoir*, written by General Wetmore. His "Legends of the Rocks," and more than sixty miscellaneous Odes and Sonnets, were published in 1827. In 1850 " The Immortal" and other poems, prefaced with a Memoir by General George P. Morris, were given to the public, from the press of Stringer & Townsend, and in 1859 " The Romance of the Ring " and several minor poems were published.

No. 857.—*May*, 1818. Jacob Vanderbilt, Principal for many years of Hackensack Academy, N. J.

No. 897.—*June*, 1819. Samuel E. Sproulls, upon graduating (1824) engaged with Inglee, Fuller & Co., 127 Maiden Lane, Shipping and Commission Merchants. 1827, was sent in a vessel owned by the firm to Matanzas, Cuba, with consignment of cargo and letters of credit. In the following year he accepted an offer made him by Spofford, Tileston & Co., with whom he remained until January, 1831, when, by their advice, he went to Charleston and entered into co-partnership with Baker, Gregory & Co. 1833, the firm became Baker, Sproulls & Co. They also established a house in this city, 117 Maiden Lane. 1838, sold out his interest, and became a member of the firm of Rankin, Sproulls & Co., connected with Rankin, Duryee & Co., a wealthy concern of Newark, N. J. 1846, dissolved partnership and became a member of the firm of Hurral, Sproulls & Co., Wholesale Saddlery and Harness, 119 William Street. 1853, removed to 27 Chambers Street, and continued the business under the firm name of Sproulls, Meeker & Co. until June, 1863, when the co-partnership expired, and he retired from mercantile pursuits. While in Charleston, was a member of the New England Society and of the Chamber of Commerce. Was a member of the Chamber of Commerce, New York ; of the Historical Society, and a life member of the Society of Mechanics and Tradesmen, 1856. 1851, became a Trustee of the Mutual Life Insurance Company, and still holds that office. 1855, was instrumental in organizing the Importers and Traders' Bank, and served as Director until February, 1866, when he became President of the Merchants' Exchange Bank. February 1, 1870, resigned as President, but continued as Director until 1872.

No. 996.—*May*, 1822. George S. Conover, Superintendent Market Street Sunday School 1833 to 1853. Member of the Board of Managers N. Y. S. S. Union 1845 to 1856. Vice-President N. Y. S. S. Union 1856 to 1862.

No. 1,019.—*March*, 1823. Theodore Frost, Searcher in the Tax Office, New York. Was appointed August, 1843, when the office was created, with General Henry T. Kiersted as Collector, and still maintains his connection with it. 1848-9, Trustee of Common Schools, Eighth Ward.

No. 1,160.—*June*, 1827. William Anderson, after graduating from the School, and while preparing for the Ministry at New Brunswick, his health failed. Became a Civil Engineer, and as such, among other important works, assisted in superintending the construction of the Croton Aqueduct from Fordham to the Forty-second Street Reservoir. Having regained his health, after graduating at the New York University, he entered the Theological Seminary at New Brunswick. 1849, was licensed to preach, and became pastor of the Church at Peapack, N. J. 1856, was settled at Fairview, Ill. 1859, was settled at Newtown, L. I. 1866, removed to East Greenbush, near Albany. 1877, removed to Fordham, N. Y., where he still remains, having one of his sons as Assistant Pastor.

No. 1,216.—*September*, 1830. John H. Chambers. 1845-6, Deputy City Inspector. 1848-9, Assistant to Clerk of Common Council. 1849, appointed Secretary of the Board of Health by Gov. Morgan. Drs. Alexander F. Vache, William P. Buel, Isaac Greene, Ovid P. Wells, John M. Lawrence and Henry M. Whittlesey, Physicians at the various Cholera Hospitals, at the close of the year presented Mr. Chambers with testimonials of the valuable services rendered by him during the prevalence of the epidemic. From among the many testimonials received by him we append only the following :

MR. JOHN H. CHAMBERS—*Dear Sir :* Having been, as the Medical Advisers of the Board of Health, the daily witness of your conduct as Secretary of the Sanitary Committee, it gives us great pleasure to bear our testimony to the uniform courtesy, zeal and ability which you displayed in the discharge of your duties. During the prevalence of the cholera those duties were peculiarly arduous, and we acknowledge, with grateful feelings, the prompt and efficient assistance rendered by you on all occasions where your services were called into requisition. With our sincere wishes for your success in life, we remain very truly yours,

RICHARD L. MORRIS, M. D.,
Health Commissioner.
JOHN B. BECK, M. D., }
JOSEPH M. SMITH, M. D., } *Medical Advisers.* SETH GEER, M. D.,
SAMUEL W. MOORE, M. D., }
Resident Physician.

1850-52, Assistant Deputy Clerk of Common Council. 1852 to 1858, Deputy Clerk of Common Council. 1861, Collector of Assessments for Central Park. 1863 to 1869, Librarian and Registrar of New York Free Academy—College of City of New York. April, 1875, to date, Water Registrar, Croton Aqueduct Department.

No. 1,285. *October*, 1832. Henrietta Gains, an Assistant-Teacher in the School from May 1, 1843, to November 1, 1846.

No. 1,336. *April*, 1834. William H. Burras, Trustee of the Common Schools (Fifth Ward) eight years, from 1865 to 1872, inclusive. For the last twelve years has been Secretary of the Apprentices' Library, supported by the General Society of Mechanics and Tradesmen, New York City.

No. 1,444. *October*, 1837. John Henry Magonigle, Assistant-Teacher in the School from February 1, 1845, to May 1, 1852.

No. 1,543. *September*, 1841. Cornelius T. Downs, for three years in the 69th Indiana Regiment, and was in twelve hard-fought battles.

No. 1,544. *September*, 1841. John S. Downs, Captain of the First Scott Life Guards, so distinguished himself during the first year of the Civil War as to be complimented by his senior officers. He fell at the battle of Sharpsburgh, September 17, 1862. Officers and privates, detailed for the purpose, escorted his remains to his home, at Dayton, Ohio, and the interment was with high military honors.

No. 1,572.—*April*, 1842. Rachel A. Mickens, Assistant-Teacher in the School from November 1, 1847, to May 1, 1851.

No. 1,573. *April*, 1842. Sarah C. Mickens, Assistant-Teacher in the School from November 1, 1847, to August 1, 1851.

No. 1,582. *June*, 1842. William H. Storrs, Teacher and Vice-Principal in the Common Schools of this city. For twenty-three years was Principal of Schools in New Jersey and New York, and with great success. Since February 20, 1872, has been a preacher of the Gospel in the Methodist Episcopal Church.

No. 1,614. *June*, 1843. James W. Purdy, Physician, Brooklyn.

No. 1,656. *September*, 1844. Matthew Pettiner, Graduate (1861) of the " Eclectic School of Medicine," Cincinnati, Ohio.

No. 1,705. *March*, 1846. Jacob Powles, member of 48th New York Volunteers, August, 1862, was engaged at Morris Island, Battery Wagner, Olustee, Florida ; Bermuda Hundreds. Severely wounded at Coal Harbor, June, 1864. Honorably discharged at the close of the war.

No. 1,712.—*June*, 1846. George Clendenin, after the commencement of the war, joined the Rhode Island Volunteers, was rapidly promoted and served as First-Lieutenant throughout the Peninsular campaign. Subsequently became Captain, Major and Lieutenant-Colonel, and previous to his decease (February 8, 1882) was stationed at Fort Benton, Montana, bearing the rank of Colonel and Assistant Adjutant-General.

No. 1,715.—*June*, 1846. Elsie J. Nicholson, Assistant-Teacher in the School from August 1, 1851, to June 1, 1859.

No. 1,718.—*September*, 1846. William H. Maverick, for fifteen years previous to his death (1877), was engaged in the Ministry. Was Missionary in the South, and subsequently was settled at Waverley and Farmingville, L. I.

No. 1,734.—*March*, 1847. Samuel G. Jelliffe, Attorney and Counselor-at-Law. Commissioner of Common Schools, New York, from May 16, 1877, to January 1, 1880.

No. 1,754.—*September*, 1847. William D. Jones, Attorney and Counselor-at-Law, New York.

No. 1,790.—*April*, 1848. Henry Vehslage, ordained and installed, July 23, 1861, as Pastor of the Reformed Dutch Church, Irvington, N. J., where he still remains.

No. 1,796.—*April*, 1848. Catharine E. Yereance, Assistant-Teacher in the School from December 1, 1853, to November 1, 1863.

No. 1,815.—*October*, 1848. Henry E. Roth, Graduate of the College of Physicians and Surgeons, New York. 1863, appointed Apothecary of U. S. Steamer *Mercedita*, under Rear-Admiral George M. Ransom. September 1, 1864, Joined the 39th Regiment New Jersey Volunteers, and participated in the whole Petersburgh, Va., campaign from that date. Detailed by General Potter to take charge of the medical supplies of First Brigade, Second Division, Ninth Army Corps, following the Army of the Potomac until the close of the war. Was wounded at Port Royal. At present, practicing Physician, Harrison, N. J.

No. 1,826.—*February*, 1849. Charles Ruston, Attorney and Counselor-at-Law, New York.

No. 1,828.—*February*, 1849. Henry S. Sproull, Commercial Reporter, New York.

No. 1,832.—*April*, 1849. Thomas E. Babb, Pastor of Congregational Church, Eastport, Maine, from September, 1868, to April, 1871. Pastor of Congregational Church, Oxford, Mass., from May, 1871, to May, 1877. Pastor of Presbyterian Church, Victor, N. Y., from October, 1877, to June, 1883, when he accepted a call to the Congregational Church, West Brookfield, Mass.

No. 1,856.—*November*, 1849. Joseph Pettiner, member of the 14th (Brooklyn) Regiment, was in the battles of South Mountain, Antietam, and in every battle in which the regiment was engaged up to Gettysburgh. Was furloughed on account of severe illness. When recovered, joined 75th New York Regiment. Fought under Sheridan in the Shenandoah Valley, at Martinsburgh, Winchester, etc. Was taken prisoner, incarcerated in Libby Prison for five months, and, after being exchanged, was mustered out, having served three and a-half years.

No. 1,891.—*February*, 1850. Charles R. Munson, participated in seventeen battles, 112th Illinois Volunteer Infantry, between August, 1862, and June 20, 1865, when he was mustered out with the rank of Sergeant. Joined consecutively the 10th, 17th and 22d Regiments Infantry, guarding the frontiers of Texas, Dakota and Montana. Was promoted rapidly from Corporal to Sergeant-Major, and retired to civil life in 1878.

No. 1,896.—*March*, 1850. Lydia A. Arkills, Assistant-Teacher, Grammar School No. 15, from October, 1859, to June, 1879.

No. 1,899.—*March*, 1850. Daniel J. Haring, August, 1862, to June, 1863, in 22d Regiment New Jersey Volunteers. Was in the engagements at Fredericksburgh and Chancellorsville, with First Army Corps.

No. 1,915.—*July*, 1850. David Ferdon, served in the Third Army Corps from August, 15, 1862, with 11th New Jersey Volunteers. Was engaged at Fredericksburgh, Chancellorsville, Gettysburgh, Whapping Heights, James City and elsewhere. Taken prisoner October, 1863. Suffered many hardships in one of the Libby prisons, in Andersonville and other places until released in Florida, April, 1865. Honorably discharged, June, 1865, after a service of two years and ten months.

No. 1,933.—*November*, 1850. Peter Palmer, on President Lincoln's proclamation and first call for 75,000 men, served with the 7th Regiment at Annapolis and Washington from April 19, 1861, to June 1st. April 30, 1861, while quartered at Washington, appointed First Sergeant. September 13, 1861, elected Second Lieutenant. When Stonewall Jackson drove General Banks into Maryland and threatened the Capitol, served again at Washington from May 25 until August 29, 1862. During the campaign was elected First Lieutenant, and was appointed Acting-Adjutant of the Regiment. Served again in defence of the Capitol in 1863, when Lee crossed the Potomac, leaving New York in command of the Company in the absence of Captain (now Colonel) Emmons Clark. June 30, 1864, elected Captain, and resigned September 23, 1867. Is now a veteran of the 7th.

No. 1,938.—*January*, 1851. John K. Demarest, graduated New York University June 18, 1863. Graduated Theological Seminary, Princeton. N. J., 1866. Ordained and installed Pastor Presbyterian Church, Palisades, N. Y., October, 1866. Installed Pastor, Owensboro, Ky., December, 1869. Installed Pastor Westminster Church, Twenty-second street, New York, 1872. Installed Pastor, Gettysburgh, Pa., 1875, where he still remains.

No. 1,946.—*February*, 1851. Mary C. Vanderbilt, Teacher in Grammar School No. 35, from March 14, 1859, to March, 1863.

No. 1,947.—*February*, 1851. Sarah L. Vanderbilt, Assistant-Teacher in the School from March, 1853, to December 15, 1856, from which date she was an Assistant-Teacher, Grammar Department, Grammar School No. 35. Appointed Vice-Principal of Primary Department May 16, 1859, and was Principal from March 5, 1863, to November 1, 1863.

No. 1,959.—*April*, 1851. Sarah A. Van Orden, Teacher in Grammar School No. 35, from May 7, 1863, to September, 1868.

No. 1,975.—*September*, 1851. Alexander F. Kircheis, Attorney and Counselor at-Law, New York.

No. 1,976.—*September*, 1851. Charles A. Kircheis, Attorney and Counselor-at-Law, New York.

No. 1,977.—*September*, 1851. William H. Kircheis, Attorney and Counselor-at-Law, New York.

No. 2,002.—*May* 12, 1852. N. I. Marselus Bogert, graduated from the Theological Seminary, New Brunswick, 1867. Pastor Reformed Dutch Church, Metuchin, N. J., October 1, 1867. Resigned on account of his health, February 1, 1870. April 1, 1876, to June 1, 1881, Pastor Presbyterian Church, White Haven, Luzerne County, Pa. At latter date became Pastor of the Presbyterian Church, Bellport, Long Island. Received into the Classis of Philadelphia, Oct. 21st, and installed Pastor of the Reformed Dutch Church at Clover Hill, N. J., November 12th, 1884.

No. 2,011.—*May*, 1852. Louis P. Kircheis, Attorney and Counselor-at-Law, New York.

No. 2,039.—*March*, 1853. Thos. W. McKee, served in civil war in famous 5th Michigan Cavalry for three years; exposed to great perils in Mississippi Valley, and took part in Sherman's "March to the Sea." Prisoner also in Andersonville.

No. 2,053.—*September*, 1853. John Jacob Diehl, Oct. 1, 1853, enrolling officer for the 15th New York Volunteers, Heavy Artillery, by Special Order No. 4,536, Head-quarters, State of New York, Adjutant-General's Office, Albany. February 19, 1864, mustered in as Second Lieutenant at Arlington, Va., by Captain Van Horn. Aug. 22, 1864, acted at the battle on the Weldon Railroad as Aide-de-camp on staff of Brigadier-General R. B. Ayres, by Special Order, No. 47, Head-quarters Second Division, Fifth Army Corps. Oct. 14, 1864, Aide-de-camp, by Special Order No. 75, Head-quarters Second Division, Fifth Army Corps. Nov. 23, 1864, mustered in as First Lieutenant in the field at Petersburgh, Va., by Captain W. Gentry. March 13, 1865, Brevet-Captain United States Volunteers for gallant and meritorious services before Petersburgh and on the Weldon Railroad. April 1, 1865, Brevet-Major United States Volunteers for gallant conduct at Battle of Five Forks, Va. With 15th Regiment New York Volunteer Heavy Artillery, participated in the battles of the Wilderness, Spottsylvania, North Anna, Tolopotomy, Bethesda Church and Petersburg, and on the staff of Major-General Ayres, Weldon Railroad, White Oak Road, Hatcher's Run, Chapel House, Five Forks, Dinwiddie Court House, and at surrender of Lee. September 2, 1865, discharged (at the age of 19) by Special Order No. 194, Headquarters, Department of Washington, D. C.

No. 2,059.—*September*, 1853. William M. Kemp, Physician, New York.

No. 2,072.—*November*, 1853. Olivia Wendover, Assistant-Teacher in the School from December 1, 1856, to October 1, 1864.

No. 2,105.—*October*, 1854. Louis E. Genin, Assistant-Manager Union Mutual Life Insurance Company, New York.

No. 2,123.—*February*, 1855. Emil Walser, Merchant in London, with a large manufactory for white embroidered goods in Switzerland. A leading Elder in the Reformed Dutch Church.

No. 2,127.—*March*, 1855. James R. Hitchcock, Colonel of 9th Regiment from February 1, 1875, until his decease, April 12, 1878.

No. 2,137.—*May*, 1855. Charles Roth, Pharmacist, Harrison, N. J.

No. 2,138.—*June*, 1855. Euphemia Powles, Assistant-Teacher in the School from December 1, 1864, to April 1, 1867.

No. 2,154.—*December*, 1855. Julia Ostrom, Artist. Her paintings have been awarded premiums at Academy of Design, San Francisco. At present, Professor of Drawing, Music and Penmanship of State Normal College, Los Angeles, Cal.

No. 2,159.—*May*, 1856. Kate E. Jones, Teacher in Grammar School No. 35 from January 9, 1860, until June, 1871.

No. 2,162.—*June*, 1856. Ann E. Mabie, Assistant-Teacher in the School from November 1, 1863, to December 1, 1864.

No. 2,167.—*September*, 1856. Robert H. T. Leipold was three years in the Civil War, and served in battles at Hanover Court House, Gaines's Mills, Charles City C. R., Malvern Hill, Second Bull Run, Antietam (was promoted for gallantry at this battle), Fredericksburg, Gettysburg, Brandy Station, Spottsylvania Court House, North Anna River, Coal Harbor, Wasilian Station and Petersburg. In Libby prison five months and at Belle Island. As Corporal he was Orderly and Despatch-Bearer under Generals Kearney, McClellan, Porter and Locke. Horse shot under him at battle of Second Bull Run. Left the army June, 1865, and entered the Treasury Department, Washington, 1872, Chief of the Division of Public Moneys. 1874, Chief of the Division of Warrants, Estimates and Appropriations; selected as one of the three Commissioners for settling the affairs of the Freedman's Savings and Trust Company, June, 1874, which office he filled for seven years. Now Attorney and Counselor-at-Law, Washington, D. C.

No. 2,169.—*September*, 1856. Sarah C. Mott, Assistant-Teacher in the School, from January, 1870, to the present time.

No. 2,187.—*April*, 1857. Henry F. Lippold, Attorney and Counselor-at-Law, New York.

No. 2,197.—*May*, 1857. George H. Lehmkuhl served in the Navy through the war. Was at the capture of Forts Gaines and Morgan, Mobile Bay. Returning home at the close of the war, the vessel was wrecked off Hatteras, and he lost his life.

No. 2,206.—*July*, 1857. William Cleverley, June, 1862, joined 12th Regiment New York State Militia. Sept., 1862, taken prisoner at surrender of Harper's Ferry. His parole declared invalid by the Government. Joined 176th New York State Volunteers. Again a prisoner, at surrender of Brashier City to the Confederates, April, 1863. When mustered out of the service, November, 1863, he received, by a vote of the officers, a gold medal, on which was inscribed, "To the best and most faithful soldier of the 176th N. Y. S. V.," and on the reverse, "Presented to Sergeant William Cleverley by Major M. Morgans, Jr."

No. 2,215.—*December*, 1857. Wm. L. Van Dyke, Pharmacist, Brooklyn.

No. 2,226.—*May*, 1858. Helen A. Little, Assistant-Teacher Grammar School No. 41 since 1878.

No. 2,252.—*January*, 1859. John P. Krechting, Pastor of German Lutheran Church, Amsterdam, N. Y., 1870 to 1879. Since then, of the English Lutheran Church, New Germantown, N. J.

No. 2,285. *September*, 1859. Peter I. Ackerman, Company C, 22d New Jersey Volunteers. On guard at Washington, Acquia Creek, etc, in First Army Corps, for nine months, from September 1st, 1862.

No. 2,366.—*April*, 1861. John E. Willard, Evangelist, England.

No. 2,415.—*November*, 1861. Rachel A. Van Voorhis, Vice-Principal in the School from December 1, 1865, to September 1, 1875.

No. 2,463.—*February*, 1862. John H. Stoutenburgh, Attorney and Counselor-at-law, New York.

No. 2,474.—*April*, 1862. John A. Steele, Attorney and Counselor-at-Law, Albany, N. Y.

No. 2,482.—*May*, 1862. Daniel H. Smith, Physician, New York.

No. 2,524. January, 1863. Bloomfield Littell, Attorney and Counselor-at-Law, New York.

No. 2,530.—*February*, 1863. Mary Lowe, Assistant-Teacher in the School from November, 1864, to November, 1870.

No. 2,538.—*March*, 1863. Walter Van Emburgh, D. D. S., Yonkers, N. Y.

No. 2,545.—*May*, 1863. Lewis R. McCulloch, Attorney and Counselor-at-Law, Hoboken, N. J.

No. 2,556.—*September*, 1863. Agnes A. Brennan, Vice-Principal Pullman City Institute for Young Ladies, Illinois.

No. 2,576.—*October*, 1863. Edward V. Thornall, Attorney and Counselor-at-law, New York.

No. 2,592.—*January*, 1864. Julius H. Wolff, June, 1874, graduated from German Theological Seminary, Newark, N. J. July, 1874, licensed and ordained. In charge of Fourteenth Street Mission, New York, June, 1874, to May, 1875, when he was settled over his present charge—Third German Presbyterian Church, Newark.

No. 2,396.—*February*, 1864. Samuel H. Mabie, Telegraph Reporter, Gold and Stock Exchange since 1873.

No. 2,610.—*May*, 1864. Francis Z. Demarest, Attorney and Counselor-at-Law, New York.

No. 2,695.—*September*, 1865. Samuel J. Oerter, Professor of Music, New York.

No. 2,709.—*November*, 1865. Clarissa Allason, Teacher Common Schools since 1878.

No. 2,721.—*December*, 1865. John U. Crygier, graduated June 10, 1879, as Cadet Engineer United States Naval Academy, Annapolis, Md. June 10th, 1881, Commissioned Assistant-Engineer, with rank of Ensign.

No. 2,742.—*May*, 1866. Martha W. Allason, Principal of Private School, New York.

No. 2,871.—*September*, 1868. Walter B. Styles, Missionary to the Hoonyah Indians, Alaska, and Postmaster at Sitka.

No. 2,937.—*September*, 1869. William R. Chapman, Organist, Church of the Covenant, New York. Teacher of Music in sixteen schools and Conductor of the Bank Clerks' Musical Association, and of the *Musurgia*.

No. 2,944.—*September*, 1869. Mary Frances Lowe, Assistant-Teacher in the School, from September 1, 1871, to September 1, 1875.

No. 2,957.—*October*, 1869. J. Harrison Brownlee, Government Surveyor and Civil and Mining Engineer, Brandon, Manitoba; and Foreign Corresponding Member of the American Geographical and New York Historical Societies.

No. 2,972.—*January*, 1870. Charles H. De Lamater, D.D.S.; N. Y.

No. 2,998.—*April*, 1870. Archibald G. Brownlee, Quartermaster's Department, Fort Yates, Dakota Territory. Since May 30, 1883, in the Assistant Adjutant-General's Office, Head-quarters Military Division of the N. W., Chicago, under General Sheridan.

No. 3,021.—*June*, 1870. Matilda C. De La Croix, Principal of Home Industrial School, No. 10, New York.

No. 3,179.—*October*, 1871. William J. Burns, Pharmacist, New York.

No. 3,222.—*March*, 1872. Willard Parker Beach, Physician, Brooklyn, N. Y.

TWO HUNDRED AND FIFTIETH ANNIVERSARY

OF THE

SCHOOL.

As early as 1881 the initiatory steps were taken by the Board of Trustees for celebrating the quarter-millennial of the Institution. This celebration was held in the Collegiate Dutch Church, Fifth Avenue and Twenty-ninth Street, on the evening of Nov. 22, 1883, a large and appreciative audience being in attendance.

The pulpit was occupied by the senior pastor, Rev. Thomas E. Vermilye, D.D., LL.D.; the presiding officer, Rev. Talbot W. Chambers, D.D.; Rev. Edward B. Coe, D.D.; Rev. Sullivan H. Weston, D.D.; Samuel G. Jelliffe, Esq., and Mr. Henry W. Dunshee, the Principal of the School.

Among the clergy present were :

Rev. John A. Lansing, D.D.; Rev. William V. V. Mabon, D.D.; Rev. G. H. Mandeville, D.D.; Rev. John L. See, D.D.; Rev. Roderick Terry, D.D.; Rev. Paul D. Van Cleef, D.D.; Rev. J. Howard Suydam, D.D.; Rev. A. R. Van Nest, D.D.; Revs. William Anderson, Graduate 1831 ; Henry De Vries, Elijah S. Fairchild, Isaac E. House, Charles Parker, John Ruston, William H. Storrs, Graduate 1847 ; Abraham Thompson, Henry Vehslage, Graduate 1848 ; and Oliver H. Walser.

The Board of Trustees was fully represented by :

Messrs. Henry W. Bookstaver, Chairman ; James Anderson, M.D., Frederick R. Hutton, Ralph N. Perlee, Robert Schell, Abraham V. W. Van Vechten, and Augustus S. Whiton.

The Ex-Trustees and Consistory by :

Messrs. Richard Amerman, William Bogardus, Abraham Bogardus, William L. Brower, John S. Bussing, Charles A. Colby, William H. Dunning, Peter Donald, James S. Franklin, John Graham, David Gillespie, William P. Glenney, William C. Gifting, George S. Stitt, John Van Nest, Henry Van Arsdale, M.D.; James Voorhis and Peter R. Warner.

The St. Nicholas Society by a delegation consisting of :

Messrs. John D. Wilson, Chauncey M. Depew, Robert G. Remsen, James H. Beckman, Frederick J. De Peyster, A. R. Macdonough, Benjamin L. Swan, Jr.; William H. De Launay, Edgar De Peyster and Thomas Storm.

Among other gentlemen present were :

Messrs. Samuel E. Sproulls, Graduate 1824 and Ex-President of the Merchants' Exchange Bank ; Frederick W. Devoe, Commissioner of Education ; Thomas Dickson, President Delaware and Hudson Canal Company ; Col. Thomas F. Devoe, William M. McLaury, M.D.; Prof. David B. Scott, of the New York College ; Henry B. Dawson, Historian ; representatives from the

Vestry of Trinity Church, the Historical and Geograpical Societies, and other invited guests, who occupied the pews on either side of the pulpit and in the body of the church.

The interior of the church was tastefully draped with the colors of Holland and the United States, the former of which was loaned for the occasion by Hon. John R. Planten, Consul-General of the Netherlands. Back of the pulpit, standing out conspicuously above the colors of the two nationalities, was set a beautiful floral piece, representing the coat-of-arms of William of Orange, quartered in red, orange, pink and white. Directly facing this was festooned, in front of the organ, the motto of the school, *Ora et Labora*.

The programme for the evening was as follows :

1. ORGAN VOLUNTARY AND PROCESSIONAL.
2. ANTHEM, "I will Give Thanks"—*Barnby*.
3. PRAYER, *Rev. Thomas E. Vermilye, D.D.*
4. SOLO AND CHORUS, "Incline Thine Ear"—*Himmer*.
5. HISTORICAL ADDRESS, *Rev. T. W. Chambers, D.D.*
6. ADDRESS, *Merrill Edward Gates, Ph. D., LL.D.*
7. ANTHEM, "Great and Marvelous are Thy Works"—*Farmer*.
8. ADDRESS, *Samuel G. Jelliffe, Esq.*
9. ADDRESS, *Rev. Sullivan H. Weston, D.D.*
10. DOXOLOY.
11. BENEDICTION, *Rev. Edward B. Coe, D.D.*

The music was rendered by a choir of twenty-four graduates of the School, with Mr. Frederick W. Steins as Conductor, and Miss Mary P. Dunshee, the Vice-Principal of the School, as Organist ; and the ushers were also from among graduates of the School.

Mrs. Sarah McFarran, a lady of ninety-one years, the oldest surviving graduate of the School, which she left in 1805, after completing the course, was one of the earliest ladies at the Church. That she gathered around herself a number of friends on that occasion can easily be comprehended, and that she was, too, the subject of the warmest congratulations.

HISTORICAL ADDRESS,

BY REV. TALBOT W. CHAMBERS, D.D.

The historical address of Dr. Chambers opened with an allusion to the state of affairs in Europe at the time when this school was founded, two and a half centuries ago. Cardinal Richelieu was at that time ruler of France. The Thirty Years' War was raging through Germany, leaving broad tracks of devastation which can be recognized to this day; and Gustavus Adolphus of Sweden, "the Lion of the North," had but recently yielded up his life on the plain of Lutzen, when a chaplain and a schoolmaster were dispatched from Holland to the young settlement of New Amsterdam—a fair indication of the spirit of the Home Government, and the principles on which they proposed to rely for the success of their Colonial venture. One of these is finely illustrated in one of Carlyle's essays, where he contrasts moral and physical forces by referring to the famous Tartar pyramid of skulls (something like that of Gizeh), which struck terror in every direction, while at that very time there was a boy playing in the streets of a German city, whose fertile brain would produce an invention to last through all time, and change the face of the world. The builder of the former was Genghis Khan, the prince of butchers; the other was Gutenberg, the foster-father of the art of printing. Firmly convinced, as the Hollanders were, that the pen is mightier than the sword, the Dutch Government, in founding the new settlement, laid learning and religion side by side as its corner-stones.

Three years after the opening of the school in New Amsterdam, Harvard College began its great career, starting amid the penury of the early settlers, and going steadily on to success and wealth, until it to-day counts its resources by millions of dollars, and, in the character of its students and the number of its instructors, can take rank with the famous seats of learning in the Old World. The Dutchmen, however, had in view no such career for their little enterprise. They founded it as a primary school, and, although the course has been greatly extended in the lapse of these two and a half centuries, the school has ever been content to remain "a school."

The records of the early history of our Church in this country are exceedingly meagre, and there is, consequently, very little in the way of detail that can be ascertained in regard to the first years of its progress. We have, however, the names of the seventeen masters of the school, beginning with Adam Roelantsen in 1633, and closing with the present Principal, Mr. Henry W. Dunshee, who has been in office since 1842. It is pleasant to note that in the past 110 years there have been only four schoolmasters.

Passing on to the scholars who had received instruction in the institution, Dr. Chambers mentioned the fact, that in the audience was a lady, now in her ninety-first year, who was graduated at the school in 1805, and whose great-grandson is now one of its pupils. Colonel Egbert Benson, an honored member of one of the old families of our city, records that the early years of his life were passed in the School of the Collegiate Dutch Church. During the last forty years twenty-three hundred pupils have been taught and trained, the history of 1,100 of whom can be traced to-day. Of these 1,100, 58 per cent. are now in the full communion of the Christian Church. Many of them have gone into business, where they bear honorable records. Ten are engaged in the ministry of the Gospel, and there is now one in training for the sacred office. Fifteen are in the practice of the law. Nine have become physicians. Nor is there lacking a creditable "war record." During the Civil War seventy of its graduates went to the front, and not a few of them laid down their lives in defence of their native land. The theory of the school is, that the children shall be taught in the principles of our holy religion, as those principles are formulated in the Heidelberg Catechism. A Christian atmosphere has always pervaded the exercises, so that, while the idea of the institution, as one in which knowledge is imparted and the mental faculties are trained, has been kept steadily in view, this has ever been carried on amid such surroundings and under such influences as would tend to develop traits in the child which would incline him or her in maturer years toward the paths of righteousness and truth.

THE STUYVESANT PEAR TREE.—*Vide* p. 28

PRESIDENT GATES' ADDRESS.

The Influence of Christianity upon Education.

In turning over the leaves of translations of the Chinese classics, one is sadly impressed by the constant responsibility which the Chinaman seems to feel for the proper burial of the aged. Page after page takes up the subject, discussion after discussion, starting with other themes, inevitably ends in a melancholy relapse to this sad topic, until the conviction forces itself upon you that the whole life of the Chinaman is overshadowed, and his whole being oppressed by the responsibility of deciding how properly to dispose of the poor mortal remains of his aged relatives and friends.

Is not this symbolic of the awful pressure upon China of a lifeless past? And may we not find a perfect and a joyous contrast to it in the wide-spread, deep-felt interest in the life of *the young* that marks our own land and our own age?

Your presence here to-night is an illustration of this interest. As a nation, we are enthusiasts in matters of education. The maxim, "Come, let us live for our children," seems to have permeated American life.

This interest in education is in part the cause and in part the effect of our steady looking toward the *future*. As a people, we are systematically and persistently hopeful. As a nation, our attention is too constantly fixed upon the material interests of the present, upon the particular piece of work we may have immediately in hand. When our thoughts are not on the busy PRESENT, we look forward and not backward, to the future and not to the past. So fixed is this habit of mind that we are somewhat surprised when we find that *we have a past!* Even this last decade of "centennial celebrations" has hardly convinced us that we have a history. There is no such gratifying novelty with us as a genuine flavor of antiquity. And an occasion that commemorates any event connected with a church or a school *two hundred and fifty years old* is indeed a novelty among us. There are but half a dozen places in the land where such an anniversary is possible.

A historic address, such as that to which we have just listened, should remind us afresh that to the Dutch who settled this part of the country we owe, among many debts, one for the awakening and preserving of a HISTORIC CONSCIOUSNESS among us. They had a dress, an architecture, a language and social customs, strange alike to us now, and to that Mother-England, with whose earlier history ours so naturally blends. The Dutch houses, with their gable-ends to the streets—built of the little Holland-baked bricks, and filled with Dutch furniture, and perhaps with Dutch portraits—these things have helped always, and still help, to give us as a people a sense of historic perspective, a vivid consciousness of colonial days, and a direct connection with *Continental Europe.* Our early associations are not confined to insular England, noble a heritage as is our share in England's past.

Thus the history of this Dutch Church School takes hold on three centuries and on two hemispheres. The especial significance of this school and its history seems to me to lie in two facts:

I. It was established as a free school, the first free school on the territory of this State, if not the first in the country.

In these days, now that a place is fully conquered for the free-school system, it is almost impossible for us to understand the difficulties which were encountered by the early friends of free schools. All honor to those who first vindicated and applied the principle here in our Western land.

But, with the general establishment of free public schools, the lack, the radical defect in any system of education which makes no provision for moral and religious training has become clearer and clearer to all thoughtful minds.

This school, by steadily giving such moral and religious training, has emphasized this need by contrast.

And this brings us to that other aspect of this school and its work, which I wish to notice:

II. It has always been a school supported by a Christian Church, distinctively as a piece of *Christian* work.

For this reason its history has an especial interest. And the occasion naturally suggests the question: What are the interacting influences of Christianity upon education, and of education on Christianity?

I submit, then, that *true religion, Christianity, uniformly does and should stimulate and broaden the intellectual life.*

Our time has seen the publication of certain attempts at a philosophy of history, based upon a purely mechanical interpretation of statistics, minimizing spiritual forces as much as possible, and belittling the influence of great souls and strong wills on the world's history. These writers attempt to explain all the revolutions and reforms the world has witnessed by the physical agencies of climate and race impulses, and to avoid belief in a directing Providence by recourse to unexplained "tendencies of the age." The influence of these books has

been great, especially among people who like to appear to
themselves and to others to be philosophical, but who have not
the ability to detect fallacies, or to distinguish between demonstrations and mere assumptions, between intelligent discussion
of the modes in which clearly discernible forces act, and vague
general terms so used as to veil the absence of proof under a
show of the love of logic.

The extreme form of such teaching allies itself on one side
with agnosticism, and on the other, with that gross physiological
philosophy which is summed-up in such epigrams as Feuerbach's
German pun : "*Mann ist was er isst.*" "Man is what his food
makes him ;" and that other celebrated dictum : "The brain
secretes thought, as the liver secretes bile." Speakers and
writers who hold such opinions are notoriously active in disseminating them, and are loud in denouncing Christianity and
Christian institutions as utterly opposed to intellectual progress,
and especially to the "true scientific spirit." This charge has
been so often reiterated, that many well-meaning Christians
seem to take it for a truth. And it sometimes seems as if many
of the attempts which certain preachers in Christian churches
are persistently making to " reconcile " religion and science were
especially calculated to perpetuate this mistaken idea, that
science and religion are natural antagonists.

Against this idea, alike, the finest minds of all ages, and the
deliberate common-sense verdict of all Protestant nations, most
decidedly protest.

Look at the history of the world since the Reformation !

Not all the efforts of those philosophers who "patter a thin
agnosticism," or adopt a gross materialism ; not all their glittering generalities regarding a spontaneous awakening, the necessary
result of the tendencies of the times ; not all the polished
sophistries and the casuistic pleading of any orators, American or
English, who attempt to explain away the man Luther ; not one
nor all of these can blind us to the fact, that, for these last four
hundred years, since Luther, with unshakable faith and indomitable courage first exposed the evil of enforced ignorance on
spiritual matters, and, Bible in hand, dared to withstand the
power that tried to enforce such ignorance, it is the *spirit of* THE
GOSPEL that has lifted Europe and the world upward and forward. No "tendency of the times," no illumination from
natural science, will explain the mighty changes !

It was the illumination that broke from God's Holy Word,
held in every man's hand, read in every man's house, and
binding, without interference of priest, on every man's conscience,
and every man's life — it was *this* that worked, and still works,
the transformation !

Say the German sceptics and their English followers: "'T was 'the Zeitgeist,' the Spirit of the Age!"

"No," cries the true philosophical student of history and the true believer; "no 'spirit of the age' can account for these results. It is the Spirit of God!"

And wherever the knowledge of God's truth has made men free, science and education have prospered.

If one wishes to understand the difference, in their effects on learning and education, between Christianity, God's truth, and a false religion, let him visit, as it was my fortune to do, three or four years ago, the greatest Mohammedan University of the world, at Cairo, Egypt.

You all know that for several centuries Mohammedans led the way in the study of mathematics and the natural sciences — were the teachers of Europe — of the world. We cannot name algebra, key to all the higher mathematics, without bearing witness in its first syllable, the Arabic article, to its Arabic origin; and chemistry, most widely ramifying of the natural sciences, is the Arab al-chemy developed by instruments of precision, and by sound hypotheses and careful experiment, unto an exact science.

Now, what has a false religion done for natural science and education among the Arabs? Let us see.

The University of Cairo, by far the most important Mohammedan university in the world, with its 300 professors and 10,000 students, gathered from the four quarters of the Mohammedan world, with courses of study filling from three to six years, has shown what progress? 'T was founded 900 years ago. What is its course of study to-day? Arabic grammar and a course of theologic instruction founded on the Koran. Then a course in law, divided into the religious law of Islam, which deals with the unity of God, and the doctrine that Mohammed is His prophet, the duty of repeating the canonical prayers, of giving alms, of fasting, and of going on a pilgrimage to Mecca; and a course in secular law, also based on the Koran and its interpreters. The works of all these commentators on the Koran are committed to memory. Any criticism or independent thought, deviation of any kind from the accepted views, is not for a moment tolerated. Beside these principal branches of instruction, there are brief courses in logic, rhetoric, the art of poetry, rules for the correct pronunciation of the letters and for intoning the Koran. This is all! So far are they from intellectual progress, that even geometry, algebra and astronomy, in which they were once so honorably pre-eminent, have long ago fallen into utter oblivion. For natural science, they have a supreme contempt.

Against such influences as this, science may well protest. But in Europe and America, and wherever Christianity prevails, nothing can be wider of the truth than the assertion that Christianity has been opposed to the intellectual life, and to the development of science. Here in America, especially, natural science has been cradled and nurtured at Christian colleges. American churches have always fostered education. Since our land was settled, Christian churches have cherished our colleges ; and our Christian colleges have been the nursing mothers of natural science. As a rule, Christian men have given the money for buildings and laboratories, for scientific libraries and illustrative collections. Christian men have led, and still lead the way in scientific research. The very ministry, for whose broad education so many of our colleges were explicitly founded, while they have opposed, and must ever oppose, the sensualizing tendencies of that science, falsely so called, which sinks to gross materialism, have been among the most earnest advocates of the spirit and work of true scientific investigation. The churches which have laid the most emphasis on the need of an educated ministry, have been quick to see that there is no work which the Creator has sent fit to do, which is not worth the painstaking study of the reverent Christian. And while those studies which deal distinctively with man as a rational, moral and religious being, have always received, as they always should receive, the first place in a course of liberal study, our Christian colleges have been the homes in which the physical sciences have grown to their present proportions.

Most of our colleges have been founded since the Revolution. Among the hundreds of institutions in our land that bear the name of college or university, Rutgers is one of the few (only nine all told) which were founded before 1776. And this century has seen the growth, one might almost say the birth and growth, of the natural sciences. Lavoisier's work in organizing the science of chemistry on a truly scientific basis, belongs to the last years of the last century. Dalton's law of chemical equivalents and definite proportions was first given to the world in 1808. Cuvier's works on "Fossil Bones" and the "Animal Kingdom," published in 1812 and 1817, made Zoölogy a systematic science. Geology was taking form at the same time—through the systematic study of the earth's strata, by William Smith and others. Mineralogy and Botany in their present form were taking shape during this same first quarter of our century. As late as 1805, the whole mineralogical and geological collections of Yale College went in a single small box from New Haven to Philadelphia, that they might be classified and labeled by Dr. Adam Seybert, "then fresh from Werner's School at Freiburg," the only man in the country capable of performing this work. Under such reverent Christian scholars as the elder Silliman and Hitchcock and Dewey, laboratories were equipped and collections gathered at our Christian colleges, and Chemistry, and Geology, and Botany became departments of research and study. The natural sciences had not much strength or many followers in America then ; but all the strength they had was developed at Christian colleges, which then and always since have cherished their study, hailed their new discoveries and supported their most costly experiments.

In our Sister Dutch city, old Fort Orange, up the Hudson, I had the honor of presiding for twelve years over an institution of learning, founded and always maintained as a *Christian* institution, round the walls of which are still to be traced the marks of the circuits of wire, two miles or more in length, through which Dr. Joseph Henry, that distinguished Christian man of science (whose early experiments there in electricity and whose later labors in the Smithsonian Institute have given to his name a worldwide fame), was sending his electric-bell signals, for some time before Morse's successful experiments in telegraphy. At this and at other Christian institutions of learning, early experiments were laying the foundations for that marvelous development of the powers and laws of electricity which has wrought such changes in our modern life. Electricity, this latest-summoned of the slaves of the Lamp of Science, who now keeps the world agog and tiptoe, wondering at what has already been done, and tantalized by long-delayed promises of vast revolutions in all our motive powers and mechanical appliances—this subject of electricity, from Franklin's day and Henry's earlier experiments down to our own time, has been the object of study and experiment at our Christian institutions, where have been made many of the most brilliant discoveries of its laws and its useful applications.

Let it not be said, then, in our land, that Christianity has sought to fetter and cripple science, or that one department of God's truth is hostile to another! Would that the name of science were never used to cover atheistic assaults upon the existence, the rightful authority and the revealed word of the God whose will has fixed and now maintains that universal order which alone renders science possible! Would that the agnostic might no longer waste his time, wreck his manhood and wrong his reason in the effort to construct an artificial haze of speculation, which shall be dense enough to blind him to the rays of divine truth! Those rays, "shining in their own light," will still smite upon the vision of his conscience, will ever make him doubt his own sophistries, and with such awe as Kant expressed, see God in "the starry heavens above and the moral law within."

Christianity has ever laid a sublime emphasis upon the *knowing* powers, used in the light and along the line of God's revealed will. Mere training of the intellect is not enough. But an intellect, trained to do God's will, acting along the line of that holy will, and impelled to action by that most forceful moral dynamic, *God's love*, what a power for good it is! To form such characters, is the aim of Christian education.

The work of such a school as this one, in whose interest we are met to-night, goes on silently, almost unnoticed in a great city like New York! How slight the attention it attracts! How quiet its work when compared with the bustle and din of a noisy factory, or the hurrying throngs that press in and out of the busy centres of trade!

Yet we all know, in these days of eager competition, that even in trade the essential question is not of the numbers who enter the store, or admire the stock—is not even a question of the number of customers and of the volume of sales—but it is the question of the quarterly and yearly *balance sheet* that is vital. What is the outcome of all this display, and hurry, and toil? On the whole, profit, or loss?—that is the question!

So, in reply to deeper and higher questions, we must answer, not length of days, not mere busy-ness, not popularity, not newspaper fame, *not these*—but actual acquirements in goodness—the effective use of opportunities and the steady preference of the best thoughts and the highest aims—*these* it is that give to life its true value and significance.

To train minds to this intelligent apprehension and achievement of nobility of character is the highest work in which men are allowed to engage.

When we ask ourselves, then, what satisfactions, in the use of time and property, are keenest and most lasting, we must say that none surpass the satisfaction found in giving time or money to the work of Christian education.

In what material will you do your life-work? In that which perishes with the using and changes with the changing fashions; or, in that which lasts for eternity, in soul, in character?

This church has done well to direct some of its giving along the line of educational work. Christian education works for eternity, on undying souls. Every dollar spent for Christian education is so given that it works at an immense leverage. It works on those who are to work on others. Its force continues to be felt through all time, and beyond time; and it makes the best citizens by preparing them for a citizenship above and beyond this life.

For our country's sake, as well as for the sake of our Divine Redeemer, this work of Christian education should go forward.

In His Providence God has left one continent free—one quarter of the globe in which the education of the law-making, governing *sovereign*, the people—is in the people's own hands. Let us see to it that our Christian churches are loyal to their trust, and so far as it is in their power, that they hold this nation true to God and Christianity by the wise and generous use of all the educating forces and charities of a Christian people.

ADDRESS OF MR. SAMUEL G. JELLIFFE,

Representative of the Alumni.

On Monday next we celebrate the Centennial Anniversary of the Evacuation of the City of New York—the visible sign, the accomplished fact of American Liberty. And in the emotions of gladness that filled the hearts of the inhabitants, not the least, we may be sure, was the feeling that they were free not only from the grosser exactions of tyranny, but from that spirit which had transformed the church, reared by their ancestors to the ministry of holy things, into a riding-school for the exercise of cavalry.

It is fitting that here and now we celebrate the anniversary of the founding of this venerable institution of learning, a visible sign of the idea which made that evacuation possible and logical.

The intimate connection between education and freedom was early seen and acted upon. Sparta had her schools; and Pericles, as a means of preserving and developing Athenian independence and supremacy, established a system of universal education broad and deep—such as Jefferson and the Fathers deemed essential to the perpetuity and prosperity of our Republic. Discerning minds in all ages have seen that education is the very sap of the Tree of Liberty, whose flower is peace and whose fruit is blessedness.

In the addresses delivered in this place five years since by the senior pastor, on the celebration of the founding of the Dutch Church in America, the particular causes and circumstances which made Holland at the period of the Reformation the leading country in the world in many respects, particularly in that of education, were pointed out and, in a measure, dwelt upon, and the sublime origin of the University of Leyden was detailed.

The revived study of the classics in the Universities and elsewhere, recalling the experience of Greece, the teachings of Solon, Socrates, Aristotle and Plato, impressed the mind with a sense of the importance of public education, if on no higher ground, on that of expediency. The very building of Holland, the keeping out the aggressive sea, was not the brilliant fiat of Pope or King or Emperor, but the result of the combined effort of the many individual units, each active and intelligent. Eternal, intelligent vigilance was the price not of liberty only, but of existence itself; thus the Common School system was established in Holland and her colonies. It is true that before the fifteenth century there had been schools established in connection with cathedrals, with the larger churches and with the convents, the instruction being under the charge of the Catholic clergy.

All honor to the Church for these schools. Thankful are we this day because of them, for in these institutions was preserved and transmitted much that is important for the welfare of mankind.

But these schools thus established, such schools even to this day, have a special distinctive character of their own from the nature of the Catholic polity, from its underlying and energizing idea. The instruction was and is directed more to manners, to discipline and method, in order that the select few might become able "to rise to the dignities of the Church, fitted out with ecclesiastical erudition and spiritual weapons," and to this point was all instruction directed, rather than to the enlargement of the powers of the mind or to the gain from the great ocean of the unknown, the firm and fertile ground of definitely ascertained and eternally verifiable fact. And it is a sufficient answer to the claims of that Church as an educator of mankind and as a promoter and protector of Schools, Colleges and Universities, to point to the condition, intellectual and moral, of Europe at and just prior to the Reformation, as depicted by such good Catholics as Chaucer in England and Erasmus on the Continent. And to-day, wherever the claim of that Church to the exclusive education of the young is conceded, in Italy, in Spain, in Portugal, in Mexico, Cuba and South America, the crass ignorance of the people at large and the prevalence of superstition, even as to matters not connected with religion, proclaim the failure of that Church as a teacher of the ascertained and agreed-on truths of even the physical world. And in the moral world what city under Popish teaching in all history shows such practical fruits of Gospel Teaching, in the high probity of its merchants, the general intelligence and sobriety of the great mass of its mechanics and laborers, the clean, moral life of all but a small fraction of its population, the earnest life of its Churches, and, above all, the spirit of active benevolence which has earned the title of "The City of Charities," as this, our own, city, founded by the Dutch, growing with Dutch principles of toleration and hospitality, and educating its children under a system which, starting with our own as the first "Free Public School," the first Common School in America, has, during the last year, given instruction to nearly

200,000 children. Some may style these Godless Schools, but they have been *the* schools of this city for nearly a century, and if the influence of schools is to be judged from the character of the life which surrounds them, where in all history beside will you find such goodly or Godly results? Side by side with the development of the Common School system of New York was that of New England. Go back with me for a moment to that City of Leyden prior to 1620. The same spirit which moved the inhabitants of Leyden to choose a University rather than a fair, their practical application of the text

> How much better it is to get wisdom than gold,

made them welcome alike the Pilgrims from Stamford and the Huguenots from Amiens and Abbeville, the Walloons from Avesnes and Artois. It is needless in this company to call attention to the French origin of so many of what we call the early Dutch settlers. Near the University was the Walloon or French Church, and attached to this church was a school. Prominent among the members of this Church were the names of Jesse De Forest and John Montagne. The former was a prominent man among the workers of wool; the latter a physician and student at the University, and who ultimately married a daughter of De Forest. I mention these names because they were the ancestors of at least two of the early teachers of this our School, Jan Montagne, Jr., also a doctor, and Barent De Forest, and because the name of De Forest is identified with Yale College through a descendant of Jan De Forest. There is abundant evidence that the Walloons and the Huguenots, under De Forest and Montagne, and that the Pilgrims, under Brewster, Carver and the rest, made simultaneous efforts to effect arrangements with the Virginia Company, and also with the Dutch West India Company, whereby lands might be obtained in this New World for a settlement.

Within sight of the University was the house of Pastor Robinson, where gathered the Pilgrim Fathers "to receive the Word of Life, and to enjoy sweet and delightful society and spiritual comfort together." Many of the Pilgrim band worked side by side with the carders and weavers and dyers who ultimately came to New Amsterdam. It is no mere imagining to see these founders of New England and New York together. To both, Holland was but a resting-place, a refuge from actual and anticipated persecution, a workshop and a study.

Thus working and worshiping together in Leyden, the Pilgrims and the Fathers of this Church and School exchanged the secrets of trade and the treasures of each others hearts. Both came to this country, the one to New England, the other to New Amsterdam.

Their Common School systems developed side by side. In 1633 this our School was established, the first Common School in these colonies. In 1637 was the first effort at founding a University or College in New England, and in 1647 was the first order for a Common School in New England.

Thus the settlers of New Amsterdam were united with those of New England in Holland, the ideas of each acting and re-acting on the other. Both coming to the new country, both by the circumstances of the growth of a new country developing those traits of independence which had started them in their new career, both appreciating the necessity of schools, and wherever they went establishing churches for the study of the Word of God and schools for the study of the works of the Almighty, we cannot wonder that New York and New England should stand side by side at Monmouth, Saratoga and Yorktown, and that together they should enter this redeemed and purified city. To break that union formed in Leyden and continued in America was the one consistent policy of Great Britain during the Revolutionary War. To keep that union intact is the best guarantee for the preservation of what is of most worth in our national life.

I have thus spoken of our School to show you its relation to the Common School system of the country as its first type and example. May it be allowed a graduate of this School to say a few words, as to the work of the School, from personal experience, and to express hopes for its future which, I trust, will find echo in your hearts. I came into the School at the age of nine, having previously attended one of the schools of the Public School Society, and remained there some four years. At the time I entered, the School was located in the basement of the Church in Ninth Street. Subsequently the School was removed to the building in Fourth Street, near Sixth Avenue, and in close proximity to Washington Square—naturally our play-ground. How many delightful associations come to many here at the mention of that locality. In that locality was the bulk of the members of the Dutch Church. There were some of its strongest churches, where our parents attended, to the Sunday Schools of which we were attached. In that old American quarter most of us lived. The friendships formed there have been largely maintained in after years. Of the instruction there given I can only say that it was without severe labor and was a constant pleasure. Not only were all the studies there pursued that obtained in other schools, but others since added to the curriculum of the Common Schools—physiology, the elements of natural science, drawing, music, and for those who chose, Latin, French, algebra and geometry. What was enjoyed was not only the direct teaching of the subjects required, but the suggestive leading out into new fields of thought and new methods apart from those set out in our books of discussing problems. In later years it has become my duty to examine into many of the so-called new methods in teaching under technical terms, "pedagogics," "object teaching," "Quincey methods," and the like. Well, I found many good ideas, but I cannot now recall one single one of any value that had not already, prior to 1852, been put in successful practice by Mr. Dunshee in our School. I have mentioned his name, and I can never mention it but with feelings of deepest affection and respect. The Ministers and Trustees we respected and liked, but in Mr. Dunshee each one of us found and kept a friend whom we loved with deepest affection. I have seen many well-known noble teachers, but only of him can I say that each of his scholars has found in him a particular and personal friend. As to the practical results: The School is but a small one, never more than 200 attended at any one time; most of us left by the time we were fifteen. But in its long history the school has sent out earnest, thoughtful doers of work; lawyers, physicians, clergymen, printers, merchants, mechanics of all kinds, who have done, I am sure, fully their part in keeping a clear stream of usefulness running through the currents of the life of our city and country. It may not be out of place to here mention two names—that of Daniel Ayres and General Henry T. Kiersted, both recently deceased. It would not be proper not to touch upon one subject, which is the one dearest to the hearts of most of you as connected with this School, I mean the subject of personal religion. That subject was not omitted, it was not obtruded, it was not made a matter of routine or cold formality, but at a fitting moment, privately, where heart could go out to heart, and in a tenderness which has given a meaning to the word saintly not otherwise derived, Mr. Dunshee would talk to us of those themes of tremendous import; of God; of death; of eternity; of Christ; never I know without making us realize the solemn sense of those words, never without causing noble resolves, and never without sending us on our knees in humble, earnest prayer. That he has felt, that after all, his great work was to win the souls of his scholars to God; that the sweet relations established here might be interrupted for a while, but never sundered; this has borne him up amid all his trials and griefs; has made him a welcome visitor in our homes at all times and kept him, as he seems to us, a model of earnest Christian manhood. Of those who were contemporary with me, or nearly so, the great majority have acknowledged Christ for their Saviour and exemplar; three are earnest ministers in this or the cognate Presbyterian or Congregational Churches, and in all, even among those who have not realized his and your dearest hope, I trust you will find some measure of the "Fruit of the Spirit in all

Righteousness, Goodness and Truth." So much for the School of the past. It is, I know, permitted for me here to say a word as to its future. So far as I am known at all in this community, I am known as an earnest advocate of Common Schools, and of a purely secular education. Yet here to-night, without abating one jot or tittle of my convictions, that the teaching of all history is that ecclesiastical control and teaching is destructive alike of personal religion and intellectual vigor, yet I plead for this distinctively denominational School. Its 250 years of past and useful history give it a right to persist. The original spring of our Common School system, it should not be choked up; this testimony of the founders of this Church and State as to their large liberality of mind, their perception of the necessity of educated intelligence to social, business and political welfare should be kept. It is here in the City of New York; but the building is not where it should be; its first home was alongside of the church; so it was in the beginning; so it was in Garden Street; so it should be in the future. Even now it has an excellent class of children in attendance, notwithstanding it is in a neighborhood the least favorably situated for a school of almost any in the city, and the attendance is still representative of the city and the Church. I cannot believe that the oldest Church in this State will fail to maintain its School, while the youngest Church, the great bulk of whose members earn less than one-half of the amount earned by the poorest member of this congregation, not only adds on school to school, but purposes to establish here in New York a University to find the parallel of which we are referred to a period so remote as to appear that of a fable. But the first step to develop your School is to bring it near where you worship, and not remote from where you live. One great work it should perform is in connection with your College. Rutgers College has, under the able presidency of the reverend gentleman who preceded me, taken a large step forward; but from New York, as the home of the greatest number of members of the Dutch Church, must come a large share of its students. Let your School, therefore, be the Preparatory School for your College. Do not change its distinctive features. In the beginning it was a School for all—it was a Free School. Your Dutch ancestors never founded Church or University or School except free ones, and you alone, while the Public Schools of England have been wrested from their original purpose, and even the school of your neighbor, whose eloquent representative is to follow me, has not entirely escaped the clutch of what a clergyman of Dutch lineage has called the "dangerous classes;" you, alone, of all who have founded schools, have it to-day as it was in the beginning, free and open to all. *So keep it.*

The last speaker of the evening was the Rev. Dr. Sullivan H. Weston, of the Episcopal Church, who, speaking to those of the scholars and graduates of the School who might or had become teachers, told some amusing pedagogic experiences of his own, when, at the head of a school in Massachusetts, after leaving college, he reformed unruly boys, the terror of the school, into the most obedient scholars. His remarks were of an encouraging nature to the teachers and Trustees, whom he congratulated on their success in imparting an education which combines the moral and spiritual with the intellectual, and in conclusion bade them God speed in their glorious work.

The exercises closed with the Doxology, "Praise God from whom all Blessings Flow," and the Benediction, by Rev. Edward B. Coe, D. D.

RE-UNION OF THE GRADUATES

AND

UNVEILING OF A TABLET.

In connection with the public exercises commemorative of the 250th Anniversary of the School, the Graduates held a re-union at the School-rooms on Thursday evening, December 13, 1883, and signalized the occasion by the unveiling of a Tablet, presented by them to the Board of Trustees.

The commodious chapel was crowded to its utmost capacity. Here were assembled from far and near—one even from Alaska— children and, in a few instances, children's children who had been educated under the auspices and by the liberality of the Mother Church.

Among those present were:

Rev. Talbot W. Chambers, D.D.; Revs. William Anderson, Henry Vehslage, William H. Storrs and John P. Krechting, Graduates of the School, Rev. G. H. Mandeville, D.D.; Rev. John L. See, D.D.; Rev. Abraham Thompson; Rev. Isaac W. Brinkerhoff; Messrs. Henry W. Bookstaver, Ralph N. Perlee, Robert Schell and Abraham V. W. Van Vechten, of the Board of Trustees; Ex-Trustees Peter R. Warner and George S. Stitt; Messrs. Charles A. Colby, John Graham and William C. Giffing, members of Consistory; Samuel E. Sproulls, Ex-President of the Merchants' Exchange Bank, and a Graduate of 1824; John H. Chambers, Registrar of the Croton Aqueduct Department, and a Graduate of fifty years' standing; Mr. William F. Van Wagenen, a descendant of Gerrit Van Wagenen, the Schoolmaster from 1733 to 1743, and many others.

The memorial Tablet is of white marble, is seven feet long and four feet three inches high.

It contains the Coat-of-Arms of William, Prince of Orange, on either side of which are the dates 1633-1883.

The lower half of the Tablet contains the names of the masters who have been at the head of the School since the date of its establishment.

Above it, suspended from a festoon of smilax, was the number 250 in evergreen.

When all were assembled the entire audience arose and testified their respect to the oldest living graduate of the School, Mrs. Sarah (Ayres) McFarran, who entered leaning on the arm of Mr. Dunshee, by whom she was escorted, amid applause, to the seat reserved for her upon the platform.

The exercises were opened by Mr. Charles Ruston, President of the Alumni, who remarked that on an occasion such as this one would naturally expect the presiding officer to be one who had made a nearer approach than he to the age of the institution itself. This commemoration, he said, brings once more to mind the incalculable influence exerted during 250 years by such a school as this in the formation of character, whether we look at the secular or the religious aspect of its work. We are here, however, we Graduates of the School, not so much to make or to hear speeches as to grasp one another by the hand and to greet our beloved teacher, Mr. Dunshee, who for forty-two years has been the Principal of the School, and who has won the warm regard of every pupil whom he has ever touched. And we desire to leave to-night on the schoolroom wall, as a slight testimonial of our love for the School and our appreciation of its work, a tablet containing the names of the Masters since Adam Roelantsen took the School under his charge.

ADDRESS OF REV. HENRY VEHSLAGE,

ON PRESENTING THE TABLET.

Mr. President, Ladies and Gentlemen:

Our gathering this evening brings to mind many various lines of thought. We can note the zeal and energy of the men and women who, with us, occupy the field to-day, enlisted in the great philanthropic movements which mark the age. But as we meet here, our attention is withdrawn a little while from the busy present—to think of men whose memories we cherish, and the fruits of whose labors we inherit and enjoy. The Alumni have had prepared a memorial tablet, in which appear the coat-of-arms of the Prince of Orange, and the names of the principals of our school from Adam (1633) down to the present time. No one in this audience will take exception to our admiration of him whose fame is inseparably joined with the history of that grand and protracted struggle of Protestant Holland with Papal Spain. With intense interest we read the story again and again, following the course of this young man, who, at an early age, became a page in the family of that Emperor who prided himself, above all other gifts, in the power of reading and of using men. So the Prince was brought up behind the curtain of that great stage where the world's dramas were daily enacted, and at the age of 21 was general-in-chief of the army on the French frontier, and acquitted himself in a manner which justified his appointment. While in Philip's service he heard the unfolding of the plot for the massacre of all the Protestants in France and the Netherlands—because, as the French king protested, his conscience would never be easy, nor the State secure, until his realm

could be delivered from "that accursed vermin." Horror-struck
and indignant at such a revelation, the Prince controlled himself
—the King had no suspicion that he had thus warned the man
who had been born to resist his infamous scheme—and though
shuddering at the iniquity so proposed, he gave no intimation, by
word or look, to the monarch, of the enormous blunder, and so
gained the name of "William the Silent." But a grand purpose
took possession of him. The unflagging devotion and self-denial
which marked his whole course, made it seem only natural for
him in 1568 to part with his precious jewels, his old vessels of
silver and gold, his tapestries, and all that he valued most, to
raise money for the national cause. No wonder that a medal was
afterwards issued, having on one side his coat-of-arms, surrounded
by the collar of the Order of the Golden Fleece, and on the other
side a pelican, with her young, whom she is feeding with blood
from her own breast—a favorite emblem of the Prince—often
placed on his battle flags.

But we cannot tarry on this history, stirring and captivating
as it is—nor need I detain you to explain the various armorial
bearings that appear in these shields and quarters. We turn
away, to look upon the names of men whose achievements were
not in the council-rooms of kings, nor on the field of battle. We
trace the names on this honored list, and mark the terms of their
service—we recall that early period when, with limited numbers
and slight equipment, the early settlers planted the school as
soon as they had established the Church, and we remember with
mingled pride and joy the faithful labors of the men who did
such good work in the noble profession of teacher—with special
regard holding him to whom so many of us are indebted for
wise counsel and help from the year 1842 down to the present
time. And our grateful joy does not overlook the fact that the
old church, for two centuries and a half, has never failed to care
for this enterprise—providing for its ample maintenance, and
that, as a return she has been permitted to welcome so many of
the graduates into her own embrace, or to see them enter, as
intelligent Christians, into the fellowship of other Evangelical
churches. Most gratifying and encouraging has been the result
of this generous and protracted outlay of love and wealth by the
Church—and it amply justifies the perpetuation of this agency,
which supplies a religious education, and so successfully, to those
whom it provides with the other preparation needed for the active
duties of life. If the number now in process of instruction seems
small, it will be all the better, if thereby attention is directed to
the need of giving the school a new and better location, free
from the difficulties which do now deter many from attendance,
who would gladly avail themselves of the privileges and advan-

tages of our school. And with this change of location might well come the consideration of the duty of making an adequate provision for the continuance of the school, which is in some minds a doubtful question. I am certainly justified in saying that this marble, which we present to the Board of Trustees, is in *no* sense to be considered as a mural tablet of the school, as if its work were finished,—as if in this exercise we were to speak of a past, but now exhausted efficiency, and at the same time forewarn the Board that in a short time their occupation will be gone. *No*—instead of this we anticipate a career of larger usefulness and power, by reason of what has already been so wisely and so cheerfully done by our Collegiate Church, and we venture the hope that in some way an endowment may be provided—by the liberality of an individual, or otherwise—looking to a complete equipment for the future need, placing the school so that it may be regarded as, and become an unfailing source of supply for our College and Theological Seminary.

Permit me, in closing, to suggest that in this direction may be found a line of holy work to which the love of the Master may direct some servant of His who wishes to concentrate the wealth entrusted to him. So will he be brought into the choice fellowship of all those who, out of love for Christ, have been anxious to know how their service may be most effective. The gifts and labors of the many have contributed to the record of these 250 years, in which we rejoice. Of this result, many facts we can trace, and we are sure that where our vision fails, another eye discerns the deed and notes the motive. Happy are all they who, in any place, and to their best ability, seek to advance the cause of our blessed Lord.

"A century since, in the North of England stood an old cathedral, upon one of the arches of which was a sculptured face of wondrous beauty. For a long while it was hidden, until one day the sun's light through a slanted window revealed its matchless beauty. And ever after, year by year, on the days when, for a brief hour, it was thus illumined, crowds came and waited to catch a glimpse of that face. It had a strange history. When the cathedral was in process of construction, an old man, broken with the weight of years and care, came and besought the architect to let him work. Out of pity for his age, and yet fearful lest his failing sight and trembling touch might mar some part of the fair design, the master set him to work in the shadows of the vaulted roof. Gladly he took his place, but one day they found the old man asleep in death, the tools of his craft laid in order beside him, the cunning of his right hand gone, his face upturned to this other marvelous face—which he had wrought there—the face of one whom he had loved and lost in his early manhood.

And when the artists, and sculptors, and workmen from all parts of the cathedral came and looked upon that face, they all said : 'This is the grandest work of all—love wrought this.'"

In the great cathedral of the ages which is being builded for an habitation of God, may we all be found co-working, and may the inspiration of our toil always be love—which gives grandeur and permanence to every work.

Having touched the fastenings that held the flags of Holland and the United States, they fell apart and disclosed to view the Tablet, which the speaker, in behalf of the Alumni, formally presented to the Trustees of the School.

Mr. HENRY W. BOOKSTAVER,

THE CHAIRMAN OF THE BOARD OF TRUSTEES,

in accepting the Tablet, replied as follows :

Reverend Sir, and Graduates of the Collegiate School :

It is my pleasant duty on behalf of the Board of Trustees to accept the very appropriate memorial, your liberality and affection have induced you to present to the school.

Sir, you have spoken of one whom every Dutchman reveres, and men everywhere respect and honor. You have alluded to the Emperor's power of reading and using men. It recalls one of the most pregnant events in the world's history. It recalls the 25th of October, 1555—the splendid palace of the Dukes of Brabant, the assembled dignitaries of the German Empire and of Spain, and the abdication of Charles V.

Of all that august assembly, the one the Emperor chose as the staff on which to lean, during that ceremony, was the man you have named—William, Prince of Orange—and during the remainder of his life he was the staff and stay of his country, which never failed it.

Great in every way, he was more than all else a religious man, and yet without cant, or ostentation of piety. No one ever heard him speak of a heavenly mission, or of being the instrument of the Almighty ; but when the vindictive Granville and the crafty Philip put him under the ban, declaring his property forfeit to any who would take it, and offered a reward for his life, he could, with calm simplicity and trust, say : "I am in the hands of God ; my worldly goods and my life have long since been dedicated to his service. He will dispose of them as seems best for his glory and my salvation."

His firmness was near akin to his piety, and he illustrated the motto his friends applied to him: *Sævis tranquillus in undis.* His courage sprung from both, and while he knew what fear was, yet dared despise it for the cause of God and truth.

Never was a warrior called on to battle single-handed and alone with greater odds; yet Alva, Don John, and Alexander, the greatest generals of his time, failed to overcome him, and he managed to wrest perfect victory even from his defeats.

As a statesman he has had few equals in any age, and was without a peer in his own. In the midst of war, internal confusion, and in the face of the most persistent and relentless monarch of his time, he founded upon the morasses of his native country an enduring government, which continues to this day.

In an age when eloquence was rare he was master of

Thoughts that breathe and words that burn,

yet his eloquence was not that of smooth, flowing sentences and flattering compliment so common in his age, but, he used it as an instrument of earnest endeavor, and it was always direct, truthful, and convincing, carrying all before it. His "Apology" in answer to the king's "ban" should be in the hands of every student of eloquence. Who can forget its conclusion, addressed to his countrymen? "If then, my masters, you judge that my absence or my death can serve you, behold me ready to obey. Command me—send me to the ends of the earth, I will obey. Here is my head, over which no prince, no monarch, has power but yourselves. Dispose of it for your good and for the preservation of the Republic."

On such a theme one delights to linger, but I wander from the matter in hand. This tablet—whose are the names engraved on it? Why should they be thought by you worthy of such honor? All, indeed, were inspired with the same religious faith which animated William the Silent, and they all acknowledged the same Master, but they were neither statesmen, nor warriors, nor orators. Their exploits are not recorded in history; their biographies are unwritten; the world has not crowned them with laurel; and yet they are worthy of all and more than you have done for them.

The social fabric is so fitly framed together, that no member can be taken from it without causing a shock to every part. Its order and stability depend on each member and on all. Smiling infancy and hoary age, are alike necessary to its completeness. Each acts on and is acted upon by all. And in this sense is the saying, that "none of us liveth to himself and none dieth to himself," profoundly true.

As in the enduring temple there are the foundations, and the walls, base and column, and capital, architrave and frieze, perityle and adytum, places holy and common, things of necessity and use, and things of ornament and beauty, so in the social fabric, all parts are not equally important or useful. But by whatever standard we judge the relative importance and usefulness of men's labor, the office and work of the teacher must ever hold a foremost rank, as it has ever held among thinking and farsighted men. Hear what Marcus Aurelius says he owed to his teachers and learned from them :

From my grandfather, Verus, I learned good morals and the government of my temper.

From the reputation and remembrance of my father, modesty and a manly character.

From my mother, piety and beneficence, and abstinence ; not from evil deeds only, but even from evil thoughts. * * *

From my governor, non-partizanship, endurance of labor, to want little, to work with my own hands, and not to meddle with other people's affairs, and not to be ready to listen to slander.

From Diognetus, not to busy myself about trifling things. * * *

From Rusticus, I received the impression that my character required improvement and discipline. * * *

From Apollonius, I learned freedom of will and undeviating steadiness of purpose and uniformity of temper under all adversity.

From Sextus, a benevolent disposition, the example of a family governed in a fatherly manner, and the idea of living conformably to nature. * * *

From Alexander, the grammarian, to refrain from fault-finding. * * *

From Fronto, I learned to observe what envy and duplicity, and hypocrisy are in a tyrant. * * *

From Alexander, the Platonic, * * not continually to excuse neglect of duty * * by alleging urgent occupations.

From Catulus, not to be indifferent when a friend finds fault, even if he should find fault without reason. * * *

From my brother Severus, to love my kin, and to love truth, and to love justice. * * *

From Maximus, I learned self-government and not to be led aside by anything. * * *

All this and much more, he says, he learned from his teachers, and all these things it is necessary the teacher should teach. How great and manifold are his duties, and how many-sided and composite a creature is man. And then consider that to the teacher is committed the race when the mind is plastic and easily influenced, and that it passes from his care with a direction and bent which will determine all its after development ; "Even the light of the eternal world will take a tint from the colors with which the teacher shall tinge the windows of the soul." Consider also, that this influence does not end with the scholar so taught, but that each mind so trained and bent, becomes a new centre of force and influence, shaping the destinies of others who shall again impress the minds of generations yet unborn, and you will appreciate something of the importance and dignity of the teachers' office. If the magnitude of the work, the good accomplished, and the far-reaching power and permanence of the result is to be the standard of honor, then, Graduates of the Collegiate School, you have done well in erecting this monument to your teacher and those who have preceded him as schoolmasters here. Although their lives are unwritten and unsung, they still live in the minds of the thousands they have taught and their influence shall never die. In the words of Pericles, we may say of them, "signalized not alone by the inscription on the monument in their native land, but in lands not their own, by the memory which remains of the *spirit* even more than the *deed.*"

The Church of Holland—the Church under the Cross—has ever been the friend of learning, and sought to make it the handmaid of religion. At the close of the long struggle for independence, Holland lead the whole of Europe, not in navigation only, but in her knowledge and application of all the natural sciences and the arts that civilize and uplift mankind. Whereever she planted her colonies she sent not only her ministers but her schoolmasters.

"The Church under the Cross," so bitterly tormented that she could not hold her first Synods within the borders of Holland, but was compelled to go to Wessels and Embden for safety, even then, a mid the fires of persecution, took thought for the Christian education of the young : and when better days came the famous Synod of Dort, in 1618, enacted that schools should be instituted "not only in cities, but also in towns and country places where heretofore none have existed" * * * "and especially that the children of the poor should be gratuitously instructed, and not be excluded from the benefit of the schools."

This we believe to have been the first provision for free schools for the poor. It was in this spirit and under this Church that this school, your school, was founded, the oldest in America.

1633-1883—then and now. What a contrast these two dates present. How one is tempted to compare the trading post in the wilderness and its handful of sturdy self-reliant Dutchmen with the metropolis of a continent and its million inhabitants. How much this school has done to promote that wondrous growth none can tell, but of this I am sure, its influence for good has been mighty. Its graduates have gone forth to illustrate and sustain all that is good and noble in our fair city.

All but one of the men whose names you have engraved on this tablet, having moulded and bent the generations under their care, have finished their labors and gone to their reward. Yet their work lives after them and shall not die.

One alone of all that list is with us to-night. For more than forty years has he been schoolmaster here. His work has been a labor of love, love for his scholars and the school. Surely in this audience, so largely composed of his former pupils, there can be no need of calling attention to his virtues. All of you know and love Henry Webb Dunshee. You know his worth. You are the best witnesses of his ability as a teacher, his patient care, his unobtrusive but sincere piety. How many of you have been led to the service of the blessed Saviour by his precept and example, and in the time to come you will be the crown of his rejoicing.

It is with a lively sense of the worth of the men you have thus commemorated, and whose names you thus propose to hand down to posterity, that I, in behalf of the Board of Trustees and the Consistory of the Collegiate Church, accept this tablet, not only as a memorial of them, but also as a testimonial of your affection for them and the school.

Sir, you have referred to this marble as a mural tablet ; it certainly is that, but it is neither given nor accepted as in any sense a mortuary tablet.

I do not know why any should consider the continuance of this school a doubtful question. To-day, more than ever before, is there need for just such schools as this. It is claimed by unbelievers that the Church is afraid of science, but the charge is unfounded, and the entire history of our Church refutes the assertion. Even if time permitted it would be unnecessary to review that history here ; you all remember the heroic defence of Leyden, and the founding of its illustrious University as a reward for its heroism. But there are men of science who seem to be afraid of religion and claim there is an irreconcilable conflict between the two, and in the name of science attack the Church. As long as these attacks continue must these schools be maintained, to teach the great truth that all of God's laws are in harmony, and to point out the way by which we can be restored to that harmony with God and his laws which has been lost through transgression, by showing us how great our sins and miseries are, how we may be delivered from our sins and miseries and the gratitude we owe to God for such deliverance.

We therefore hope and trust with you that a more convenient location may be found for it, and that it may be greatly increased in usefulness and power. To this end we would gladly welcome any endowment that God may move any of His servants to make for the better equipment of the School. But, in the meantime, you, the graduates of the school, may do much for it by showing in your daily walk and conversation the value of the instruction here given, and by unwavering loyalty to your *Alma Mater.* Let us determine to do all we can for it, and let each one of us, in our attitude toward the school, adopt the motto of William of Orange, *Je Maintiendrai,* and it will be maintained.

ADDRESS OF
REV. TALBOT W. CHAMBERS, D.D.

Dr. Chambers began his remarks with a playful story once told him by a relative who attended a meeting of Friends in Chester County, Pa., where he saw a man arise in the gallery, and make the following speech: "Friends, when I left home this morning it was impressed on my mind that I must say something at the meeting. When I reached this house it was impressed upon me that I must say something at the meeting. When I sat down in the gallery, here, it was impressed upon me that I must say something at the meeting. And now, since I have gotten up and said something at the meeting, I'll just sit down." Dr. Chambers said that he felt very much like imitating this gentleman and taking his seat forthwith, since, considering what had been said and what was yet to come, there was no need of further utterances to do justice to the occasion. Yet there was one point which of late had so pressed itself upon his mind that he could not refrain from bringing it before the assembly. This was teaching, as a profession. In a country where so much is continually said in the public press, and on the platform, and in legislative halls about the value of education and the necessity of free schools, as if no topic in the world were more sure to secure popular favor, it strikes me as very strange that the office of the teacher is so lightly esteemed. People at large show this in various ways. They look upon the occupation not as belonging to the liberal professions but as that of a mere hireling, and they pay accordingly. The wages of even accomplished instructors are less than those of skilled handicraftsmen. The chief cook of a first-class hotel gets a larger salary than the president of any one of our colleges. Such, too, is the tone of society. Ask an acquaintance about persons whom you may meet, and the answer is, "Oh, it is only a school-teacher," or "She, why she is nothing but a school-marm." And this is said of those who do not deal in silks or satins, in gold or jewels, in products of art or taste, but have to do with immortal minds in the plastic period of their lives, and therefore exert an influence for good or for ill to continue long after the sun and moon have ceased to be! Alas for the grievous misreckoning of popular opinion. But teachers themselves have some share of the blame for it. So many of them all over our land look upon the vocation as one in itself by no means dignified or desirable, but only to be adopted as a stepping-stone. Young men temporarily at a loss for employment fall back upon school-keeping until something better turns up, meanwhile chafing at their hard lot. Young women enter the ranks of the profession with the determination to remain only till a husband makes his appearance over the horizon. In thousands upon thousands of instances teaching is a mere makeshift, taken up for lack of any opening elsewhere, and to be dropped at the first convenient opportunity. Is it any wonder that the public takes teachers at their own estimation, and regards them accordingly? In other countries it is not so. There the teacher is a recognized and permanent part of the social organization. There is corresponding respect and remuneration, and both the holders of the office and others look upon it, not as a temporary substitute for something else, but as a fitting and important life-work.

In Germany a university is not deemed complete in its equipment unless it has a department of Pedagogics—one devoted to the theory and practice of the art of giving instruction and training minds. And something of this kind is greatly needed here. We shall never, in this country, reach the right position of things until we reverse current notions, lift up the profession, magnify its importance, increase its emolument, and give the world to understand that he who fills this function faithfully is doing a work that ranks second only to that of the minister of God. Such a work ought to command a price that bears some proportion not only to its delicacy and difficulty, but to its immeasurable importance in shaping the destiny not only of individuals here and there, but of the whole community; nay, the nation itself. These men whose names are inscribed on this monumental stone—here the speaker pointed to the tablet—contributed largely to the formation of that character which carried us safely through the perils of the Revolution and through the far greater perils of later days. In the Old Testament the figure of the Church was the magnificent candelabrum of beaten gold in the temple; and in the vision of John the divine, the Lord revealed Himself as one who held the seven stars in His right hand and walked among the seven golden candlesticks. It is *light* which is connected with the civilization that springs from the religion of the One God, and of no other religion that ever arose in the earth is this true. Is, then, a profession which typifies the spirit of Christianity to be any longer considered a mere stepping-stone? The names on that tablet ought to excite a thrill of surprise, admiration and gratitude for the past and of purpose for the future, a determination to lift up this honored profession, to put it where it ought to be, to establish its status, to raise the school to such a position that it shall be felt to be an honor to have come under its care or to have been connected with its history. Let the whole country understand that we, at least, recognize that those who do the work of this school do it as benefactors of the race and as servants of the living God.

The last speaker of the evening was Mr. Dunshee, who cordially welcomed the graduates and friends of the School. He reviewed, briefly, the history of the School from its commencement, and with deep emotion expressed his gratitude to God that he had been called to be a schoolmaster, and that he had been spared to meet and to greet so many of his former scholars, some of whose children, also, had been taught by him, and who were now occupying positions of trust and honor in the Church and in the world.

Letters of regret were received from the Sandwich Islands, Europe, and from the far West and South, where the scholars are to be found. Two of these letters from pupils who graduated in the early part of this century were read.

One closed with the remark that the only relic of his school-days which still remained to him was his Bible (presented to him when he graduated), which had been as a beacon to him all his life, and Judge Thomas H. Locke, of Yates Co., described the quaint little post-office of that day, and told how when the city was threatened by the British in the war of 1812, the boys of the School, and he among them, went over to Gowanus to assist in throwing up earthworks.

The following hymn, written for the occasion by the Principal, was sung by the entire audience, to the tune of "Creation:"

> GOD of our fathers, Thee we praise
> That Thou, to them, did'st give the grace
> To open for their rising youth
> This Fountain of Eternal Truth
> From whence the streams of knowledge flow,
> Two cent'ries and a half ago.
>
> Their sons and daughters here could drink
> Refreshing waters from its brink,
> To fit them to be useful here
> And happy in the Heavenly sphere,
> Through Him, whom it is Life to know :
> Two cent'ries and a half ago.

> Down through the ages here they've come
> And near this Fountain found a home,
> Received the blessings it imparts
> To form their minds—renew their hearts,
> From streams which here began to flow
> Two cent'ries and a half ago.
>
> And may the Mother Church still hand
> This Fountain from the Fatherland
> Down through the coming ages, free,
> A source of Light and Purity,
> To many a heart and many a home
> For many centuries to come.

A Poem, entitled "Retrospect," written by Mrs. Mary (Latschar) Lutz, a graduate of 1852, was read by Mr. Charles Ruston, President of the Alumni Association.

The remainder of the evening was spent in greetings among old schoolmates around the Tablet and in relating pleasant reminiscences of their school-life around their photographs, which are suspended on the walls of the Chapel and in the supper room below.

COAT-OF-ARMS OF JOHN HARPENDING.

DESCRIPTION

OF THE

COAT-OF-ARMS ON TABLET.

DESCRIPTION OF THE COAT-OF-ARMS.

The three shields constitute the Coat-of-Arms of William the Silent, Prince of Orange, under whom the Netherlands achieved her civil and religious independence. The Princes of Orange were also Counts or Lords of the other Principalities represented. The first quarter of the *large shield* bears the arms of Nassau. It has a lion rampant, on a red field surrounded by seventeen dots, indicating the union of the ten States of the Netherlands, with the seven States of Holland, under William. The second quarter represents Katzenelnbogen, and has a crowned lion, red on a golden field. In his right paw is an elevated sword, ready for defence, and the left holds seven arrows, denoting the union of the seven States. The third quarter represents Vianden, and has two running lions on a blue field. The fourth quarter, blue banded with gold, is the shield of Dietz.

The first and third quarters of the *smaller* shield, bearing diagonal bands of gold, represent the Principalities of Chalons. The second and fourth quarters, with a horn or bugle suspended on an orange field, that of Orange. These martial horns symbolize the courageous leadership of those who took up arms against the Moors and Saracens.

The *smallest* shield is that of Geneva, the city of John Calvin. It bears the Helvetic cross, and was added by William to his Coat-of-Arms in token of his Protestant faith, and his adherence to the principles of the great Reformer.

The *crown* which surmounts the shield represents the Emperor, Charles the Great, who, while Sovereign of the Netherlands, granted them the right of carrying the imperial crown above the Coat-of-Arms. The motto, *Nisi Dominus Frustra* (Psalm cxxvii, 1), "Without the Lord all is vain," fitly expresses the deep religious convictions of the Dutch and their sincere trust in God while struggling for a home and a Church.

The legend in Dutch, *Een-dracht maakt macht*, signifies " Union makes Strength," and was the rallying cry in times of despondency.

EXPLANATORY.

Montagne taught in a *branch* school, established by the Deacons, in the City Tavern—1652—probably until the Capitulation, 1664 (*vide* page 24).

Hoboocken was transferred in 1661 to a *branch* school organized on the Governor's Bouwery (*vide* page 29), and was superseded by Keteltas in the main school, near the Fort.

De La Noy and Van Dalsem taught in a *branch* school in Cortlandt Street (*vide* page 46) from 1743 to 1757.

1705. The Deacons' Minutes during the period from 1687 to 1726 cannot be found. They would undoubtedly furnish the required name. The nomination of a Schoolmaster, by the Deacons, *in the ordinary way*, and the action of the Great Consistory, in connection therewith, in 1705, show that the school was in operation at that date. *Vide* p. 38.

1633.   1883.

Een-bracht maakt macht

ADAM ROELANTSEN		1633 1639
JAN STEVENSEN		1639 1648
JAN CORNELISSEN		1648 1650
WILLIAM VERSTIUS		1650 1655
JAN MORICE DE LA MONTAGNE		1652 16..
HARMANUS VAN HOBOCKEN		1655 1664
EVERT PIETERSEN KIEFTLAS		1661 1687
?		1705
BARENT DE FOREEST		1726 1733
GERRIT VAN WAGENEN		1733 1743
ABRAHAM DE LA NOY		1743 1747
HUYBERT VAN WAGENEN		1743 1749
WILLIAM VAN DALSEM		1747 1757
DANIEL BRATT		1749 1755
JOHN NICHOLAS WELP		1755 1773
PETER VAN STEENBURGH		1773 1791
The School was interrupted by the Revolutionary War.		
STANTON LATHAM		1791-1810
JAMES FORRESTER		1810 1842
HENRY WEBB DUNSHEE		1842

Barent deforeest

The Schoolmeester, 1726–1732.

Latham, teacher

1791–1810.

Daniel Ayres

Graduate of 1802.

Sarah (Ayres) McFarran

Aged 93–Graduate of 1805.

John DeLamater

Graduate of 1805.

H. T. Kiersted

Graduate of 1808.

Sam'l E. Sproulls

Graduate of 1824.

INDEX.

	PAGES
ABEEL, David	97, 99
" Gerrit	98
Abrahamse, Jacob	97
Abrahamze, Andries	95
Abramse, Anthony	100
" Jacob	100
Academy and Classical School	33, 60
Ackerman, John	104
Act of Incorporation of R. P. D. Church	37
Additions and Corrections	xv
Adriance, John	106
Amerman, Peter	101
" Richard	90, 105
Anderson, James, *M. D.*	xx, 106
Anniversary, 250th	246
" Rev. T. W. Chambers' Address at	248
" Merrill Edward Gates, *Ph. D.; LL.D.*, Address at	250
" Mr. Sam'l G. Jelliffe's Address at	257
" Rev. Sullivan H. Weston's Address at	263
Anthony, John	99
" Nicholas N	66, 99
" Theophilus	104
Attendance of the Scholars on the Sabbath	83
Ayres, Daniel	xiv, 237
" " Autograph of	280
BALDWIN, Jesse	70, 102, 103
Bancker, Adrian, Jr.	98
" Evert	98
Banker, Adriaen	97
" Christoffel	96
Bassett, Francis	99
" Mary, Legacy of	85
Bayard, Balthazar	94
" Nicolaes	94, 97
" Petrus	94
" Samuel	96
Beadle, Edward L.	xii, 105
Beekman, Gerardus	96
" James	56, 98
" James W	87
Benson, Egbert	24, 46, 109
" Robert	97
Bleecker, Leonard	66, 100
Bloodgood, Abraham	103
Boelen, Abraham	96
" Jacob	94
Bogardus, Abraham	86, 105
Bogert, Abraham	102
" Cornelius	98
" Fac.	98
" Hendrick	98
" Jan	97
" Nicholas	98
Bookstaver, Henry W.	xx, 105
" " Address of, at Unveiling of Tablet	268
Boyd, Thomas, *M. D.*	102
Bratt, Daniel	47, 48, 59
Breestede, Andries	97
Brevoort, Elias, Legacy of	84
" Jan	47

	PAGES
Brevoort, John	98
Brinckerhoff, Abraham	70, 103
" Dirck	56, 98
" Joris	97
" Seba	101
Brouwer, Abraham, Jr.	101
" Jeremiah	98
" John	99
Brower, Abraham	46, 109
" John I.	104
Brown, Jacobus	100
Bruen, Matthias	102
Buck, Robert	105
Byvank, Evert	97
CALHOUN, John C	81, 105
Catalogue of Scholars	109
Catechetical Instruction. 30, 36, 70, 71, 73, 74, 76.	
Chambers, Rev. T. W., *D.D.*	v, 89
" " Address at 250th Anniversary	248
Chambers, Rev. T. W., *D.D.*, Address at Unveiling of Tablet	273
Childs, Abraham	101
Church School, Bethel Baptist	77
" " Congregational	77
" " Episcopal	61, 65
" " " Schoolmasters of	61
Church School, Grace	77
" " Presbyterian	73, 75
City Tavern, School at	24
Clark, John	104
Clarke, John, *M.D.*	103
Clarkson, Cornelius V., *M. D.*	106
" Matthew	97
Clock, Ancient, in the School	71
Clopper, Cornelius, Jr.	98
" Pieter	98
Coerten, Henry	97
Cole, Peter	100
Consistory, Letter from, to Holland	48
Cornbury, Lord, Opposition to Dutch Schools	37, 58
Cornelissen, Jan	20, 21, 32
Cortlandt, Stephanus	94
Crol, Sebastian Jan, *Zieken-trooster*	14
Crolius, John	100
" John, Jr.	100
Currency of New Amsterdam	33
Curtius, Alexander Carolus, *Latin Schoolmaster*	33
Cutrier, Hendrick	94
Cuyler, Hendrick	96
DAM, Jan	18
Darvall, John	94
De Bow, Garrit	101
De Foreest, Barent	38, 42, 59
" " Contract with	39, 41
" " Declaration Concerning	40
" " Autograph of	280
De Foreest, Isaac	95
" " John I	104
De Kay, Jacobus	94
" " Theunis	94
De Lamater, John	237
" " Autograph of	280

T 2

INDEX.

	PAGES
De Lamater, Samuel	101
De La Montagne, Jan Morice	24, 32, 36
De La Noy, Abraham	xv, 36, 46, 59
" " Pieter	94
Demaray, Joseph	101
De Motte, Mortimer	xi, 86, 104
De Peyster, Cornelius	95
" " Isaacq.	95
" " Johannes	95
" " Sarah, Legacy of	85
" " Willem	98
" " William	99
De Reimer, Isaac	95
" " Peter	100
" " Pieter	94
Devoe, Charles	104
De Vries, Captain	18
Dey, Anthony	70, 103
De Witt, Rev. Thomas, D.D., Historical Sketch	1
De Witt, Rev. Thomas, D.D., Address	89
Dickinson, Charles	100
Doughty, Samuel	101
Duiken, Gerrit	95
Dumont, Peter, M. D.	102
Dunning, William H	105
Duryé, Jakob	98
Duryee, Charles	100
" Jacob	56
" Richard	70, 71, 102, 103
" Richard, Chairman	72
" Richard, Decease of	79
Duyckink, Gerardus	56
Ebbing, Hieronymus	94
Elsworth, John T	100
" William J	99
Elting, John	100
Evertson, Nicholas	101
Forbes, John	99
" William G	100
Forrester, James	71, 79, 80
Free Grammar School	60
Free School, Latin, Greek and Mathematics	62
French, Philip	97
Gates, Merrill E., Ph.D., LL.D., Address at 250th Anniversary	250
Gilbert, William W	98, 99
Goelet, Jacobus	38, 95, 97
Graat, Johannes	97
Groesbeck, Johannes	97
Haight, David I	104
Ham, Coenrad W	99
" Wandle	101
Harberding, Jan (Harpending?)	94
Hardenbrook, Abel	47, 53, 97
" Johannes	95
Hardenbrook, John	98
" William	66, 99
" William, Jr	103
Harmony Hall, School at	77
Harpending, John, Coat-of-Arms	276
Harsen, George	100
" Gerrit	97, 99
" Jacob	110
Herring, Elbert	102
Heyer, Cornelius	102
" Isaac	70, 103
" William	99
Hinds, Joseph	71

	PAGES
Hinton, John W	102
Historical Sketch of Parochial School System in Holland	1
Hitchcock, Daniel	101
Hoffman, Nicholas	99
Holmes, Obadiah	103
Hoog, Thomas Andrew	99
Hopper, Andrew	100
" Garrit	101
Huigen, Leendert	95
Hunter, Charles F	105
Hutton, Frederic R	xx, 106
" Timothy	103
Huyck, Jan, Zieken-trooster	14
Hymn, Sung at 250th Anniversary	275
Irving, Washington, Letter of	xiv
Janeway, George	99
Jelliffe, Samuel G	241
" Samuel G., Address of, at 250th Anniversary	257
Jeremiah, Thomas	81, 86, 90, 104
Johnson, Isaac	99
" Jeromius	103
Julien, Alexis A	106
Kane, John	103
Keese, John D.	103
Kerfbyl, Dr. Johannes	38, 94
Keteltas, Abraham	96
" Evert Pietersen (Vide Evert Pietersen)	32, 58
Keteltas, Gerrit	96
" Pieter	98
Kieft, Director William	18
Kiersted, Henry T	xiv, 238
" Autograph of	280
King, William	101
Kip, Abraham	100
" Henry	98
" Isaacq	95
" Isaac I	101
" Jacobus	95
" Jacobus, Jr	95
" James H	101
" Johannes	94
" John H	100
Knapp, Benjamin S	102
Knox, Calvin E	105
" Henry E	106
Kruger, Johannes	95
Kuyter, Joachim Pietersen	18, 94
Labagh, Abraham	101
" John I	102, 104
Laidlie, Rev. Archibald, D.D.	52
Lansing, Jacob J	100
" John G	98
Latham, Stanton	63, 69, 71
" Autograph of	280
Latin School	33, 60
Latin and English Grammar School proposed	52
Laurenszen, Thomas	94
Lawrence, James V. H	104
Lefferts, Abraham	96
" Dirck	98
Le Foy, Thomas	100
Leixsler, Jacob	94
Lent, John A	103
Le Roux, Charles	96
Letter from Directors W. I. Co. to Stuyvesant	27

INDEX. 283

	PAGES		PAGES
Limberger, John	104	Richard, Paul	96
Lispenard, Leonard	98	Ringo, Albertus	95
Little, Charles S.	105	Roelantsen, Adam	15, 16, 17, 32
Livingston, John	98	Roeloiszen, Boole	94
" Philip	98	Romer, Henry	99
" Robert, Jr.	97	Rous, Gerrit	97
Locality of School	85	Roosevelt, Isaac	98
Locke, Frederick T.	105	" James	101
Lott, Abraham P.	56	" James C.	103
Louw, Cornelius	96	" Jan	96
Low, Pieter	97	" John J	99
Luerson, Carlton	95	" Nicolas	95
Luyck, Rev. Ægidius	34	" Theodore, Jr.	98
Lynsen, Abraham	97	Rosehoom, Willem	96
		Roseveldt, Jacobus	96
McFarran (Ayres), Sarah	238, 247, 264	Ruston, Charles, 241—Address of, at Re-union	264
" Autograph of	280	Rutgers, Antony	96
Madam's School	69	" Harmanus	96
Maerschalk, Andrew	98	" Harmanus, Jr	97
" Andries	95	" Petrus	97
" Francois	97		
" Johannes	97	Schell, Robert	106
" Pieter	97	Schieffelin, Samuel B	90
Malcolm, Alexander, *Principal of Free School.*	62	Scholars, Alphabetical List of	217
Man, Adriaan	96	" Catalogue of	109
Manley, Robert	99	" *Notes pertaining to*	237
Manly, John	101	" Re-union of	264
Marius, Pieter Jacobus	94	School, Aid from State Fund	72, 73, 77
Mathews, Rev. James M., D.D.	89	" 250th Anniversary of	246
Maybee, Frederick	101	" Course of Study in	91
Middle Dutch Church built	xviii	" Evening	57
" " " used as riding school	64, 257	" "Honors" of	92
Minthorne, Philip	99	" Hymns sung in	68
Moene, Dr. Jacob	96	" Legacies to	85
Montagne (*Vide De La Montagne*)	24	" Locality of	46, 77, 78, 85
Myer, Ide	97	" Officers of	94
		" on the Governor's Bouwery	29
Narbury, Jan	95	" Opening exercises in Fourth Street	87
Nevius, Peter I	103	" Opening exercises in Twenty-ninth Street	89
New Kirck, John	101	" Pay Scholars in, 43, 44, 49, 57, 66, 69, 71.	
Nexsen, Elias	66, 99	" Psalmody taught in	51, 70
" John	103	" *Public, Free* or *Low Dutch*	65
Nine Men	18	" Qualifications for admission to	91
Nitchie, John, Jr	70, 72, 100, 103	" Revenue of	84
North Dutch Church built	52	" Sewing and needlework taught in	79
" " " used as prison	64	" Trustees	xx, 94, 103
" " " pulpit and pews of	64	Schoo house built 1748	47
		" " 1773	57
Officers of the School	94	Schoolmaster, last in Dutch language	63
Oliver, James D	104	Schoolmasters, Private, prior to 1664	23, 32
Oothout, Henry	xii, 105	" " 1664 to 1785	60
" John	69, 104	Schoonmaker, Michael	103
		Schuyler, Brandt	94
Parochial School System in Holland	1	" Philip	96
Perlee, Ralph N	xx, 106	Sebring, Isaac	101
Pietersen, Evert (*Vide Keteltas*), 14, 27, 28, 29, 30, 35, 36.		Sickels, John	69, 99
Pieterszen, Adolf	94	Simmons, James	104
Polhemus, Abraham	101	Slidell, Isaac, Legacy of	85
Post, Anthony	56, 101	Smith, Gamaliel G	105
Proudfoot, Lawrence	101	" Stephen	101
Provost, David, Jr.	95	" William Wheeler	106
" William	96	Snyder, Henry	105
Public School, fund for erecting and maintaining, by Consistory	54	Solinger, Henry M	100
		South Dutch Church built	47
Rapelye, Gerrit	56, 98	" " View of	xix
Ray, Richard	98	Spratt, Jan	95
Re-union of Scholars	264	Sproulls, Samuel E	239
Reyke, Hendrick	97	" " Autograph of	280
Reynders, Barend	95		

INDEX.

	PAGES
Staats, Samuel	95
Stagg, John	66, 99
" John, Jr	101
" Peter	104
Stevensen, Jan	17, 20, 32
Steymets, Frederick	100
Stitt, George S	105
Storm, Thomas	100
Stoutenburgh, Isaac, *Chorister*	42, 47
" Isaac	69
" Isaac	95
" Isaac	98
" Jacobus	53
" John	70, 72, 101, 103
" Peter	94
Streets, Ancient and Modern names of	107
Stryker, John	100
" Rev. Peter, *D.D.*	90
Stuyvesant, Gerardus	97
Suydam, James	104
Syoerts, Olphert	95
TABLE OF CONTENTS	iii
Tablet, Unveiling of	264
" Description of	278
Teachers, 1883	xx
" Assistant, Names of	236
" of Private Schools	23, 32, 60
Teller, James	100
" Olivier	96
Ten Eyck, Abraham	97
" Anthony	98
" Coenraadt	97
" Dirck	93
" Elizabeth, *Teacher of Madam's School*	69
" Jacob	96
Tiebout, Albert	98
" Teunis	98
Trinity School	61
Trustees of Collegiate Church School, appointed	70
Trustees, Names of	xx, 94, 103
Turck, Cornelis	97
Turk, Ahasuerus	99
Turk, Jacob	47, 98
VAN ARENAM, John, *Chorister*	43, 45, 47
Van Antwerp, Jacobus, *Voorsanger*	52, 54
" " James	100, 104
" " Nicholas	100
" " Simon	103
Van Benschoten, James	105
Van Brunt, Stephen	104
Van Cortlandt, Jacobus	95
" " Philip	96
" " Stephen	100
Van Courtland, Frederick	96
Van Dalsem, William	xv, xvi, 51
Vanderbilt, John, Jr	101
Van der Heul, Johannes	96
Van der Linden, Peter, *Voorleeser*	20
Van der Sman, Adrian, *Catechist*	48, 53, 52
Van der Spiegel, Hendrick	96
" " Jacobus	95
Van De Water, Valentine	104
Van Dolsem, William	100
Van Dyck, James	101
Van Dycke, John	100
Van Fricht, Gerrit	94

	PAGES
Van Gelder, Abraham	100
" " Hermanus	96
Van Giessen, Johannes	95
Van Hoboocken, Harmanus	23 to 35
Van Hoorn, Gerrit	95
" " Joan	96
Van Horne, Abraham	96
" " Cornelius	97
Van Imburg, Gysbert	95
Van Kleeck, Baltus	99
" " Isaac	94
Van Kleek, John L	101
Van Nest, Abraham	102, 103
" " John	xii, 105
Van Orden, John	101
Van Pelt, Reuben	104
Van Ranst, C	98
" " Petrus	97
Van Steenburgh, Peter, *Call to teach in Dutch and English*	56, 59, 64, 68
Van Tilburg, Pieter	95
Van Vechten, Abraham V. W.	105
" " John	103
Van Vleck, Abraham	96
Van Wagenen, Gerrit, Contract with	43, 45, 59, 109
" " Huybert	45, 46, 47, 53, 59, 109
" " Huybert	103
" " Huybert, Jr	105
Van Wyck, Theodorus	47, 98
Van Wyk, Abraham	96
Van Zandt, Tobias	99
" " Wynant	97
Varick, John	101
" John V. B.	101, 103
" Joseph V	124
Vehslage, Rev. Henry	241
" " Address of, at Unveiling of Tablet	265
Verplank, Gulian	97
Verstius, William	22, 23, 32
Vroom, Guysbert Bogert	102
WALDEGROVE, Garrit	101
Waldron, Alexander Phœnix	101
" John	101
Wanshaar, Jan	95
Ward, James	104
Warner, Peter R	xii, 86, 104
" " Donation to Library	87
Welp, John Nicholas	50, 51, 53, 54, 55, 59
Wendover, Peter H	101
Wessels, Hendrick	94
Westervelt, James J	101
" John	101
Weston, Rev. Sullivan H., *D.D.*, Address of, at 250th Anniversary	263
Wetmore, Noah	81, 88, 104
Whitlock, Thomas B	101
Whiton, Augustus S	106
Wilhemszen, Reynier	94
Wilson, Peter	69
Wood, William	105
Wright, John	101
Wyckoff, Cornelius P	101
" Henry J	103
Wynkoop, Benjamin	95
YOUNG, Isaac	103, 237
ZABRISKIE, George	105